Tribes into Nations

Other books from The Letterworth Press
by Laurence Bristow-Smith

A History of Music in the British Isles:
Vol. 1 From Monks to Merchants
Vol. 2 Empire and Afterwards

and

Harold Nicolson: Half-an-Eye on History

Tribes into Nations

The Early History of the British Isles

Laurence Bristow-Smith

The Letterworth Press

Published in Scotland by the Letterworth Press
http://www.TheLetterworthPress.org

Text set in Augustin
Printed by Ingram Spark

© Laurence Bristow-Smith 2022

ISBN 978-1-3999-3283-7

3 5 7 9 8 6 4 2

For Ezra and Adam

who are discovering history

Contents

Acknowledgements	xiii
Groundwork	1
1 A Sense of Perspective	14
2 Settling the Archipelago	22
3 Paths across the Sea	32
4 Marks upon the Land	46
5 Structures on the Ground	59
6 Ritual in the Landscape	72
7 Beakers and Bronze	87
8 Walls and Weapons	102
9 Hoards and Water	113
10 Iron and Settlement	123
11 Sounds and Speech	135
12 A Question of Identity	144
13 Culture and Language	154
14 Belief and Ritual	166
15 Invasion and Influence	183
16 Invasion and Conquest	194
17 Romans in the North	206
18 Romans in the South	221
19 Over the Wall and across the Sea	236
20 God and the Gods	249
21 The Crumbling Façade	265
22 Chasing Shadows	277
23 Spreading the Word	292
24 Building Kingdoms	307
25 Saints and Warriors	317
26 The Land and the Law	331
27 Words and Images	341
28 The Third Wave	352
29 Kingdoms in the North	368
30 Kingdoms in the South	382
31 England	395

32	War, Peace, and More War	411
33	Beyond England I	428
34	Dynasties and Directions	446
35	Beyond England II	460
36	Power Struggle	477
37	Conquest	491
38	Transformation	506
39	Scotland and the Isles	520
40	Wales	538
41	Ireland	551
	Closing the Dig	560

Notes	565
Sources	584
Index of Places and Events	593
Index of Persons	602

Maps

Map 1	Regions of the Archipelago	12
Map 2	A Sense of Perspective	20
Map 3	Settling the Archipelago	28
Map 4	Paths across the Sea	38
Map 5	The Early Neolithic Period	51
Map 6	Cursus Monuments, Tombs, and Long Barrows	61
Map 7	Henges, Stone Circles, and Sacred Landscapes	73
Map 8	The Spread of Beaker Culture	91
Map 9	Beaker Culture in the British Isles	95
Map 10	Bronze Age Land Use and Settlement Patterns	107
Map 11	Hoards and Water	120
Map 12	Iron Age Zones of Settlement	127
Map 13	Rounds, Brochs, Crannogs, and Hillforts	132
Map 14	Language and Identity	148
Map 15	The Spread of Celtic Language and Culture	163
Map 16	Tribes of Great Britain, c.50 AD	192
Map 17	The Roman Conquest	212
Map 18	The Roman Occupation	234
Map 19	God and the Gods	261
Map 20	The Roman Provinces of Britain	270
Map 21	The Kingdoms of the British Isles, c.500 AD	284
Map 22	Spreading the Word	302
Map 23	The Kingdoms of the Heptarchy	310
Map 24	Saints and Warriors	324
Map 25	Anglo-Saxon Law, Language, and Art	342
Map 26	The Arrival of the Vikings	366
Map 27	The British Isles in the 9th Century	381
Map 28	England in the 10th and Early 11th Centuries	412
Map 29	Ireland, Scotland, Wales, and Kingdom of the Isles in the 10th and Early 11th Centuries	443
Map 30	England Conquered and Transformed	503
Map 31	The British Isles in the 12th and 13th Centuries	539

Acknowledgements

Above all, I am indebted to Peter Winnington for designing and editing this book. Adam Bristow-Smith did a great job producing the maps. Damian Leeson's challenges, suggestions, and proof-reading were invaluable. Stan Calder also read the text and accompanied me on trips to the National Museum in Edinburgh, Stirling Castle, and other key locations. The Rev. Nigel Gibson explained issues of religious doctrine and terminology with characteristic directness. Professor James Stephens Curl offered informed advice on architecture and Ireland. Alan Prosser checked my Welsh history and spelling.

Retrospective thanks are due to Mr J.A. Williams who taught me Latin at the Skinners' School, and to Professor Richard Bailey and John Frankis who taught me Old English and Old Norse at the University of Newcastle-upon-Tyne.

I am grateful to the BBC for permission to quote from Simon Schama's *A History of Britain* and Douglas Adams' *A Hitchhikers Guide to the Galaxy*. Curtis Brown gave permission to quote from Winston Churchill's *A History of the English Speaking Peoples*. Yale University Press kindly allowed me to quote from Ronald Hutton's *Pagan Britain*.

Some of the quotations from Classical sources are my own translations; others are taken, with permission, from the Loeb Classical Library or Project Gutenburg. Similarly, quotations from Anglo-Saxon sources are either my translations or taken, with permission, from Everyman's Library or Project Gutenberg.

Every effort has been made to contact the copyright holders of all quotations and images; where this has been unsuccessful, 'fair usage' has been assumed.

Laurence Bristow-Smith
Glenholme, Kirkcudbright
2022

Groundwork

I

The writing of history is essentially personal. Every historian selects, organises, and emphasises particular aspects of the available data. From that process emerges a personal interpretation of history, a personal reconstruction of the past.

This is particularly true in the case of the distant past – that shadowy region generally referred to as 'prehistory', a term with connotations which will be discussed in due course. The further back into the past one delves, the less certainty there is. As a consequence, in order to produce a coherent picture of the lives of the men and women who lived so very long ago – and, what is more important, the ideas and aspects of behaviour they have passed down to us – the historian has to do more, to try harder to join up the dots of whatever archaeological or documentary records are available.

This process inevitably involves speculation and imagination. Equally inevitable is the fact that historians (myself included) will interpret the past in the light of their own preconceptions and prejudices, which are shaped by acceptance or rejection of the norms and orthodoxies of their own age and society. The historian's responsibility is to recognise this: to apply imagination, logic, and reason in pursuit of objectivity while knowing full well that it can never be attained. Therein lies the challenge, the interest, and the fun, but also many difficulties and contradictions. For example, the archaeologist Francis Pryor has characterised the latter part of the Bronze Age in Britain as peaceful and egalitarian. Two other experts in the field, Timothy Champion and Christopher Darvill, have seen it as a time when a warlike aristocracy dominated society. All three were working from the same basic information. None of them is wrong. They just assessed the material differently and reached different conclusions. This study, it should be added, inclines to the latter view, but that is simply my personal assessment of the available evidence.

History in this second sense is closely allied to identity – the historian's sense of personal identity, and the broader cultural identity of the society within which, and for which, he or she is writing. Identity may be racial, national, regional, or personal, but it is almost always defined as a mix of present qualities or characteristics that derive from the past. Historical identity can be useful in promoting understanding of the present. Equally, it can be dangerous. It can be slanted or distorted and used to justify partisan political or social actions. The best the historian can do is interpret the historical data – I am deliberately avoiding the word 'facts' – as they appear at the time and without conscious bias. The word 'conscious' is important because, ever since written records began, historical bias and misrepresentation has been used to flatter the great, to blacken the enemy, to drive home political arguments, and to justify everything from tax rises to racist pogroms.

On the positive side, history is open to different interpretations; it can be told in different ways and from different points of view; and that is its attraction. I have always found that history grows with you, perhaps because it is never static. New documents may be discovered. Known documents may be reinterpreted in the light of new knowledge. Accounts of events or descriptions of individuals – written, recorded, or filmed – may turn out to be partial or inaccurate. In recent years, archaeology has been the most exciting area. New sites have been discovered and new science-based techniques, such as dendrochronology and isotope analysis have allowed archaeologists to probe their new discoveries, and reassess old ones, with much greater precision.

Humility, therefore, is required. The single most important thing for the historian is to remember that he or she does not *know*; that whatever he or she might believe – and however passionately that belief may be held – it can never ultimately be proved. There will always be a chance that it did not happen that way, that things could be explained differently.

This book is thus a contribution to a debate which can never be concluded. It tells the story of that archipelago, consisting of something over six thousand islands and situated off the north-western shore of mainland Europe, which we nowadays call the British Isles. It begins with the first traces of humanoid creatures that we can identify, and it ends in the high medieval period – there is no precise end date because different parts of the archipelago developed in different ways – by which time most of the racial groupings and political entities that we recognise today had been established. The timescale is immense, and for all but the last fraction of the period, dating is rarely more than approximate. In the same way, for all but that last fraction of time, documentary sources are non-existent. This is where speculation and imaginative reconstruction play their part.

To give a sense of the passage of time is not always easy. Nor is it necessarily helped by the now traditional segmentation of prehistory into Ages – Palaeolithic, Mesolithic, Neolithic, Bronze, Iron, and so on. Human prehistory is generally defined as the period from the first appearance of man right up until the invention of writing and the existence of written records. The term was coined in French – *'préhistorique'* – in the 1830s by the French chemist and archaeologist, Paul Tournal (1805–72). It was first used in English by the Scottish antiquarian Daniel Wilson (1816–92) in his *The Archaeology and Prehistoric Annals of Scotland* (1851). How relevant is it today? Why should 'history' begin with the appearance of the written word – especially in an age where the scientific techniques that support both geology and archaeology can give us increasingly detailed information about the evolution of the land and its peoples? These sources can often provide us with information that is more reliable than that contained in early documents. The written word is the basis of modern civilisation, and there is a temptation to give too much weight to early written sources precisely because they are written – a temptation encouraged in the past by the fact that Latin and Greek authors assumed what many would now see as a disproportionate importance in the British educational system. That said, written sources do have the effect of humanising our view of the past. They offer us names and characters, descriptions of how people behaved, of their religious practices, of what was important to them. Coins give the names of kings and tribes. Inscriptions tell us who built a particular monument or structure, which legion was stationed where. Such sources undoubtedly have their value, but they must be used with caution. In this study, the terms 'prehistory' and 'prehistoric' will continue to be used in the accepted manner simply as a matter of convenience, but with the caveat that their use should not be taken to imply that there is any hard-and-fast division between 'prehistory' and 'history'.

In the 1820s, ninety years after Tournal's invention of prehistory, Christian Jürgensen Thomsen (1788–1865), Director of the Royal Museum of Nordic Antiquities in Copenhagen, divided it into three. In his view, the archaeologists of the time did not pay sufficient attention to the context of their finds, to what objects were found together and what that implied, so he came up with the Three Age System – Stone, Bronze and Iron – as a workable chronological framework. Forty years later in 1865, Sir John Lubbock (1834–1913), the English banker, politician, botanist, ethnologist, and archaeologist – in fact, a classic example of the Victorian polymath – published *In Pre-Historic Times*, which became one of the most influential archaeological books of the nineteenth century. Lubbock's contribution was to divide the Stone Age into an early period when man lived alongside now extinct animals, the Palaeolithic (or Old Stone Age), and a later period, the Neolithic (or New Stone Age), characterised by polished stone tools.[1] A few years later in 1872, the Irish archaeologist, Hodder M. Westropp, introduced the term Mesolithic (or Middle Stone Age) to define a recognisably separate phase of human development between the Palaeolithic and the Neolithic.

The Three Age System remains the generally accepted way of segmenting prehistory, but, of course, the transition between one developmental phase and the next not only took a long time, it took place at different times in different places. Neolithic culture, for example, emerged in the so-called Fertile Crescent by 10,000 BC or perhaps earlier. It arrived in Greece about 6800 BC and then spread across Europe at a rate which has been estimated at one kilometre a year. In terms of the geographical region we are considering here – those lands which eventually became the British Isles – the Palaeolithic Age covered the period from mankind's earliest beginnings until about 9600 BC. The Mesolithic, marked by smaller, more closely-worked stone tools and a more defined hunter-gatherer lifestyle, lasted until about 4200 BC. The Mesolithic led into and overlapped with the Neolithic, which continued until about 2500 BC, and was characterised by the spread of arable farming, the domestication of animals, and the use of more sophisticated tools and technologies. The later stages of the Neolithic overlapped with the Bronze Age. This overlap, when both metals and stone tools were in use, may have lasted for anything up to five hundred years, from 2500 to 2000 BC. Some archaeologists insert an extra period here, which they call the Chalcolithic Age, referring to those centuries when copper was smelted, but before it was combined with tin to produce bronze. In general usage, however, the British Bronze Age is held to have begun about 2500 BC and to have lasted until about 800 BC, when it gave way to the Iron Age. The Iron Age then lasted until the coming of the Romans in 43 AD – at which point 'prehistory' gave way to 'history'.

These divisions are understood by most lay readers and fixed within the compass of the educational system; and they have their uses. Given that the vast span of prehistory cannot be divided up by kings or dynasties, they provide useful reference points, charting the stages of human development. They also provide a framework for archaeologists and others engaged in the more detailed task of relating one set of finds to another, of dating and categorising the archaeological record. However, their utility has its limits. Many archaeologists now see the later Neolithic and the early Bronze Age as having more in common with each other than with the preceding or succeeding periods. And they see the late Bronze Age, early Iron Age and middle Iron Age as constituting a single definable period, while the Late Iron Age is then attached to the Roman period which followed. In the light of current research, these ideas make sense.

Again, the conventional Ages of prehistory will be used in this study as a matter of convenience, to indicate broad periods of time and the general characteristics associated with them. However, it must be emphasised that these terms are not only generalisations, but also retrospective: they only make sense to us because we know what happened next. The risk is that they suggest a rigid, artificial structure focussed on change and transformation. They create a temptation to see each new stage of social or technological development as a sudden burst of progress, after which nothing much happened until the next Age came along. The fact is, of course, that human society is constantly changing and evolving – just like the view of it taken by historians – even when it moves slowly. Most of the cultural changes of prehistory took place over hundreds, even thousands of years, so to the population of the time the reality would have been one of continuity and slow transition. This becomes particularly important when we consider the process or processes by which change came about.

The traditional view – which developed as archaeology itself developed in the eighteenth and nineteenth centuries – was that the major cultural changes in the prehistory of the British Isles were brought about by successive waves of invaders and immigrants coming from the Continent. Invasion theory, as it is known, sees first Neolithic peoples, then Bronze Age peoples, then Celts, all arriving on these shores, bringing new tools and technologies, new art and new languages, and crucially, so the argument goes, replacing the existing inhabitants. Such a view remained widely current until the second half of the twentieth century, when a battery of new techniques – radiocarbon dating, dendrochronology, isotope analysis, and the use of computers to process vast amounts of data – enabled archaeologists and historians to take a more scientific approach to excavation and to challenge accepted ideas. Invasion theory was regarded as too simplistic, and a much larger role accorded to acculturation: the process by which ideas, technologies, fashions, and even languages are transferred from one population group to another through extended contact, whether that contact is the result of trading relationships, 'political' exchanges, kinship visits, intermarriage, or any other form of interaction. Such an approach still allowed for immigration, and even invasion – albeit on a much smaller scale than previously assumed – but it argued against the idea that major prehistoric cultural changes necessarily involved the wholesale displacement and replacement of one population by another.

However, nothing – not even prehistory – stays still, and in recent decades the advent of increasingly sophisticated techniques of DNA analysis have transformed our understanding of at least two crucial stages in the cultural and racial development of the British Isles. DNA extracted from skeletal remains now suggests that the arrival of Neolithic peoples towards the end of the fifth millennium BC, and the arrival of the Beaker People in the middle of the third millennium, were both marked by population change on a significant scale, although there is nothing in the archaeological record to suggest that either change was characterised or accompanied by a large-scale invasion. The new evidence appears convincing, although given what has gone before, we should perhaps add the caveat that DNA analysis is a relatively new technology and larger-scale studies with broader sampling will be required before it can be considered wholly conclusive. All one can say is that each period of the prehistory and early history of the British Isles needs to be approached on its own terms and with an open mind.

Traditional invasion theory may have been overtaken by science, but it is worth exploring because it helps explain how and why, in the past, British prehistory was interpreted as it was. Scientific archaeology, as opposed to amateur digging and object collecting, developed only slowly over the course of the nineteenth and twentieth centuries. It built on the work of men such as Thomsen, Lubbock, and Westropp, and established both a structure and a chronological framework for prehistory. Antiquarian writers and early archaeologists, with no such framework and no detailed archaeological record to guide them, had to rely on a combination of deduction and guesswork. The written sources available to them were a mixture of ancient documents and 'histories', many of which contained as much fantasy as fact – and sometimes more. And, of course, they relied also, as we all do, on the intellectual orthodoxies of their time.

The first descriptions of Britain and the British are found in the works of Greek and Roman authors, to whom Britain was a remote and difficult land, populated by people with whose lives and culture they had no point of connection. By the sixteenth century, the study of classical literature was an essential part of every gentleman's education and had a profound cultural influence, so that when Caesar, Cicero, Tacitus and others wrote that the Britons were savage, painted and ignorant, their opinions went unchallenged. And when, for example, James VI and I (r. in Scotland, 1567–1625; in England, 1603–24) commissioned the architect Inigo Jones (1573–1652) to carry out a study of Stonehenge, it was self-evident that such a vast monument could not have been built by the savage barbarians described by Roman authors. The Romans themselves, Jones concluded, must have been responsible. Others suggested that it was the Saxons, or the Danes, or even the Phoenicians. But the message was clear: the native Britons (and precisely who they might have been is something we will explore in due course) were too primitive to have built it. The expertise must have come from abroad. Even the writer John Aubrey (1626–97), who did correctly attribute Stonehenge to 'the Britons', struggled to square their ability to build such a complex and sophisticated structure with the received picture of savages dressed in skins.

Another aspect of the difficulties faced by early archaeologists in establishing a reliable model for prehistory is illustrated by the story of William Buckland (1784–1856) and the Red Lady of Paviland. Buckland was a figure of immense authority in the world of geology and archaeology at the beginning of the nineteenth century. He became Oxford University's Reader in Mineralogy in 1813 and its first Reader in Geology in 1819. He was the first man to write a full description of a fossilised dinosaur which he called a Megalosaurus. He was also a clergyman – later to become Dean of Westminster – who was insistent that archaeological discoveries could only be interpreted in the light of the story of man as told in the Bible.[2] In 1823, excavating Goat's Hole Cave, one of the Paviland Caves on the Gower Peninsula in Wales, Buckland uncovered a partial skeleton which had apparently been dyed with red ochre and buried with seashell necklaces and ivory jewellery. From the decoration, he assumed the remains to be female. As a good Christian of his time, he accepted the biblical chronology of Bishop Ussher (1581–1656), which dated the Creation to 4004 BC and the Flood to 2349 BC; and, as no human could predate the Flood, he came to the conclusion that the skeleton was Roman. Putting the two assumptions together, he hypothesised that the remains were those of a Roman prostitute, or possibly a witch. What he had in fact discovered was a man's body, dating from c.31,000 BC, and the oldest evidence of ceremonial burial yet found in Western Europe. What Buckland demonstrates is not only the ingrained assumption that anything new or complex or out of the ordinary was too sophisticated to be native to Britain, but also the added complication of trying to reconcile empirical observation with religious orthodoxy.

The idea that the native Britons were essentially ignorant savages was deeply entrenched; it was reinforced by the Three Age System which offered a simple, progressive chronology for prehistory; and a combination of the two ideas produced invasion theory, which seemed to offer a clear explanation for the process underlying that chronology. Each new stage of development *must* have been brought from Europe, because it could not have originated in the British Isles; and because the natives were primitive barbarians, it must have been imposed upon them by culturally superior invaders. Some progress was made during the course of the nineteenth century – the work of John MacEnery (1796–1841) and William Pengelly (1812–94) swept away Bishop Ussher's biblical chronology – but it was surprisingly little. As late as 1899, Professor John Meiklejohn of the University of St Andrews, could describe the 'pre-Celtic inhabitants' of Britain as 'stunted savages, whose tools and weapons were of flint, wood, or bone; who dressed in skins, painted their bodies with red ochre and blue woad juice.'[3]

Invasion theory was the product of the collective wisdom of archaeologists and historians at a particular time. At the time, it was a useful tool, allowing them to structure their ideas more clearly than before. Yet it also reflected the broader political and ideological temper of the age in which it was formulated. Britain was the hub of a huge and expanding empire. The study of prehistory was still in its infancy, but historians had developed a clear-cut scheme of early British history from the arrival of the Romans onwards. This scenario – which was still being taught in British schools as late as the 1980s – was also constructed around a series of invasions. Romans, Angles, Saxons, Norwegians, Danes, and Normans – so the theory went – all invaded and all brought with them their own particular racial characteristics. From the resulting mixture, so the argument continued, emerged the unique British character which went on to win and to rule the greatest Empire the world had ever seen. Unlike other contemporary European theories of national character, this one did not depend or dwell on racial purity. Rather, it saw the English – not the inhabitants of other parts of the British Isles who were by that time branded as Celts – as super-mongrels: superior because they possessed all the virtues of all the races that had invaded over the centuries. Invasion theory effectively extended this approach backwards into prehistory, and thus became a means of reinforcing the concept of British exceptionalism.

It will, I hope, be apparent from the above that this history is social and political in the broadest sense of those terms. It begins with the earliest traces of mankind yet found in the British Isles. It follows the emergence of new societies with new patterns of settlement, new technologies, and new ways of recording their presence on the landscape. It examines the linguistic and racial composition of the British Isles when they became part of recorded history with the arrival of the Romans. It explores the turbulent post-Roman period when new peoples arrived from the Continent, raiding and invading and establishing new kingdoms. And it takes the story to the point where we can identify the foundations of the nations and polities of the British Isles as they exist today. Art, literature, and other forms of cultural expression are, of course, part of the story. Neolithic stonework and polished stone axes, Bronze Age daggers and Irish goldwork, illuminated manuscripts from Celtic monasteries, the heroic tales of Irish and Welsh heroes, Anglo-Saxon art and poetry: all these are key signifiers of group, regional, national, and even political identity, and all feature in these pages. That said, given the problems and preoccupations of our present time – the United Kingdom's role in relation to Europe and immigration being not the least of them – I feel there is much to be gained from re-examining both the origins of the nations that today inhabit the British Isles and the way in which the historians of previous centuries have interpreted that story. In particular, given the Anglocentric approach of so many historians in the past, I devote more space to Scotland, Ireland and

Wales, as well as to such defunct polities as the Kingdom of the Isles and Alt Clud, whose contribution to the overall shaping of the social and political complexion of the British Isles is equally important.

I hope that in due course the development of the creativity, the intellectual and imaginative structures, and the individual drive and intelligence that have played a major part in driving all forms of change since the early medieval period will be the subject of a companion volume, but that is for the future.

II

Some terminology needs to be examined and, as far as possible, defined at this point. How should one refer to areas, regions, and places as they existed during the prehistoric period? It is important for the reader to be able to locate Goat's Hole Cave, Callanish (Calanais), or Stonehenge on his or her mental map of the world. The obvious solution is to provide the necessary references by using contemporary names, but such a course has its risks. Associating locations from the distant past with modern-day political, civic, and administrative entities and boundaries is both anachronistic and potentially misleading. Equally, avoiding contemporary names may well prove disorientating for the modern reader. In one sense, that might serve a useful purpose. The tribe who buried one of their number with some ceremony in Goat's Hole Cave would have had a race memory, but no developed sense of history. They were travelling, nomadic peoples, but they had no maps. They would have had a sense of direction; they would have had a knowledge of the main features of the lands across which they moved; and they would presumably have named those features – the seas, rivers, mountain ranges, peaks and headlands – in their own language. What those names were, we can never know; nor can we assume that the names used by one tribe would have been the same as those used by another. In such a context, it may be appropriate for the modern reader to experience a slight sense of uncertainty, and it is probably less misleading than using names that take their significance from peoples and events of later ages.[4]

A compromise is necessary. While using contemporary names and locations to identify specific prehistoric sites, the first part of this study will use other terms for larger geographic entities:

The Western Lands: Western Europe including the British Isles
The Continental Lands: Western Europe, excluding the British Isles
The Peninsular Lands: that area, then still connected to the Continent, which eventually became the British Isles
The Archipelago: the British Isles once they had become islands
The Main Island: Great Britain
The Lowland Zone: Great Britain south and east of a line drawn between the Bristol Channel and the Tees, excluding Devon and Cornwall
The Upland Zone: Great Britain north and west of the same line
The Western Uplands: Wales
The High North: Scotland north of the Central Belt
The South-Western Peninsula: Devon and Cornwall
The Western Channel: the Irish Sea
The Western Isle: Ireland
The Halfway Isle: the Isle of Man
The Outer Isles: the Outer Hebrides
The Northern Isles: Orkney
The Far Northern Isles: Shetland

Such a scheme may sound awkward or simplistic, but it is intended to remind – indeed, to emphasise – that these lands had an existence in the minds of the peoples who lived in them long before the emergence of the ethnic and cultural identities and political entities by which they are now defined.

Once we reach later ages where documentary sources are available, names of people and places pose a particular problem. It is impossible to be wholly consistent or to satisfy everyone. Latin names are easier to deal with because Latin texts have been studied over the centuries and Latin spelling largely standardised. However, where British names appear in Latin texts – and many such names are known to us only from Latin sources – the spelling will be an approximation of what a Celtic-language name sounded like to the scribe or his informants. And, of course, later historians have made their judgements and choices on the basis of what the Latin scribes wrote. For example, Iceni is the commonly accepted spelling of the British tribe who inhabited East Anglia at the time of the Roman invasion. However, the name has on occasion been spelt Eceni, and first century AD coins from the area use the spelling Ecen. The queen

Map 1   Regions of the Archipelago

of the Iceni, who mounted possibly the most dangerous rebellion against Roman rule, was for many years spelt Boadicea. More recently, the spelling Boudicca has been preferred as being closer to what is thought to be the original Celtic root.

With Irish, Scottish, and Welsh names, whether found in Celtic-language manuscripts, or transliterated into Latin or English, we find an almost infinite variety of alternative spellings. Here, the problems of transliteration are complicated by the fact that the scribes may be trying to interpret regional differences in pronunciation or to write down names from versions of P- and Q-Celtic that they themselves did not speak. Scottish kings in particular are sometimes referred to by their Gaelic name, and sometimes by its anglicised version. Cináed MacAlpín thus frequently appears as Kenneth MacAlpin; Domnall mac Ailpín (*sic*) as Donald I; and Causantín mac Cináeda as Constantine I. In such cases, I have listed the main alternatives when the individual first enters the story, and then used the version of the name that seems to me most appropriate in the context of the overall narrative.

With Scandinavian names, the situation is still more complicated – especially when we come to those individuals who played a part in the story of both Viking Ireland and Viking Jórvik. Most of them had both an Old Norse and an Irish name The two names are often not obviously similar, and there is frequently also a defining nickname. For example, Amlaíb Cuarán, as he is referred to in this text and most commonly referred to in literature dealing with the period, was twice King of Dublin and twice King of Jórvik. Cuarán is a nickname meaning sandals. His name in Irish Gaelic was Amlaíb mac Sitric, and in Old Norse he was Olaf Sigtryggsson. There are also two or three alternative anglicised versions of his name. As before, I have listed the most common alternatives when individual first appears and then chosen what seems to me to be the most appropriate version.

Anglo-Saxon also requires the author to make choices. Should it be King Ælfred or King Alfred? King Eadward or King Edward? Harald or Harold? For the most part, I have chosen the spelling that is closest to the Anglo-Saxon version of the name. I have, however, varied this practice where I felt the need to distinguish between two characters with the same name. Thus, Harald Haradrada retains the contemporary spelling, while Harold Godwineson uses the later Anglicised spelling. And I confess to having indulged one of two personal preferences. My use of Godwineson, rather than the much more common Godwinson, is a case in point. It is closer to the Anglo-Saxon, and I prefer the sound it makes.

In all cases where names and their variants are concerned, I have been guided by my sense of what is appropriate to the cultural character of the narrative, and a concern that the reader should be able to follow the twists and turns of the story and its actors without undue difficulty.

1 A Sense of Perspective

The village of Happisburgh – pronounced 'Hazeboro' – sits on the cliffs on the north-east coast of Norfolk, looking out onto the North Sea roughly halfway between Cromer and Great Yarmouth. It is a small village of some nine hundred inhabitants. It has a pub, a handful of houses, a fifteenth-century church, a lighthouse, a lifeboat station, and a coastline that is being rapidly eroded by the sea. Eight hundred and fifty thousand years ago (give or take fifty thousand) the geography of the area was very different. The land where the village now stands formed part of the north bank of the estuary of a large river, a precursor of the Thames, flowing eastwards to the sea. To the north of the estuary, the coastline ran north-south. To the south, it followed a south-easterly course until it reached a point in the middle of what is now the North Sea, some distance offshore from Den Haag. There, it turned north again, creating a large north-facing gulf into which this proto-Thames emptied itself.

The coastal erosion that is pushing the coastline back is of great concern to the residents. Over the years, it has caused a number of houses to collapse into the sea, but it has also led to some spectacular archaeological finds. As long ago as the 1820s, local fishermen, hauling in their nets, were bringing up the antlers, bones, horns, the teeth of long extinct, prehistoric species. Storms battering the coast revealed fossilised tree-stumps and the shapes of leaves imprinted in layers of sedimentary rock. Large quantities of bison bones suggested that early man might well have been active in the area, but it was not until 2000, when a retired policeman walking his dog on the beach found a black flint axe head, that there was actual evidence of a prehistoric human presence.

The discovery led to the area being explored and excavated. Archaeologists uncovered more than eighty flint tools, together with animal bones bearing marks that suggested the animals had been butchered by men using stone tools. Then, in 2013, a period of stormy weather swept away all the sand from part of the beach, revealing the compacted silts which had once bordered the proto-Thames. There, in the silts, were some fifty fossilised footprints. They were only exposed for a few hours at low tide, and scientists had to work quickly to record the details before, within a fortnight of their appearance, they disappeared, eroded by the same tidal scour that had exposed them. Careful study suggested that the footprints had been made by of a group of five individuals, whose height – calculated from the length of the prints – varied between 0.93 and 1.74 metres, indicating the presence of children as well as adults. The strata in which the footprints were found were also analysed. The magnetism of the rocks, together with the flora and fauna preserved in them, gave a date of between 800,000 and 900,000 BC, making the footprints the earliest traces of humankind yet found in northern Europe.

Who were these people and what were they doing? Palaeontologists have built up a picture of a grassy river valley surrounded by dense coniferous forests, inhabited by a bestiary of now extinct or locally extinct animal species – mammoths, woolly rhinos, hippos, giant deer, sabre-toothed tigers, lions, wolves, and other potentially dangerous species. Climatologists, working from the evidence of fossilised plants and insects, have suggested that the climate would have been roughly equivalent to that of southern Scandinavia today. This means that the Happisburgh group must have had the ability to clothe themselves – presumably in skins – to build some kind of shelter, and to keep warm in winter. They were apparently walking southwards, away from the mouth of the river. What were they doing? Collecting shellfish? Or edible plants from the water's edge? Were they looking for a place to cross the river? Would they have made a camp in the forest? Or on the riverbank? Or on an island which could offer protection from predators or enemies? All sorts of ideas can be advanced, but they remain at best educated speculation. As Happisburgh has not yielded any human fossils, we cannot even be sure to which species or sub-species of humans this group belonged – although there is a broad consensus that they were probably *Homo antecessor* or 'Pioneer Man' and, as such, representatives of the first wave of humans to move into, explore, and settle the lands which now form the European Continent.

Despite the uncertainties and the impossibility of knowing who these people were, how they lived their lives, or how they thought, this first sighting of man in northern Europe is important because it gives a sense of perspective. Most of this book deals with the ideas, beliefs, and actions of men during the last 6,000 years because they are to a greater or lesser degree accessible; because one can trace or speculate on their visual, psychological, and even political legacy as it affects life in the British Isles today. Nonetheless it is worth recognising that those 6,000 years represent just over half of one percent of the time that has elapsed since the Happisburgh group left their footprints on the bank of the river that would one day run through London, under the Millennium Bridge and past the Tower of London to the Thames Barrier.

The Happisburgh footprints belong to the early Palaeolithic Era. They were made at a time when sea levels were lower than they are today, so while we know almost nothing of the Happisburgh group and whatever tribe they may have belonged to, we can be sure that they lived not on an island, but on a peninsula. The southern shore of the gulf into which the proto-Thames drained also formed the northern shore of a broad, chalk isthmus. Technically referred to as the Weald—Artois Anticline, but more commonly known as the Land Bridge, this isthmus connected the Peninsular Lands with the main body of the Western Lands, allowing men and animals to move freely back and forth. For the next 400,000 years, the Peninsular Lands appear to have been sparsely but more or less continuously inhabited by nomadic bands of humans who moved with the seasons, following the migration routes of the animals which provided their food. *Homo antecessor* was succeeded by *Homo heidelbergensis*, whose fossilised remains have been found in Eartham Pit, a disused quarry near Boxgrove in Surrey. Dating from 500,000 years ago, they are the oldest human remains yet found on the western side of the Land Bridge. Then, about 478,000 years ago, there came a period of intense glaciation during which the ice sheets advanced to cover some three-quarters of the land area of the Peninsula. Early man either died or moved south in search of a warmer climate. Towards the end of this glacial period, about 425,000 BC, the Land Bridge was breached, probably by a massive outburst flood, when a vast reservoir of glacial melt water suddenly burst through the ice sheets which had held it back. The Peninsula became an island, although only for what was – at least in geological terms – a short period. The climate warmed and the Land Bridge, though much eroded, reappeared. Movement to and from the Peninsula became possible again, and those who came belonged to a new species of human.[5]

Many traces of early man have been discovered relatively close to the western end of the Land Bridge, and the earliest Neanderthal remains yet found on the Peninsula were discovered at Swanscombe in Kent in the 1930s. They date from c.400,000 BC. Further Neanderthal remains, dating from c.225,000 BC were found in Bontnewydd near St Asaph in North Wales. They represent the most northerly evidence of Neanderthal habitation in the Western Lands. Neanderthals were skilled at making and using stone tools; they were capable of hunting big animals, such as mammoths; they knew how to butcher what they killed in a comparatively sophisticated manner; they could catch dolphins, sharks, crabs, and other seafood; and they used fire. Fossil records from across Europe allow us to reconstruct their physical way of life to a limited degree – though to a greater extent than any previous human species. Yet we can barely guess at their inner life. How closely did it approach that of modern man? Archaeological evidence indicates that they had some kind of social organisation. How did it work? They must have had a language that enabled them to cope with the practical tasks of hunting and surviving. How far beyond that did it go? Archaeological finds in Spain suggest that they used body paint, perhaps even make-up. In Spain, there is also evidence that they painted shapes on cave walls. Does this mean that they were capable of the kind of abstract thought which finds expression in art? What were they doing in those deep, dark caves in the first place? They must have had belief systems and rituals. One school of thought suggests that some cave art may be the product of the shamanic rituals involving psycho-active drugs; and drug residues have been identified in some centres of cave art. Does that explain their presence underground? Or were their beliefs based on the seasons? On the stars and astronomy? Or on fertility? Analogy with other so-called primitive tribes elsewhere in the world would make any or all of these ideas possible – even probable – but we cannot really know.[6]

Somewhere around the time of the Bontnewydd Neanderthals, the Land Bridge was again briefly severed by another outburst flood. It reappeared and, over the next twenty or thirty millennia, expanded or contracted in rhythm with the advances and retreats of the ice sheets and the consequent fluctuations in sea level. About 180,000 years ago, the ice sheets advanced once again, and the climate deteriorated to the point where the Neanderthals, like their predecessors, either died or moved south. There are no human fossils or traces of human life in the Peninsula for the next 120,000 years. The Neanderthals did return, but only – again in terms of the timescales we are considering here – for a comparatively short period.

Homo sapiens first emerged in Africa over 150,000 years ago. It took them over 100,000 years to reach the Continental Lands, and another 4,000 to reach the Peninsular Lands. The first evidence of their presence is the fossilised remains of a jawbone found in a cave in Devon and dated to approximately 41,000 years ago. At this stage *Homo sapiens* and Neanderthals overlapped. The nature and frequency of contact between the two species remains a mystery, but modern DNA analysis suggests that at some stage, or perhaps at several different stages, they interbred. What evidence we have, however, indicates that the two coexisted for a comparatively short time, after which the Neanderthals disappeared. The cause or causes of their extinction continue to be a matter for debate. Did they compete with *Homo sapiens* for hunting grounds? Did competition for food lead to physical confrontation and violence? It is possible, but in a sparsely populated landscape this can hardly explain the demise of a whole species. Or, like the Spaniards arriving in Mexico, did *Homo sapiens* bring new diseases to which the Neanderthals had no immunity? Recent research has raised the possibility of a link between the extinction and the eruption of the volcano Campi Flegrei, not far from present-day Naples. Volcanologists consider that the eruption, which took place between 39,200 and 39,400 years ago, was the biggest in Europe in the past 200,000 years. It threw some two hundred cubic kilometres of ash into the atmosphere with devastating effects on the climate. This scenario is persuasive in so far as there are no known Neanderthal sites in the Western Lands after 39,000 years ago, but it begs the question as to why *Homo sapiens* proved more resilient in the face sudden climatic change. Whatever caused the extinction, *Homo sapiens* was left the sole surviving human species.

The ice sheets advanced again and the consequent drop in sea levels was massive. The seas to the east of the Peninsular Lands simply disappeared. In their place was now a broad plain across which *Homo sapiens* chased the herds of giant deer and mammoths on which he relied for food. To the north and west of the Peninsula, the seas also receded so that the entire continental shelf became dry land. The Peninsula was no longer a peninsula, but part of a broad and gently undulating addition to the northwestern edge of the Western Lands, which included Orkney and Shetland

and stretched far out into the Atlantic. Only the southern third of what had been the Peninsula remained free of glaciation, and it was during this period that the 'Red Lady' of Paviland was buried in Goat's Hole Cave. Who he was, or what he was – tribal chief, elder, warrior, hunter, spiritual leader – we shall never know. However, his remains do give us a very brief glimpse of early *Homo sapiens*, what used to be called Cro-Magnon man, although archaeologists these days prefer the term 'European early modern human'. The fact that he was singled out for a special, ceremonial burial indicates a collective response and shared values among those who buried him. It also implies a sense, inculcated by some kind of belief system, that humankind exists in relation to time.

Glaciation intensified again about 25,000 years ago, and the Western Lands were once again abandoned. The Last Glacial Maximum, as it is known, buried most of the Main Island and the Western Isle under an ice sheet 1.5 kilometres thick. It was 10,000 years before the ice melted and humans returned. When they did, they hunted mammoth, red deer, reindeer, and wild horses, as well as smaller mammals such as hares and foxes, across what was probably a treeless, tundra-like landscape. Ivory weapons, tools, and beads, together with stone knives and axes, all dating from this period were found in Gough's Cave in the Cheddar Gorge. The same site revealed both animal and human bones. The human bones had had the flesh carved from them. Excarnation – the stripping of the flesh from the bones of the dead – was common throughout prehistory, but the fact that it appears to have been done in the same way and with the same stone tools used to butcher animals may well suggest cannibalism. If it does, then we have to ask whether this was 'everyday' cannibalism: cannibalism for food? Or was it cannibalism as a ritual associated with death: cannibalism as a means of ingesting and somehow sharing the experience or the courage or the wisdom of the dead? We cannot be sure, but it is worth noting that Gough's Cave also contained skulls apparently fashioned into drinking bowls, a practice in later times and in other parts of the world associated with tribal rituals.

An even more important discovery was made in 2003 in Robin Hood's Cave at Creswell Crags, a limestone gorge on the Nottinghamshire-Derbyshire border. Until then, no cave art had been discovered at any Palaeolithic site in the Peninsular Lands and the assumption was that, for whatever reason, there was none to discover. A simple and delicately

Map 2   A Sense of Perspective

beautiful outline engraving of a horse's head on a piece of rib, known as 'The Ochre Horse', had been discovered in the same location as long ago as 1876, but it had been categorised with other items of worked bone, such as beads and needles, and not as cave art. Now rough bas-reliefs of animals (stags, bison, horses, bears) and birds (notably an ibis) were identified on the walls and ceiling of the cave. Further research then identified the figures of dancing women, and marks which were taken to be stylised representations of female genitalia. Some of these identifications, made in the excitement of discovery, may have been a little enthusiastic and have subsequently been questioned. The cave was evidently a place of significance, but the nature of that significance remains obscure. Why, for example, should one drawing be made so deep inside the cave that it would have required artificial light to create it, and in a place where only one person at a time could see it, and then only by lying on their side in a confined space?[7] Could it represent some kind of shamanic test or initiation? Or an attempt to get close to the spiritual otherworld? The discovery of the Creswell carvings, which have been dated to 11,000 BC, was followed by the identification of a mammoth carved on the wall of Gough's Cave, and a reindeer on the wall of a cave in the Gower Peninsula, both dating from more or less the same period. None of these works bear comparison with the spectacular colour and detail of the cave art at Altamira in Spain, or Lascaux and Niaux in France, which date from between 15,000 and 17,000 years ago, but they do indicate some level of common culture among the widely-spread inhabitants of the Western Lands.

Reporting the Creswell discovery in 2004, the *National Geographic News*, said: 'The finding proved for the first time that ancient Britons were capable of producing artwork similar to that of their Palaeolithic (early Stone Age) counterparts on continental Europe'[8] – a statement which highlights the difficulties inherent in trying to describe 'prehistory' and its peoples. The Creswell carvers did not have any counterparts on Continental Europe because the lands across which they hunted were an integral part of the same continental land mass – which was not shaped like the European land mass we know today and was certainly not called Europe. For the same reason, while they may be described as 'Palaeolithic', 'Early Stone Age', or 'Ice Age' people, they cannot be called 'ancient Britons'. Britain did not exist. They were, as far as we can tell, just the same as any other group or tribe of seasonal hunters who roamed the Western Lands.

About 12,900 years ago, the temperature, which had been rising, dropped again quite suddenly – possibly because cold water from the melting ice sheets interrupted the Gulf Stream. This cold snap lasted about 1,300 years and the hunter-gatherer tribes who left their traces at Gough's Cave and Creswell Crags probably abandoned the area for most of that time. About 11,600 years ago, a slightly different group of hunter-gatherers made a brief appearance. Their main contribution seems to have been the introduction of the bow and arrow, and their main prey was reindeer, but after two or three hundred years they, too, were driven away by falling temperatures.[9] Another two or three hundred years and the climate began to recover again. Beginning somewhere around 9000 BC, fresh nomadic groups began to arrive. It was not a rapid process: the settlement – or resettlement – of the north-western edges of the Western Lands lasted some 5,000 years, but whatever climatic conditions or other difficulties they faced, these new people seem to have had the ability to adapt. Not only have the Peninsular Lands been continuously inhabited since that time, but DNA evidence suggests that the new arrivals made a significant contribution to the current gene pool. Their contribution has naturally enough been diluted over the millennia, but they remain the distant ancestors of many present-day British people.

2   Settling the Archipelago

Where did they come from, these new groups of hunter-gatherers?

The ice caps were melting, sea levels were rising, and the shape of the land was changing. The sea was encroaching from both north and south, reclaiming low-lying lands that had been sea in the past, so that the Peninsular Lands became a genuine peninsula once again, connected to the Continent by a new Land Bridge. The northern coast of this new Land Bridge stretched eastward from what would become the Wash, until it reached an unsubmerged area of the North Sea, known to archaeologists as Doggerland that was still connected to the Continental Lands. Doggerland, of course, survives as the shallow area of the North Sea known as the Dogger Bank. The southern coast of the Land Bridge was the head of a large estuary into which flowed both the proto-Thames and the proto-Rhine. Many of the new hunter-gatherers would have migrated from the Continental Lands, following the herds of reindeer and wild horses and populating the eastern side of the Peninsula. However, at much the same time, rising sea levels also had the effect of creating a new north—south channel on the western side of the Peninsular Lands, splitting off a new Western Isle from the main body of the Peninsula. Here, settlement followed a different pattern. DNA-based evidence emerging in recent years suggests that a significant proportion of the hunter-gatherer peoples who settled the Western Isle during the millennia following 9000 BC – and they seem to have favoured its east coast – came from northern Iberia, the Pyrenees, and the south-western corner of what is now France. Which means that they would have come by sea.

Once the Land Bridge was finally breached – probably between 5800 and 5400 BC – the sea would become of fundamental importance to life in the new Archipelago. Yet it is clear that even 2,000 years earlier there was an established channel of migration and communication running the length of Atlantic coastal waters, from Iberia to Armorica in the south to the coasts of the Western Isle and beyond, as far as the Northern and Far Northern Isles. Sea levels have risen significantly since then, and the remains of coastal camps, temporary settlements, and the boats on which their inhabitants depended for transport have long since disappeared under water, so archaeological evidence is lacking. However, there is nothing impossible in the scenario of groups of hunter-gathers making their way northward up the western shore of the Continental Lands, following the fishing grounds and shellfish beds, moving slowly, even taking generations on their journey. It is difficult otherwise to explain the appearance of settlements such as Mount Sandel in Coleraine, or Druimvargie near Oban, or on the Isle of Ulva in the Inner Hebrides – all of them dating from between 7000 and 4400 BC – or to explain the strength of the genetic link between these areas and Iberia. Over the millennia, the Atlantic seaways and their natural link to the Western Channel and the whole western side of the Archipelago would have a profound impact on the pattern of settlement and development of the Archipelago as a whole.

The coastal waters were rich in food. The excavation of middens on the Isle of Oronsay suggests that, unusually for Mesolithic times, people may have lived there all year round, or, perhaps more likely, returned for lengthy periods on a regular basis, relying on fish and seafood to sustain them. And the land was as food-rich as the sea. Indeed, the whole post-9000 BC colonisation of the Peninsular Lands may well have come about because of new and abundant sources of food resulting from climate change. What had been open tundra became pine forests and extensive woodlands of birch, alder, and hazel. What had been frozen ground became large expanses of boggy wetland. The forests were full of elk, roe deer, red deer, boar, and aurochs. The wetlands offered fish (although the archaeological absence of fish bones has led to suggestions that freshwater fish may have been taboo), as well as beavers and many kinds of birds: heron, stork, mallard, and other species of duck. Here were riches, but they had to be hunted in a different manner from reindeer and wild horses on the open plains. The hunters adapted. They developed tools for shaping wood to make better spears, harpoons, and arrows; and they used tips or blades with barbed edges to improve their chances of making a kill.

Up to this point, man had apparently been seasonally nomadic, migrating as the animals he hunted migrated. Now, for the first time anywhere in the Western Lands, we have evidence of longer-term settlement. Oronsay has already been mentioned. At Star Carr in Yorkshire, excavations of a two-hectare site on the edge of what was once a lake have revealed the remains of a structure some three-and-a-half metres wide, with a floor apparently lined with moss and reeds. It dates from over 10,500 years ago, making it the oldest man-made structure yet identified in the Peninsular Lands, and it was inhabited for somewhere between two hundred and five hundred years. A similar structure, dating from 7600 BC and inhabited for at least a hundred years, was found at Howick in Northumberland. Another house of roughly the same age, oval in shape with thirty uprights probably supporting a large conical roof, was found at East Barns, near Dunbar. At Mount Sandel, positioned on a hilltop overlooking the River Bann in County Londonderry, archaeologists have uncovered what is at present the earliest known human settlement in the Western Isle. Excavations here revealed evidence of circular wood-framed structures up to five metres in diameter, as well as pits for storing food. Radiocarbon dating locates it in the middle of the eighth millennium BC, somewhere between 7900 and 7600 BC. Were such sites inhabited permanently? Or were they bases from which the hunters set out on seasonal migrations? And did these sites also have some spiritual or ritual significance? Whatever the case, the discovery of these house-like structures has challenged the long-held assumption that Mesolithic hunters were wholly nomadic; and it has also moved back by up to 4,000 years the date at which men in the Western Lands were thought to have built houses and created longer-term or semi-permanent settlements.

Sea levels continued to rise – sometimes faster, sometimes more slowly – narrowing the Land Bridge and flooding many coastal valleys. Around 6000 BC, one such valley on the southern coast of the Peninsula was home to a thriving seasonal or semi-permanent community. The sea which submerged it and the silt which covered it, have preserved much organic evidence that would not have survived on land of how people lived at the time. The valley where the community lived has become the Solent, the strait separating the Isle of Wight from the mainland, and the archaeological site at Bouldnor Cliff, near Yarmouth, is now eleven metres below sea level. It was first identified when a diver saw flint tools being ejected from a lobster's burrow. Despite the difficulties posed by the depth and the strong coastal current, the site has produced some striking finds. There are worked timbers, suggesting the construction of dwellings, shelters, and also boats – making it the earliest known boat-building site in the world. There is a wooden pipe, perhaps for water; and there are fibres twisted to form what appears to be string. All this indicates that the people who lived in the valley were developing skills and employing tools in a way not previously thought to have been current until the beginning of the Neolithic period, some 2,000 years later. The same site has also yielded grains of wheat, the earliest to be found in the Peninsular Lands, and DNA extracted from them matches strains originating in the Near East.[10] It seems unlikely that people living on the southern edge of the Peninsula 8,000 years ago were in direct contact with tribes living far away across the continental land mass, but it is certainly possible that they were at the end of a chain of communication along which goods were traded or exchanged.[11]

We do not know when rising sea levels made Bouldnor Cliff uninhabitable, but an event that may have played a part occurred around 5800 BC. Geological evidence suggests that a massive submarine landslide somewhere off the north-west coast of Norway – perhaps caused by an earthquake – triggered a huge tsunami, which swept southwards inundating much of Doggerland, breaking through the Land Bridge and swamping many coastal areas. Once the flood waters receded, the Land Bridge re-established itself, but not for long. One imagines a gradual process with the sea rising and advancing, changing the character of the low-lying lands, creating salt marsh, cutting new channels and widening estuaries. Perhaps in the later stages the connection was reduced to tidal mud flats or sand bars, allowing men and animals to cross only at low tide. Once the barrier was breached, tidal currents would scour the shallow waters, deepening and widening the narrow channel and turning it into a broad seaway. However and whenever it happened, we can be certain that there was a moment towards the end of the Mesolithic Era, when the Peninsular Lands became an offshore archipelago.

What can this story tell us that is relevant to our lives today? In terms specific to the British Isles, very little, beyond the obvious fact that the

2 Settling the Archipelago

origins of the British Isles and its people are inextricably bound up with those of the European Continent and its inhabitants. The idea that Britain and the British (or just as often England and the English) are somehow different by virtue of their separation from the Continent has a long history. It is there in the pronouncements justifying the English Reformation; Shakespeare draws on it in John of Gaunt's 'this sceptred isle' speech; it was accepted by many as the legitimising basis of Empire; and it came to the fore in the debate surrounding the United Kingdom's departure from the European Union. It is a theme we shall examine in this study, but we can say at the outset that it has no basis in prehistory. We cannot know what a *Homo sapiens* of the time would have thought as he stood looking across a narrow stretch of water to an opposite shore: a shore which in his father's time, or perhaps during his own childhood, had been accessible on foot, but now required a boat. In all likelihood he would have felt more connection than separation. In terms of species and race and – we can only presume – culture and language, he would have been little, if at all, different from members of the tribes on the opposite shore.

The people of the new Archipelago gathered in small communities, groups or tribes. Most would have migrated seasonally – perhaps from a winter home camp to spring and summer hunting grounds, or from low to high ground – following their sources of food. Logic, supplemented by anthropological observation from elsewhere in the world, suggests that the extended family would have formed the basic organising principle of tribal society. Archaeologists have estimated that Mesolithic settlements in the interior of the Main Island could have supported populations of between twenty-five and fifty inhabitants, while those closer to the coast where food was easier to come by could have supported between one and two hundred. Beyond that, we can only guess as to how these people organised themselves socially or politically. Their settlements show evidence of communal and collective activity. Hunting was clearly a cooperative business. Someone had to make decisions and give the orders. Was it a patriarch, a tribal chief, a group of elders, the senior hunter or hunters? And was the practical decision-maker supported by a spiritual leader? We do not know how one tribe related to another; whether hunting grounds were claimed by a particular tribe, shared with others, or contested. Nor do we know how big the population was. Estimates, which are little more than guesswork, range from as few as 3,000 to 20,000 or more, but even

20,000 may still be a conservative figure. As more sites are identified and research continues, so we are being brought to the realisation that our ancestors were in many respects more sophisticated and probably more numerous than was previously assumed.

The word 'ancestors' is chosen deliberately. In 1903, a complete male skeleton was found in Gough's Cave, the oldest complete skeleton found in the Peninsular Lands. It has been dated to about 7150 BC and subsequently nicknamed 'Cheddar Man'. In 1997, DNA testing showed that Adrian Targett, a retired history teacher from Somerset, born in 1955, shared a maternal ancestor with Cheddar Man. Further testing and analysis have led scientists to conclude that members of the current British population who do not have a recent history of immigration share approximately ten per cent of their ancestry with the population to which Cheddar Man belonged. Few other skeletons from this period survive from burial sites in the Peninsular Lands, perhaps adding weight to the theory that the dead were usually dismembered, and the flesh cut from their bones. Aveline's Hole, a cave in the Mendip Hills, was discovered at the end of the eighteenth century and excavated in 1860. Unfortunately, many of the finds have been lost, but we do know that the cave contained the bones of some fifty individuals and two full skeletons. Recent tests on some of the bones that remain indicate that they were, on average, around 1.52 metres tall, and had a life expectancy of less than thirty years. Traces of red ochre (recalling the Red Lady of Paviland) and the presence of carefully placed ammonite fossils show that at least some of the bodies had been decorated or adorned, and we can speculate that the placing of their remains in the cave was accompanied by some kind of ceremony or ritual. Given the apparent rarity of such burials, we can only suppose Aveline's Hole was site of particular religious or spiritual significance.

The lives of Mesolithic people will inevitably remain largely closed to us. They are too far away. The archaeological data are often difficult to interpret, and we can never do more than speculate upon their thought processes, rituals, and beliefs. The fact that some of the surviving cave markings have been interpreted as representing female forms or female genitalia, coupled with analogous discoveries in the Continental Lands, suggest a focus on fertility – although one cannot assume that all tribes held the same beliefs and observed the same ritual practices. The moon may also have been a focus of attention. At Warren Field in Aberdeenshire,

Map 3 Settling the Archipelago

archaeologists have excavated twelve pits, dating from around 8000 BC, which, it has been claimed, are arranged in such a way as to act as a lunar calendar – though this interpretation has been disputed.[12]

In this context, it is worth noting that, while modern societies would separate the religious function of such a monument from the practical function of marking the passing of time and the changing of the seasons, prehistoric societies are highly unlikely to have made – indeed, probably could not have made – such a distinction. Nor should we conclude that the combination of images connected with fertility and an interest in the moon indicate the kind of matriarchal religion or goddess cult often attributed to early societies, such as the Minoan civilisation in Crete. The concept of matriarchal religion, like invasion theory, has its origins in the mid-nineteenth century and is now widely challenged, if not discredited.[13] It is much more likely that the rituals practised across the Western Lands were broadly shamanistic in nature. At Star Carr, for example, headdresses made from red deer skulls with the antlers still attached have been discovered, suggesting some sort of shamanistic ritual designed to ensure the continuing fertility of the animal which made up a significant part of the local diet. Other finds at Star Carr seem to confirm that it was a centre of ritual activity. The discovery of a large, wooden platform at the lake edge – quite possibly the earliest evidence of carpentry in the Western Lands – may also indicate ritual activity. As we shall see, right up to the Roman occupation and beyond, water, particularly fresh water, was a recurring element in religious belief and ritual.

Archaeologists and historians frequently fall back on ritual to explain facts or phenomena which they cannot interpret in any other way. At the same time, it does seem – and studies of analogous pre-technological cultures confirm – that for prehistoric peoples, as for many people in early historical periods, the spiritual world was an ever-present feature of their lives. The moon, the seasons, the fertility of the natural world, water: all probably had a place in their belief systems – along with the ancestors, and the animals they hunted and ate. Excarnation seems to have been a common method of dealing with the dead. Yet, as we have seen, some individuals were apparently singled out for special treatment, their corpses decorated or adorned but otherwise left untouched. What was the purpose of this? The association between art and beauty and religion was understood in Egypt under the pharaohs. It is there in the great temple complexes of Cambodia and Indonesia; in the glorious churches and mosaics of Byzantium; in the great masterpieces of Islamic art; even in the Church of England under Charles I and Archbishop Laud, and during the Oxford Movement in the nineteenth century. It is a human universal; and it is not too fanciful to see its distant beginnings in the Mesolithic Era.

However, given what we know of other pre-technological societies, it is equally reasonable to assume that the adornment of the dead would have a deeper purpose than simply honouring their achievements in life. It would also have reflected a need to propitiate the spirit of the dead person which, in death, might still have had the ability to influence the living. Most attempts to reconstruct early belief systems see death as marking a transition from the world of the living to the world of the ancestors. In terms of the Mesolithic era, this is speculation, but the concept is implicit in the way the Egyptians treated their elite in death, and it is explicit in some of the earliest Greek and Roman documentary sources. It is not unreasonable to assume that the ancestors remained a central element in belief systems from the earliest times right up to Roman times and beyond. However, given that we are talking about a period of several millennia, it is equally likely that the role and function of the ancestors, and the manner in which they were propitiated, evolved and changed as society developed.

Beliefs and belief systems are created by humankind: they represent an intellectual and emotional response to the world about us, to things we cannot otherwise explain or understand. Art is also an intellectual and emotional response to the world as we perceive it. There is very little art surviving in the Peninsular Lands from the pre-Neolithic period (see Chapter 1). The oldest item, discovered as recently as 2015 at Star Carr, is a shale pendant engraved with incised lines, some parallel, some crossing each other. These have been subject to various interpretations: an abstract pattern; a stylised representation of a tree; a conceptual map of the structures of the Star Carr settlement. In the end, the pendant may well have been a purely decorative item, but we cannot be sure. What about the bison and the ibis on the wall of Creswell Crags? Are they simply mimetic? Are they the work of a hunter relaxing and celebrating after a successful hunt? Or is the mimesis a form of communication? If so, what is the message and who is it for? Is it addressed to the spiritual otherworld, perhaps offering thanks for the bounty of the kill? More prosaically, might it tell other hunters passing that way what food can be found in the surrounding region? Or is it for the tribe itself? Could it be a kind of hunting *aide-memoire* for the next time they found themselves in the region; or a teaching aid for the children and younger members of the tribe, a guide to what is dangerous and what can be eaten?

Whatever the answers to these questions, the belief systems and the art of Mesolithic man – however little we know of them, and however difficult it is to interpret what we do know – mark the beginning of the spiritual, intellectual, creative and artistic history of what would become the British Isles. That they were shared to a greater or lesser extent with tribes across the narrow sea on the main body of the Continent does not alter or diminish that fact. It only emphasises the fact that our intellectual and artistic heritage, like our racial and technological heritage, is a shared one.

Between 1919 and 1920, H.G. Wells published his *Outline of History* in twenty-four fortnightly instalments, which were later collected and published in book form. It sold over two million copies and was hugely influential, offering a fascinating overview of historical thought at the beginning of the twentieth century. The illustration on the cover of the second part depicts two naked, hairy, savage-looking figures at the entrance to a rush-strewn cave that has bones and a skull on the floor. In a wholly different context, Douglas Adams' *Hitchhiker's Guide to the Galaxy*, first broadcast in 1978, includes a radio station announcer somewhere in the galaxy saying 'and we'll be saying a big hello to all intelligent life forms everywhere … and to everyone else out there, the secret is to bang the rocks together, guys.'[14] The traditional image of early man as cave man – primitive, physical, driven by instinct rather than reason – is long established and dies hard. William Golding's *The Inheritors* (1955) attempted to project a more subtle image but gained little traction. Perhaps we like to think of our remote ancestors as primitive because we can then flatter ourselves how far we have come.

The truth is somewhat different. Certainly, practical technologies took a long time to develop and be adopted – a very long time indeed when compared to the pace of change which seems normal to us in the twenty-first century. Yet archaeologists are constantly being surprised at how early certain skills and technologies made their appearance, and, as a consequence, have been forced to reassess and adjust their overall view of the period. The situation would have varied from tribe to tribe and from region to region across the Archipelago but, on the whole, while they may have lacked what we consider the essential amenities of life, the Mesolithic population lived relatively ordered, relatively comfortable lives. They also appear to have had a varied diet and been relatively healthy. They may well have skirmished with neighbouring tribes, but theirs does not appear to have been a society ruled by violence. They would have had linguistic skills of some sophistication and a set of spiritual or religious beliefs, including honouring the dead, which were expressed in ritual activity, potentially of some complexity. They were not cave-dwelling savages living on the edge of starvation.

3   Paths across the Sea

From the severing of the Land Bridge somewhere in the middle of the sixth millennium BC until Friday, 7 January 1785 AD, the only way to travel between the Archipelago and the Continental Lands was by sea. On that day, the French inventor, Jean-Pierre Blanchard, and his American colleague, the scientist and surgeon John Jeffries, flew in a hydrogen balloon from Dover to Guînes in the Pas de Calais. It was an achievement for the record books, but not one which had an immediate, broader impact. It was over a hundred and twenty years later, in 1909, that Louis Blériot took off from Calais in his Type XI monoplane and made the first powered flight across the Channel. During the First World War, German Zeppelins made return crossings in order to drop bombs on England. Then, after the war, progress was rapid. Commercial air passenger services began in 1919, growing steadily and, during the 1920s and 30s, beginning to exercise a cultural and, to a lesser extent, economic influence. By the 1970s air travel had become the norm for most people leaving or arriving in the Archipelago. But for 7,500 years access to the Archipelago was wholly dependent on sea travel. People, animals, goods, books, papers – everything had to travel by sea.

In the twenty-first century, travel usually means the motorway, the train, or a scheduled flight. It is easy to forget that for thousands of years – from the time mankind learnt to paddle a hollowed-out tree trunk until the coming of the railways in the nineteenth century – sea travel was faster and more efficient than travel over land. In the 1,500 years between the final severing of the Land Bridge and the arrival of the first representatives of Neolithic culture in the Archipelago, sea levels rose. Tidal currents eroded the coasts and scoured the seabed, widening and deepening the seaways. Nonetheless, it is clear that the seafaring abilities of those who inhabited the coastal areas of both the Continent and the Archipelago kept pace with the changes. The world's oldest known boat is the Pesse canoe, a hollowed-out tree trunk, found in Holland and dating from approximately 8000 BC; we have seen evidence of boat building at Bouldnor Cliff about 6000 BC; and a dugout dating from the end of the fourth millennium BC was found in the Boyne Valley in Ireland. We can assume that dugouts – usually referred to as logboats – would have been the craft used for the earliest river travel and the earliest inshore travel up and down Atlantic coastal waters. Ordinary logboats, propelled by paddles, may have risked deeper waters, and there is some evidence that they could have been fitted with outriggers, or that two or three logboat hulls may have been connected side-by-side. Either method would have given them greater stability and increased their seaworthiness, but logboats would not really have been suitable for longer sea journeys. Nonetheless, such journeys were made – precisely how, we shall discuss later in this chapter – and we can say with certainty that the final severing of the Land Bridge did not result in the new Archipelago being in any sense isolated or cut off.

Everything we know about Mesolithic people has been pieced together from fragmentary archaeological remains. They left no marks on the landscape; they left no written records; and we have no way of knowing anything about their language. The archaeological record indicates the presence of social organisation and religious belief, which in turn suggests relatively sophisticated linguistic skills – although in the absence of evidence that must remain an inference. With the exception of a few enigmatic cave drawings and the equally enigmatic Star Carr pendant, they left no images to explain or comment on their world. With the coming of what is often known, in a convenient piece of historical shorthand, as the Neolithic Revolution, at least some of that begins to change. Neolithic people remain remote from us. We still have no knowledge of their language or languages or of what they thought, but we can at least see – and try to interpret – the results of their thoughts and actions carved into or built upon the landscape.

Reduced to essentials, the Neolithic Revolution marked a change in human behaviour from a nomadic, hunter-gatherer lifestyle to one characterised by settlement and agriculture, both the growing of crops and the domestication and breeding of animals. It was radical and, in the Archipelago at least, it was rapid, thereby perhaps justifying the use of the term 'revolution'. Indeed, the Neolithic Revolution may represent the greatest change in human lifestyle and the human condition in the history of our species. The Communication and Information Revolution which began with the steam engine and continues into our own time with the internet and nanotechnology may well run it close, but that remains to be seen.

The idea and the practice of agriculture appears to have developed independently in several different regions of the world – among them, the so-called Fertile Crescent in the Middle East, the Yangtze and Yellow River Valleys in China, central Mexico, the north-west of South America – all within a millennium or two of each other. The agricultural techniques that eventually made their way to the Archipelago originated in the Fertile Crescent about 8000 BC. Whether through migration, acculturation, or a mixture of both, they spread westwards through the Levant and westwards again across the expanse of the Continental Lands. In very broad terms, we can trace two branches of Neolithic culture, both of which eventually arrived in the Archipelago. The first travelled across the Mediterranean to the Italian Peninsula, the south of what is now France, and Iberia, before following the Atlantic coast northwards until it reached Armorica. The second branch spread up the Danube Valley, into the North European Plain and eastwards to the Channel and North Sea coasts, where it arrived a century or two later. The important point here is that the Neolithic culture which reached the western shores of the Continent was not necessarily homogenous – and here, we have to assume that acculturation played a role. Either the existing coastal population absorbed Neolithic culture, or, perhaps more likely given what we now know of Neolithic origins, those who brought Neolithic culture to the Continental coasts absorbed maritime culture. One or the other must have happened. Otherwise, Neolithic ideas could not have made the crossing to the Archipelago.

The first wave or phase of Neolithic culture reached the shores of the Archipelago between 4300 and 4200 BC – although there are isolated instances of earlier Neolithic settlements. Increasingly accurate radiocarbon dating techniques now indicate that Neolithic culture spread more rapidly than previously thought. By 3800 BC, it had had a significant impact and had become the dominant cultural strain in many, if not most, parts of the Archipelago. Exactly how this occurred, how Neolithic ideas and practices were transmitted and how they achieved the dominance they did, has been the subject of much debate.

Advocates of invasion theory seem to have envisaged an aggressive mass migration which overran the existing Mesolithic peoples and their culture. This idea was widely discredited and replaced with theories based on acculturation (see 'Groundwork'). New concepts and practices, it was suggested, would have been transmitted in the course of regular exchanges with tribes on the Continent – exchanges combining elements of trade with kinship and 'political' visits – and those exposed to Neolithic ideas in this way would then have passed them on to their families and their neighbours. However, in 2019, a study led by London's Natural History Museum concluded that the Neolithic Revolution in the Archipelago was, after all, driven by migration. The study was based on DNA extracted from six Mesolithic skeletons (including Cheddar man) and forty-six Neolithic skeletons. Its central finding was that Neolithic migrants had largely replaced the previous population; or, more precisely, that after the arrival of Neolithic migrants, the genetic legacy of the existing hunter-gatherer population was very significantly diminished.[15] Moreover, the DNA extracted from the Neolithic skeletons makes it clear that migration to the Archipelago was dominated by people who had their distant origins in the Aegean. They belonged to that branch of Neolithic culture which crossed the Mediterranean to southern France and to Iberia; and from there they moved northwards to the Archipelago. This mirrors the route taken by those early Mesolithic peoples who settled the Western and Northern Isles and emphasises the vital importance of the western seaways as a channel of communication and cultural transmission – something we shall see time and time again. The second group, belonging to that strand of Neolithic culture which migrated up the Danube Valley and across the Western Lands, reached the Archipelago from the east. However, DNA evidence suggests that this group was smaller and less genetically influential. These results confirm archaeological evidence that Neolithic culture arrived earlier in the west of the Archipelago than the east – and this, in turn, fits with our understanding of the broader movement of Neolithic peoples across the Continent

What drove these migrants? Were they searching for a climate and soils suited to agriculture? Or were there pressures of some kind in the Continental Lands encouraging or forcing migration? We can only guess at the numbers involved, but they must have been substantial – at least relative to the population of the Western Lands as a whole – and the impact on the genetic make-up of the Archipelago may well be explained simply by numbers. Estimates of the Mesolithic population of the Archipelago are largely conjecture (see Chapter 2), but even if the true figure were three times current estimates – say, 60,000 people – a steady flow of migrants over several centuries would have a significant genetic impact. Such a scenario does away with the need to suppose that the existing population was displaced or replaced. They may have integrated with the new arrivals, become fully acculturated, but in the end been overwhelmed by sheer numbers to the point where they left only a much-reduced genetic legacy. Several questions then arise. Did the migrants and the Mesolithic population share a common language? (The issue of language is one to which we will return.) Did they mix? Did they interbreed? Current DNA evidence suggests probably not, or not much. What little we know suggests that Mesolithic people were darker skinned with blue eyes, whereas the Neolithic arrivals were lighter skinned with brown eyes. However, these results cannot yet be considered conclusive, as studies based on larger samples may well reach different conclusions. Once again, the explanation may lie in the disparity in size between the two groups. The evidence we have today – and it is limited – tends to support the idea that the existing population was swamped rather than destroyed.

Neolithic society was radically different from that of its Mesolithic hunter-gatherer predecessors, but certain components of Neolithic culture were, albeit to a limited extent, already present in the pre-Neolithic way of life. We have identified a number of long-term settlements. There is evidence for the loose herding of animals – where the herd is followed and observed, but not closely penned in what we would regard as the traditional manner and only tended at certain times of year. There is also evidence for the management of woodland, such as pruning to produce crops of hazelnuts and coppicing to produce withies. To some extent, therefore, Neolithic ideas would have required the elaboration and development of things already partially understood rather than the imposition of wholly new concepts. Several sites have been found where evidence of Neolithic habitation overlies that from the Mesolithic period, suggesting that they remained in use during the period of cultural transition. This, in turn, suggests continuity rather than upheaval or dislocation. So, too, does the fact that Neolithic practices were not adopted wholesale or uniformly across the Archipelago. Many areas were cleared and used for crops and grazing, but it is clear that hunter-gathering did not die out completely or immediately. It continued in areas where there was an abundance of natural supply. Along the western shores of the High North, where communities lived close to the shore and relied heavily on fish and seafood, it took a millennium or more for the Neolithic Revolution to take hold. Francis Pryor, in *Britain B.C.*, draws attention to coastal communities on either side of the Western Channel which adopted certain useful components of Neolithic culture, such as pottery and polished stone axes, but otherwise saw no reason to modify what appears to have been a stable and sustainable lifestyle.[16] Given the distance in time and the limited amount of evidence available, definitive conclusions are impossible, but the evidence we have – and the new, scientific archaeology is increasing our knowledge all the time – does indicate that the Neolithic Revolution in the Archipelago was in large measure driven by migration.

In his examination of the spread of Neolithic culture, Barry Cunliffe has identified several maritime contact zones between the Archipelago and the Continent.[17] This study will use a slightly simplified version of his scheme – and in defining the zones we must necessarily use modern place names to avoid confusion.

• The Atlantic Zone linked Iberia, the coast of the Bay of Biscay, Brittany, and the Cotentin Peninsula with the western side of the British Isles: South-West England, South Wales, the western coast of Great Britain right up to Orkney and the Shetland Isles, and the whole of Ireland.

• The Channel Zone linked the French coast from the eastern side of the Cotentin Peninsula to Dunkirk with southern England from the Isle of Wight to the south side of Thames Estuary.

• The Southern North Sea Zone linked the European coast from Dunkirk to the north of Holland with the north side of the Thames Estuary to the north Norfolk coast.

• The Eastern Zone, open to influences from Holland, Denmark and Scandinavia, stretched from north Norfolk all the way to Orkney and the Shetland Isles.

These zones were dictated by coastal geography, but their influence and their importance were increased by ability of migrants to penetrate inland by travelling upriver from the sea. So, in both Neolithic times and later ages, those arriving across the Southern North Sea Zone and the Eastern Zone were able to navigate the Thames, Great Ouse, Nene, Trent

1 Limavady
2 Boyne Valley
3 Ferriter's Cove
4 Brigg

Map 4   Paths across the Sea

and Derwent right into the centre of the Main Island. We cannot tell precisely when links across these zones were first established. It would be natural to assume that the shorter and safer routes across the Channel Zone developed first in the aftermath of the disappearance of the Land Bridge, but we have already seen how the Atlantic Zone was an effective channel of movement and communication from the earliest times. Nor can we tell with what frequency voyages were made, although given what we now know about the scale of Neolithic migration, they were evidently more than occasional. What is clear, however, is that these routes remained in use and remained influential throughout the Neolithic period and into subsequent eras. More important still, the differences between the zones left a legacy, most notably an east-west divide on the Main Island that had, and arguably still has, a significant cultural impact.

One of the earliest Neolithic sites in the Archipelago is Ferriter's Cove, a small bay situated at the furthest point of the Dingle Peninsula in the far south-west of the Western Isle. It was a site visited by Mesolithic people regularly over a long period of time, but there is also clear evidence of

Neolithic occupation, including the bones of sheep and cattle not native to the Western Isle and dating from *c.*4350 BC. So how did they get there? Clearly, they came by sea – the date is far too early for Neolithic culture to have spread across from the Main Island – but how?

Logboats with outriggers could certainly have carried a handful of individuals from the Continental Lands to the Archipelago. They could also have carried a few sacks of grain, enough to sow a small area which, given a season or two, might have given enough seed corn or barley to sow a few fields. But it would have been difficult for logboats to carry cows, sheep, or pigs, especially in the numbers necessary to start a breeding herd. Rafts – either tree trunks lashed together with leather ropes, or planks laid across three or more logboats to form a stable platform – are one possibility, but they would have been difficult to steer and would have had limited freeboard. The earliest known raft found in the Archipelago dates from a much later period, between 860 and 820 BC, and would not have been seaworthy. It was discovered at Brigg in Lincolnshire and probably served as a ferry to cross the River Ancholme.

A more advanced kind of prehistoric craft was the sewn-plank boat, constructed of thick oak planks sewn together with yew withies, caulked with moss, and finished with oak laths. Seven of them have been discovered in the Archipelago: three at Ferriby on the north shore of the Humber estuary, one at Kilnsea on the farthest tip of the same estuary, one at Dover, one on Southampton Water, and one on the Bristol Channel. They all date from between 2030 to 1500 BC, so again we have no evidence of their use in Neolithic times. The best-preserved example, known as Ferriby 1, would have been 13.1 metres long and 1.7 metres wide. The Dover boat was probably about the same length, although only 9.5 metres of it survives, but, with a beam of 2 metres, it was wider. Both would have had room for eighteen men with paddles. Replicas have been made and launched, but questions remain about the seaworthiness of such craft, especially about their freeboard when fully laden or in rough water, and their distribution strongly suggests that they were used for estuary and coastal work. The Dover boat, with its slightly broader beam and pointed prow, would probably have been capable of making the journey back and forth across the Channel in calm weather conditions, but it is unlikely that sewn-plank boats could have crossed the North Sea safely or made longer voyages in the exposed Atlantic seaways.

Neolithic sea crossings of any length or duration were probably made in wooden-framed, hide-covered boats. No remains of any craft of this type dating from the Neolithic period have been found, but this is not surprising, given that they were made from easily degradable materials. However, researchers extrapolating from other evidence have concluded that hide boats may well have been in use in parts of northern Europe as early as 9500 BC.[18] There is also documentary evidence for the use of hide boats, although admittedly from many centuries later. Chronologically, the first actual reference is by the Greek historian, Timaeus (c.350–260 BC). Writing in the third century BC, he describes boats made of osier covered with skins stitched together and says that people he calls 'the Britons' made voyages of six days to reach the Continent. This was not first-hand knowledge: Timaeus was born in Sicily and, as far as we know, never went further afield than Athens. He was probably drawing on a now lost work by Pytheas (c.350–285 BC), a Greek geographer who, some years earlier, probably about 325 BC, made a voyage of exploration during which he may have circumnavigated the island he called *Prettanikēi*. This is a voyage to which we shall return. In 55 and 54 BC, during his raids on what was by that time called Britannia, Julius Caesar took careful note of how the ships of the Britons were built and rigged. A few years later in 49 BC, while on campaign in Spain, he told his legionaries to build boats 'of the kind his knowledge of Britain a few years earlier had taught him. First, the keels and ribs were made of light timber, then the rest of the hull ... was made of wickerwork and covered with hides.'[19] Pliny the Elder, in the first century AD, and Solinus, in the third, also refer to sea-going craft covered in skins. So, too, does Avienus, in his poem *Ora Maritima* (*Sea Coasts*), which, although written in the fourth century AD, is probably based on information from a Greek *periplus* or seafaring manual from the sixth century BC. Then there is St Brendan who, in the early years of the sixth century AD, set out with his companions in a leather-covered boat on a voyage which we are told lasted seven years – although the details of this expedition were not recorded until the ninth century AD. In the west of Ireland, such boats, known as *currachs* (or *curraghs*) are still in use, although they usually stretch canvas rather than animal skins over the wooden frame. Elsewhere in Ireland, and in Scotland and Wales, small circular or oval craft of similar construction, known as coracles, are still used for fishing in lakes and rivers.

Hide- or leather-covered boats of sufficient size to make a sea voyage were evidently a well-established part of life on Atlantic coastal waters in the first millennium BC. They would have had sufficient beam and freeboard to transport men and animals between the Continent and the Archipelago. The question is whether they were in use three thousand years earlier. Literary evidence cannot help here and may even be misleading. The documentary sources quoted above were written by men to whom the Atlantic seaboard in general and hide-covered boats in particular were new and unfamiliar. They recorded what was to them unusual, even surprising, and can give no indication of the history of such craft. However, given the extent and frequency of communication between the Continent and the Archipelago during the Neolithic era, some kind of craft significantly larger than a logboat must have been in use long before the first millennium BC. Despite the lack of archaeological evidence, hide-covered boats offer the most practical and seaworthy solution. Such boats may even have been in use before the arrival of Neolithic culture – their size, safety and seaworthiness no doubt improving with the passing millennia – but we have no way of knowing.

How were the boats which travelled between the Archipelago and the Continent propelled? And how were they navigated? If weather and sea conditions were reasonable, experienced mariners could have paddled logboats with outriggers across the Channel Zone. They could also have paddled the shorter routes across the Western Channel, perhaps using the Halfway Isle as a staging point. Where the longer sea crossings of the Atlantic and Southern North Sea Zones are concerned, we have to assume they sailed. In 1896, two ploughmen working in a field near Limavady in County Derry, not far from the shore of Lough Foyle, uncovered a collection of gold objects known as the Broighter Hoard. The most striking item was a model of a hide-covered boat. It dates from the first century BC, so we cannot assume that it represents the vessels that brought Neolithic culture to the Archipelago 4,000 years earlier, but the evident sophistication of its design suggests a well-established technology. The model is 18.4 centimetres long and 7.6 centimetres wide. Broad in the beam, with nine thwarts and positions for eighteen oarsmen, it has a stern-mounted steering oar, and a mast and spar indicating that it would have carried a square-rigged sail.

We know that the Phoenicians were sailing square-rigged ships into the Atlantic and making their way as far north as Galicia in the north-west of the Iberian Peninsula by the eighth century BC. It has been suggested that their example taught the inhabitants of the Atlantic-facing coasts how to use sails, but wind and tide are powerful forces in Atlantic waters – more powerful than in the Mediterranean – and it must be probable that sailing and navigational skills developed independently along the shores of the Atlantic Zone. Without the ability to cross the seas in relative safety, Neolithic culture could not have migrated to the Archipelago. It is difficult to believe that hide-covered boats travelling back and forth between Armorica and the South-Western Peninsula or the Western Isle in the third and fourth millennia BC, possibly loaded with live animals or sacks of grain, were propelled only by oars or paddles. Neolithic peoples were practical and sophisticated. They must surely have developed their own seagoing craft with square-rigged, hide or leather sails.

Similar considerations apply to navigation. On a clear day, the shortest routes between the Continent and the Main Island, or between the Main Island, the Halfway Isle, and Western Isle, are navigable by eye. Coastal or river travel, both essential for the spread of Neolithic people and culture in the Archipelago, would have posed few problems. However, longer voyages would have taken the boats and their crews out of sight of land for three or four days at a time. Again, Ferriter's Cove provides a good example. The Neolithic elements of the settlement pre-date the earliest evidence of Neolithic settlement on the Main Island, so the animals, the pottery and other objects discovered there must have come from the Continent, probably from Armorica. We can imagine a number of small boats hugging the coast as far as Ushant, before crossing to the South-Western Peninsula. From there, they might again hug the coast until they could cross to the Western Isle, and then follow its southern and western coasts until they reached their destination. Such a course would have minimised the amount of time out of sight of land, but it would still have been a daunting voyage in an open boat of whatever kind.

A group of Neolithic mariners crossing the Southern North Sea Zone, whether east-west or west-east, had at least the certainty that they would make landfall at some point. The Atlantic Zone, with much more powerful currents and the possibility of being swept out into the open ocean, presented a much greater challenge. How could open boats have made voyages lasting four, even five or six days without any navigational tools that we would recognise today? The magnetic compass was known in China in the third century BC, but it was not used for maritime navigation in either China or Europe until the twelfth century AD. An early astrolabe was invented in Greece in the second century BC, but it was not used for navigational purposes until the fourteenth or fifteenth century AD. Yet if we look at the barrows, tombs, henges, and stone circles of the Neolithic period, their design, orientation, and alignment all indicate that there were people in Neolithic society who had a deep and practical understanding of astronomy – an understanding that certainly extended to the position of sun, moon and visible stars and the timing of solstices. The fact that their astronomical knowledge found expression in these monuments strongly suggests that it was linked to their belief systems: it may even have been the perquisite of some elite brotherhood or priestly caste. And it is clear that, if applied to navigation at sea, the level of astronomical understanding displayed on land would have made longer sea voyages a practicable proposition.

An ability to set or estimate a course by the stars, by the rising or setting of the moon and sun, would have been essential for such voyages. Other skills would also have been necessary: a knowledge of tidal flows and major currents; an ability to read cloud formations, to interpret the flight of birds and other natural signs; the capacity to recognise and distinguish particular landfalls. Such skills would have been passed down from one generation of seafarers to the next. The mariners who launched their boats into the rough waters of the Atlantic or the North Sea had to have both ability and courage. The sea is dangerous; there were enormous risks and no doubt many perished; yet many more must have made the journey successfully. The archaeological evidence is indisputable: a whole new way of life was transported to the Archipelago and spread northwards along its eastern and western shores. Navigation has always had an aura of mystery about it, a sense of man probing the secrets of the universe. That sense is present in the narratives of the great fifteenth- and sixteenth-century voyagers – Cabot, Columbus, da Gama; in Jules Verne's *Great Navigators of the Eighteenth Century* (1880); even in Frank Herbert's science fiction epic, *Dune* (1965), where those who navigate the cosmos have exceptional, drug-induced powers. The Neolithic seafarers who understood both the mysteries of the sea and the mysteries of the stars may well have been an elite, a caste apart.[20]

This extended discussion of boats and navigation is relevant in two ways. Firstly, and at the risk of labouring the point, the sea was the only means of access to the Archipelago; coastal waters allowed Neolithic people to move easily between different parts of the Archipelago; and river travel was the best way of reaching the interior of both the Main Island and the Western Isle. By 3700 BC, Neolithic settlers had reached the Northern Isles – which became a major hub for later Neolithic culture and the site of some of the most spectacular Neolithic monuments in the Archipelago, if not the world (see Chapter 6) – and reached the Outer Isles and the Far Northern Isles soon afterwards. One example of the northward spread of Neolithic culture throws an extraordinary light on the maritime capability of Neolithic people, as well as on the enduring impact of their husbandry. Red deer were an important source of food from the earliest times through the Neolithic period and beyond. Studies have shown that they were introduced into the Northern and Outer Isles between 3500 and 2500 BC. The distance from the mainland to either group of islands is too far for deer to swim, so they must have been introduced by man. However, recent DNA analysis indicates that the deer found in the islands are not related to those found in the rest of Scotland or, for that matter, in Scandinavia. Neolithic settlers evidently not only understood the potential for deer to thrive in the islands but were also capable of transporting red deer in sufficient numbers to form a breeding herd all the way from the Continental Lands. The herd expanded and was managed as a source of food and skins, while antlers and other bones were used as tools. Its descendants roam the islands to this day.[21]

Secondly, there is a psychological dimension. For many centuries, the British saw themselves as a maritime people. It was central to their sense of identity, their culture, and their myth of themselves, although it manifested itself differently in different parts of the British Isles. In England, it found expression in those stories every schoolchild was supposed to know: Drake and the Spanish Armada; Nelson at Trafalgar; Dunkirk; the sinking of the *Bismarck*. In Scotland, the islands of the west, Orkney and Shetland, all still remember the sea kingdoms of a thousand years ago; while the east coast holds more recent memories of the great fishing fleets of the nineteenth century; and Clydeside was the biggest shipbuilding centre of the British Empire. In Ireland, the same idea is present, though in a different form. There are heroic stories – the voyage of St Brendan; the exploits of Gráinne Mhaol, the Pirate Queen; the west coast fishermen whose lives achieved almost mythical status in the 1934 film *Man of Aran* – and many great passenger liners from the *Titanic* to the *Canberra* were built in Belfast. But perhaps the strongest memory of the sea in modern Ireland concerns the hundreds of thousands of emigrants who took ship for the United States in the nineteenth century.

Whether these are true stories or have been elevated to the level of cultural myth is less important than the fact that they have exercised, and in some cases still continue to exercise, a powerful influence as cultural reference points. They reflect a consciousness of the sea as fundamental to the national psyche. That consciousness must have begun somewhere and – although this is speculation – it is at least possible that its origins lie in the Neolithic Era, at a time when the people living in the Archipelago understood how much the sea contributed to their existence, their survival and, indeed, to their character. The sea and seafaring has retained its psychological hold throughout the long history of the Archipelago, but, in recent years, its importance has declined significantly. Over the last fifty years, the predominance of air travel has broken our dependence on the sea and ships – has in fact broken a link with prehistory – and changed the way our society thinks about travel. Even in the 1960s, passenger liners connected the British Isles with the rest of the world, linked London, Liverpool and Southampton with New York, Cape Town, Sydney, Singapore, and Hong Kong. Most of the shipping lines that ran the great ocean liners – Cunard; Union Castle; P & O; Shaw, Saville & Albion – are now defunct. Those that still exist operate cruise liners or short-distance ferries. In the 1960s, cargo ships came right up the Thames into the Pool of London; banana boats from the West Indies unloaded their cargoes onto the dockside at the Isle of Dogs. Nowadays, if freight does not come by air, it comes in containers which are offloaded at deep water ports. The process is less visible and more remote from daily life. The Royal Navy is a fraction of the size it was in the decades after the Second World War – or even at the time of the Falklands War in 1982. The fishing fleet is massively reduced, largely because of regulations and quotas designed to prevent overfishing and help fish stocks recover. As late as 2000, there were six ferry routes operating between the United Kingdom and Scandinavia. At the time of writing, there is only one. Technological developments and economic factors make such changes inevitable; and changes in culture and psychology naturally follow on. One cannot turn back the clock. In this particular case, however, the result of change has been to weaken our link with the distant past and with our origins; and thereby weaken our natural understanding of a key factor in the history of the British Isles.

4 Marks upon the Land

By 3700 BC, Neolithic people had settled much of the Archipelago and had left their mark on its environment. In many areas, large stands of forest and woodland had been cleared to provide grazing and arable land. Cattle, sheep, and goats were being herded, bred, and used for both milk and meat. Red deer were also being herded, although probably in a looser manner. Wild boar had been domesticated and were being bred for meat. Wolves had long since been domesticated as hunting dogs, but now they fulfilled new roles: herding animals and guarding settlements. Grain and seed corn had transformed both landscape and diet. On the Western Isle, wheat and barley were the main crops. In the Upland Zone, along the damp, western margins of the Main Island, barley also flourished.[22] In the Lowland Zone, wheat and barley were grown alongside peas, beans, and bitter vetch. The archaeology suggests that much of the population were now settled in permanent or semi-permanent villages, although there were still some who maintained their seasonal or longer-term migratory lifestyle, at least for a time. Only five hundred years after the first Neolithic arrivals, the life and culture of the pre-existing hunter-gatherer population was on course to be swamped or swept aside.

In terms of the previous history of the Archipelago, these changes were rapid and far-reaching; in terms of change as we understand it in the twentieth-first century, they were gradual and left plenty of room for regional variation. Once again, a sense of perspective is essential. The initial phase of the Neolithic Revolution – the period of migration and initial settlement – took place over a period which, if it were reaching its final stages now, would have begun about the time Henry VIII came to the throne in 1509. The population of the Archipelago increased during the early stages of the Neolithic period. Food security was probably a factor. Changes in diet may also have played a part, though this has been disputed.

Even so, the total numbers involved remained relatively small, at least by modern standards. It is unlikely that the population of the Archipelago as a whole reached one million before the middle of the Bronze Age, about 1400 BC. Clearing land was hard work. There were no machines and no metal tools. Trees were cut down with flint axes. The land was broken up either by hand, using hand tools made from wood or bone or flint, or by simple wooden ploughs, known as *ards*, drawn by oxen. Where the ground was stony, complex wall systems might be built as a way of clearing the land and dividing it into fields. A spectacular example of this kind of Neolithic walled field system is Céide Fields in the west of the Western Isle, in use between 3700 and 3200 BC, where approximately one thousand hectares were cleared in this way.[23] Yet while large areas of land were cleared for farming and grazing, equally large expanses of forest and woodland remained in their original state – some perhaps left as a source of timber.

The hunter-gatherer lifestyle was, on the whole, comparatively low risk. Weather or disease might cause occasional shortages; there might be incidents of famine; but hunter-gatherer tribes relied on a wide range of plants, animals, birds, and fish for their diet; and because they were essentially nomadic, if they felt their food supply to be seriously at risk, they simply abandoned their camp and moved to a new area. The Neolithic lifestyle increased the amount of protein in the daily diet but significantly reduced the range of foods – fruits, grains and meats – that made up their diet. The reliance on a reduced number of foodstuffs, coupled with the fact that growing crops and herding livestock demanded a more settled lifestyle, increased the level of risk. Bad weather, drought, crop or animal disease could create serious food shortages. Such incidents would inevitably have occurred on an occasional and regional basis, but there was one period, around 2500 BC, when economic and agricultural life in the whole Archipelago seems to have taken a step back. There were regional differences, but we can see that across the Archipelago settlements were deserted and many areas previously cleared for farmland were abandoned and woodland allowed to return. We do not know the cause or causes of this setback. Climate change, crop disease, an epidemic affecting livestock, disease among the population, even inter-tribal wars have all been suggested. However, when the Neolithic farming lifestyle worked, it worked well. It meant that a farming-based community – a tribe, a settlement, or the inhabitants of a particular region – could look beyond subsistence. A good year or series of good years could see them fed and clothed and living with a sense of security unknown to their hunter-gatherer predecessors. Surpluses of grain or meat or cloth could be exchanged or traded with neighbouring, or even more distant communities, and this led to a new kind of prosperity.

The transition from nomadic, hunter-gatherer subsistence to a more settled, agriculture-based lifestyle had implications which went well beyond diet and food security. It brought important conceptual and philosophical changes, the echoes of which are still with us. Nomadic hunter-gatherers understood the cycle of the seasons and responded to it. In tune with the seasons, they gathered different plants, hunted different animals, or moved to different hunting grounds. Neolithic farmers also followed the cycle of the year: they planted, grew, and harvested their crops; they bred, reared, and slaughtered their animals. This process was focussed on the future, on future reward for present labour; and, as such, it required them to plan ahead over a comparatively long period. They harnessed the changing seasons rather than simply responding to them, and in this sense – which is characteristic of the Neolithic Revolution as a whole – they exercised, or sought to exercise, control over their environment.

All societies, no matter where they sit on the developmental ladder, require and create roles for their members. Anthropological observation suggests that in hunter-gatherer societies, the relative simplicity of their lives means that those roles are few in number and simple in content. Some roles, such as those involving hunting larger or dangerous animals, may be regarded as specialised, but most roles can be exchanged among members of the group or tribe. Neolithic society was more complex in its structure and in the way it functioned. Permanent settlement, the demands of agriculture, and a surplus-orientated economic model led to the creation of more closely defined social roles. The tasks involved – clearing the land, growing the crops, tending the animals, maintaining and protecting the settlement, making tools, processing and storing food, making clothes – were more various, often more specialised, and less easily exchanged. This, in turn, strengthened the connection between labour and reward. Studies of Neolithic dwellings appear to show differences in size, reflecting differences in wealth and status, suggesting that the social and economic system may well have created inequalities within communities.²⁴ And, as part of the same process, it may also have defined separate roles for men and women.

Permanent settlement naturally led to the creation of permanent buildings. The remains of wooden halls have been unearthed across the Archipelago. In the Western Isle alone, some eighty have been identified on fifty different sites – among them the earliest so far found in the Archipelago, dating from c.3795 BC – again indicating the importance of cultural transmission along the Atlantic Zone. The halls vary in size but are generally rectangular in shape and up to twelve metres long and eight metres wide. Two notable exceptions to this are in the High North, at Balbridie in Aberdeenshire, and a little further south at Dreghorn in North Ayrshire. Here, the buildings are on an altogether larger scale: twenty-six metres by thirteen, and twenty-three by five respectively. Most of these halls appear to have had a frame constructed from solid posts, with walls of heavy oak planks or wattle and daub. A number had distinctive curving end walls. The roofs may have been thatched, although the solidity of the foundations and frames suggests that they could have supported heavier structures. We do not know. These halls, sometimes also termed longhouses, are found in almost all parts of the Archipelago, and the fact that in size and construction they are similar to halls on the Continent indicates that they represented an established tradition of building that was characteristic of early Neolithic culture.²⁵ Inside, there is often evidence of partitions and hearths, possibly indicating a domestic space for members of an extended family. However, most larger halls seem to have had an open area where people may have gathered for meetings or other communal purposes.²⁶ Perhaps the hall represented the centre of the village, the seat of the head man or chief, while other villagers lived in smaller, often circular, huts set around it. Perhaps it had several functions. Yet the existence of such buildings points to the fact that Neolithic villages were cohesive social groups; that villagers worked together digging foundations, felling trees, cutting posts and planks and so on, to build them. In doing so, they were creating a place which asserted their existence as a group and, again, exercising control over their environment.

Permanent or long-term settlements, a more complex system of food production with the need to store quantities of grain, fruit, and meat, led to the beginning of a material culture. This is most obvious in the appearance of the first pottery, in the form of what are known as carinated bowls:

simple hand-formed bowls that have a shoulder or sharp change of angle between the neck and body of the vessel, and a rim that is often folded or rolled over. These bowls were introduced from the Continent between 4000 and 3800 BC and were used for cooking and storage. They are significant in that they were the first objects to be *manufactured* in the Archipelago – using heat to change the nature of a raw material, rather than simply reshaping a source object with stone knife or axe. Sealed kilns were not introduced until Roman times, so bowls were fired by being buried in a mound or a lined pit of combustible material. Experiments have shown that firing to between 600 and 800° C produced usable but brittle pots, while peat firing could reach temperatures of up to 1100° C and resulted in better quality products.[27][28] The realisation that heat had the potential to alter the properties of raw materials was a crucial step forward in human development. As time went on, carinated bowls were followed by other kinds of pots, such as Mildenhall Ware, which first appeared around 3700 BC, and Peterborough Ware, from about 2700 BC. These featured more sophisticated shapes and more elaborate, incised, decorative patterns of dots and lines.

A settled culture and a larger population engaged in building and farming needed tools. It also needed to defend itself, its lands, and its animals – which required weapons. Both tools and weapons were frequently made of flint, and the management of the supply of flint illustrates just how different Neolithic culture was from what had gone before, as well as the capacity of Neolithic peoples for organisation. Flint mines dating from this period have been discovered across the Continental Lands – from Krzemionki in south-western Poland to Spiennes, just south of Mons in Belgium, where the mines cover an area of about a hundred hectares. More than seventy possible mining sites have been identified across the Main Island, although not all have been investigated. The earliest and densest group is on the South Downs, where mining began about 4000 BC. The mine sites are recognisable as large, crater-shaped hollows. These are the remains of partially back-filled shafts, which descended anything up to twelve metres and branched out into galleries, giving access to bands of flint running through the chalk. The men who went down the mines hacked at the chalk using picks made from the antlers of red deer. About the time the mines on the South Downs were abandoned – roughly 3000 BC – another equally impressive complex was opening up in an area now

Map 5   The Early Neolithic Period

known as Grime's Graves in Norfolk. Here, the remains of some four hundred and forty shafts have been identified, some of them up to fifteen metres deep and covering an area of thirty-seven hectares. These mines were also in use for about 1,000 years and overlapped with the period when Bronze Age technologies were being introduced.

Flint tools came in an array of shapes and sizes, and with a range of different purposes. There were scrapers: hand-held pieces of flint with a sharp edge that could be used for skinning animals, cleaning hides, and shaping wood. There were long, thin flints used as knives. There were burins: flints with chisel-like edges for engraving wood or bone. Arrowheads, spearheads, and harpoons could be made out of a single piece of flint or from a number of microliths, small fragments of flint, sharpened and set into a wooden shaft to make a composite weapon. And there were axes, the Neolithic tool which, for very good reasons, has tended to attract the most attention.

The western edges of the Archipelago offered surface outcrops of rock which meant that flint could be quarried rather than mined. One of the largest Neolithic quarries was on the high fells above Great Langdale in Cumbria. For a thousand years, beginning about 4000 BC, it was a major source of greenstone and hornstone axes. Another large quarry centred on an outcrop of igneous rock at Graig Lwyd, near Penmaenmawr in Conwy; and there were several quarries on the South-Western Peninsula. In the Western Isle, porcellanite was quarried at the foot of a mountain called Tievebulliagh in County Antrim; and there was another major quarry and production area on Rathlin Island, off the Antrim coast. Of the many thousands of axe heads found at these and other quarries, most are what are known as 'roughouts': pieces of stone chipped from the parent rock and subjected to preliminary shaping so that they are recognisably axe heads, but not yet finished. In some places, roughouts were taken from the quarries to other locations where different kinds of rock, such as sandstone or millstone grit, were available to grind and polish them into their final shape and condition. At least some of the roughouts from Great Langdale were taken to North Walney some thirty kilometres away on the Cumbrian coast and polished there;[29] while on the Isle of Rum, bloodstone roughouts were quarried at Guirdil Bay in the north-west of the island before being transported across the island and then ferried to Kinloch on the Isle of Skye for finishing.[30]

Most axes were tools or weapons, made for daily use. Others had no practical function. They were either too big to be used as tools or made of rock that would chip or shatter on impact, yet they are nonetheless carefully shaped and highly polished. Time and labour were invested in creating them – in some cases it has been estimated that the polishing alone would have taken a hundred hours – and they were probably the most valuable objects in human society until the coming of gold. Their precise function is uncertain. They probably denoted wealth and status; they may well have featured in kinship or diplomatic exchanges between tribes; and they also appear to have had another, more conceptual function. Given that for prehistoric people the spiritual world was as ever-present as the material one, the centrality of axes to Neolithic society appears to have given them a role in the interplay between the two worlds. Both everyday axe heads and what we may call the ceremonial kind, denoting wealth and status, are frequently found in the beds of rivers or lakes, or at other sites that seem to have had a religious significance. They appear to have been deposited as offerings, but beyond the fact that they were objects of value, the precise significance of axes in this context remains obscure.

Demand for axes was widespread and sustained; and at least as fascinating as the scale of the mining and quarrying operations that produced them is their distribution. The Tievebulliagh axes, as one might expect, are found in heavy concentration in the north-east of the Western Isle, but scattered examples have been found right across the Main Island and as far north as the Far Northern Isles. Graig Lwyd axes are found mainly in the Lowland Zone. Cornish axes are also found mainly in Lowland Zone, but they are present in greater numbers in those southern and central areas where there is a concentration of Neolithic monuments. The Langdale quarries account for a remarkable twenty-seven percent of all polished stone axe heads so far found in the Archipelago. Perhaps surprisingly, given the location of the quarries, they appear not have crossed the sea to the Western Isle in any quantity, but they have been found in significant numbers in most parts of the Main Island except the Western Uplands and the High North – the densest concentration being in areas adjacent to the Lake District and the northern half of the Lowland Zone. Some examples of Langdale axes have been found on the Continental Lands, as far away as modern-day Poland, while axes from the Continental Lands – flint from Spiennes and Brittany, jadeite from the Alps – have been found in the Archipelago. All of which suggests that as early as 4000 BC Neolithic man had evolved the basis of an industrial or business model which we can still recognise today. Raw material was mined or quarried and went through a first-stage manufacturing process on site; the semi-finished product might then be sent away for finishing; and the final product was distributed across the Archipelago and beyond.

Modern methods of transport make it all too easy to forget the importance and efficiency of water transport in previous ages (see Chapter 3). Two hundred years ago, the coastal waters of the British Isles were crowded with vessels of all shapes and sizes transporting raw materials, agricultural produce, and manufactured goods between the great seaports, such as London, Bristol and Liverpool, and the hundreds of smaller ports and harbours on which thousands of small towns and villages depended for their supplies. Inland water transport was equally crucial. The canal network was an essential part of the infrastructure which allowed the Industrial Revolution to transport its raw materials, its coal, and its manufactured products cheaply and in bulk. In Neolithic times, logboats would have played a significant role in the transport and distribution of goods. While their low freeboard would not have been suited to the open sea, they would have come into their own when it came to estuary and river travel.

In 2004, the remarkably well-preserved remains of a logboat were found in the mud at Greyabbey on the shore of Strangford Lough. It consists of a single, hollowed out trunk of an oak tree with a shaped prow and stern, and has been dated to between 3499 and 3032 BC. It would have been 9.35 metres long and could have carried a cargo of over three tons, including a crew of five. Fully laden, it would have had a draft of fifty centimetres.[31] Such craft would have been ideal for river travel, and most of the preserved logboats so far discovered in the Archipelago have been found close to estuaries, rivers, and lakes. They would have been able to navigate any of the major rivers and to penetrate the larger tributaries as well. Of course, rivers in Neolithic times were very different from those we see today. The main channels were less defined and were bordered by expanses of wetland, marsh, and bog, but river systems such as the Thames, Severn-Avon, Trent-Derwent, or the Shannon would still have allowed logboats to make their way a considerable distance inland.

Logboats would have been paddled, and the archaeological record contains numerous paddles, some dating from Mesolithic times. They are long, with relatively narrow blades, and carved from single pieces of wood. Four or five men kneeling on the floor, with cargo spaced evenly between them along the length of the vessel, could have propelled a logboat at some speed, although care would have been required to avoid capsizing when manoeuvring. Arriving at its destination, the logboat's cargo would have been offloaded at a suitable riverside location, and there is evidence that, in some places, riverbanks were reinforced with tree trunks or heavy planks to make docking and unloading easier. Riverborne trade, based on the catchment areas of the major rivers, using logboats to transport anything from axes, grain, and animals to stones and building materials, was a recognised part of life.

Where water transport was not possible, Neolithic man established paths and trackways. These were another essential part of Neolithic culture, and networks existed across both the Main Island and the Western Isle, linking settlements to each other and to the coast, and providing access to centres of religion and ritual, where we find the great monuments, henges, and stone circles of the age (see Chapters 5 and 6). The most famous trackway on the Main Island is the Ridgeway, which crosses the Lowland Zone following a broadly south-west/north-east course, linking the Dorset coast with the Wash. The Harrow Way had two eastern terminal points – corresponding to Rochester and Dover – and ran westwards from Kent to Seaton on the south Devon coast. The end points of both these paths were probably entrepôts, where boats carrying cargoes of varying sorts arrived from and departed for different parts of the Continent. Further north, routes such as the Tyne Gap, the Stainmore Gap, and the Aire Gap, all of which cross the mountainous spine of the Main Island, were all identified and used during the Neolithic period, and many of the routes established at that time have remained in use ever since, often featuring as part of today's road network.

Goods transported over the network of long-distance trackways would probably have been carried on pack animals. These would not have been horses. Wild horses appear to have been present on the Main Island, but probably not in the Western Isle, since the final severing of the Land Bridge. It is not certain when they were first domesticated; extrapolating from developments on the Continent, it was probably somewhere around 2500 BC. The earliest actual evidence of domesticated horses in the Archipelago comes from Newgrange in the Western Isle at the beginning of the Bronze Age about 2400 BC.[32] Even then, they were rare and valuable beasts, reserved for warriors and members of the political or religious elite – certainly too valuable to be used for daily tasks.

Nor was wheeled transport an option. A ceramic pot unearthed at Bronocice, not far from Kraków in southern Poland, and dated to between 3635 and 3370 BC, features what is widely believed to be the earliest known depiction of a wheeled vehicle. It is a stylised representation, repeated five times, of a four-wheeled cart with axles and a shaft to which the draft animals – presumably aurochs, the skeletal remains of which were found beside the pot – were attached. If this interpretation of the drawing is correct (and it has been disputed), it suggests that wheeled waggons were in use comparatively early during the Neolithic period in central and eastern Europe. This is supported by the fact that the oldest wooden wheel yet discovered, dating to between 3340–3040 BC, was found at Ljubljana in Slovenia.[33] However, a lack of similar finds in the lands to the west of Slovenia until much later suggests that the wheel as a technology may have been slow to spread – perhaps the paths and tracks were simply too rough and rugged for carts or waggons to be practicable. The earliest fragmentary remains of a wheel yet found in the Archipelago date from the middle of the Bronze Age, c.1300 BC.

Aurochs with panniers on their backs and led by ropes tied around their horns are likely to have been the pack animals of choice – skulls have been found with grooves in their horns, apparently caused by the abrasions of rope. Progress, determined by the speed of the aurochs, would have been slow, and a journey from, for example, the quarries of Great Langdale to the east coast, north of the Humber, where a large number of Langdale axes have been found, would have taken many days. The travellers would have been in a group because travelling alone in a land inhabited by wolves, bears, wild boar and wild aurochs could be dangerous. Their road would take them along the rocky but well-established path over the Aire Gap, where many stone axes have been found. They would have worn at least two layers of clothes: an inner layer perhaps of rough, woven fabric, an outer layer of skins or furs, fastened with bone pins. On their feet, they would have worn either bast shoes, woven from birch fibres, or more likely, short leather boots stuffed with grass or hay. Ötzi, the late Neolithic hunter whose remains were discovered in a glacier on the Italian-Austrian border, had shoes which consisted of a string net stuffed with straw, covered with deerskin on the uppers and bear skin on the soles.

Where possible, Neolithic paths followed higher ground and watershed ridges, avoiding the potential dangers of densely forested or swampy, low-lying areas, although waterlogged ground was not in itself a barrier to Neolithic roadbuilders. Timber trackways appear to have been in widespread use across the southern half of the Main Island and in the Western Isle – although those so far discovered in the Western Isle are of a later date. Two of the oldest in the Archipelago are the Post Track and its successor, the Sweet Track, which ran for about two kilometres across the Somerset Levels to Westhay, then an island in the middle of a lake or swamp. Dendrochronology allows us to date construction of the Post Track to 3838 BC and the Sweet Track to 3806. Archaeologists have calculated that the Sweet Track, the better preserved of the two, contained 2,000 tons of stakes and planks – all cut and shaped by stone axes. Supporting the trackway are pairs of wooden stakes driven at angles into the waterlogged ground and bound together to form a long line of 'X' shapes. The path itself was created by fastening oak planks horizontally in the angle above the crossing point of the two stakes.

Other ancient trackways have been found to the east of London – at Silvertown (3340–3910 BC), north of the Thames, and at Belmarsh (c.4000 BC), to the south.[34] These are simpler structures, known as corduroy trackways, where vertical piles have been driven into the boggy ground to support heavy logs laid crosswise and lashed together. In 2004, a similar structure, a forty-five-metre trackway leading from dry land across wetland to an offshore platform, was discovered at Lindholme in South Yorkshire. In 2018, archaeologists working ahead of the installation of new electricity cables near Woodbridge in Suffolk, found an almost perfectly preserved thirty-metre wooden trackway which had once been surrounded by water from nearby springs and had acted as the focal point of a large henge.[35] Similarly, in the Western Isle, an early trackway has been found around the Hill of Tara – which in later ages was claimed to be the seat of the High Kings of Ireland, but during Neolithic times was topped by a large wooden henge – while a network of wooden tracks and platforms has been found in the wetlands around the town of Edercloon (Eadarchluain) in County Longford.

Trackways served a variety of purposes. The primary function of the Post Track and Sweet Track was no doubt to improve communication across the Somerset Levels. Similarly, much of the London Basin would have consisted of wetlands during the Neolithic era and the trackways may well have been built by communities to assist their hunters for whom the wetlands were a rich source of food. However, whatever their practical purpose, given the central part played by water in Neolithic belief systems, all such trackways are likely to have had held a spiritual significance for those who used them. The lakebed along the length of the Sweet Track was found to be littered with objects and artefacts – including an exceptionally valuable and unused jadeite axe head originating from the French Alps. There were far too many items to be explained as accidental losses, so archaeologists have concluded that they were ritual offerings deliberately deposited.

The pictures of men paddling a logboat and foot sloggers leading an aurochs are, of course, speculative, although consistent with the available archaeological evidence. However, it is clear that rivers, tracks, and trackways allowed not only for communication and transport, but also for trade. The question of trade in the Neolithic era requires a cautious approach. We noted that the process of making, finishing, and distributing axe heads formed the basis of what is, to us, a recognisable economic model. And from a twenty-first century viewpoint, it is tempting to see the logboat crew and the land travellers as precursors of those eighteenth century merchants who collected their stock of knives and scissors, or silks and ribbons, from the point of manufacture and sold them as they travelled through rural communities; or of today's white van man, who will load up with surplus carpets or garden furniture from factory or wholesaler and sell them at weekly markets or car-boot sales. Neolithic man, this scenario says, was not so different from us. There may be some truth in this, but for Neolithic man, the economic element of the exchange would have been only one part of a more complex, multi-layered mechanism of social interaction.

Although not conclusive, the archaeological remains of Neolithic settlements suggest that certain things, such as the animals, agricultural produce, and food, were probably held in common. Individual villagers would then have contributed their labour or their particular skills – weaving, making pots, or knapping flint – to the common good and received food, clothing and protection in return. Neighbouring villages probably exchanged their surplus produce – grain, meat, young animals, smoked fish, cloth, salt, skins and so on – and we know from the distribution of archaeological finds that other goods – notably, but not solely, stone axes – were traded or exchanged over long distances. What is important here is the context. If axe heads were given in return for sacks of grain or a young, healthy aurochs received, the context was 'exchange', which may not have been quite the same as 'barter' and certainly not the same as 'payment'.

In our society, all goods and services have a monetary value, and must be paid for. Possessions are assessed in monetary terms. Monetary worth is a key factor in judging the status or success of an individual. We do not know what drove Neolithic man, but it was not – it could not have been – money. Money did not appear in the Archipelago until the second century BC. Susan McCarter has divided Neolithic exchanges of goods into several different types – direct, reciprocal, redistributive, and longer-distance exchange conducted in several stages.[36] And we have already noted that exchanges beyond the village or settlement may well have taken place within the broader context of kinship visits and the maintenance of friendly relations between tribes. The picture we are building here is of a society in which material goods had a very different value from that assigned to them in our society – which may explain why even the most valuable could be dropped into the water as an offering. In so far as we can reconstruct philosophical and religious beliefs from the archaeological record, that difference stems from the fact that the dominant factor in Neolithic life was a constant interplay between the material and the spiritual world, between the living and the dead, between the living and the ancestors.

5 Structures on the Ground

Unlike their predecessors, the Neolithic inhabitants of the Archipelago left an obvious and visible legacy. From the South-Western Peninsula to the Far Northern Isles, and across the length and breadth of the Western Isle, there are massive earthworks and monumental assemblages of stone which attest their presence, their skill, and their organisation. These structures take many forms and clearly fulfilled a range of different functions – even though we often cannot be sure precisely what those functions were. Both form and function naturally changed over the two millennia of the Neolithic period, yet in all the great man-made structures of the age we are conscious of a sense of assertion. This is more than a matter of scale, and more than an appreciation of the vast collective effort that was required to build them. It is a sense that here was a culture expressing its identity and its beliefs with absolute conviction and self-confidence. These great Neolithic monuments are, in their way, comparable with the towering castles and cathedrals of the Norman era, the supreme architectural masterpieces of the Renaissance, or the viaducts and vaulting termini of the

Victorian railways. They demonstrate a mastery of design and technique, and both the shared purpose and the collective will required to realise that mastery. In doing so, they express the prevailing values and belief systems of the day. So, in the absence of written records, any attempt to understand what those values and beliefs were, or might have been, must turn to archaeology and the nature of monuments that were built.

Some of the earliest large-scale structures to appear in the Archipelago were causewayed enclosures, also called causewayed camps. These were more or less circular areas surrounded by a ditch, which could be anything up to six metres deep and fifteen metres across, inside which was a bank made up of the heaped spoil dug from the ditch. The ditch and bank were discontinuous. Some narrow sections were left undug, allowing access to the centre of the enclosure – hence the term 'causeway' – and dividing the outer structure into segments. Sometimes the bank was topped by a palisade or fence. On the Continent, causewayed enclosures are a recognised part of Neolithic culture from c.4500 onwards. Over a thousand sites have been identified across a broad area from the River Oder to the Pyrenees;[37] more than a hundred of them are in the north and west of what is now France. About eighty causewayed enclosures have so far been identified in the Archipelago. Almost all of them date from between 3750 and 3350 BC, and the majority are located south and east of a line drawn between the Wash and the Severn Estuary, suggesting that the concept, and possibly the builders, migrated across the Channel and Southern North Sea Zones to the south-east of the Main Island.

Yet what appears to be the earliest causewayed enclosure in the Archipelago is located not on the Main Island, but at Magheraboy in County Sligo in the Western Isle, one of only two examples found there. Built between 4115 and 3850 BC and in use for the next seven hundred years, in its early date and its remote location it recalls the farming settlement at Ferriter's Cove. Again, we can perhaps imagine a group of Neolithic pioneers setting off over the seaways of the Atlantic Zone, making their way up the coast of the Western Isle until they found a site which suited their needs on the edge of the rich wetlands between Lough Gill and the sea. Here, once their colony was established, once their crops were growing, once their numbers were increasing, they dug their ditch, piled up the spoil, and created their enclosure as their culture dictated.

But why? Causewayed enclosures evidently had a purpose, and it was

Map 6   Cursus Monuments, Tombs, and Long Barrows

of sufficient centrality and importance to Neolithic culture to survive as that culture migrated first westwards across the Continental Lands and then across the sea to the Archipelago. The existence of palisades has led to suggestions that the purpose may have been defensive. At Magheraboy, the bank was topped by a fence which appears to have been two metres high,[38] and in the south-west of the Main Island there are four causewayed enclosures – Carn Brea in Cornwall, Hembury in Devon, Crickley Hill in Gloucestershire, and Hambledon Hill in Dorset's Blackmore Vale – which appear to have been attacked and burnt.[39] Intertribal raiding and violence was probably common enough in Neolithic times, and while it is conceivable that causewayed enclosures could have provided the local population with a place of refuge in times of trouble, it seems unlikely that their primary purpose was defence. The concept of an interrupted bank and ditch militates against the idea, making it more difficult to deny access to an attacking force; and while some enclosures were small enough to be defensible, many others encompassed large areas of ground. Hambledon Hill in Dorset, for example, extends over nine hectares. It has a perimeter of over a kilometre and would have been impossible to defend without large numbers of armed and organised men. Some enclosures – such as Knap Hill in Wiltshire, Windmill Hill near Avebury, and Hambledon Hill – were built in commanding hilltop positions: some – such as Crickley Hill in Gloucestershire, and Maiden Castle just outside Dorchester – were later turned into Iron Age hillforts; yet at least as many others were built on low-lying ground or in river valleys. In several locations two or more enclosures have been found close together. In Kingsborough on the Isle of Sheppey, for example, there are two small enclosures within three hundred metres of each other, something which would surely have weakened rather than strengthened defensive capability.

Excavations at causewayed enclosures have thrown up many finds – from flints, pottery and quernstones, to animal bones and human remains – but only rarely evidence of huts or dwellings or long-term middens. The conclusion drawn by archaeologists is that the enclosures were used regularly but were not inhabited on a long-term basis. In the late 1950s, the prehistorian Isobel Smith conducted her own detailed excavation at Windmill Hill, while at the same time making a thorough reassessment of the records of digs conducted there in the 1920s and 30s. Her conclusion was that causewayed enclosures were places where, at certain times of year, communities met to exchange breeding stock and agricultural produce; to hold initiations, betrothals, and weddings; and to conduct ritual celebrations based around fertility, the seasons and the agricultural year.[40] Such activities would naturally have been accompanied by feasting, which would explain the presence of animal bones. Francis Pryor, basing his views on his excavation of the causewayed enclosure at Etton in Cambridgeshire, adds an extra dimension which offers an explanation for the segmentation of the ditch and bank. Each segment, he suggests, was dug by, and thus belonged to, a particular family group; and he sees the small, filled pits, found in association with most ditch-and-bank segments, as the equivalent of gravestones, commemorating particular individuals. If he is correct, one important function of causewayed enclosures would have been as a place to conduct those rituals which marked the passing of family members from the world of the living to that of the ancestors.[41] Although they retain an element of speculation, these explanations do combine three elements which most archaeologists judge to be central to Neolithic society: an emphasis on the family, on collective activity, and on the need to acknowledge and honour the ancestors.

If causewayed enclosures are difficult to interpret, cursus monuments are all but impossible. A cursus is a long – sometimes very long – narrow enclosure. Some shorter and earlier examples have sides that are defined by parallel lines of pits or postholes which would have held vertical posts or planks. Longer and later ones have ditches and banks. Many long cursus have narrow, causeway-style entrances at various points along the sides, while the ends (often called terminals) are usually closed off in the same manner as the sides – although there are some examples where the terminals are left open. Beyond that basic structure, cursus monuments, unlike causewayed enclosures, exhibit no standard pattern. The cursus associated with the great Neolithic passage tomb at Newgrange in County Meath in the Western Isle is no more than a hundred metres long. The Lesser Cursus, the smaller of two associated with Stonehenge, is four hundred metres long and sixty wide. Its companion, the Greater Cursus, is fully three kilometres long and between a hundred and a hundred-and-fifty metres wide. The so-called Stanwell Cursus, discovered and excavated in the late 1990s during the construction of Heathrow Airport's Terminal 5, is four kilometres long, making it the second longest in the Archipelago, although with a width of only twenty-two metres, it is much narrower than most – the spoil from the ditches having been thrown inwards to create a kind of raised pathway. The Dorset Cursus, apparently constructed in two stages, is eighty-two metres wide, flanked by a shallow, one- to two-metre-deep ditch, and stretches for nearly ten kilometres across rolling chalk countryside, making it the longest by far.

Unlike causewayed enclosures, cursus monuments seem to have originated in the Archipelago. There are no continental examples or precedents. The earliest examples are found in the High North, in a band stretching southward from Aberdeenshire, through Angus and Perthshire, to Lanarkshire and Dumfries. These include the pit-defined structures mentioned above and have been dated to between 4000 and 3600 BC. Once established, the concept appears to have moved southwards and, in the process, the scale on which new monuments were conceived grew significantly, with simpler method of ditch-and-bank construction replacing timber-lined sides. The highest concentration of cursus is in the Lowland Zone of the Main Island, which, then as now, was more heavily populated. The majority of these appear to have been dug between 3600 and 3300 BC. Only a handful of examples have so far been identified in the Western Isle, one of them, as noted above, at Newgrange. Because they have been damaged by erosion and ploughing over the years, cursus are often difficult to identify on the ground. Some, such as the Greater Cursus at Stonehenge, have been known about since the eighteenth century, but it is only since the advent of aerial surveys that the true number and the extent of these structures have been realised, and it is likely that more will be discovered.

Most cursus were dug after causewayed enclosures. This is confirmed not only by the radiocarbon dating of finds, but also by their positioning in the landscape. A number were evidently aligned on existing enclosures and long barrows, while one or two actually cut through the earlier structures. Did cursus monuments in some way succeed or take over from causewayed enclosures? Once again, we are in the realms of speculation because we have no idea what purpose they served. We can, on this occasion, be sure they were not connected with defence or warfare, but that is as far as certainty goes. The name was coined by the eighteenth-century clergyman and antiquarian, William Stukeley (1687–1765), who thought that the Greater Cursus at Stonehenge resembled the kind of running or chariot-racing track found in the classical world. Arrowheads found at the terminals of some cursus have led to theory that ritual hunting may have taken place; that deer or other game may have been driven up the cursus towards the enclosed end, where there would have been no escape from the waiting bowmen. Another theory is that they were zones where, at certain times of year, ceremonial processions would take place. There is no clear archaeological support for either theory. One problem is that excavations of cursus monuments have yielded very few finds of any kind, too few to suggest a clear pattern of usage. This has given rise to the idea that they were areas which were deliberately left empty; that they were reserved for the ancestors, and only entered by the living on specific ritual occasions. That many cursus are associated with water may strengthen the idea of a ritual connection – most are located in river valleys, on flood plains, or at the confluence of rivers. Some, notably the Dorset Cursus, are actually constructed across rivers or watercourses, while the Old Montrose (or Powis) Cursus in the valley of the South Esk in Angus appears to have been dug in such a way that it would become an island when the river flooded.

Causewayed enclosures and cursus monuments were earthworks, dug using picks made from antlers, and shovels made from wood or the shoulder bones of cattle or deer. They would have required planning and organisation, but not the kind of complex engineering techniques demanded by stone-built monuments. Lack of convincing alternative explanations has led to a general (if, in some cases, reluctant) acceptance that they fulfilled some kind of function in relation to the dead and the ancestors but, despite the occasional skeleton or bone-filled pit, they were clearly not tombs or burial sites. They were, however, contemporary with several types of stone-built tombs, which offer a different perspective on Neolithic attitudes to death and the dead. Unlike cursus monuments, these different kinds of tomb all have models or precedents on the Continent, but their distribution within the Archipelago again describes an east-west division consistent with transmission over different contact zones.

The simplest structures are known as portal tombs – or dolmens, or sometimes cromlechs – although, again, only the lack of a plausible alternative explanation has caused them to be designated as tombs. They consist of three or four upright stones with a flat capstone placed on top. Two of the stones are usually placed so that they create an entrance or portal leading into a simple, rectangular chamber. Quite how they functioned is once again not clear. One interpretation is that what we see is the inside of an earthen barrow or tumulus, a stone framework long since denuded of earth by weathering and erosion. The advantage of this theory is that it offers a simple and practical explanation of how the capstone could be put in place without having to lift it off the ground. One alternative view is that the dead body or bodies were placed in the open chamber and left there to decompose or be eaten by animals and birds. A second is that the dead were placed on top of the capstone to be scavenged by birds in a manner equivalent of a Tibetan sky burial. The very simplicity of these structures, and a lack of associated archaeological finds, makes them difficult to date, but where associated items have been found, they generally date from between 3800 and 3200 BC. Over four hundred such tombs – if that is what they were – are known in the Archipelago, mostly in the west, with the heaviest concentration in the north and east of the Western Isle and smaller clusters on the coast of the Western Uplands and the South-Western Peninsula.

A more complex burial structure was the court tomb. Again, over four hundred examples are known, most of them in the northern half of the Western Isle, while a variant form, the Clyde-Carlingford or horned cairn, is found in Argyll and across Dumfries and Galloway, indicating close contact across the Western Channel. Court tombs, which almost always face east, consist of a simple, chambered grave under a mound or barrow with a clearly defined entrance. The name derives from what would have been an open area or courtyard, often paved, in front of the entrance to the burial chamber. This courtyard area was in some cases flanked by curved, stone or wooden 'horns'.

Court tombs are sometimes referred to as gallery graves to distinguish them from the passage graves, which, as the name implies, have an extended passage leading from the entrance into the heart of the mound, where there are often multiple burial chambers. Passage graves are distributed throughout the western side of the Archipelago, from the South-Western Peninsula to the Far Northern Isles, and across the Western Isle. Given such a wide distribution, size and design naturally vary widely. In the Outer Isles, numbers of small, early passage graves are often found clustered together in what are, in effect, cemeteries, while in the Western Isle and the Northern Isles, there are individual examples which are both spectacular and monumental.

The first, modest passage graves may have been constructed as early as 4000 BC and are found on both sides of the Western Channel. As with cursus monuments, the passing of time saw a widening area of distribution and a significant increase in scale. Newgrange, built between 3200 and 3100 BC, is quite simply massive. The mound has a diameter of over eighty metres and a height of almost twelve. The total weight of earth involved has been estimated at more than 200,000 tons; and some of the stones used in its construction have been transported over fifty kilometres from their place of origin. Placed around the base of the mound are ninety-seven 'kerbstones', all carved with elaborate spiral or serpentiform patterns – although it has to be added that the external appearance of the tomb has been damaged by the 'restoration' of a white quartz retaining wall around the base of the mound, which appears to owe more to the architecture of the 1960s than to the Neolithic period. Above the main entrance is a rectangular, stone portal or 'box' through which, at the winter solstice, sunlight shines directly down the passage and into the central chamber. Beyond it, the passage extends nineteen metres into the mound to a central chamber nearly six metres tall with a spectacular corbelled roof and flanked by three smaller chambers. The orientation of Newgrange is paralleled by that of the passage grave of Maes Howe on the largest of the Northern Isles, which also has a spectacular central chamber, and is also aligned to catch the midwinter sun; while Bryn Celli Ddu in Anglesey catches the light of the summer, rather than the winter, solstice. Inside Newgrange, there are more carved stones, some displaying spiral patterns, others exhibiting angular and linear designs. These carvings, together with those on the stones outside, and over two hundred more found at the large-scale passage grave at Knowth just a kilometre away, have been seen as purely decorative, as symbolic representations of the Neolithic cosmos, and as evidence that the Neolithic rituals involved mind-altering, hallucinogenic drugs. Any or all of these explanations could be valid. Given its scale, the complexity of its construction, and sophistication of its decoration, it is worth emphasising that Newgrange predates not only Stonehenge, but also Mycenae and the Pyramids.

Portal tombs, court tombs, and passage graves all appear to have arrived across the Atlantic Zone. However, long barrows appear to have arrived from the east, across the Channel and Southern North Sea Zones, again indicating an east-west cultural divide on the Main Island. Over 40,000 long barrows have been found on the Continent, from Turkey to Spain and from Spain to Sweden. Over three hundred have been identified in the Archipelago, from Aberdeen in the north all the way south to Kent and Sussex, and westwards across the Lowland Zone to Gloucester, Somerset, and Dorset. Most of them appear to have been built between

3800 and 3400 BC. The most obvious difference between long barrows and passage graves is that they take the form not of a circular mound, but of a rectangular or wedge-shaped one. Coldrum Long Barrow in Kent is one of the oldest, built in two phases, the first somewhere around 3900 BC, the second some two hundred years later. Both the early date and its location, close to the Medway and Thames Estuaries, point to transmission across the Channel Zone. It consists of a rectangular mound, aligned east—west, with stone revetments on the outside; a burial chamber at the eastern end; and a well-defined entrance with uprights and a large capstone. Like many long barrows, Coldrum contained the remains of numerous bodies – in this case at least twenty-two, from a new-born baby to elderly men and women.

Some of the best-known long barrows form what archaeologists call the Cotswold-Severn Group. Wayland's Smithy in Oxfordshire, located close to the ancient Ridgeway track and first built c.3590 BC, is one of the most interesting. The name, of course, comes from a later age: it was coined by the Saxons, but it is an indication of cultural continuity in spiritual matters that, 4,000 years later, they should have accepted the site as sacred and chosen to associate it with one of their own gods. The barrow was built in two phases. The first consisted of a wooden mortuary structure with a stone floor and large split tree trunks at either end. It contained one male skeleton, buried in a crouched position, and fourteen other skeletons, all of which had been excarnated and disarticulated. All the remains had been deposited within a comparatively short period, probably between ten and fifty years. The tomb was then 'closed' by being covered with earth to create a twenty-metre-long barrow. About a hundred years later, probably c.3450 BC, a large, stone mortuary was built on top of the first barrow. It had a terminal chamber and two side chambers, giving it a cruciform shape, and contained the disarticulated remains of eight more skeletons, one of them a child. After another comparatively short period, perhaps fifty or sixty years, this tomb, too, was closed by being covered with earth, forming the longer, wedge-shaped barrow that we see today.

There were other long barrows, such as West Kennet in Wiltshire, dated to c.3650 BC, another of the Cotswold-Severn Group, where the earth mound was an integral part of the mortuary structure from the beginning and not a means of closing the barrow. In such cases, closure was effected by putting massive blocking stones across the entrance to prevent further access. Most long barrows exhibit the same basic structure: a forecourt area, perhaps flanked by stone or timber wings, a well-defined entrance, and beyond the entrance a mortuary area with one or more burial chambers, usually roofed with wood or stone.

These monumental stone-built structures from the early Neolithic period are all connected with death and its associated ritual observances, and the same may well be true of the great earthen structures – causewayed enclosures and cursus – although we cannot be sure. Yet the entire Neolithic population could not have been buried in monumental stone tombs or in the segments of causewayed enclosures. The remains of most of the Neolithic population, when they survive at all, are found in pits under or close to the remains of huts, on the edge of villages, in open ground beyond the village, or even down flint mines. Who then was buried in the tombs? The short answer is that we do not know. It is tempting to see the tombs as reserved for members of elite groups or elite families – elite, in this context, meaning those exercising political or religious authority within the tribe – but unlike elite Iron Age burials, Neolithic barrows contain no grave goods to indicate status. The arrangement of the first Wayland Smithy barrow, with one complete skeleton separated from other disarticulated ones, may suggest that a particular individual was being honoured; and medical studies of the remains at Coldrum indicate that all the dead may have belonged to a single-family group. Beyond such possibilities, we are back in the realm of speculation.

The people who lived in the Archipelago in early Neolithic times were not 'primitive'. We do not know how their society was organised, but clearly it *was* organised. They were capable of establishing and maintaining a social order, and of planning their activities in tune with the annual, agricultural cycle. The mechanics of their daily life – what they grew, what they ate, how they dressed, where they lived – can be described and, to some extent at least, imagined, because they probably did not differ greatly from any other agrarian society. However, Neolithic society was also capable of planning and executing construction projects on a scale that would be regarded as challenging even today. Without modern technology, simply putting the capstone on a portal tomb would have required significant cooperative effort. Digging a ten-kilometre cursus or shifting 200,000 tons of earth to build a passage grave, would have needed cooperation on a grand scale, and a shared understanding of and belief in the purpose and necessity of whatever was being built – as well as some kind of coordinating intelligence, whether an individual or a team. What little evidence we have suggests that Neolithic society was cooperative and collaborative, but alternative structures are possible. It might be, for example, that society was dominated by powerful authoritarian elites, who used slave labour to build cursus monuments, passage graves and long barrows as the pharaohs built the pyramids. It seems unlikely, but – as so often with the distant past – certainty remains elusive.

Attempting to reconstruct the spiritual beliefs of Neolithic people is a way of establishing the first links in a chain of connections that leads from them to us. The different kinds of early Neolithic tomb all feature the idea of a door or an entrance. A twenty-first century mind might see the door as a symbol, a concrete representation of a metaphorical passing into another world. For Neolithic people, the door was of real importance. It was more than just a hole through which the living could pass in order to dispose of corpses. The scale of these entrances, with massive pillars and with flanking wings, all drawing attention towards the door itself, is significant. So, too, is the fact that these entrances were not collapsed or destroyed when tombs were closed. They may have been blocked or buried, but they were left in place. Neolithic people would almost certainly have seen passing through the door as a literal transition to another world.

The other constant is water. We have seen that causewayed enclosures and cursus monuments were frequently located near water; and that trackways across water were regarded as having ritual significance, even when their primary purpose was practical. Too many items of value – some, like jadeite axe heads, of immense value – have been recovered from the course of trackways and from the beds of rivers for their presence to be a matter of accident or chance, and we should not underestimate the significance of this behaviour in a culture where the range and supply of material goods was limited. In our culture, we still throw coins into fountains or wells and, if pressed, will probably say we were doing it for good luck. Why did Neolithic people do it? Almost certainly to reach out to and propitiate their ancestors. This matches our knowledge of peoples in similar societies elsewhere in the world, where the ancestors are feared and respected in equal measure, where they can influence the world of living for good or ill. There may also have been nature spirits of gods of place who needed to be propitiated or worshipped as well. We cannot know. However, it does seem that water represented another doorway, another access point to the world of the dead and the ancestors, the otherworld.

Then there is the actual treatment of the dead body. Early Neolithic practice was far from uniform. Away from the big, stone-built tombs, there were cremations and burials of different kinds. Many of the tombs, however, display evidence of excarnation, secondary burial, and disarticulation. In other words, corpses were stripped of their flesh, perhaps sometimes by animals or birds but also certainly by members of the tribe. Bodies might be dismembered, and skeletons disarticulated. If not excarnated they might be buried, then dug up and reburied a few months later, sometimes before the flesh had completely disappeared from the bones. In some tombs, notably those of the Cotswold-Severn Group, skeletal remains were sorted and arranged so that legs are in one place, arms in another, skulls in another, and so on. This sounds gruesome and, by our standards, it is. Yet, as Alice Roberts notes in her book on the Iron Age Celts – who also frequently decapitated and dismembered their dead – our own tradition of burning the bodies of our loved ones at 1,000 degrees centigrade for anything up to three hours, and then pulverizing what is left into powder, can appear equally weird if you think about it.[42] Gruesome or not, we have to assume that the Neolithic treatment of the dead outlined above was normal; that it represented accepted practice. If, again by our standards, the process seems an extended one, this is because each procedure marked a stage in the dead person's journey from our world to the world of the ancestors. It may be that continued involvement with the dead comforted the living. Our funerals are over in a few hours at most. Neolithic man would be shocked.

The evidence does not allow for firm conclusions, but we can attempt a picture of what Neolithic people might have thought and believed. We can imagine that death for them was ever-present and very real. Average life expectancy for Neolithic people was no more than their late twenties. There was a strong belief in the reality of a world beyond death – a world that could, as it were, come back to haunt the living if the correct rites were not observed. This otherworld, inhabited by the ancestors, could be 'reached' through water. The vital importance of the ancestors is evident in the number and the nature of the offerings that were made to them; in the number and the scale of the monuments apparently dedicated to them; and in the amount of effort society felt compelled to invest in the construction of such monuments. We can perhaps take this further and suggest that the rites and ceremonies surrounding death, the ancestors and the otherworld were not just important, but were in fact the central purpose of Neolithic society. This is an idea with which the twenty-first century might struggle, but it would not seem odd or unreasonable to the medieval mind, to the monks on Mount Athos, or to a Tibetan lama before the Chinese takeover in 1959. So, in the absence of any other evidence of a political or social structure, we may ask whether early Neolithic society was a theocracy. Did those who mediated contact between the living and the otherworld also have the temporal authority to decide upon and control the construction of a Newgrange or Maes Howe? We cannot know the answer, but the question is a legitimate one.

None of this might seem to take us very far forward in understanding the Neolithic mind; but it does at least establish a baseline. One of the things we shall see as our story unfolds is a remarkable continuity in certain aspects of belief relating to death and the ancestors. That does not mean that beliefs and the rituals surrounding them did not change – far from it – but rather that there was a coherence, an evolutionary quality to that change; and the early Neolithic period is where we get our first sighting of those beliefs.

6 Ritual in the Landscape

The first phase of the Neolithic period in the Archipelago was characterised by ideas which had come from the Continent. Farming, land use, and (except for cursus monuments) the massive structures which were dug or built in all parts of the Archipelago all followed models which had evolved and developed on the Continent. But Neolithic society was not static, and, from somewhere around 3100 BC, the people of the Archipelago began to build new kinds of monuments – and perhaps to practise new forms of ritual to go with them. These monuments were circular – henges, circles of wooden posts, stone circles – and they were built in large numbers, apparently expressing a new sense of shared cultural identity which diverged from that observable on the Continent.

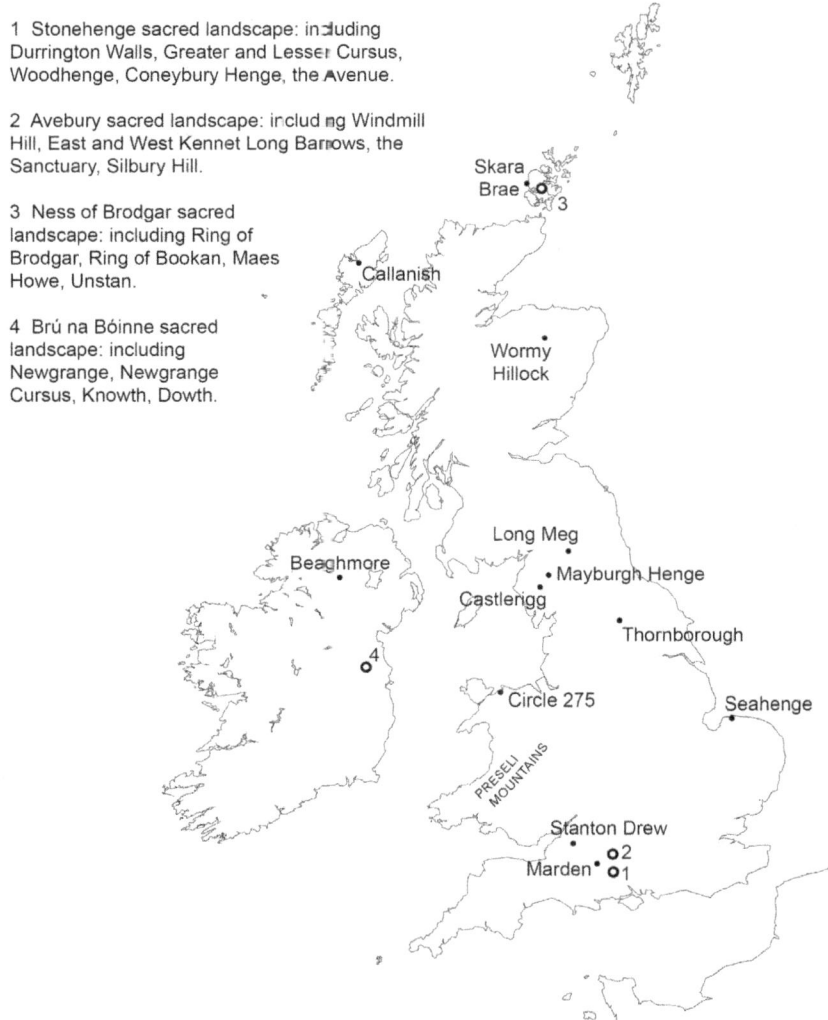

Map 7 Henges, Stone Circles, and Sacred Landscapes

The terms 'henge' and 'stone circle' are often used interchangeably, but there is a distinction – even though it is one that archaeologists themselves often ignore. The word 'henge' is what linguists call a back formation. It comes from the name Stonehenge, which is itself derived from the Old English *stan*, meaning 'stone', and either *hencg* meaning 'hinge', or *hengen*, meaning 'hanging' – either of which could describe the great arches, the trilithons, that are unique to Stonehenge. 'Hinge' might refer to the join between the uprights and the lintels; while 'hanging' is more likely to take the meaning 'supported' than that of 'gallows' – although the discovery of a decapitated seventh-century corpse has led to the suggestion that Stonehenge may have become a place of execution in Saxon times.

Despite this derivation, by the eighteenth century the word 'henge' had come to mean a ditch-and-bank earthwork enclosing a circular area of ground, with the ditch, in most cases – and in contrast to causewayed enclosures – inside the bank. Such a broad definition leaves scope for many variations. In some henges, such as the three, enormous, aligned circles at Thornborough in North Yorkshire, or the three Priddy Circles in Somerset, the circular, central areas appear to have remained empty. Others, including some of the best known, such as Avebury Ring in Wiltshire, the Ring of Brodgar and the Stones of Stenness in the Northern Isles, contained one or more stone circles. Woodhenge, not far from Stonehenge, contained six concentric rings of wooden posts; while nearby Durrington Walls housed both a village – the only henge to show evidence of extensive habitation – and several post circles. Size, too, varies enormously: Marden, again in Wiltshire, is 530 metres across, while the wonderfully named Wormy Hillock in Aberdeenshire is no more than six metres in diameter.

Stone circles and wooden-post circles exhibit similar variations. Most are circular, although some are elliptical or egg-shaped. Some have stone-lined approach avenues, or arrangements of stone at their centre. Others are simply circular monuments. Avebury, the biggest stone circle in the world, is 347 metres in diameter, while the smallest, known as Circle 275 and standing on a headland overlooking the sea above Penmaenmawr in Gwynedd, is three metres across and consists of just five stones. Stone circles are found throughout the Archipelago, but those in the Western Isle tend to be smaller than those on the Main Island.

On the western fringes of the Continental Lands, there are isolated examples of standing stones and stone arrangements that pre-date similar constructions in the Archipelago. One complex arrangement of stones in Portugal, known as the Almendres Cromlech, may date back as far as 6000 BC, and seems to have included several stone circles. At Carnac in Brittany about 4000 BC, over 3,000 stones were carefully arrayed, not in circles but in a series of straight lines. And on the tiny island of Er Lannic in the Gulf of Morbihan, only a short distance from Carnac, there are – or were, because one is now submerged – two stone circles, both dating from c.3000 BC and each consisting of sixty stones. It is just possible that these examples show the slow northward movement of a basic idea which eventually crossed the Atlantic Zone to the Archipelago, but they appear more like isolated experiments. Wherever it originated, the concept of stone circles fired the imagination of the people of the Archipelago – over a thousand examples have been identified.[43]

There are a handful of stone circles outside the Archipelago, but henges are found nowhere else at all. When and where they originated is not entirely certain. The earliest example appears to be the Stones of Stenness, just half-a-kilometre south of the religious centre of Ness of Brodgar on the largest of the Northern Isles. The henge and stone circles at Stenness, and Ness of Bodgar itself, were already under construction before 3100 BC, two or even three hundred years before the first phase of Avebury or of Stonehenge. Many henges in the south of the Main Island were built, or at least begun, around 3000 BC or shortly afterwards. The evidence we have at present indicates that the henge-and-stone-circle concept originated in the Northern Isles and – in a manner similar to cursus monuments – moved southwards, although we still lack secure dating for many henges.

Henges are found in all parts of the Archipelago, with the exception of the Far Northern Isles. They were built in large numbers, although they are less common in the south-eastern part of the Main Island. While there are regional variations in size and structure, the east-west divide which we saw in the distribution of different types of tombs has, if not disappeared, at least significantly diminished. This may imply improved communications within the Archipelago, perhaps based on a greater degree of linguistic homogeneity than earlier or it may imply a greater homogeneity of belief and ritual behaviour. The existence of a greater degree of shared culture than earlier in the Neolithic period is suggested by the distribution of Grooved Ware, a kind of flat-bottomed, straight-sided pottery, decorated with incised lines and dots. Grooved Ware is mainly associated with henge monuments and ritual sites and was current from about 3400 BC for about a thousand years. It is found throughout the Archipelago but, again, the earliest known examples are found in the Northern Isles.

As with earlier Neolithic monuments, the great henges and stone circles immediately impress with their scale and the immense collective effort that must have been required to build them. The three Thornborough henges and their connecting avenue make up a single monument which stretches for some 1.7 kilometres. The outer circle of the complex Avebury monument consisted of ninety-eight sarsen stones – a particular kind of sandstone block found on Salisbury Plain – each weighing anything up to forty tons. The bluestones which make up one of the inner rings of Stonehenge were quarried in the Preseli region in the Western Uplands. There were probably eighty of these stones, each about four metres long and weighing about four tons. Archaeologists have identified the exact location where they were quarried and confirmed that they originally formed a stone circle near the quarry site. Somewhere between 3000 and 2755 BC, they were transported the 225 kilometres to Stonehenge where they were re-erected as part of the first phase of construction.[44] [45] The great sarsen stones, which make up both the arched, sarsen circle and the horseshoe of even larger trilithon arches, may well have weighed up to sixty tons before being shaped. They were transported from the Marlborough Downs, 32 kilometres to the north-west. Quite how stones of such size and weight could be transported over such distances has been a matter of debate and experiment – including the ill-fated Millennium Bluestone Project designed to transport a bluestone (christened Elvis Preseli) from its source to Stonehenge. The first stage of the journey was successfully accomplished using a wooden sledge, but when the four-ton stone was being loaded onto two replica Neolithic boats, it slipped and sank in fifteen metres of water. Nonetheless, at Stonehenge, at Avebury, and at sites throughout the Archipelago, enormous stones were successfully transported, frequently over considerable distances, and were successfully raised into position.

Stonehenge is unique. It is unique in its design, using lintels to span between uprights in both the sarsen circle and the trilithons; in the extent to which its great stones were shaped; and in the fact that it continued to be used, reshaped and remodelled for nearly 1,500 years. It is unique also in that it has entered the national consciousness: everyone knows its name and what it looks like. It has been the subject of innumerable theories – both serious and crackpot. It has also been studied more intensely than almost any other prehistoric monument, and what has been learned gives us a sense of Neolithic design and construction as a mixture of the amazingly sophisticated and the grindingly basic. The big sarsen stones were delivered to the site having been very roughly shaped. They then had to be squared off and shaped with sufficient precision to take their place in the circle. Huge amounts of stone had to be chipped and ground away using nothing but other stones. The lintels of the sarsen circle and the trilithons are held in position using mortise and tenon joints. As Julian Richards points out in his *Stonehenge: The Story So Far*, hollowing out the mortise holes in the lintels would be bad enough, but the amount of stone needing to be removed and the effort required to leave the tenon protruding on top of the uprights is almost inconceivable.[46] Once shaped and finished, the stones had to be raised into an upright position – a task which had to combine sufficient force to lift some forty tons of deadweight with the ability to position it precisely, so that the curve of the circle was maintained and the lintels connecting each stone to its neighbours were exactly level. Moreover, Stonehenge sits on a slight, north-facing slope. The builders were aware of this and adjusted the height of the uprights accordingly so that the circle of lintels remained level.[47] This level of technical achievement is matched only by the passage grave at Maes Howe, where the stones of the central burial chamber have been cut, shaped, and fitted together with mathematical precision.

Stonehenge, Avebury, Stenness, Brodgar, Thornborough, Callanish in the Outer Isles, Beaghmore in County Tyrone – these and all the other major henge-and-stone-circle monuments raise the same question: how were they built without what we would see as essential tools? Without theodolites, tape measures, levels, and – above all – without the written word and the ability to draw plans on paper? The Scottish engineer, Alexander Thom (1894–1985), came up with the theory that there was a standard 'Megalithic yard' – 83 centimetres – used in the planning and construction of Neolithic monuments.[48] On the whole, this seems unlikely: Thom's yard can be just as easily explained as the length of a pace. A more probable explanation is that Neolithic builders designed and constructed their monuments using measuring rods of equal length. Circles could have been marked out using a rope attached to a central stake; and levels could have been maintained by using water-filled troughs. And we can imagine plans or rough designs being chalked on a rock or cut into the turf with an antler or a stone knife. Even then, the Neolithic architect, unable to write down detailed measurements and specifications, must

6 Ritual in the Landscape

have been able to hold a staggering amount of information in his head. This leads to an important point about the pre-modern mind. Centuries of books and libraries, and now decades of computers and databases mean that the modern mind – actors, opera singers, and concert soloists perhaps excepted – tends not to store large quantities of structured information. Rather, it knows where to find information, and how to synthesise and apply it once it is retrieved. The pre-modern mind stored information differently. We are familiar with the idea that ancient poets, whether Greek or Anglo-Saxon, would memorise immense quantities of poetry for public recitation. Similarly, monks in Anglo-Saxon times were required to memorise the entire *Book of Psalms* as well as hymns, introits, antiphons, and other music for performance in church. The builders of henges and stone circles would have needed to commit plans and dimensions to memory in the same way – and to share them with their fellows, probably by recitation. It would have been important to do so: construction took place over long periods; information had to be communicated over long distances; and life spans were short.

This brings us back to the question, what was it all for? Looking at causewayed enclosures, cursus monuments, and other structures from the early Neolithic period, we established certain parameters. Henges and stone circles seem to mark not so much a change as an expansion or an intensification of ritual behaviour. This is not just because of the number that were constructed – but also because they often form a central part of what have become known as ritual or sacred landscapes. These are areas that contain a concentration of Neolithic and often also early Bronze Age monuments. They are found throughout the Archipelago, although there is a concentration in the Wessex region, with no less than nine within a 100-kilometre radius of Stonehenge. Many, though not all, sacred landscapes appear to have begun with a causewayed enclosure. Over time, other monuments were built, some standing alone, others linked by directional alignment, sightlines, or avenues of stone, but all connected with the beliefs and the rituals surrounding the dead and the ancestors that we have postulated as central to Neolithic society. As Cunliffe has said: 'You could not go far without confronting a sacred location: the entire landscape seemed to belong to the gods.'[49]

The great henge and stone circle at Avebury were constructed in several stages between *c.*3000 and *c.*2600 BC. The outer circle is familiar from photographs, but recent geophysical surveys have shown that, within the main circle, there was a square arrangement of large stones, and at the central point of the whole monument was some form of hall or house, which predates the rest of the structure. This arrangement, complex in itself, sits at the centre of a collection of other extraordinary monuments, all within two kilometres. The oldest, to the north, is the causewayed enclosure of Windmill Hill, dating from c.3800 BC. West Kennet long barrow to the south, c.3650, also pre-dates the henge. So, in all probability, does East Kennett (*sic*) long barrow, also to the south, although it has never been sufficiently excavated to determine a date. To the south-east, on Overton Hill, lies the remarkable and complex monument known as The Sanctuary. Originally consisting of a simple post circle, begun c.3000 BC, more post circles and finally a large stone circle were added over the next few hundred years. About the time it was completed, it was connected to the main Avebury henge by a two-kilometre-long avenue of stones, known as West Kennet Avenue. A second stone-lined avenue, Beckhampton Avenue, leads west from Avebury main henge and connects with an arrangement of stones called the Longstones, only two of which remain standing. These are set on the edge of a large enclosure, badly damaged by ploughing, possibly constructed c.2900–2700 BC. The Avebury sacred landscape also contains a number of smaller stone alignments and many Bronze Age barrows, as well as the great bulk of Silbury Hill. This was last of the main monuments to be built, somewhere between 2400 and 2300 BC, probably in several stages. It is nearly forty metres high, making it Europe's (and possibly the world's) largest man-made hill – so large, in fact, that archaeologists have estimated that, given the technologies available at the time, Silbury Hill would have taken five hundred men working for fifteen years to complete.

 Stonehenge is part of a sacred landscape which has two centres: the henge itself and Durrington Walls. It includes the mysteries of the Greater and Lesser Cursus, the concentric circles of Woodhenge, Coneybury Henge, and the three-kilometre long, semi-circular Avenue connecting Stonehenge with the River Avon. In the Western Isle, the Brú na Bóinne (Bend in the Boyne)[50] sacred landscape is one of the densest in the Archipelago. At its centre is the dominating presence of Newgrange, but there are some forty other passage graves, including Knowth and Dowth, as well as the Newgrange Cursus and half-a-dozen henges, one of which was only discovered during the drought in the summer of 2018. Yet the most spectacular sacred landscape in the Archipelago is to be found in the Northern Isles.

The Northern Isles were probably settled between 4000 and 3800 BC by people moving up the western side of the Main Island, and they were soon – by Neolithic standards – densely populated. Almost 3,000 Neolithic sites have been identified across the islands. One of the best known is the preserved village of Skara Brae. It was occupied for six or seven hundred years until *c*.2500 BC, after which it was buried in earth and sand for four-and-a-half millennia. The inhabitants were makers of Grooved Ware, and their eight houses with their stone-slab beds and dressers, cupboards and water channels give a unique insight into the domestic lives of a group of Neolithic families. Ten kilometres south-east of Skara Brae is a narrow strip of land known as the Ness of Brodgar, separating the sea loch of Stenness from the freshwater Loch of Harray. Today, there is a narrow channel linking the two lochs but in Neolithic times this might not have been the case. The Ness, we now know, was the cultural focus of the Northern Isles and in all likelihood of a much larger area. To the north we find the Ring of Brodgar, over a hundred metres in diameter and originally consisting of sixty huge stones; a massive henge, known as the Ring of Bookan; and a number of barrows, cairns and standing stones. To the south lie the Stones of Stenness, the oldest-known stone circle in the Archipelago; the superb passage grave of Maes Howe; and a Neolithic village known as the Barnhouse Settlement, which consisted of some fifteen structures, including a building aligned on Maes Howe which archaeologists consider was used for ritual or ceremonial purposes.

Excavations began on the Ness of Brodgar itself only in 2003, when what had been thought to be a ridge of glacial moraine was discovered to be the remains of a huge Neolithic settlement. The results have been nothing short of a revelation. Called *Ness of Brodgar* after its location, the village or township covered at least 2.5 hectares and was inhabited between *c.*3500 and *c.*2300 BC. To date, over thirty buildings have been uncovered and there are thought to be many more. Discoveries have included the first Neolithic roof slates, and the first evidence that Neolithic people painted their walls, some early stone steps, and some unique stone spatulas. While, as usual, it is difficult to determine precisely how individual buildings were used, the settlement was not solely a domestic one. At its heart is a building known as Structure Ten, twenty-five metres long and nineteen metres wide, with walls four metres thick – dubbed by the media a 'Neolithic cathedral'. While we cannot tell precisely how it was used, there is no doubt that it acted as some kind of temple or centre of ritual. It was probably built before 2900 BC and remained in use until c.2450 BC. Like other Neolithic monuments we have looked at, it was not abandoned but formally closed. Whatever 'closure' involved, it certainly included a massive feast: the bones of some four hundred cattle were found in the passage surrounding the building. Putting a temple or ritual site beyond use was not a new idea. There are precedents dating back as far as the beginning of the Neolithic period when the vast complex of Göbekli Tepe in Anatolia appears to have been deliberately buried. Ness of Brodgar is the best and largest example in the Archipelago.

Sitting at the heart of what is probably the most impressive of all sacred landscapes, the sheer scale of the Ness of Brodgar settlement is unparalleled in the Archipelago. It was clearly a major religious centre with connections that went far beyond the Northern Isles. We noted earlier how henges, stone circles, and Grooved Ware pottery, appear to have originated in the Northern Isles. Current excavations at Ness of Brodgar support the idea that the whole second phase of Neolithic culture in the Archipelago, with religious and ritual observance at its core, had its origins in the Northern Isles, and developed sufficient momentum to migrate rapidly southwards. This idea has been contested in some quarters, perhaps in part because almost all the new cultural concepts of the last three millennia have come from the Continent, arriving in the west or south of the Archipelago, so that the idea of an indigenous and northern origin for an important cultural shift is difficult to accept.

The Ness of Brodgar sits in the middle of a wide circuit of low hills. It is a beautiful location, and most sacred landscapes are similarly positioned in areas of natural beauty. This does not appear to be accidental. The monumentality of the great henges and stone circles is impressive in itself, and a big, open setting would have increased the drama and power of the rituals conducted there, creating a connection between the monuments built by man and the natural world which belonged to the gods. Sacred landscapes consist of monuments of different kinds built at different times, probably indicating the evolution of ritual practice within a common and accepted belief system. Yet some important sacred landscapes appear not to have been what we might term greenfield sites. They are located in areas that seem to have been regarded as sacred in earlier times. The areas around Stonehenge and around Thornborough were in use, probably for ritual purposes, during the Mesolithic period; while at Avebury, Stanton Drew in Somerset, and Brú na Bóinne in County Meath there is evidence of Mesolithic activity, though we cannot be sure of its purpose. As elsewhere, this kind of continuity is a feature of human behaviour in the Archipelago. The Anglo-Saxons accepted the sacredness of Neolithic sites, among them Wayland's Smithy (see Chapter 5), and when their time came, Christians would build churches in locations previously given over to the worship of heathen gods.

None of this takes our understanding of how the henges, stone circles, and the other monuments were actually used much further forward. Of course, there is no reason to suppose that henges had a single purpose, any more than a cathedral, although dedicated to the Christian religion, conducts only one kind of service. Much has been made of the alignment of henges and stone circles in relation to the sun and the moon. We have seen how both Newgrange and Maes Howe are positioned so that the midwinter sun shines into the burial chamber. So much has been written about Stonehenge, and so many theories advanced and countered, that it is not possible to go into detail. The case for a relationship between the position of the stones and the rising and setting of the sun on the midwinter and midsummer solstices is undeniably persuasive. Elsewhere in the Stonehenge landscape, the entrances to both Woodhenge and Coneybury appear to be aligned towards sunrise at midsummer. In Cumbria, Mayburgh Henge, Castlerigg stone circle, and the stone circle known as Long Meg and her Daughters, all appear to have equinoctial or solstitial alignments. The dog-leg arrangement of the three, linked Thornborough henges has been seen as intended to mirror Orion's Belt. Alignments involving the sun, the moon and the stars have been claimed for many other henges and circles throughout the Archipelago.

Although some of these ideas may be more fanciful than others, there is no reason to regard the alignment of monuments in relation to the sun, moon, and stars as surprising. To a society based on farming, where the fertility of the animals and the fields was all-important, the movement of the sun and the cycle of the seasons was life itself. What could be more natural than marking and celebrating the solstices? Neolithic people were certainly capable of making the necessary observations and calculations. Again, what could be more natural than to incorporate the movement of the sun into the structure of one's temples and rituals? Most Christian churches face east. People of Jewish faith face Jerusalem when praying; Muslims face Mecca. Positioning entrances and stones to align with lunar cycles or astronomical observations would require more detailed calculations, but similar calculations would have been necessary when navigating a boat across the Atlantic Zone or the Eastern Zone (see Chapter 3). We are constantly being surprised by the feats of engineering and the craftsmanship of which Neolithic people were capable, and this may well be another example of how sophisticated they were. However, that emphatically does not mean that Stonehenge or any other stone circle was intended to be a calendar, nor yet, as it was described in the book *Stonehenge Decoded*, a 'Neolithic computer'.[51]

Henges and stone circles were connected with the spiritual beliefs of their builders, with the focus on death and the ancestors which we identified in the earlier Neolithic period. And there can be no doubt of the immense amount of planning, organisation, and effort which went into building these monuments. Beyond that, we must again speculate. Is circularity a clue? Was a circle intended to mirror the shape of the sun or the moon? Or was it a symbolic entrance to the otherworld? Was it both? If it was an entrance to the otherworld, is the fact that so many circular monuments are approached by an avenue significant? Were the dead carried along a ceremonial route to a symbolic entrance to the world of the ancestors? Are the cup and ring markings found throughout the Archipelago and across the Continental Lands linked in conceptual terms to wood and stone circles? Is it just coincidence cup and ring markings almost all take the form of concentric circles with a single line, like an avenue, cutting through to the central point?

What happened in the circle itself? Given the alignments discussed above, it may well be that ceremonies and rituals were conducted to mark the solstices and other key moments in the solar or lunar cycles. Some have suggested that the stones were places of healing, that they were considered to have magical properties. Others have seen them as places of sacrifice. Human sacrifice – often with women or children as the victims – is well attested in primitive religions in many parts of the world, but evidence for the practice in the Archipelago is limited. There are a number of instances which suggest human sacrifice, but we have no way of knowing how common it may have been. The body of a child in a crouching position and with a split skull was found at the centre of Woodhenge. Some archaeologists have seen this as evidence of a dedication rite conducted to mark the completion of the henge, although that interpretation has been challenged. At Stonehenge, there are a large number of cremation pits, all containing the remains of men between twenty-five and forty. The age range suggests that they were specifically chosen for burial in that particular place. The consensus is that they were probably leading members of local tribes or families, and that the location reflects their status, but we know so little of the rites and ceremonies of the time that they could conceivably be the victims of sacrifice.

Another equally plausible theory, which again sees the circle as an entrance to the otherworld, is that henges and stone circles were used for the equivalent of sky burials; that the bodies of the dead were carried to the centre and there exposed for excarnation, either by members of a priestly caste, or by birds and animals. This theory received support with the discovery in 1998 of Seahenge on the north Norfolk coast. Seahenge was uncovered by tidal action on the beach, although it had originally been built on an area of salt marsh. It consisted of fifty-five split oak trunks, felled – according to dendrochronology – in the spring or summer of 2049 BC, and set closely together in a circle. In the centre of the circle was a large oak tree placed upside down so that its roots spread out to create a platform which would have been suitable for the exposure of bodies. Speculation can always take us further. The vast bulk of Silbury Hill has no obvious purpose. Ceremonies involving a lighted beacon might have been held on its summit, thus connecting with other communities which would have been able to see the fire from a distance. Or was the circular summit plateau used for the exposure of bodies?

A more complex theory was proposed, also in 1998, by the British archaeologist Mike Parker Pearson and his Madagascan colleague, Ramilisonina. They compared the contemporary Madagascan practice of erecting standing stones as a symbol of death with the arrangement of Neolithic monuments in landscape around Durrington Walls and Stonehenge. They concluded that the area around Stonehenge was divided into a domain of the living, associated with wood (Durrington and Woodhenge); a liminal or transitional zone, represented by a passage down the River Avon, through which the dead had to pass on their journey to join the ancestors; and a domain of the dead or the ancestors, associated with stone (Stonehenge). It is a fascinating theory, and the summary above is inevitably a huge simplification. It has the merit of being applicable to other sacred landscapes, not just to the Stonehenge area; and it also emphasises the evident importance to Neolithic society of the symbolic journey made by the dead on their way to join the ancestors. In the end, however, it seems a little too compressed, and a little too comprehensive – an attempt, in a single theory, to explain a complex reality which evolved over many hundreds of years.

If asked, in the absence of the written word and documentary evidence, to interpret the cathedrals and churches scattered across the British Isles, or to explain the concentration of churches found in places such as Canterbury or York, what would we say? Some churches date back to Anglo-Saxon times. Many of the great cathedrals were begun under the Normans. Gothic styles flourished during the thirteenth, fourteenth and fifteenth centuries. Abbeys were demolished and statuary defaced during the Reformation. Hundreds of parish churches were restored by the Victorians. Many churches built after the Second World War feature concrete, steel, and glass, and are wholly different in design from those built fifty or a hundred years earlier. Churches belong to different denominations, sects, and splinter groups, from the Russian Orthodox to the Scottish Free Church. They are dedicated to saints as various as St Peter and St Rumwold, even to historical figures such as King Charles the Martyr. Churches reflect the constant evolution of the Christian religion over 2,000 years. The era of henges and stone circles lasted 1,500 years. Why should we expect its history to be any less diverse or complex?

There are no hard and fast answers. We have to admit that we do not know how henge monuments were used. It is natural for us to want to see the Stones of Stenness, or Callanish, or Avebury as the equivalent of churches: sacred buildings where ceremonies were held to mark special events – the cycle of the year, the harvest, deaths, perhaps even marriages. These are our preconceptions and expectations, and we may be wrong, but research at the University of Salford has revealed one interesting connection. By building a scale model of what Stonehenge might have looked like with all the main stones in place and reconstructing its acoustic properties, researchers found that it reflected and amplified sound.[52] Although there were gaps between the stones and no roof, the voice of a priest or an orator, the sound of drums and chanting, would have carried to hundreds, even thousands, of people gathered within the compass of the circle. Not only would this have had a practical value in terms of communication, it would also have been a sound unlike anything they had ever heard. In a world before concrete and brick, where the only buildings were of wood or wattle-and-daub, it would have had a magical, mystical quality. In the same way, in the centuries that followed the Norman Conquest, those who gathered to attend Mass in the great Romanesque and Gothic cathedrals would have heard the sound of the choir and the organ echoing through the soaring volumes of the nave. It was something they would not and could not have experienced anywhere else, and we know that this experience was often interpreted as mystical or religious.

We do not know what Neolithic people believed, and we do not know how they expressed their beliefs. We do know that the henges and stone circles appear to be one of the first significant cultural movements to have originated in the Archipelago, and their number and distribution suggests that whatever they represented in terms of belief was understood and shared by most of the population. In that sense, they may have expressed a cultural unity, however qualified, which we have not seen before. We know also that henges and stone circles appeared at a time when there was a thriving and prosperous society in the Northern Isles, which may well have originated the forms and ideas which spread across the landscape of the late Neolithic period and produced some of the most startling and impressive architecture of the age.

What happened next demonstrates the connection and continuity between the later Neolithic and the early Bronze Age, and the danger of regarding such divisions as in any sense rigid. Somewhere around 2500 BC, the so-called Beaker People began to arrive in the Archipelago, bringing with them a range of new ideas, including metal-working technology. This marked the beginning of the next significant cultural change, but it did not mark the end of henges and stone circles. They remained in use for most of the next millennium. Both the building of Silbury Hill and the later modifications to Stonehenge took place at a time when Bronze Age culture was rapidly changing the face of the Archipelago; and, given the date of its construction, Seahenge can be considered as belonging to the Bronze Age. No doubt the rites and rituals that were performed in such places altered and evolved as Beaker ideas and new technologies took root. Yet it was not until c.1500 BC that there was a detectable decline in the use of henge and stone circles. From that time onwards, and within no more than a century or so, they seem to have been largely abandoned.

7   Beakers and Bronze

From about 3100 BC, for about six or seven hundred years, the people of the Archipelago dug their henges, built their stone circles, conducted their rituals, and lived their lives without any significant influence or interference from their Continental neighbours. They were not isolated. The exchange of goods continued, and political and kinship visits presumably continued as well, but – allowing for regional variations – there was a broad cultural alignment within the Archipelago which differed in certain key areas from the Continental Lands. In part, this was because the Continent itself was going through an extended period of cultural upheaval. New people, new ideas and new patterns of behaviour were sweeping across a vast swathe of land from the Tagus to the Vistula, but they had not yet reached the Archipelago. To understand what was happening, and what eventually happened in the Archipelago, requires a digression.

We do not know when copper was first smelted in the Iberian Peninsula. Nor do we know whether the tribes of southern Iberia developed copper-smelting technology independently or whether it was transmitted across the Mediterranean Basin: its first known occurrence was in what is now Serbia between 5500 and 5000 BC. However, by 3200 BC we have clear evidence that copper was being smelted and that copper tools and weapons were being produced in two major centres: the Tagus Valley on the Atlantic coast of what is now Portugal, and the Almería region of southern Andalusia. Then, somewhere between 2800 and 2700 BC in the lower reaches of the Tagus Valley, the local people began making what are known as 'bell beakers' – so-called because, although they have a flat base, they look like upside down bells. These early beakers were probably a fusion of local Iberian styles and designs which had originated in North Africa. They soon evolved into the Maritime Bell Beaker – one of two classic beaker types, and identifiable by horizontal bands on their outer surface, decorated with patterns made by combs or pieces of cord pressed into the clay before firing.

Bell beakers and basic copper-working technology are the two key markers of the Beaker People and the so-called 'Beaker Package', which spread across the Continental Lands with remarkable speed in the middle centuries of the third millennium BC. The beakers themselves were probably status symbols. They are most commonly found in burial sites. Some have been shown to contain the residues of beer and mead, both of which were discovered, or at least introduced into the Continental Lands, about this time; and it is possible that their association with alcohol may help explain their rapid spread. They are also frequently found in locations associated with the smelting of copper and gold. The presence of Maritime Bell Beakers is a key marker which allows us to trace the initial diffusion of Beaker culture from southern Iberia – the word 'Maritime' indicating that cultural transmission followed coastal trade routes. And those routes led in two directions: north and east.

The northern route followed the Atlantic seaboard. Maritime Bell Beakers have been discovered in northern Galicia, and on the southern coast of Armorica, particularly in the region around Carnac and the Gulf of Morbihan, which we have already noted as a centre of Neolithic culture. It was from Armorica that this strand of Beaker culture crossed the Atlantic Zone to reach the Western Isle. The eastern route took Maritime Bell Beakers from southern Iberia into the Mediterranean. They spread across the sea to the Balearic Islands, Corsica, Sardinia and Sicily; and they spread along the northern littoral, eventually reaching the Italian Peninsula and the Po Valley. There was a particular concentration of Beaker activity in what is now the south of France, from Languedoc to Provence. It was from here that Beaker culture migrated northwards up the Rhône—Rhine Corridor, and in the Rhine Valley it came into contact with another cultural package known as Corded Ware culture.

The origins of Corded Ware culture lay far to the east, on the Pontic or Ukrainian steppes. This vast expanse of open grassland, stretching from the area north of the Black Sea to the northern shore of the Caspian, was the home of a web of interrelated tribes, known as Yamnaya (or Yamna). The Yamnaya were semi-nomadic people, their lives based around domesticated horses, ox-drawn waggons, and herds of sheep and cattle. Like the southern Iberians, they knew how to smelt copper and make copper axes, and they also knew how to decorate their pots – which were more bulbous and less elegant than bell beakers – in their case by pressing lengths of twisted cord into the unfired clay. They also buried their dead in individual graves, frequently beneath round barrows, and often with grave goods.

Somewhere between 2900 and 2700 BC, the Yamnaya began to migrate westwards. They followed the coast of the Black Sea as far as the Danube Delta and then moved up the Danube Valley, eventually reaching the open grasslands of the Great Hungarian Plain, a landscape not unlike the one where they originated. The tribes themselves appear to have halted at this point, but aspects of their culture – individual burials, round barrows, and grave goods – were adopted by their new neighbours and continued to spread northward and westward, taking a new name from the distinctive cord-decorated pots which characterise their burials. Along the middle and lower reaches of the Rhine, Corded Ware culture moving west met and interacted with Beaker culture moving north. The resulting hybrid eventually reached the coast and, somewhere between 2500 and 2400 BC, began to cross the Channel and Southern North Sea Zones to the Main Island.

There is a danger in treating the movements of cultures across the Continent like the movement of ocean currents across the face of the deep. It can reduce complex interactions between people and ideas to mere arrows on a map. At the same time, it is important to convey the physical and temporal distance travelled by the cultural, economic, and demographic forces that shaped society in the Archipelago at the beginning of the Bronze Age. Beaker culture was never a single or unified culture. At its core, it mixed technological and social change with a strong element of material culture, although that mixture varied from region to region. When it reached the Archipelago, it did so as a result of a kind of pincer movement – not unlike the pattern of Neolithic migration – with one strand arriving in the Western Isle and the western side of the Archipelago, while a second, slightly different strand arrived in the south and east.

The movement of Beaker culture northwards along the Atlantic seaboard may have been stimulated by the search for new sources of copper as local supplies became depleted. The sea was the easiest means of finding and transporting raw materials. There were copper-bearing rocks in northern Galicia and some, though fewer, in Armorica. However, the mariners of Armorica knew the western seaways; and it seems likely that representatives of Beaker culture sailed north from the Carnac region to the Western Isle. The word 'representatives' is deliberately chosen for this was in no sense a migration. Communication across the Atlantic Zone was well established. The Western Isle was a known quantity. We can imagine an expedition, a small flotilla of boats, manned by experienced seamen but including a few men who understood the mysteries of metallurgy, setting off in search of copper. They found it on Ross Island – today a peninsula rather than an island, sticking out like a claw into the middle of Lough Leane in County Kerry.

Copper is a soft metal. It needs to be alloyed with other metals to give it strength. The copper ore mined at Ross Island produced arsenical copper, stronger than pure copper, though not as strong as the bronze – a tin-copper alloy – which later replaced it. Mining began about 2400 BC. Shafts and galleries were dug; fires were lit so that the heat would crack the rock face; and stone hammers were used to detach lumps of rock. The rock was crushed, processed, and smelted in crucibles. Ross Island continued to produce copper for five hundred years. During that time anything up to 35,000 tons of ore was extracted. For the first two or three hundred years, it was probably the only copper mine in the Archipelago. Almost all the copper axes from this period found in the Western Isle, and those found along the western coast of the Main Island, are made from Ross Island copper. By 2100 BC, copper had been found in the Western Uplands and surface mining was taking place at Copa Hill near Cwmystwyth, some twenty kilometres inland from Abersytwyth. By 1800 BC an impressive deep mining operation was under way at Great Orme's Head near Llandudno. This was the biggest Bronze Age mining complex anywhere in the Western Lands, with some five kilometres of galleries and shafts at least seventy metres deep. It has survived to become a twenty-first century tourist attraction.

The ability to smelt, work, and cast copper represented a step change in human development, even though it took time for the possibilities of the new technology to be fully realised. In Anatolia, and in several regions on the Continent, communities were experimenting with differing copper alloys, but it was in the Western Isle and the South-Western Peninsula that bronze began to be produced in significant quantities. The main reason for this was the ready availability of tin: the strongest bronze consists

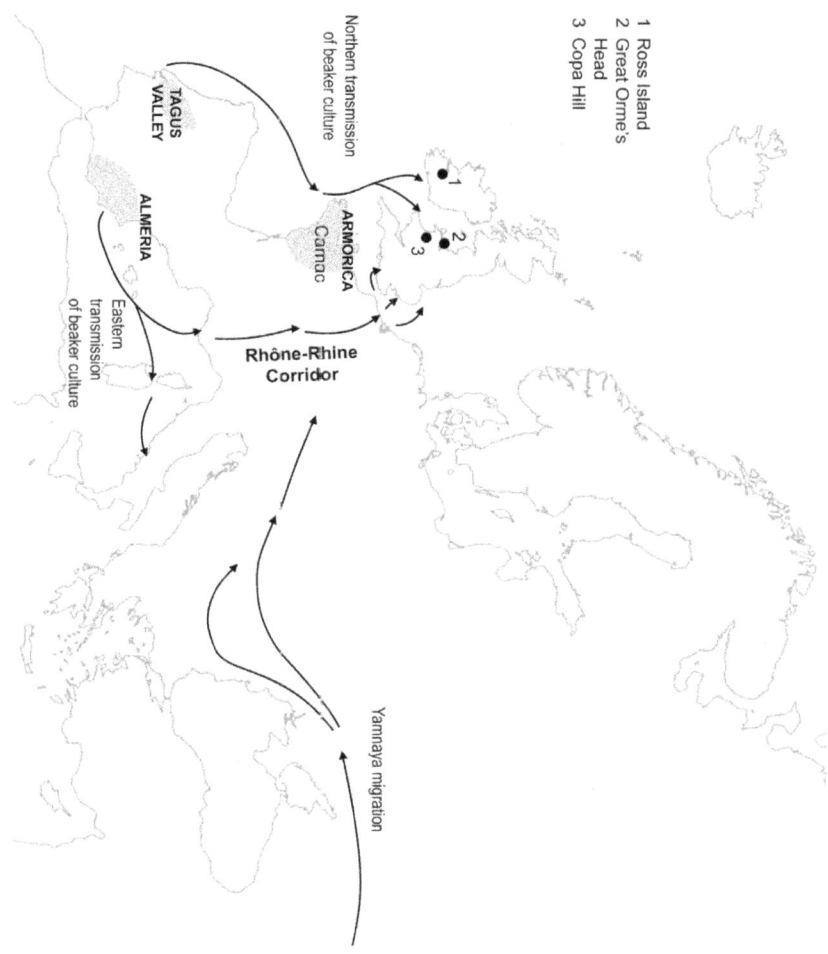

Map 8   The Spread of Beaker Culture

of 90 per cent copper and 10 per cent tin. While there was enough tin in the Western Isle for the coppersmiths to experiment and get production under way, the main source was what is now Cornwall, where mining began about 2150 BC. The advantages of bronze were obvious, and in the Archipelago the transition from arsenical copper to the new, stronger alloy took place over a comparatively short period: it seems to have spread to most areas by 2000 BC. The same change across the Continental Lands took another two hundred years.

Neither copper nor bronze immediately replaced flint. There were some tasks, such as hunting, or cutting and shaping wood, for which bronze axes, daggers, spearheads, and arrowheads were immediately recognised as more efficient. The first site where we can be certain that metal axes were used is in the Western Isle, on on one of the older corduroy trackways, underlying the famous Iron Age trackway at Corlea in County Longford, and dating from about 2250 BC. The first site on the Main Island was Seahenge in 2049 BC. For other tasks, notably mining and shaping stone, flint was more durable and less valuable. Compared with their Neolithic predecessors, the Beaker people appear to have shown an increased regard for material possessions – a characteristic maintained during the later Bronze Age. However, there is an interesting continuity in that, just as some of the most beautiful Neolithic stone axe heads were never used, so some of the most impressive copper and bronze axes and daggers were also kept as objects of display, probably to demonstrate their owner's status, prestige, and power.

Gold also began to be mined, smelted, and worked at this time. The immediate source seems to have been the Wicklow Mountains in the east of the Western Isle. Other sources were soon discovered, notably in the Western Uplands and the South-Western Peninsula, but the Western Isle seems to have been home to the most skilled goldsmiths. Of the two hundred and fifty gold objects from the early Bronze Age found in the Archipelago, two thirds come from the Western Isle. Among the most beautiful items are lunulae – thin sheets of gold shaped like a crescent moon, often decorated along the edges, and designed to be worn as a neckplate or collar. Of the one hundred or so lunulae found across the Western Lands, the Western Isle accounts for over eighty. Two other notable gold items come from the Western Uplands. The Banc Ty'nddôl disc, a small gold circle apparently representing the sun, was found near the site of the copper mines at Copa Hill; and the spectacular Mold Cape, a ceremonial cape made of hammered gold, designed to cover the shoulders and upper arms, and probably intended for a woman, was discovered at a burial site near Mold in Flintshire. The lunulae and the Banc Ty'nddôl disc probably date from between 2200 and 2000 BC, while the Mold Cape was probably made two or three hundred years later. With gold, as with copper, early Bronze Age activity was concentrated on the western side of the Archipelago, reflecting the accessibility of sources of ore and the fact that the technology to exploit them was transmitted across the Atlantic Zone.

Beaker culture, as it arrived in the Western Isle, was defined principally by metal-working technology. The strand of Beaker culture which arrived on the eastern side of the Archipelago was more varied and more malleable, having evolved and absorbed other influences as it spread northwards and then westwards across the Continent. It also employed a slightly different method for smelting copper. The first wave of these Beaker people consisted of three main groups, perhaps based on different tribes or extended families. The beakers they brought with them belong to the second classic beaker style known, for obvious reasons, as Overall Decorated. We can distinguish the three groups from one another by the nature of the decoration, and this also indicates the part of the Continent where each group originated. Those migrants who crossed the Channel Zone from Brittany and the Pas de Calais to the south coast of the Main Island favoured a style close to the original Maritime Bell Beakers, at least in so far as they used combs to decorate the external surface. Those who crossed the Southern North Sea Zone from the area between what is now Belgium and the Rhine Delta to Essex, Suffolk and East Anglia used knives and fingernails to incise decorative patterns on their beakers. Those who crossed the Eastern Zone from north of the Rhine Delta to the coast of Lincolnshire and Yorkshire brought beakers that are completely covered with the impressions of twisted cord.

The Beaker migration to the east of the Main Island became a mass migration, but, despite having a significant cultural impact, in its early stages it probably involved comparatively small groups of people. While we can identify the different groups by their beaker styles, the actual number of early burials is limited. At the same time, they are very visible and distinct from other burials of the period, taking the form of round barrows. This may indicate that the earliest Beaker arrivals attained or were accorded a high social status, perhaps because they possessed skills not previously known in Neolithic society. The nature and contents of these graves also illustrate the cultural differences between the new arrivals and the existing Neolithic inhabitants. The fact that burials were individual rather than collective – a practice which has persisted ever since, and which our society regards as 'normal' and as a demonstration of respect – suggests a change in attitudes towards individuality. In the few instances where they exist, Neolithic grave goods have a symbolic quality, as if expressing tribal or social identity, or perhaps some association with the otherworld. By contrast, the goods found in early Beaker graves – such as small gold ornaments, stone wrist guards (to protect the wrist when firing arrows), arrowheads, copper or flint daggers – seem more like personal possessions. That personal quality, the fact that we can believe they belonged to a particular individual who used or displayed them in daily life, has the effect of bringing him or her closer.

The most famous early beaker burial is that of a man who has been described by one archaeologist as 'the poster boy for the Beaker people.'[53] Aged between thirty-five and fifty, he is more formally known as the Amesbury Archer. The name derives from the village in Wiltshire near which his grave was discovered – in 2002, during the construction of a new primary school – and from the fifteen arrowheads that were buried with him, together with an unprecedented range of other objects including no less fewer five beakers, two gold hair ornaments, three copper knives, two wrist guards, and a cushion stone used for metalworking. The grave dates from c.2300 BC, and its contents clearly indicate a high social status – perhaps because he knew how to work copper. Yet he was not a native of the Archipelago: dental isotope analysis shows that he probably grew up in the Alps. Even more remarkably, a second grave discovered nearby contained the remains of another, younger man, probably in his twenties at the time of his death, whose grave goods also included two gold hair ornaments. Medical evidence revealed a shared, usually hereditary fusing of bones in the feet, suggesting they were probably father and son, and dental isotope analysis indicated that the son had grown up, not in the Alps, but in Wiltshire. We are, of course, only dealing with two individuals here, but we can propose a narrative, the outline of which could have applied to others. A skilled metalworker from the Continent migrates to the Main Island. He may be an adventurer seeking an opportunity to better his lot; or he may be invited through a network of kinship or tribal connections. Amesbury is only four kilometres from Stonehenge, so his metalworking abilities are employed in an area of spiritual and social importance. He settles there. His craft and his ability gain him social recognition and wealth, and he has a son who shares at least some of his father's prestige and wealth. He has an accident, badly damaging his left knee, and resulting in an infection in the bones which may have led to his death. When he dies, his possessions are buried with him.

Map 9   Beaker Culture in the British Isles

The introduction of metalworking marked a permanent change in human society, and for a period put the Western Isle in the forefront of developing technical expertise. And there were other major changes. Domesticated horses made their appearance in the Archipelago – the earliest evidence coming from Newgrange about 2400 BC (see Chapter 4). Initially, they were probably status animals, reserved for members of the elite, and, although we cannot be certain, they were probably ridden bareback with a simple rope bridle. It is not until the middle Bronze Age that copper and bronze bridle and harness fittings begin to appear, often as grave goods and notably in chariot burials – seeming to confirm that the possession of horses was an indicator of prestige and possibly membership of an aristocratic or a warrior elite. At the same time, by the turn of the second millennium, there is evidence to suggest that horses were beginning to be used as draft animals. The importance of the domestication of the horse cannot be overestimated. For the next four thousand years, the horse was to be fundamental to all aspects of human society: military, agricultural, commercial, social. As with sea travel, it is only in the recent past, within the last hundred years, that this link has been broken and the internal combustion engine has superseded the horse in daily use. Wheeled vehicles also made their appearance during the Beaker period, initially pulled by oxen, and then later by horses. The animal-drawn plough was also introduced with obvious implications for crop yields and land use. Weaving had begun in Neolithic times, often using vegetable fibres and upright wooden looms with clay warp weights. From the early Bronze Age, metal tools made for better looms, while the introduction of new breeds of sheep with better wool led to the production of good quality woollen cloth.

There were, as always, regional variations. On the east coast of the Far North, between Inverness and Aberdeen, there is a very early concentration of Beaker settlement and round barrows. Many of the grave beakers found in this area have been decorated with a white powder made from pulverised bone not known elsewhere. Moreover, when analysed, the bronze discovered along this coast was found to be the earliest yet discovered in the Main Island. Copper from the Western Isle and tin from the South-Western Peninsula had apparently been smelted and cast using methods originating in the Rhine Delta, suggesting that the area was a hub or meeting point for transport routes across the North Sea and along the Great Glen. In the south of the Main Island, a number of coastal burials have been found to contain a distinctive delicately crafted kind of cup, with a handle. These are clearly valuable items, made of gold, silver, amber or shale, not found elsewhere in the Archipelago, although examples have been found in Brittany, suggesting a maritime origin or cross-Channel links. In the Western Isle, with its earlier strand of Beaker culture and where it seems likely that there were fewer migrants, individual burials and round barrows were adopted, but grave goods are simpler, less valuable items, such as food vessels. There are no beakers, no axe heads, no wrist guards, nor any gold items, even though these items were produced locally.

This transformation of society was balanced by significant continuities, many of them concerning ritual behaviour and the disposal of the dead. Individual burial under round barrows was a mark of Beaker culture, but other ritual practices, including excarnation, remained widespread. There was continuity, too, in the use of ritual sites. The land was scattered with sites long regarded sacred. The Beaker people accepted the spiritual significance of such sites and continued to use them, while modifying and developing them over time. We do not know what they believed, whether they shared a single belief system, or how their beliefs differed from the pre-existing Neolithic population, but they adopted the indigenous practice of building henges and stone circles with evident enthusiasm. It is even possible that the construction of such monuments may have increased during the Beaker period. A number of stone circles in the Inverness-Aberdeen area are contemporary with early Beaker culture there. Beaker fragments have been found in and around the Callanish stones. Both Woodhenge and Seahenge date from the Beaker period – shaping wood was easier with bronze axes – while Silbury Hill and the later stages of Avebury and Stonehenge are contemporary with the spread of Beaker influence (see Chapter 6).

The Wessex region, with its concentration of Neolithic ritual landscapes and monumental structures, was immediately accepted by the incoming Beaker people as an area of particular spiritual importance. There are hundreds of round barrows dating from c.2000 to c.1500 BC scattered across the landscape. Among these are a series of extremely rich burials, the most impressive being Bush Barrow, less than two kilometres from Stonehenge. The grave goods from Bush Barrow include two lozenge-shaped pieces of sheet gold, decorated with hexagonal patterns; a bronze dagger, the hilt of which was embedded with 140,000 tiny gold studs (at a density of over one thousand per square centimetre); two of the longest bronze daggers ever found; the remains of a bronze knife which would have been at least two hundred years old at the time it was buried; and other valuable items.

Bush Barrow was exceptional, but it was not unique. One of the barrows in Amesbury's Solstice Park, another barrow known as Amesbury 61a, and the grave of a cremated woman at Upton Lovell – all have yielded rich finds of grave goods. In total, more than a hundred wealthy burials have been found in the Wessex region. Who were these people? They were evidently prosperous, but does that mean they were powerful as well? Did they belong to a ruling class or a political elite? What of those buried in the hundreds of other round barrows with more modest grave goods? Whoever they were, they were important enough to be buried individually under a mound, with all the work and effort that entailed. Were they less wealthy members of Beaker families? Or less important members of the ruling elite? As so often, because we do not know how society was organised, there are no conclusive answers.

From the limited amount of evidence available, it does not seem that Neolithic society was marked by major social divisions. It may not have been egalitarian: there may well have been certain castes or groups set apart from the rest of society and exercising authority in one area of activity or another – someone had to decide to build a new stone circle, how much food to store over the winter, what course to set for Iberia – but there is no indication of a political elite. In Beaker culture, we sense an increased concern for individuality which may suggest greater social stratification. The rich graves probably indicate that Beaker incomers attained a high social status. Whether high social status translated into political power is arguable. Beyond grave goods, there is little evidence for it, but as we shall see in the later Bronze Age, elite structures did eventually develop (see Chapter 8). It is possible that Beaker individuality laid the groundwork for later social change.

Wessex was a centre of ritual and religion and probably a place of pilgrimage. Copper, tin, and gold were beginning to move around the Archipelago more freely and in greater quantities than before. So, too, were items that could be displayed in order to demonstrate status and prestige. Wessex, with the sacred landscapes of Stonehenge and Avebury at its heart, was an area where important communication routes converged. The already ancient Ridgeway passed nearby, linking the Thames Valley, and ultimately the East Anglian coast, with Dorset, where

Hengistbury Head was becoming a port of consequence, and where more wealthy graves have been found. Routes westward led to the sources of tin in the South-Western Peninsula, and to the Bristol Channel and the Western Uplands, which offered maritime links to the sources of copper and gold in the Western Isle. In such a context, traders and merchants, and those who transported goods, could well have amassed significant wealth without necessarily belonging to a political elite. What impact that wealth might have had on the development of political and social structures remains an open question.

Wessex was unique in its concentration of wealth, but round barrows containing valuable grave goods can be found in most parts of the Main Island – though not, as noted earlier, in the Western Isle. Copper daggers, bronze axes, and gold ornaments feature prominently, but there are also other valuable items. Amber – washed up on the east coast of the Main Island or brought across from Jutland – is found in the form of beads, necklaces, or raw, unshaped lumps. Faience, a glass-like, ceramic compound with a rich turquoise colour and produced on the Main Island, was used to make beads.[54] There was jet from the North Yorkshire coast, used for buttons, beads and necklaces. One of the most impressive finds from the period, now in the National Museum of Scotland, is a jet necklace consisting of ten strands of beads with flat spacers, which was discovered on the island of Inchmarnock off the western coast of Bute in the Firth of Clyde. Lunulae, gold ornaments, decorated daggers and axes, amber necklaces, faience beads, jet necklaces, jet buttons, bone belt rings, even the detailed decoration of burial beakers, all testify to an increased interest in and availability of manufactured goods – in other words, a more material culture.

The distribution of grave goods in relation to their area of origin (or presumed origin) is one of a number of factors indicating that goods were moving within the Archipelago and between the Archipelago and the Continent with greater frequency and in greater quantities. Beaker culture, like Neolithic culture, had arrived in the Archipelago by sea, and the sea was crucial to maintaining it. A culture with more interest in material possessions was a culture that required an efficient communication and distribution system. Ox- or horse-drawn waggons would have improved the efficiency of land transport. Metal tools brought improvements in boat-building technology through greater precision in cutting and shaping wood, and the number of boats operating at sea and in coastal waters seems to have increased. Bronze Age wrecks off Salcombe on the south Devon coast have provided proof that both heavy finished articles, such as axe heads and swords, and raw materials such as copper and tin, in the form of ingots, were being transported by sea. It was the tin trade and the South-Western Peninsula that put the Archipelago onto the maps and into the books of literate men from southern Europe (see Chapter 11).

Given previous time scales, the Beaker phenomenon – at least as represented by its most distinctive feature, the beaker itself – did not last very long. By c.2250 BC, Beaker burials had become widespread, but the beakers themselves displayed much greater variation in shape and decoration, suggesting a diffusion from the original immigrant groups to a wider population. By c.1950 BC, barrow burials were becoming poorer and scrappier, and beakers had begun to disappear, being replaced by coarser pottery which harked back to earlier pre-beaker styles. Only in areas where there was a concentration of wealth, such as central Wessex, did rich burials and traditional beaker styles continue. By c.1600 BC, some nine hundred years after the influence of beaker culture had first made itself felt, society in the Archipelago was entering a new phase.

The Beaker people who crossed the Atlantic Zone to the west of the Archipelago did so earlier and apparently in smaller numbers than those who arrived in the south and east of the Main Island. For many years, while invasion theory was the accepted wisdom, it was assumed that the numbers of migrants arriving in the south and east were sufficiently large to displace the existing population. As attitudes altered and the importance of acculturation in cultural change gained broad acceptance, estimates of the number of migrants were reduced. It was accepted that there must have been some migration, for acculturation alone could not explain the rapid diffusion of a new culture which depended to a significant extent on technological innovation. At the same time, the idea that acculturation could work in both directions was helpful in explaining why the Beaker incomers had so readily adopted the henge- and stone-circle-based rituals that had not featured as part of their Continental background. However, in 2017, a major shock was administered by a team from Harvard Medical School which had conducted a study of DNA taken from Neolithic and early Bronze Age skeletons.

The study compared samples from the remains of four hundred and five individuals: two hundred and fifty from the Continent and a hundred and fifty-five from the Archipelago. Of those from the Archipelago, fifty-one were from the Neolithic period, dating from between 4000 and 2500 BC; and one hundred and four from the early and middle Bronze Age, dating from between 2450 BC and 1000 BC. The results showed that the arrival of the Beaker people led to a profound demographic transformation. The researchers admit that the uneven geographic distribution of samples within the Archipelago, coupled with the fact that immigrants and locals adopted different burial practices, may have biased the results against the pre-existing population. Nonetheless, they concluded that the genetic evidence indicates very substantial migration from the Continent to the Archipelago beginning around 2400 BC, which replaced 90 per cent of Britain's Neolithic gene pool in the space of just a few hundred years. The study also concluded that the main body of immigration came across the North Sea from the area around the Rhine Delta. These people were fairer-haired and lighter-skinned than their predecessors, and it is their genes that make up the major part of the heredity of the present-day population of the Archipelago.[55]

These results completely overturned our previous understanding of what happened during the early Bronze Age. The geographical distribution of samples was not completely uniform, so the results cannot be applied with quite the same degree of confidence to the Western Isle or the High North, but the overall picture is clear. There is nothing in the archaeological record to suggest that the Beaker people conquered the Archipelago by force of arms, or that they systematically killed off the existing inhabitants. Burial evidence certainly indicates that some Beaker people acquired wealth and a high social status. At the same time, however, evidence suggesting that they were culturally distinct from the existing population is matched by evidence of continuity in other areas, most notably the use of existing ritual sites and the construction of new ones in line with precedents dictated by the pre-existing culture of the Archipelago.

So what did happen? Could Neolithic society have been in some kind of general decline at the time the Beaker people arrived? We know that the major centre of Neolithic culture at Ness of Brodgar fell out of use about 2300 BC. Elsewhere, at much the same time, there is evidence of farmland being abandoned, settlements being deserted, and woodland re-establishing itself. Could this have been caused by changes in climatic conditions (see Chapter 4)? There is evidence that the north in particular was wetter than average during the period from 2500 to 2200 BC.[56] But this by itself is not enough to explain the wholesale substitution of one population by another. An alternative theory is that the Beaker people brought a disease, possibly bubonic plague, with them, and that this decimated the Neolithic population in much the same way as the Spanish *conquistadores* are said to have brought disease to Central America and decimated the Aztecs. This is certainly plausible and to some extent supported by the evidence for depopulation. At the same time, it does not explain the fact that henges and stone circles continued to be built and used for nearly a thousand years, or the intensification of sea and coastal transport associated with the growth in the trade and circulation of valuable commodities. A further question concerns those people who, as the archaeological record clearly demonstrates, transmitted copper-smelting up the Atlantic seaways. They were fewer in number than those arriving from the east. What happened to them? Were they simply swamped by the arrivals from the east? Yet again, there are no clear answers. We can only speculate and hope that future studies will offer clarification.

8   Walls and Weapons

The Beaker period was a time of technological innovation – metalworking, the wheel, the animal-drawn plough – and, as we now know, population change. By contrast, the middle and later Bronze Age – the period from 1500 to 700 BC – was a period of structural change. The land was used differently; society organised itself differently; people lived differently, and expressed their religious beliefs differently. Such broad generalisations gloss over a range of exceptions and variations, but they highlight the fact that from somewhere around 1500 BC the Archipelago and its people underwent a slow transformation, and the context of the changes was a further increase in and intensification of those cultural and kinship exchanges across the Channel and Southern North Sea Zones which had been the main route for Beaker immigration.

In previous chapters, we have seen Ness of Brodgar as the focal point of later Neolithic culture in the Archipelago; we have seen Wessex and its sacred landscapes as a centre for ritual and religious observance; and we have seen a period when the Western Isle led the way in metalworking expertise – particularly in gold-working. In the later Bronze Age, the cultural leadership of the Archipelago passed decisively to the southern part of the Main Island. The Archipelago, as we have noted before, was never cut off by the sea, and sea transport, despite its dangers, was quicker and more efficient than transport over land. There had never been a time when communities on either side of the Channel Zone had not maintained some level of contact with each other. Now, however, those contacts became a sea-based social interaction which bound the communities together. The culture of the southern part of the Lowland Zone shows close similarities with that of the coastal regions of the Continent from the Brittany Peninsula to the Rhine Delta. These similarities go beyond those of the Beaker period, which centred on prestige objects, such as the beakers themselves or items of copper, bronze, or gold, to include more basic elements such as settlement patterns and everyday items of pottery.

This new and remarkable degree of mobility and connectivity gradually extended beyond the Channel Zone to other parts of the Archipelago. It can be seen in the development and distribution of those basic items which characterise later Bronze Age society – and it shows influence moving in both directions. Bronze cauldrons and buckets (often known to archaeologists by the Latin term *situlae*) originated on the Continent, somewhere to the east of the Rhône—Rhine corridor. They reached the Archipelago and were then produced in the south-east of the Main Island. From there, production spread not only westwards to the Western Isle, where large numbers have been found, but also southwards across the Atlantic Zone and down the western seaboard as far as Iberia. Bronze flesh-hooks, used for lifting cooked meat out of cauldrons, appear to have originated along the coast of the Bay of Biscay. They, too, began to be made in the south-east of the Main Island from where they spread both westwards and northwards. By contrast, gold hair rings, like the gold ornaments we saw earlier in the Bronze Age, were made in the Western Isle and exported. Examples have been found in the High North, in Wessex, and along the south coast of the Main Island, as well on the Continent in the Seine and Rhine Valleys. Distribution patterns of this nature have many possible explanations – exchange-based trade, tribute gifts, kinship gifts, personal use by high status individuals, the elite or dynastic marriages – but above all they bear witness to increased connectivity.

Weapons also testify to increased mobility and the existence of expanding distribution and exchange networks. The earliest versions of the carp's tongue sword, a bronze weapon with a broad blade that tapers down to an elongated, narrow tip – and thus suitable for both slashing and thrusting – came from around Huelva in southern Iberia, probably c.1000 BC. They spread north along the Atlantic seaboard to Armorica, and to the region around Nantes, where a variant form was produced around 950 BC. In the past, the natural channel of transmission, perhaps reflecting kinship ties, was northwards, across the Atlantic Zone to the South-Western Peninsula and the Western Isle. In this instance, however, transmission followed the coastal route to Brittany and Normandy, before crossing the eastern end of the Channel Zone to the south-east of the Main Island.

An example of transmission in the opposite direction is the basal-looped spearhead. These are simple enough objects: bronze spearheads cast in a two-part clay mould, with two metal loops at their base through which a cord or a strip of leather could be threaded to secure the head to the shaft. They probably originated in the Western Isle, but examples have been found right across the Archipelago and beyond. We can trace a pattern of distribution from the south-east corner of the Main Island to the Continent, where they spread as far north as Schleswig-Holstein and as far south as Aquitaine, with a high concentration in the Seine Valley. They penetrated inland as far as the upper Rhône and the upper Ems Valleys, while direct transmission from the Western Isle took them to the Nantes region of Armorica, down to Galicia and south to the Huelva region of southern Iberia.

The items listed above – and many others, such as Ballintober swords, sickles, and torcs, that could be added to the list – are found across the Archipelago and throughout the western Continental Lands. Reconstructing their distribution is a complex process, dependent on analysing the archaeological context of hundreds of individual finds. It may be that, as with the DNA analysis, future techniques will challenge or overturn current conclusions in individual cases. However, the broad picture of later Bronze Age society exhibiting an unprecedented level of mobility and interconnectedness, leading to an extraordinarily wide distribution of manufactured items, is unlikely to be challenged. The intensification of cultural connections across the Channel Zone was new and significant but did not develop at the expense of other routes and relationships. Although the evidence clearly shows the Thames Estuary and the Kent coast becoming the most important channel of communication and trade, the Atlantic Zone retained its importance as a link between the western seaboard of the Continent and the western side of the Archipelago. Within the Archipelago, the level of communication and exchange of goods between the Western Isle and western regions of the Main Island appear to have grown steadily throughout the period. There are many possible reasons for this general expansion. The Beaker people and their descendants may well have had closer kinship-based relations with the Continent than their Neolithic predecessors. The population of the Archipelago was growing, and with it the demand for prestige items made from copper and bronze, as well as other commodities. This led to a need to transport both more raw materials and more finished goods. This in turn created a demand for more boats, which, with the advent of metal tools, could now be built more easily. More boats meant more people sailing them and thus more contact with more people on the Continent.

Any attempt to put an accurate figure on the population of the Archipelago at this time – or any other time in prehistory – is fraught with difficulties. The best estimates we have suggest that by the middle of the second millennium BC it was growing strongly. By 1400 BC the population of the Main Island may have reached one million, and that of the Western Isle 200,000. Population growth may go some way to explaining the changes in land use that began around 1500 BC. Here again, modern archaeology has been transformed by new scientific techniques, such as the analysis of pollen sequences, which have made it possible to establish a basic narrative of how land use developed. Neolithic farmers began the process of clearing the land for crops and for grazing animals, as at Céide Fields, the early Neolithic complex of walled fields in the Western Isle (see Chapter 4), or at Fengate in Cambridgeshire, where a pattern of late Neolithic field boundaries has been uncovered. But these are isolated examples, and elsewhere it is difficult to get a sense of how Neolithic farming communities were organised on the ground.

From the middle of the second millennium BC onwards, we see less effort being directed towards the construction of henges, stones circles and other monumental structures, and more effort being put into structuring and managing the landscape. Land clearance increased and field systems with defined boundaries were widely constructed throughout the Archipelago. On the South-Western Peninsula, traces of many field systems have survived, some of them still forming the basis of present-day field boundaries. From the Lizard Peninsula to Bodmin Moor, both in lowland areas and on higher ground, we find small enclosures of irregular, oblong shape – often referred to as 'brick-shaped' fields – divided by banks made of stones cleared from the surface of the land. Elsewhere, often on the edge of higher, more open ground, are what are known as 'coaxial' field systems: laid out on a common axis with parallel boundaries, creating much more regular fields.

Further east, on Dartmoor, a vast system of field boundaries, known as 'reaves', was laid out about 1300 BC. In scale, it was equal to any Neolithic or early Bronze Age monumental construction. It enclosed approximately 10,000 hectares with over two hundred kilometres of dry-stone walls on a broadly coaxial pattern, and it divided the enclosed land into ten areas of more or less equal size and equivalent land type. Further east still, in Wessex and on the chalk downlands that span the south-east of the Main Island, coaxial systems were again widespread, with field boundaries marked by ditches running long distances across the open landscape. Windy Dido, a ninety-hectare area on the Hampshire chalklands, is one of the best examples. In time, the fences that may originally have topped the spoil from the ditches were replaced by hedges, which in many cases still mark boundaries laid down three-and-a-half thousand years ago. Both on the chalklands and in the fenlands of East Anglia, where ditch-based coaxial systems are also in evidence, it is noticeable that field boundaries are aligned in such a way as to respect burial and ritual sites dating back to Neolithic times and beyond.

One characteristic of this period was the clearance of upland areas – such as Dartmoor, the Yorkshire and Northumberland Moors, and the Border Hills – that had not been farmed before. This was made possible, at least in part, by warm and dry climatic conditions, which made the growing of wheat and barley possible up to a height of around four hundred metres. While there were no great stones to be transported over long distances and fewer technical challenges, the physical task of dividing up vast swathes of the landscape in this manner would have involved the same degree of planning and the same mobilisation of labour as the construc-

Map 10   Bronze Age Land Use and Settlement Patterns

tion of a stone circle. Even in the mountainous High North and the northern archipelagos, there are widespread traces of land clearance and agriculture dating from the middle and later Bronze Age. Field systems here are on a smaller scale and often less clearly defined than those further south. Drumturn Burn in Perthshire is well preserved, and one of few in the north where all four sides of the fields remain defined. Elsewhere, widespread evidence of stone banks, clearance cairns, and lynchets (ledges formed on a hillslope by repeated ploughing), shows that the intensification of agriculture and the desire to divide up the landscape was extended even to the remoter parts of the Archipelago.

This period of expansion lasted for two or three hundred years before going rapidly into reverse. The climate may have begun to cool around 1100 BC, but the process was accelerated in 1159 BC when the Icelandic volcano, Hekla, began an eruption which lasted some nine years. An estimated 7.3 cubic kilometres of volcanic debris was thrown into the atmosphere. The climatic impact lasted at least eighteen years and was felt throughout the whole of the Northern Hemisphere: it has even been blamed for famines in Egypt under Ramesses II. Across the Archipelago, it led to a series of poor growing seasons. In the High North, pine trees died. Across the Upland Zone, many of the newly-cleared upland areas became uncultivable, and the wetter climate began the process of turning many of them into the peat bogs that still exist today. It is possible that there was famine in parts of the Archipelago, and that many of the inhabitants of the High North migrated southwards. Some historians have seen migration and social breakdown in the wake of this rapid climatic downturn as responsible for the emergence of a more hierarchical, warrior-led society.

The task of marking out and dividing the land was accompanied by an equally important change in the nature and organisation of settlements. Central to this was the roundhouse, a type of dwelling not widely found on the Continent, but characteristic of settlements in the Archipelago from the Bronze Age right through the Roman period and, in some areas, for several centuries afterwards. Bronze Age roundhouses usually consisted of a circle of wooden uprights and walls made of wattle-and-daub panels – though in upland areas or out among the islands, where the supply of timber was limited, the walls were made of turf or stone. The roofs were conical and thatched, with wide eaves to keep rainwater well away from the base of the walls. Understanding of the importance of roundhouses has grown in recent years. As late as 1970, only two hundred had been recorded. Now, well over 4,000 have been excavated. The earliest known examples, dating from somewhere around 2300 BC, have been found in Dumfries and Galloway, but the design soon spread throughout the Archipelago.

Some of the best-preserved Bronze Age buildings ever found are the roundhouses on the edge of a quarry at Must Farm in Cambridgeshire.

Part of the site has been lost to quarrying, but five roundhouses remain, all in an extraordinary state of preservation due to the wet ground. At the time, the area was a wetland environment, and the roundhouses, clustered close together, were built on piles over water, making this the only Bronze Age lake village yet discovered in the Archipelago. On the edge of the site, in an ancient riverbed, archaeologists discovered no fewer than eight perfectly preserved logboats. The village evidently caught fire, causing the inhabitants to flee and the houses to collapse into the water and mud, which then preserved them. Because the villagers had to run for their lives, they left behind all their possessions and an unsurpassed record of their daily lives – including complete pots, some containing half-eaten food; quantities of bronze tools, such as socket axes and sickles, some of them still sharp; weapons, such as swords and spearheads, again still sharp; large quantities of beads, some of them coming from as far away as the Mediterranean; delicate textiles and coarsely-woven nets and baskets made from plant fibres, and with them a full set of spinning and weaving tools; as well as the oldest complete wheel yet found in the Archipelago.

The village was surrounded by a palisade of heavy wooden stakes driven deep into the mud, which can only have been defensive in purpose. We cannot tell whether the fire that destroyed the village was the result of an attack by a hostile tribe, or whether it was simply an accident. However, some of the swords found at the site have notched blades, suggesting they had been used for fighting, not just display, and the villagers never returned to rebuild their houses. The site was abandoned. Again, we do not know why, but the idea that they were driven out and subsequently unable to return is certainly plausible.

Elsewhere, on dry land, it was becoming increasingly common for settlements to be enclosed. Banks, ditches, palisades, walls of turf and stone were all used to separate the homestead from the surrounding fields, depending on the geography and geology of the region. There was great variation in both the number of roundhouses enclosed – anything from one to half-a-dozen – and in the scale and shape of the enclosure, but the idea of enclosed settlements spread to all parts of the Main Island. The drive to divide the land into smaller, more defined units and to enclose the homestead may reflect a growing sense of family or group identity and of ownership – an extension of the increased sense of individuality that we saw in Beaker period burials. At the same time, enclosed settlements may well have had a defensive purpose, reflecting changes in the wider structure of society that were designed to counter increased violence and instability – changes which would eventually lead to each family or homestead owing allegiance to an overlord or regional chieftain. As suggested by Must Farm, and as we shall see again shortly, later Bronze Age society shows every sign of being less stable and more violent than preceding eras.

Throughout much of the Archipelago, there is evidence of Bronze Age settlements which were significantly larger than enclosed homesteads. In the north of the Main Island, the first hillforts were appearing. The earliest rampart and settlement at Traprain Law, in East Lothian, dates from about 1500 BC. At Eildon Hill in the Borders, construction of what was to become a large hillfort began about 1000 BC. These may well have been regional centres of power, occupied by a ruling elite at the top of a more stratified society than we have seen before. An alternative explanation is that they began life as gathering points, where the tribe or community could gather for ritual or social occasions – although, as Cunliffe points out, the two explanations are not mutually exclusive.[57] From the beginning, both forts were conceived on a large scale, enclosing thirteen and sixteen hectares respectively, but were subsequently expanded, remaining in use throughout the Iron Age and the Roman occupation, when they certainly did have a military purpose.

In the Western Isle, where enclosed homesteads seem to have been less common, circular hillforts were appearing. These, too, were on a large scale, and often feature two or more widely spaced circular ditch-and-bank ramparts – creating what archaeologists call a 'multivallate' structure. The presence of large hillforts at places such as Rathgall in Wicklow, Cashel in Tipperary, Mooghaun in County Clare, and Armagh probably indicates that these were regional centres of power. Clashanimud – the name means 'the trench of timbers' – was constructed around 1200 BC and is among the oldest hillforts in the Western Isle. Sitting on a hilltop sixteen kilometres west of the city of Cork, its position gives it a commanding view over the landscape in all directions. Two massive earth and stone ramparts enclosed an area of over eight hectares. The outer rampart, more than a kilometre long, was topped by a wattle palisade; while the inner rampart, eight hundred metres in circumference, consisted of three hundred and eighty enormous wooden uprights joined together by heavy wooden planks. Presumably built by a local warlord with hundreds of men at his command – it has been described by some as the first proper capital of Cork – the immense effort involved in building Clashanimud was in vain. It was burnt to the ground shortly after its construction in what has been described as 'a deliberate act of war'.[58]

Smaller forts, circular in shape, and with one or two ramparts, are found in the east of the Main Island. Known as 'ringforts', they are concentrated in an area which runs from Yorkshire to Kent. They are certainly bigger and grander than enclosed homesteads – the one at Thwing in Yorkshire is a hundred metres in diameter; that at Springfield Lyons in Essex about fifty metres – and it is possible that they were the dwellings of local chiefs or leaders. Another kind of hilltop enclosure, broadly on the same pattern as enclosed homesteads, but significantly larger, covering areas of up to a hectare or more, is found across the southern region of the Main Island. These, too, have been seen as the residences of the elite.

What we appear to be seeing here are regional differences, not in ritual or in material culture, as has been the case up to now, but in 'political' structures – in how the land was ruled, who owed allegiance to whom, and in the scale of the areas ruled by different chiefs or families. We may also be seeing regional differences in social conditions – particularly levels of violence. In the Western Isle, for example, both Clashanimud and Cashel hillforts were burnt to the ground in large-scale episodes of violence which have been described as 'warfare at an interregional level.'[59] The rise of violence in society, and the parallel rise of a warrior elite who were presumably responsible for it, is evidenced not only by the construction of forts and the charred remains of battles, but also by the vast amount of weaponry found in the archaeological record.

Swords were a Bronze Age invention. The production of daggers, knives and halberds came first – the earliest examples in the Archipelago date from the last centuries of the third millennium BC – because they required less technical expertise. (A Bronze Age halberd was a broad, dagger-length blade mounted sideways at the end of a wooden shaft that could be swung in the direction of an enemy.) Swords, cast in two-part clay moulds, and then hammered into shape and sharpness, began to appear between 1350 and 1300 BC. Carp's tongue swords and Ballintober swords were mentioned earlier in the context of trade and communication routes, but archaeologists have listed many other kinds and categories.[60] Well over a thousand Bronze Age swords have been found on the Main Island, and another six hundred on the Western Isle, including short, thin-bladed swords for stabbing, as well as broader, heavier weapons for thrusting and slashing. Some had bone handles, some had wood handles, some had decorated handles of cast metal. Many are badly damaged, or just fragments, but the numbers indicate the importance of the new weapon, and probably the level of violence in society.

Spearheads, too, came in different shapes and sizes. Looped spearheads – such as the basal looped type referred to earlier – were tied to the spear shaft. Others were secured to the shaft by a bronze or wooden peg. Small ones would have been thrown like javelins; larger and heavier ones were used for thrusting in battle; while very large, decorated spearheads would probably have served for display and ceremonial purposes. Shields are another item of a warrior's equipment which are widely found, at least in the Archipelago – on the Continent, perhaps surprisingly, they have been found only north of the Rhine Delta. Some were made of thick moulded leather – a reminder that leather would have been an effective source of protection, and much lighter than metal – but the majority are of bronze. Nipperwiese shields,[61] dating from about 1200 BC, are particularly sturdy, with a heavy, central boss and three or four concentric, circular ridges to give them strength. One example found in Oxfordshire has a lozenge-shaped hole in it, probably made by a spear thrust. The most commonly found shield in the Archipelago is the Yetholm type, named after the village in the Borders where three examples were recovered from a peat bog. Twenty-six examples have been found, all in the Archipelago except for one in Denmark, dating from between 1300 and 975 BC. They are made of bronze which has been hammered to a thickness of around 0.6 of a millimetre and are between 55 and 70 centimetres in diameter with a hemispherical central boss surrounded by twenty to thirty concentric ridges. The circular depressions between the ridges are decorated with small bosses approximately four millimetres in diameter, hammered out from the reverse side. Despite the elaborate detail and the workmanship, these do not appear to have been prestige or display items. At least one has been punctured by a spear, and several others show signs of repair, suggesting use in combat.

9 Hoards and Water

So what changed? How did what appears to have been a comparatively peaceful society during the Beaker period, become one where warriors roamed the land and many of the defining characteristics appear to be linked to warfare and violence? Concepts of individuality and ownership have already been mentioned. So, too, has the impact of the eruption of Hekla and the climatic downturn that followed. Agriculture remained the dominant economic force. Although we do not know how agricultural produce was divided up or shared, the fact of physically dividing the landscape – while it may have had some benefits in terms of stock management – does suggest a move away from the common holding and management of land. Agriculture itself was also changing. New crops – millet, peas, and beans – provided extra nutrition and were suitable for preserving over the winter. The number of storage pits and storage huts increased. There is evidence of transhumance, which would have improved grazing for cattle and increased the supply of meat. Meat had long been preserved by smoking, but there is evidence that it was now salted as well. The salt industry at Droitwich in Worcestershire and Middlewich in Cheshire probably had its origins during this period. Another Bronze Age development was a significant improvement in weaving technology (see Chapter 7). Both on the Continent and across the Archipelago, demand for woollen cloth led to an increase in both wool production and weaving. Woollen clothing became all but universal. Archaeologists have identified woollen tunics, woollen skirts, woollen cloaks, and lengths of woollen cloth intended to be wrapped around the body like traditional highland plaid.

A general increase in population; a growing sense of individuality and ownership; greater demand for manufactured bronze products; an agricultural system increasingly geared towards the production of surpluses; increased possibilities for travel thanks to wheeled vehicles and better boats; closer relations with distant communities both within and beyond the Archipelago – all these point to a more connected society, to an economy ever more geared towards trade, and also to the likelihood of competition with other communities based on trade. In such a situation, new social institutions would inevitably develop, both to protect community interests and to manage external relationships. Precisely how leadership structures developed we can only speculate. They would certainly have varied from place to place. We can infer from the marked differences in defensive settlements that large-scale, regional overlordships probably developed in the Western Isle before they did in the wealthy, southern parts of the Main Island. Most social structures would have been based on a system of allegiances: the villager or farmer offering labour or some proportion of the year's produce in return for protection. To maintain his position – and, in all likelihood, that of his kinship group – the leader or overlord would have had to fulfil his part of the bargain. Even in the Bronze Age, gifts, trade agreements and marriage alliances seem to have been the common currency of diplomacy. They were the tools tribal leaders could use to establish stable, mutually beneficial relationships with other communities, whether near or far. The tribal leader might enrich himself and his family in the process, but in the last resort the community and its land had to be protected – by force if necessary. That force took the form of warrior bands or a warrior elite.

The swords, the spearheads, and the shields all point to the existence of a warrior class. But who were they? Were they full-time warriors? Were they ordinary men, farmers and landowners protected by an overlord, who strapped on their leather armour when danger threatened? We do not know. Perhaps, over the course of time, ordinary men might become warriors if circumstances demanded. How much actual fighting they did we do not know. Hillforts, ringforts, and enclosed homesteads suggest that communities felt themselves vulnerable to attack. Two skeletons found at Tormarten in Gloucestershire and another at Dorchester-on-Thames attest to some degree of violence in society at the time. All three were speared.[62] But three bodies do not make a raid, and there is only limited evidence of violence on a larger scale, repeating a pattern we have seen before: some of the most elaborate pieces of weaponry that have been discovered seem to have been intended for display rather than combat. A regional chief may well have wanted an elaborate sword or shield to enhance his prestige. Or we can imagine that a warrior band, dependent on its finery and its outward show for at least part of its impact, might have wanted such weapons as deterrents, even if they were never used.

These social changes reflect a more basic shift in middle and late Bronze Age society: a transfer of power from the priests to the men of bronze; from those with spiritual authority to those whose authority rested on their position in society and their ability to enforce their will.

Between about 1700 and 1400 BC, the spiritual and ritual life of the Archipelago underwent a profound change, although, as ever, it is not possible to know exactly what happened and why. Henges and stone circles – the traditional places of spiritual observance and ritual activity for the previous 1,500 years – fell out of use. Avebury may have been abandoned as early as 1800 BC. The last significant modification of Stonehenge took place around 1600 BC. The stones may well have remained in use for some time without leaving any archaeological traces, but by 1400 BC the site was probably deserted. Callanish, which had been a focus of activity during the Beaker period, shows a marked decline in use from 1500 BC, and was completely abandoned before 1000 BC. Burial practices were also changing. Collective burial had given way to individual burial, often under round barrows, during the Beaker period. From around 1700 BC, cremation became the most common method of disposing of the dead. Burial remained individual, with the ashes placed in a pot or urn, again under a barrow, and often accompanied by grave goods. This pattern soon changed again so that by 1400 BC, the cremated dead were buried close together in what are effectively cemeteries, and without grave goods. In the Western Isle and much of the Main Island, these cemeteries take the form of burial mounds, usually raised for the purpose, though sometimes the flanks of earlier, existing mounds were used. In the south-east of the Main Island, flat areas known as urnfields were preferred, with the urns buried close together in individual pits. That said, while cremation was the main method of dealing with the dead, instances of bodies being preserved by evisceration, smoking, and mummification have all been identified, and excarnation was almost certainly still practised in some areas.

In the past, proponents of invasion theory sought to link these changes to the radical shift in population which they saw following on from the arrival of the Beaker people; suggesting, in effect, that once the Beaker immigrants replaced the Neolithic population, becoming the dominant cultural and racial group, they simply adhered to their own cultural norms. Although we now accept that there was a massive population shift in the second half of the third millennium BC, this solution does not work chronologically. Beaker immigration occurred much earlier than the changes in ritual and burial practice outlined above, so we must look to broader social developments for an explanation.

By the second half of the second millennium BC, the population was not only much larger, roles were becoming more specialised. It seems likely that the number of men (and it would have been men) earning their living as a member of what we might call professional groups – traders, merchants, sailors, metalworkers, and warriors – increased. In many cases, their roles would have allowed or required them to travel, and we have seen how cultural links across the Channel Zone and in other directions intensified and how trading and distribution networks for manufactured goods expanded. However, the vast majority of the population still worked the land, and for them this may well have been a period of reduced mobility. Agriculture was becoming more intensive, and farming units, based on enclosed fields and whether owned or worked by family groups, were becoming smaller. Collective effort was focussed on building walls rather than henges, perhaps because people were less inclined, or less able, to take the time and bear the cost of long pilgrimages and huge ceremonies. The archaeology suggests that the rites and ceremonies surrounding death and the ancestors were no longer as central to people's lives as they had been in Neolithic times. If the priests no longer led society, that was understandable. Their temples, their centres of power, and their rituals would have had less relevance. Ritual and belief undoubtedly remained important, but the focus had changed. To understand how, we need to look at two key elements: deposition and water.

In December 1959, Arthur Houghton was ploughing a low-lying field on the farm at Little Isleham in Cambridgeshire, which he worked with his brother, when he turned up a number of bronze objects. Excavations revealed a pit, roughly a metre in diameter and a metre deep, dug on the edge of what had been a water course or channel, and containing a huge earthenware pot packed with bronze objects dating from around 1000 BC. There were swords, axe heads, palstave axes, knives, odd bits of armour and horse gear, and pieces of sheet bronze – a total of some 6,500 items weighing almost ninety kilos, making it even now the largest hoard ever discovered in the Archipelago. The Isleham hoard consisted solely of bronze; whereas the St Andrews hoard, discovered in 1990, and dating from just a few years later than Isleham, probably between 950 and 750 BC, contained a variety of materials. There was bronze, but also gold from the Western Isle, jet from Yorkshire, amber from the Baltic, and, because ground conditions favoured preservation, the remains of textiles – yarn, string, even a rare fragment of Bronze Age wool – raising the possibility that other hoards may have included organic material which has not survived. Isleham and St Andrews date from near the end of the Bronze Age, but the Migdale hoard, discovered in 1900 by workmen at Bonar Bridge on the north bank of the Kyle of Sutherland, is at least a thousand years older. It contained a bronze axe head, hair ornaments, fragments of a woman's headdress in North European style, solid bronze bangles (or possibly anklets), sheet bronze, beads, and buttons made of jet and cannel or bituminous coal. Although separated by a full millennium, these hoards all demonstrate the connectedness of Bronze Age society, the way items could move between regions. The sense of close cultural links between the Archipelago and the Continent is reinforced by the Near Lewes hoard, discovered in Sussex in 2011. Buried, like the Isleham hoard, in an earthenware pot, the hoard consisted of seventy-nine items, most of them ecorative pieces. Some, such as Sussex loops (single lengths of bronze twisted to form a particular kind of bracelet), are clearly of local provenance, while others have a more distant origin. There are gold appliqué discs of a kind usually found in France; special *tutuli* mounts (pins with heads shaped like miniature shield bosses) from Germany; and amber beads probably from the Baltic. One other hoard which should be mentioned here was found in the parish of Mooghaun North in County Clare, unearthed in 1854 by workers building a railway line. Buried just two kilometres from Ireland's largest hillfort, it weighed over five kilos, making it the largest collection of Bronze Age gold ever found north of the Alps. It probably consisted of several hundred items but, unfortunately, most were sold or melted down at the time. The twenty-nine that remain – bracelets, torcs, collars – all date from around 800 BC and are made of gold originating in County Down.

In the nineteenth and early twentieth centuries, archaeologists finding large quantities of valuable Bronze Age objects buried in the ground or deposited in a river or lakebed, assumed that someone had hidden them there – perhaps during an episode of violence – and intended to come back and reclaim them later. It was a natural assumption, which appeared to explain hoards of coins, plate, jewellery and other items dating from Roman, Norman, and medieval times, so why not those from the Bronze Age? Today, more weight is given to the idea that many Bronze Age hoards represent ritual deposition – although we should be cautious in suggesting that there was only one motive for the deposition of hoards. This change in interpretation is, in part, due to the sheer number of Bronze Age hoards that have been discovered – in the age of metal detectors, the British Museum is dealing with more than thirty new discoveries a year – and in part, to the application of new scientific techniques which have given us a better understanding of the period as a whole. A key site in this respect is Flag Fen in Cambridgeshire, just two kilometres north of the lake village of Must Farm.

In 1365 BC – the date supplied by dendrochronology – the inhabitants of Flag Fen began building a trackway out over an area of wetland. It stretched from Fengate on the edge of the dry land, to Northey Island. By the time it was finished, it was a kilometre long, seven metres wide, and consisted of over 60,000 stakes and planks. The wood was carefully chosen. Some of the timbers were oak, but as oak trees did not grow in the area, they were – like the stones of Stonehenge – bought some considerable distance to the site, perhaps because they do not rot as fast as other timbers, perhaps because they had some kind of spiritual significance, or perhaps both. Practical considerations aside, the whole idea of making a connection across water between the shore and the island clearly had symbolic and spiritual implications for the community that built it. Many Bronze Age round barrows have been found on Northey – quite possibly the burial sites of chiefs or warriors – and there are many instances of cremations and secondary burials in and around the barrows. The accumulation of valuable items deposited in the water along the length of the causeway includes swords, axes, spearheads, daggers, brooches, clasps, pins, rings, earrings, even a set of chisels, but it differs from the hoards discussed earlier in that it was deposited over the course of more than a thousand years.

We have noted the importance of water in the ritual behaviour of Neolithic people, how they would deposit items of value along the length of trackways such as the Sweet Track (see Chapter 4). That practice reached its apogee in the Bronze Age. We do not know how many hoards or depositional sites there were, but the number must run into thousands. We do not know what proportion of available bronze was taken out of circulation – it may have been considerable – nor what economic effect this may have had. In theory, given that in a pre-monetary society bronze probably functioned as a medium of exchange, the removal of a significant percentage could have had a marked deflationary effect. We do know, however, that from 800 BC onwards, with the coming of iron working technology and the associated cultural changes, the size and number of hoards soon fell away to almost nothing. Scattered instances of what may have been ritual deposition have been identified in the later Iron Age and even in the Roman period, but the apparent fervour exhibited during the middle and later Bronze Age never revived.

Analysis of what was deposited, and where, appears to confirm that deposits were made according to a set of rules or preferences. It seems that bronze and gold were rarely deposited together (the St Andrews hoard is an exception in this respect). Bronze hoards are found in or near water, or occasionally at the edge of settlements. Gold was almost always buried at some distance from villages, field systems, or other areas of human activity (as is the case with the Mooghaun North hoard). Single weapons, usually complete, and usually rapier-style or flat-bladed swords, are found in river channels and flowing water. By contrast, weapon fragments are found on dry land. Traditional hoards – that is, those containing collections of mixed metal and other objects – are generally found in still water, in bogs or marshes, or on dry land close to the edge of lakes or wetlands. Moreover, the objects contained in these hoards often appear to have been deliberately damaged or broken before being deposited.

We can only guess at the beliefs underlying these differing practices. Were the complete swords the property of warriors thanking the gods for their victories? Were they the equivalent of grave goods – the property of warriors or tribal leaders whose cremated ashes were thrown into the moving stream at the same time as the sword? There is some indication that swords were deposited close to fords. Was this because fords marked a liminal place between the water and the land? Because they were territorial boundaries? Or, more prosaically, because they were strategic locations and therefore likely battle sites? And what of the mixed bronze hoards? Were they deposited by individuals or families? Did they represent propitiation or thanksgiving? Does an edge-of-water location imply some transition between the world of the living and the world of the dead, similar to that which may have applied to henges and stone circles? Or, as has also been suggested, is their location connected to the fact that water levels are known to have been rising during the later Bronze Age? Were these offerings intended to persuade the gods to hold back the waters? Any or all of these explanations could have some validity.

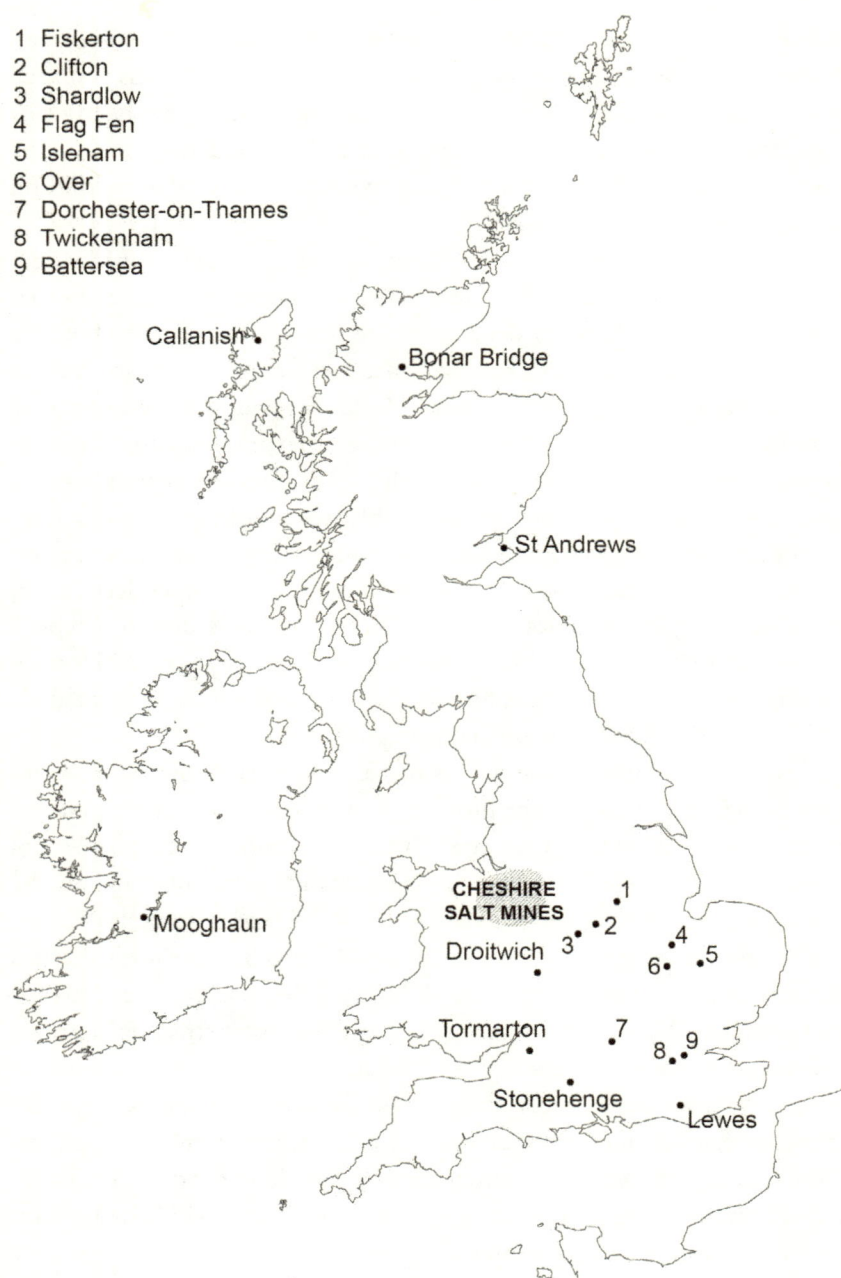

Map 11   Hoards and Water

Water as an element was clearly of importance to Bronze Age religious practice, but some lake or riverine locations were clearly more sacred than others. Flag Fen was one, but while exceptional in terms of what was preserved there, it was not unique. The remains of a causeway and large quantities of associated depositions, including swords, rapiers, spearheads and even logboats, have been found in the River Trent at Clifton on the edge of Nottingham. Proof that causeway-related deposition continued into the Iron Age has been discovered at Fiskerton in the Witham Valley in Lincolnshire, where a sword, a complete spear, a dagger, some bronze fittings and two boats have been recovered from the peaty soil. Certain stretches of river also appear to have had particular significance. East Anglia is rich in archaeology, but even by local standards, the Godwin Ridge near the village of Over in Cambridgeshire is remarkable. Once a sandy island about six hundred metres long in the middle of the braided stream of the Great Ouse, it now sits on flat, drained fenland. Excavations have revealed a history of continuous usage, though probably not habitation, from the Mesolithic period into the later Iron Age. Over 70,000 artefacts of different kinds have been uncovered, ranging from skulls to weapons to ornate brooches, and while only a proportion of these can with any certainty be categorised as votive offerings, it was clearly a place of ritual deposition for many centuries.[63] The area around the confluence of the Rivers Trent and Derwent, near the village of Shardlow in Derbyshire, shows evidence of habitation from the Mesolithic right up to the Iron Age and is a site marked by dense votive deposition of Bronze Age weapons – mainly rapiers, palstaves and socket axes.[64]

A popular deposition site that has been more intensively studied than most is the River Thames. Polished Neolithic mace heads of an apparently ceremonial kind have been recovered from the river at Twickenham, but the stretch between Waterloo and Battersea seems to have had particular ritual or spiritual significance, perhaps because it was a ford or crossing place, or possibly because it was a frontier where tribal lands and the tribes that controlled them met. Dredging and bridge-building during the nineteenth century led to the discovery of many Bronze Age artefacts, including swords, axes, and other weapons, as well as human remains. That ritual deposition continued into the Iron Age is evident from the spectacular Battersea shield, dating from sometime after 350 BC, and the horned Waterloo helmet, probably dating from after 150 BC. Both are made of delicately-worked bronze and neither is suited for use in battle. As so often, we cannot tell why such objects should have been deposited in the water, but their value, their number, and their distribution all indicate that they were deposited deliberately, as votive offerings, not merely lost or discarded. The continuity of offerings made in the Thames is remarkable. Romans threw coins into the river. Medieval pilgrims, returning from Canterbury, threw their pilgrim badges into the Thames as a thank offering – hundreds have been found around London Bridge. Even today, in a much changed and multiracial United Kingdom, the river retains its sacred quality for some people: Hindu communities use the Thames as they would the Ganges. They drop small, metal and soapstone statues of Ganesha, Hanuman, and Shiva into the moving stream, as well as offerings of flowers, beads, coconuts, ghee lamps and even jewellery.

Whether on land, in water, or on the edge of water, ritual deposition was a salient feature of middle and later Bronze Age life. Causeways of the kind seen at Flag Fen, Clifton, and Fiskerton were major construction projects. Although perhaps not requiring the same level of engineering skill as Stonehenge, Avebury, or Callanish, they certainly required planning and collective effort on a significant scale – which argues that whatever spiritual or religious beliefs they represented were broadly shared across the wider community. Such major sites are likely to have been under the supervision of a priesthood or priestly caste – even if the priests themselves did not enjoy the same level of authority in wider society as their Neolithic predecessors. However, the scattered nature of so many hoards and depositions suggests that individuals or families may have conducted their own rituals. One possible reading of the broad shift from stone circles to deposition is that deposition, particularly in water, represented an increased emphasis on 'direct' contact with the otherworld and its gods or spirits, indicating a reduced emphasis on formal and public ceremonies as a way of contacting the ancestors. This is speculation, but it does seem to parallel the wider changes in society. If the gods of the otherworld – often referred to as the chthonic deities – provided rain, a good harvest, healthy animals, even plentiful supplies of the copper and tin ores that underpinned social structures, then their generosity needed to be reciprocated. In this sense, deposition becomes a mixture of propitiation and tribute – not unlike the relationship that we have suggested might have existed between villagers and farmers and their overlord.

10 Iron and Settlement

Iron was probably first smelted in the southern Caucasus, where artefacts dating from the latter part of the third millennium BC have been discovered – although there is also evidence of early iron working in central Anatolia, not far from Ankara, about 2200 BC. Smelting iron requires more heat and therefore more energy than smelting tin, gold, or copper. Its melting point is 1530° C, so that while early metal workers could smelt tin (230° C), gold (1060° C), and copper (1080° C) using much the same equipment and many of the same basic techniques as they used to fire pottery, iron required the construction of a special furnace. These early furnaces, known as bloomeries, had a vertical shaft where the ore was melted and reduced, an opening at the base to act as an air intake, and a pit where the slag collected.[65] The molten iron, or bloom, was removed from the bloomery, cooled rapidly to make it hard and brittle, then tempered by reheating and hammered into whatever shape the smith desired.

Because it took time to develop and refine the process, it was only in the second millennium BC that iron working technology began to spread from its region of origin. It spread in all directions, but moving westwards, it reached the Balkans around 1200 BC and continued to spread westwards up the Danube Valley and across the Continent. Whereas Neolithic and Beaker culture reached the Archipelago as the result of a kind of pincer movement – crossing the Atlantic Zone in the west, and the Channel and Southern North Sea Zones in the east – on this occasion, the Atlantic Zone does not seem to have come into play to any significant extent. The new technology arrived by the most direct route, reaching the southern and eastern shores of the Main Island about 800 BC, before moving gradually north and west, reaching the High North about 700 BC and the Western Isle about 500 BC.

Given the sophistication of Bronze Age weapons and tools, and the comparative complexity of iron working technology, it was natural that the transition between the two should have been lengthy – and, in the case of the Main Island, it was some two hundred years before iron became the dominant and preferred metal. Those two hundred years, from 800 to 600 BC, were a period of gradual change. The process of bringing more land under cultivation and dividing it up into fields continued. So, too, did the construction of enclosed, defensible homesteads, although many of these were larger than before, centring on roundhouses with a diameter of anything up to fifteen metres – so large, in fact, that they may even have had an upper floor. Roundhouses of this type have been found throughout the Archipelago and probably represent the dwellings of regional chieftains or overlords. While copper was usually smelted close to where it was mined, it seems that iron – which was much more widely available – was smelted and worked at the homestead level, giving local chiefs the ability to produce their own weapons, tools, and horse gear.

At about the same time, we see the development of a new kind of hilltop enclosure: usually areas of between ten and fifteen hectares enclosed by a simple ditch and bank. About thirty have so far been identified, mainly in the Lowland Zone of the Main Island – although some will undoubtedly have disappeared under the plough, while others were transformed into hillforts at a later date. Among those which can be positively identified and were not subsequently restructured are Balksbury and Walbury in Hampshire, The Lawley in Longnor in Shropshire, and Camp Hill at Woolton outside Liverpool. These enclosures are distinct from hillforts in that their structure clearly suggests containment rather than defence. Soil analysis confirms that animals were kept there over a long period of time but has revealed little or no evidence of habitation. Enclosures of this kind may have resulted from the spread and intensification of animal husbandry. They were probably used at key moments in the agricultural year: at lambing and calving time; when animals were herded together for exchange or slaughter; or when seasonal or annual tributes had to be paid. In an agricultural society, such occasions would have brought people together and would have had an added social dimension, providing opportunities to exchange produce, pass on news, to arrange and celebrate marriages, and – something that was clearly important in both Bronze Age and Iron Age society – to indulge in large scale feasting.

The beginning of the Iron Age also saw changes in ritual behaviour. The deposition of hoards, which was such a feature of the later Bronze Age, shows a marked and rapid decline. Across most of the Main Island, the practice seems to have come to a halt around 800 BC. Only in the south and south-west do hoards – although reduced in size – continue to feature in the archaeological record beyond 800 BC, and even here they drop off abruptly after *c.*650 BC. This short transition period is known as the

Llyn Fawr Phase, taking its name from a remarkable hoard, dating from between 750 and 650 BC, discovered at the bottom of a lakebed at Llyn Fawr, near Rhigos, in the southern part of the Western Uplands. The Llyn Fawr hoard is an indicator of cultural change in that it contains a mixture of bronze and iron items, including socketed axes, chisels, sickles, horse gear, a spearhead, a sword, and a massive bronze cauldron. The continuing close cultural relationship between the people living in the south of the Main Island and their Continental neighbours is illustrated by the fact that many of the socketed axes found in hoards dating from the Llyn Fawr Phase came from Armorica, probably imported through the ports at Mount Batten on Plymouth Sound and at Hengistbury Head. These axes add an extra dimension to the conundrum of deposition. In Armorica, deposition remained a central part of ritual activity much longer than in the Main Island, reaching its peak between 800 and 600 BC. Socketed axes were manufactured in vast quantities – an estimated 40,000 were buried in Armorica and Normandy alone – yet the bronze used had such a high lead content that they were too soft to be of any practical use. It seems they were manufactured with the sole purpose of being 'sacrificed', of being buried or deposited in order to propitiate the gods. In the Western Isle, hoards continued to be deposited for longer than in the Main Island – the most impressive being the spectacular Dowris Hoard from County Offaly, containing twenty-six bronze horns, some of the earliest musical instruments to have been discovered in the Archipelago. Then, around the turn of the sixth century BC, deposition drops off almost completely.

As we do not know the precise motivation for deposition in the first place – beyond the fact that it seems to have been an attempt to communicate in some way with the otherworld – we cannot tell why it stopped. In both the Main Island and the Western Isle, the timing of the change coincides with the arrival of iron working technology, so there may have been a cultural reason for the change, but more than that we cannot say. Nor is there any evidence to explain why deposition appears to have revived in popularity, though never reaching Bronze Age levels, during the Roman occupation.

In previous chapters, we have seen how the transmission of goods and ideas across different contact zones, coupled with the geography of the Archipelago itself, led to an east-west divide and other regional variations in everything from ritual behaviour and tomb construction to the distribution of weapons and pots. Evidence of such variations increases in importance as the Iron Age progresses. Continuing population growth leading to more complex social and political structures may well have played a part. The middle centuries of the first millennium BC, from 600 to 400 BC, marked the beginning of major changes in regional settlement patterns that imply the development of regionally distinct socio-economic systems. Barry Cunliffe, whose expertise in Iron Age society is unparalleled, has divided the Main Island into four zones.[66] The first, from the Thames to the Humber, was characterised by villages and open, unenclosed settlements. The second, stretching north from the Humber as far as the Tweed and across to the Lake District was a zone of enclosed homesteads, much like those we saw in the later Bronze Age. The third comprised a broad band extending from Kent to Dorset which turned north up the Severn Valley to the north coast of the Western Uplands, as well as a second area stretching north from the Solway across to the Firth of Forth and the Firth of Tay. Here, hillforts were dominant – as they were also in the Western Isle. The fourth zone, running the full length of the western coast of the Main Island, from the South-Western Peninsula to the Northern and Far Northern Isles, was marked by settlements which varied greatly in size and nature, but were all apparently constructed with a strong emphasis on defence.

It is tempting to see Cunliffe's four zones as reflecting differing levels of violence and instability – or at least differing levels of fear of violence and instability. Increased instability and insecurity may explain the emergence of an overlordship-based society and warrior elites in the later Bronze Age, but there is no evidence to suggest that the situation during the early centuries of the Iron Age was any worse. The changes in regional settlement patterns appear to have been largely evolutionary, developing models which had existed during the Bronze Age or before, rather than a radical transformation. It seems likely that the changes in social organisation that had begun during the Bronze Age simply continued but diverged, leading to the development of regionally distinct social and political systems which reflected local conditions, such as physical security and relations with neighbouring (or rival) tribes. Geography, too, would have played a part. In an agrarian society where soil and climate were determining factors, the nature of farming would have differed widely (as it still does). The differences between the damp, flat landscapes of East Anglia,

Map 12   Iron Age Zones of Settlement

the broad, open chalklands of the south and centre, and the rocky coastal regions of the west would have determined the relative economic strength of the regions, the amount of power exercised by local chieftains, and thus the way in which society was organised.

The defended settlements strung out along the western edge of the Main Island take a range of names and forms. In the south-west, they are known as 'rounds'; in the Western Uplands 'raths' or 'ringworks'; in the High North and the Islands, they are 'wheelhouses' or 'brochs'; and where they appear in the Western Isle they are 'raths' or 'ringforts'. They all represent an expansion and intensification of the principle of the enclosed homestead. Some 2,500 Cornish rounds have been identified, many of them situated in the middle of field systems that suggest mixed agriculture. Typically, an area of about a hectare was enclosed by an earth bank, often faced with a stone revetment, through which there is a single entrance or gateway. Within the enclosure, there may be up to half-a-dozen roundhouses with additional byres and storehouses. The first rounds probably appeared during the fifth century BC, but they continued to be built, rebuilt, and inhabited right up to – and in some cases beyond – the Roman period. Like so much else in Iron Age society, rounds can be subject to more than one interpretation. Some archaeologists point to the labour involved in digging the ditch and bank, to the heavy stone revetments and the single gateway, as indicating a need to defend the settlement against attack. Others see the fact that rounds remained central to the social organisation of the region for a thousand years as evidence of an extended period of peace and social stability.

Much of Cunliffe's fourth zone, particularly in the north of the Archipelago, has few trees and only thin soil. Stone was the natural building material and provided the best protection against the wet and windy climate. In these areas, defended settlements were massive, dry-stone constructions. Wheelhouses, such as those at Jarlshof in Far Northern Isles, or Cnip and Grimsay in the Outer Isles, consisted of a large circular chamber – a communal living area with a central hearth – surrounded by a ring of smaller rooms or bays leading off it. Brochs, of which some five hundred survive, were double-walled, tower-like structures with two or three internal floors. There may also have been a ring of wooden huts attached to the outer wall. Most wheelhouses and brochs are found by the sea, by loch sides, or on islands. Promontory, cliff top, or island locations may have been chosen because they were defensible in times of trouble, but they could equally be taken as indicating yet again the primacy of sea and water transport, particularly in the more remote and isolated areas. Dun Ringhill broch on the Isle of Skye is one of several that have ramps leading down to the water's edge where boats would have docked. If long usage is evidence of stability, Dun Ringhill must have been a particularly peaceful region: it was occupied from the first millennium BC until the nineteenth century. The Broch of Burrian, situated on the southernmost tip of the isle of North Ronaldsay, also has an entrance on the seaward side, but on the landward side there are traces of four earthwork banks. Substantial earthworks on such a small island seem incongruous. We do not know when they were dug – such archaeological finds as have been unearthed have not provided a secure date – so they may be the remains of an earlier enclosure, but the builders of the broch evidently both adopted and adapted them, though whether as genuine defences or to make a statement about ownership and power is unclear.

Another type of defended settlement was the crannog. These are lake villages, but unlike Must Farm where the houses were suspended over the water, crannogs were built on artificial islands just offshore in a lake or a river. They were anything between ten and thirty metres across, and usually consisted of one or two roundhouses, a causeway or bridge linking the crannog to the mainland, and a mooring for boats. Crannogs had good defensive potential but, given the significance of fresh water in early belief systems, their location may have added a spiritual dimension. The sites of some 1,200 crannogs have been identified in the Western Isle, while in the north-western part of the Main Island – today's Argyll, Dumfries and Galloway, and the Hebrides – there are nearly six hundred more.

The earliest crannogs are in the Outer Isles and date back to Neolithic times. Eilean Dòmhnuill on Loch Olabhat in North Uist was occupied from between 3650 and 2500 BC, while some of the timbers belonging to crannogs on Loch Bhorghastail in Lewis have been dated to around 3500 BC. These early examples predate not only Stonehenge, but also the great settlement at Ness of Brodgar. The idea of the crannog was evidently an old one, and, like cursus monuments and stone circles, it may perhaps have originated in the north. However, it was only towards the end of the Bronze Age that crannog building caught on. While many of the known sites have yet to be dated, the data we have so far indicate that the majority were built and in use between about 800 BC and 200 AD. And with crannogs, as with brochs, there are instances of an essentially prehistoric type of dwelling being lived in and remaining in use for many hundreds of years. In the Western Isle, records show crannogs being used as defensive locations in the late 1500s; while in the Outer Isles and the north of the Main Island, we read of crannogs being inhabited into the early years of the eighteenth century.

Hillforts exist in all parts of the Archipelago, although in higher concentrations in certain areas. In 2017, Oxford University published an online atlas listing all the known hillforts in the British Isles.[67] It records a total of 4,147 examples. This breaks down – and because of the way the Oxford atlas is structured, we must use modern names – as 30 in the Isle of Man, 509 in Ireland, 690 in Wales, 1,224 in England, and 1,694 in Scotland. Even allowing for some dispute as to what precisely constitutes a hillfort, the numbers speak for themselves. The earliest, as noted earlier, have their origins in the later Bronze Age, while a small number continued to be built or substantially modified up until about 700 AD. As with crannogs, many hillforts have yet to be dated, but the great era of hillfort construction, in the Main Island at least, seems to have been between 600 and 400 BC. The question, of course, is why the inhabitants of large areas of the Archipelago felt the need to pepper the landscape with these massive constructions?

Hillforts are not unique to the Archipelago. They are found right across the Western Lands, with higher concentrations in the west and north and fewer examples in the central and Mediterranean lands, reflecting the cultural changes brought about by population movements (see Chapter 11). Within the Archipelago, although they vary widely in location and size, hillforts fall into two broad categories. Most were surrounded by one or more ditch-and-bank structures of sufficient width and height to indicate a defensive purpose; the outer banks were usually faced with timber – or sometimes stone – revetments to create a vertical rampart; and there were two entrances, usually on opposite sides of the enclosed area. The second category comprises what are known as promontory forts. Built of stone and, as the name suggests, found on cliff tops or headlands overlooking the sea, they are positioned so that the cliffs made a hostile approach from the sea impossible. This reduced the length of rampart required to make the site secure. Promontory forts are found in Brittany and up the length of the western side of the Archipelago – from the South-Western Peninsula to the Northern Isles, including the Halfway Isle and the Western Isle (where there are over two hundred). This may indicate a sharing of ideas across the Atlantic Zone, or it may reflect the geology of the coastline, the difficulty of digging earth ramparts in stony ground, and the abundance of stone as a building material.

Like the henges and stone circles of the Neolithic period, hillforts demonstrate a capacity for organised and collective effort on a significant scale, but the context is different, quite clearly social and political rather than spiritual. That distinction, coupled with the nature and location of these structures, suggests a competitive rather than cooperative environment. It seems likely that they served to assert control over a given territory and, in doing so, also asserted the identity of the tribe or community that built them. Many of the best-known hillforts – British Camp on Herefordshire Beacon in the Malvern Hills, Cadbury Castle in Somerset, Eildon Hill in the Borders, and the vast complexities of Maiden Castle in Dorset – loom over the landscape in an almost threatening manner, which may be what their builders intended. Hillforts such as these had the capacity to serve a defensive purpose – and some of them did – but they were built as statements of strength, not admissions of weakness. The nature and identity of the communities responsible is unclear, but they probably consisted of one or more extended kinship groups. What we do know is that archaeological finds of luxury goods and items of horse gear suggest an association between hillforts and elite groups. This returns us to the idea that the political structure of such communities may have been based on reciprocal allegiances – tribute in exchange for protection – perhaps building on the structures that developed in the middle centuries of the Bronze Age, although there would no doubt have been wide regional variation.

Hillforts such as Maiden Castle – the largest in the Archipelago – and Danebury, in Hampshire – painstakingly excavated under the direction of Barry Cunliffe over several decades – encapsulate the changes that took place during the middle and later centuries of the first millennium BC across much of the Main Island. Both are hilltop sites that had a long history of use before the construction of the fort. In the case of Maiden Castle, archaeologists have identified the remains of a causewayed enclosure dating from about 4000 BC and abandoned some 600 years later. The early history of Danebury is less definite, but there are pits and the remains of standing timbers that could be evidence of a Neolithic henge. The first phase of Maiden Castle began around 600 BC. It consisted of a single ditch enclosing an area of about six hectares, and ramparts that were at least

Map 13   Rounds, Brochs, Crannogs, and Hillforts

eight metres in height. Over the next century-and-a-half, the ramparts were repaired and strengthened at least once, and the two eastern entrances made more defensible by the construction of complex outworks through which the path to the gates twisted and turned. Then, somewhere after 450 BC, we see the beginning of a new phase of rebuilding and expansion. Over the next two hundred years, the fort tripled in size. New ramparts and new entrance passages were constructed, resulting in the complex, multivallate structure we see today. The development of Danebury followed a similar pattern: an initial ditch and rampart enclosing some five hectares, begun about 550 BC, which was repaired and strengthened over a period of two hundred and fifty years. Danebury did not undergo expansion on the scale of Maiden castle, but from around 310 BC it was rebuilt as a multivallate fort with a single entrance passing through two gateways and protected by massive hornworks.

As first constructed, both Maiden Castle and Danebury were more or less standard hillforts, in both size and design. Over a hundred similar examples have been identified in the southern hillfort zone, apparently indicating that the land was now being divided up into small, discrete territories, among people who shared a broadly similar cultural background. The second phase of construction – which saw Maiden Castle expand massively, and the defence works of both hillforts achieve monumental proportions – coincided with a period in which other hillforts in their vicinity were abandoned. This seems to have been a widespread phenomenon, although not always on the scale observable at Maiden Castle and Danebury. The most likely explanation is that power was becoming centralised; that the extended family groups controlling those forts which continued to be used had conquered or taken control of neighbouring forts and their associated lands. The enlargement and aggrandisement of Maiden Castle and Danebury was a declaration of power and status, and both show signs of strong, central control during this period. Roundhouses, which in the earlier phase appear to be randomly sited, were now organised in rows to create streets; separate areas were reserved for storehouses and storage pits. At a later stage, one area of Maiden Castle was set aside for smelting iron and, presumably, the production of iron tools and weapons. It became one of the largest iron working sites in the south of the Main Island, bringing in supplies of ore from outside the area – probably from the Weald. There is also evidence of iron working at

Danebury. Settlements such as these were probably still too small to be called towns. Cunliffe has calculated the population of Danebury was probably somewhere between two hundred and three hundred and fifty,[68] while Maiden Castle and British Camp might have been a little larger. Nonetheless, they exhibit certain features – defined boundaries, an ordered internal structure, a system of governance – that would become key characteristics of the first towns when they did develop in the first and second centuries BC. Other hillforts may have been larger – the population of Eildon Hill, for example, may have approached 2,000 – but they do not show the same evidence of internal organisation.

The evidence suggests that the period from 1500 BC onwards was marked by smaller tribes, quite possibly based on kinship groups, gradually coalescing into larger groupings, impelled by population growth, shared location, and shared interests or marriage alliances. These larger groupings seem to have provided the structural basis for society throughout much of the Archipelago during the second half of the first millennium BC. How they functioned we can only guess. Leadership may well have been based on the ability of the chief and his followers to deliver wealth and offer physical protection to those who owed him allegiance and paid him tribute. These were tribal chiefs, not kings, and in such a context it seems probable that the eruptions of inter-tribal violence – which undoubtedly did occur – were focussed on raids with the objective of stealing cattle and booty, and perhaps also taking prisoners to be sold as slaves. As far as we can tell, the idea of territorial conquest seems to have been less important.

Prestige and status were one way of deterring attacks, and the monumentality of Maiden Castle and Danebury was an important statement of the power of those who ruled within. But both were built with a practical eye on resisting attack. The ramparts which today – while still impressive – appear as gentle slopes, would have had vertical, timber-fronted outward faces. The elaborate outworks around the gates were intended to slow the approach of any attack, and to funnel the enemy into a confined space where they would be exposed to the fire of the defenders. Large quantities of sling stones have been found near the gates in both forts. Yet, despite such precautions, the gates of Danebury were burnt down twice. On the first occasion, between 500 and 450 BC, they were rebuilt, and the outer works strengthened. On the second, probably around 100 BC, they were not. A hundred or more bodies with what appear to be spear and sword injuries suggest a major confrontation and the probability that the defences were overwhelmed. Danebury's fortunes went into rapid decline and most of the inhabitants moved away. About the same time, Maiden Castle also went into decline, although in this case there is no evidence of violent attack. The regular street pattern gave way to more random settlement and the population thinned. The site remained in limited use well into the first century AD – it may even have been used as a base by Roman forces – but, like Danebury, it was a shadow of its former self.

In terms of big archaeology – types of settlement, patterns of settlement, land use – the period from 600 BC onwards presents a complex but coherent picture of evolutionary change and regional divergence. In terms of population and cultural change, the picture is equally complex but less clear. One important reason for this is that the second half of the first millennium BC brings us, for the first time, within range of early documentary sources. Most of these sources have been known and studied, often uncritically, for centuries. They have also been used as the foundation stones for contemporary cultural and political identities. However, new archaeological knowledge which has emerged in recent decades is challenging previously accepted associations between culture, language, and ethnicity. As a result, much of the story of the closing centuries of prehistory has had to be rewritten.

11 Sounds and Speech

What did the prehistoric world sound like? We can be sure that birds sang, dogs barked, and children cried, but anything else is a matter of guesswork and speculation, although we do have a few clues. The physical form of stone circles and the avenues that lead to them suggests processions and ceremonies, and it is difficult to imagine either without some kind of music – slow, echoing drumbeats; the deep chanting of the priests; an occasional blaring of horns. We know that the tribes who came together in their hilltop enclosures and hillforts marked their gatherings with the slaughter of cattle and feasting into the night. Such events must surely have been accompanied by singing and dancing, strongly rhythmic music, creating an emotional response, and perhaps even driving the dancers into a Dervish-like trance state.

No society has ever existed without music. Drums made of wood and animal skin would have long since decayed, but in the Continental Lands the remains of flutes made from mammoth and bird bones dating back many thousands of years have been found. In the Archipelago, the oldest musical instrument yet discovered is a set of six, yew-wood pipes, unearthed at Greystones in County Wicklow. They date from *c.*2000 BC and probably formed a set of panpipes or an early pipe organ. We do not know when stringed instruments first appeared. Ancient Irish texts suggest that they accompanied songs and recitations at the courts of semi-mythical Irish kings many centuries before the arrival of Christianity, but because these texts were not written down until early medieval times, we cannot be sure. The earliest evidence for stringed instruments in the Archipelago – in fact, in the Western Lands – is a wooden fragment discovered in a cave on the Isle of Skye, dated to *c.*300 BC and identified as the bridge of a lyre.

With trumpets and horns, we are on slightly firmer ground. As late as the first century AD, the Roman cavalry were still using trumpets made of wood and covered with leather rather than bronze or brass, which suggests that such instruments could well have appeared much earlier, although no examples have been found. The ability to smelt and work metal led to the development of bronze horns known as *trompa* or *trumpa*, some of them remarkably sophisticated. Over a hundred of these instruments are known have survived. Most come from the Western Isle, where they first appeared *c.*1500 BC and where they probably continued in use for two thousand years. Some smaller examples, like one found at the bottom of a well in Battle in East Sussex, have a simple, curved shape, not unlike the traditional idea of a hunting horn. Some were end-blown in the traditional manner; some were sounded through an aperture on the side, like a modern flute, while others were held in an upright position, with the bell above the player's head. Four instruments of this type, dating from *c.*100 BC were discovered in 1794 at the ancient hillfort of Emain Macha (known today as Fort Navan) in County Armagh. Three are now lost, but the one that survives consists of two curved bronze tubes which fit together to form a vertically-held horn, two metres long and with a flat, decorated, bronze disk around the bell. The bronze has been worked to a thickness of half a millimetre, so that the instrument weighs only one kilo. Another variety of upright horn is the *carnyx* (sometimes *carynx*). Ten of these spectacular instruments survive – one of the earliest was found at Deskford in Banffshire. Made up of four or five bronze sections, they are up to three metres tall, topped with an elaborate boar's head – or in one case a serpent's head. They seem to have been in use between about 300 BC and 200 AD and are of particular importance because they give us an actual sonic connection to the past. Replicas have been made, producing a sound that is booming, raucous, and very loud. They give at least a distant impression of what prehistoric ceremonies might have sounded like, or the noise and clamour of opposing warrior bands trying to intimidate each other.

Music is one thing. Language in pre-literate societies is quite another. We may recreate the sound of horns on the edge of battle, but we cannot tell what the warrior bands shouted at each other. We have no idea what language or languages were spoken in the Archipelago until the islands were named and described in the writings of men from the literate world of the Mediterranean – and even then there are problems of interpretation. The earliest reference to the Archipelago is probably traceable through the work of the fourth-century AD poet, Avienus. His poem *Ora Maritima* suggests that he made use of material from a Greek *periplus*, or navigation manual, written nearly a thousand years earlier by a Carthaginian navigator named Himilco (see Chapter 3). Avienus says that it is two days by ship from the islands of the Oestrymnides to the land of the Hierni, which 'the ancients' used to call 'the Holy Island', and that the land of the Hierni is near the island of the Albiones.[69] Avienus seems to have muddled two groups of islands, for Oestrymnides is the usual name for the islands off the north-west coast of Galicia. In this context, however, the Oestrymnides are almost certainly Ushant, Île-Molène and the islands off the coast of Brittany. Whatever the case, *Hierni* and *Albiones* appear to be the first direct references to the islands and the populations of Ireland and Britain. The names are likely to derive from Continental informants rather than from the inhabitants of the Archipelago, but even so, examining their origin may give us an insight into linguistic prehistory.

The word *Albiones*, together with related forms such as *Albion* for the island of Britain, and *Alba*, the still current Gaelic name for Scotland, are probably of Celtic or proto-Celtic origin. One theory is that they derive from a non-Indo-European root *alb*, meaning 'hill' or 'mountain' (as in the

Alps), but it is generally accepted that they stem from the Celtic root, *albiū*, meaning 'white'. It was the Austrian-born librarian, translator and editor, Alfred Holder (1840–1916), who in 1896 first translated Albion as 'white land' and suggested that the white cliffs of Dover, often visible across the Channel, were the origin of the name.[70] Because it harnessed the iconic status of the white cliffs at a time when the British Empire was at its zenith, this idea was immediately and widely accepted. Perhaps surprisingly, it has rarely been challenged since.

To put forward an alternative, we need to explore how and why the Archipelago attracted the attention of men from the literate south. Tin was, as we know, essential for the making of bronze, and it was not plentiful on the Continent. It was tin that attracted Bronze Age merchants to the South-Western Peninsula. They came from Brittany, from Galicia, even from as far south as Gadir (modern Cadiz). Gadir, originally founded by the Phoenicians, was part of Tartessos, a rich and culturally influential kingdom, centred on the Guadalquivir Valley, which flourished between about 1200 and 550 BC. Tartessos was a centre of metalworking, and sought ores, particularly tin, from the lands along the Atlantic coast. Gadir became an important entrepôt, linking those trading routes which extended beyond the Pillars of Hercules with Phoenician, and later Greek, settlements around the Mediterranean, supplying them with much of their tin.

In the fifth century BC, Herodotus, apparently responding to some kind of rumour or statement, says that he does not 'know of any islands named Cassiterides, whence comes the tin we use,' and that he has been unable to obtain a first-hand account of 'any sea existing on the far [western] side of Europe.'[71] The name Cassiterides comes from the Greek *kassíteros*, and actually means 'Tin Islands'. Posidonius and Diodorus Siculus, both writing in the first century BC, treat the existence of the islands as a fact and say that they are off the north-west coast of Iberia. Strabo, in the first century AD, agrees and goes further, saying there are ten islands, one of them a desert, and that they are further from the Continent than from Britain. We do not know where this information came from. Voyagers along the western seaboard no doubt had tales to tell, although the Gadir merchants are likely to have muddied the waters in order to keep knowledge of the trade routes and sources of tin to themselves. Writers such as Posidonius, Diodorus, and Strabo tended to recycle the contents of earlier manuscripts, without checking their facts. And yet, in a general sense, they were right: tin did come from somewhere beyond the Pillars of Hercules and to the north. The idea of the Cassiterides, however muddled, may be the first reference to the Archipelago.

About 325 BC, Pytheas the Greek set off on an unprecedented journey. From his hometown of Massalia – present day Marseille – he made his way, probably overland, to the Gironde estuary and from there to Brittany. He then circumnavigated Britain and perhaps managed to get as far as Iceland. His chronicle of the voyage, *On the Ocean* (*Peritou Okeanou*), written about 320 BC, included much geographical and scientific information that was entirely new to the Greek and Mediterranean world. Unfortunately, no copy survives. Here, however, the habit of classical writers of borrowing from one another comes to our aid, and we can reconstruct at least some of his text from the works other writers who made use of it over the next nine hundred years. Although Pytheas had a scientific interest in the tides and in measuring the latitude of the places he visited, the quest for tin may have played a part in his journey. The established economic order which had seen Massalia grow into a major trading centre, was under threat from the rise of Carthage to the south and disruptive tribal migrations in the north. Discovering more about the sources of tin could have been a lucrative project.

Diodorus Siculus' massive *Bibliotheca Historica*, written c.40 BC, contains the classical world's fullest description of tin mining in Britain. He draws heavily on the work of another Greek historian, Timaeus, who wrote c.280 BC, but neither he nor Timaeus ever travelled far beyond the Mediterranean, and certainly never went as far as the Channel coast, so we can be reasonably certain that *Bibliotheca Historica* preserves the observations of Pytheas – and thus quotes or paraphrases the first written description of Britain and its inhabitants. He gives a geographical summary of surprising accuracy mentioning Cantium (Kent), Belerium (Cornwall), and the Horcas or Orcades (Orkney). He describes the 'indigenous people', their use of chariots in war, their thatched houses, and the cold climate in which they live. He then says that

> The inhabitants of the British promontory of Belerium, because of their dealings with merchants, are more civilised and courteous to strangers than the rest of the population. These are the people that produce the tin, which with a great deal of care and labour they dig out of

the ground; but because the ground is rocky, the metal is mixed with some veins of earth, so they melt the metal; then refine it; then beat it into square pieces like knuckle-bone dice, and carry them to a nearby British island, called Ictis. At low tide, because the passage between the shore and the island is dry, they can transport large quantities of tin across in waggons. But what is peculiar to these islands which lie between Britain and Europe is that at high tide they appear to be islands, but at low water they look like so many peninsulas. From there, the merchants transport the tin they buy from the inhabitants over to Gaul; then it is carried on pack horses for thirty days across Gaul to the mouth of the river Rhone.[72]

The geographical description of Ictis fits St Michael's Mount off Marazion in Cornwall, but archaeological evidence seems to favour Mount Batten in Plymouth Sound, which could have been a tidal island in the fourth century BC – although Pliny the Elder, claiming to quote Timaeus, complicates matters by saying 'There is an island called Mictis lying inwards six days' sail from Britain, where tin is found, and to which the Britons cross in boats of wickerwork covered with stitched hides.'[73]

Long before Rome expanded into the lands known as Gallia, or Gaul, southern Europe knew about Britain and about the South-Western Peninsula in particular, because it was a source of tin. And given the concentration on tin, it may well be that the white element of *Albiones* came, not from cliffs – there are white cliffs along the south-western coast, but they are not distinctive enough to characterise the land – but from the Latin for tin, *plumbum album,* or white lead. This would allow *Albiones* to take the meaning 'white metal land' or 'white tin land' which would, in effect, be a translation of the Greek, Cassiterides.[74] This is to some extent supported by the name Belerium which is traditionally associated with Belenos (also Belenus, Belinus), a Celtic god associated with light and fire – both words having proto-Celtic origins that support the idea of pale, white and shining.[75]

If the term *Albiones* as used by Avienus does come from a sixth-century BC *periplus,* it represents the first known name for Britain. The second, originally coming from Pytheas, is *Prettanikēi*. Diodorus uses *Prettanikē nēsos* for 'the islands of Britain' and *Prettanoi* for its inhabitants. Strabo uses *nēsoi brettaniai*, 'the Britannic islands', and subsequent writers used variants of the same form. Ptolemy, writing in the second century AD, in his mathematical work, *Almagest*, uses *megale Brettania* for Great Britain and *mikra Brettania*, literally 'little Britain' for Ireland. However, in his *Geographia*, he refers to *Aluion* and *Iwernia*, describing both of them as *nēsos Bretanikē*. Clearly, the terms had become interchangeable.

The traditional view has long been that the Greek *Prettanikēi* and the Latin *Britannia* derive from the Celtic word *Pritani*. The meaning, usually given as 'form' or 'figure' or 'shape', is taken as referring to the British habit of tattooing their bodies with blue dye made from woad, and thus developed to mean 'the painted people'. While there is some logic in this, there are also problems. Tattooing was common among the Gauls, Dacians, Sarmatians, Germans, Helvetii and many other tribes in the Continental Lands, so to describe the British as the painted or tattooed people would hardly have differentiated them from many of their Continental counterparts. An alternative to the Celtic derivation of *Prettanikēi* has been proposed by Theo Vennemann, a German linguist with a reputation for controversial alternative theories and an interest in Semitic, non-Indo-European languages. He has drawn attention to a first millennium BC papyrus where the Semitic form, *pretan*, means tin. This is supported by fact that the Coptic form *pithran* (πιθραν) also means tin.[76] The Phoenicians, who spoke a Semitic language, dominated trade in the Mediterranean Basin between 1300 and 700 BC, and traded tin from the mysterious Cassiterides right across the Mediterranean to Egypt and the Levant. This raises the possibility that *Prettanikēi* and *Prettanoi* could represent the original Phoenician terms, and that their equivalents, *Albion* and *Albiones*, were adopted by the Greeks when they challenged Phoenicia's commercial dominance. Such an idea links the two sets of terms commonly used by classical writers when referring to the British Isles, giving them a common meaning and maintaining the emphasis on the importance of tin.

The word *Hierni*, which Avienus uses for inhabitants of Ireland, is often considered to be of Celtic or proto-Celtic origin. In Ancient Greek, Ireland is *Iernē* or, later, *Ivernia*, which became the Latin *Hibernia*. It is usually accepted that they derive from the Celtic root, *Īweriū*, meaning 'fertile land'. *Īweriū* is also associated with the Irish mother goddess Ériu, who is the origin of the name of Éire, the official Irish language name for the Republic of Ireland. However, this chain of derivation has been challenged, again by Vennemann, who points to a number of place names, particularly in the south of Britain – among them the River Itchen, the Solent, the

Scilly Isles – that are believed to be of pre-Celtic origin. He suggests that *Hierni*, *Iernē* and *Ivernia* derive from a non-Indo-European and probably Semitic form, *ywe-ri'um*, which would give the meaning 'copper island'.[77] Ireland was an important early source of copper (see Chapter 7), and this derivation would again link the name of the land and its inhabitants to their importance as perceived by people in the wider world.

The connectedness of the prehistoric world, and the cultural interchange between the Archipelago and the Continent, has been a recurrent theme in this study. The Mesolithic inhabitants of Bouldnor Cliff would have had an awareness of the existence of other lands. The builders of Ness of Brodgar and Avebury would have known that far-off lands were the source of unusual and valuable artefacts. Their monuments may have attracted pilgrims from distant places. The Amesbury Archer came from the Alps. Bronze Age chiefs and warriors knew that swords, spears and ornaments, the source of prestige and status, were exchanged and traded beyond the bounds of the Archipelago; that marriage alliances with their Continental neighbours could offer power and security. Contacts with the Continental Lands may have varied in intensity, but they were a constant factor in the development of the Archipelago's culture and society. But if the lands across the Channel were a known quantity, the Mediterranean and the distant lands beyond, while known as the source of rare beads and other decorative objects, would have been the stuff of mystery and myth.

Reversing this scenario, Phoenician civilisation, at its zenith between 1300 and 700 BC, may have dominated trade and created a network of settlements the length and breadth of the Mediterranean, but neither the Phoenicians nor any other Mediterranean people had more than a minimal knowledge of north-west Europe. As late as the first century AD, Strabo was ridiculing Pytheas, calling him a liar for reporting things that were actually true. The Phoenicians knew that their tin came from islands somewhere in the north-west, but they did not trade directly with its producers. Despite claims dating back as far as the eighteenth century, there is no evidence of Phoenician traders reaching Cornwall or any other part of the Archipelago. This is another myth that gained credence at a time when Britain saw itself as the world's dominant political and trading power. Pytheas' voyage, and his description of tin being carried overland from the coast of Gaul, post-date the decline of Phoenician power. The Phoenicians were seafarers. They traded through the Tartessians and perhaps also through the mariners of the Armorican coast, neither of whom would willingly have volunteered information about the source of their most valuable commodity. In this, it would have been natural for the Phoenicians to give these distant islands names in their own language. Later, when the Greeks began to set up their own trading colonies, such as Massalia, Pytheas' native town, those names would have transferred into Greek usage – and when Pytheas set off on his travels, he naturally used those terms.

Etymologies based on manuscripts which may be anything up to two thousand years old, and may also involve scribal errors, are never going to be definitive. However, the suggestion that the earliest names for Britain and Ireland were related to the metals they exported is not far-fetched. These names exist in documents originating in the literate Mediterranean world, written at a time when north-western Europe and its islands were the subject of outlandish tales and rumours, and when the strange languages spoken there did not yet exist in written form. It would not be surprising if travellers and writers from the Mediterranean bestowed names which reflected the principal function of those lands as perceived in their world. Hence *'white tin land'* and *'copper island'*.

We have no record of what the inhabitants of Britain and Ireland called themselves, but we can be certain that Pytheas got his information from natives of Gaul, or possibly southern Britain. The Celtic languages of north-west Europe divide into two groups: Q-Celtic (today's Irish, Manx, and Scots Gaelic) and P-Celtic (today's Breton, Cornish, and Welsh) – a division we shall explore further (see Chapter 13). One of the defining differences is between the initial 'p' and 'k' sounds. Thus *Pritani* would be P-Celtic, while the Q-Celtic equivalent would be *Kuttenikē*. As Norman Davies points out, had Pytheas been talking to a Q-Celtic speaker, we might be talking of the 'Cruttish', not the 'British' Isles.[78]

There is, of course, much speculation in all this. Nonetheless, the issue of linguistic prehistory – who spoke what language and when – is of real significance in that it laid the foundations for cultural differences and divisions which are still visible today. Moreover, what the Mediterranean lands knew and understood about the Archipelago is the essential background to the arrival of Julius Caesar and his legions on the Channel coast in the middle of the first century BC.

12   A Question of Identity

We have names for the main islands of our Archipelago – which may or may not have been those used by the inhabitants. We have the first descriptions of the geography of the Archipelago. We have the first observations about the society and economy of the Archipelago – direct observations rather than interpretations of the archaeological record. But what of the inhabitants? For centuries they were known simply as 'Ancient Britons', which is logical, but not very helpful. They lived in tribes; they built hillforts; they sometimes fought with one another. Their society had its rituals and traditions. They could work bronze and iron with great skill; they traded among themselves, and, probably through intermediaries, with more distant parts of Europe and North Africa. But who were they? Where did they come from?

Until the end of the first millennium AD, documentary records dealing with the British Isles are thin on the ground. Those that have survived did so by chance not selection, so they do not offer a coherent or comprehensive picture of society at the time. Until the arrival of the Romans, Britain was a pre-literate society, and Ireland, for the most part, remained so until the arrival of Christianity in the fourth century. The druids deliberately rejected literacy in order to preserve the secrecy surrounding their rites and practices (see Chapter 14). The Greek and Roman authors whose works contain the earliest references to the British Isles wrote at a distance from their subject: their knowledge was at best limited, and they tended to repeat – not always accurately – what others had written several hundred years earlier. Only when the legions of the Emperor Claudius landed on British shores in 43 AD did literacy arrive in Britain.

Roman society depended on the written word. Orders were written; reports despatched; purchases listed; payments documented; invitations issued; letters sent home. So when the Romans arrived in Britain, the society they established was based on the written word, although literacy remained confined to southern Britain, where they ruled, to the Romans themselves and to those Britons who adopted Roman culture. When Romans and would-be Romans wrote about Britain, they did so from a Roman point of view – and in Latin, which remained a foreign language as far as most of the population was concerned. Those who ruled in the

Roman-occupied areas, and those who served in the army or were granted lands to settle there were, as a rule, contemptuous of the inhabitants; while those who had never been to Britain were simply ignorant.

In 54 BC, Cicero wrote that there was no silver in Britain, no hope of any booty beyond slaves, and that the slaves could not be expected to know anything of letters, music, or poetry. He had never been there. He was drawing on letters from his brother, who was in Britain with Julius Caesar's legions, and on letters from Caesar himself. Condescending and disdainful, and not based on personal experience, his view reflected Roman prejudices against people who did not share their culture: people they termed 'barbarians'. Writing in the third century AD, Cassius Dio could claim that the inhabitants of northern Britain were able to 'plunge into the swamps and exist there for many days with only their heads above water.'[79] And as late as the sixth century AD, Procopius could write that north of Hadrian's Wall 'it is actually impossible for a man to survive there even a half-hour, [because] countless snakes and serpents and every other kind of wild creature occupy this area as their own.'[80] Britain was on the edge of the world: the climate was hostile, and the people were ignorant savages.

Both Julius Caesar's *Gallic Wars*, written in the middle of the first century BC, and Tacitus' Agricola, written at the end of the first century AD, contain more measured descriptions, perhaps because both had served in Britain. Yet neither is strictly neutral or objective. Both have subtexts. Caesar is concerned to justify and exaggerate what he achieved during his two not-wholly-successful raids on Britain. Tacitus is intent on eulogising Agricola, his father-in-law, and refuting those who questioned his record as governor of Britain. We need to be cautious about what Roman and Greek authors say about the Ancient Britons, not least because classical literature was for so long the core of the British educational system and the assertions of many classical authors have been absorbed into the fabric of historical writing without sufficient examination or criticism.

Julius Caesar briefly addresses the origins of the British:

The interior of Britain is inhabited by people whose traditions, it is said, maintain that they were born in the island. The maritime area is inhabited by those who crossed from the lands of the Belgae to plunder and wage war ... and, having done their fighting, stayed on and began to cultivate the land. The population is too numerous to be counted; the

12 A Question of Identity

number of buildings, which are for the most part like those of the Gauls, is enormous; and the amount of livestock is great…

The most civilized of all these nations are the people who inhabit Kent, which is a wholly maritime district. Their customs do not differ much from those of Gaul.[81]

Tacitus goes into a little more detail.

As is usual among Barbarians, who the original inhabitants of Britain were – whether indigenous or foreign – is not well understood. Their varying physical characteristics allow certain conclusions to be drawn. The inhabitants of Caledonia have red hair and large limbs, pointing to German origin. The Silures have dark complexions and their hair is usually curly. This, and the fact that the coastline opposite them is Spain, is evidence that, in the past, Iberians came across and settled these regions. The Britons who live nearest the Gauls are also like them, either because of the enduring influence of shared origins, or because, in countries which are so close together, the climate has produced similar physical characteristics. On the whole, it seems likely that the Gauls established themselves on a nearby island. Their rites can be traced in the superstitious convictions of the British. Their dialect is not very different. They show the same boldness in facing up to danger and, when it comes, the same timidity in shrinking from it.[82]

Both writers assert the existence of an indigenous population, supplemented by migration from different parts of the European Continent. 'Indigenous' in this context presumably means only that their origins were beyond tribal memory. Caesar confidently asserts that the population of the 'maritime area' came originally from the land of the Belgae, the area between the Seine and the Rhine. His 'maritime area' was probably the south-eastern quadrant of Britain, from East Anglia to Dorset – the area he would have known from contacts with tribal leaders before his raids, and from personal experience during the raids. Caesar's claim chimes with Tacitus' statement that the areas of Britain nearest Gaul had been settled by Gauls, and significant cultural and ethnic transference in those areas closest to the Continent is exactly what we would expect.

Tacitus makes two further assertions: that the inhabitants of Caledonia originated in Germany, and that the Silures were of Spanish origin. It is only with the arrival of the Romans that we learn the names of the various tribes inhabiting Britain but locating the territories of particular tribes is an uncertain business. Our main tool is the first known map of the British Isles, included in Ptolemy's *Geography*, written about 150 AD. Ptolemy, undoubted polymath though he was, lived in Alexandria and had no first-hand knowledge of Britain. Unsurprisingly, the map offers no more than a broad approximation of the actual geography of the British Isles; and we must be cautious about accepting Ptolemy's location of individual tribes. On the other hand, there are few other sources to help us.

The Ptolemaic map shows a dozen tribes north of the Forth—Clyde line. One of them, located on the Great Glen, is the 'Caledonii', but in Roman usage the terms 'Caledonia' and 'Caledonian' are not clearly defined. When Tacitus and other writers use the term 'Caledonians', they seem to refer to a confederation of northern tribes which came together to resist Roman incursions. Only Cassius Dio is a little more specific (see Chapter 17). Similarly, 'Caledonia' is used to refer to those areas of northern Britain beyond Roman control. When Tacitus writes about his father-in-law's attempts to push that Roman control northwards, his Caledonia probably meant north of the Forth—Clyde line. For most of the Roman period, however, it meant north of Hadrian's Wall. It may be that the Caledonii were the first northern tribe with which the Romans came into contact and, not greatly caring which tribe was which, they simply applied the name to the region and everyone in it.

The Silures are easier to locate, although little is known about them beyond the fact that they were unquestionably warlike. According to the Ptolemaic map, their territory stretched from present-day Herefordshire and Gloucestershire to Carmarthen, although it may possibly have extended as far as Dyfed. The uncertainty arises from Ptolemy's identification of a tribe he calls the Demetae, which he locates to the west of the Silures. However, the words *de metae* can be interpreted to mean 'from the border', so Ptolemy may have misunderstood his source – and it is true that the name appears nowhere else.

The earliest information about Ireland also comes from Ptolemy's map which gives some forty river, place, and tribal names – some confirmed by later sources, some not – presumably provided by sailors and merchants trading across the Irish Sea. Beyond that, we have to look to the ancient Irish legends. These were originally part of an oral tradition intended to preserve tribal history, probably dramatised in order to flatter a ruling chief and entertain an audience, and then centuries later, written

Map 14   Language and Identity

down, usually Christianised, romanticised, and often bent out of shape for social, political, or religious purposes. Ireland is unusual where such myths are concerned. For over a thousand years, it enjoyed greater social and cultural continuity than much of Britain. It did not suffer the disruption of Roman invasion and occupation. It was not subject to the cultural and political upheaval brought about by the Anglo-Saxons and Danes. As a result, Irish settlement myths seem to have survived better than those from other parts of the British Isles, so although we cannot rely on them for an accurate picture of what happened, they may contain traces of earlier memories which it is unwise to ignore.

The key text is *Lebor Gabála Érenn*, known in English as *The Book of Invasions*. The earliest surviving version dates from the eleventh century, although much of the material clearly comes from a pre-existing oral tradition. It begins with the descent of the Irish people – called here the Gaels – from Japeth, the son of Noah, and the creation of their language, Gaelic, at the time of the Tower of Babel. It tells the story of the Gaels' expulsion from Egypt at the same time as the Jews, how they settled in Scythia, to the north of the Black Sea, and how they moved slowly westwards until they reached and conquered Iberia. It goes on to chronicle the six invasions or occupations of Ireland, the last of which was carried out by the Milesians, who came from Iberia and are presented as the forefathers of the existing Irish population. The whole story is a mixture of pseudo-history drawn from early medieval Christian texts, and pre-Christian mythology; and it was designed to give the Irish a biblical heredity – a recognised characteristic of medieval pseudo-history – and an epic, heroic past. *The Book of Invasions* is a morass of complexities and contradictions, but we cannot ignore the repeated references to Iberia. Roman written records give descriptions of actual people, their behaviour, and their society; they give us a sense of cultural expectations and differences, what one group thought of another. The Irish legends offer a different perspective, less concise, more poetic, but no less valuable. In this case, they share the conviction that the west side of the Archipelago was settled from Iberia, a version of tribal origins preserved in the oral tradition over several millennia which modern DNA analysis has now confirmed (see Chapters 2 and 7).

The Book of Invasions describes the Irish as Gaels, which is obviously related to the word 'Gauls', used by Caesar and Tacitus to describe the people who had settled in the south-east of Britain. 'Gauls' was the name commonly used by the Romans for the tribal peoples they encountered across a vast swathe of territory: from Galicia in north-west Spain to Galway in Ireland; from Galloway in Scotland to the other Galicia, shared between Poland and Ukraine; from the city of Galati in Romania to Galatia in central Turkey. The derivation of the name is uncertain. It probably comes from the Greek word *Galatai*, meaning 'heroic' or 'brave', but later, in Irish Gaelic and other western languages, it came to mean 'foreigners' or 'immigrants', and in the *Book of Invasions* it may have that connotation.

The Romans also described the same sweep of tribal peoples as 'Celts'. The word was first used by the Greek historian, Hecataeus of Miletus, in the sixth century BC as an ethnic descriptor – *hei keltikei*, 'the Celt people' – for the population along what is now the south coast of France; and he states that among the Celts there are different tribes, such as the *Narbaioi*, the inhabitants of Narbonne.[83] Celt derives from the Greek *Keltoi*. Again, the original meaning is uncertain, although 'to strike' and 'to exalt' have been proposed. The term was later adopted by Herodotus and continued to be employed throughout the classical period. Most classical writers use the terms Gaul and Celt interchangeably, and they evidently see the Gauls/Celts as a separate ethnic group, which can be distinguished from Romans, Greeks, Persians, and the Germanic tribes beyond the Rhine. In this context, it is significant that no contemporary or near-contemporary source – none of the classical authors on whom we depend – ever refers to the inhabitants of the British Isles as Celts. They are always referred to as Britons. Caesar and Tacitus suggest that the people of south-eastern Britain are most like those in Gaul, noting similarities in language and culture, but that is as close as it gets. Pytheas states that it is several days' sailing from *Kantion*, or Kent, to *Keltikē*, the land of the Celts. We may question his geography or speculate that he sailed along the Channel to Armorica,[84] but it is clear that he does not include Britain – not even Kent – as part of the land of the Celts.

Leaping forward to the nineteenth and twentieth centuries, we find that view has changed radically, and the pre-Roman populations of both Britain and Ireland are almost universally held to be Celts. By that time, archaeologists and historians had evolved a view that the Celts were a distinct ethnic group, consisting of a number of related tribes, which had originated somewhere in central or east-central Europe, and, at some time in the eighth century BC, begun a massive expansion and migration. Over the next five or six hundred years, they were supposed to have conquered and controlled a vast arc of territory extending from Poland to Asia Minor in the east, and from Iberia to the British Isles in the west. According to this model, the first wave of Celts reached the southern coasts of Britain and Ireland somewhere between 600 and 500 BC, bringing their language and culture with them (see Chapter 13). Two further waves followed later, bringing different versions of Celtic language and culture, sweeping all before them until they had displaced or overwhelmed the pre-existing population and conquered the entire archipelago.

This, of course, is a version of invasion theory; and it was widely accepted as accurate from the mid-nineteenth century until the later decades of the twentieth – and it is still accepted in some quarters. It was the view which informed the excavations and writings of eminent Celtic scholars and writers from Donald MacKinnon (1839–1914) and Sir John Rhys (1840–1915) to Nora Chadwick (1891–1972) and Kenneth Jackson (1909–91). It was also the story taught in British schools – when early British history was taught at all – until the 1980s. The trouble with this version of 'Celtic Britain' is that it assumes that ethnicity, culture, and language are coterminous – an assumption encouraged by the theories of racial and social Darwinism which emerged in the later nineteenth century, but now widely discredited in the face of new archaeological discoveries, the reinterpretation of existing evidence, and new technologies, above all DNA.

The advent of DNA sequencing and analysis has transformed our ability to understand the origins and movements of prehistoric populations. DNA analysis works by tracing the Y chromosome, which is transmitted through the male, and mitochondrial DNA, which is transmitted through the female. By tracking the variant forms and mutations of these key elements, we can trace the heredity, the interrelationships, and the movement of groups of people back to the early days of humankind. For the archaeologist and the historian this represents a huge leap forward, but DNA analysis is a complex science, and made more complex by the sheer scale and diversity of human migrations over the millennia. The conclusions published by scientists depend on a range of factors, such as the size of the sample, the way in which the data are interrogated, and, of course, their interpretation of the results. Consequently, DNA analysis often gives us not a simple truth, but a complex, multi-layered picture. In 2012, Peter Donnelly, Professor of Statistical Science at Oxford University, conducted a study which concluded that the Cornish and the Welsh were among the most genetically distinct groups in the British Isles. Three years later, in 2015, looking at the same issues from a different perspective, a second study concluded that, although the Cornish were genetically distinct from their Devonian neighbours, they still had more in common with the rest of the population of England than with the populations of Scotland and Wales.

DNA evidence is crucial in helping us determine the composition and origins of the population of the British Isles before the arrival of the Romans. The traditional story is that Celtic tribes from the Continent invaded, conquered, and displaced the existing population. The Romans then invaded, conquered a little less than half the land area of the British Isles and governed a little more than half the population, but they did not displace the existing inhabitants. When the Romans left, the Anglo-Saxons forced the Celts westwards and northwards until the they were left with Cornwall, Wales, Scotland, the Hebrides, Orkney, and Ireland – those territories now known as 'the Celtic fringe'. If this scenario were correct, then we would expect to find a degree of genetic similarity between the inhabitants of what, for want of a better term, we shall continue to call the Celtic fringe. But this is not the case.

Analysis of DNA samples from people inhabiting the Celtic fringe, and excluding recent immigrants, shows a population characterised by genetic diversity rather than similarity. For example, the Hebrides are genetically distinct from the rest of Scotland, a circumstance probably determined by their isolation and distance from the mainland, which has allowed the early population to maintain its distinct identity. Orkney and Shetland each have populations which are distinct from each other and also strongly differentiated from the rest of the British Isles, probably for the same reasons. In these areas, leaving aside the later Norwegian overlay, it is even possible to detect genetic differences between the populations of individual islands.[85] Elsewhere in Scotland, genetic divisions appear to follow the borders between early medieval kingdoms, but do not appear to reflect major population change during the supposed Celtic period. The genetic make-up of mainland Scotland is particularly diverse; and within that diversity there is even the possibility that a group of young males, originating in what is now Germany, arrived in what is now Scotland about 3000 BC, settling along the east coast, and bringing with them early farming techniques, including grass-derived crops such as oats. If proved true, this would not only vindicate Tacitus' view of the origins of the Scots but might also – according to the writer and historian Alistair Moffat – explain the origins of porridge and its identification with Scotland.[86]

Further south, a genetic division has been identified between the inhabitants of North and South Wales, but at the same time the Welsh appear to be distinct from the other groups in the British Isles, perhaps having the closest connection with the early hunter-gatherers. Ireland shows a distinct genetic connection with Iberia, but within Ireland itself there is a broad division between east and west, probably reflecting early settlement patterns; and there are also clear genetic borders, notably between Munster and Leinster, apparently reflecting a tribal division that goes back to prehistoric times and subsequently took political form.[87] Ireland, however, is not genetically isolated from the rest of the British Isles: there are clear links across the North Channel to Cumbria and Dumfries and Galloway.

Professor Donnelly's 2015 study of DNA from populations across the British Isles was, at the time, the most detailed ever carried out. The data were interrogated according to criteria that allowed researchers to filter out the impact of immigration in the last 1,000 years and concentrate on the pre- and post-Roman periods. The conclusions were surprising to many but unambiguous. The population of the British Isles was much more genetically diverse than had been thought. Later incoming populations, such as the Anglo-Saxons and the Danes, had left a localised genetic imprint in those parts of the isles where they had settled, but that imprint was smaller than anticipated. Above all, it was clear that, in the British Isles at least, there is no such thing as a distinct Celtic ethnic group – meaning that there were no waves of Celtic invasion during the first millennium BC, and consequently that there was no radical displacement of the existing population.[88]

This last point may comfort archaeologists, who have not been able to identify any evidence of a rapid or widespread population shift at the time when waves of Celtic invaders were supposed to have been arriving on Britain's shores. However, the fact that the populations of the Celtic fringe are not linked by a shared ethnicity leaves unanswered the question with which we began this chapter: who were the inhabitants of Britain and Ireland when the Romans arrived? Who were the Ancient Britons? And it also poses a second question. Why do we talk so readily of and have a clear sense of what is meant by concepts such as Celtic languages, Celtic music, Celtic art and – in the 1990s – of the Irish economy as a 'Celtic tiger'?

13 Culture and Language

Just as no classical writer ever called the inhabitants of the British Isles Celts, so before the eighteenth century the word 'Celt' was never used except in the context of classical studies. That changed with the publication of two books: *Antiquité de la nation et la langue des Celtes, autrement appellez Gaulois* (1703) by Paul-Yves Pezron; and *Archaeologia Britannica* (1707)[89] by Edward Lhuyd. Pezron was a Breton by birth, and Abbot of La Charmoie in the Champagne region of France. Lloyd was a Welsh polymath and Keeper of the Ashmolean Museum in Oxford. The two men worked independently, and, although Lhuyd did try to make contact with Pezron, they never met. Both died soon after the publication of their respective works: Pezron in 1706; Lhuyd in 1709.

Pezron was more of an historian than a linguist. He identified the Breton people as the survivors of the Gauls and Celts described by Roman writers. On that basis, and recognising the similarities between the Breton, Cornish, Welsh, and Irish languages, he postulated the existence of a common ancestral tongue spoken by the ancient Gauls/Celts, which had transferred from Brittany to the British Isles. Lhuyd's approach was more empirical and more sophisticated. He travelled widely in Brittany and in the west and north of the British Isles, and he divided the languages he found there into two groups: Goidelic, comprising Irish, Manx, and Scots Gaelic (nowadays Q-Celtic), which he saw as originating in Iberia; and Brythonic, comprising Breton, Cornish, and Welsh (nowadays P-Celtic), which he believed came from Gaul. Believing these languages were of Celtic origin, he made the short – but as we now realise false – step of assuming that the people who spoke them must therefore be Celts. Thus the link was made, and Lhuyd's suggestion that the two varieties of Celtic languages arrived by separate routes laid the foundation for the theory that there were two waves of Celtic invasion from the Continent.

Identifying the populations of Scotland, Wales, Ireland, and Cornwall as Celtic did not have an immediate impact on the British cultural imagination. The 1715 and 1745 Jacobite rebellions, and the continuing political and religious problems in Ireland, created a distinct sense that the Scots and the Irish were somehow 'other', but they were not yet defined as Celtic. Towards the end of the eighteenth century, however, the emergence of the Romantic movement with its focus on nature, on the past, and on the quest for the sublime, led to increased interest in the Celtic fringe.

A key event in this respect was the publication, in 1760, of *Fragments of Ancient Poetry Collected in the Highlands of Scotland*. The poems were published by the Scottish poet, James Macpherson, who claimed they were translations of Gaelic poems from an original manuscript written by an ancient bard named Ossian. The authenticity of Ossian himself, and of Macpherson's translations, was challenged at once by no less a figure than Dr Johnson, but that did not prevent the 1760 volume and those which followed – *Fingal* in 1761, and *Temora* in 1763 – from having an extraordinary impact throughout Europe and across the Atlantic. Both Napoleon and Thomas Jefferson were Ossian enthusiasts. Goethe, Walter Scott, and Wordsworth were all influenced by the poems. Thomas Gray's poem, *The Bard*, was directly inspired by Macpherson's work, and was itself the inspiration for John Martin's famous painting of the same name. Ingres and François Gérard painted scenes from the poems. Schubert set some of them to music, and they provided the impetus for Mendelssohn's visit to the Hebrides which led to the overture, *Fingal's Cave*. There was even an *Ossian* opera by Jean-François Le Sueur, premiered in Paris in 1804 in the presence of Napoleon. By 1800, the poems had been translated into all the major European languages, including Finnish and Russian.

Of course, Dr Johnson was right. Ossian was a fiction, and the poems were Macpherson's work, although they are now recognised as based on genuine Scottish songs and folk tales that he had collected. Authentic or not, the poems powerfully stimulated awareness of the landscape, myths, and culture of the Celtic fringe. They helped create a sense of Celtic identity, which grew and gathered momentum as the nineteenth century progressed. The Irish historian, Caoimhín De Barran, has shown how the word 'Celtic' appeared only rarely in print at the beginning of the nineteenth century, but in the 1840s it suddenly began to feature more often. By the 1850s its use had doubled, and by the 1880s it had doubled again.[90]

13 Culture and Language

Against the background of this new, widespread, and highly romanticised vision of the Celts – which appeared to stand in opposition to the rapidly industrialising world of the nineteenth century – two important archaeological discoveries were made. In 1846, in the small Austrian village of Hallstatt, fifty kilometres south-east of Salzburg, Johann Georg Ramsauer, the manager of the local salt mine, stumbled upon a large Bronze and early Iron Age cemetery, which eventually yielded the remains of some 2,000 individuals. It soon became apparent that salt had been mined in the area continuously ever since 5000 BC. Subsequent excavations revealed an elaborate complex of mine workings where the salt had preserved many organic items – leather bags, shoes, and caps, rope, textiles of different weaves and design – that would not have survived in earth or water. These discoveries defined 'Hallstatt culture', which was seen as the dominant cultural strain in central and western Europe from about 1200 to 450 BC, spanning the transition between the Bronze and Iron Ages. Hallstatt culture was concentrated on sixteen or seventeen hillforts – some of them, such as Heuneburg on the banks of the Danube, densely populated enough to be considered cities – and its heartland stretched from south-eastern France across southern Germany to Austria. It was clearly a prosperous culture, marked by long-distance trading connections; by princely burials including finely worked bronze and iron grave goods; and by distinctive pottery, in the later part of the period thrown on a potter's wheel.

The second discovery – potentially even more important – was made in 1857, at La Tène, on the edge of Lac de Neuchâtel in Switzerland, six hundred kilometres to the east. A local fisherman named Hansli Kopp was scouring the foreshore for relics. Drought had lowered the level of the lake and Kopp noticed several rows of wooden piles sticking out of the water. Investigating, he immediately found some forty iron objects – swords, pieces of scabbards, spearheads. That was just the beginning. Subsequent excavations revealed the existence of two wooden bridges, each a hundred metres long, crossing the River Thielle (or Zihl) at the point where it enters the lake. The site has produced over 2,500 Iron Age items, most of metal, many of them weapons, and a large proportion apparently unused. The lakeside location, the nature of the finds, and the absence of any large settlement in the vicinity, all suggest that La Tène was a votive site of some importance, although it may also have functioned as a trading post.

La Tène has given its name to the phase of European culture which succeeded Hallstatt culture, lasting from c.450 BC until disrupted by Germanic invasions and Roman military conquests beginning at the end of the first century BC and continuing into the first century AD. La Tène culture is distinguished by high quality metalwork, evidently developed from the techniques used to produce Hallstatt artefacts, and by what is sometimes called its 'vegetal style'. While Hallstatt art tends to mix circular and geometric forms, La Tène art is predominantly curvilinear, characterised by knotwork, spirals, intertwined plant forms, stylised palmettes and garlands, and elongated animal figures.

Hallstatt art and culture spread into Gaul and across the Channel to Britain, but only to a limited extent, and it did not reach Ireland at all. La Tène had a much wider influence, spreading both east and west from its area of origin. Examples from Britain include the Wandsworth and Battersea shields found in the River Thames in the mid-nineteenth century; the Snettisham torc, a kilo of solid gold, from Norfolk; and the remarkable pony cap, topped with two curious horns, found at Torrs in Dumfries and Galloway. In Ireland, the items which made up the Broighter Hoard (see Chapter 3) show strong La Tène influence, as does the superb Petrie crown with its spirals and interlaced decoration, discovered in County Cork. La Tène style is easily recognisable, and has endured and developed. It can be seen in the illuminated manuscripts, crosses, and religious artefacts of the early Middle Ages; in the Celtic Revival of the nineteenth and early twentieth centuries; and in the many 'Celtic' T-shirts, posters, necklaces, rings, and earrings that are on sale today. It is the basis of what we generally recognise as Celtic art.

The comparative proximity of the discoveries at Hallstatt and La Tène convinced archaeologists and scholars that they had found the heartland of the ancient Celts, the region from where they had set out on their migrations and conquests. This conviction was strengthened by the fact that a number of Greek and Roman writers seem to suggest that the Celts came from central Europe. Herodotus, for example, says that:

> the Ister [Danube] flows through the whole extent of Europe, rising in the country of the Celts, who are the most westerly dwellers in Europe, except for the Cynetes, and flowing thus right across Europe it issues forth along the borders of Scythia.[91]

Scholars seized on the first part of this statement. Herodotus said that the

Danube rose in the country of the Celts. The Breg and the Brigach, the two sources of the Danube, both rise in the Black Forest, less than five hundred kilometres from Hallstatt and two hundred from La Tène. The discoveries at both sites therefore had to be Celtic. Subsequent research into the spread of Hallstatt and La Tène cultures appeared to offer confirmation – even though the core La Tène region was later located between the Seine and the Rhine, further north than La Tène itself. La Tène-style objects were found in those lands to the west where 'Celtic' languages were still spoken. And, of course, the existence of two different but related 'Celtic' cultures appeared to support Lhuyd's idea of two waves of Celtic warriors, sweeping across Europe, each speaking a different Celtic language.

The problem here was that, just as Pezron and Lhuyd equated language with ethnicity, so nineteenth-century scholars – influenced, no doubt, by the social dogmas of their time – equated culture with ethnicity. The tribes which developed Hallstatt and La Tène cultures were probably among those whom the Greeks and Romans called Celts. They probably spoke one of the many different Continental Celtic languages – languages which, while part of the Celtic language family identified by Pezron and Lhuyd, were at some distance from the Celtic languages spoken in the British Isles. However, as DNA evidence has made clear, neither the Celtic languages, nor what we call Celtic culture, arrived in the British Isles as a result of invasion or immigration by peoples with a common ethnicity (see Chapter 12).

We have seen that in the British Isles, the period after 600 BC – the traditional date for a Celtic invasion – was one of rapid and radical change. Tribal society reformed and reorganised itself. Many smaller tribes were absorbed into larger groups. In some cases, this may have happened peacefully, but violence appears to have been on the increase, and this was reflected in the construction of large numbers of defensible settlements – hillforts, crannogs, and brochs. Political and social upheaval does not preclude cultural change. It can often stimulate change, and it was during this period that La Tène culture began to appear in the British Isles. It seems to have arrived by the pincer movement that we have seen before, with one arm crossing the Atlantic Zone from Armorica to the South-Western Peninsula, Wales, and Ireland; while the other crossed the Channel and the Southern North Sea Zones to the south and east of the Main Island.

A number of small bronze bowls, with wide, flared rims and decorated in the La Tène style, have been found at sites in Cornwall, Devon, Wales, and Ireland. The design appears to have originated in the Bourges area of France, travelled down the Loire to Armorica, probably in the fourth century BC, and then crossed the Atlantic Zone to western Britain and Ireland. On Anglesey in 1942, during the construction of an RAF airfield on the edge of a lake called Llyn Cerrig Bach, workmen uncovered a hoard of Iron Age metal work. It consisted of one hundred and eighty-one items, including swords, spearheads, the remains of over at least twenty-two chariot wheels, parts of a shield, a bronze trumpet, horse gear, and two cauldrons. Some objects were manufactured locally, others came from Ireland and some possibly from southern England, but the La Tène influence is clear. Anglesey was the centre of the druidic power in Britain, so it is no surprise that the items appear to have been deliberately broken and deposited in the lake as votive offerings. They date from between 300 BC and the first century AD, when the Romans conquered Anglesey and slaughtered the druids. In Northern Ireland, eight La Tène-style scabbards from the second or first century BC were retrieved from the River Bann and the bog of Lisnacrogher. These appear to show direct Continental influence modified by the kind of native craftsmanship that we saw with Irish goldsmiths in the Bronze Age. Some scholars have seen similarities of design with scabbards found in Yorkshire and suggested an east-west transference of ideas. This is possible but goes against what we have seen as the established routes by which styles and ideas were spread.

The intensity of contact across the Channel and Southern North Sea Zones was naturally greater than that across the Atlantic Zone. We see this in the way La Tène influence affects even mundane objects. There are close similarities between painted pottery and coarse ware pottery found in Kent, the Thames Valley, and East Anglia and that found in the Pas de Calais, Belgium, and the Rhine Estuary. We can also see cultural transmission in terms of funerary behaviour. La Tène culture in the area between the Seine and the Rhine featured sky-burial-style exposure of the dead, allowing the bones to be picked clean by birds and animals. Earth burial, when it took place, was a haphazard affair with complete skeletons or random collections of bones dumped into old storage pits or other holes in the ground. During this period, there are hardly any ordinary burials in south-east Britain, but there are many examples of bone-filled pits.

Another example of cultural transmission on the east side of Britain concerns chariot burial – where a high-status individual, probably a warrior or a tribal chief, was buried with his chariot, his horse gear, and associated grave goods. Chariot burials belong to a sub-group of Le Tène called Arras culture. They are relatively common across an arc of territory from the Upper Rhine and Mosel valleys to the Middle and Lower Seine, and they also occur in Britain, but – with one exception – only in eastern Yorkshire. This same area of eastern Yorkshire is also home to nearly eighty square barrows bounded by ditches, another characteristic feature of Arras culture on the Continent but otherwise unknown in Britain. It may be that high status individuals, quite possibly warriors fighting on behalf of a kinship group, or acting as mercenaries, crossed to this part of what is now Yorkshire and brought their culture with them. Although we have ruled out mass immigration, there must have been *some* groups crossing the North Sea to settle and intermarry – big enough to leave a cultural imprint, but small enough not to disturb the overall DNA pattern.

The only British chariot burial which occurs outside Yorkshire is also the oldest, having been radiocarbon dated to between 475 and 380 BC. Discovered in 2001, close to a burial mound at Huly Hill, just next to Edinburgh Airport, it consists of an upright chariot with a rider, also buried in an upright position. Even more recently, in 2017 and 2018, excavations at a large burial site at Pocklington in Yorkshire, have uncovered two chariot burials with both riders and horses. The first chariot was dismantled before burial, but the other was buried intact, together with two upright horses, as if ready to leap ahead and pull the chariot out of the ground. The grave goods associated with this second burial included a spectacular shield – on which the body had been placed – which has been described as one of the most important finds of the last hundred years. These two burials come closest to Continental practice, but, as Cunliffe has pointed out, there are differences. Most Continental burials include horses, upright chariots, and bodies which are stretched out horizontally. In Britain, only Newbridge and Pocklington include horses; most chariots were dismantled before the grave was closed; most bodies were arranged in a crouched position; and almost all contain grave goods which, while in the La Tène style, were made in Britain. Equally important is the fact that such burials are surrounded by settlements in the British style, featuring traditional roundhouses, rather than the rectangular dwellings characteristic of La Tène culture on the Continent.[92]

DNA evidence proves that Celtic culture did not arrive as a result of mass immigration, so we can set aside the nineteenth-century notion that 'the Celts' arrived in the middle of the first millennium BC bringing new customs, traditions, and languages as a combined ethnic and cultural package. We can accept that there was some, limited immigration, concentrated in those areas with easiest access to the Continent, and no doubt a fuller picture of the transference of La Tène culture to Britain and Ireland will emerge in time, but we can say with some certainty that it spread principally through acculturation. Which brings us back once again to the same question: who were the inhabitants of the British Isles when the Romans arrived?

Before the first millennium BC, the last major population shift – and thus genetic shift – was the arrival of the Beaker people in the second half of the third millennium BC (see Chapter 7). As our knowledge stands at present, this appears to have been the greatest genetic shift in the history of the British Isles. We cannot know in detail how it occurred, but we can imagine slow and cumulative immigration spanning several centuries, perhaps with settlement initially concentrated in one or two regions, with pockets where Neolithic bloodlines may have survived for longer in more remote areas. But the DNA evidence as we understand it today indicates a genetic continuity between the Beaker People and the 'Ancient Britons'. The warriors who fought Julius Caesar's troops on the beaches and in the forests of Kent in 55 and 54 BC; the Druids slaughtered by the Romans on Anglesey in 60 AD; the warriors of Calgacus who fought Agricola's legions at the Battle of Mons Graupius somewhere in what is now Scotland – these and the vast majority of the population of the British Isles would have been descendants of the Beaker people.

In their enthusiasm to establish a central European origin for the Celts, the archaeologists and scholars of the nineteenth century either overlooked or ignored a number of key statements. They took no account of Hecataeus of Miletus, who, as early as the sixth century BC, asserted that Narbonne was a Celtic town. They ignored Herodotus when he said that the Celts lived 'beyond the Pillars of Hercules',[93] and they seem to have ignored the second half of his statement, quoted above, that the Celts were 'the most westerly dwellers in Europe, except for the Cynetes.' The Cynetes are known in classical texts by at least ten alternative names, and the precise extent of their territory is uncertain. However, we know that they lived in the far south-western corner of the Iberian Peninsula – before it came under Roman control, the area we know today as the Algarve was called Cyneticum – and we know that during the third and second centuries BC the Cynetes were under pressure from their northern neighbours, who were described as Celtic tribes. Strabo, writing in the first century AD, says that 'Amongst the Kelts the most famous place is Conistorgis.'[94] Described elsewhere as the chief city of the Cynetes, Conistorgis was located in the Algarve, suggesting that, by the time Strabo was writing, the Celts had become the dominant force in the region. Strabo also quotes Ephorus, the fourth-century-BC Greek historian, as saying that 'Keltica' includes 'most of what we now designate as Iberia, as far as Gades [Cadiz].'[95]

All this indicates that, from an early stage, classical writers understood the Celts to be a western people who had a strong presence in Iberia. Aspects of later Hallstatt culture appeared in north and western Iberia, probably from the mid-seventh century BC onwards, but the area remained on the periphery. It was never part of the core Hallstatt region. Certain features of La Tène culture reached northern Iberia in the third century BC, though not its characteristic curvilinear and knotted design forms. So these Iberian Celts did not share what we would recognise today as Celtic culture. There appear to have been numerous different, perhaps related, groups or tribes – classical writers give them an assortment of names: Celtiberi, Celtici, Gallaeici, Turduli, and Turdetani, among others – but they were not a distinct ethnic entity. What probably united them was language. That is not to suggest that the whole Iberian Peninsula spoke a common language, rather that Celtic languages predominated throughout the region. Two now extinct languages have been studied in some depth: Gallaecian, once spoken in the north and north-west, and Celtiberian, spoken in the centre and north-east. Both appear to have belonged to the Goidelic, or Q-Celtic branch of the Celtic languages, and it is worth recalling that Edward Lhuyd claimed that the Q-Celtic languages still spoken in the Celtic fringe originated in Iberia.

A third Iberian language that has attracted increasing attention in recent years is Tartessian, the language associated with the rich, metal-working and trading kingdom Tartessos, whose merchants we met seeking tin up and down the Atlantic seaways (see Chapter 11). Tartessos was centred on the Guadalquivir Valley and is thus 'beyond the Pillars of

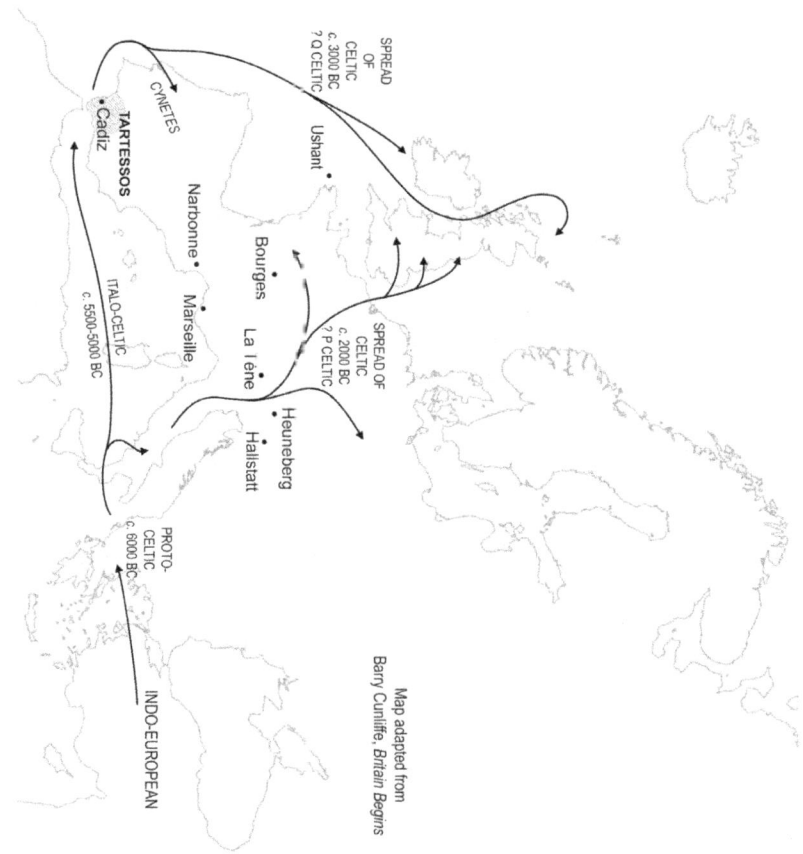

Map 15 The Spread of Celtic Language and Culture

Hercules' where Herodotus said the Celts lived. So were the Tartessians Celts? If we define Celticness as a collection of peoples or tribes and peoples unified by language rather than culture and ethnicity, the answer may well be yes. Across the Tartessian region – from Cadiz to the town of Lagos, close to the south-western tip of modern Portugal – archaeologists have uncovered nearly a hundred inscriptions on stone stelae marking graves. At first sight, the script looks like a mixture of Nordic runes and Irish ogham, but philologists have concluded that it is in fact a Celtic language written in Phoenician script. The earliest of these stones date from the early or middle part of the seventh century BC – making Tartessian the earliest known Celtic language – and the inscriptions are neither primitive nor simple. Although translation is difficult with such a small corpus, some of them evidently employ sophisticated, even poetic, language to describe and honour the dead.

As Cunliffe observes, if a language of such maturity could be spoken and written in the seventh century BC, it must have evolved much earlier.[96] Working from this basis, he has developed a model for the origins and spread of Celtic languages which attempts to combine archaeological, philological, and genetic evidence. In essence, he believes that some form of Indo-European, proto-Celtic language arrived in the Aegean and the southern part of the Balkan peninsula – roughly the area comprising Greece, Albania, and Northern Macedonia – during the seventh millennium BC. Over the next thousand years, it evolved into what is known as Italo-Celtic, and whether driven by trade or migration, moved westward across the Mediterranean basin eventually reaching the south coast of France and the southern third of Iberia. From southern Iberia, Celtic developed into the *lingua franca* of the Atlantic Zone, with the sea, as ever, providing the quickest and most effective route for cultural transmission. By 3000 BC it had established itself in north-western Iberia, Armorica, Brittany, Ireland, and along the western side of the Archipelago. In this model, the rapid transmission northwards from Iberia of new technologies – such as those employed in building passage graves or smelting metal – would have been accompanied by the Celtic language. Such technologies were sophisticated for their time and would surely have required explanation and instruction for ideas to pass successfully from one group and another. This version of Celtic, which presumably replaced earlier languages in the same way that the Beaker Package replaced Neolithic culture, became the basis for Goidelic or Q-Celtic. A little later, Bell Beaker culture began to spread along the northern shore of the Mediterranean, and then northwards up the Rhone—Rhine corridor, taking a Celtic family language with it. This, Cunliffe suggests, was how Celtic penetrated and spread across central Europe. By 2000 BC, it had reached as far as Poland and Hungary in the east; while in the west it spread to France, Belgium, Holland and, of course, the eastern half of Britain. And the language which reached Britain in this way became, in due course, Brythonic or P-Celtic.[97]

Cunliffe's model remains speculative in that the dates are no more than broadly indicative and there is much that cannot be proved. It does, however, sit comfortably with the facts as we understand them today. In terms of the British Isles, it demonstrates again the importance of transmission along the sea routes, and of the east-west divide which we have seen as a determining factor in other contexts. It observes in language the same pincer movement that we have seen as the basis of population movement and cultural transfer in Neolithic times and in the early Bronze Age. Cunliffe's analysis completes a picture which offers a coherent alternative to the traditional view of Celtic Britain. Having examined ethnicity, culture, and language separately, we can see that the society that had evolved in the British Isles by the second half of the first millennium BC was far more complex, with roots that were often older and certainly more varied, than has traditionally been supposed. This will naturally affect our understanding of the evolution of British and Irish society as we go forward. However, it worth stressing that, while we can deconstruct historic Celticness, this does not mean that our present concepts of Celtic identity and Celtic culture have no validity.

Popular interest in Celtic culture – as represented by myths, folk tales, folk songs, and Celtic-flavoured poetry and prose – grew strongly through the nineteenth century, culminating in the Celtic Revival which lasted well into the twentieth century. It may have begun with language and culture – particularly literature, and particularly in Ireland – but the Celtic Revival soon became a spur to nationalism, again particularly in Ireland. And it took on an international dimension with the Celtic populations of the British Isles receiving support and encouragement from emigrant Celtic communities around the world. The fact that there were, and are, communities in places as diverse as Canada, Argentina and New Zealand which identify themselves as Celtic is a testament to the power of the Celtic idea. The basis of this idea of Celticness may, in historical terms, be mistaken or misguided, but that does not alter its subsequent and current importance. On St Patrick's Day, one of the fountains in front of the White House is dyed green. So, too, is a lot of beer in the bars of New York. In 1972, the IRA announced that they would not carry out attacks on their 'Celtic brothers' in Scotland and Wales. The annual Celtic Connections festival in Glasgow attracts Celtic musicians from all over the world. In 2019, the leader of Plaid Cymru spoke in favour of setting up a Celtic Development Bank. These are just a few manifestations of an idea which, whatever its historical accuracy, looks set to exercise an important cultural and political influence for the foreseeable future.

14 Belief and Ritual

The prehistoric population of the Archipelago held spiritual and religious beliefs that we will never be able to reconstruct. The closest we can get to the spiritual context of their lives is by examining the physical locations where those beliefs were expressed and celebrated. Ritual sites divide into two broad categories: those primarily connected with earth and water, and those associated with the sky and the movement of celestial bodies. The long barrows and passage graves scattered across the Archipelago, and the many deposition trackways and platforms, all suggest a connection with earth or water. Henges and stone circles – from Stonehenge to the diminutive Wormy Hillock – all mirror celestial shapes and point, often literally, to the sky. But the distinction is not absolute. We have seen how passage graves such as Newgrange and Maes Howe are orientated in relation to the winter solstice (see Chapter 5), and there are instances of burial in the vicinity of stone circles (see Chapter 6). The abandoning of henges and stone circles in the middle of the second millennium BC, and the parallel increase deposition in both earth and water, was a major shift in ritual practice which seems to reflect a movement away from the sky gods towards placating the chthonic deities. However, the exposure and excarnation of corpses – either by man, or by birds and animals – remained commonplace, and from somewhere around 1700 BC, cremation appears to have become the most common funerary rite: both seeming to indicate some continuing orientation towards the sky gods. The relationship between sky and earth-water rituals is unclear, but they do not appear to represent radically different belief systems. It may be that shifts in emphasis between the two indicate change, development, or even schism, within a common framework of belief – as if we were following the archaeology of Christianity through the Great Schism, the Reformation, and the dissolution of the monasteries.

Like most religious belief, prehistoric religion appears to have centred on belief in, and attempts to communicate with and influence, the otherworld. It seems to have placed particular emphasis on appeasing and propitiating the controlling gods or spirits, who were regarded as active and potentially dangerous, with the ability to intervene in daily life. Comparative anthropology tells us that tribal cultures commonly believe that the gods will reward the dutiful and visit disease, death, ill fortune, or a bad harvest on the neglectful. And, of course, the idea that God will punish man for his failure to obey the commandments is common to all three Abrahamic religions. The consensus among archaeologists is that in Neolithic times, it was the ancestors who were the focus of this propitiation, and that the primacy of deposition in the second millennium BC indicates that the ancestors had become less central to ritual activity, perhaps losing out to new deities whose names and nature we do not know.

Propitiation clearly took various forms. Ceremonies at henges and stone circles might offer celebration and praise. Death rituals varied: they could involve excarnation, exposure, disarticulation, reburial, and cremation in various combinations – indicating that the passage of the dead to the otherworld was an extended process, each stage accompanied by specific rituals. Later funerals, whether cremations or burials, might be accompanied by grave goods. Sometimes these were small, everyday items buried in or around a beaker of ashes, or sometimes thrown into a disused storage pit along with the bones of the dead. Some grave goods consisted simply of food and drink. Elsewhere, high-status individuals were buried under individual mounds or barrows surrounded by rare and valuable items, chosen to emphasise their wealth and prestige. Again, and as with the burial of the Egyptian pharaohs, the implication is that the transition to the otherworld was an extended process or journey that could be assisted by the presence of grave goods. Propitiation also underlies the deposition of objects in earth or water – some of the items deposited were extremely valuable – but the concept of transition is less evident. Deposition into flowing water may have been associated with the scattering of cremated ashes (see Chapter 9), and many river and lake deposition sites – the Thames in London, the Trent near Clifton, Flag Fen in Cambridgeshire, Llyn Cerrig Bach in Anglesey – had been regarded as sacred since earlier times, suggesting that water continued to be seen as a gateway to the otherworld.

Another form of propitiation requires examination at this point. Sacrifice undoubtedly played a part in prehistoric ritual. How important it was is difficult to assess, but when the Romans conquered southern Britain it assumed a political and moral dimension in the context of their attitude to the British tribes and their religious practices. Animal sacrifice was current during the Neolithic period and the Bronze Age, but appears to have become much more common during the Iron Age, the Roman period, and the early medieval period.[98] Animal remains associated with burials may suggest sacrifice, but in archaeological terms it is not always possible to distinguish one type of offering from another. The presence of whole skeletons seems to indicate a sacrificial rite. Dogs are among the most commonly found animals. Horses, too, were sacrificed, although it is usually just the head and the bridle that are found in the grave. A willingness to sacrifice horses, animals of great practical and prestige value, shows how seriously these rituals were taken. Were these animals chosen because they belonged to the dead man or woman? Because they were his or her favourites? Or did they have some symbolic or spiritual significance for the journey to the otherworld? Pig bones are also commonly found in burials. They are generally interpreted as food offerings intended to help the dead person on their journey to the otherworld, but there are instances, such as the late Iron Age shrine at Hallaton in Leicestershire, where the presence of skeletal remains of pigs which had not been butchered strongly suggests sacrifice. As so often, there are no definitive answers.

The prevalence of human sacrifice is even more difficult to determine. We may find human remains; we may determine that the individuals concerned were deliberately killed; but determining why they were killed is much more difficult. The child whose body was found in the centre of Woodhenge certainly looks like a sacrificial victim, though other explanations have been advanced (see Chapter 6). The dismembered remains of another child, found at Wandlebury hillfort in Cambridgeshire, also suggest sacrifice. The hillforts of Danebury and Cadbury Castle show evidence of animal sacrifice, and at both sites human burials have been found at the level of the foundations, again raising the possibility of human sacrifice as a ritual consecration of the ground before construction. One indicator of possible sacrifice is what archaeologists call overkill: where the injuries inflicted on a body are in excess of what would have been needed to cause death. The disarticulated remains of a boy of about twelve discovered in South Uist, and the mutilated bodies of two women, one found at Lowbury Hill camp in Oxfordshire and the other at Dunstable in Bedfordshire, are among a number of examples that seem to fit these criteria. The remains of the two women date from the Roman period, so if they were the victims of sacrifice, it would cast doubt on the assumption that human sacrifice ceased during the Roman occupation, but, once again, we cannot be sure.

One specific version of overkill that occurs regularly in both Celtic and Germanic mythology – it may ultimately be of Indo-European origin – concerns the threefold death of kings. A tribal chief or king was held responsible for the well-being of his people. If things went wrong – if battles were lost, if there was an outbreak of disease, if the crops failed – he was ritually killed. The death was not a simple execution, but a sacrifice in which the victim was put to death by three different methods. It is a scenario which occurs in Welsh legend with the story of Merlin or Myrddin, and in Norse mythology with Odin. It features in Lucan's first-century epic, *Pharsalia*, and in Adomnán's seventh century *Life of Saint Columba*.

A number of bodies recovered from peat bogs in Britain and Ireland appear to offer *prima facie* evidence of threefold death. The remains of one such individual were found at Croghan in County Offaly, at the foot of an isolated hill known to have been used for tribal ceremonies. Old Croghan Man, as he is known, was evidently a member of the elite, for his hands were soft, showing no sign of manual labour, and his diet was rich in meat. He was also between 1.91 and 1.98 metres tall, almost a giant for his time, and died between 362 and 195 BC. His death was probably caused by a stab wound to the chest, but he had also been decapitated and the lower half of his body had been detached from the upper half. His arms had been pierced and hazel withies passed through the holes – perhaps to drag him along – and his nipples had been sliced through. Another victim, Clonycavan Man, found in a bog in County Meath, was probably only about 1.50 metres tall, but he, too, shows signs which can be interpreted as evidence of ritual killing. Not all of his body was recovered, but he was evidently disembowelled, struck three times over the head and once in the body with an axe, as well as having his nipples sliced. That idea that Old Croghan Man and Clonycavan Man were kings or chieftains is supported by the fact that in ancient Ireland the act of sucking the king's nipples was a recognised gesture of fealty and submission. Eamon Kelly, Keeper of Antiquities at the National Museum of Ireland, has suggested that cutting the nipples was a symbolic indication that the king could no longer nourish his people; that he had been effectively 'decommissioned.'[99] Another male body retrieved from a peat bog, this time at Lindow in Cheshire, has been dated to between 2 BC and 119 AD. He was about twenty-five years old, with short, clipped hair and a beard, and so well preserved that it was possible to analyse the contents of his stomach, revealing that he may have ingested mistletoe, perhaps as a drink. He had apparently been killed by a blow to the head which penetrated his skull, by being garrotted with a leather strap, and then being thrown face down in the waters of the bog.

Given the way in which these three individuals appear to have met their deaths, it is not surprising that their remains should have been seen as confirmation that threefold death, and thus human sacrifice, were a part of ritual religious practice in Iron Age Britain. However, doubts have been cast on this interpretation. In her book, *The Celts: Search for a Civilization*, Alice Roberts expresses concern about the relationship between the archaeological record and those classical texts, myths, legends and folktales which describe Iron Age ritual behaviour. She sees a danger of circular interpretation: that we interpret fragmentary or potentially ambiguous archaeology – such as the wounds on the bodies of Croghan, Clonycavan and Lindow Man – in the light of information gleaned from documentary sources, which themselves may not be completely trustworthy; and then claim that the archaeology confirms the accuracy of the documentary sources. Ronald Hutton in his book, *Pagan Britain*, goes further. He refutes the idea of a ritual explanation for Lindow Man's death point by point. He suggests that there was not enough mistletoe in his gut to indicate consumption of a drink; that the leather garrotte was in fact a decayed necklace; and that the cut to the throat was inflicted after death, perhaps by a peat harvesting machine.[100] Hutton's characteristic approach is one of demystification. He argues that, even given today's much improved archaeological techniques, it is often impossible to distinguish between normal, daily behaviour and ritual, and that modern scholars are too prone to interpret as ritual things for which they cannot find an alternative explanation. This is a salutary warning, although Hutton's analysis of certain sites and finds can sometimes suggest that he is straining the evidence to prove a point. As far as threefold death is concerned, we must await new research or new discoveries before we can reach a firm conclusion.

All ritual activity, including sacrifice – whether animal or human – would have been conducted or supervised by what up to this point we have called a priesthood or a priestly caste. However, by the end of the Iron Age, and thanks to those classical authors with an interest in Britain, we can give them a name. That the priests of the Celtic-speaking British Isles were called 'druids' is perhaps the one thing about pre-Roman Britain that everybody knows. Yet we have very little information about them, and what we have comes not from the druids themselves, but from external, often hostile sources. Julius Caesar's account in the *Gallic Wars* stands out because it is detailed, contemporary with the events it describes, and, for the most part, based on his personal experiences during the conquest of Gaul between 58 and 51 BC. Caesar's understanding of the druids was also helped by his friendship with Diviciacus (also Diviaticus), who is often claimed to have been a druid himself. At the same time, it is worth remembering that Caesar was describing Gaul, not Britain, and there may well have been important societal differences between the two of which we are unaware.

Describing the society of Gaul, Caesar dismisses the common people as little better than slaves, and states that there are only two classes of people of 'dignity and account'. These are the knights (*equites*) – by which he means tribal leaders and warriors whose social status entitles them to a following of liegemen – and the druids. He notes that the druids are responsible for the interpretation and conduct of all religious matters, including public and private sacrifices, and makes it clear that their authority also extends to matters that we would regard as within the secular sphere. Like medieval bishops, they adjudicated on crimes, including murder, and on inheritance and boundary disputes. If their judgement was not respected, the offender was shunned by other members of his community and forbidden to take part in sacrifices – in effect, excommunicated. Caesar states that human sacrifices were regarded as a necessity to propitiate the gods in the event of battle, imminent danger, or severe illness. He also describes the wicker man phenomenon, where huge effigies woven from osiers were filled with live men and then burnt – the victims were usually criminals, but ordinary people could be sacrificed if no criminals were available. The druids themselves did not go to war, nor did they pay tribute. They trained for up to twenty years, memorising huge numbers of verses concerning philosophical matters, the size of the world, the movement of the stars, the nature of things, and the powers of the gods. All this had to be learnt by heart because writing things down would imperil the secrecy of druid lore. They had one supreme leader. If there was a pre-eminent candidate, he was chosen by acclamation if not, he was chosen by election among the other druids. Caesar adds that the contest was occasionally decided by force of arms. He also notes that druidism was said to have originated in Britain before spreading to Gaul, and those seeking to understand the subject in depth had to travel to Britain to study.[101]

Did druidism begin in Britain? Traces of the earliest reference to druidic practice may perhaps be found in Diodorus Siculus' *Bibliotheca Historica*, written in the first century BC, and they may refer to the British Isles – although the chain of connection is tenuous. Diodorus relates what he calls the legendary accounts of the Hyperboreans. He describes a fertile island with a temperate climate about the same size as Sicily, and far to the north, beyond the land of the Celts. The inhabitants worshipped Apollo – whom the Greeks understood as the god of the sun, and of knowledge, medicine, and oracles – and on the island there was both a city dedicated to the god and a sacred precinct with a circular temple adorned with votive offerings. According to Diodorus, the moon, when viewed from the island, seemed only a short distance from the earth, and the rituals of the island were based of the nineteen-year lunar cycle, known as the Metonic cycle.[102] Diodorus, we know, draws heavily on Timaeus, but in this case he is quoting from *On the Hyperboreans*, a lost work by the fourth-century BC Greek historian Hecataeus of Abdera.[103] However, the details given by Diodorus suggest first-hand knowledge, and it seems likely that Hecataeus, like Timaeus, drew on Pytheas' lost *On the Ocean*. We know that on his journey around Britain, Pytheas made measurements of the height of the sun in order to gauge how far he had come from Massalia. One of these measurements appears to have been taken from the Isle of Lewis.[104] If this is the case, we can speculate that the circular temple may have been Callanish. Diodorus does not use the word druid – he calls the kings and the priests of the precinct 'Boreadae', descendants of the Boreas, the north wind – but if the passage does refer to them, it means that druidic belief and practice was fully established in the Outer Hebrides by the fourth century BC. Lost works by both Aristotle (384–322 BC) and Sotion of Alexandria (early second century BC) are quoted by the third century AD writer Diogenes Laertius (180–240 AD). Both refer directly to druidic practice and belief – notably to the transmigration of souls, which appears to have been central to druidic doctrine and was also an essential element in Mediterranean and Neoplatonist philosophy. Neither Aristotle nor Sotion travelled anywhere they could have had contact with druids – nor did Diogenes Laertius, who came from Cilicia in Anatolia – but their work indicates that druidism and its central tenets were sufficiently well known and understood to be written about as far away as Athens and Alexandria several centuries before the Romans conquered Gaul and Britain. Which, in turn, means that druidism must have developed and established itself among the Celtic-speaking peoples at a much earlier stage.

Another faint clue may be found in Roman attitudes to the island which they called Mona and we call Anglesey. The Roman conquest of Britain was a slow process. The Roman governors and their legions were constantly having to subdue tribal rebellions, particularly in the north and west. In 60 AD, seventeen years after Emperor Claudius' troops had landed on British soil, the then governor, Gaius Suetonius Paulinus, launched an attack on Anglesey. It was not a simple operation: special flat-bottomed boats had to be built to ferry his soldiers across the Menai Strait, while the cavalry had to swim across beside their horses. Describing the attack, Tacitus says only that Anglesey had become a haven for refugees, but the implication of the passage as a whole is that the druids, not the refugees, were the real target. And it is noticeable that the first thing the victorious Romans did was to destroy the island's sacred groves.[105] Suetonius Paulinus had to abandon Anglesey almost at once in order to suppress Boudicca's revolt (see Chapter 15), but when Agricola, who had served with Suetonius Paulinus' army during the Anglesey campaign, became governor in 77 or 78 AD, one his first objectives was to re-conquer and occupy Anglesey. The implication – which has also survived in Welsh folklore – is that Anglesey was a stronghold, probably the headquarters, of the druids in Britain. This does not prove that druidism began in Britain, but that Anglesey should be a target twice, and that the Romans should feel they had to break the power of the druids in order to complete their conquest of Britain, does indicate the centrality of druidism in British tribal life and the power it exercised.

The traditional assumption was that the druids and their religion arrived in Britain with the supposed waves of Celtic invaders in the middle of the first millennium BC – and it was on this basis that scholars and archaeologists ruled out any connection between the druids and Stonehenge, despite the fervent assertions of latter-day druids, who adopted 'the stones' as their temple as long ago as the eighteenth century. Given that the Celtic invasion hypothesis is no longer tenable, we need to look elsewhere for the origins of the druids and druidism. We have already noted a number of continuities in the spiritual or religious sphere. We have seen that the apparent changes in religious practice from Neolithic times into the Iron Age were paralleled by significant continuities, suggesting evolution within an enduring framework of belief. In this context, druidism may conceivably have been the latest (and, as it would turn out, last) manifestation of the indigenous beliefs and practices that had evolved and changed over the previous three or four millennia. Another possibility is that druidism, or a set of beliefs from which it developed, arrived at the same time as Beaker culture. This would link the advent of druidism to a time of cultural and population change in the Archipelago and with the Celtic language. Either explanation would delight modern-day druids in that it would open the possibility that the great henges and stone circles might have druidic connections – although the abandoning of Stonehenge and the subsequent gulf of some 1,300 years before the first documentary reference to druids would still require explanation. Cunliffe prefers to see druidism emerging in the middle of the second millennium BC, a time he characterises as the end of the Neolithic cycle of development. He points to the abandoning of megalithic monuments and collective ancestral tombs, and to an increased emphasis on individual burial, on deposition, and on more intensive land use as evidence of a cultural shift sufficiently radical to be accompanied by an equally radical shift in belief systems. And he sees the society that emerged from that period of change as likely to reflect and respond to druidism's apparent emphasis on the passing of the months and the seasons.

What the druids believed is, again, something we can only attempt to piece together from classical sources, myth, and folklore. The word 'druid' appears in Latin as *druidae*, in Scots Gaelic as *draoidh*, and in Irish Gaelic as *draoi*. Several derivations have been suggested, including the Persian *duru*, meaning a good or holy man, but the most widely accepted draws on a combination of two proto-Celtic roots: *deru* or *daru*, meaning 'tree' and often 'oak tree'; and *wid* or *witt* meaning 'to know'. Trees, each species with its special magical or healing properties, feature prominently in the myth and folklore of the Celtic fringe. Pliny the Elder (23/24–79 AD) suggests that the oak was the most important. It is possible that the Welsh poem, 'Cad Goddeu' ('The Battle of the Trees'), in which a Welsh magician, Gwydion, brings the trees of the forest alive to become his army, preserves fragments of druidic tree lore. Although the poem first appears in a fourteenth-century manuscript known as *The Book of Taliesin*, it was almost certainly composed much earlier. Taliesin himself, who is credited with the composition of several other poems in the manuscript, lived in the sixth century.

Druidism was evidently a nature cult, but it had other important characteristics. Caesar does not mention trees, but he does stress the druids' concern with philosophical matters, particularly the transmigration of souls – something which fascinated the Greek writers. Where Caesar touches on doctrine, he uses the names of the Roman gods whose divine remit is closest to the gods of the Gauls he is describing – presumably to make his narrative more accessible to a Roman readership. Thus, when he says that the Gauls worship Mercury in particular, regarding him as the originator of the arts, he is referring to Lugh (also Lug and Lugus), the most prominent member of the Celtic pantheon, even though the analogy is not particularly close. Lugh was a king and warrior, associated with the tree of life, and given the epithet *samildánachi*, meaning one who is skilled in all the arts. It is Lugh, who gave his name to the Celtic harvest festival Lughnasa, and who may well have given his name to places such as Lyon, Leiden, Luton, Lothian, possibly London, but certainly Ludgate Hill in London. Similarly, when Caesar says that druidic tradition claims that all Gauls are descended from Dis, the god of the underworld, he may be referring to the horned god known as Cernunnos, sometimes also seen as guardian of the treasures of the otherworld, but again the analogy is far from exact (see Chapter 20).

Caesar's account of the Gauls and their religion is notable for its matter-of-fact tone. He gives his opinion that the Gauls are devoted to superstitious rites, but even when discussing human sacrifice, he is not condemnatory. The same approach is taken by Diodorus Siculus, writing in the first century BC; by Strabo, in the early decades of the first century AD; and by the Greek philosopher, Dio Chrysostom, at the end of the first century AD. Strabo goes further than Caesar, listing three groups of men who are held in exceptional honour: the Bards, the Vates and the Druids. The Bards are singers and poets; the Vates, diviners and natural philosophers; while the Druids, in addition to natural philosophy, also study moral philosophy.[106]

All three writers emphasise the intellectual status of the druids, their philosophy, and their decision-making role in society.

Furthermore, since they cannot always be ruled by kings who are philosophers, the most powerful nations have publicly appointed philosophers as superintendents and officers for their kings... The Celts appointed men they call Druids, who are also devoted to the prophetic art and to wisdom in general... The kings were not permitted to do or plan anything without the assistance of these wise men, so in truth it was they who ruled, while the kings became servants and ministers of their will, even though they were sitting on golden thrones, dwelling in great houses, and feasting sumptuously.[107]

The most detailed – and picturesque – accounts we have of druidic rituals come from Pliny's *Natural History*. His most famous description is of cutting mistletoe.

> The druids — for that is what [the Gauls] call their magicians — believe nothing more sacred than mistletoe and the tree on which it grows, particularly if that tree is an oak. They select oaks to form whole groves, and none of their religious rites is performed without the use of oak branches.... Mistletoe is only rarely found on oaks, but, when it is, it is gathered with rites full of great reverence. This is done particularly on the fifth day of the moon ... because the moon, although not in the middle of its course, already has considerable power and influence. They call mistletoe a name which in their language means all-healing. Having made all necessary preparations for the sacrifice, and for a banquet beneath the trees, they bring up two white bulls, the horns of which are bound for the first time. The priest, clad in a white robe, climbs the tree and cuts the mistletoe with a golden sickle, and it is received by those below in a white cloth. They then sacrifice [the white bulls]...[108]

This passage with its oak tree, mistletoe, moon, white robes, and sickle, has probably had more influence than any other on the way subsequent ages have visualised the druids. But Pliny describes other ceremonies as well.

> In summertime, numberless snakes become artificially entwined together, and form rings around their bodies from the viscous slime they exude from their mouths, and from the foam they secrete. The Druids tell us that the serpents eject the eggs [formed from the rings] into the air with their hissing, and that a person must be ready to catch them in a cloak, so as not to allow them to touch the ground. They say,

too, that he must immediately flee on horseback because the snakes are sure to pursue him until he crosses a river that will act as a barrier between them.[109]

Care is taken to gather [the herb known as *selago*] without using iron, and with the right hand being passed through the left sleeve of the tunic, as if the person gathering was in the act of committing a theft. His clothes must be white, his feet bare, and he must have made a sacrifice of bread and wine before gathering the herb. It should be carried in a new napkin.[110]

The Druids have also given the name *samolus* to a certain plant which grows in humid places. They say that it must be gathered while fasting and with the left hand, as a protection against the disease which affects swine and cattle. The person who gathers it must also be careful not to look behind him, nor must it be put anywhere except in the troughs from which the cattle drink.[111]

Quite where Pliny got his information from is unclear: perhaps from Pytheas' lost *On the Ocean*, or perhaps from the work of the Greek polymath Posidonius (c.135–c.51 BC), who we know travelled in Gaul. Unfortunately, most of Posidonius' work is also lost. Pliny offers far more detail than any other writer and, while acknowledging that the episode of the snakes includes an element of folklore, many commentators have accepted his descriptions as essentially true. However, given the fantastic nature of some of the detail – which would not be out of place in Gormenghast – it seems likely that either Pliny, his source, or his informants have embroidered reality to present the druids in a particularly bizarre and outlandish light for the benefit of their readers.

Pliny also differs from Caesar, Strabo, Diodorus, and Dio Chrysostom in adopting a strongly moralistic tone when discussing the druids and their rituals.

We cannot too highly appreciate the obligation that is due to the Roman people, for having put an end to those monstrous rites, in accordance with which, to murder a man was to do an act of the greatest devoutness, and to eat his flesh was to secure the highest blessings of health.[112]

Pomponius Mela, writing in the middle of the first century AD, talks about 'abominable rites' and 'outright slaughter'.[113] At the beginning of the second century AD, the historian Suetonius (not to be confused with the governor Suetonius Paulinus) lists the abolition of the druids' 'barbarous and inhuman religion' as one of the achievements of the Emperor Claudius.[114] Tacitus, describing Suetonius Paulinus' attack on Anglesey in 60 AD, goes even further. The druids are supported by a band of women 'in black attire like the Furies, hair dishevelled, and waving brands.' The druids scream 'dreadful curses'. The groves of trees are destroyed because they are devoted to 'inhuman superstitions' and contain 'altars [covered] with the blood of captives' where the druids consulted 'their deities through human entrails'.[115]

Cunliffe identifies a perceptible change in Roman attitudes following the fall of the Republic and the establishing and subsequent expansion of the Empire in the first century AD.[116] The power of the druids extended beyond the spiritual and into the temporal realm. Their word was law. They could sanction rebellion. They could influence, even overrule, the decisions of kings. To conquer and control the lands where they exercised authority, Rome had to break their power. For the emperor, it was useful to have the enemies of Rome denounced as murderous savages, devoted to bloody and inhuman ceremonies. It justified him in the eyes of his people and his army, and it would justify him in the eyes of history. The Romans themselves had only outlawed human sacrifice in 97 BC (three years before Caesar's birth) and were still happy to throw prisoners to the lions and stage gladiatorial fights to the death. Nonetheless, the fact that the druids performed human sacrifices was used to emphasise their status as 'barbarians' and show how far their practices were at odds with 'civilised' Roman values. It is interesting that none of these writers makes any reference to the threefold death of kings. Had Pomponius Mela or Tacitus heard of it, they would surely have added ritual regicide to their list of the druidic crimes.

These glimpses of the druids give us our first direct information of how society in Britain was organised, and how its power structures operated. It seems probable that the earlier writers, who took a less judgemental view, are more reliable. Caesar may have been blowing his own trumpet in the *Gallic Wars*, but he was not seeking to make propaganda by demonising the enemy. This is not to deny that druidism may have involved human sacrifice and other abhorrent practices – it almost certainly did – but rather to seek the most objective view available of the society in which such practices evidently played an important and accepted part.

We have already asked whether early Neolithic society could be described as theocratic (see Chapter 5). We now can ask the same of the pre-Roman Iron Age. As before, while there is some evidence to support the idea, we cannot really tell. Caesar, Diodorus, and Dio Chrysostom all state that the druids wielded great power; that their judgement on religious and legal matters was law. Yet it is equally clear that there was a secular structure consisting of 'kings' (tribal leaders) and 'knights' (warriors). What the relationship was between the two groups, we can only guess. Dio Chrysostom presents the druids as the power behind the throne. That kind of informal relationship may have worked in particular places and at particular times, but it is unlikely to have applied everywhere. It could be that there were incidents of conflict between, in effect, church and state. Such incidents have occurred throughout history and in all parts of the world. There is no reason to suppose Iron Age Gaul and Britain were any different. Perhaps a more relevant question is how much – if at all – contemporary belief systems and social structures allowed for a distinction between the sacred and the secular. We can only extrapolate from the few surviving texts, and the few, often ambiguous, clues offered by the archaeological record.

Those sources we have considered so far relate only to Gaul and to that part of Britain which was eventually occupied by the Romans. It is reasonable to assume that druidism was also the religion of northern Britain – although the more remote areas and the islands could have maintained an earlier belief system – and Ireland. Beyond the Solway—Tyne line, along which Hadrian's Wall would eventually be built, we know the names of some of the tribes and the approximate area in which they lived, but little else. We know almost nothing of how society functioned. Most of the tribal hillforts are found south of the Forth—Clyde line, which suggests some socio-political similarity with southern Britain. We know that there was a prehistoric village on Iona; and there is some evidence that the island may have been a sacred site before the arrival of St Columba in the sixth century AD (see Chapter 23) – in which case it could possibly have been a druidic site, but that is speculation. Tacitus goes into detail about Agricola's military expeditions into Caledonia and about the opposition he faced but says nothing about druids. However, he does not say that the Caledonian tribes were in any way different from those in the south.

In Ireland, we are on slightly firmer ground. Tacitus says that the Irish were much like the British, and we know that the Irish tribes, unlike those in Caledonia, were recognised as traders. Long before the Romans arrived in Britain, there were established trade routes between Ireland and Iberia, probably based on the port of Galway. Once southern Britain was occupied, trade across the Irish Sea boomed, much of it apparently based on Drumanagh, just north of Dublin, where Roman merchants appear to have set up a trading post (see Chapter 19). Traders no doubt added to the store of Roman knowledge about Ireland, although they may also have exaggerated the dangers to deter competition. Diodorus Siculus insists that cannibalism was common in Ireland; Strabo says the men ate their fathers and had sex with their mothers and sisters; Pomponius Mela says the grass grew so richly that cattle would burst if they were not stopped from eating it; but none of them mentions druids. Ireland had no tradition of literacy before the arrival of Christianity, so we must rely on documents that were written much later, between the fifth and twelfth centuries AD: the law tracts, the lives of the saints, *The Book of Invasions*, and the Irish sagas. Apart from the lives of the saints, all these sources have their roots in the pre-Christian oral tradition, but when they were written down it was by Christian scribes who would naturally have been biased against druidism and pre-Christian religion. Nonetheless, we can get a sense of the social and religious structures of Iron Age Ireland.

There appear to have been about one hundred and fifty *túatha* or tribes, each with its own king; and there were three levels of kingship: king of a single tribe, king of several tribes, and overking or provincial king. Within this society, there were the unfree and the free; and among the free were the *nemed* or privileged ones, including kings, lords, bards, and members of whatever priesthood existed. Such a clear-cut hierarchy may perhaps reflect the reality of the times, or it may have been tidied up by early medieval scribes with their passion for order and lists. Cunliffe points to the fact that *nemed* is cognate with *nemeton*, meaning sacred place, and may suggest a religious origin or underpinning for the privileged ones. Elsewhere, we learn of a distinction between druids, seers (or *fili*), and bards, which appears to replicate Strabo's division between druids, vates and bards.

Irish sources also tell us how the year was divided into quarters, each marked by a particular festival. These festivals, adopted and adapted by the early Christian church, are still recognised and marked two thousand years later. Imbolc, halfway between the winter solstice and the spring equinox, marked the beginning of spring. In the Christian calendar, this is St Brigid's Day: Brigid was probably an Irish goddess, and St Brigid possibly the druid responsible for converting her cult to Christianity. A trace of Imbolc survives in the fire festival of Up Helly Aa in Shetland – although a nineteenth-century invention, it evolved from the ancient practice of running lighted tar barrels through the streets. Beltane came halfway between the spring equinox and the summer solstice, marking the beginning of summer. It survives in the many Mayday ceremonies and celebrations across Europe and elsewhere. The druids would light Beltane fires and drive the cattle between them, and domestic hearths would be put out and then re-lit from the Beltane fires. Lughnasa, halfway between the summer solstice and the autumn equinox, was a celebration of the harvest, transformed by Christianity into Lammas Day, Lammastide, or Harvest Festival. Samhain, halfway between the autumn equinox and the winter solstice, marked the onset of winter. This was the time when the border between our world and the otherworld was at its thinnest. People left out offerings for the spirits. The druids lit fires and offered sacrifices to ward off incursions from the spirit world. Samhain survives as All Hallows' Eve or Hallowe'en when the dead are remembered, and ghosts walk. Today's pumpkin lanterns would have been illuminated skulls to keep the spirits from entering the houses of the living. People dressed up, disguising themselves as protection from wandering spirits – the origin of today's mummers and guisers.

It seems likely that the druids fulfilled a broadly similar spiritual role across Gaul and the British Isles, although their political influence may have varied from region to region. By the time the Irish texts were written, druidism was a mere shadow of the force it had been. In southern Britain, it had been targeted and suppressed by the Romans. What survived had probably gone underground, perhaps resurfacing briefly in remote areas when the Romans left before fading into folklore with the coming of Christianity. In Ireland, where the process of conversion to Christianity was slower (see Chapter 23), the druids were a focus of resistance. The story of St Patrick, one of the earliest missionaries to Ireland, dramatises the struggle between the old and new faiths. In one episode, Patrick calls on God to strike down a druid who opposes him, and God obliges. In another, Patrick's follower Benignus (sometimes Benineus) undergoes a competitive ordeal by fire with Cruth (sometimes Lucat), the druid of King Laoghaire. Needless to say, Benignus survives unscathed, while nothing is left of Cruth but ashes.

By the seventh century – perhaps even earlier – druidism had ceased to be an active force anywhere in the British Isles. The office and idea of the bard, someone whose skill with words gave him special powers deserving of respect, continued, but the spread of Christianity reduced druidism itself to folk magic and superstition. Only during the Renaissance, with the rediscovery of classical texts dealing with Britain, did the idea begin to grip the British imagination. The antiquarian and historian, William Camden (1551–1623) was the first to revive mention of the druids in his *Britannia* (1586), although he dismissed the druids' religion as 'a dismal and confused heap of superstition'.[117] The Reverend Henry Rowlands of Anglesey (1655–1723) conjectured that the druids had inherited the religion of Abraham, which, in the Old Testament, calls for human sacrifice.[118] John Aubrey (1626–97) first linked Stonehenge with the druids, and his ideas influenced a number of people, including Edward Lhuyd and John Toland (1670–1722), whose *History of the Celtic Religion and Learning Containing an Account of the Druids* was published posthumously in 1726. Aubrey also influenced William Stukeley, who gave cursus monuments their name (see Chapter 5).

Stukeley began by making topographical observations and measurements in a manner which marked him as a genuine pioneer of archaeology. Unfortunately, he became obsessed with druidism, claiming that it was the precursor of Christianity, and had been introduced to Britain by Hercules, whom he declared was a Phoenician druid. He also adopted the pseudonym Chyndonax, after a chief druid whose tomb was discovered near Dijon in 1598. Absurd and unlikely as it may seem to a modern readership, in its day Stukeley's work was extremely influential. William Blake's fascination with bards and druids owes much to Stukeley. The clergyman and historian, Thomas Maurice (1754–1824), drew on Stukeley's writings when he developed his theory that the druids were originally Indian Brahmins. So, too, did the clergyman and antiquary, John Bathurst Deane (1797–1887), in his study *The Worship of the Serpent* (1830) which linked the serpent in the Book of Genesis with snake worship in pre-Christian Europe and with other polytheistic societies as far away as China and Mexico.

As the eighteenth century progressed, interest in druidism continued to grow and, in 1781, the Ancient Order of Druids was founded – or, as its members would have it, 'revived' – in the King's Arms on Poland Street in London's Soho. A plaque on the wall commemorates the occasion. For the next, and probably crucial, phase in the rise of latter-day druidism Edward Williams (1747–1826) was responsible. Williams, who preferred to use his self-chosen bardic name, Iolo Morganwg, was a Welsh poet, antiquarian, and collector of manuscripts. He was also a forger. A native of Glamorgan, Morganwg had convinced himself that the bardic traditions of his home region contained the essence of ancient, esoteric, druidic law. In 1792, on Primrose Hill, London's highest point, he and some companions performed a rite which he had devised called the Gorsedd of Bards. The climax of the ceremony involved unsheathing a sword while standing at the centre of a magic circle of stones and reciting 'traditional' bardic verses. Williams/Morganwg told the *Monthly Register*: 'It is not a little remarkable that the order, or hierarchy of the *ancient British Bards* has been continued in regular succession from remotest antiquity down to the present day, without any interruption…'[119]

From these disingenuous beginnings, latter-day druidism has never looked back. The Romantic and Celtic Revivals saw a succession of white-robed figures performing rituals at historic sites – most notably Stonehenge – and inventing ever more. The emphasis placed on nature and spirituality meant that the movement flourished as part of the counterculture of the 1960s and 70s; and today it is a recognised and accepted part of the spectrum of neo-pagan belief.

15 Invasion and Influence

In 55 BC, the history books tell us, Gaius Julius Caesar launched his first invasion of Britain – although it was actually a large-scale raid. Caesar had been governor of Gaul since 58 BC and had proved himself skilled and ruthless. He had conquered and subdued the Celtic-speaking tribes of what is now Belgium and central and northern France and had defended the Rhine frontier against Germanic tribes seeking to cross into Gaul. Rome was still a republic, and the Senate was still its most powerful political institution, but the process that was to undermine it and create the

15 Invasion and Influence

Roman Empire had already begun. In 60 BC, three of Rome's most powerful individuals, Julius Caesar, Gnaeus Pompeius Magnus (Pompey the Great; 106–48 BC), and Marcus Licinius Crassus (115–53 BC), had reached an informal understanding, agreeing to work together to further their respective ambitions. Pompey was the greatest soldier of the age and, as such, adored by the populace. Crassus was the richest man in Rome and wanted the political power and military glory to match it. Caesar, a more obviously political figure, had served in a variety of military and administrative posts in both Rome and in Hispania. He had also been elected to the influential position of Pontifex Maximus, effectively chief priest of the Roman religion. There was little genuine common ground between them, and they were distrusted by much of the Senate. Working together, however, they were all but irresistible. Later historians dignified them with the title 'The First Triumvirate', but the contemporary writer, Varro (116–27 BC), preferred to call them 'the three-headed monster'.[120] Their informal agreement came to an end in 53 BC when Crassus died ignominiously fighting against the Parthians, and by 49 BC Caesar and Pompey were fighting each other. Nonetheless, their short-lived alliance enabled Caesar to become governor of Gaul, and to extend his tenure to an unprecedented nine years. It also provided the context for his decision to invade Britain.

That context is important because, had things been otherwise, Rome might never have invaded Britain at all. Gaul was the perfect place for Caesar to grow his reputation as a military leader, but he needed to undertake exploits daring and successful enough to keep his name in front of the senate and the Roman public. Technically, it was illegal for Roman governors to mount military operations beyond the borders of their provinces unless there was a serious threat to security. Almost as soon as he became governor, Caesar engineered such a threat on Gaul's eastern frontier, allowing him to cross the Rhine and mount operations against the Suebi. Then, in 57 BC, his armies moved into north-western Gaul. After some resistance, the leaders of the Bellovaci tribe, who occupied the land between the Seine and the Somme, fled to Britain. The following year, when a revolt broke out among the Veneti, a seafaring tribe who lived on the southern coast of Brittany, British tribes apparently sent them assistance. Neither circumstance could realistically have threatened Caesar's position in Gaul, but they offered the excuse he needed.

Beyond enhancing Caesar's reputation, it is difficult to see any other reason why the Romans should have invaded Britain. Writing in 54 BC, the year of Caesar's second invasion, Cicero was dismissive of Britain and the British (see Chapter 12). The Romans knew Britain as a source of tin but, perhaps surprisingly, neither Cicero nor anyone else mentions tin as a motive for the invasion. Grain would later become important: Britain was a fertile country, and the Roman army always needed grain to feed its soldiers, but again this was not mentioned at the time. The main driver was Caesar's ambition. But if he was ambitious, he was also willing to take risks. The Roman army was a land army. Never before had it attempted a seaborne operation on the scale required to invade Britain. Such maritime experience as he and his men had was derived from the Mediterranean – which, as they would soon discover, was very different from the Channel, with its rapidly changing weather patterns, powerful tidal currents, and a tidal range as much as twenty times greater than they were used to. The weather was a particular risk. By the time Caesar had made his preparations, the summer was almost over. It was late in the year for such a major military operation, and autumn storms would pose a threat.

Nonetheless, on 23 August 55 BC, Caesar set sail from Portus Itius – probably Boulogne – with eighty transport ships carrying two legions. Eighteen more transports carrying his cavalry set sail from another unidentified port, possibly Ambleteuse in the Pas de Calais. In total, he probably had about 10,000 men. The whole venture was very nearly a disaster. As part of his preparations, Caesar had collected what intelligence he could about Britain and its tribes from the traders who worked across the Channel. They been unable or unwilling to tell him much, but the exercise had alerted the Britons to his intentions: some tribes had even sent delegations pledging allegiance and offering hostages, presumably hoping to escape the full force of Roman military might. When the Roman fleet came in sight of Dover, where Caesar was hoping to land, the cliffs were lined with a mass of armed tribesmen. The fleet sailed further up the coast and made a landing at a more open location, probably Pegwell Bay, but the draft of the loaded transports meant they could not be beached close to the shore. Caesar's men had to wade through deep water while under attack from the tribesmen who had followed them up the coast. Eventually, supported by ballistae and catapults fired from the ships, the soldiers established a beachhead and drove the tribesmen back. Meanwhile, the ships carrying the cavalry had been driven back to Gaul by a storm and adverse winds. Then gale force winds and the high tides played havoc with the main fleet. Ships drawn up on the beach were swamped and damaged, while those anchored offshore were driven against each other and some of them sank. A foraging party was ambushed by the British tribesmen and only saved from annihilation when dust stirred up by the fighting was seen from the main camp and reinforcements swiftly despatched. Only when the British made a tactical error and mounted a frontal assault on the Roman camp was Caesar was able to secure something he could claim as a victory. The Britons sued for peace and promised hostages. Caesar assembled his remaining ships and headed back to Gaul. The brief campaign had been anything but a success, yet by the time news reached Rome, he was praised for conquering the sea and going beyond the limits of the known world. The senate decreed twenty days of public thanksgiving. Political spin is nothing new.

Caesar returned to Britain the following year, but this time he was better prepared. His army was much larger — perhaps as many as 27,000 men — and his new fleet included many ships with a wider beam and shallower draft to make them easier to beach. Much of the previous year's fleet had been propelled by oars alone, but many of the new ships had sails, making them more manoeuvrable in Channel conditions. Caesar also ensured that his troops were trained in how to counter the British tactic of using chariots to move quickly in and out of the battle line — a tactic the legions had not previously encountered, and which had caused much confusion the previous year. Politically, too, he was better prepared. Mandubracius, son of the king of the Trinovantes, whose territory included what is now Essex, had fled to Gaul when his father had been killed by a neighbouring tribe, the Catuvellauni. He had provided Caesar with information about the geography and politics of southern Britain and would also prove a useful political lever.

The British knew he was coming. An army of tribesmen had assembled, but for some reason — perhaps because of internal disagreements, or because of the size of the Roman army — the landing went unopposed. Caesar and his men began to move inland. They crossed the River Stour and repulsed a British attack. They had successfully stormed a hillfort at Bigbury Wood, just west of Canterbury, when Caesar received news that, in a repeat of the previous year's disaster, a violent storm had wrecked forty of his ships. Putting things right caused a delay. The British tribes regrouped and organised themselves, putting Cassivellaunus, king of the Catuvellauni, in overall command of their forces. Cassivellaunus fought a guerrilla campaign, allowing the Romans to move forward, but harassing them all the way. Only once did he risk a frontal attack on the three advancing legions. He lost, and his men were pursued by the Roman cavalry. Caesar crossed the Thames, probably near London, and drove the Britons from the north bank. The British adopted a scorched earth policy. Caesar's men also burnt all the villages they came across, but their supply line was becoming dangerously extended. Cassivellaunus tried to take advantage of this by pressing the leaders of the Kentish tribes to attack the Roman fleet. They did, but the attack was beaten off. A stalemate had been reached. Autumn was approaching and Caesar needed to return to Gaul. Terms were agreed. Cassivellaunus promised not to attack the Trinovantes, who accepted Mandubracius as their king. The Catuvellauni and their allies agreed to give hostages and pay an annual tribute to Rome. All things considered, the terms were light enough, but could be made to sound better when Caesar's despatches reached Rome.

In the *Gallic Wars*, the source of most of our information about the invasions, Caesar does not hide the fact that he suffered setbacks, but he does not address what the text implies: that he seriously underestimated the strength and tenacity of British resistance. The first invasion may have been a raid or large-scale reconnaissance, but the second looks like a failed attempt at conquest. Whether he would have returned again had the tribes in Gaul not staged a major revolt, first under Ambiorix and then under Vercingetorix, which took several years to suppress, is something we cannot know. In the event, it would be ninety years before Roman soldiers again landed in Britain, but Caesar's departure did not mean that the situation reverted to what it had been previously. The relationship between Britain and Rome had changed.

Caesar may have managed to enhance his reputation on the strength of limited military success, but in the longer term his real achievement was probably making Rome aware of Britain as a real and accessible place, rather than as a distant and unknown land beyond the sea. This had consequences for both parties. In Britain, the impact of Caesar's invasions was naturally greatest in the south-east, although knowledge of what had happened would have spread to other regions, as would some of the economic and political repercussions. Trade patterns shifted. Hengistbury Head had long been a major trading port, growing prosperous on its links with Armorica. Suddenly, it went into decline. This may have been due to the bloody repression Caesar had visited on the Armorican tribes when they rebelled in 56 BC; or it may have been because he granted favourable trading terms to the Trinovantes, who had pledged allegiance to Rome. The focus of trade shifted dramatically to the Thames estuary, north Kent, and the Essex coast. These were the lands opposite Belgic Gaul, where the tribes were becoming increasingly Romanised. The Trinovantes certainly prospered: Roman goods, notably wine amphorae, are found in large numbers in their territory, often as grave goods. Another tribe, the Atrebates, who inhabited parts of what is now Berkshire, Wiltshire, and Oxfordshire – and whose king, Commius, had assisted Caesar in 55 BC – also maintained connections with Rome and prospered as a result. From around 20 BC, there is evidence of increasing quantities of Roman goods arriving in their territory. We do not know the terms of the relationship between these tribes and Rome. They may simply have been granted trading privileges. Alternatively, they may be early examples of what historians call 'client kingdoms' – the Romans preferred 'friends of the Roman people' – which, in practical terms, meant that as long as their rulers maintained order, they were given protection, usually trade privileges, and sometimes gifts.

The first coins to circulate in Britain appeared about 150 BC. They were gold staters, imitations of Macedonian coins depicting Philip II, and came from Belgic Gaul, although whether they were used as a medium of exchange or as prestigious gifts is uncertain. The first coins actually minted in Britain were imitations of coins from Massalia and were used as a medium of exchange. They were known as 'potins', and were cast, not struck, from a tin-rich bronze of the same name. They began to circulate between 80 and 60 BC, initially among the Cantii (or Cantiaci) tribe, who gave their name to Kent. Soon after this, the first British gold coins appeared. These were gold staters, imitations of Gallic models, minted by the Durotriges tribe, whose capital was probably Dornovaria, modern-day Dorchester. The Durotriges' prosperity was to a significant extent based on the fact that their territory included Hengistbury Head, and the staters appeared when trade in and out of Hengistbury was at its height, just before Caesar's invasions. As the port declined in the second half of the first century BC, so the currency became progressively debased.

The nature of Caesar's invasions suggests that his men would have been more likely to forage, loot, and pillage than to purchase goods from the local population. Nor were the legions there long enough to inject much cash into the local economy. Nonetheless, in the aftermath, more tribes began to mint coins, and these, following Roman models, featured the head and name of the tribal ruler responsible. The Trinovantes minted coins from their capital at Camolundum – modern Colchester – under a series of shadowy rulers with names such as Addedomarus and Dubnovellaunus. The Atrebates began to mint coins at their capital, Calleva Atrebatum – modern Silchester – allowing us to establish that three brothers, Tincomarus, Eppillus, and Verica, ruled in sequence between 25 BC and 40 AD. Both Eppillus and Verica called themselves *Rex*, a title the Romans reserved for client kings. They may indeed have been client kings, but it is equally possible that they adopted a Roman-style title as a matter of prestige.

Increased trade and their connections with Rome brought the Trinovantes and the Atrebates wealth and prosperity, but it also made them the target of aggression. It was the Catuvellauni who had attacked the Trinovantes prior to Caesar's second invasion and their king, Cassivellaunus, who led the British resistance. During the last decades of the first century BC, the Catuvellauni, under a new king, Tasciovanus, embarked on another period of expansion and again attacked the Trinovantes. Tasciovanus is known only from coins minted during his reign. These first appeared at the Catuvellauni capital of Verlamion – later Verulamium, today St Albans – suggesting that he came to power between 25 and 20 BC. However, between 15 and 10 BC coins bearing his name were struck in the Trinovantes' capital of Camulodunum. Whether this means he had replaced the Trinovantes' king – probably Addedomarus – or was exercising some kind of overlordship is not clear. Later coins, again minted at Verlamion, feature the Celtic word *Ricon* (sometimes *Rigonos*), meaning king but do not use the Latin *Rex*. This may simply indicate a wish to avoid Roman styles and titles, or it may suggest that he now saw himself as a regional overking, leading resistance to Roman influence.

Tasciovanus' son, Cunobelin or Cunobeline – Shakespeare's Cymbeline – took a different approach. He did use the title *Rex* on his coins. He also used iconography copied from Roman models: images of Jupiter Ammon (Jupiter with horns) and of lions; laurel chaplets to signify military victory; ears of wheat to signify prosperity. He came to power in 9 AD, apparently ruling from Camulodunum, and reigned for thirty-two years, during which time Catuvellauni power continued to grow. In the 30s, Adminius, one of Cunobelin's sons, conquered the Cantii, giving the Catuvellauni control of Durovernum (Dover), which even then appears to have dominated cross-Channel trade. In or around 39 AD, Adminius was banished – we do not know why: perhaps he allowed the Cantii to rebel, or perhaps because he tried to rule on his own account – and fled to Rome.

This led to the strange and still uncertain incident of the Emperor Caligula's 'invasion' of Britain. Caligula seized on Adminius' account of his ill usage by his father as a reason to invade. He raised an army and set off for the Channel coast where he arrived probably in the spring of 40 AD, having plundered parts of Gaul on his way. What happened next is unclear. Of the three surviving accounts, Suetonius and Cassius Dio, writing in the second and third centuries respectively, say that he ordered his men to gather seashells, while Sextus Aurelius Victor, writing in the fourth century, says he ordered them to gather cockles and mussels. All three agree that the shells were to be sent to Rome as the spoils of his victory over the ocean. Suetonius adds that he built a lighthouse as a further celebration of his success. What actually happened, whether Suetonius was seeking to discredit Caligula and the others followed him, or whether there was a mistranslation, has been much discussed.[121] It is enough to note that, while Caligula did not invade, Britain was again – some ninety years after Caesar – attracting attention as a potential target.

Cunobelin's son had conquered the Trinovantes and, in the 20s, his brother, Epaticcus, began the conquest of the Catuvellauni's other great rivals, the Atrebates. Somewhere around 25 AD, he took control of their capital, Silchester, and started issuing his own coinage there. When he died in c.35 AD, his place was taken by Caratacus, another of Cunobelin's sons. Caratacus completed the conquest of the Atrebates, ousting their king, Verica, who fled to Rome, no doubt proclaiming – with some justice – that his tribe had always been friendly to Rome, and thus providing the Emperor Claudius with his excuse to invade Britain. Cunobelin died, probably in 41 AD, and his third son, Togodumnus, succeeded as king of the Catuvellauni. Both Caratacus and Togodumnus went on to play important roles when Claudius' invasion came in 43 AD.

Despite his aggressive policy towards neighbouring tribes who traded and remained friendly with Rome, Cunobelin also seems to have remained on reasonably good terms with the Romans, at least until the last years of his reign. Throughout his thirty years in power, trade continued to grow steadily with Camulodunum one of the main centres for imports. Archaeological finds include platters, cups, and other tableware from Belgic Gaul; amphorae from the Italian peninsula that would have held wine; Iberian amphorae that would have contained olive oil; beads, bronze brooches, and other jewellery, much of it also from what is now Italy, but some from further afield. The inhabitants of Camulodunum even seem to have developed a taste for *garum* – the strong, fermented fish sauce, which was an essential ingredient of Roman cuisine. If the British were becoming ever more interested in luxuries, the Romans were beginning to find Britain useful as a source of more basic commodities. Strabo lists grain, gold, silver, iron, cattle, hides, slaves, and hunting dogs as the principal exports.[122] The growth of trade was closely connected with the growth of markets and the growth of towns, or *oppida* as they are known. Given what we know of how Roman traders operated beyond the frontiers of the empire in other parts of Europe, it is more than likely there were groups of them already living and working at ports such as Hengistbury and Dover, and in the major trading centres such as Camulodunum, Verlamion, and Calleva Atrebatum.

Once the Romans controlled Gaul, some cross-Channel influence would have been inevitable, but the creeping Romanisation of tribal culture – or, at least, of tribal elites – and the deepening of economic ties were undoubtedly stimulated by Caesar's invasions. Yet it is worth emphasising that these changes were, understandably, concentrated in the south and south-east. We can piece together a picture of what happened in these areas from Roman and Greek sources, supplemented by the archaeological record. Elsewhere, we are largely limited to the archaeology. On the east coast, we know that the Iceni, who lived in the Norfolk area, and the Corieltauvi (sometimes Corieltavi, or even Coritani), who inhabited a broad area including Lincolnshire, Nottinghamshire, Leicestershire and Northamptonshire, were minting coins before Caesar's invasions. So, too, were the Dobunni, whose territory centred on what is now Gloucestershire. Tribes such as these, on the periphery of the newly prosperous areas in the south and south-east, no doubt benefitted from a general increase

Map 16   Tribes of Great Britain, *c.*50 AD

in trade and wealth, but further north and west these developments had less impact; and both Ireland and the northern half of Britain – more than half the land area of the British Isles – remained unaffected.

One aspect of British society highlighted by the early Roman writers is slavery: Cicero, Strabo, and Tacitus, all refer to slaves coming from Britain. Slavery was common to almost all societies at the turn of the millennium, but it had a particular role in Celtic-speaking societies, in part because they practised partible inheritance: that is, the estate of the deceased was divided equally between all the heirs. In a society of extended families where land was the main and most valued possession, this could and did cause friction. Slaves provided labour but had no claim on the land. Slavery as practised in the Celtic lands and in Rome was not the racially-based institution it became in the seventeenth and eighteenth centuries. In both societies, despite their structural and cultural differences, being a slave was essentially a question of legal status. In Ireland slaves were listed as a social class, albeit the lowest, the unfree (see Chapter 14). That does not excuse slavery, but it points to the fact it was an accepted part of life. It was also profitable

While some slaves were probably prisoners-of-war, captured during an inter-tribal conflict and made to labour on behalf of the victors, most were probably seized as children or teenagers by slave raiders, who sold them on to households of all social ranks in a different and probably distant part of the Archipelago. Most slave raids were probably seaborne. The sea allowed for surprise and a quick escape. In later centuries, there is evidence of slave raids along the western coast of Britain and across the Irish Sea. St Patrick, whose story dates from the first half of the fifth century AD, claimed to have been captured by Irish pirates and sold into slavery at the age of sixteen, but there is little doubt that slave raids had become common – even normal – practice for hundreds of years before that. One of the items retrieved from Llyn Cerrig Bach in Anglesey was an iron chain used for shackling slaves together. Its date is uncertain, but it could be as early as 300 BC. There are stories of slaves bonding with their owners and eventually being freed – this was a recognised phenomenon in Rome – but most slaves were simply a commodity to be bought and sold. Even before Caesar's invasions, Roman traders in and around Britain were probably buying slaves from local gangs, or even from tribal leaders, and shipping them off to the Continent, to Rome, or to wherever they thought they could make the greatest profit. We have no way of knowing how many victims were captured and sold at any one time but given that slaves were listed as one of Britain's main exports, the number must have been considerable. And it is not unreasonable to suppose that, as the trade and economic relationship between Britain and the Roman-ruled lands on the Continent deepened following Caesar's invasions, the number of slaves traded across the Channel increased.

16   Invasion and Conquest

For Claudius, as for Julius Caesar, the decision to invade Britain was a matter of political expediency, but in almost every other respect the background could not have been more different. Rome was no longer a republic. It was an empire. The first Emperor, Augustus (27 BC–14 AD), had given Rome stability after an extended period of civil war. His successor, Tiberius (r.14–37 AD), was a military man whose reign began well, but ended in treason trials, executions, and stories of sexual depravity. Tiberius' adopted heir, Caligula (r.37–41 AD), had no experience of war, diplomacy, or government, and his short reign has been characterised by tales of whimsical cruelty, more sexual depravity, and by the squandering of vast sums of money. Whether or not he was the monster he has been painted, it is certain that Claudius, who was proclaimed Emperor by the Praetorian Guard after they had assassinated Caligula, was entirely different. Although a member of the ruling family – Tiberius' nephew, and Caligula's great-uncle – he had been kept out of the spotlight because of his disabilities, which included a stammer, a limp, and slight deafness. Denied a public career, he came to the throne, like Caligula, without any practical experience of government. However, he was a student of history and had written books about Carthage, the Estruscans, and the reign of Augustus, giving him an extensive theoretical knowledge that he was able to apply administering the Empire. What the study of history could not give him was the military glory the Roman people demanded of their emperors. The growth of political connections and trading relationships across the Channel meant that by 43 AD Rome was a great deal better informed about Britain than it had been at the time of Caesar's invasions. Claudius would have been aware that there were economic benefits – the metals, cattle, grain, and slaves listed by Strabo – to be had from conquering Britain. But it was his political profile, and thus his survival as Emperor, that was the main motive for his decision to invade.

Roman legions generally consisted of ten cohorts. Each cohort was made up of eight centuries, and each century comprised eighty (not a hundred!) men – although the first cohort of any legion was usually double the size of the others. There were significant variations in both structure and numbers over time and in different parts of the Empire. Numbers might be increased by the addition of extra personnel or units of auxiliaries made up of native troops from other regions of the Empire. They might be lowered when detachments (known as vexillations) were transferred to other legions or assigned to duties outside the legionary structure. An average legion probably consisted of a core of somewhere between 5,000 and 6,000 men, although when auxiliaries were included, the figure could be as high as 10,000 or even 11,000. There were also cavalry units, or *alae*, usually consisting of about five hundred men, that could be attached to an army, depending on the nature of the campaign. Legions had both a number and a name. The numbers – although not names – are often duplicated, because the system kept changing. This can lead to confusion but keeping track of individual legions can be important because inscriptions indicating the presence of a particular legion at a particular place are among the few clues we have to the movement of military forces around Britain during the Roman occupation.

Claudius' invasion force was commanded by Aulus Plautius, who had been Governor of Pannonia, a province comprising the middle Danube valley and what is now central Hungary. He certainly had four legions under his command – IX Hispania, which he brought with him from Pannonia; II Augusta from Strasbourg; XIV Gemina from Mainz; and the XX legion from Neuss – and possibly also all or part of VIII Augusta, also from Strasbourg. There was a considerable body of auxiliary troops, including cavalry, so that his total strength was probably in the order of 40,000 men. That Claudius felt able to withdraw so many troops from the German frontier suggests that the tribes there – which had caused trouble in the past and would do so again in the future – were temporarily quiescent, so the invasion of Britain was made possible, in part, by their docility.

Claudius' invasion is not well documented. Our main source is Cassius Dio who, although usually reliable, did not write his *Historia*

16 Invasion and Conquest

Romana until nearly two hundred years after the event, and never travelled north of Pannonia. Nonetheless, the outlines are clear. Plautius brought his army across the Channel in three separate flotillas, with the intention of landing at different locations and dividing the British forces. In the event, the tactic was unnecessary. The landings were unopposed, and he set off across Kent in search of the British, whose resistance was probably led by the Catuvellauni. In two battles – we do not know where – he defeated one force led by Togodumnus and another led by Caratacus. A third battle took place during which German auxiliaries swam across a river – possibly the Medway – in full armour to gain surprise. A fourth battle saw the British fight hard, but they were eventually forced to withdraw beyond the Thames. Again, the Germans surprised them by swimming the river, while another detachment of Roman troops crossed an undefended bridge. The British were defeated, but managed to disappear into the marshes, where they could adopt guerrilla tactics and the Roman troops could not follow them. Plautius pushed on and then, just at the point where he was ready to attack the Catuvellauni capital, Camulodunum, he paused his advance, in part no doubt to secure his supply lines and consolidate his hold on those territories he had conquered, but also to allow Rome's triumph over the barbarians to be presented in the most appropriate way.

Claudius himself arrived in August, bringing with him a number of elephants, presumably the first ever seen in Britain, to overawe the natives. He took command of the troops and launched the assault on Camulodunum. It was a spectacular success, and he was – apparently spontaneously – hailed *Imperator* by the troops, the traditional way for the legions to express their support for an emperor. The military victory was accompanied by a diplomatic one when he received the – apparently voluntary – submission of eleven British kings. Details of this appear in the inscription of the triumphal arch that was built in Rome to celebrate his triumph, and on a replica at Boulogne, where he had embarked.

> The Roman Senate and People to Tiberius Claudius Caesar Augustus Germanicus, son of Drusus, Pontifex Maximus, Tribunician power eleven times, Consul five times, Imperator 22 times, Censor, Father of the Fatherland, because he received the surrender of eleven kings of the Britons defeated without any loss, and first brought barbarian peoples across the Ocean into the dominion of the Roman people

Claudius had achieved the reputation for military glory that he sought. It was, of course, a put-up job, as was the submission of the eleven kings. He spent only sixteen days in Britain, which allowed no time for such a gathering to be organised without advance warning, let alone for negotiations. We do not know which kings were involved. We can guess that they included the kings of tribes which had already been defeated by Plautius' legions, such as the Cantii, as well as kings of tribes which had had a long-standing friendship with Rome. And there may well have been others who saw advantages in submitting to Rome before they were confronted with military force.

One oddity concerns the King of Orkney. Both Flavius Eutropius in his *Breviarium Historiae Romanae* (*Brief History of Rome*), written in the middle of the fourth century, and Paulus Orosius in his *Historiarum Adversum Paganos* (*History against the Pagans*), probably written at the very end of the fourth century or the beginning of the fifth, claim that Claudius added 'the Orcades islands, situated in the ocean beyond Britain',[123] to the Roman Empire. For years this was regarded as bravado, intended to boost the patently untrue claim – recorded by Suetonius among others – that Claudius reduced the greater part of Britain to submission in a matter of days. However, archaeologists have discovered more and more evidence of Roman trade with Orkney. While much of this is difficult to date, one amphora, discovered at the Broch of Gurness, is of a type which had become obsolete by 60 AD. Did the King of Orkney travel over a thousand kilometres to Colchester to bend the knee before Claudius? It would have needed advance planning, probably predating the invasion. How was contact made? Probably not directly. Was there a network of inter-tribal and trading contacts stretching to the far north that could have negotiated an Orcadian presence? What, in practical terms, did the submission of such a distant tribe mean? We do not know the answers, but it remains a fascinating puzzle.

Claudius returned to Rome in glory. South-eastern Britain was declared a province of the Empire with its capital at Camulodunum and Aulus Plautius its first governor. No one records what happened to the elephants. The legions pressed onwards, and by the time Plautius was recalled to Rome in 46, they had reached a line from the Humber estuary to Lyme Bay in Dorset. Plautius was succeeded by Publius Ostorius Scapula who, over the next five years until his death, in 51 or 52, extended

Roman control over most of the South-Western Peninsula and up to the borders of Wales. It was a hard-fought progress. One of the principal obstacles was Cunobelin's son, Caratacus. He had been defeated by Plautius, probably on the River Medway, but had escaped. He now reappeared leading a confederation of the Silures from South Wales and Ordovices from North Wales and conducting a guerrilla campaign against Ostorius' forces. After several years, Ostorius manoeuvred him into a set-piece battle somewhere on the Welsh borders. The result was a crushing defeat for the British. Caratacus' family were captured, but he himself escaped again and fled to the territory of the Brigantes in modern-day Yorkshire and County Durham, where he threw himself on the mercy of their Queen Cartimandua. She may have been one of those who had submitted to Claudius, and certainly seems to have been one of the early client rulers, for she enjoyed some degree of Roman protection. She was loyal enough to turn Caratacus over to Ostorius in chains. He was then famously taken to Rome and paraded before the crowds during Claudius' official triumph. According to Tacitus, he made such a noble speech that Claudius pardoned him. Cassius Dio also portrays Caratacus as heroic and defiant with words that strike a chord in the post-colonial world: 'Why do you Romans, with all your wealth, still covet our poor huts?'[124]

Another aspect of the early stages of the Roman occupation is illustrated by the story of Togidumnus or Togidubnus, one of the early client kings who is often, though without definitive proof, associated with the palace uncovered at Fishbourne in West Sussex – the largest Roman-period residential building yet found in Britain. He was given Roman citizenship by Claudius and took the Roman name Tiberius Claudius Togidumnus – or sometimes Tiberius Claudius Cogidubnus. An inscription found in Chichester names him as *Rex Magnus,* or great king, which supports Tacitus' claim that he was the ruler of several *civitates*, or tribal territories. Was this Caratacus' brother, Togodumnus? The two were clearly contemporary. The differences in spelling mean nothing, reflecting only the difficulties the Romans had in attempting to transcribe unfamiliar names in a foreign, and to them barbarian, language. Cassius Dio, writing in Greek nearly two hundred years after the event, says that Togodumnus 'perished'.[125] Several commentators, among them Cunliffe, have suggested that this may be a mistranslation or misinterpretation of a Latin source and that it should read 'defeated'. Could Caratacus' brother simply have changed sides, thrown his lot in with the Romans and reaped the rewards? We shall probably never know, but the story of Togidumnus, as opposed to that of Caratacus, shows the advantages of cooperating – or collaborating – with the Romans.

The conquest continued, but only slowly. Ostorius was faced with a rebellion among the Iceni of East Anglia. They had voluntarily submitted to Rome, but when Ostorius broke his earlier undertakings and demanded they give up their weapons, treating them on the same footing as other, hostile tribes, resentment led to violence. They not only rebelled but encouraged neighbouring tribes to do the same. The revolt was put down, but it was a warning – which the Romans did not heed – that the British could be dangerous if not treated fairly. Elsewhere, it was equally hard going. The *legatus* or commander of the II Augusta legion was Titus Flavius Vespasianus, later to become the Emperor Vespasian (r.69–79). Suetonius says that he fought thirty battles, took control of twenty towns, and conquered two tribes. The only named location is Vectis, the Isle of Wight, but after Vespasian's return to Rome, Exeter (Isca Dumnoniorum) became the headquarters of II Augusta, so it seems likely that his troops subdued the south-west, storming the hillforts of Maiden Castle and Ham Hill, and defeating the Dumnonii and Durotriges.

When Ostorius died, Aulus Didius Gallus became governor. His main target was the Silures in South Wales. He failed to make much headway, but his campaign in the region has been linked with the founding of Cardiff – the name perhaps deriving from *Caer Didius*, the fort or castle of Didius. He also sent troops to support the client queen Cartimandua of the Brigantes, whose husband, Venutius, had decided to break his allegiance to Rome. Tacitus criticised Didius for being too defensive, but criticising the actions and attitudes of other governors is one of the techniques he uses in order to show his father-in-law, Agricola, in the best possible light. In 57, Didius was replaced by Quintus Veranius, who died within the year. His replacement was Gaius Suetonius Paulinus, a much more dynamic character. Suetonius Paulinus took control of most of Wales and, in 60, launched his dramatic attack on the druids in Anglesey (see Chapter 14), but almost immediately things began to unravel.

When King Prasutages of the Iceni died, control of the kingdom passed to his widow, Boudicca. Female succession was normal among British tribes. Before his death, however, he had appointed his two daughters and Emperor Nero as his joint heirs. This was a recognised form of client king behaviour. It reaffirmed loyalty to Rome, while safeguarding the position of the ruling family within the kingdom – or so Prasutages thought. Nero took a different view. Roman law stated that when a client king died, the emperor had the final say in who inherited what, so he ordered the procurator Catus Decianus – effectively the finance minister of the province of Britain – to take possession of the whole Icenian kingdom, both land and property. Prasutages had apparently accepted subsidies from Claudius in order to make his kingdom more Roman. Decianus seems to have interpreted these subsidies as loans and demanded that Boudicca repay them, secure in the knowledge that she would not be able to do so and that he would then have a justification to intervene. Whatever the legal niceties, Decianus' treatment of what was supposed to be a friendly tribe was severely heavy-handed. Resistance was met with force. The Iceni aristocracy were particularly badly treated, evicted from their houses and some even sold into slavery, but it was the treatment of Prasutages' family that provoked the greatest outrage: Queen Boudicca was flogged, and her two daughters raped by Roman soldiers. Whether this was done on Decianus' orders, or whether it was the result of indiscipline, we do not know. Whatever the case, it led to the first real challenge to Roman rule in Britain.

The Iceni rose in revolt. The Trinovantes joined them – their lands around Camulodunum had been heavily settled by Roman veterans, which may have led to tensions – and we can reasonably assume that others did so as well. Tacitus says that as Suetonius Paulinus marched south from Anglesey to confront the rebels he did so in the midst of the enemy.[126] Neither Queen Cartimandua and the Brigantes in the north, nor the tribes owing allegiance to Togidumnus in the south, seem to have joined the uprising. Had they done so, Tacitus would surely have remarked on their disloyalty.

In the seventeen years since the invasion, three towns had been developed along Roman lines: Camulodunum, Londinium, and Verulamium (the Roman name for Tasciovanus' capital, Verlamion). Politically, Camulodunum was the most important. It was the administrative capital and the most potent symbol of Rome's presence in Britain, with a huge temple to the now deified Claudius, built to celebrate his victory, at its centre. It was the natural first target for the rebels. Decianus sent two hundred, poorly armed troops to reinforce the garrison, but they could do nothing. The town was sacked and burned. Civilians and soldiers alike barricaded themselves inside the Temple of Claudius. After two days, Boudicca's warriors broke in, slaughtered everyone, and destroyed the building. Some of IX Hispania legion, under the command of Quintus Petillius Cerialis marched south, probably from their headquarters in Lindum Colonia, today's Lincoln, but they met a large force of British warriors, suffered heavy losses, and were forced to retreat. Meanwhile, Suetonius Paulinus had reached Londinium with the XIV Gemina and the XX legions. He had sent messages to the camp commandant of II Augusta in Exeter, Poenius Postumus, ordering him to send reinforcements but, for reasons we do not know, Postumus did not obey. Suetonius Paulinus realised he did not have enough men to defend Londinium against the approaching British and withdrew. Boudicca's army swept into what was already the biggest commercial and trading centre in the country, killing everyone who had not already fled. They hanged, they burnt, they crucified. According to Cassius Dio, they impaled people on wooden stakes and mutilated women. They quite simply destroyed the city, burning and demolishing everything they saw. In 1955, excavations ahead of a new road found a layer of burnt daub and ash at least thirty centimetres thick. Verulamium suffered the same fate.

Eventually, Suetonius Paulinus brought the British to battle, probably in the Midlands, somewhere along the Roman road known as Watling Street. Boudicca's forces heavily outnumbered Suetonius Paulinus' legions, but they were no match for the disciplined and tactically superior Romans and were routed. It is difficult to get a clear sense of how many people were involved. Cassius Dio claims that there were 230,000 British warriors in the final battle. Tacitus claims that 80,000 British troops died, as against four hundred Romans. He also claims that when the British sacked Londinium and Verulamium, they left 70,000 dead. But Tacitus frequently exaggerates numbers to make Romans victories look more impressive and enemy atrocities more barbaric. What the true numbers were we simply cannot tell. Cassius Dio says that after the battle Boudicca became ill and died.[127] Tacitus says she took poison.[128] The fate of her daughters is unknown. Hearing of the victory, Poenius Postumus committed suicide, presumably rather than face accusations of cowardice. Suetonius Paulinus began the task of re-establishing control, meting out harsh treatment to almost all the British tribes. He was eventually recalled to Rome and replaced by Publius Petronius Turpilianus who, according to Tacitus, took a more conciliatory approach.

Boudicca's revolt was a short episode, which has attained an iconic status in traditional accounts of British history: the defiant native queen, standing tall in her chariot, leading her people against the armies of the Roman oppressors. This view sits oddly alongside the other traditional narrative that it was the Romans who brought order, justice, and civilisation to Britain. Both views are, of course, products of their time. Boudicca's name was not widely known until the revival of interest in all things Celtic in the eighteenth century; and it was only in the second half of the nineteenth century that she was elevated to heroic status. Boudicca became a female national figurehead, at first a prototype and then a mirror of the status accorded to Queen Victoria as the embodiment of the nation. Interestingly, the name Boudicca – and its numerous variant forms, the most common being Boadicea – derives from the feminine form of a Proto-Celtic adjective, *boudīkā*, meaning victorious, so that the names Boudicca and Victoria have the same meaning.[129]

The contention that the Romans were the fount of civilisation has a longer pedigree. As early as the late fifth or early sixth century, the British cleric, Gildas, in his polemical sermon *De Excidio et Conquestu Britanniae* (*On the Ruin and Conquest of Britain*), lamented the passing of the Roman age and the barbarism of his own times. From the Renaissance onwards, the rediscovered texts of the classical authors formed the core of a gentleman's and a gentlewoman's education, which meant that the educated classes viewed history through Greek- and Roman-tinted spectacles. The coming of the Romantic Movement, and then the Celtic Revival, qualified, but did not materially change the situation. If Boudicca could be seen as a precursor to Queen Victoria, then – despite the inherent contradictions – the Roman Empire could be seen as a precursor of the British. Boudicca fought oppression, but it was the Romans who brought the light of civilisation to barbarian peoples. Although there were those who questioned the moral basis of the Empire in the aftermath of the First World War, this view remained current until well after the Second, and it was not until the 1960s and 70s that the primacy of the Classics in the British education system was ended. A fascinating example of conflicting attitudes is contained in an 1848 translation of Gildas by the Reverend J.A. Giles. Gildas describes Boudicca as a 'deceitful lioness [who] put to death the rulers who had been left among [the Britons] to unfold more fully and to confirm the enterprises of the Romans.' He adds that the Romans rapidly took 'vengeance on the crafty foxes.'[130] The Reverend Giles felt it necessary to add a partisan footnote:

> The Britons who fought under Boadicea were anything but 'crafty foxes.' 'Bold lions' is a much more appropriate appellation; they would also have been victorious if they had had half the military advantages of the Romans.[131]

From a twenty-first century viewpoint – no doubt reflecting our own preconceptions – we are more inclined to see the Roman attempt to civilise the Britons as subordinate to their overall aim of imposing structures of power and control that would allow them to exploit the wealth and the resources of their new province. With the possible exception of Caesar, whose interests may have reflected his strategic and military concerns, there seems to have been little attempt to understand the Britons. Despite a century of closer contacts and increasing trade, Roman attitudes towards the British did not change between Cicero's letters, written at the time of Caesar's invasions and the inscription on Claudius' triumphal arch. It was these attitudes, both patronising and contemptuous, that led to Boudicca's revolt, the first – and for the next three centuries, the only – real challenge to Roman control of southern Britain.

To the Roman soldiers patrolling outside their legionary headquarters at Lindum Colonia or Isca Dumnoniorum, the British must have seemed a genuinely barbarian lot. The Roman Empire could not have worked if its soldiers and administrators had not felt a sense of engagement with its aims. The concept of citizenship and its importance to native-born Romans and to those subject peoples to whom it was later extended is proof enough of this, but in Britain the Romans saw nothing that might resemble a polity or a unifying ideology. Tribal loyalties were paramount, and the tribes themselves allied or fought with each other on the basis of shifting patterns of self-interest. Of course, the Romans themselves often behaved in the same way, but to them it was the context that was important. They simply could not see anything of intellectual or moral value emerging from the barbarian surroundings of Britain – or indeed Germany. One or two tribes stood by their commitments to Rome, but among the rest there was sufficient disaffection and double-dealing to confirm the Romans in their opinion: the British were simply not to be trusted. These same patrolling legionaries would also have heard horror stories of how the druids conducted human sacrifices, choosing an individual and then plunging

> a dagger into him in the region above the diaphragm, and when the stricken victim has fallen they read the future from the manner of his fall and from the twitching of his limbs, as well as from the gushing of the blood.[132]

They would have heard how when their enemies fell in battle, the British would

> cut off their heads and fasten them about the necks of their horses ... [and] carry them off as booty, singing a paean over them and ... these first-fruits of battle they fasten by nails upon their houses, just as men do, in certain kinds of hunting... The heads of their most distinguished enemies they embalm in cedar-oil and carefully preserve in a chest, and exhibit them to strangers.[133]

In the end, while it was Roman brutality that provided the spark for Boudicca's revolt, once the fire was lit, the British proved themselves every bit as brutal and bloody as the Romans suspected.

At this point, it is worth considering the oft-repeated claim that Celtic warriors went into battle naked. It appears in Polybius, Diodorus Siculus, and Dionysius of Halicarnassus.[134] Caesar, who had more direct experience of Celts than any of them, talks about the Suebi wearing nothing but skins, but does not mention naked warriors.[135] The famous statue of the 'Dying Gaul' depicts a warrior wearing only a torc around his neck, but we have plenty of archaeological evidence for Celtic armour. Some Celtic warriors may have gone into battle naked – perhaps the equivalent of Norse beserkers – but not the majority. The emphasis placed on the idea by Greek and Roman historians with no personal experience of the matter was another way of emphasising the sheer barbarity of these enemies of Rome.

The suppression of Boudicca's revolt was followed by a period of rebuilding and stabilisation. Records are so scarce that it is difficult to know what happened under Petronius Turpilianus (governor from 61 to 63) and his successor, Marcus Trebellius Maximus (governor 63 to 69). It may have been very little. In those areas that supported the rebellion, retribution was probably severe. Many men will not have returned to their villages. Some of those who did will have been executed or sold into slavery. We can only guess at the effect on communities and on their ability to farm the land. Trebellius began the reconstruction of Camulodunum, while Londinium seems to have been rebuilt more quickly than the other towns, though whether by the Roman authorities or by the merchants and traders who gained their livelihood from the port we do not know. It may have been during this period that Londinium became formally recognised as the capital of the province.

In 69, following the murder of Nero, the Empire descended into civil war. It was the Year of Four Emperors. First Galba, then Otho seized power. In Britain, the XX legion – now with the additional title Valeria Victrix, possibly as recognition of its role in suppressing Boudicca's revolt – declared for Vitellius, whose power base was among the legions on the Rhine, and forced the governor, Trebellius, to flee to the Continent. By the end of April, Vitellius was in control in Rome and had been recognised as Emperor by the Senate. He appointed one of his own supporters, Marcus Vettius Bolanus, as governor of Britain. Tacitus claims that Bolanus was ineffective. Whether he was or not, he certainly had a baptism of fire. The men of XIV Gemina, who had been marched from Britain to the Balkans, from the Balkans to Turin, and then back to Britain were disaffected and could not be trusted – they were withdrawn to the Rhine and replaced by II Adiutrix. Venutius, one-time husband of Queen Cartimandua, was stirring up unrest among the Brigantes. Bolanus sent auxiliaries to rescue Cartimandua, but he was not able to dislodge Venutius. By this time, the situation in Rome had changed again. Forces loyal to Vespasian had defeated Vitellius and, although the civil war continued in parts of the Empire for another year, Vespasian was recognised as sole Emperor. Policy towards Britain changed immediately, presumably influenced by Vespasian's own experience of serving with II Augusta and, as with Claudius, by a new emperor's need to prove himself a conqueror. Bolanus retained his position as governor until 71, but Gnaeus Julius Agricola was appointed as the new commander of XX Valeria Victrix, and it was clear that expansion was once again the order of the day.

Bolanus' replacement was the same Quintus Petillius Cerialis who had commanded IX Hispania during Boudicca's revolt. He arrived in Britain fresh from putting down a revolt on the Rhine and at once embarked on a campaign against the Brigantes. What sources are available suggest that

Cerialis led his troops, probably his old legion, IX Hispania, up the east coast, while Agricola led XX Valeria Victrix up the western side of the island. The advantages of having two leaders who had both served in Britain must have been considerable. We know no details of the campaign, beyond the fact that the power of the Brigantes was effectively broken. The legions reached the Solway—Tyne line and may have penetrated further north. Luguvalium, modern day Carlisle, had long been an important settlement, possibly the capital of the Carvetii tribe, whose territory comprised much of the present-day Lake District. Dendrochronology dates the Roman fort there to 72 or 73. The first camp at Eboracum, today's York, also dates from this campaign.

In 73, Agricola left Britain, having been promoted to become governor of Gallia Aquitania. Later the same year, or perhaps in 74, Cerialis was replaced by Sextus Julius Frontinus, of whose term in office we know only the broadest of outlines. Rather than move further north, he seems to have sought to consolidate south of the Solway—Tyne frontier. He is credited with conquering the Silures in South Wales; he campaigned against the Ordovices in North Wales; and he presumably continued the task begun under Cerialis of pacifying and garrisoning the Brigantes. He may also may have been responsible for founding the legionary fortress at Chester (Deva Victrix), as a base for XX Valeria Victrix.

17   Romans in the North

In 77 or 78, Agricola returned, this time as governor, a position he retained for an unprecedented period of nearly seven years. Tacitus' biography of his father-in-law contains no firm dates and few identifiable place names; it is also highly flattering; yet without it, we would know almost nothing of Agricola's term as governor, or of the history of Britain at that time. Immediately on his arrival, although it was late in the year for campaigning, Agricola completed the conquest of the Ordovices and retook Anglesey. The next year, he probably sought to consolidate Roman control of the territory of the Brigantes; and he may have begun operations north of the Solway—Tyne line. In his third campaigning season – either 79 or 80, depending when he arrived – he moved decisively north, up the east coast as far as the Tay estuary and possibly beyond. When the season ended, he established a line of camps which were garrisoned throughout the winter months, denying the British tribes the opportunity to access winter food supplies, or to reoccupy territory lost during the summer. These camps became the basis of what is known as the Gask Ridge system: a line of so-called glen-blocking forts, designed to impede or at least give early warning of tribesmen coming down from the mountains to raid the lowland areas.

The fourth season was one of consolidation. Agricola established a temporary frontier based on a string of turf-and-timber forts, known as *praesidia*, across the Forth—Clyde isthmus, and created a network of strategic roads, in many cases still visible in today's system of trunk roads and motorways. These roads, lined with forts no more than a day's march from each other, enabled him to a keep close watch over the territory of several hostile tribes, and to move troops and supplies quickly in case of need. His western supply line ran north from the newly-established legionary headquarters at Chester and through the territory of the Brigantes and the Selgovae to Carlisle. North of Carlisle it divided, with one branch following Nithsdale and the other following Annandale, before they rejoined each other at the fort of Crawford in the Clyde Valley. The eastern supply line, later known as Dere Street, ran north from York, bridged the Tyne at Corbridge, and crossed the Cheviots to reach Newstead in the Tweed Valley, and Elginhaugh near Edinburgh. Newstead (also known as Trimontium) was of particular strategic importance. Located below Eildon Hill North, where the troublesome Selgovae maintained their capital, it was positioned so as to prevent them from sweeping down and cutting the Romans' north—south supply line. Running east—west between Corbridge and Carlisle and connecting these two routes was the Stanegate, which followed the border between the territory of the Selgovae to the north and the Brigantes to the south.

Tacitus says that Agricola's fifth campaigning season concentrated on the west coast, but we do not know whether that means Dumfries and Galloway, the lands of the Novantae, or north of the Clyde. He may even have contemplated invading Ireland at this point (see Chapter 19). The following year, he switched back to the east. His army marched north beyond the Firth of Forth, shadowed offshore by the fleet which brought supplies and sometimes moved ahead of the advance, raiding and burning coastal areas. Agricola may have been trying to provoke the British into full-scale confrontation, but they continued to use guerrilla tactics, melting away into the mountains and glens when threatened. Only when Agricola feared he might be surrounded and split his forces into three did they risk an attack. The British targeted IX Hispania, which they apparently knew to be the Romans' weakest link, but were driven off, again disappearing into the hills where the Romans could not pursue them.

Agricola's seventh and last campaigning season culminated in the battle of Mons Graupius. Like Boudicca's revolt, Mons Graupius has probably attracted much more attention than it deserves. No one knows where it took place – indeed, whether it took place at all has been questioned. Agricola's army again crossed the Firth of Forth and took a route through the eastern lowlands, but we do not know how far north it reached. In his account of the battle, Tacitus invents an eve-of-battle speech for Calgacus (the name translates as 'The Swordsman'), the leader of the Britons, who says 'there are no tribes beyond us, nothing indeed but waves and rocks.'[136] In a parallel, and equally fictitious, speech to his troops, Agricola says 'we now occupy the last confines of Britain.'[137] Both statements are intended to suggest that the battle took place at the extreme north of mainland Britain, thus supporting Tacitus' claim that his father-in-law completed the conquest of Britain. This is extremely unlikely. Camps capable of accommodating Agricola's army – two legions, three thousand cavalry, and eight thousand auxiliaries – would normally have left at least some traces on the landscape, yet no camps of any size have been identified north of the Great Glen. However, a camp of the right size has been identified at Durno, near Inverurie in Aberdeenshire. The surrounding landscape fits Tacitus' description of the geography of the battle, with the isolated hill of Bennachie as Mons Graupius, but no supporting archaeological evidence has been discovered.

According to Tacitus, the battle was a triumph for Agricola, ending only when night fell, and leaving 10,000 British dead compared with just three hundred and sixty Romans. The number of British dead is almost certainly one of Tacitus' exaggerations, but despite such inflated claims he cannot disguise the fact that the victory was not followed up. The next morning there was no enemy to be seen. The British had once again disappeared into the mountains. Roman supply lines were already stretched. It was late in the season. There was neither the time nor the logistical support to march the army into the Highlands. Agricola turned south, taking hostages along the way, and encouraging his men to loot and burn as they went. He also ordered the fleet, which had supported his march northwards, to sail all the way round Britain to demonstrate that it really was an island.

Agricola was recalled to Rome that winter. This was not surprising – he had already served twice as long as any previous governor – but, again according to Tacitus, the Emperor Domitian gave him a cool reception. He received a formal kiss of welcome but no other mark of recognition. Agricola's achievements entitled him to expect the governorship of a major province, but he never received another appointment, and lived the last ten years of his life in retirement. Was Domitian jealous of his success and suspicious of his motives? Or did the Emperor believe Agricola had exaggerated his achievements in Britain? Some writers have suggested that Mons Graupius was a fiction, invented by Agricola to boost his reputation. Tacitus is the only author to mention it. It has left no trace in oral tradition or folklore. It does not feature in the histories of IX Hispania and XX Valeria Victrix, the two legions that were present. It is not commemorated by any monuments or inscriptions. Nor is there any archaeological evidence. On the other hand, for Agricola to invent a major battle when none took place would surely have risked his whole reputation, if not his life. Men who had served with him would surely have come forward to refute the claim. An encounter of some kind probably took place, although how big and how significant remains an open question. Pollen analysis indicates a decline in farming activity across the Aberdeenshire region in the first century AD, which could perhaps be attributable to the aftermath of a battle in which many local people died. What is clear is that Mons Graupius was not the decisive battle Tacitus claimed it to be. The Britons were defeated, but not conquered. Agricola had penetrated further than any previous governor; he had extended, even doubled, the area of Britain under Roman control; but he had not conquered the whole island.

Agricola's campaigns – not only maintaining the frontline soldiery, but also building and garrisoning of over sixty new camps and forts, and constructing 2,000 kilometres of new roads – inevitably placed huge demands on reserves of manpower and resources. We can only presume that he reduced the size of garrisons in the south, bringing men north to support his advance and maintain control of the newly conquered areas. In theory, the Roman Empire maintained an army of twenty-eight legions, plus auxiliaries and cavalry. The four legions stationed in Britain – a small, new province in the north-west of the Empire – represented 15 per cent of the core of the official Roman army. Including auxiliaries and cavalry *alae*, Roman military strength during Agricola's term as governor probably exceeded 40,000 and may have reached 50,000. Even by Roman standards these were large numbers.

Agricola's Mons Graupius campaign was the high-water mark of Roman control of British territory. On his march north, he had marked down Inchtuthil as a suitable location for a fort. On a plateau overlooking the Tay and strategically placed to control access to and from the Highlands, it was to be the headquarters of a legion responsible for maintaining control in the north. Work began in 83 or 84, but was abandoned, probably in 86, before the fort was completed. Domitian himself seems to have taken the decision to abandon Agricola's northern conquests. He did so because he needed men. The army of the Kingdom of Dacia had crossed the Danube and taken the Romans by surprise, wiping out one entire legion. The II Adutrix was withdrawn from Britain and marched rapidly to the Balkans. With only three legions, it was not possible to maintain a military presence in the north, and the army moved back to Agricola's turf-and-timber frontier across the Forth—Clyde isthmus. 'Britain was conquered, then discarded,' says Tacitus.[138] This is something of an exaggeration, but the decision to abandon the north did mark a moment of retreat, possibly the first time that the armies of Rome had been forced to admit that they could not hold on to a given region.

We have little information about the next period of the Roman occupation. We know that at the time of Domitian's assassination in 96, the Romans still controlled what is now southern Scotland and Northumberland; and the archaeological record tells us that by 105 they had withdrawn to the Solway—Tyne line. The new frontier probably extended from Gateshead in the east to the Solway Firth in the west, its central section following the Stanegate with its line of forts built by Agricola thirty years earlier. What caused this second withdrawal? A tribal insurrection or a sustained series of attacks are the most likely explanation. Six forts – including Newstead, and one at Corbridge on the new frontier – show evidence of burning. When forts were no longer needed, it was normal for the legions to dismantle them and burn everything that might be of use to an enemy, but these forts appear to have been demolished and burned in a less than orderly manner. At Newstead numerous severed heads and large quantities of damaged equipment have been found, while Corbridge, guarding a strategic crossing place on the Tyne, was the only one of the six to have been immediately rebuilt, suggesting an urgent need to re-establish a secure frontier. About this time, the Romans strengthened their position by concluding a treaty with the Votadini, who occupied the coastal lands between the Tyne and the Forth. Votadini territory became an independent buffer state allied to Rome and reaped considerable rewards as a result. Those northern tribes who maintained their hostility to Rome – the Selgovae, and their northern neighbours the Damnonii, the Novantae – probably lacked the strength to force the Romans back from the Solway—Tyne line, but they may have mounted an insurrection sufficiently disruptive for the Romans to conclude that, with manpower now limited, the hostile and largely unproductive lands between the isthmus and the Stanegate were not worth holding on to.

The withdrawal to the Stanegate may have gained the Romans a short period of peace, but the northern tribes were not ready or willing for peaceful co-existence. Although we have no details, it seems that there was a serious outbreak of trouble on the northern frontier, and perhaps also in Wales, shortly after the accession of the Emperor Hadrian in 117. Some time after that, Britain was reinforced by three thousand men drawn from the legions in Spain and Germany, suggesting that the tribes continued to be troublesome. We do not know when they arrived or where they were stationed, but the most likely scenario is that they immediately preceded or accompanied Hadrian when he visited Britain in 122.

Hadrian probably arrived at the Roman quayside in Newcastle in July 122, possibly on a ship called *Radians*, the only Roman trireme in British waters. He had already appointed Aulus Platorius Nepos as the new governor of Britain and, accompanied by a retinue of troops and court officials, the two of them reconnoitred the course of what would become Hadrian's Wall. Hadrian is recorded as camping out and drinking wine with the soldiers, determined to demonstrate that an Emperor could be just as tough as they were. When he succeeded Trajan in 117, the Roman Empire was at its greatest territorial extent. He ruled twenty-six provinces and controlled thirty legions and ten fleets. From the beginning of his reign, he decided against further expansion. His policy was to define and consolidate the Empire's borders in order to build prosperity within. In Germany,

Map 17   The Roman Conquest

he transformed Domitian's line of watchtowers into a solid fence made of some 250,000 oak trees; in North Africa, he built sections of wall across tribal transhumance routes; in Britain he went further, building a wall from one side of the island to the other.

Hadrian's Wall stretched for 117 kilometres from Wallsend in the east to Bowness-on-Solway in the west. It included fourteen forts and eighty milecastles, and its northern face was painted with white lime mortar, making it visible from a considerable distance. In the west, it was extended by a line of five forts following the Cumbrian coast from Bowness to (probably) Ravenglass, connected by a track and a shallow ditch and bank. The project must have been close to completion by 126 when Platorius Nepos left Britain, and the Wall itself seems to have been operational over most of its length by 128. Even today with modern machinery and technology at our disposal, six years would be an impressively short time to complete such a project, but, given that every stone had to be quarried and shaped by hand, transported on ox- or horse-drawn waggons, and then hoisted into place, it was a truly remarkable effort. The fact that the last forty-eight kilometres were initially built of turf, because of a shortage of lime mortar, and only rebuilt in stone a few years later, does not diminish the achievement.

The Wall had many functions. It was not a city wall, intended as an unbreachable boundary, although its core function was clearly defensive. Its sheer scale probably deterred some attacks, and an assault anywhere along its length could be held off long enough for reinforcements to be summoned from neighbouring forts and milecastles. The Wall allowed patrols, both cavalry and infantry, to monitor the activities of tribes to the north. A handful of outlying forts to the north – Bewcastle, Birrens, Netherby in the west, and later High Rochester and Habitancum in the east – evidently fulfilled the same function. The Wall also allowed for the monitoring and control of those passing into and out of Roman-controlled territory. It divided the Selgovae from the Brigantes, both of whom the Romans considered hostile, and could serve as a barrier preventing them from joining together or coordinating their attacks. The Wall would also have acted as a customs post. There is ample evidence of Roman goods circulating north of the Wall, and little doubt that the northern tribes would have wanted to sell their goods in the secondary settlements that grew up along the length of the Wall to the south. The Romans did not object to trade as long as it could be taxed. The Wall did not permanently overawe the northern tribes, who continued to press and attack the Romans whenever they saw an opportunity, but the archaeological record indicates a significant improvement in agricultural production, both

17 Romans in the North

arable and livestock, south of the Wall, perhaps attributable to a reduction in levels of raiding and violence.

In 138, Hadrian died and was succeeded by Antoninus Pius. Shortly afterwards, in 139 or 140, Antoninus ordered the governor, Lollius Urbicus, to retake the lands north of the Wall that had been given up some thirty-five years earlier. No one knows why. Antoninus was not a soldier, so he may, like Claudius, have been seeking military glory to enhance his image in the eyes of the Roman people, yet he seems to have been a largely pacific emperor. The only other example of him pursuing an aggressive policy was in response to a revolt among the Moorish people of Mauretania in 152. There is no evidence to indicate widespread or severe fighting around the time of Antoninus' accession, but it seems likely that the decision was taken because of continued attacks on the Wall or on the Roman forts to the north of it. The northern frontier had only ever been peaceful for short periods and would continue to be troublesome until the end of the Roman occupation.

There must have been resistance to Lollius' northern campaign, for it took him two or three years to reoccupy the lands up the Forth—Clyde isthmus. Almost immediately, probably in 142 and on the orders of the Emperor, work began on the construction of the Antonine Wall, along the line of Agricola's frontier. The isthmus is the narrowest part of Britain, and the new wall was only 63 kilometres long, half the length of Hadrian's Wall. It was built of turf blocks, not stone, and took between six and twelve years to complete. It included twenty-four forts, plus one outlying fort to the west, one north of the Wall to the east, and an unknown number of smaller buildings, similar to the milecastles on Hadrian's Wall. Some forts that had been built by Agricola, among them Newstead to the south, were rebuilt and enlarged, while others were added. If the number of forts is anything to go by, there was a greater need to protect lines of communication than previously.

Somewhere between 155 and 158, there seems to have been trouble south of the new frontier. The evidence is sparse and sometimes ambiguous, but we can guess that the Brigantes were, as usual, restless, and it is possible that the Carvetii from the Lake District – an area that had been largely bypassed by the Romans – were involved. We do not know what happened, nor what its impact was, but somewhere towards the end of his reign, possibly in 158, Antoninus ordered his wall to be abandoned. We do not know why he decided to move the frontier north, and we do not know why he chose to withdraw from it. He had ordered its construction less than twenty years previously and it had been operational for less than a decade. We can only assume that continual unrest among the tribes made it untenable in terms of resources. The forts were dismantled, and materials burned, this time in a careful and orderly fashion. The frontier returned to Hadrian's Wall, where the archaeology shows that neglected forts, milecastles, and other building were restored, and defences along its whole length repaired and strengthened. To the north of the reinstated frontier, Newstead and a number of strategically important forts were retained and garrisoned.

According to the *Historia Augusta*, a compilation of thirty biographies of Roman Emperors probably dating from the fourth century, there was more unrest in Britain in the 170s. No archaeological traces have been found, but Emperor Marcus Aurelius, who was heavily involved in wars on the Danube, sent first some German cavalry, and then 5,500 Sarmatian cavalry to Britain. The Germans and at least some of the Sarmatians were based at Ribchester in central Lancashire, suggesting that the tribes in that region – the Brigantes (again) and the Setantii (or Segantii), who lived on what is now the Lancashire coast – may have been causing trouble. There was more trouble in 180, during the reign of Emperor Commodus (r.180–192). Tribes from the north swept across Hadrian's Wall, creating havoc and killing 'a certain general and his soldiers'.[139] A new governor, Ulpius Marcellus, led the fight back. He seems to have abandoned the outlying forts and concentrated on conducting a series of punitive raids. He may have concluded some kind of peace treaty with the tribes immediately to the north of the Wall, though this is not certain. In 184, Commodus was hailed *Imperator* in Rome, and took the additional title of Britannicus, suggesting that Marcellus had reported the situation under control, but another problem arose almost immediately when all three legions under Marcellus' command mutinied. The mutiny appears to have been provoked by what the legions considered Marcellus' excessively severe discipline, but whatever the cause it was serious enough for some 1,500 soldiers to march to Rome to put their grievances to the Emperor. Such a situation could scarely have been kept secret from the British – especially given the reduction in manpower – and can only have further weakened Roman authority. Commodus acted quickly, replacing Marcellus with Publius

Helvius Pertinax, who brought the mutinies under control, but made himself so unpopular in the process that he, too, had to resign and return to Rome, probably in 187.

The Emperor Commodus was assassinated on the last day of 192. Pertinax became Emperor, but lasted barely three months before he, too, was assassinated. He was followed by Didius Julianus, who had organised the murder of Pertinax and paid the Praetorian Guard to put him on the throne. He lasted only nine weeks. There followed a civil war between three rival claimants: Gaius Pescennius Niger, who was Imperial legate in Syria; Septimius Severus, who was governor of Pannonia Superior; and Decimus Clodius Albinus, who had been appointed governor of Britain in 191. Severus was nearest to Rome and seized control. He appeared to conciliate Albinus by offering him the title 'Caesar', implying that he would be next in line of succession, and allowing him to mint his own coins. In 194, Severus defeated Niger and had him beheaded. With the Senate favouring Albinus, a clash between the two remaining claimants was inevitable. Albinus had been hailed as Emperor by the legions of Britain, and when he crossed to Gaul in 196, he took with him as many soldiers as he could, including a significant number from the Wall. He gained more support as he moved south through Gaul, but not enough. In February 197, he and Severus faced each other just outside Lugdunum, modern Lyon. Cassius Dio claims there were 150,000 on each side,[140] unquestionably an inflated figure, but there is no doubt it was a bloody battle. In the end, Albinus realised he was defeated and committed suicide. Severus had his head impaled on a stake and sent to Rome.

Severus was now sole emperor. Britain may not have been his main priority – his principal concern seems to have been to return to Rome and extract a fearsome revenge on all who had opposed him – but it still posed serious and immediate problems. The three legions stationed there were desperately under strength. At least half of their men – and very probably more – had followed Albinus to Gaul, and many will have been lost in the fighting at Lugdunum. Severus could hardly have regarded them as trustworthy, but nonetheless he sent them back, for the British had taken advantage of their absence. Some of the northern tribes had swept south over the Wall, while others to the south were in open revolt.

We do not know which tribes were involved. Cassius Dio says that there were two tribal confederations living north of the Wall: the Maeatae and the Caledonians. The Maeatae probably controlled the area north of the Votadini, between Stirling and Perth, and the name Dumyat Hill in Ochil Hills is often held to derive from *Dun Maeatae*, the fort of the Maeatae. According to Cassius Dio, the Caledonii lived further north.[141] This seems to confirm the evidence of Ptolemy's map that they lived in the Grampian region as far north as the Great Glen (see Chapter 12). The Maeatae certainly crossed the Wall, possibly in company with the Selgovae and the Novantae. The Caledonii do not seem to have joined in at this stage. South of the Wall, the Brigantes were certainly involved and probably responsible for the destruction of forts at Ilkley and Bainbridge in Yorkshire.

How far south of the Wall the trouble spread and how much damage was done is difficult to judge, but we know that when the new governor, Virius Lupus, arrived in 197, he found a province in chaos. For perhaps as much as a year, there had been no governor to command and hardly any troops to keep order. Forts and other buildings had also been destroyed in Wales, and there may have been localised disorder elsewhere. We do not know how quickly the troops that had followed Albinus returned, whether Severus had made up their numbers, or how they were deployed when they arrived, but none of this would have happened immediately. According to Cassius Dio, the Caledonii were about break 'their promises' – perhaps the agreement they made with Ulpius Marcellus in the early 180s – and support the Maeatae.[142] As a result, Lupus was forced to buy off the Maeatae to gain time and secure the release of the prisoners they had taken. The process of restoring order and rebuilding the military infrastructure evidently took a long time, although we do not know whether this was due to a lack of manpower and resources, or to continued resistance on the part of the tribes, or perhaps both. Archaeological evidence suggests that the rebuilding of forts along the full length of Hadrian's Wall did not begin until 205.

In 208, the Emperor Severus, his wife, and his two troublesome sons, Caracalla and Geta, set off from Rome for Britain. Cassius Dio says this was because he wished to get his sons away from Rome, and because the legions were idle.[143] Herodian agrees that he disliked the life his sons were leading, but states that the governor at the time, probably Lucius Alfenus Senecio, had asked for reinforcements or an imperial visit because 'the barbarians were in revolt, overrunning the country, looting and destroying almost everything...'¹⁴⁴ The two accounts seem contradictory. Herodian is not always the most accurate of chroniclers, and he does tend to exaggerate. Nor is his version of events backed up by archaeological evidence. Yet the claim is interesting in that it assumes that at any given time Roman Britain was likely to be in the throes of trouble with the barbarians.

Severus established his headquarters at York and, in 209, marched north taking his son Caracalla with him. Geta was left at York and charged with the civil administration of the province. Cassius Dio says Severus wanted to conquer the whole island, but he may only have intended a major punitive expedition. The tribes were clearly alarmed when they heard of his approach and offered terms. Severus, having evidently set his sights on military glory, was not interested. Like Agricola, Severus marched his army up the east coast, shadowed by the fleet offshore, but we do not know how far he advanced. Agricola probably reached the Moray Firth, but it seems unlikely that Severus progressed far beyond modern-day Aberdeen. Even if he did, Cassius Dio's claim that 'he approached the extremity of the island ... [where] he made most accurate observations of the variation of the sun's motion and the length of the days and the nights' cannot be true and probably stems from an inadequate knowledge of geography.¹⁴⁵

The campaign was far from an unqualified success. Cassius Dio lists the problems the army faced. They were unused to the demanding terrain. They were subject to sustained guerrilla tactics. The enemy would place sheep and cattle as a lure for Roman foraging parties, make a sudden attack, and then disappear into the hills and forests. He says that 50,000 Romans died – obviously an exaggeration – and that Severus failed to bring the tribes to battle, but then makes the surprising statement that the Emperor 'forced the Britons to come to terms' and 'give up a large part of their territory.'¹⁴⁶ What happened? Did the Romans starve the tribes into submission by destroying their crops and farmland? Or is this the kind of spin we saw with Caesar and Agricola, designed to boost Severus' reputation in Rome? Whatever was agreed did not last for long. By the time Severus was back in York, the Maeatae were again in revolt, but by now he was too ill to command the army himself and, in 210, sent Caracalla north with orders that can only be described as genocidal. The legionaries were to kill everyone they met; they were even to kill babies in their mothers' wombs. How far these orders were executed we do not know, but the revolt continued, with the Caledonii now joining in with the Maeatae. Severus was preparing a third northern expedition when he died in York in February 211.

In 212, Caracalla returned to Rome. He became sole Emperor by ordering the murder of his brother, Geta, and secured his position by killing some 20,000 people he thought might not display the loyalty he expected. However, in 211, before leaving Britain, he conducted one last campaign north of the Forth—Clyde isthmus. Again, we have no details, but he concluded treaties with the tribes that proved more effective and longer-lasting than any previous agreements. Given his character and subsequent events, it is difficult to see how this could have been achieved without another murderous campaign. Caracalla withdrew the frontier to Hadrian's Wall where it stayed. The zone to the north was patrolled by Roman forces, and several outlying forts were reoccupied and maintained for their use. The tribes may have given hostages; they may have allowed the Romans to recruit from among their people; and they may also have received subsidies. Whatever the terms agreed, on this occasion they were adhered to for over eighty years. Information is sparse but, while there were almost certainly occasional raids and localised disturbances, there were major no outbreaks of violence on the northern border until 296.

It took Caesar just over seven years to conquer Gaul. It took a succession of Roman governors and emperors one hundred and sixty-eight years to accept that they could not conquer the northern part of Britain. Of course, the two regions are not directly comparable. Northern Britain offered far fewer rewards and presented far greater difficulties. It had none of the strategic and economic value of Gaul. The climate was hostile, especially for those used to the Mediterranean, and any invading force was faced with formidable logistical difficulties. The west and centre were mountainous, and any advancing army risked ambush or attacks on its rear. Even the eastern route, preferred by both Agricola and Severus, was swampy and thickly forested. Nowhere were there crops or animals sufficient to feed a large army, so food and other necessities had to be transported up an extended supply line or brought in by the fleet. And the tribes were unremittingly hostile.

As far as the Romans were concerned, the constant hostility of the tribes could be explained simply: they were barbarians and that was how barbarians behaved. The tribes saw things differently. It was natural for them to defend their territory when the Romans invaded, and it is clear from their guerrilla tactics that they understood from the beginning that they might wear down the legions but could not actually defeat them – the only pitched battle during those hundred and sixty-eight years was Mons Graupius and, as noted earlier, the scale of that is disputed. Given that understanding, we have to ask why, once the Wall was built and the frontier established – and allowing for a period of comparative peace following Caracalla's 211 campaign – they continued their attacks, breaching the Wall when they could, even at times when they were not directly threatened. The Votadini, like Togidumnus in Sussex, cooperated with the Romans and reaped the benefits. Compared with their neighbours, the ever-troublesome Brigantes, their lands show few signs of military activity. To judge from the archaeology, notably at Traprain Law, they had access to wine and other Roman luxury goods, and they may also have received subsidies. Why then did the other tribes regularly renew their attacks? Were they looking for plunder? Was the attraction the stockpiles of food, weapons, and other equipment held on the Wall and in its associated settlements? Did the lands south of the Wall offer the prospect of cattle and sheep? These were, after all, the lands ravaged by the Border reivers between the thirteenth and seventeenth centuries. Or did an attack on the Wall become a kind of challenge or ordeal that every tribal leader had to undergo?

One legacy of the Roman failure to conquer the northern tribes is the concept of a border between the north and south of Britain. The present border between England and Scotland does not follow Hadrian's Wall or the Antonine Wall: it runs from the western end of Hadrian's Wall to the east coast just north of the Tweed Estuary. It is a border that has been fought over, moved, extended, and bent out of shape in various ways. There have been times, particularly between the end of the Roman occupation at the beginning of the fifth century and the defining of Scotland's territory in the ninth, when it might have disappeared. The dividing line has at different times been tribal, linguistic, cultural, political, or a combination of any of those elements; but ever since the Roman occupation – indeed, ever since Agricola – there has been a border between the polities of the north of Britain, however divided, and those of the south.

18 Romans in the South

The guiding philosophy of the Roman Empire was power; and the basis of power was control. Economic factors were a secondary consideration, which usually came into play only after a territory had been conquered. Had it been otherwise, it is quite possible that Britain would never have been invaded. There was considerable mineral wealth and there were rich agricultural lands, but in economic terms it must be doubtful whether Roman Britain ever offered a return on the investment of men and materials required to conquer and retain it. Similarly, the only justification for advancing into the lands north of Hadrian's Wall was the never-achieved glory of conquering the whole of Britain. Some chroniclers argue that the northern campaigns of Agricola and Severus were necessary to ensure the security of the rest of the province – in much the same way as the British in the nineteenth century argued that their invasions of Afghanistan were necessary in order to secure the Indian Empire. Whether true or not, there was certainly no economic advantage to be gained.[147]

Roman control was pragmatic. It did not necessarily involve the wholesale disruption or subjugation of an existing society. Indeed, the Roman authorities could be remarkably tolerant. In Britain, provided tribal leaders and their families bowed the knee and caused no problems, they were often left in place and allowed to exercise a degree of circumscribed power. On matters of religion, too, the Romans were tolerant. They made no attempt to interfere with local cults and practices, except where these assumed a political dimension. The druids were destroyed because of their capacity to incite resistance rather than their 'abominable rites' (see Chapter 12). Christianity, as we shall see in due course, was also suppressed, at least at first, because it was held to constitute a danger to the Roman state. Nonetheless, Roman civilisation was wholly different from that of the British tribes, and the imposition of foreign rule did mean the imposition of foreign governmental and social structures, foreign concepts, and a foreign language.

British society was based around the tribe. Each tribe had its territory, in Latin its *civitas*; its ruler, who could be male or female; and its ruling family. While Roman writers called these rulers 'kings' and 'queens' as the most convenient way of translating foreign concepts of tribal leadership for their readers, the terms risk giving the modern reader an exaggerated sense of the grandeur and the stability of such positions. At the time of Claudius' invasion, most tribal chiefs ruled their *civitas* from fortified locations, which are often termed 'capitals', but, again, the term suggests a greater degree of scale and splendour than was actually the case. Most were essentially no more than large villages centred on a wooden hall and a collection of roundhouses which served as the headquarters of the local warlord and his family. In the north and west, most capitals were located in hillforts. In the south and east – those areas most exposed to Continental influence – hillforts were gradually being superseded by other kinds of fortified settlement. These consisted of a perimeter marked by a ditch and bank, not on the scale of a hillfort but sufficient to prevent the passage of a chariot. Within the perimeter were collections of huts, mainly roundhouses – some for domestic use, others associated with smelting, metalwork, and pottery – and an area of agricultural land for growing vegetables or grazing animals prior to slaughter. The Roman term for a settlement of this nature was *oppidum*. Five pre-Roman tribal capitals – Canterbury, St Albans, Chichester, Leicester, and Winchester – displayed this structure. Whether they were large and structured enough to be called towns is a matter of debate, but they certainly did not approach the architectural, organisational, and administrative sophistication of the towns that grew up under Roman rule, and on which Roman civilisation was based.

In the broad system of Roman civil administration, the *oppidum* was the lowest tier of local government. The second level was the *municipium*, responsible for administering both itself and a *territorium* comprising all or part of the surrounding tribal lands. Only one *municipium*, St Albans, has been confirmed in Britain, although Colchester may briefly have enjoyed the same status before it was elevated to the third and highest level, *colonia*. *Coloniae* were established by formal charters, which mirrored the constitution of Rome itself, and were often distinguished by the presence of large numbers of Roman veterans who had been granted land there. There is documentary evidence for the existence of just four *coloniae* in Britain – Colchester, Lincoln, Gloucester, and York – although London was almost certainly granted the same status at some time. *Oppida*, *municipia*, and *coloniae* had different powers and privileges, but central to all three was the existence of a council, or *ordo*, nominally consisting of one hundred members, or decurions. Their role was to supervise the collection of taxes, to find the funds necessary for public works, festivals, and games, and to oversee the maintenance of public order. It was from among their number that public officers, such as magistrates, were chosen.

These structures and the concepts they embodied would have been wholly foreign to the British, and it is difficult to assess how they reacted. No doubt many found this new world confusing, and many will inevitably have resented the changes. However, it is worth recalling the creeping Romanisation we saw affecting the tribes of the south and east in the years between Caesar and Claudius (see Chapter 15). Certain aspects of the Roman way of life – particularly the material aspects – would probably have made their way to Britain eventually, whatever happened. Silchester, the capital of the Atrebates, suggests how Roman culture might have influenced southern Britain if Claudius had not invaded. The Atrebates' appetite for all things Roman went well beyond wine, olive oil and *garum*. About 30 BC – over twenty years after Caesar's invasions – they laid out a new town on a distinctly Roman model, with a grid system of paved streets, stone buildings, and even a bath house. Of course, there is a difference between choosing something and having it imposed, and such imitations of Roman style would not have happened everywhere. Nonetheless, the example of Silchester does suggest that we must consider carefully how willing or unwilling the southern British would have been to adopt a Roman way of life.

Three-and-a-half centuries of Roman occupation meant that life in southern Britain developed, evolved, and changed. Strange ideas became familiar. Generations grew up with no memory of life before Roman authority. Britons were recruited into the Roman army. Many became Roman citizens. Some will have adopted Roman modes of dress. Some will have learnt to speak Latin. Some will have learnt to read and write. However, despite much research and debate, there is still no clear consensus on how deep and widespread the Romanisation of British society was. Most of the archaeological evidence, and all the documentary evidence, comes from the upper echelons of society, which were Roman or Romano-British. What they tell us would not necessarily have applied to the numerically larger remainder of the population. Nonetheless, the issue of Romanisation is important, both in helping us understand how society functioned at the time, and because it can shed light on what happened later, in that confused period after 400 when Roman authority collapsed.

18 Romans in the South

The army was the dominant factor in the social and political order the Romans imposed on southern Britain. The military led the conquest, built the roads, maintained order, and patrolled the borders. The military set up the camps and built the forts that became the nuclei of civilian settlements; and these in time grew into towns which survive to this day – Cardiff, Chelmsford, Chester, Doncaster, Exeter, Gloucester, Lancaster, Newcastle-upon-Tyne, Southampton, York, and others. Until the beginning of the fourth century, governors held both civil and military authority, but it was by their military exploits that Roman public opinion and chroniclers such as Tacitus and Cassius Dio judged them. And if they lost the confidence of the legions, as was the case with Ulpius Marcellus and Publius Helvius Pertinax, their authority was undermined to the point where they could not continue in office.

The basic structure of Roman civil government, as outlined above, applied in Roman and Romanised towns, and it brought with it a further set of new concepts embodied in the Roman legal system. Roman law consisted of a number of different codes – civilian law, foreign peoples' law, natural law, common law, public law, and so on – more than one of which might be applicable in any given case or dispute. Indeed, the system became so complex that Vespasian decreed that all provinces in the Empire should have a legal legate (*legatus iuridicus*) to act for the governor in legal matters. Precisely how Roman law was applied and enforced in Britain is difficult to judge, but its all-embracing nature would certainly have been foreign to those Britons who came within its orbit. Equally foreign would have been the context of its administration – the formal setting; the defined roles of the officials involved; the stage-by-stage procedure; and, of course, the Latin language in which proceedings would have been conducted.

Although there is no conclusive evidence, it seems likely that in at least some of the smaller, traditional settlements, known to the Romans as *vici*, tribal systems of government and law still obtained to some extent. Yet here, too, there was change. Even if the druids had administered justice among the British tribes, as Caesar says they did in Gaul, within thirty years of Claudius' invasion, their power was broken. It is probable that local tribal leaders took responsibility for the initial dispensing of justice, although their authority would have been limited. Where there was any overlap or conflict of interests, Roman law would have taken precedence;

and any case involving a Roman citizen would have been dealt with under Roman law.

Social organisation and social structures in Roman-occupied Britain were not static. They evolved to meet the changing political environment as Roman control was established, strengthened, and then gradually declined. Nor were the Romans able to impose the same degree of control in all parts of occupied Britain. Roman control and cultural penetration was greatest in the 'Civil Zone,' roughly equivalent to what we have called the Lowland Zone. Geography made the area more accessible to the Roman armies at the time of the invasion, more suitable for settlement and economic exploitation afterwards, and thus easier for the military and civil authorities to maintain effective control.

North of the Civil Zone was the hill and moorland territory of the perpetually troublesome Brigantes, and beyond them and beyond the Wall, the savage, 'barbarian' tribes that Rome was unable to conquer. There was a pause in hostilities during the third century, but even when not actively resisting Roman rule, the northern tribes remained unimpressed by Roman culture – with the exception of its currency. To the west, in what is now Wales, forts and military roads lined the coasts and followed the river valleys, but the mountainous interior made military operations and civil penetration more difficult. Roman interest in Wales was largely confined to exploiting mineral wealth – lead, copper, and gold – and most Roman remains are military in character. The inhospitable terrain, particularly the lack of flat land suitable for agriculture, apparently dissuaded the Roman authorities from greater involvement in the region, so that even though the tribes, once conquered, offered no significant resistance to Roman authority, Romanisation was limited. In the south-west, tin remained important – especially after the third century when the supply from Iberia was exhausted – but, apart from its tin mines, the South-Western Peninsula appears to have been regarded as remote and unprofitable. It was formally under Roman control and, as with Wales, there are no signs of significant tribal resistance, but once beyond the inhospitable bulk of Dartmoor, signs of Roman presence are few and far between.

Society in Roman-occupied Britain was a spectrum, with Latin-speaking, fully Roman towns at one end and Celtic-speaking, still-traditional villages and farming settlements at the other. Although there were settlements and institutions which mixed Roman and British elements, a society encompassing such disparate extremes was never going to be cohesive; but social cohesiveness was not a Roman priority. However, there were certain aspects of policy and practice that sought to connect the two extremes, or at least render them less unfamiliar to each other.

Even before Claudius' invasion, the Romans had begun to strike agreements and alliances with certain tribes. The Atrebates were among those who assisted Caesar during his 55 BC raid, subsequently maintaining their pro-Roman stance and choosing not to oppose Claudius' forces. The Trinovantes, who also assisted Caesar in 55 BC, remained loyal to Rome until their lands were overrun by the Catuvellauni. The Dobunni,[148] who lived to the north of the Atrebates, also seem not to have opposed Claudius' legions. Although well outside the Civil Zone, the Votadini became allies of Roman not long after the invasion, probably under Agricola. With Roman support, they acted as a buffer state, reducing the threat to the northern frontier, and managing to maintain their status as independent – if sponsored – supporters of Rome until the end of the occupation in the fifth century. These rulers of client kingdoms avoided military confrontation and were able to show their people economic and material benefits – which helped keep them in power – while their neutrality allowed the Romans to concentrate on the resistance offered by more aggressive tribes. These were cases where Roman policy worked, exercising what we would now call soft power to remove potential obstacles to their broader ambitions.

In other cases, the policy was less successful. In the early stages of the conquest, the Romans established close relations with the Iceni and the Brigantes, both of them among the most warlike tribes and occupying strategically important areas. The Iceni, alienated first by governor Ostorius' heavy-handed attempts to make them give up their weapons, and then by procurator Decianus' brutal treatment of Boudicca and her daughters, staged what was probably the most violent rebellion of the Roman occupation (see Chapter 15). The Brigantes seem not to have supported Boudicca's rebellion, but relations soured soon afterwards. More than once, the Romans intervened to support Queen Cartimandua, with whom they had made their agreement, against her anti-Roman husband, Venutius. Although they rescued the Queen, they were unable to dislodge Venutius, and under his leadership and that of later leaders, the Brigantes went on to cause endless trouble.

It was probably under Vespasian (r.69–79), who had personal experience of Britain, that the Roman authorities instituted a policy of defining the boundaries of each tribal *civitas*. Within the Civil Zone at least, this had the effect of putting an end to the intertribal territorial disputes that had characterised pre-Roman Britain. Further north, and in those areas beyond Roman control, intertribal conflicts continued – except when the tribes joined together to fight the Romans. This division may well have had a longer-term impact, so that when Roman authority finally broke down, the southern tribes, having become used to civil administration and unused to intertribal wars, were less able to adapt to the return of instability than their northern neighbours.

At the time the borders of the *civitates* were defined, the Roman authorities appear to have encouraged the construction of new *oppida* to act as tribal capitals. We have no documentary record of such a policy, but it is difficult otherwise to account for the foundation of so many new tribal capitals, and the redevelopment of the five with pre-Roman origins, within a period of just twenty-five years. Many of these *oppida* established themselves in the shadow of Roman military camps or forts; and many of them prospered, surviving the vicissitudes of the next two thousand years to become familiar English towns: the capital of the Cantii became Canterbury; that of the Durotriges, Dorchester; the Belgae, Winchester; the Corieltauvi, Leicester; and so on. Given that the Iceni were the driving force in Boudicca's rebellion, it is not surprising that their new capital, Venta Icenorum – near Caistor St Edmunds, just south of Norwich – was slow to establish itself. Despite being in the heart of a rich, agricultural district, it never achieved the economic and political stature of other tribal capitals and did not survive to become a modern town.

Tribal *oppida* became central to the Roman system of government. They were self-governing in so far as each had an *ordo* or council, but in matters of policy they were subordinate to the central, provincial government. The process suggests that the Roman authorities hoped that Romanisation would lead tribal civil government to evolve to the point where it could replace direct military control. Quite how the development of new *oppida* was financed remains unclear. Were they paid for by central government subsidies? By the ruling families and their associated elites? Or by merchants who had prospered under the Roman commercial regime? A mix of all three seems most likely. The towns were built in the

Roman manner, laid out on a grid system with paved roads and stone buildings. Most had a forum and a basilica where Roman-style government was administered, and justice dispensed. There were colonnades, baths, even amphitheatres. London's basilica measured one hundred fifty metres by thirty-six, larger than any found in Gaul; both Verulamium and Cirencester had a forum bigger than that in Paris; the amphitheatre at Chester had a capacity of 7,000. And, of course, they were connected by a network of paved roads. The physical face of southern Britain changed radically in a short period of time.

Town dwellers obviously accepted the new *oppida*, and to a greater or lesser degree shared in the wealth they created. What is harder to gauge is the impact of Romanised environments and lifestyles on the rest of the province. Estimates of the population of Roman-occupied Britain vary between two and four million – the population of England at the time of the Norman Conquest was about two million, and under Elizabeth I about three million. London was rebuilt rapidly after Boudicca's revolt. It was a port and a trade hub. Seagoing ships could make their way up the river to unload at a point where the Thames was bridged and their goods could be distributed. It soon became the biggest town in the province, and although – or possibly because – it had never been a tribal capital, it became the provincial capital early in the second century, probably at the time of Hadrian's visit in 122. London's population may, by the most generous estimate, have reached 50,000, the same size as Dover, Durham, or Dunfermline today, but without the surrounding suburban sprawl. At the end of the second century, Cirencester, usually cited as the second-biggest town, may have had a population of 15,000 to 20,000. Other major towns, such as Lincoln, Verulamium, and Colchester probably reached between 10,000 and 15,000. Other *civitas* capitals are unlikely to have exceeded 3,000 or 4,000, with some, particularly in the north, being significantly smaller. Other Romanised or semi-Romanised towns, usually classified as those with town walls, probably had populations of between a few hundred and a thousand.

Although these figures are estimates, and uncertain ones, when seen in relation to England and Wales today, with a population of fifty-nine million, and eighty-one towns and cities with over 100,000 inhabitants, they do give a sense of perspective. In 2020, more than 81 per cent of the population of England and Wales was defined as 'urban'. Comparison is difficult because in Roman Britain 'urban' included settlements of no more than three or four hundred, but the comparable figure may have been as low as 10 ten per cent and is unlikely to have exceeded 15 per cent. Roman Britain was an overwhelmingly rural society

If we accept that Roman-occupied Britain had a population of three million, how would the two-and-a-half million people living in the countryside have interacted with the almost half-a-million living in the towns? Decisions taken by the *ordo* of their *civitas* would have had an impact on their lives. The *ordo* would have consisted of both Romans and members of the Romanised British elite – with a larger proportion of British members in the smaller and more remote *oppida*. Their deliberations presumably took place in Latin: few Romans would have spoken Celtic, and the laws were written in Latin. Decisions concerning taxes, land and property disputes, and other issues with implications for rural communities would, we must assume, have been communicated to those in rural areas in the local Celtic language, perhaps by some lower-ranking official responsible for overseeing payment, implementation, or whatever other action was required.

Following the conquest and after the upheaval of Boudicca's rebellion, southern Britain settled down and began to grow wealthy. Villas began to appear in the Civil Zone, although the modern connotations of the word must be set aside. A Roman villa was not a holiday home or a country retreat. It was usually a large house arranged around a courtyard with a farm and other residential buildings attached. It was the hub of a large agricultural estate, both the owner's residence and the administrative centre, and, as such, the heart of a small rural community. In that sense, Roman villas may perhaps be compared with certain eighteenth-century English country houses. Some villas were linked to an industrial operation – such as pottery, tile-making, or mining; a handful have no obvious commercial *raison d'être* and may, indeed, have been residences of the rich; but most were agricultural in origin and function. They would have been owned mainly by Romans; although some may have belonged to wealthy Britons, members of the tribal elites whom the Romans had cultivated, or to merchants and businessmen who had benefitted from the Roman-style economy. They represented an extension of urban values into the country, not the adoption of urban concepts by the rural population.

Villas varied in size from elaborate, almost palatial complexes, to smaller, although still substantial, stone buildings. The range of domestic features – mosaic floors, painted walls, hypocausts, baths, swimming pools, even temples – bear witness to a quality of life that was probably not equalled until the time of the Tudor gentry or the Georgian squires. The first villas appeared towards the end of the first century and are found close to those towns that developed soon after the conquest. The villas at Boxmoor, Northchurch, and Gadebridge, for example, are all within twenty-five kilometres of Verulamium. Although Gadebridge went on to become a much larger and grander establishment than the others, all three show a similar pattern of development. Beginning as what were essentially wooden farmhouses, they were rebuilt on three or four or more occasions over the next three hundred years – each rebuilding displaying the owners' increased wealth and sophistication. The second century saw villas spreading more widely, mainly across the Civil Zone, while in the third and fourth centuries they reached new heights both in grandeur and in number, beginning to appear in other parts of the province as well. Despite occasional tribal disturbances, and incursions across the Wall by the northern tribes, or across the North Sea by Germanic raiders, Britain – southern Britain in particular – was prosperous and stable, at least when compared to many Continental provinces. Wealthy Roman families felt sufficiently secure to invest in land and property. So, too, did upwardly mobile and newly prosperous Britons. And they were joined by affluent families who chose to move to Britain from Gaul and the Lower Rhine, again for reasons of security. Only following the so-called Barbarian Conspiracy in 367 (see Chapter 21) did villa building decline, and when it did, it did so rapidly.

By that time, there were between six and eight hundred villas in Britain. Where they existed, they were a powerful force for the Romanisation of rural areas, but distribution tells a tale. There were none north of Hadrian's Wall. There were none in Lancashire and only one in Cheshire – the territory of the Brigantes. There were perhaps twenty north of York on the eastern side of the Pennines; another thirty scattered across Wales; and a mere handful in Devon and Cornwall. The majority, as noted earlier, were in the Civil Zone, and within the Zone they were concentrated in the rich agricultural areas of today's Somerset, Gloucester, and Hampshire, as well as in the territories of Rome's allies, such as the Atrebates and the Dobunni. In these areas, it seems, agricultural businesses could prosper, and Roman or Romano-British owners feel safe.

The villa community would have been largely self-supporting, breeding its own horses; rearing its own cattle, sheep, pigs, and poultry; producing its own milk, cheese, and beer – and wine, too, in the south; growing its own vegetables; providing tallow for candles, leather for shoes, aprons and harnesses; weaving its own cloth. The villa itself, the estate, and the business of the estate would have required a substantial workforce: managers, overseers, accountants, builders, maids, cooks, household servants, grooms, gardeners, and agricultural labourers of various kinds. Villa communities varied considerably in size. Estimates put their size as ranging from thirty to forty up to three or four hundred in the larger, more palatial establishments. Slaves would have provided much of the labour, but some of the more responsible positions would have been filled by local, Celtic-speaking inhabitants who, together with their families, would have lived in or around the villa complex. Here again the issue of language becomes important. Who spoke what and to whom? In Romano-British households, we might assume the local Celtic language would be favoured – except perhaps among social climbers. Where the owners were Roman, we can imagine a scenario similar to that in British and French colonial possessions with the owners speaking Latin among themselves and a limited pidgin Celtic to their servants. Among the estate workers, there would be managers or supervisors who had learnt Latin, and whose value was increased because they could communicate the owner's wishes to the workforce. The labourers and slaves would have spoken Celtic but may have understood enough Latin to respond to familiar orders in familiar situations. There will also have been some Romans who took the trouble to learn Celtic; and the number of Romans speaking Celtic would have increased the longer their family stayed in Britain; just as the number of Britons speaking Latin would have risen over three-and-a-half centuries of occupation.

Trade in Roman goods between Gaul and south and south-east Britain was well established even before Claudius' invasion. It was well organised, since Strabo says that the Britons paid taxes on both imports and exports,[149] and it was focussed on 'allied' tribes. After the first stage of the conquest, once Roman control was established across the southern part of what became the Civil Zone, the policy of political sticks and economic carrots evolved swiftly into a broader policy of cultivating tribal elites, most of whom were members of or were connected with the ruling families. Imported foodstuffs, manufactured and luxury goods – wine, olives, olive oil, sesame oil, *garum*, figs and dates, jewellery, glassware, textiles (including silks and cottons from Asia), crockery, metal tools, pots and pans – were powerful levers in persuading wealthy British elites of the benefits of Roman rule. They were also the commodities demanded by expatriate Romans used to living a comfortable Roman life; and with military personnel, civil administrators, and veterans allocated land in the *coloniae*, that population was growing rapidly. There were almost certainly Roman businessmen and entrepreneurs working in Britain before the conquest, and a wave of traders and merchants followed in its wake. While 'Roman' in that they operated within the Roman economic system, many of them were from the German provinces, Gaul, Iberia, or even the Levant. Although their influence could be seen as cosmopolitan rather than Romanising, they made their money by satisfying the demand for Roman foodstuffs and luxury goods created by the new ruling class; and they and the goods they imported were closely associated with Roman rule and Roman society. Among the British, at least in the century or so following the invasion, it is unlikely that these goods would have circulated far beyond the elite groups who could afford them. That would not have worried the Romans. Theirs was not a *mission civilisatrice*: it was a mission of control, and anything that drew ruling elites deeper into the cultural and economic orbit of Rome increased that control.

As time went on, a more settled trading pattern evolved. Foodstuffs and luxury goods from all over the Empire continued to be imported, while exports developed as a result of new investment, increased stability and improved links with the Continent. Britain was a source of lead, which was in demand throughout the Roman world for pipes, tanks, and roofs. Screw pump technology allowed for the development of lead mines in the Pennines and Wales, which were considered sufficiently important to remain under military control. Iron ore was sourced from the Weald and the Forest of Dean, and gold from Wales. Slaves, grain, hides and hunting dogs have already been mentioned. Wool and woollen products became valuable exports for the first time – and would continue to remain so for the next 2,000 years. An indication of just how effective Roman transport systems could be is that oysters from Britain could reach the Imperial Court in Rome in good condition.

Cross-Channel trade grew rapidly. Initially, the ports of Pevensey, Hastings, Lympne, Dover, Reculver, Rochester, and London were all involved, but by the end of the second century Dover had outstripped them all. Direct trade with the Rhine provinces across the North Sea, and with Brittany and Iberia up and down the Atlantic seaboard, also grew. So, too, despite the emphasis frequently placed on the efficiency of Roman roads, did trade in British coastal waters. There were new and developing towns to be supplied, legions in their bases and garrisons along the Wall to be supported. This led to investment in a string of ports along both the eastern and western coasts – Brancaster, Lincoln, Scarborough, South Shields, Newcastle-upon-Tyne; Gloucester, Caerwent, Chester, Lancaster, Bowness. Demand stimulated trade, and trade stimulated demand, but how far the goods traded and the wealth created permeated the wider, rural population remains uncertain.

Coal was widely mined and used. It smelted iron in the Weald; it was used for crop drying; it heated bath houses on Hadrian's Wall and in Bath – although most baths and hypocausts were heated with wood. The salt industry expanded. Roman soldiers were paid partly in salt: it was their *salarium* or salary. Salt pans and other archaeological traces have been found in Cheshire, Worcestershire, Somerset Lincolnshire, Essex, Kent, and Sussex. In a world before rubber or plastic, the tanning industry was of fundamental importance. Shoes, gloves, belts, straps, capes, caps, buckets, shield covers, shield straps, scabbards, saddles, harnesses, bridles, reins and a hundred other items in daily use were made of leather, and the remains of tanneries have been found in many Roman towns. The redevelopment of existing towns and the foundation of the new *oppida* created a major demand for building stone. Kentish ragstone, Bath stone, York limestone, Chester red sandstone, and Pennine millstone grit were all quarried and transported by waggon, usually to building sites in their region, but also by boat round the coast to other parts of the province. Rarer, higher value stone, such as marble or porphyry, had to be imported. Heavy or large-scale industries such as these were almost certainly developed by the Roman authorities themselves or by merchants or businessmen using capital from outside Britain; and their development would have had an impact on the local population in terms of employment, increased wealth, and exposure to Roman industrial practices and record keeping.

1   Caistor St Edmunds / Venta Icenorum
2   Leicester / Ratae Corieltauvorum
3   Gloucester / Glevum
4   Colchester / Camulodunum
5   Caerwent / Venta Silurum
6   St Albans / Verulamium
7   London / Londinium
8   Silchester / Calleva Atrebatum
9   Winchester / Venta Bulgarum
10 Chichester / Noviomagus Reginorum
11 Exeter / Isca Dumnoniorum
12 Dorchester / Durnovaria

Map 18   The Roman Occupation

We have only limited information about how commerce in Roman Britain functioned at a local level. Individual shops have been identified at military sites, such as Housesteads and Vindolanda on Hadrian's Wall, and at Maryport on the Cumbrian coast, but most evidence of commercial life comes from the south of the Civil Zone. In the *coloniae* and other towns located on, or close to, the strategic road network shops were often grouped together in arcades to give security and protection against the weather. In the larger towns, such as London and the legionary headquarters of Gloucester and Lincoln, shops may also have had living accommodation upstairs, like the traditional shophouses of Singapore or Malacca. In the countryside, away from the road network, life probably continued in a more traditional manner. Basic goods and foodstuffs would have been bought and sold or exchanged within the village and its environs. We can imagine itinerant merchants bringing their wares from the towns to the villages and more isolated communities; and we can be reasonably sure that there was a network of rural markets, probably dating back to pre-Roman times, which changed and adapted as town-based commerce grew in importance.

Economic change in Roman Britain was underpinned by the development of a money-based economy. Coins minted by British tribes were in circulation as early as the first century BC (see Chapter 15), but these coins and their successors were of different types and values and not necessarily interchangeable. Roman coinage was standardised and dependable. An accepted and reliable medium of exchange acted as a stimulus to both external and internal trade, which naturally increased profits. These benefits were readily understood, and Roman coinage was quickly and widely adopted, bringing a Roman-style monetised economy in its wake, although exchange and barter transactions no doubt continued. As ever, these developments had greater impact in the Civil Zone. However, even in the troublesome north, and beyond the Wall, the advantages of Roman currency were understood. Roman coins were in circulation as far north as the Great Glen.

Three-and-a-half centuries of Roman occupation inevitably transformed the face of southern Britain and affected all aspects of life. The existence of a central authority reduced the power of tribal leaders. It also altered the relationship between the tribes themselves. These changes were reinforced by the existence of an occupying military force, which could be called upon to enforce the will of the central authority if required. Beyond the political and military sphere, towns developed; stone buildings became commonplace; villas and estates dotted the countryside; farming became more efficient; new industries started up; old ones expanded, often because of new technologies; an effective transport infrastructure was established, involving ports and a network of roads that had both military and economic value; the population increased significantly; a standardised coinage was introduced; literacy became, if not widespread, at least more common; people ate different food, and wore different clothes.

Yet Romanisation remained an essentially urban phenomenon, based on wealth. Its impetus came from the Roman ruling class, who lived in towns or in villas, and to a lesser extent from the military. It was embraced by the tribal elites, by British members of their town's *ordo*, by new money – the manufacturers of pottery, the smelters of lead, the traders and merchants who benefitted from the new trading environment – by all those who had invested socially or financially in the new order. They, too, were mainly town dwellers. Outside this circle, if members of the rural population wanted to adopt a Roman lifestyle, they are unlikely to have had the opportunity to do so. The urban Briton had greater exposure to Roman culture than his rural counterpart, although neither would have been able to ignore, or to remain unaffected by the taxes, edicts, regulations, and other dictates of Roman authority. While Roman rule continued, Roman influence was inescapable, and the attractions of the Roman lifestyle reinforced Roman systems of control, but to judge how deep and lasting Roman influence really was, we need to look at what happened when Roman authority failed.

19 Over the Wall and across the Sea

Roman Britain, the area south of Hadrian's Wall, amounted to some 52 per cent of the land area of the island of Great Britain, and 30 per cent of the land area of the British Isles as a whole. Yet ever since the rediscovery of Greek and Roman literature during the Renaissance, it is Roman Britain, not Celtic Ireland or what, for the sake of convenience, we shall continue to call Caledonia, that has attracted the attention of writers and historians and captivated the public imagination. Roman society could not have existed had it not recorded its internal workings and chronicled its activities. By contrast, tribal society in Ireland and Caledonia remained pre-literate until the spread of Christianity from the fourth century onwards. As a consequence, all our contemporary and near-contemporary documents come from Roman sources, which deal with Ireland and Caledonia only when Roman interests are involved, and they do so, inevitably, from a Roman perspective. For many years, archaeology took a similarly Rome-centred approach, concentrating on sites such as Hadrian's Wall, Fishbourne Palace, and the theatre at Verulamium. The danger is that because we know so much more about it, we may regard events in Roman Britain as more important than what happened in Ireland or Caledonia, and that we use our knowledge of Roman Britain to judge the tribal societies beyond its borders – in other words, we begin to judge Celtic tribes by Roman standards.

Happily, the situation has changed significantly in recent decades. The Irish historian, Dáibhí Ó Cróinín, the Scottish writer, Alistair Moffat, and the anthropologist and television presenter, Alice Roberts, are among those who have refocussed attention on non-Roman society, on the tools and artwork, and on the brochs, crannogs and hillforts that provide evidence of tradition and continuity among the Celtic-speaking tribes. This is important because, in historical terms, the Roman occupation was comparatively brief. The Romans introduced much that was new and technologically advanced, and Roman luxury goods were used and consumed in parts of Ireland and Caledonia as well as in Britannia. Yet in the longer term, very little of what the Romans brought survived. By contrast, while the Celtic-speaking tribes cannot be said to have defeated Rome and the Romans, in the end it was their society, culture, and language that survived and outlasted the Roman presence. And it is the legacy of the Celtic tribes, not the Romans, which in various modern incarnations remains visible in parts of the British Isles today.

The Romans never invaded Ireland, although Tacitus suggests Agricola may have thought about it. He collected information about Irish ports and seaways from the merchant community. He welcomed an exiled Irish chief and kept him in the gubernatorial entourage to use as a political lever should he decide to invade – much as Caesar used Mandubracius in 54 BC. He also gave his opinion that a single legion and a few auxiliaries would be sufficient to conquer and occupy Ireland.[150] An ambiguous passage has given rise to claims that Agricola did make a reconnaissance visit to Ireland. An elaborate medieval version of this story – verging on conspiracy theory – links the unnamed exiled chieftain with the shadowy figure of Túathal Techtmar, supposedly the son of a deposed High King of Ireland, and suggests that the Romans invaded Ireland in order to restore him to power. There is no evidence for any of this. However, there is evidence of a Roman presence on the peninsula of Drumanagh, just north of Dublin. Drumanagh is a flat area of some sixteen hectares, with three defensive banks, possibly dating from the Bronze Age, on the landward side. Roman pottery, coins, copper ingots, and other items have been discovered on the peninsula itself and in the neighbouring area. It is unlikely to have been a military base – there are no rectangular forts, straight roads, or other characteristic signs of a Roman military presence – but it could have been a Roman trading post, either permanently inhabited or the site of an annual fair, and it is just possible that a detachment of legionaries may have accompanied the traders in order to protect them. We know that there was significant trade between Ireland and Roman Britain, as well as political contacts, which were probably no more than occasional, between Irish tribal leaders and the Roman authorities.

Trade across the Irish Sea had been a fact of economic life for millennia, and it was common for Roman merchants to trade, and sometimes live, beyond the confines of the Empire. Yet it is often assumed that contacts and the spread of Roman influence across the Irish Sea were limited or constrained by Irish hostility. No doubt the Irish feared a Roman invasion, and those fears were probably heightened by refugees fleeing from the occupied parts of Britain. Equally, the Romans resented and sought to curb the activities of Irish raiding parties. However, the archaeological record shows that the Irish Sea was just as porous a border as Hadrian's Wall. Ireland was, if not awash, then at least well supplied with Roman artefacts: pottery, ingots, weapons, silver plates, brooches, rings and other jewellery, and coins have been found in most areas, although naturally concentrated on the east coast. Of course, we cannot tell how or when these items came to be there. Some will have been traded directly, either purchased or bartered as payment for slaves, hides, grain, woollen cloth, or other goods. Some may have been gifts brought by representatives of British tribes visiting their Irish counterparts. Some may have been brought by pilgrims from Britain visiting sacred sites such as Newgrange or the Hill of Tara. Some may have been looted from Britain in the later stages of the Roman occupation. However these items arrived, there are enough of them to show that Roman culture, in its material aspects, was familiar to a significant proportion of the Irish population, although that familiarity would naturally have been greater among the tribal elites.

Tracing Ireland's social and political development during the early centuries of the first millennium AD is difficult because we have hardly any information. Ptolemy's *Geography* and its map gives us some basic geographical information – the names of headlands, estuaries, and settlements – as well as the names of sixteen tribes with a general indication of where their territories lay. Ptolemy is generally reliable where the physical features of Ireland are concerned, but with the sixteen tribes it is difficult to know how accurate, or how up to date, his information was. Some of the tribes he names do not appear anywhere else and have never been identified; and the map gives only a general indication of where tribes and their territories were located. This information presumably came from merchants and seafarers who regularly crossed and re-crossed the Irish Sea. It is even possible that the information Agricola collected when considering an invasion of Ireland in 80–81 made its way slowly to Alexandria and was the source on which Ptolemy relied when drawing his map some seventy years later. However, we can say with certainty that the original source or sources on which Ptolemy drew were not Irish. Ptolemy's Greek is a translation of a Latin transcription of Celtic, and the phonetic evidence indicates that the original informants were P-Celtic-speakers, and thus Britons, not Irish, Q-Celtic-speakers. The accuracy of Ptolemy's map as it comes down to us may be affected by the fact that the earliest surviving manuscripts date from the thirteenth and fourteenth centuries, and are thus copies of copies, so we cannot tell what scribal errors may have crept in. Beyond Ptolemy and occasional references by other classical authors – Paulus Orosius, writing at the beginning of the fifth century, added a seventeenth tribe – the documentary history of Ireland only begins with religious and legal texts in the eighth century. There is a wealth of myths and legends and king lists, but they were not written down until early medieval times and recount events that may or may not have taken place hundreds of years earlier. They may give us clues, but they cannot be relied upon.

Ptolemy's map, even if accurate, would not have been a representation of the political structure of Ireland. Rather, it would have indicated that there were sixteen areas where the population acknowledged some degree of broad common identity. These areas would have been subdivided among the smaller tribal units known as *túatha,* creating a complex territorial patchwork. Some archaeologists, basing their findings on pollen data, have identified a decline in human activity and agricultural productivity between the first and the third century AD, which could have stimulated political change. Whether this is true or not, at some time during the first half of the millennium – perhaps between 250 and 350 – tribal structures began to change, merging and coalescing into larger groupings. This was a complex process, lasting several centuries, which eventually led to the formation of regional kingdoms and sub-kingdoms that played such a major part in later Irish history (see Chapter 23).

High King was a recognised title in early medieval Ireland, but the origins and significance of High Kingship are less clear. As so often with early Irish history, we have to look to various uncertain or unreliable sources. There are medieval texts, such as *The Book of Invasions*, *The Book of Leinster*, and *The Yellow Book of Lecan*. There are two seventeenth-century compilations – *The Annals of the Four Masters*, compiled by four Franciscan friars, and Geoffrey Keating's *Foras Feasa ar Éirinn* (*The Foundation of Knowledge on Ireland*) – both of which consist mainly of much earlier material. Most of these sources accept that Ireland was ruled by a High King (*ard ri*) from the earliest times. Some give names and regnal dates stretching back to the beginning of the second millennium BC. Most of this we can safely regard as invention, but from the first century AD onwards, the situation is complicated by the inclusion of people we know, or judge, to be real, such as Túathal Techtmar, mentioned earlier as a possible, if unlikely, candidate for the Irish chieftain who was held at Agricola's court. Túathal may have been real; he may have been the son of a High King called Fíacha Finnolach; but the idea that he fought a hundred and ten battles, subdued the whole of Ireland, and became High King in his own right is obviously fiction.

The current consensus is that the concept of a High King was invented, probably in the eighth century, by scribes and chroniclers seeking to justify the power and status of the ruling families who employed them. Providing kings and their families with glorious and extended genealogies was a recognised practice in Ireland as elsewhere. History in the early medieval period was not expected to be objective. Inventing two thousand years' worth of High Kings was no different from the Welsh monk, Nennius, in his *Historia Brittonum* (*The History of the Britons*), linking the origins of the British to Aeneas and Noah. However, it is just possible that at times the chroniclers are recalling – and exaggerating – a distant but real process which saw Ptolemy's sixteen tribes coalesce into regional kingdoms and certain families emerge as powerful regional overkings. High Kings and regional kings both remained a feature of Irish political life until the arrival of the Normans in the twelfth century.

The law codes of the seventh and eighth centuries recognise degrees of kingship from the ruler of an individual tribe, through the overlord of several tribes, to the regional king (*rí ruirech*). And in the ninth century, we have High Kings whose existence we can verify, although the title reflected a claim of precedence and overlordship, rather than actual control. That claim may first have been made by the chiefs of the Uí Néill clan, and spread by their bards and clerks, to boost their prestige. From the ninth century onwards, we have names and regnal dates that are broadly reliable, and as the centuries progress, more accurate information about the seemingly endless raids and wars between the kingdoms. To be acclaimed and accepted as High King was clearly something that the Irish kings regarded as prestigious and important, but it was not until the eleventh century and the advent of the best known of all Irish kings, Brian Bóruma, anglicised as Brian Boru (r.1002–14), that anyone managed to wield political control over the whole island.

All sources claim that the ancient High Kings – those we might regard as mythical – ruled from the Hill of Tara in County Meath. Tara had been a sacred site since Neolithic times and was traditionally supposed to be the home of the legendary warrior queen, Maeve or Medb. Early Irish kingship almost certainly had a spiritual aspect to it,[151] so associating the High King with Tara – whenever and however it happened – was a logical step. It elevated the High King's status by adding a spiritual dimension to political power; it associated him with a shared legendary past; and it promoted an underlying concept of Irish unity. Accepting that High Kingship was an eighth-century invention, then what was the significance of Tara before that time? It evidently retained considerable importance. Who lived there? Who exercised power there? Given that the druids remained a powerful religious force in Ireland, could Tara have been a centre of druidic religion? It would be neither unprecedented nor unusual for the early Christian scribes, the authors of the chronicles and king lists, to reinvent the past, downplaying or even denying the existence of pre-Christian religion and its priests. Although speculative, it would be consistent with what we know happened elsewhere if they had sought to write the druids out of history, replacing their spiritual authority with the concept of political overlordship exercised by a mythical High King.

When Caesar wrote that it was the druids who were responsible for administering justice in Gaul, he was talking of the first century BC. Whether they had any similar role in Ireland, we do not know. The earliest knowledge we have of Irish law comes from a document known as the *Senchas Már*, possibly written as early as 438, by which time it was administered by the Brehons, a class of people enjoying high social status, whose role was a mixture of judge and arbitrator. Most of the law codes were not written down until the seventh and eighth centuries, and they contain the collective, accumulated experience of the Brehons transmitted orally from one generation to the next. Early Irish law is often known as Brehon Law. The written texts were produced after the arrival of Christianity and the influence of Christian teaching is visible in many places, but both linguistic evidence and the fact that some laws are in direct conflict with Irish canon law clearly indicate pre-Christian origins.

Brehon law was comprehensive, progressive, and practical – at least by comparison with Roman law. It was also more favourable to women. Both men and women could be Brehons and, while denied complete equality, under Brehon law women enjoyed greater rights – at least in theory – in relation to marital conduct and divorce than British women did until the twentieth century. The laws list the strata of society in precise detail. The king is at the top, although it is explicitly stated that he is not above the law. Then come the aristocracy, and a descending scale of different groups and professions, ending with the slaves. Each group was carefully divided into sub-categories: the clergy according to the seniority of their position; bards and poets according to their skills and qualifications; craftsmen – everyone from blacksmiths to the makers of chariots – according to the value placed on what they produced. The legal provisions relating to each group and each sub-group depended on their 'honour', and the 'honour price' to be paid to them in the event of injury, or to their family in the event of their death. Every eventuality was provided for – there were payments for wounding, and payments made to the victim to sustain him during his recovery. Capital punishment was discouraged. Complicated, and usually partible, inheritance procedures were laid out, and their implications for land rights and land tenure made explicit. Once the Brehon had made his or her decision, a three-level system based on sureties and guarantors was used to ensure implementation. Payment might be made in goods or in kind; land might be held as a bond; and in the last resort the offender might be held hostage until the debt could be discharged.

These Irish laws evidently evolved during the first four or five centuries AD, a period when the workings of Irish society otherwise went almost completely unrecorded. The Romans were not deeply interested in Ireland: they lacked curiosity about other civilisations unless they impinged on the fortunes of the Empire. So, we can construct only a rough outline of what life was like. There are enough tales and legends to make it clear that violence and inter-tribal raiding were common practice, and they would remain so for the next thousand years or more. Irish society was no utopia, but, in theory, it was based on sophisticated concepts of order and legally-defined social hierarchies. And it worth noting that these ideas, however often they were in reality breached or ignored, had evolved internally: they were not foreign concepts, imposed from without. None of this makes the Irish moral paragons, but it does mean that whatever the Romans chose to think, and whatever Diodorus Siculus and Strabo may have said, the people of Ireland were not incestuous and cannibalistic barbarians.

The tribes to the north of Hadrian's Wall were obviously more directly affected by the presence of the Romans than the Irish. Full-scale invasions, such as those mounted by Agricola, Lollius Urbicus, and Emperor Severus, and regular minor expeditions by Roman forces designed to punish or pre-empt tribal incursions inevitably created a sense that the Romans were the natural enemy. On the other hand, the flow of trade back and forward through the Wall, regular patrols, gifts to tribal leaders, and other diplomatic attempts to establish friendly relations allowed the two communities to become familiar with each other. In this scenario, the Votadini sit a little oddly. Having decided at an early stage that an alliance with Rome would be to their advantage, they kept to the terms of their agreement and became Rome's longest-lasting client kingdom in Britain. We can only guess at the impact this had on their relations with other tribes, but, while their loyalty contradicted the Roman assumption that British tribes were unreliable barbarians, it did not lessen Roman contempt for the British in general. A stone tablet from the end of the first century discovered at Vindolanda Fort on Hadrian's Wall uses the disparaging term

'*Brittunculi*' – 'horrid, little Brits' – to describe them; and the poet Claudian, writing *c*.400, personifies Britain as a female figure 'dressed in the skin of some Caledonian beast, with her cheeks tattooed.' However, the Caledonians were capable of holding their own in such matters. Cassius Dio reports a conversation between the wife of a Caledonian chief, Argentocoxus, and Julia Augusta, wife of the Emperor Severus. The Empress made fun of the free sexual morals of British women. The reply came back: 'We satisfy the demands of nature better than you Roman women. We go openly with the best men, you let yourselves be debauched in secret by the worst.'[152]

As with Ireland, our knowledge of Caledonia during the early centuries of the first millennium comes from a mix of Roman sources and texts written after the arrival of Christianity but containing information handed down through the oral tradition. How tribal structures evolved over the period is not clear. Roman support strengthened the position of the Votadini – who mutated into the Gododdin in the post-Roman period – and at least one new political entity came into being. The kingdom of Alt Clud (Al Clud, Alcuith), later to become the Kingdom of Strathclyde, was based on Dumbarton Rock – Dumbarton meaning the fort of the Britons – and was probably established by the Damnonii, whom Ptolemy places in the Clyde Valley. Although little known today, it existed for at least six hundred years and played a significant part in the territorial and cultural struggles that engulfed northern Britain from the fifth century onwards.

There is some evidence that, as in Ireland, tribes were coalescing into larger groupings. The speech which Tacitus puts into the mouth of Calgacus on the eve of Mons Graupius implies a degree of unity among the northern tribes. These are Tacitus' sentiments, not those of a genuine Caledonian, but we know that faced with Roman aggression, the tribes were able to form a confederation under a single leader and make strategic decisions, so they were no mere rabble. Whether or not they shared any sense of unity or common identity beyond that arising from the need to confront a common enemy, we cannot tell. The Roman threat stimulated cooperation, but in doing so may have delayed the inter-tribal conflicts and territorial readjustments that took place when the threat was lifted – although by that time there were new factors and forces involved.

Documentary sources relating to Caledonia are even scarcer and more fragmentary than those concerning Ireland – in part because Christianity, and thus literacy, arrived later and took longer to embed itself – and there are the usual issues of invented or 'legendary' material, and scribal error or distortion. The gap in time between events taking place and being recorded also has greater significance because the northern tribes moved, migrated, and re-settled far more than their Irish counterparts, so the scribes and chroniclers found themselves faced with stories handed down orally that bore little or no relation to the situation they saw about them. This may explain why the names of certain tribes appear and disappear with no explanation. Another complicating factor is that names of all sorts – tribal, personal, geographical – vary in form and spelling because they are transliterations of P- or Q-Celtic, often mediated through Latin, and copied, often inaccurately, by early medieval scribes. These issues are particularly significant in the story of the Picts, whose influence was at its greatest in the post-Roman period, but whose emergence as a cultural and political force began much earlier.

The Picts are not named in Tacitus' account of Agricola's campaigns north of the Forth—Clyde line; they do not appear on Ptolemy's map; and they are not mentioned in Cassius Dio's report of Severus' northern campaigns. The name first appears in *Panegyric VI*, delivered by the orator Eumenius in praise of the Emperor Constantius I (Constantius Chlorus) in 297. He praises Julius Caesar but says that he did not conquer 'the forests and swamps of the Caledonians and the other Picts.'[153] Eumenius is talking about events that took place three hundred years earlier, and his statement could be an anachronistic reference to a tribe that was unknown at that time. On the other hand, Eumenius evidently regarded the Picts as a grouping that included the Caledonians, suggesting that 'Picts' had become a general catch-all description of the northern tribes, perhaps using an indigenous term – much as the nineteenth century's Persians are today's Iranians.

The word 'Picts' is generally assumed to mean 'painted people', a reference to tattooing, and perhaps originating as a derisory nickname applied by Roman soldiers. The same meaning, applied to the word *Pritani*, the earliest term for the inhabitants of Britain, was challenged earlier and an alternative derivation suggested (see Chapter 11). In the case of the Picts, the etymological link to Latin (*pictus*, painted) and Greek (*pyktis*, picture) is more direct; and the fact that the Q-Celtic word *cruthin* or *cruithin*, used by the Irish to refer to the Picts, means 'figure' or 'shape' strengthens the derivation. There is evidence that tattooing with woad was more intense among the northern tribes, and that it lasted much longer as a cultural marker. Writing at the beginning of the seventh century, the scholar and archbishop, Isidore of Seville (c.560–636) wrote that the name Picts derived from their bodies; and half-a-century later in 787, while attending a synod in Northumbria, Bishop George of Ostia expressed the Pope's disapproval of the northern pagans and their heavy tattooing.[154] As with Alice Roberts' concerns about the three-fold death of Celtic kings (see Chapter 14), the danger here is that having settled on the idea that 'Picts' equals 'painted', we seek evidence of tattooing to prove the point and create a circular, self-affirming argument. An alternative is to see the essential difference of the Picts – the art of their carved stones and their still largely inaccessible language – as representing the survival of an older, but still 'Celtic', family. This view would see Pictish cultural influence spreading out from their homeland in north-eastern Scotland in the early and middle centuries of the first millennium, perhaps at a time when the Caledonii and Maeatae had been weakened by their conflict with Rome; and it would argue for 'Pict' deriving from the P-Celtic word *pecht* or *pegh*, which would give a meaning closer to 'the ancestors' or 'the old ones'.[155]

The few Pictish settlements that have been identified and excavated suggest that, beyond the fact that they lived in the north of the Main Island, there is little to distinguish the Picts from other Iron Age tribes in Britain. Most lived in roundhouses or longhouses in small, stockaded communities. Some lived in crannogs. Most of them were farmers, raising cattle, sheep, and pigs, and planting wheat, barley, oats, and rye. They grew flax to make oil and linen, although most of their clothes were of wool. What differentiates the Picts from other Iron Age communities are more than two hundred carved stones bearing highly distinctive designs. Known as symbol stones, they are concentrated in the Pictish heartland of north-eastern Scotland but are also found as far north as Shetland and as far south as Gatehouse of Fleet in Galloway, an indication of the extent of the lands that, at one time or another, shared elements of Pictish culture.

The symbols that appear on the stones fall into two broad categories: outline carvings of fish, birds, and animals (salmon, goose, eagle, horse, deer, boar, wolf), and abstract or semi-abstract symbols (the so-called Z-rod and V-rod, the double disc and Z-rod, the crescent and V-rod, the comb and mirror, the triple disc and cross bar, the disc and rectangle). These symbols are not only distinctive, they are also surprisingly consistent across the range of stones. It is possible that they had a talismanic quality – and they may have been replicated in the tattoos borne by the Pictish warriors – but scholars now believe that they represent a written form of the Pictish language, albeit a form that we cannot yet interpret.[156] If so, it would not be unique – there were other attempts at writing, such as the Irish ogham script, in the lands bordering the Roman Empire– but it would be further evidence that the Picts were not the barbarians that the Romans claimed.

Symbol stones divide into two categories: Class I, which are wholly Pictish in that they do not features crosses or any other form of Christian iconography, and Class II, which mix Pictish and Christian symbols. Dating either category with any accuracy is difficult. The earliest surviving symbol stones are probably those found on the rugged sea-stack of Dunnicaer, off the coast of Aberdeenshire, where they have been set into a rampart dated to the third or fourth century. Some of the symbols show a close stylistic affinity with designs found on metalwork from northern Caledonia during early centuries of the millennium. At Rhynie, also in Aberdeenshire, archaeologists have recently excavated a Pictish royal centre that was inhabited from the fourth to the sixth century. Among the finds were eight Class I stones, and another quite remarkable slab featuring the carved outline of an axe-carrying warrior, perhaps a Celtic god. Another stone, from Sanday in Orkney, seems to date from about the same time. Although precise dating is impossible, we can at least be sure that the birds, beasts, and geometric symbols which define Pictish art are pre-Christian in origin. The conversion of the Picts to Christianity is largely undocumented and, given both the terrain and the tribal nature of society, may well have been patchy. It began in the sixth century, and it was probably during the seventh century that Christian iconography began to appear alongside Pictish symbols. Class II stones probably date from between the seventh century and the end of the ninth when the Picts disappear from the historical record.

In the nineteenth and twentieth centuries, when invasion theory held that the Celts were a distinct ethnic group that invaded in waves from the Continent, the position of the Picts seemed more perplexing than it does today. Various explanations for their presence were advanced, including the idea that they were the descendants of the Neolithic peoples who had inhabited the north-east of the British mainland. The Pictish language is long extinct. What little we know of it has had to be pieced together from personal names, place names, as yet indecipherable symbols, and scraps of information from medieval manuscripts. Nonetheless, Sir John Rhys, the doyen of early Celtic studies and first Professor of Celtic at Oxford University, was convinced that it was a non-Aryan (that is, non-Indo-European) language overlain by loan words from two separate Celtic dialects. The present-day consensus that Celtic languages and Celtic culture arrived in the Archipelago much earlier than previously thought, allows us to take a different and simpler view. It is now generally accepted that the Picts were not an ethnically distinct people, but rather a tribe or confederation of tribes living in the far north-east of Britain, with their own version of Celtic culture and their own Celtic language. In archaeological terms, as noted earlier, there is little to distinguish them from other Caledonian tribes, and their language, we now believe, was a version – quite possibly an early version – of P-Celtic, the language type found throughout most of Caledonia at this period.

Naturally enough, many questions remain. Ptolemy's map places several tribes in north-eastern Caledonia: the Venicones, the Taexali, the Vacomagi, the Decantae. Were these tribes Picts – in the sense that they shared Pictish culture? Were they the early components of what became a Pictish federation? And what of the Caledonii, whom Ptolemy places along the Great Glen, and after whom the Romans initially named the whole region? Were they Picts? Or should we ask, did they become Picts? How did the Picts organise themselves politically? A list of Pictish kings survives in the *Pictish Chronicle*, one of seven texts contained in the fourteenth-century Poppleton Manuscript, probably compiled in Hulne Priory near Alnwick. It begins in 311 with the thirty-year rule of King Vipoig, but nothing it says before the middle of the sixth century can be relied upon. Appealing stories such as Nechtan Morbet being raised from the dead by Saint Boite and Drest I ruling for a hundred years and fighting a hundred battles are clearly the stuff of legend. Nonetheless, at some time during the early centuries of the first millennium, the Picts went from being a sub-regional culture to becoming the principal force opposing the Romans in northern Britain. Exactly when and how this happened remains unexplained, but we are now closer to understanding their supposedly mysterious disappearance in the ninth century (see Chapter 29).

We cannot follow developments in Ireland and Caledonia as closely as we follow the events of Roman Britain. We lack the documentary sources, which means we lack knowledge of how the tribes organised themselves and of individuals and institutions. We have no detailed chronology, only a broad narrative outline. Yet we can still sense the stirring of forces and the building of pressures – to some extent autonomous, to some extent conditioned by the massive presence of Rome – that would later burst onto the stage of recorded history. From the fourth century onwards, as Roman power declined and new ethnic and cultural players entered the arena, these forces would play a critical part in shaping the social and political structure of the British Isles. However, before we look at the post-Roman phase of British history, we need to consider the advent of an entirely new and transformational ideology which still influences the daily life of many in the British Isles.

20 God and the Gods

Religion as practised by the Celtic-speaking tribes of Britain at the beginning of the first millennium AD was polytheistic and affirmed the immortality of the soul. There were major gods who presided over key aspects of life and the natural world – love, fertility, war, victory, hunting, thunder, agriculture, death, the underworld; there were minor deities associated with people, animals, or things – blacksmiths, merchants, dogs, horses, pigs and boars, meadows, wells and springs; there were local deities responsible for a particular river, hill, or forest; and central to the propitiation of all these gods and spirits was the act of sacrifice. Amid the profusion of names and possibilities, establishing the identities and attributes of individual gods and goddesses is an uncertain process. The druids wrote nothing down. The Romans tended to identify Celtic gods with their nearest Roman equivalent, which may have been convenient for Roman readers, but can be confusing for the historian (see Chapter 14). Most of our information comes from medieval legends and romances – the Welsh *Mabinogion*, the Irish *Lebor na hUidre* (*The Book of the Dun Cow*), *The Yellow Book of Lecan*, and *The Book of Invasions* – with all the uncertainties such texts bring with them. There is also the added complication that nineteenth and early twentieth-century Celtic scholars, chief among them Sir John Rhys, synthesised all the relevant information from the British Isles, Gaul, and elsewhere to create a unified pantheon of Celtic gods and goddesses, which certainly did not exist at the time. The result is fascinating but artificial and misleading.

Cernunnos is a case in point. He is known as the horned god of Celtic mythology, and features prominently in books on the subject, but there is considerable uncertainty about his name, his identity, and his role. The figure of a horned god has a long history and many manifestations, but the name Cernunnos was only applied in the nineteenth century. It was taken from a damaged inscription on a first-century monument, the Pillar of Boatmen, found in 1710 under the nave of the Cathedral of Notre Dame in Paris. Underneath a carving of a horned figure, with torcs on his horns and sitting cross-legged in a position suggesting meditation, is the word '*ernunnos*'. The first letter is missing. The 'C' was added by Celtic scholars because of a perceived link with the proto-Indo-European *krn/ker-no* and the Celtic root *kornu/kernu*, both meaning 'horn'. The name appears nowhere else. It does not feature in any legends, rhymes, or folktales. Nonetheless, within the context of Celtic culture, whenever there is a depiction or a description of a horned figure, it is frequently – and without supporting evidence – identified as Cernunnos.

The origins of the horned figure appear to lie in Mesolithic times, with the men who wore shamanistic, antlered, red-deer headdresses, such as those found at Star Carr. This may explain why he is seen as the guardian of the under- or otherworld. Several millennia later, the horned god became a recognisable part of the iconography of the Celtic tribes. There are numerous images and carvings in northern Gaul, notably around Paris and Reims. Most replicate the horns-and-torcs motif and may reasonably be associated with the figure on the Pillar of Boatmen. Similar carvings have been found in Iberia, although the details are not always the same. The most detailed image of a horned god, surrounded by snakes and animals and with a torc in his hand rather than on his horns, features on a silver cauldron from the first or second century BC found at Gundestrup in Denmark. This may be Cernunnos, although differences in iconography have led some scholars to identify him as Lugh. In Britain, three possible horned god images have been found – on a coin found near Petersfield, a carving from Cirencester, and a miniature sculpture found in Cambridgeshire – but none of them can be securely identified. An image from Clonmacnois in County Offaly in Ireland has also been associated with Cernunnos, but the identification seems wishful rather than likely.

As soon as scholars associated the name Cernunnos with the figure of the horned god, he began to appear in studies of Celtic mythology, and he continues to feature in contemporary books on the subject. He has been adopted by the modern, neo-pagan Wiccan religion. In such contexts, he has a range of attributes: he is a nature god, linked to animals and snakes; he is the god of the hunt; he is the god who guards the otherworld. These attributes derive from descriptions and depictions drawn from folklore and early documentary sources, from carvings and metal objects, such as the Gundestrup cauldron. But their association with Cernunnos is the result of a complicated and insecure process of reverse accretion – another circular argument – whereby images of a horned figure are identified as Cernunnos and all the attributes associated with those images are then credited to Cernunnos.

Similar uncertainties affect Maponos/Maponus, a god of music, healing and prophecy; Nudd/Núadu/Nodens, a god of war and the sea; Lugh/Llew/Llwch, the god of skills and mastery; and most of the other major Celtic deities. These gods were real enough in the minds of the people who honoured and worshipped them, but there is an essential difference between the Celtic and Roman pantheons. The hierarchy of the Roman gods (deriving, of course, from the Greek pantheon) is relatively clear cut – to the point where it can be presented as a genealogical diagram. Classical authors could allude to relationships, feuds, and squabbles among the gods with every expectation of being understood by their readers (as, indeed, could writers and poets right up to the twentieth century). This reflects Rome's status as a literate culture, with a unified and ordered (if unstable) polity, and a central religious authority. By contrast, the British Celtic tribes and their European counterparts were pre-literate and in no way unified – which is reflected in the way they recognised, honoured, and propitiated hundreds of different deities, who existed in a complex, even chaotic, spiritual landscape. Moreover, the gods they recognised, the powers they attributed to them, and the way in which they were worshipped almost certainly varied from region to region and tribe to tribe. When approaching the Celtic gods, it is better to start with an image and assess the function that the deity appears to fulfil in the context of that image, rather than giving the image a name and shoehorning him or her into a neatly structured pantheon which did not exist in the minds of worshippers at the time.

The Romans brought their own gods: that august pantheon which, because of centuries of emphasis on the classics in British education, is more familiar to most British and Irish people than their own 'native' gods. Like the Celts, they ascribed to each god influence over a particular aspect of human endeavour or the natural world, and they communicated with their gods through rites and sacrifice. Statues, carvings, and inscriptions show that Jupiter, Mars, and Mercury were the deities most widely honoured in Britain, with Hercules, Venus, Diana, Silvanus, and Minerva close behind. The temple complex constructed in Colchester in honour of the deified Claudius was the centre of the imperial cult in Britain – which was then spread across the province by merchants who established subsidiary branches in London, York, and Lincoln. The Romans also brought with them several so-called mystery cults devoted to individual gods, such as Mithras or Dionysus, or to pairs of gods, such as Cybele and Atys or Isis and Serapis. Unlike most Roman religious observance, the activities of mystery cults took place behind closed doors, involving initiation rites and other ceremonies designed to emphasise the mystical aspects of religion. The cults appear to have been favoured by the legions, by officials, and by others who moved around the Empire. Membership has been likened to a kind of Freemasonry.[157] In Britain, the all-male cult of Mithras, with its origins in Persian Zoroastrianism, seems to have had a strong following, particularly among soldiers. Of four known Mithraic temples, one is in London, one in Caernarfon, and two on Hadrian's Wall.

In the Roman world, honouring – or being seen to honour – the traditional pantheon was necessary for anyone seeking to climb the social ladder or obtain a senior public appointment. At the same time, it was normal for people to have a private religious life as well. It was not unusual for officials, soldiers, traders, and others serving or working in distant parts of the Empire to adopt local gods and, when they returned home or were posted to another part of the Empire, to take the gods and the associated rites and rituals with them. The cult of Toutatis, whose name means 'protector of the people', was imported to Britain from the Rhine and Danube valleys, presumably by legionaries who had been stationed there.

His image is found on Hadrian's Wall, in Hertfordshire, and on a number of rings, many of them found close to the legionary headquarters in Lincoln. The cult of the Matres, a trio of ladies associated with fertility and childbirth, originating in the Rhineland, was also probably introduced to Britain by the legions: some fifty images have been discovered, mostly on military sites.

Once settled in Britain, the Romans embraced a range of local deities. Codicius, a god associated with war, hunting and forests, had a temple at Bewcastle in Cumbria, and was worshipped across the northern part of Roman Britain, particularly along Hadrian's Wall. Coventina, a goddess of wells and springs, is known principally from a collection of inscriptions at Carrawburgh (Brocolita) Fort also on Hadrian's Wall. Antenociticus had an altar at Benwell and seems to have been the centre of a cult that attracted senior military officers. Belatucadrus, the 'bright slayer', was another Hadrian's Wall god, apparently worshipped by people of lower social status. Verbeia was the goddess of the River Wharfe in Yorkshire; Belisima/Belisama of the River Ribble in Lancashire. Our knowledge of most of these deities is limited to a handful of inscriptions indicating that the local Roman and Romano-British population honoured them, and we know nothing of what their cults involved. Nevertheless, the evidence indicates that it was not unusual for local deities to be adopted in this way.

Sometimes, a local god or goddess would merge with his or her Roman counterpart, a phenomenon known as syncretism. So we find inscriptions to Mars Codicius and Mars Belatucadrus, but the best example is found at Bath. Just as Neolithic arrivals accepted the sacredness of Mesolithic sites, and the Beaker people continued to venerate Neolithic sites, so the Romans were quick to make use of sites deemed sacred by the Britons. The principal attraction of Bath was, of course, the hot springs, which the local Celtic tribes held sacred to Sulis, a goddess of fertility and healing. The Romans erected a temple on the site as early as 60–70 AD, before Wales and much of the north had been conquered, but rather than impose Minerva, their own goddess of healing – and also of wisdom, poetry, and crafts – they fused the two goddesses into one, so the statue of Sulis-Minerva presided over the baths until they were destroyed, probably in the sixth century. The baths were a magnet for Roman society, but the Celtic element remained strong. Most of the famous curse tablets – small pieces of metal inscribed with requests that the goddess visit punishment on those guilty of stealing items, such as a cloak, a bathing suit, or money – were addressed to Sulis; and the town that grew up around the baths was Aquae Sulis, not Aquae Minerva.

It was against this religious background – crowded, complex, colourful, and above all flexible, with plenty of scope for personal choice – that Christianity arrived in the British Isles. Christianity was a fundamentally different *kind* of religion. It was monotheistic. The one God was omnipotent, omniscient, and omnipresent. He was abstract and unknowable. He may have taken human form in the figure of Jesus, but he did not have the human characteristics, or the failings and frailties, of the Celtic and Roman gods. Divisions between piety and impiety, legality and illegality, duty and neglect, obedience and disobedience were swept aside and replaced by a single cosmic opposition between good and evil, and its correlative: sin. All other gods and religions were pronounced false, their followers and celebrants damned. Where Christianity offered choice, that choice was binary. Such an unambiguous approach may have been familiar to the Jews and Persians, but to the inhabitants of the Mediterranean Basin and western Europe, it contradicted everything they had ever known.

Another fundamental difference was that Christianity was based not on ritual, but on the written word, on sacred texts revealing the will of God and passed down directly from God to man. For Greeks, Romans, and Celts religious observance was separate from philosophical speculation. For Christians, if God was omnipotent and omniscient, then the sacred texts contained all wisdom and the sacred texts revealed the purpose of the universe and of life itself. This was the basis of theology, a new discipline which, in many respects, replaced philosophy and changed the nature of western thought for the next millennium-and-a-half. It was during the Roman occupation that this new creed – simple, but dogmatic and challenging – began to make inroads into the dominance of the disorganised, colourful array of polytheistic gods, but how and when that happened is uncertain.

Christianity originated in Judea and spread rapidly, following the trade and transport routes that held the Roman Empire together. In Rome in 64 AD, less than forty years after the Crucifixion, the Emperor Nero launched the first major persecution of Christians. It was probably intended to divert attention from Nero's own misdeeds, but it shows that there were enough Christians in the city to provide a target. Somewhere around 200, the early Christian writer, Tertullian, claimed that 'regions of Britain which have never been penetrated by Roman arms have submitted to Christ.'[158] Is he implying that Roman Britain was already Christian? And which were the other 'regions'? Is he referring to southern Caledonia? Or the west coast? He cannot mean the Picts, for we know that they were not converted until after the end of the Roman era. Could 'Britain' mean 'the British Isles', suggesting that Christianity had already reached Ireland? Then about 240, Origen, one of the early Church Fathers, asked rhetorically 'when, before the arrival of Christ, did the land of Britain agree together in the worship of the one God?'[159] Again, this suggests that most of Britain had already been converted, but both Tertullian and Origen were writing at a time when Christianity was still not a legally authorised religion within the Empire.

Like the Jews, Christians refused to sacrifice to the gods and refused to worship the emperor. Worse still, they claimed that Christianity was a universal religion. Such claims were interpreted as a direct challenge to the Roman state and were the ostensible basis for periods of persecution – although the persecution of Christians, like that of Jews in later ages, was often scapegoating, and backed up by wild allegations that the Eucharist involved drinking blood and eating human flesh. Despite the claims of later Christian propagandists, persecution was sporadic rather than constant, and Christianity was not the only sect to be outlawed. The cult of Bacchus was suppressed on grounds of drunkenness and violence, and that of Magna Mater, or Cybele, because it encouraged outlandish behaviour and self-castration. Attitudes towards Christians were conditioned by the attitude of the emperor, of provincial governors, and by local circumstances. In 260, the Emperor Gallienus formally decriminalised Christianity, yet in 303 Diocletian unleashed a wave of savage attacks on believers. This policy was continued by Galerius, ruler of the Eastern Empire, until 311 when, suffering from illness and fearing death, he issued the Edict of Toleration. If he was hoping for divine intervention, he was to be disappointed: he died within a matter of weeks, and his son Maximinus II (also Maximinus Daia) reverted to a policy of persecution.

The crucial change came in 313 when co-Emperors Licinus and Constantine I issued the Edict of Milan, formally ending persecution in the west and granting Christianity full legal status. The Empire remained a mixture of faiths. Although he declared himself a Christian, built churches, and gave Christians financial privileges, Constantine did not renounce the title of Pontifex Maximus. He built a new and supposedly Christian capital at Constantinople but did not prohibit the construction of temples and statues to the old gods. In the early 360s, the Emperor Julian – known as the Apostate – attempted to reverse toleration and reinstate full paganism, but he was killed in Persia before his policies could have a lasting impact. In 380, by which time Christianity had spread widely across the Empire, the Emperor Theodosius outlawed sacrifice, divination, and all other pagan practices, and declared Christianity to be the official Roman religion.

It was probably merchants and traders who first brought Christianity to Britain and Ireland. Legionaries arriving from areas where Christianity was already established may have played a part – although most of them appear to have worshipped Mithras. Another possibility may be glimpsed in the story of Lucius, who is styled a king but was evidently a tribal leader. The Venerable Bede, writing his *Historia ecclesiastica gentis Anglorum* (*An Ecclesiastical History of the English People*) in the early decades of the eighth century, says that in the year 156

> whilst the holy Eleutherus presided over the Roman Church, Lucius, king of Britain, sent a letter to him, entreating that by a mandate from him he might be made a Christian. He soon obtained his pious request, and the Britons preserved the faith, which they had received, uncorrupted and entire, in peace and tranquillity until the time of the Emperor Diocletian.[160]

Historia Brittonum (*The History of the Britons*), an imaginative work, usually dated to around 830 and credited to the Welsh monk Nennius (although the attribution has been questioned), also tells the story but gets it wrong. It says that in 167 'King Lucius, with all the chiefs of the British people, received baptism, in consequence of a legation sent by the Roman emperors and pope Evaristus.' In the first place, the Pope (or Bishop of Rome, at the time) would have been Eleutherius (or Eleutherus; r.c.174–189), not Evaristus (r.c.99–c.107). Secondly, and more important, the co-emperors, Lucius Verus and Marcus Aurelius, would surely not have agreed to send a legation on behalf of a religious group that was not recognised by the Empire – especially as Marcus Aurelius was generally unsympathetic towards Christians.

In 1817, the Reverend William Gunn, who edited and translated *Historia Brittorum*, complicated matters by claiming, though on what evidence is not clear, that Lucius was the great-grandson of Caratacus. Gunn argues that Caratacus and his family learnt about Christianity during their exile in Rome and points out that St Paul's *Epistles to the Romans* would have been received while Caratacus was living in the city. He suggests that this knowledge was passed down the generations to Lucius and explains his wish to convert.[161] While this makes for human interest, the whole Lucius story is probably an invention designed to show the British elites as having seen the Christian light at an early stage. Bede's reference to Diocletian's persecution of Christians is historically accurate and could be interpreted as an attempt to explain why, if Lucius did indeed take the lead in converting the Britons, so many of them needed to be converted again later. The real significance of both Bede and Nennius telling the story of Lucius is that it shows they had no alternative narrative to explain the early spread of Christianity. They both lived in the post-Roman era, when it was not uncommon for a ruler to accept baptism and require the rest of his kingdom to follow his example. Including the Lucius story allowed them to apply a phenomenon familiar in their own time to an unexplained happening in the past.

On the Continent, we find stories of burnings and massacres and of missionaries being hunted down. In Britain, we have the names of three martyrs and the story of one, and in Ireland none at all. The name of St Alban, the first British martyr, appeared in a now-lost manuscript *Martyrologium Hieronymianum*, compiled in 362 – its contents were reproduced in a still extant Syriac manuscript known as *The Martyrology of 411*. Our main source for the little we know about his life is *Passio Albani* (*The Passion of St Alban*), probably written by Germanus, the Bishop of Auxerre, in the 440s. Germanus says that when a detachment of Roman soldiers was searching for a priest, Alban disguised himself and gave himself up, and was killed, thus allowing the real priest to escape. One manuscript dates the story to the persecutions under Severus c.209,[162] while Bede places of Alban's death in the years between Diocletian's decree of universal persecution in 303 and the Edict of Milan in 313. Alban gave his name to modern-day St Albans, where his cult was established, but he may have been killed in London. It is even possible that, like Lucius, the whole story is fiction invented for proselytising purposes. Of Saints Aaron and Julius, we know even less. Gildas says they were from Carlisle, although he may mean Caerleon. Bede says they were citizens of 'the City of the Legions', which is usually taken to mean Caerleon, but could also mean Chester. He also states that they were tortured, and their limbs mangled but gives no other details. Their martyrdom is usually associated with Diocletian's persecutions at the beginning of the fourth century.

Beyond the three martyrs, we have only a handful of documentary references to Christianity in Britain before the end of Roman rule. In 314, the year after Christianity became legal under the Edict of Milan, three British bishops – Restitutus of London, Eborius of York, and Adelfius of Lincoln – attended a council in Arles to discuss the Donatist heresy. In 359, three British bishops attended the Council of Ariminum (Rimini) to discuss the Arian heresy. Shortly after the end of the occupation, probably in 429, Germanus of Auxerre and another bishop, Lupus of Troyes, were sent to Britain to confront those British clergy who had embraced the heresies of Pelagius. Germanus, we are told, lacked any local support, but nonetheless soundly defeated the Pelagians in debate because of his superior rhetoric and wisdom. This intellectual victory was followed by a military one. He took command of a British army facing a force of Saxons and Picts. On the eve of the battle, he baptised the British soldiers *en masse* and taught them to shout 'Allelulia' as a battle cry. Germanus and his men were, of course, victorious. These stories are recounted in the late fifth century *Vita Germani*, one of the few contemporary sources of information on post-Roman Britain, and one of the least disputed. They reveal that by the mid-fourth century, Christianity in Britain was organised enough to have its own episcopal structure, and sophisticated enough to play a full part in the theological disputes of the day.

The early life of St Patrick gives a glimpse of church organisation on a smaller scale. Patrick says that his father was a deacon of the Church, a member of the *ordo* of his *civitas*, and the owner of a small country estate. Looking at the names in Patrick's text and considering his abduction by Irish slavers, it is probable that the *civitas* in question was Carlisle (but see Chapter 23). Patrick also states that his grandfather, Potitus, was an ordained priest. St Patrick was probably active in Ireland from 430s onwards – the *Irish Annals*, although not always reliable, date his arrival as 432. From this, we get the picture of a wealthy, well-connected Christian family living on a country estate somewhere near Carlisle and belonging to a church that was sufficiently organised and established to ordain its own priests, somewhere towards the end of the fourth century.[163]

The archaeological record adds very little to our understanding of the spread of Christianity. In 1930, the philosopher and archaeologist, Robin Collingwood stated that 'relics of Christianity in Roman Britain are very rare.'[164] In 1953, Professor Jocelyn Toynbee published a study which concluded that there was evidence of widespread Christian activity.[165] The process of time has seen many new sites discovered and many old ones reassessed, much new evidence uncovered, and many new – often contradictory – conclusions reached. Writing in 2013, Ronald Hutton summarised the situation with characteristic directness: 'Four centuries of the most diligent and intelligent scholarly investigation have failed to establish any consensus concerning the extent, nature and success of the Christian faith in Roman Britain.'[166]

If we are correct that the legionaries were not a major channel of transmission for the new religion, then most early Christians are likely to have been people of wealth and status: officials, members of the *ordo*, landowners, members of tribal elites, merchants, and people with connections on the Continent. Elsewhere, converts were usually members of the urban poor, but in this respect Britain seems to have diverged from the rest of the Empire, probably because it was an island. Initially, Christians would have worshipped in private houses, villas, or any building with sufficient space – a practice unlikely to leave significant archaeological traces. Later, as their number grew and Christianity was no longer actively persecuted, there would have been purpose-built churches, but while some possibilities have been identified, no churches and only one chapel have been positively identified. Hutton draws attention to Nettleton Shrub in Gloucestershire where, in the middle of the fourth century, a temple complex dedicated to the syncretic Apollo Cunomaglus was replaced by a cross-shaped building. This could have been a church, but the only evidence is the shape of the building.[167] At Uley, also in Gloucestershire, a shrine to Mercury was demolished during the 380s to make way for a building with internal structures that have been interpreted as stone altars, although this has been questioned.[168] In Gloucestershire, Wiltshire, and Somerset, modest stone buildings that could have been churches were erected on the site of cult shrines. From the 380s onwards, some pagan temples were falling into disuse or being demolished, while others, notably to syncretic Romano-Celtic gods, continued in use or were refurbished, and some new ones were built. Hutton sees such contradictory evidence as reflecting the political and social uncertainties of Roman Britain at the time. Christianity was growing less tolerant of other religions, but the increasingly frequent attacks of war bands from Ireland, from north of the Wall, and from across the North Sea were weakening the Roman authority on which Christianity in Britain depended.[169]

Graveyards are another source of information. Christians insisted on bodies being buried intact, on their backs, with their feet facing east so that they could rise to face the Last Judgement. They did not allow grave goods; but they allowed infants to be buried in their cemeteries, which pagans did not. Using these criteria, a number of cemeteries have been identified as Christian – with a higher density in what is now central southern England. Unfortunately, across the province as a whole, many burials meeting these criteria also occur in known pagan cemeteries; and, over the course of the fourth century, the number of pagan burials relative to Christian burials appears to increase.[170]

Even with images or artefacts, similar problems exist. The Chi-Rho symbol ☧, a monogram made up of *chi* (X) and *rho* (P), the first two letters of the Greek *Khristos* (Christ), was used throughout the Empire as a mark of the Christian faith. It appears in mosaics and frescos, on gravestones and sarcophagi, and on objects such as coins, rings, and cutlery. The difficulty here is that, after Emperor Constantine's decision to embrace Christianity, the Chi-Rho began to feature in images of the emperor to symbolise the fact that he ruled with divine authority, so not all Chi-Rho denote the presence of the faith. So the remarkable mosaic image of a male figure with a Chi-Rho behind him discovered at Hinton St Mary in Dorset, could be a representation of Christ, or it could be an image of Constantine or another emperor.[171]

The puzzle of Christianity in Roman Britain is summed up by Lullingstone Villa in Kent, which contains the only securely identified chapel or house-church in the British Isles. There are images of worshippers with raised hands, and three Chi-Rho symbols, one of them the centrepiece of a unique fresco, which also incorporates the Greek letters, Alpha and Omega, an allusion to the Book of Revelations. However, this house-church was constructed on the floor above a temple-room dedicated to local water nymphs, and the temple was renovated in the middle of the fourth century, suggesting that both the Christian church and the pagan temple were in use at the same time. Were the family just hedging

Map 19   God and the Gods

their bets and following both faiths? Were they Christians who feared the return of paganism and persecution? Were they divided, with the older generation following the old gods, and the younger ones following the new religion? We shall never know.

In the lands north of Hadrian's Wall, we have clues and legends, but no relevant documentary sources before John of Fordun's *Chronica Gentis Scotorum* (*Chronicles of the Scottish People*) in the fourteenth century, and

Hector Boece's *Historia Gentis Scotorum* (*History of the Scottish People*) in the sixteenth – and both need to be treated with considerable caution. Fordun and Boece drew on sources which are lost – or imaginary – and their writings inform those of two seventeenth-century historians of the Scottish church, David Calderwood (1575–1650) and John Spotiswoode, Archbishop of St Andrews (1565–1639). Calderwood claims that there were 'many Christians' among the population before the conversion of King Donald – 'as there were among the Britons, before the conversion of King Lucius'.[172] Spotiswoode dates the conversion of 'King Donald with his Queen and divers of his Nobles' to 203. He goes on to say that King Cratilinth came to the throne in 277 and 'made it one of his first works to purge the Kingdom of heathenish superstition, and expulse the Druids', a task made easier by an influx of Christians fleeing from the persecutions decreed by Diocletian.[173] The idea that Christians fled north to Caledonia to avoid persecution is appealing, and may contain a kernel of truth, but it is unlikely that King Donald or King Cratilinth existed. Once again, we are probably looking at stories designed to promote the image of early piety among the rulers of north Britain.

Two further clues from the end of the Roman era are worth considering, both demonstrating the porous nature of the northern frontier. In 1919, Alexander Ormiston Curle, at the time Director of the National Museum of Scotland, uncovered a hoard of Roman silver at Traprain Law. It weighed over twenty-two kilos and contained more than two hundred and fifty items, most of them crushed or deliberately broken, perhaps preparatory to being melted down. Some pieces, mainly items of tableware, are engraved with traditional Roman images, but some feature biblical scenes, outline drawings of fish – often used to represent Christianity – and Chi Rho symbols. The horde has been dated to the beginning of the fifth century, contemporary with the collapse of Roman power. The silverware is of a type known to have been in use in Britain, so it could have been loot, brought back from a raid south of the Wall, but Traprain Law was the seat of the Votadini, Rome's allies, so it could equally have been a payment to ensure that the Votadini did not raid south of the Wall. In any event, it is evidence there was a Christian community in Roman Britain wealthy enough to have collected so much silver.

On the other side of the country, we have St Ninian. Although doubts have been cast on his authenticity, including the suggestion that he is a scribal error for 'Finnian', he probably did exist. He is mentioned by Bede; he is the subject of an anonymous and fanciful eighth-century poem, *Miracula Nynie Episcopi* (*The Miracles of Bishop Ninian*), and of *Vita Sancti Niniani* (*A Life of Saint Ninian*), written by Ælred (or Ailred) of Rievaulx about 1160. Ninian was probably of British origin, possibly the son of a Christian tribal leader. He studied in Rome and was instructed by the Pope to convert people whom Bede calls the 'southern Picts'.[174] However, it seems that there were already Christians in the area and, in addition to his missionary work, Ninian may have acted as their first bishop. There is clear evidence of an early Christian presence in Carlisle and along Hadrian's Wall, and there is no reason why Christianity should not have passed beyond the Wall and spread among the local population. Ninian began his mission in Galloway in the 390s and built a church of stone – something unusual among the British. He dedicated it to his patron, St Martin of Tours, probably after St Martin's death in 397. The church became known as Candida Casa, the white house, which translates into Old English as *hwit-aern*, giving its name to the town of Whithorn in Wigtownshire, where there is evidence of an early Christian community. The Latinus stone – 'We praise thee as Lord! Erected by Latinus, aged thirty-five, and his daughter' – Scotland's oldest Christian monument, dated to c.450, was found in Whithorn, and during the sixth century Whithorn monastery was actively training monks as missionaries to northern Caledonia and to Ireland.

Christians living in Galloway and other areas north of the Wall were not ruled by Rome and not part of the organisational structure of the Church to the south. Nonetheless, they would undoubtedly have been aware of Roman towns, Roman temples, and the complexities of Roman polytheism and its syncretic absorption of many Celtic gods. In Ireland, the situation was simpler. There was no Roman presence, and no Roman religion to complicate the spiritual context. In theory, conversion should have been a straightforward choice between Celtic polytheism and monotheistic Christianity, but we know little about it. Christianity may have arrived with the merchants and traders crossing the Irish Sea. Slaves may have brought the new religion with them. St Patrick, writing in the second half of the fifth century, says that thousands of people were abducted from Britain and taken to Ireland as slaves, as he was himself. Some of them may have been Christians. There may have been missionaries from Britain during the fourth century. There were increasing numbers of Christians in both Gaul and Iberia, so we cannot rule out some transmission up the Atlantic seaboard. We simply do not know.

The first, indeed the only, verifiable information we have dates from 431, after the collapse of Roman power in Britain. The chronicler Prosper of Aquitaine states that a man called Palladius, from a noble family in Gaul, was commissioned by Pope Celestine in 431 to become 'the first bishop to the Scotti believing in Christ.'[175] The term Scotti during this period usually refers to the tribe who held lands in both north-east Ireland and the western part of the British mainland to which they gave their name (see Chapter 23). In this context, however, it seems likely to apply to the Irish in general. Prosper's information is almost contemporary with the events it describes (he died c.455). It contains references which can be checked and is generally credible. Thus 431, when we are told Palladius and his three companions – Auxilius, Secundinus, and Iserninus, all of whom were later canonised – landed at Arklow in County Wicklow, is the first verifiable date in Irish history. They were driven off by hostile tribes and made their way to Leinster, where Palladius founded three churches and left relics of St Peter and St Paul before being banished by the King of Leinster for reasons unspecified. He then spent the next twenty years as a missionary in Caledonia. Later scribes either confuse, or deliberately conflate, his exploits with those of St Patrick, who probably began his ministry in Ireland just a few years later, and whose cult rapidly eclipsed that of Palladius. It is only recently that Auxilius, Secundinus, and Iserninus have been recognised as companions of Palladius, not Patrick. The essential point, however, is that Pope Celestine's commission indicates that there were sufficient Christians in Ireland before 431 to merit the services of a bishop.

Over the course of the second half of the first millennium, Christianity played a pivotal role in the cultural, political, and ethnic struggles that swept across the British Isles. Its monotheistic nature and its – in principle – unified organisation, allowed the new religion to exert an influence that was unprecedented for a non-political entity. Roman Britain became the object of hostile forces attacking from the outside, which, when the Romans left, strove for mastery, at first against each other, and then against new waves of invaders. The Church emerged as a different kind of force, with God's blessing or condemnation as its principal weapon. Whether it worked with or against kings and tribal leaders, it remained essentially independent because it dealt in spiritual and moral imperatives, and because its leaders – though divided at times – saw themselves as representing a supranational body which it was beyond the ability of secular leaders to control. Consequently, the Church was a significant force in shaping almost all aspects of life in the post-Roman British Isles.

21 The Crumbling Façade

> In the early part of the year 410 – the very year when Rome was besieged and taken – the Emperor Honorius wrote letters to the British cities, releasing them from all allegiance to the empire; and the Britons were left to themselves to guard their towns against the Caledonians.
> — Professor J.M.D. Meiklejohn[176]

> By the beginning of the fifth century all the legions had gone on one errand or another, and to frantic appeals for aid the helpless Emperor Honorius could only send his valedictory message in 410, that 'the cantons should take steps to defend themselves'. — Winston Churchill[177]

> In 410, the Emperor Honorius responded to requests for help from Britain by writing to the leading citizens of Britannia that from now on they would have to defend themselves from their own resources…
> — Simon Schama[178]

Professor John Meiklejohn writing in 1899, Winston Churchill in 1956, and Simon Schama in 2000, all focus on Honorius writing to the British in 410 as the definitive moment in the last stages of Roman Britain. They are not alone. Generations of schoolchildren – including the present author – were taught that the Romans 'left' Britain in 410. Yet the story of Honorius' letter is based on a single half-sentence in the *Nova Historia* of the Greek historian Zosimus, a man notorious for his inaccuracy in names and geography, writing a hundred years after the event, and taking his information from the now lost *History* of Olympiodorus.

Writing of Alaric the Visigoth, who had been enlisted to help Priscus

Attalus become emperor and was rampaging across northern Italy, Zosimus says:

> Alaric ... proceeded with his army to all the cities of Aemilia, which had refused to accept Attalus as their sovereign. Some of these he speedily reduced, but having besieged Bononia, which resisted him many days, without being able to take it, he advanced towards Liguria, to compel that country likewise to acknowledge Attalus as its emperor. Honorius, having sent letters to the cities of Britannia, counselling them to be watchful of their own security, and having rewarded his soldiers with the money sent by Heraclianus, lived with all imaginable ease...[179]

Honorius may possibly have been responding to frantic calls for help from Britain, but there is no mention of them here – or anywhere else. They are the presumption of historians. Nor is there any mention of releasing the British from their allegiance to the Empire. Moreover, the half-sentence to which such importance has been attached is sandwiched between the wars in northern Italy and mention of Heraclianus who was in North Africa. This has led to suggestions that 'Britannia' is a transcription error for 'Bruttium', which was sometimes written 'Brettia', or even for 'Raetia'.[180] Unfortunately, Bruttium, in present-day Calabria, the southernmost province of Italy, is nearly as far from Liguria as Britain, and was not – at the time – threatened by Alaric; while, even allowing for scribal errors in Greek cursive script, Raetia is some orthographic distance from Britannia. However, it is worth noting that even the chief defender of the 'Britannia' reading concedes that Zosimus is 'the worst of all extant Greek historians of the Roman Empire' and that Book VI, containing the disputed passage, 'swarms with errors and confusions'.[181] A plausible alternative may be found in the fact that later in 410, after the sack of Rome, Alaric did go on to threaten Bruttium. In fact, he died there, in the city of Cosenza, that same year. Zosimus' *Nova Historia* comes to a sudden halt just a few pages after the Britannia passage, and before the sack of Rome. He may well have died at this point. It is possible that the crucial sentence is simply out of chronological order and describes (accurately or otherwise) something that happened later.

Whatever the truth of the matter, this single, disputed half-sentence clearly cannot bear the weight of the interpretation that has been put on it. What it has done is to provide historians and students with a fixed reference point for the 'end' of Roman Britain, and in so doing fundamentally distorted understanding of the period. Roman power came to Britain only slowly. Caesar's two abortive invasions brought Roman influence, but it was another century before Claudius began the process of conquest. And it was another century before the Romans discovered how much of the island they could realistically hold and rule. The Roman departure from Britain was a similarly extended and even more complex process, due as much to the breakdown of the Roman political system and to social and economic upheavals within the Empire as to the predations of the Irish, the Picts, and Germanic tribes from across the North Sea.

Politically as well as geographically, Britannia was on the edge of the Empire. It was not unimportant, but it was not at the centre of the internal upheavals convulsing the Empire, nor was it in the front line of the migrations and invasions that assailed the Empire from the east. It was probably Caracalla who decided to divide the province in two. To the north, Britannia Inferior was poorer and less stable. Caracalla's agreements with the tribes meant that the northern frontier remained relatively peaceful until the end of the third century, but small-scale raids across the Irish Sea and the North Sea continued. To the south, Britannia Superior was wealthy and secure, although the construction of a line of forts along the eastern and southern coasts – among them Brancaster, Burgh Castle, Richborough, and Lympne – suggests that raids were becoming more common. In the fourth century, these forts were incorporated into the defensive system known as the Saxon Shore. Nevertheless, while the Empire suffered an unparalleled series of political crises and invasions, Britain remained comparatively peaceful.

Caracalla campaigned successfully against the Alemanni on the Upper Rhine in 213–14, and then less successfully against the Persians in 216–17, when he was assassinated by a soldier whom he had refused to promote. There were three emperors in the next six years, each assassinated by soldiers loyal to the next. Severus Alexander (r.222–235) brought a degree of stability but faced with simultaneous invasions by the Persians and the Germanic tribes, he was forced to buy off the Germans in order to gain time. The army, growing less and less amenable to discipline, regarded this as shameful and murdered him, marking the beginning of an extended period of chaos, which only ended with the accession of Diocletian in 284. During the intervening fifty years, Rome was constantly at war with itself. Some twenty-seven emperors and co-emperors came and went, often with breath-taking speed: there were no fewer than six in 235 alone. Most were murdered by their own soldiers, a handful died in battle, two died of plague, and one is reported to have been struck by lightning. At the same time, there were continual tribal incursions. The Goths invaded through the eastern Balkans. The Alemanni twice reached northern Italy before being defeated. Smaller tribes, such as the Juthungi, Chaibones, Salians, Frisians and Burgundians, also crossed into the Empire to grab their share of the spoils. In the east, Persian armies under Shapur I invaded Syria and Mesopotamia. The demands on Roman manpower and resources were immense. And as if civil war and foreign invasion were not enough, between 249 and 262 the plague swept across much of the Empire. There is no evidence that it reached the British Isles, but at its peak 5,000 people a day were reported as dying in Rome, while in Alexandria sixty per cent of the population may have died. These unprecedented strains meant that the complex network of internal trade routes, one of the Empire's great strengths, began to break down. There were shortages in some provinces, and gluts in others. Food, wine, and manufactured products were all affected. The merchants and traders who were essential to wealth creation and the economic health of the Empire began to suffer.

Invasion, instability, and disruption meant that Rome could not provide adequate military support to everyone, so some parts of the Empire began to look out for their own interests and rely on their own resources. As far as Britain was concerned this manifested itself in the Gallic Empire. In 260, alarmed and frustrated by the inability of Rome to prevent further invasions, the troops on the Rhine proclaimed the regional governor, Marcus Cassianius Latinius Postumus, as Emperor. Initially at least, this was not a usurpation. Postumus sought to maintain the security and integrity of the western provinces. He ruled his breakaway provinces – two in Germany, Gaul, Hispania, and Britain – in a thoroughly Roman manner. He did not attempt to invade Italy or dethrone the Emperor Gallienus in Rome. Geographical reality meant that Britannia had little option but to join the breakaway state. However, by 269 Postumus' Gallic Empire had become victim to the same political instability that it was set up to counter, and he was killed by his own men. It staggered on for a few years under a series of short-lived rulers, but by 274 the Emperor Aurelian had completed the process of reintegrating it into the Empire. If Britain suffered any consequences, they are not recorded.

Zosimus claims that there were two political rebellions in Britain during the reign of Probus (r.276–282) but gives no details. In 284, the Emperor Carinus (r.283–285) took the title *Britannicus Maximus*, suggesting a successful military campaign, but whether to counter a political rebellion or a tribal incursion is unknown. A more serious challenge came in 287: Maximian, ruler of the Western Empire, ordered the arrest and execution of one Marcus Aurelius Mausaeus Valerius Carausius, a former pilot who had risen to become commander of the *Classis Britannica*, the Roman fleet based in the Channel, and tasked with putting an end to increasingly frequent raids by Frankish and Saxon pirates. Carausius responded by detaching Britain and northern Gaul from the Empire and proclaiming himself 'Emperor of the North'. He resisted initial attempts to oust him – probably setting up the network of coastal forts that became known as the Saxon Shore in the process – but the new Empire did not last long. Carausius quickly lost most of his Continental possessions and in 293 was assassinated by his treasurer, Allectus, who held onto power in Britain for three years until defeated by Constantius I, the next ruler of the western Empire, in 296.

Once Britain was reintegrated into the Empire, Constantius divided the two existing provinces into three and then, a short time afterwards, into four, in line with structural reforms being promoted by Diocletian, the ruling Emperor. Maxima Caesariensis had its capital in London; Britannia Prima was centred on either Gloucester or Cirencester; Flavia Caesariensis had its capital at Lincoln; and Britannia Secunda was probably centred on York. These four provinces were grouped together to form what was known as a 'diocese', and overseen by a *vicarius*, who reported to the Prefect of Gaul. The aim was clearly to make Britain more manageable, and to reduce the opportunity for ambitious commanders to mount a challenge for the throne.

The Roman Empire survived what has become known as the Crisis of the Third Century. Diocletian (r.284–305) and Constantine I (r.306–337) did what they could to pull the vast, disparate, and fractured edifice together, and force through much-needed reforms. It was not an easy process. Both had to fight their way to power, and the stability they achieved was at best relative. There was always the possibility of a provincial rebellion, an assassin in the Praetorian Guard, or a discontented legion proclaiming an opportunistic usurper for the sake of a few gold coins. There

Map 20   The Roman Provinces of Britain

can be no doubt that nearly a century of instability and internal conflict had encouraged Rome's enemies. Both Diocletian and Constantine were constantly fighting on the Empire's borders. Diocletian's campaigns were mainly in the east: against the Sarmatians on the Danube frontier, the Persians, and in Lower Egypt. Constantine spent thirty years fighting in Germany, Pannonia, and Dacia.

Compared with other provinces, Britain was little affected by the tramp of armies during the third century crisis. Its importance lay in its ability to feed and finance the armies that were tramping elsewhere. A panegyric addressed to Constantius after he had recovered Britain for the

Empire highlights its cereals, pastures, and tax revenues. There was trouble on the northern border in 296. Then, in 305 and 306, Constantius and his son, Constantine, campaigned beyond Hadrian's Wall, presumably in response to a tribal incursion. All we know is that they overran, but did not annexe, 'the forests and swamps of the Caledonians and of the other Picts'.[182] There may have been trouble in 343 when the Emperor Constans was lauded for his bravery in crossing the Channel in winter, but again we know no details.

In general, Britain appears to have prospered. The first half of the fourth century is often regarded as the high point of Roman rule, at least in material terms. Villas were being built; agriculture was booming; Roman-style products were widely available; Roman currency was in wide circulation; Roman governmental and legal systems functioned effectively. A further indication of the importance of British grain comes in 359–60, when the Emperor Julian re-established control of the Rhine estuary following an invasion by the Salii and Chamavi tribes. His first concern was to rebuild the granaries that had been destroyed and reinstitute grain shipments from Britain to feed his army. Despite prosperity among the elite, the life of a rural peasant remained hard – although fruit and herbs, such as apples and coriander, introduced by the Romans and widely available, had improved people's diet – but life was probably harder in those Continental provinces which had been fought over by successive claimants to the imperial throne. Moreover, the economy of Roman Britain at this time appears to have been sustainable. It was not artificially boosted by massive state spending on a huge military presence – which, at its height in the second century, exceeded 50,000 men – or on fortifications, roads, and public buildings.

However, from the 350s onwards, it all began to fall apart. The balance of causes is hard to determine. Raiding by the Picts, Irish, and Saxons was never going to cease, but it might have been held in check, had it not been for the increasingly corrosive nature of Roman politics, and what appears to have been a slow, but in the end all-pervasive economic collapse. If the escalating scale and intensity of tribal attacks and incursions was the trigger for the end of Roman Britain, the ever more apparent political and economic weakness, and the inability of the authorities to defend their territory and their people were the underlying causes.

In 350, in Autun in eastern Gaul, Flavius Magnus Magnentius, a senior army commander, was acclaimed Emperor. Britannia, Gaul, and Hispania all declared for him, but he was defeated and killed by Constantius II in 353. After his death, Constantius sent a man known as Paulus Catenus (Paul the Chain) to Britain to root out those who had supported Magnentius. According to the contemporary historian, Ammianus Marcellinus

> Paulus [was] a kind of viper ... he autocratically exceeded his instructions and, like a flood, suddenly overwhelmed the fortunes of many, making his way amid manifold slaughter and destruction, imprisoning freeborn men and even degrading some with handcuffs ... he patched together many accusations with utter disregard of the truth.[183]

We do not know who was affected by this reign of terror, but it can only have weakened the upper echelons of Roman and Romano-British society.

Ammianus states that, in 360, the Picts and the Scotti 'broke the peace that been agreed [presumably with Constantius in 306] and devastated the frontier regions.'[184] Julian sent his commander-in-chief, Lupicinus, with some lightly-armed native auxiliaries to sort things out, which, as we hear no more of the matter, we assume he did. Then in 367, came what Ammianus calls a barbarian conspiracy. The Picts overran Hadrian's Wall; the Scotti crossed from Ireland; and a slightly mysterious tribe known as the Attacotti, who may have been related to the Scotti, either crossed from Ireland or came south from the Western Isles. Small groups of Irish settlers, who had begun to colonise the coast of Wales, may also have become involved. At the same time, the Saxons renewed their attacks on Britain's east coast, while the Franks and Saxons invaded Gaul from the north. One native unit of the Roman army – the *areani*, who were probably scouts operating north of Hadrian's Wall – joined in the raiding and were disbanded once order was eventually restored. Ammianus was not alone in seeing these attacks as a coordinated conspiracy. The tribes were certainly much more sophisticated than the Romans liked to think and could perhaps have coordinated the timing of their offensive, but any broader strategic plan seems unlikely.

We do not know what Roman forces were in Britain at the time, but they were clearly swept aside. Nectaridus, possibly the first Count of the Saxon Shore and in charge of the defence of the southern and eastern coasts, was killed. Fulofaudes, the *dux Britanniarum*, or military commander, was captured and probably killed. Military discipline broke down and many soldiers deserted. What happened to the provincial governors and the *vicarius* is not known, but the civil administration also broke down. The Emperor Valentian, who was fully occupied with the Alemanni on the Upper Rhine, sent first one and then another senior general to report on the situation. Both apparently said that a large force was needed and in the autumn of 367, another commander, Count Theodosius – whose son became Theodosius the Great – was appointed to command an expeditionary force of some two thousand men. He landed at Richborough and made his way to London. There was no single army to fight, but the whole country was full of bands of warriors, raiding and pillaging at will. Theodosius proclaimed an amnesty for deserters, divided his forces, and began restoring order, perhaps assisted by naval forces along the North Sea coast. It took most of the next year to round up the raiding bands. It took longer to rebuild and reorganise the province's defences and to reform and strengthen the legions. And Theodosius' task was complicated by a revolt plotted by a well-connected criminal called Valentinus who had been found guilty of some unspecified crime either in Rome or his native Pannonia, escaped death, and been exiled to Britain.

Given the nature of the unrest, it is likely that most of the damage occurred in rural areas. Villages would have been burnt, villas and big estates attacked, and crops destroyed. We have already noted a falling off in the number of new villas being built in subsequent decades, while many others fell into disrepair or were deserted. Some towns were probably attacked, though how effectively is difficult to tell. There is some evidence of defences being rebuilt and strengthened. The Empire expended men and resources to recover the four provinces; Roman government and civil administration were re-established; but the confidence of the civilian population was shaken. The rampaging bands of tribesmen undoubtedly did significant damage, but the social and economic decline that followed had less to do with raiding tribes than with systemic economic failure.

There are few documentary sources relating to Britain in the final decades of the fourth century, but the archaeological record paints a vivid picture of social, economic and technological decline. Large-scale agriculture was a significant casualty. Most of the villas at the centre of the great estates show signs of decay. Whether the original owners remained or fled, we do not know, but many big houses seem to have had only a few rooms occupied. The grand salons were turned into kitchens or barns for storing grain. Some estates managed to maintain themselves longer than others, but the decline was countrywide and continued for thirty or forty years. By 420, most of the villas that had been Britain's glory were ruined or deserted.

The towns, too, decayed. Those areas outside the walls, usually populated by craftsmen, traders, and merchants, declined first. Within the ring of the town's defences, we find temples being dismantled, and the disciplined planning that traditionally kept the thoroughfares open ignored. Baths and theatres were used for storage or left to decay. Wooden buildings appeared among the ruins of stone ones. Baths and sewers silted up. As the towns decayed, so their administrative functions also began to fail. It became difficult to find men to serve on the *ordines* of the towns – a privilege, but an expensive one that people could no longer afford. Eventually, most of the inhabitants drifted away. There were exceptions, as we shall see, but across most of Britannia the picture was the same.

Industry also collapsed. From perhaps 360, there was a reduction in the range of pottery produced. The more elaborate and presumably more expensive designs simply disappeared. The large-scale potteries in the New Forest, Oxfordshire, London, and Lincolnshire gradually declined, and by 420, much of Roman Britain had lost the ability to manufacture pots on a wheel. In the Weald, where there had been twenty-two mines producing iron ore to feed the ironworks that made cooking pots, knives, axes, nails, and hipposandals (Roman horseshoes), production dropped off and, by 410, had fallen to undetectable levels or ceased altogether.

As the economy collapsed, so Britain's defences were undermined – initially by foreign raiders, but then by the ambition of one general after another. In 370, another Saxon invasion was repulsed, though with heavy losses. In 372, a unit of Alemanni troops, noted for its size and strength, and commanded by Fraomarius, King of the Bucinobantes, a tribe belonging to the Alemanni confederation, was sent to Britain, apparently as reinforcements. In 383, Magnus Maximus, a Roman officer from north-west Hispania, was appointed either commander of the armies in the north or possibly Count of the Saxon shore. He had previously served in Britain under Count Theodosius and was popular with the legions, who supported him when he declared himself Emperor of the West. He began well, crossing to Gaul and defeating Gratian, the existing Emperor of the West, but in 388 when he challenged Theodosius, the Emperor of the East, by invading Italy, he was himself defeated and killed.

In terms of Britain, the importance of Maximus' story is that he took large numbers of troops with him. We do not know how many, or if any of them ever returned, but by the end of the fourth century those army units still in Britain consisted principally of tribesmen, either local recruits or units, such as the Alemanni, brought over from the Continent. In the early 390s, these forces were able to fight off raids by the Picts, Irish and Saxons, but the things were growing more serious. In 398, Stilicho, a Vandal by birth but now commander of armies in the Western Empire, ordered the strengthening of Hadrian's Wall and sent reinforcements. The next wave of attacks was repelled – although probably only just – but Stilicho was forced to withdraw his reinforcements, and probably other troops as well, to join the defence of Italy against Alaric the Visigoth. Social conditions and the economy were spiralling downwards. Raids by Irish and Saxon pirates were intensifying. Germanic tribes were on the rampage through Gaul and may have begun crossing the Channel. The troops remaining in Britain knew they were too few to fight off the invaders; they saw no support coming from the Continent; and they may well have been unpaid. In 406, they rebelled.

They chose three emperors in succession. Marcus was killed because he did not do what the soldiers wanted. Gratian was killed for the same reason. Constantine survived and, in 407, crossed to Gaul to pursue his quest for the throne. Again, we do not know how many troops he took with him, but it must have been most of the available forces. The reigning emperor, Honorius, occupied fighting the Goths, first recognised him as a co-emperor Constantine III, but then in 411 had him hunted down and killed. Like Maximus, Constantine's main contribution to the story of Britain was to leave it weakened. With too few troops to mount an effective defence, when the next wave of invaders came over the Wall and across the sea, probably in 408, the British had to take decisive action.

Zosimus says:

The barbarians from beyond the Rhine attacked every province with all their power, so that the inhabitants of Britain and some of the Celtic nations rebelled against Roman rule to live on their own, no longer obeying Roman laws. The Britons took up arms and, braving danger because they were now independent, freed their cities from the barbarians besieging them.... Other provinces in Gaul copied the British example and freed themselves in the same manner, expelling their

Roman magistrates and officers and establishing their own government.[185]

This is an extraordinary passage, raising as many questions as it answers. If the British had expelled their Roman rulers, and assuming that Honorius did actually write to the British, then his statement that they should look out for themselves appears in a different light, more akin to saying 'As ye sow, so shall ye reap.' More important, however, is who could have expelled the Roman officials and what constituted independence. Although Romanised Britons had a role in governing the *civitates* and the towns, they seem to have played little part in the government of the four provinces. Who then would have taken the decision to establish a separate government? After three centuries of Roman rule, it seems unlikely that the tribal elites – where they still existed – would have had the authority. There existed an annual council where representatives from the *civitates* gathered to renew their allegiance to Rome and pay homage to the imperial cult. In theory, this body had the right to petition the emperor directly in case of need. Could it effectively have declared independence? It seems to have been a largely formal affair, but in a crisis it could perhaps have risen to the occasion. Could the British members of the *ordines* of those towns most threatened by the pirates and raiders have met to discuss how to defend themselves? Perhaps they used the Roman communication system, the *cursus publicus*, to set up the meeting, and then took matters into their own hands. Perhaps some Roman officials joined them. Or could leading merchants and traders have played a part? They had an effective network based on their guilds or trade associations. There is no definitive answer.

Whoever took the decision then had to implement it. Were the Roman officials physically expelled or just bypassed? Did some of them cooperate? If, as Zosimus suggests, the 'barbarians' were driven off, the British must somehow have raised the manpower to do it. There must have been some Roman troops left, manning the Wall and guarding strategic locations. We must assume these troops sided with the British. Was a British militia raised? Perhaps the British hired Germanic troops as mercenaries. This is all speculation, but everything we know suggests that Roman authority was succeeded by some kind of British authority. It was evidently temporary, fragile, and very soon fragmented, but for a brief period it seems to have been effective.

Hindsight can be misleading. The Britons who took matters into their own hands were not an independence party in the modern sense. They were seeking a practical and effective way of defending themselves. Consequently, what later centuries have seen as the end of Roman rule probably appeared to them as a serious but temporary hiatus forced on them by circumstances. Anyone over fifty would have remembered and wanted to avoid a repetition of 367, when civil and military authority broke down, and raiders rampaged across the country. They would have expected, and wanted, Roman authority to return.

22 Chasing Shadows

The phrase 'The Dark Ages' is unfashionable. It is held to express a value judgement on the intellectual and humanitarian backwardness of the time – although the association between Roman culture and light could equally be said to point once again to the Romano-centric bias of so much later historical writing. However if we equate lack of information with darkness, there is some justification for the term. In the period following the severance of links with Rome, we have to piece together the story of the British Isles from sources that are drastically reduced in both number and accuracy.

The archaeological record is central to our understanding of cultural change but cannot tell the story of what appears to have been a complex and rapidly evolving political situation. The documentary sources available to us are invaluable, but they are few in number, and while they do contain some historical information, they are not history as we would understand it today. In *De Excidio Britanniae*, Gildas' main purpose is to condemn contemporary rulers and the British clergy for deserting the ways of God. Their conduct has caused God to punish Britain by inflicting 'ruin', by which he means the waves of heathen Anglo-Saxon invaders. But Gildas offers no dates, few names, and is often (where we can check) inaccurate. Bede is closer to the modern idea of a historian. He gives dates where he can and cites his sources as a modern historian would. But he is writing an ecclesiastical history. He exhorts his readers 'to imitate the good ... and reject what is harmful or wrong.'[186] His narrative includes political events, but its purpose is to show how the affairs of men reveal the working of God's will, and that is reflected in its emphasis. There are also times when his personal prejudices show through. The author of *Historia Brittonum* – whom we shall continue to call Nennius, while accepting that may not have been his name – traces the origins of the British back to Aeneas on the one hand, and Noah on the other. The work claims to be compiled from a variety of sources and contains detailed versions of various events in British history, often dramatised and with the addition of dialogue. Yet it also includes much that is myth, invention, and fantasy. The *Anglo-Saxon Chronicle* is not one chronicle, but a series of texts written in different places at different times and aimed at different audiences. The material that has come down to us has been added to, amended, and reordered at various times to appeal to the courts and kings to whom it was recited. The *Annales Cambriae* exists in five versions in four different manuscripts with all sorts of later insertions and amendments. Geoffrey of Monmouth's *Historia Regum Britanniae* (*History of the Kings of Britain*), written c.1136, purports to be history – and was accepted as such for several centuries – but is largely fantasy. And so on. Any attempt to create a narrative of historical events in the British Isles during the fifth and sixth centuries necessarily involves a process of extracting historical probability from a soup of myth, legend, fantasy, and metaphor.

The connection with Rome was never restored. The civil, military, and economic structures that had held Roman Britain together, and kept it connected to the greater Empire, had collapsed. Yet for a few decades, certain aspects of Roman Britain survived – in isolated geographical enclaves where Romanised life continued; in the Church, with its Latin-based culture and connections to Rome; and, no doubt, in the minds of the older generation. However, it is worth reminding ourselves that the upheavals we have chronicled affected only 38 per cent of the land area of the British Isles and perhaps 70 per cent of the population. In what for Roman Britain was a time of mass migration and consequent cultural change, Ireland appears to have been little affected. We know that the political structure was changing, with the large number of tribes and sub-tribes coalescing into the larger, regional kingdoms. We know, too, that Christianity was beginning to take root. As far as we can tell, it was a time of gradual change. In the north-east of Ireland – modern Derry, Antrim, and County Down – lived the Scotti, whose territory spanned the North Channel to include the region we now call Argyll. Somewhere in the mid-fifth century, these territories became known as the kingdom of Dál Riata. Later, in the seventh century, the Scotti of Argyll broke away, taking the name with them. Most of the rest of modern-day Scotland north of the Forth—Clyde line was taken up by the Pictish confederation, speaking their own brand of P-Celtic, but the kingdom of Alt Clud, based on Dumbarton Rock, was beginning to gain influence and importance. The people of Alt Clud were also P-Celtic speakers; as were the Gododdin, whom the Romans had known as the Votadini, and whose lands occupied the area between the Forth and Hadrian's Wall.

South of the Wall, the Roman authorities had defined the boundaries of the *civitates* and created four provinces. (See Chapter 21; there may have been a fifth, Valentia, but no one knows where it was; or it may have been an alternative name for the London-centred province of Maxima Caesariensis.) These boundaries and the administrative structures that went with them probably continued to have some meaning into the 420s, perhaps longer in the more Romanised areas. The majority of the population spoke P-Celtic, probably with regional variations. Latin continued to be spoken among the educated and Romanised classes and was probably still used for whatever legal and administrative procedures survived, but it was a minority language and, except in the Church, its use soon declined. Along the Wall, and in other areas where there had been a significant military presence, there may have been micro-colonies of non-British tribesmen, soldiers drafted into Britain from Germany or elsewhere who had chosen, or been forced by circumstances, to stay behind when the main armies left. On the west coast of Wales, there were colonies of Q-Celtic-speaking Irish settlers; while in the east and south-east there were small colonies of Saxons, who had been brought across by the Romans during the fourth century as mercenaries. They had settled near fortified towns and coastal forts – it has even been suggested that the Saxon Shore forts took their name from these new settlers, not because they were built to defend against Saxon raiders.[187]

The episcopal structure of the Church continued, apparently unaffected, into the post-Roman period (see Chapter 20). Despite doctrinal disputes, the Church was already an 'international' body, providing a channel of communication between Britain and Rome long after political links had been severed. Its interests were, naturally enough, spiritual rather than political, but in Britain – as the story of St Germanus leading the British into battle against the Picts and the Saxons makes clear – those interests coincided with the concerns of the British in resisting incursions by people it regarded as heathens. Latin was also an important factor for continuity. The Latin-speaking, literate clergy soon became an elite, and in the longer term preserved some of the essential elements of civilisation at a time when the use of Latin among the wider population declined to nothing and literacy all but disappeared. More broadly, Christian communities worshipping together and conscious of the spiritual authority of Rome would have had their own sense of continuity.

The economy of Roman Britain was based on the production of surpluses, principally in agriculture, which could be sold and distributed to those with the means to buy them. When civic administration broke down, distribution networks failed, demand fell, production fell, and the market fragmented into regional and sub-regional areas. In the countryside, the producers suffered. In the towns, the traders were hit even harder, for the collapse of market mechanisms meant the collapse of the money economy. The producers reverted to barter and subsistence. The inhabitants of the towns drifted away into the countryside. In his study of *Britain after Rome*, Robin Fleming identifies three communities that dealt with the aftermath of Roman rule in different ways. In Somerset, the hillfort of Cadbury Congresbury was reoccupied. Pottery, glassware, jewellery, and other possessions reveal that the inhabitants were refugees from Roman-style towns or villas, but what evolved was more like an Iron Age village. They refortified their new home. A leader of some sort seems to have emerged, living in a big longhouse, while the rest of the population lived in traditional roundhouses. Yet despite the state of Britain as a whole, the community was able to trade in wine and pottery and other goods from places as far off as Rome, Greece and Byzantium. At Birdoswald on the Wall, the garrison stopped being paid in the first decade of the fifth century, but many of the legionaries stayed on. Perhaps they had married local women; perhaps they had nowhere else to go. The garrison buildings and granaries gradually crumbled and were replaced by wooden structures, but the soldiers and their descendants continued to live as a community for at least a century, possibly acting as a local defence force. Wroxeter, once a legionary headquarters and the fourth biggest town in Roman Britain, continued to operate as a town. The Roman buildings decayed, but there was evidently some form of authority that could, for example, organise the re-purposing of the old baths as a market. Later in the fifth century, as with Cadbury Congresbury, a leader emerged, building himself a large wooden dwelling and apparently exercising considerable local authority.[188]

What unites these versions of continuity is the that they begin with the psychology and the memories of those whose lives spanned what was obviously a period of momentous change. Fleming points to the fact that in 420, a large proportion of the population – he suggests a quarter – had been brought up in an era when Roman administration functioned and Britain was still prosperous. These people would have preserved the practices of Roman Britain as long as they could, keeping up habits established in early life, perhaps still hoping that the Romans would one day return. They would have passed on their memories to later generations, creating myths of a golden age which would colour the way people thought and wrote about the Roman period for the next five hundred years.

The South-Western Peninsula, where Romanisation had had only a limited impact, was perhaps the first area to take advantage of the end of Roman authority, transforming itself into an independent kingdom, known as Dumnonia and covering modern Devon and Cornwall. Its first king was Guoremor (in Latin, Vorimorus), who may have held a senior position in the Roman administration of the *civitas*. As this suggests, senior figures in the still extant, but now independent, regional administrations could take advantage of the power vacuum left by the Romans to seize control of their region. Tribal identities, dormant or suppressed under Roman rule, seem to have revived and played a part in the formation of new political entities. Evidence is sketchy, but it seems that by the 420s Roman Britain had fragmented into a dozen separate kingdoms which then divided, coalesced, and formed sub-kingdoms according to circumstances over the rest of the century and beyond.

How post-Roman Britain would have fared as a collection of independent Celtic kingdoms is impossible to say, for just as those kingdoms were forming, their existence was challenged by the great wave of Germanic immigration that would shape Britain's political and ethnic future. In the immediate aftermath of the end of Roman authority, the British had some success in defending their coasts and borders, but by about 425 the situation was deteriorating and, according to Gildas, 'a council' was called to decide how to respond to attacks by the Picts and the Scots. This could perhaps have been the annual council of leaders of the *civitates* surviving into the new era, but now consisting of the rulers of the new kingdoms. Gildas says that 'a proud tyrant' was present.[189] Bede and Nennius call him Vortigern, but Vortigern is a title rather than a personal name: it translates as 'overlord' or 'overking'. The idea that an Irish-style High King could have emerged so soon after the end of Roman rule seems unlikely. Nonetheless, Vortigern was clearly a figure of authority, and may have acted as some kind of supreme commander during the emergency.

The traditional story – told by Gildas and amplified by Bede and Nennius – is that the Romano-British made a last appeal for Roman help. Known as 'the groans of the Britons', this appeal was addressed to Agitius, usually identified as Flavius Aetius, the leading military figure in the Western Empire at the time. The terms of the Roman response are unknown, but Rome was evidently unable or unwilling to help. Vortigern and the council then turned to people that Gildas calls 'Saxons' for assistance. These Saxons – who were actually Jutes – are said to have arrived in three ships, under the leadership of two brothers called Hengist and Horsa. They are said to have landed at Ebbsfleet on Pegwell Bay, and to have been given the Isle of Thanet as a base. They immediately enjoyed a series of victories against the Picts, but quickly brought more warriors across the North Sea to join them and began to make ever-greater demands of the British. When Vortigern demurred, he found himself faced with invaders rather than allies.

Hengist and Horsa – first named by Nennius in the ninth century – may have been real or they may be the stuff of legend, like Romulus and Remus. The *Anglo-Saxon Chronicle* entries for this period, composed four hundred years after the event, feature several pairs of Germanic warriors with names such as Cerdic and Cynric, and Beda and Mela, arriving in two or three ships. However, we can accept that the new British leaders – who would have seen themselves as culturally closer to the Romans than to the Picts or the Saxons – should have chosen to engage one set of 'barbarians' to fight another. It was, after all, what the Romans had done. We can also accept the idea of mercenaries becoming greedy and seizing an unmissable opportunity to take advantage of British weakness. Yet this was not, as the chroniclers suggest, the only way in which the Saxons reached Britain. It was part of a Europe-wide process of political restructuring and mass migration.

Vortigern may also have played a part in another event that helped change the face of Britain early in the fifth century. Manaw Gododdin was a sub-kingdom of the Gododdin/Votadini located to the north of the Firth of Forth, roughly between Stirling and modern-day Fife. Its ruler was Cunedda, a Romanised Briton, whose father and grandfather both had Roman names, indicating that they were prominent enough, perhaps having defended their region against the Picts, to have been granted a Roman title. Cunedda led a large force of Gododdin warriors right across Britain to Wales, where they fought alongside local tribes against both Irish raiders and the growing number of Irish settlers. One version of this story dates these events to c.380 and suggests that Cunedda and his men made their journey at the behest of Magnus Maximus (who appears in Welsh legend as Macsen Wledig), but a more convincing version puts the date at c.430 and makes Vortigern responsible for ordering Cunedda's expedition. The Gododdin drove off the Irish – the last of whom were expelled from Anglesey by one of Cunedda's sons in 470 – but they did not go home. The expedition became a migration. They were joined by settlers from the Clyde and possibly also from Cumbria, and Cunedda is credited as the founder of the Kingdom of Gwynedd, which for many years retained a consciousness of its Romano-British origins. One significant aspect of the story is that P-Celtic-speaking tribesmen from the north should see themselves as natural allies of P-Celtic-speaking tribesmen on the other side of Britain against the Q-Celtic-speaking Irish.

Whoever ordered Cunedda's expedition, the fact that a large force of warriors could cross from one side of Britain to the other for an agreed military purpose indicates that at least in some areas there remained a capacity for organisation and strategic planning at a high level. This may point to the involvement of another shadowy figure, Coel Hen (Coel the Old), whose name is sometimes said to survive in the nursery rhyme 'Old King Cole'. Roughly contemporary with Vortigern, Coel appears to have controlled much of the north of Roman Britain; and, as Cunedda's father-in-law, he may also have had some authority over the Gododdin. Some commentators have seen Coel as the last *dux Britanniarum*, the last commander of Roman forces in northern Britain, who stayed on when Roman authority ceased to function and turned his area of command, based on York, into a kingdom. There is no documentary evidence for this, although several medieval Welsh genealogies make Coel the 'father' of

Map 21   The Kingdoms of the British Isles, *c*.500 AD

kings who ruled territories carved from what would have been his lands. In the genealogies, the term 'father' does not necessarily denote a biological relationship, but rather a figure capable of passing on authority to a new generation. Coel evidently played an important, if not fully understood, role in creating a post-Roman political structure in the north.

The territory of Bryneich (Bernicia), located between the Tyne and the Tweed, appears to have been detached during Coel's lifetime, perhaps about 440, and given to his son Germanianus. The story that Coel died in a battle at Coilsfield in Ayrshire fighting a force of Picts and Scots derives from folklore and legend but, whether true or not, after his death the rest of his lands were apparently divided into three – Ebrauc, based on York; Elmet, centred on what is now Leeds; and Rheged, a much larger entity, incorporating Cumbria and parts of Galloway and Lancashire. These territories, together with Alt Clud and the lands of the Gododdin, became known as *Yr Hen Ogledd*, the Old North: a P-Celtic-speaking region, eventually sandwiched between Q-Celtic-speaking Scots moving south and Germanic tribes moving north.

This was the Age of Migrations – the *Völkerwanderung* – a time of massive demographic change when tribes from Northern Europe and Central Asia poured across the borders of the Roman Empire. Up to now, we have used the term 'Saxons' to describe both the Germanic mercenaries deployed in Britain and the seaborne raiders across the North Sea, quite simply because that is what the Romans called them (when they did not call them barbarians). The Romans rarely distinguished between one Germanic tribe and another. Bede did, and famously says: 'Those who crossed over came from the three most powerful Germanic nations – Saxons, Angles, and Jutes.'[190] In fact, there were five groups: Jutes from what is now northern Denmark; Angles from southern Denmark; Saxons from the area of Germany fronting onto the North Sea; Frisians from northern Holland; and Franks from southern Holland. Except where it is necessary to distinguish between individual groupings, we shall use the conventional generic description, 'Anglo-Saxon'. Similarly, the many tribes living in Britain and opposed to the Anglo-Saxons will be referred to as 'the British' except where there is a need to differentiate between them.

We do not know how many 'Saxons' the Romans brought across to Britain in the course of the fourth century. It may have been several thousand, but it was not enough to make a significant social or demographic impact. A larger second wave began to cross the North Sea and arrive on Britain's east coast about 420. These new immigrants differed from those who preceded them in that they came from beyond the borders of the Empire: they had no familiarity with towns, Roman law, taxation, the money economy, or any of the other elements which, while now in significant decline, had shaped Romano-British society over previous centuries. A few of these new arrivals may have been mercenaries recruited to protect Romano-British interests; a few may originally have been pirates; but the archaeological evidence suggests that most of them were farmers. Presumably, they understood that the end of Roman rule had left a vacuum that offered them an opportunity. They would have known that Britain enjoyed the reputation of being a particularly fertile land. They came as migrants and settlers, not invaders. They built small-scale, agricultural settlements and got on with their lives. Nonetheless, as far as the British population was concerned, they were aliens, with a wholly different cultural, linguistic and religious background.

Anglo-Saxon migration was thus under way well before the events that led to Vortigern issuing his ill-fated invitation to the 'Saxons'. If the identification of Flavius Aetius as the recipient of 'the groans of the Britons' is correct, this puts the date between 446 and 454. Bede and the *Anglo-Saxon Chronicle* both date the invitation to Hengist and Horsa to 449. The period of cooperation must have been brief because, according to the *Chronicle*, by 455 they were already at war with Vortigern. The entry for that year states that Horsa was killed in a battle at Aylesford in Kent, while Hengist and his son Esc (Oisc) took over the 'kingdom'. Whether the details are accurate or not, it seems that the mercenaries had established some form of polity in what is now Kent by the middle of the 450s. Two years later, the *Chronicle* claims that the British abandoned Kent after a battle at Crayford where they lost 4,000 men. The figure is probably unreliable, but it seems that Kent had rapidly become the first Anglo-Saxon (in fact, Jutish) kingdom in Britain.

Meanwhile, groups of (actual) Saxons who had been fighting alongside the original mercenaries – possibly those recruited by the Romans and stationed around the Saxon Shore forts – continued to push the British westwards, moving up the Thames Valley to form what was to become Middlesex. About the same time, a group of Anglo-Saxons (probably Jutes, though this has been disputed) sailed up the Solent, establishing a colony in the Meon Valley and possibly also taking temporary control of the Isle of Wight. A little later, probably in 477, another group of Saxons defeated the British defenders and colonised the area around Selsey Bill, providing the core of Suth Seaxe, the land of the South Saxons, which became Sussex. A separate group, probably Jutes, landed further along the coast. They were known as the Haestingas and gave their name to Hastings.

Ironically, given its pivotal role in the formation of a united English kingdom, the beginnings of West Seaxe or Wessex are less clearly defined. The traditional story, given in the *Anglo-Saxon Chronicle*, is that in 495, a later date than for most new settlements, a Saxon tribe known as the Gewisse, led by Cerdic and his son Cynric, arrived in five ships on the coast of Hampshire. The *Chronicle*, written from an Anglo-Saxon perspective, naturally emphasises the heroism and the slaughter that accompanied the establishment of Anglo-Saxon rule. By contrast, archaeological evidence suggests a significant degree of acculturation, so it is possible that some areas were settled, or came under Anglo-Saxon control, without significant violence. It is also possible that there was a scattering of Anglo-Saxon groups in the area, perhaps farming peaceably, which joined Cerdic and his men when they arrived. One oddity is that both Cerdic and his successor, Ceawlin, have names which appear to be P-Celtic not Germanic in origin. However, British warriors did travel on the Continent, and it is possible he was of British or partially British descent.

Further north, on the east coast, the Romans had constructed a complex system of dykes and channels to turn the marshy fens into agricultural land. By the middle of the fifth century, these works had fallen into neglect. Ely was an island, and most of Norfolk was probably cut off by marsh and water. The Angles from southern Denmark, accustomed to navigating coastal waters in vessels with a shallow draught, found their way up the Nene, the Ouse, and the Cam into what is now Cambridgeshire. By c.480 they had set up a kingdom, calling it Lindesege, the Isle of Lind, which later became Lindsey. About the same time, Germanic settlers were arriving in Norfolk and Suffolk. They appear to have come in large numbers, but as scattered, apparently unconnected groups. Historians usually refer to them as Angles, which may be what they chose to call themselves when they had put down their new roots and needed to establish some form of group identity. Whatever the case, both here and in Lindisege, Anglo-Saxon settlement was evidently a gradual and peaceful process. There is no evidence of battle or slaughter.

British resistance to the spread of Anglo-Saxon control may have been hampered by conflict between two of the leading British generals:

Vortigern, whom we have already met, and Ambrosius Aurelianus. Ambrosius is one of very few individuals named by Gildas, who presents him as a representative of stability, continuity, and all the traditional virtues, the disappearance of which had led Britain to disaster and desolation. Ambrosius is the last of the Romans, a modest man of aristocratic Roman descent (his parents 'had worn the purple') and a Christian, who obtained his victories 'by the assent of the Lord'.[191] He was evidently a war leader, who masterminded a British revival against the Anglo-Saxons. According to Gildas, this revival culminated in the Battle of Mons Badonicus or Mount Badon. Gildas' text is somewhat ambiguous at this point, and it is not clear whether it was Ambrosius or his successors who led the British into the crucial battle. Nor are we told when or where it was fought. The consensus among historians is that it took place in central southern Britain – perhaps in Wiltshire or Dorset – but the date remains uncertain. Gildas, unusually precise, says it was fought 'forty-four years and one month after the landing of the Saxons, and also the time of my own nativity', which would mean 496;[192] while the *Annales Cambriae* gives the date as 516. A date nearer 516 – certainly no later – fits better with the wider narrative of events. By that time, the Anglo-Saxons controlled most of the land to the east of a line between the Humber and the Isle of Wight, as well as parts of Yorkshire and Northumberland. The assumption is that Mons Badonicus marked the high point of British resistance and stalled the Anglo-Saxon advance in southern Britain for several decades.

Bede follows Gildas on Ambrosius and Mons Badonicus. The *Anglo-Saxon Chronicle*, perhaps understandably, mentions neither. It is Nennius who adds detail but – as ever with *Historia Brittonum* – there are difficulties disentangling fact and fantasy. Leaving aside a passage where Ambrosius is introduced as a child with magical powers, Nennius promotes him to 'the great king among the kings of Britain'; suggests that Vortigern ruled in fear of him; and claims that twelve years into Vortigern's reign, there was a 'quarrel' between Ambrosius and Guitolinus/Vitalinus – who may have been Vortigern's kinsman, his successor, or a scribal error for Vortigern himself.[193] Was there a civil war among the Britons at some time before Mons Badonicus? We will probably never know, but the rapid expansion of Anglo-Saxon control during the decades after 450 could perhaps be explained by a divided opposition.

The *Historia Brittonum* does not associate Ambrosius with Mons

Badonicus. Instead, it introduces a new character: Arthur, who is not at this stage a king – it is explicitly stated that 'there were many more noble than him'. Apart from a passing reference in the seventh-century poem, *Y Gododdin* (which could well be a later interpolation), this is the first mention of Arthur, coming over three hundred years after he is supposed to have lived. It suggests that he was chosen twelve times as commander of the British armies 'by all the kings and military force of Britain', that he fought twelve battles and was victorious in all of them 'through the power of our Lord Jesus Christ, and holy Mary'. The twelve battles are named, the last one being Mons Badonicus where 'nine hundred and forty fell by his hand alone.'[194]

What are we to make of this? That a figure who enjoyed such success should go unmentioned by Gildas and Bede is surprising, to say the least, especially as he is presented quite explicitly, like Ambrosius, as a Christian leading the Britons against the heathen invaders. That Arthur should not appear in the *Anglo-Saxon Chronicle* is less surprising. The purpose of the *Chronicle* was to celebrate the deeds of the Anglo-Saxons. Very few Britons are named. The *Historia Brittonum* was written c.830. Over the next three hundred years, there are scattered references to Arthur, though none that enhance his historical authenticity. The tenth-century *Annales Cambriae*, following Nennius, says that Arthur and the Britons were the victors at Mons Badonicus, but adds that the victory was due to the fact that 'Arthur carried the cross of our Lord Jesus Christ on his shoulders for three days and three nights.' The *Annales* contain the first reference to 'the battle of Camlann, in which Arthur and Medraut fell.'[195] In the (probably) early tenth-century Welsh poem, *Preiddeu Annwfn* (*The Spoils of Annwfn*), Arthur makes a voyage to the Celtic otherworld. In the *Black Book of Carmarthen*, a collection of poems probably from the tenth and eleventh centuries, Arthur is linked by association with *Yr Hen Ogledd*, the Old North. This pre-dates Geoffrey of Monmouth in connecting Arthur with Myrddin (Merlin) the magician, and states that Arthur took part in the otherwise unrecorded and unidentified battle of Llongborth. The Welsh folktale *Culhwch and Olwen*, probably dating from the mid- to late-twelfth century, links Arthur with Cornwall. It lists the finest men, women, horses, dogs, and swords in his kingdom, and it recounts the story of the hunt for an enchanted boar. Only the *Legenda Sancti Goeznovii* (*The Legend of Saint Goeznovius*), written c.1200, presents Arthur without an aura of magic and fantasy. The text appears to suggest that Arthur was Vortigern's successor.

In the 1130s, Geoffrey of Monmouth gathered all these myths and folktales together, added a generous helping of imagination, and created the character of King Arthur as a central figure in early British history, the embodiment of patriotism, chivalry, and military glory. Geoffrey's *Historia Regum Britanniae* introduced many elements which are now central to Arthurian myth: Uther Pendragon as Arthur's father, Excalibur, Guinevere, Tintagel, Avalon. From his work descended not only the French Arthurian tradition of the twelfth and thirteenth centuries – including the *Lais* of Marie de France, and the five Arthurian romances of Chrétien de Troyes – which introduced the Holy Grail, Camelot, and the relationship between Lancelot and Guinevere as a focus for the narrative, but also the long British tradition of Arthur stories, which continues to this day.

Thousands of pages have been devoted to discussion of Arthur's historicity, the location of Mons Badonicus, the location of Camelot, and other aspects of the Arthur story. Among the many books on the subject, special mention must go to Alistair Moffat's informative, imaginative, and entertaining *Arthur and the Lost Kingdoms*, which makes a persuasive case for the reality of Arthur and for Roxburgh castle just outside Kelso as his headquarters.[196] In the end, however, we must come back to the *Historia Brittonum*, to the context in which it was written, and the terms in which it introduces Arthur. The prologue cites 'Mervyn, king of the Britons', also known as Merfyn Frych (Merfyn the Freckled), who was King of Gwynedd from about 825 to 844, and the burden of the work is that Britain rightfully belongs to the British. The tone is anti-Roman and anti-Anglo-Saxon. It uses examples from the past, and a symbolic prophecy involving a fight between a red (British) and a white (Anglo-Saxon) worm, to exhort the British to uphold Christian values and continue the fight. The Anglo-Saxon expert, Nicholas Higham, draws attention to the fact that Arthur is identified as *dux bellorum*, an unusual term, which he links to the Book of Judges and to the figure of Joshua, who is called *dux belli*. Higham also explores the biblical connotations of the number twelve, suggesting that Arthur's twelve supposed battles reflect the number of Christ's disciples, the number of pebbles Joshua picked up when he crossed into the Promised Land, and the number of the tribes of Israel. His conclusion is that Nennius' Arthur is not meant to be understood as a historical figure, but rather as a contrived, idealised hero, invented in order to inspire his contemporaries, and King Merfyn, to continue to resist the Anglo-Saxon advance.[197]

There are many other possible interpretations, but in strictly historical terms, the whole Arthur story is something of a distraction. The historical Arthur – if he existed – did not accomplish much. He may have won a famous victory over the Anglo-Saxons, but all he achieved was a brief delay in the inexorable spread of Anglo-Saxon control. More significant in the long term has been the cultural impact of the Arthur myth. Everyone knows the story of Excalibur and the Lady in the Lake – which carries within it the memory of deposition in water from an earlier age – while Arthur's life and death, as elaborated over the centuries, have come to embody the twin myths of a golden age that will never come again, and of gallant, if melancholy, failure – both of which resonate strongly in British culture.

The inclusion of Arthur in the pantheon of British hero figures is hedged around with at least as many complications and contradictions as we saw with Boudicca. Fictional or not, Arthur was a Briton, a P-Celtic speaker, a representative of a culture under threat, even on the edge of destruction. For the Welsh to adopt him as a national hero makes sense. Wales has by the far the highest density of Arthur-related place names, and the Welsh Arthur stories hold within them echoes of lost, or never-achieved, nationhood. The Old North, too, may have a claim on him. Folk legend has it that Guinevere came from Perth, and one of many traditional sites for Arthur's grave is in the Eildon Hills in the Borders, where Arthur sleeps with his knights ready to come to the aid of his country when called. Arthur stories and places names also appear in Cornwall. All three areas, it should be noted, were P-Celtic speaking. For the English, Arthur's position is more anomalous.

After the success of Malory's *Morte d'Arthur* (1485) – one of the first books printed by Caxton – the Renaissance period saw a falling off in the retelling of the Arthurian myths, though Arthur himself appeared in a number of plays as an allegorical figure of kingship. This changed with the revival of interest in the Celtic world in the late eighteenth and early nineteenth centuries. Arthur began – and has continued – to feature in an extraordinary range of poems, novels, plays, musicals, films, and operas: everything from Rutland Boughton's cycle of five very serious Arthurian operas to *Monty Python and the Holy Grail*. Yet the Celtic Revival was paralleled by a rediscovery of England's Anglo-Saxon heritage. The *History of the Anglo-Saxons*, a ground-breaking, four-volume opus by Sharon Turner appeared between 1799 and 1805. At a time when Britain was at war with France, it presented a romanticised view of noble Anglo-Saxons oppressed by tyrannical Normans. Both Walter Scott's *Ivanhoe*, published in 1819, and Charles Kingsley's *Hereward the Wake: Last of the English*, from 1866, pit Saxon nobility against Norman power. It is perhaps not surprising, then, to find that, while the mythical Arthur's character remains consistently noble, loyal, and brave – a rightful, indigenous king who is ultimately betrayed – the identity of his enemies is often obscured or glossed over. Latter-day attempts at grim realism tend to acknowledge Anglo-Saxons as his principal opponents. More often, the emphasis is on betrayal from within Arthur's court. Those who betray him are pushed to do so, sometimes by generic evil knights of unspecified ethnicity, sometimes by Anglo-Saxon kings with whom the betrayer has, in double treachery, made a pact, and sometimes by other Britons, Scots, or even Picts. What emerges is a tribute to the English ability to adopt an important cultural myth, and then modify it in such a way as to cast a veil over its inconvenient or contradictory implications.

23 Spreading the Word

It has been estimated that in Ireland between the years 450 and 750 there were about 3,000 kings of different sorts. The *Oxford English Dictionary* defines a king as 'the male ruler of an independent state, especially one who inherits the position by right of birth'. In the context of the early Irish history, and the early history of the British Isles as a whole, this needs qualification. Only a handful of the Irish kings would have been truly independent. Most would have been in an acknowledged, hierarchical relationship with a sub-regional and/or regional overking.[198] Succession was by right of birth, but not necessarily by primogeniture. When a king died, his successor was chosen from within the clan – a procedure known as tanistry. This, and the fact that, as noted earlier, Irish marriages could be dissolved with comparative ease, led to constant disputes about succession, precedence and inheritance, and contributed to the endemic instability of Irish life.

Just as the powerful, regional clans – the Uí Néill, the Ulaid, the Laigin, the Eóganachta, the Connachta – were not unitary clans but confederations of families, so the kingdoms they ruled were less centralised states than spheres of influence, groups of kingdoms held together by kinship and allegiance. Clans and kingdoms ebbed and flowed, but by the time Christian scribes began to document developments in Ireland, there were nine kingdoms of significance: in the north, the lands of the Northern Uí Néill and the Ulaid, and the kingdoms of Airgialla and Bréifne; in the centre, Meath (or Mide) and Connacht; and in the south, Leinster, Osraige, and Munster. However unstable and riven by internal conflict, these kingdoms nonetheless provided a political framework for Ireland that endured until the Norman invasion in the twelfth century.

Until the fifth century, power in the north of Ireland was concentrated in the hands of the Ulaid, the clan which gave its name to Ulster. The Ulaid's centre of power was the ancient ritual complex of Emain Macha (Fort Navan) in County Armagh. The site had been inhabited since Neolithic times, and may, like Stonehenge, have been regarded as a portal into the otherworld. Possession would have added a spiritual dimension to the authority of whoever held it. Somewhere in the 430s or 440s, it was seized and destroyed. Tradition has it that the man responsible was Niall Noigiallach, or Niall of the Nine Hostages, father of the Uí Néill clan. His name derives from an exploit in which he is supposed to have taken hostages from nine tribes of another clan, the Airgiallia (whose name means 'the hostage givers'). Niall himself was probably a historical figure: DNA evidence links the possessors of surnames associated with Clan Uí Néill to a mid-fifth century figure. Whether or not this was Niall we cannot be sure, but the destruction of the Ulaid's power base at Emain Macha undoubtedly marked the emergence of Clan Uí Néill as a major force in the north of Ireland.

Uí Néill power expanded. Soon after Niall's death c.450, another member of the clan, Cénel nEógain, seized control of the north-west of Ireland. By the 460s, another of Niall's successors, Ailill Molt, was in control of the Hill of Tara, a centre of ritual even older than Emain Macha, where the annual Feast of Tara, designed to demonstrate the power of the king and his claim to the allegiance of all who attended, again used spiritual authority to buttress political power. By the end of the century, Clan Uí Néill divided – or perhaps had always been divided – into two branches.

The Northern Uí Néill kept up their pressure on the Ulaid. About 575, they negotiated an agreement – one tradition claims the negotiator was St Columba – which led the Dál Riata territories across the North Channel to reject the overlordship of the Ulaid. In the 620s, the Ulaid were fighting back. The king of the Irish Dál Riata territories, Congal Cáech, took overlordship of the Ulaid and inflicted a series of defeats on the Northern Uí Néill. By the 630s, the Uí Néill were resurgent. In 637, they inflicted a heavy defeat on Congal Cáech and the Ulaid forces – which apparently included men from Alt Clud – at the Battle of Moira. The Argyll Dál Riata finally broke free from their Irish roots and became a separate kingdom – Irish Dál Riata survived into the eighth century, when it was eventually overrun. The Northern Uí Néill went on to take control of the Ulaid's ancestral heartlands, but this did not end the conflict between them. The Ulaid never fully accepted Uí Néill overlordship, and their lands were never assimilated into Uí Néill domains. They regularly, and sometimes successfully, pushed back against Uí Néill control, and continued to assert their separate identity right up to the Norman invasion and beyond.

Meanwhile, the Southern Uí Néill established themselves in central Ireland. Although there were smaller kingdoms in the area before their arrival, the kingdom of Meath or Mide was effectively an Uí Néill creation. They drove out another influential clan, the Laigin, who became the rulers of Leinster; they imposed their authority by demanding cattle tribute; and they adopted titles traditionally used by rulers in the area, such as King of Uisnech and King of Tara. In the sixth century, they adapted to the coming of Christianity by abandoning the traditional, pagan Feast of Tara, and replacing it with a week-long assembly to which all their subject kings and clan leaders were summoned. Known as the the Fair of Tailtiu, it was held every August and continued into the tenth century. The Southern Uí Néill did not face the same level of concerted opposition as their northern kinsmen, but they did not manage to expand their territory to the same extent: their power never extended to the south or south-west of Ireland. This may have been because they were subject to even more internal feuds and disputes about succession than most Irish clans. Nonetheless, the extent and longevity of their authority was remarkable. Like their northern counterparts, the Southern Uí Néill continued to rule until the arrival of the Normans.

The expansion and maintenance of sovereignty in early medieval

Ireland was a complex and unpredictable business. The law codes made no provision for land being forcibly transferred from one family or clan to another, so a new concept 'sword land' had to be invented. Even then, legal recognition of such a transfer would be resisted not only by the original owners, but also by their allies. And, of course, there were frequent land feuds between different branches and sub-branches of the same clan. Nevertheless, clan solidarity clearly counted for something. Uí Néill possession of Tara allowed them to lay claim to the High Kingship of Ireland, and the northern and southern branches of the clan appear to have taken the title of High King in alternation with what one historian has called 'astonishing regularity' for anything up to six hundred years.[199]

The period that saw the expansion of Uí Néill power and the coalescing of tribal territories into larger kingdoms also saw the spread of Christianity. Ireland was the first region of any size that had not been a part of the Roman Empire to become Christian. It had never had any form of centralised administration or decision-making process. This meant that Christianity had been never outlawed and Christians had never been persecuted. This may have made the process of conversion easier – certainly there were no Irish martyrs during the period – but it also meant that Christianity was never designated an official religion and Celtic religious practices were never prohibited. With no Roman legacy to inform its development – and perhaps also because continual war and instability in Britain made regular communication with Rome and with Christians on the Continent more difficult – Irish Christianity often displayed an independent spirit. It showed a tendency to make its own decisions on doctrinal and liturgical issues, which sometimes brought it into (generally good-mannered) conflict with the Church in Rome – and sometimes, given the spiritual dimension which attached to Irish kingship, with Irish kings.

When Palladius arrived in Ireland to minister to 'the Scotti believing in Christ', he did so as a papal appointee and, until banished by the King of Leinster, seems to have worked principally among Christian members of the Ulaid. By contrast, when Patrick conducted his missionary work among the Uí Néill, he was acting on his own initiative. He had grown up and been educated in the Roman Church but appears to have had no direct contact with Rome. The writer and theologian Prosper of Aquitaine (c.390–455) mentions Palladius several times but seems not to have heard of Patrick. However, despite the differences between them, they were both bishops and they both saw the Church as being organised around bishops and their dioceses – the model that obtained in fourth-century Roman Britain. The trouble was that fifth-century Ireland had no history of institutions or centralised administration. Nor did it have any real towns. There were crannogs, clusters of dwellings scattered across an agricultural landscape, and the occasional hillfort or larger settlement where the local king exercised authority. Rivers and river valleys were the main transport corridors. Large areas of peat bog and marshland, and the lack of a road network such as the Romans created in southern Britain, meant that overland travel was slow and difficult. Ireland remained essentially rural and tribal, unsuited to gathering congregations into churches or organising churches into dioceses. Founding a church thus became something more than providing a place for a congregation to worship. When St Patrick founded Armagh Cathedral, traditionally in 445, on a site barely two kilometres from Emain Macha, he was making a religious but also a political statement. He was making it clear that the old gods were dead; and he was allying Christianity with the ascendant Uí Néill cause.

Given this context, we can understand why historians have suggested that the first Irish monasteries were probably little more than Christian villages where priests and lay families, including children, lived and worshipped together. The Christian 'family' would have been recognisable as a version of the extended clan family, which remained the dominant social unit. By 550, however, there were at least a dozen monasteries as we would understand them today – communities of men who have taken religious vows – stretching from Monasterboice and Clonard in the east to Tuam and Aran in the west, and they spread to all parts of Ireland during the seventh and eighth centuries.

Christian monasticism developed in Egypt – St Anthony is widely credited as having built the first monastery in the Red Sea Mountains around the turn of the fourth century – and the idea spread rapidly. Quite how it reached Ireland we do not know, but Gaul seems a likely source. About 360, St Martin of Tours founded an important monastery at Ligugé near Poitiers, and then a few later years another, larger one at Marmoutier in Alsace. Both emphasised the ascetic aspects of monasticism which were to characterise Irish monastic life, and the two thousand monks who attended St Martin's funeral in 397 would undoubtedly have spread the word.

The most influential figure in the early development of Irish monasticism was St Finnian of Clonard (c.470–549; not to be confused with St Finnian of Movilla, c.495–589, who will appear very shortly). Finnian of Clonard was born in Leinster and into the Ulaid. He is supposed to have been baptised by Saint Abbán and may have studied at Tours. He spent many years (some sources say thirty, but this seems exaggerated given his other achievements) in study and prayer at Llancarfan in modern-day Glamorgan, before returning to Ireland where he was given land for a monastery by the King of Leinster. An undocumented tradition has it that he also founded the monastery on the rugged and inhospitable island of Skellig Michael off the coast of County Kerry – which 1,500 years later appeared in two *Star Wars* films. About 520, we are told, an angel led him to Clonard on the River Boyne in County Meath. Here, Finnian established a cell and a small church, and devoted himself to study, prayer, and isolation, but his fame spread rapidly, and large numbers of scholars, clerics, and supplicants sought out his retreat begging to receive instruction. This led him to establish a monastery based on intense scriptural study and the ascetic traditions of the first Egyptian monasteries: study, prayer, meditation, fasting, mortification, and penance. Not all Irish monasteries followed as strict a rule as Finnian imposed at Clonard, but from this period onwards, monastic life in Ireland and other areas of the Celtic fringe was often simpler, more focussed on prayer and contemplation, and also on retreat, than elsewhere in Europe.

Contemporary sources claim that at the height of his fame Finnian was instructing up to 3,000 students at any one time. This may be an exaggeration, but there is no reason to doubt that he was an inspirational teacher. Among those he instructed were the so-called Twelve Apostles of Ireland, twelve highly influential clerics, all later canonised, who went on to found monasteries and spread Christianity – and Finnian's approach to it – both within Ireland and beyond. Only two require notice here. The first is St Brendan of Clonfert (c.484–c.589; also known as Brendan the Navigator) who, once ordained, built a series of monastic cells on the coast of County Kerry before setting off on his celebrated voyage. As so often with Irish saints, it is almost impossible to separate fact from fiction. The story goes that Brendan and sixteen followers set off in a leather-covered curragh in search of the Garden of Eden. They sailed for seven years and had many adventures. They may have reached Iceland. It is even possible that they reached North America. In the end, the real significance of the voyage is that it shows just how seaworthy skin-covered boats could be. In the 1970s, the British explorer and author, Tim Severin, successfully recreated Brendan's journey, sailing a thirty-six-foot, wooden-framed boat, covered with tanned ox hides and sealed with wool grease, over 7,000 kilometres from Kerry to Newfoundland, via the Hebrides, the Faeroes, and Iceland.

The second of Finnian's students requiring comment is St Columba (521–97). Born to an Uí Néill father, possibly a great-grandson of Niall Noigiallach, and a mother descended from the ruling family of Leinster, he was originally baptised Crimthann, meaning 'the fox'. When he became a monk, he received a new name, Colum Cille, 'the dove of the Church', from which the name Columba derives. Most of what we know about him comes from the *Life of Columba*, written about a hundred years after his death by St Adomnán (*c.*624–704), one of his successors as Abbott of Iona. The lives of early medieval saints were written to inspire belief, not to record history, and have to be approached with caution. However, we do not have to believe that Columba vanquished the Loch Ness monster with the sign of the cross to accept that, like Finnian of Clonard, he was an exceptional man. His initial training was under the other Finnian – Finnian of Movilla. This Finnian was born into the Dál Fiatach clan, part of the Ulaid, and had studied at Whithorn in Galloway (though long after Ninian's death). He continued his studies in Rome before returning to Ireland to found the Abbey at Movilla in 540. After studying at Movilla, Columba – perhaps oddly – spent some time with a travelling bard called Gemman, about whom we know nothing, before moving to Clonard where he was ordained a priest.

The monasteries Columba established show how, for him, as for the rest of the Irish Church, religion and politics were closely intertwined. One was in an area called *Daire*, meaning 'oak wood', and later anglicised to Derry. Another was in Durrow in County Laois, which takes its name from *Darmhagh*, the 'oak plain'. That both names were linked to oak trees strongly suggests that these new foundations were intended to counter or replace centres of druidic ritual. That Derry was in the territory of the Northern Uí Néill, and Durrow in the lands of the Southern Uí Néill, is also significant. So, too, is the fact that he was given land to found a monastery adjoining the seat of the Uí Néill kings at *Ceanannas Mór*, the 'great fort', today known as Kells.

Monasticism spread like a wave across Ireland during the sixth, seventh, and eighth centuries. Small groups of monks, intent on isolating themselves from the rest of the world, built clusters of dry-stone beehive huts on remote promontories or all-but-inaccessible places such as Skellig Michael. Larger monasteries might consist of a slender round tower, a church, a scriptorium, a refectory, the monks' cells, workshops, and agricultural buildings, all encircled by an exterior wall. Most monasteries were administered by an abbot, often a member of the local ruling clan, while a bishop was responsible for the liturgical and sacramental life of the community. Occasionally, as in the case of Finnian of Clonard, the founder or spiritual leader of the monastery would undertake both roles.

Irish monasticism played an important role beyond the confines of Ireland itself. It was the leading force in the conversion of north Britain; and Irish monks and monasteries were instrumental in preserving the art, values, and intellectual legacy of both Christian and classical worlds when much of Europe was swamped by waves of destructive pagan invaders. Sir Kenneth Clark's iconic 1969 television series, *Civilisation*, saw Celtic monasticism as a key factor in the survival of civilised values, as he saw it, 'by the skin of our teeth.'[200] Nonetheless, Irish Christianity at this time was not wholly monastic. There was a diocesan structure of the kind promoted by Palladius and Patrick covering the whole island, but we know much less about it, and it only emerged from the shadow of monasticism to exert an influence on the shape of Irish society at a much later date.

One reason for the missionary character of Irish monasticism lies in the fact that Celtic polytheism was never proscribed. With no central authority to compel conversion, the process took longer than in Roman Britain. Monasteries were built in areas where the druids still held sway, and the monks gained experience of missionary work which they were later able to apply in more far-flung regions. Columba's decision to embark on missionary work in what became Scotland was not entirely voluntary. He copied a manuscript – perhaps the first Vulgate or Latin Bible to reach Ireland – belonging to Finnian of Movilla. Finnian claimed that the copy should also belong to him. The matter escalated, became caught up in Uí Néill clan politics and claims that King Diarmait mac Cerbaill had violated the right of sanctuary, and ended (possibly) in a bloody battle between clan factions. In the end a Tailtiu was called for the purpose of excommunicating Columba – and would have done so had not his erstwhile colleague Brendan of Birr, another of the Twelve Apostles of Ireland, spoken up for him. As it was, he either chose or was forced to leave. In 563, he and twelve companions crossed the North Channel in a leather-covered curragh either to Oronsay or to Kintyre. According to Adomnán, Columba expressed the wish to settle somewhere where his native land was not visible on the horizon. Nonetheless, the lands on both sides of the North Channel were Dál Riata territory. The clans who ruled 'Scottish' Dál Riata were all Scotti, who would have recognised Columba as an Uí Néill clansman, so this was a qualified kind of exile. And we also know that Columba returned to Ireland more than once – on one occasion founding the monastery at Durrow.

Not long after crossing the North Channel, Columba moved to the island of Iona – the usual date given is 565, although this has been disputed – and there established possibly the most famous of all religious foundations in the British Isles. Even here, however, politics intruded. Iona appears to have been disputed territory. The King of Dál Riata, Conall mac Comgaill (r.c.558–74) gave the island to Columba – perhaps impressed by his Uí Néill lineage as much as by his spiritual authority – but so, too, did Bridei I (r.c.554–c.84; Bede calls him Brude), of the neighbouring Pictish kingdom. Bridei's action is often seen as marking his conversion to Christianity, and thus the first stage in the conversion of the northern Picts, but neither Bede nor anyone else suggests that Columba converted Bridei, and it is possible that he might already have been a Christian. His headquarters were probably at Craig Phadrig, just to the west of modern Inverness. Recent excavations have concluded that a Pictish monastery at Portmahomack, sixty kilometres further north-east, was already active by 550, raising the possibility that the area might have been converted by another route before Columba's arrival. The evidence is circumstantial at best but, whatever its religious background, we can be sure that Bridei's action in giving Iona to Columba was also a political gesture aimed at Dál Riata, making it clear that he was the one who had the right to decide what happened to the island.

In Columba's time, the monastery on Iona would have been little more than a collection of wooden huts, but it soon became not only a centre of religious observance, but also of culture and literacy. Copying books had caused him problems in Ireland, but Columba never lost his belief that the written word was an essential tool in spreading the faith. He himself is supposed to have copied over three hundred books. The Church had a near monopoly of literacy, and it was a hugely important weapon in the armoury of missionary monks, for reasons which went well beyond the spiritual. Christianity was based on the Word of God as recorded in the Bible, but for kings and tribal chiefs literacy offered a boost to their secular power, allowing their words and decisions to be recorded in a permanent form. It also offered access to a wider world. When Columba moved from Q-Celtic-speaking Dál Riata to P-Celtic-speaking Pictland, he had to have an interpreter, but Latin was an 'international' language. With a monk at his side to interpret or write letters, a Pictish king could see himself as an actor on a much larger stage.

What Columba started, his successors – including Adomnán – continued. The island became both a hub of missionary activity and a focus of culture and learning. Some who set out on their missionary journeys from Iona sailed north to the Highlands, the Western Isles, Orkney, Shetland, and beyond; some travelled overland to Fife and Angus; still others reached the eastern coast of what would soon be England. Iona's position on the western sea lanes connected it with north and south Britain, with Ireland, and with other, more distant destinations. Iona's scriptorium was renowned for illuminated manuscripts of exceptional quality. Only one has survived, but that is the *Book of Kells* which, without hyperbole, can be placed among the greatest achievements of European art. It was begun on Iona sometime in the eighth century but taken to the monastery of Kells – also founded by Columba – when the island was threatened by Scandinavian raiders. To produce illuminated manuscripts such as the *Book of Kells*, with their subtly differentiated colours and their dense, interlaced, decorative detail, required not only ability but a range of specialised inks and pigments. Red ochre, yellow ochre, indigo, and verdigris, all came from the Mediterranean. Lapis lazuli (ultramarine) would have come from Badakhshan, a region now split between Afghanistan and Tajikistan. Today, we might see Iona as an isolated island off the coast of Scotland, but between its foundation in 565 and the first Viking raid in 795 it was an influential and well-connected community.

That area of Britain which had not experienced Roman occupation, north of the line of Antonine Wall, was culturally and linguistically more diverse than Ireland, but, superficially at least, less politically fragmented. The seat of the rulers of 'Scottish' Dál Riata – whom for the sake of conve-

1 Portmahomack
2 Rosemarkie
3 Stirling
4 Culross
5 Glasgow
6 Falkirk
7 Edinburgh
8 Clonard / Belfast
9 Movilla
10 Moira
11 Emain Macha / Armagh
12 Monasterboice
13 Kells
14 Hill of Tara

Map 22 Spreading the Word

nience we shall now call Scots – was Dunadd, a massive, triple-walled hill-fort on top of a steep, rugged crag at the southern end of Kilmartin Glen, just to the north of Lochgilphead. Today, the flat valley floor below the fort is a bog. In the sixth century, it was probably flooded, making Dunadd an island and even more difficult of access. The origin of the term 'Scot' is unknown. It may have been a pejorative term applied by the Romans to tribesmen crossing the Irish Sea to raid the western coasts of Britain. It may perhaps have meant 'horde', or even 'pirate'.[201] In time, the term began to be used for any Irish people who crossed to Britain, but then narrowed in scope to refer to that particular Irish tribe – or confederation of tribes – whose lands spanned the North Channel.

We do not know when the Scotti first settled on the long, ragged west coast of the land that now bears their name. The traditional idea of a migration from Ireland in the fourth and fifth centuries – a version of invasion theory – looks increasingly untenable. There is no archaeological evidence for invasion or mass migration, no changes in the pattern or type of settlement, no suggestion of major cultural change. It seems more likely that the people who eventually became the Scotti arrived during the first millennium BC, or possibly even earlier, and chose to settle on both sides of the North Channel, united rather than divided by the stretch of water between them. Irish Dál Riata emerged as a political force in the first half of the fifth century – about the time that Clan Uí Néill began to challenge the dominance of the Ulaid – controlling Derry, Antrim and County Down. Scottish Dál Riata territory originally consisted of Kintyre, Jura, and Islay, gradually expanding from the mid-fifth century onwards to include Arran to the south and Skye to the north. It is clear that, from the beginning, the Scotti were a sea people. Theirs was a sea kingdom, consisting of islands, inlets, and peninsulas. To maintain itself, any such kingdom would have needed to control its seaways, and Dál Riata possessed a powerful fleet. Looking forward, perhaps the most important aspect of the connection between the two halves of Dál Riata is that they were both Q-Celtic speaking. The Scottish part of Dál Riata was, in effect, a bridgehead, the only Q-Celtic speaking area of mainland Britain.

The conversion of Dál Riata is traditionally credited to Columba, but the lives of saints are full of traditions aimed at magnifying and glorifying the achievements of their subject. At least some of Dál Riata's population – and certainly the ruling elite – were probably Christian by the time Columba and his followers came ashore in 565. Given the linguistic, cultural, and political connections, it is reasonable to assume that Christianity crossed the sea from Irish Dál Riata at some stage during the first half of the sixth century. However, it is conceivable – for reasons we shall examine shortly – that the new religion may also have reached Dál Riata from the south, from Alt Clud, which was evidently Christian at a very early stage. Of course, conversion was not an overnight process. Even where a king converted and required his subjects to follow his example – a common enough occurrence in Anglo-Saxon England – that did not preclude the need for further missionary activity. St Catan (c.500–70), for example, spent his life proselytising among the islands of Dál Riata. It seems unlikely that Columba and his monks would have moved eastwards into Pictland if Dál Riata had still been predominately pagan. The fact that Pictland was converted from the west by Q-Celtic speaking Scots, is of considerable significance in terms of what eventually happened to the Picts, and in terms of the creation of a Scottish nation.

In his *Life of Columba*, Adomnán credits his subject with converting the Picts virtually single-handedly. That is the nature of hagiography. In reality, the process was much more complicated than Adomnán suggests. We have already noted (in Chapter 20) Bede's statement that Ninian was sent to convert the 'southern Picts', whom he defines as living to the south of some 'steep and rugged mountains'.[202] Ninian is a shadowy figure at best, but there are numerous early sites dedicated to him in the lands of the Gododdin – between Falkirk and Edinburgh and, in particular, around Stirling – suggesting he was active in the area. St Serf (c.500–83) is another shadowy figure, traditionally claimed to be the spiritual descendant of Palladius' mission to Caledonia in the mid-fifth century. He, too, seems to have been active in Gododdin territory, founding a church at Culross on the northern shore of the Forth, possibly around 528. The Gododdin, of course, were Britons, but it is possible that Bede – or his source – used 'Picts' to cover all the inhabitants of what became southern Scotland.

The same qualification also applies to Alt Clud, the P-Celtic-speaking but not Pictish entity based on Dumbarton Rock. Alt Clud appears to have become Christian somewhere around the 430s. Both the early date and geographical logic suggest transmission from Ninian's foundation at Whithorn. The early date also makes it possible that missionary activity in Alt Clud may have spilled over into its northern neighbour, Dál Riata. We can be reasonably sure that the rulers of the Alt Clud were Christian by the middle of the fifth century. Of two surviving letters written by St Patrick, one is addressed to *miles Coroticus* ('the soldiers of Coroticus'), whom it condemns for allying themselves with pagan Picts, and for slaughtering and selling into slavery newly-baptised Irish Christians. Patrick clearly intended this letter, usually dated to about 450, for the eyes of Coroticus himself – the first identifiable ruler of the Alt Clud, also known as Ceretic Guletic – in the hope that it would lead to better behaviour from his men in future. The accepted view (see Chapter 20) is that Patrick came from a small country estate near Carlisle. Norman Davies in his *Vanished Kingdoms* makes a plausible case, based in part on the terms of this letter, for Patrick being a citizen of Alt Clud.[203] Whether true or not, as early as 450 Patrick evidently felt he could address the ruler of Alt Clud, however indirectly, as a fellow Christian, and expect his soldiers to behave like Christians.

A different and just possibly complementary story concerns St Mungo (c.518–614; also known as St Kentigern). Although riddled with uncertainties and contradictions, it appears to connect the Britons of Gododdin with those of Alt Clud. Unconfirmed tradition claims Mungo as the illegitimate son of a Gododdin princess, who was brought up and educated by St Serf at Culross. At the age of twenty-five, around 423, he is supposed to have begun missionary work in the Clyde Valley, arousing the ire of King Morken (or perhaps Morgan), possibly a king or sub-king of Alt Clud, who expelled him from the region. Mungo spent several years in Gwynedd and made a pilgrimage to Rome before returning to the Clyde at the invitation of Rhydderch Hael (c.532–613), the third or fourth successor to Coroticus. He founded a church on the site where Glasgow Cathedral now stands, and in doing so founded the city itself. How much of this story one believes depends on how much one wants to believe, but it does point to an extensive tradition, with at least an underlay of fact, indicating a continuous pattern of Christian activity across southern Scotland throughout the fifth and sixth centuries.

It follows from all this that when Columba established his base on Iona in 565, the inhabitants of southern Scotland – whether we call them Picts, Britons, or Scots – were, in theory at least, Christian. Columba's missionary work, therefore, was concentrated on Pictland, the home of the northern Picts. These were the last of the Celtic-speaking peoples of the British Isles to convert to Christianity. Even here, however, Christianity had begun to make inroads. We have noted the existence of the monastery at Portmahomack, and the fact that Bridei might already have been Christian by the time Columba visited him. There is also a cluster of Christian graves, apparently dating from the fifth century, in Perthshire, just south of the River Tay. This is too far north to be Gododdin territory and may be connected with the Pictish king Nechtan Morbet mac Erp (r.c.456–c.80), who is said to have been a Christian and to have given land for a church to be built at Abernethy. There is no doubt that Columba travelled far and wide in Pictland, even founding churches in the Western Isles, but there were other Irish monks – most of them later canonised – who played an important part in spreading the word among the Picts. Columba's contemporary, St Moluog (c.530–92) founded monasteries and Christian communities at Rosemarkie in the Black Isle in Ross-shire, at Fort Augustus, at Mortlach in Moray, and on the Isle of Lismore, which was Dál Riata territory but sacred to the western Picts. St Donnán (c.550–617) was active up and down the west coast before being martyred along with fifty of his fellow monks on Eigg at the hands of a bunch of robbers hired by a Pictish queen. He had apparently upset her by settling on land where she grazed her sheep.

Columba's aristocratic background, and the apparent ease with which he mixed with kings and rulers, may have led him to assume a kind of diplomatic role, persuading Pictish rulers of the advantages of Christianity. This is speculation, though such a role is perhaps hinted at in *Amra Coluimb Chille,* a Gaelic panegyric possibly written by Saint Dallán (c.560–645; also Dallán Forgaill). Comparatively few Pictish sites have been excavated, and the archaeological record gives few clues to the process of conversion. Archaeologists have uncovered evidence of scattered Christian communities, such as the monastery at Portmahomack, the church at Rosemarkie in Easter Ross, a chapel at Parc-an-caipel near Grantown-on-Spey, and a monastery at Kenneddar in Moray. It seems likely that during the seventh century there were two bishops in Pictland, one for the north and one for the south, reflecting what may have been a political sub-division. Class II symbol stones record the gradual spread of Christianity, with Christian iconography appearing alongside traditional Pictish symbols. Even then, the stones are so difficult to date that we cannot establish a reliable chronology. All we can say with certainty is that the conversion of the Picts took over two hundred years – longer than any other region of the British Isles, and a further reason to treat Adomnán's somewhat enthusiastic claims about Columba's role as hagiography rather than history.

24   Building Kingdoms

Gildas hailed Mons Badonicus as a great British victory, but did not attempt to hide his dismay that the long-term impact of the battle was not more positive: 'Even now our country's cities are not inhabited as they used to be; they are left empty and pulled down... Our foreign wars have ceased, but our civil troubles continue.'[204] It seems that, having stalled the rapid, westward advance of the Anglo-Saxons, the British failed to follow up their advantage. This looks like a failure of leadership, and it may be – as Gildas hints – that they had begun fighting among themselves. Hostilities between the British and the Anglo-Saxons did not cease, but continued at a much lower level, allowing the Anglo-Saxons to consolidate the gains they had made up to that point, and to start the business of building kingdoms.

The leader of the Anglo-Saxon forces at Mons Badonicus was probably Cerdic, whom we met landing five ships on the coast of Hampshire (see Chapter 22). For him, the defeat was no more than a temporary setback. In 519, at Charford, half way between Worcester and Birmingham, he defeated a large British army and probably regained some of the territory lost as a result of Mons Badonicus. That same year, he assumed the title of King of Wessex. In 527, another, unlocated battle is recorded. In 530, he took control of the Isle of Wight, perhaps acting with some Jutish allies. In 534, he died. His son, Cynric succeeded, and ruled for twenty-six years. The Kingdom of Wessex had made a solid and stable start.

Further north, Mercia, too, was taking shape. Its beginnings are uncertain, but the most coherent scenario we have concerns Icil (*c*.460–*c*.535; also Icel), who was king of the Angles living in Angeln, a peninsula on the east coast of Schleswig and now part of the German state of Schleswig-Holstein. Somewhere around 515, Icil led an organised migration of his subjects, probably landing in the area of the Wash – which was much larger than today, and more of a bay than tidal mud flats. There were other groups of Angles who had already crossed the North Sea and settled in the area (see Chapter 22). These groups were in the process of coming together to form two separate groups – the North Folk and the South Folk – which would eventually combine to form the Kingdom of East Anglia in 571. Whether there was any hostility between the existing settlers and the new arrivals we do not know, but Icil's Angles moved inland to establish themselves and their own kingdom in the valley of the River Trent. By the time he died, the Mercians – to give them their new name, which translates as 'border people' – held large areas of the Trent, Avon and Nene valleys, although how securely is uncertain. Of Icil's successors – Cnebba and Cynewald – we know nothing beyond their names.

On the north-east coast were the two kingdoms of Bernicia and Deira. These kingdoms were both British in origin but were taken over by Anglian warriors. The first recorded Anglian king of Bernicia was Ida (r.c.547–59). Landing on the coast of what was then the British Kingdom of Bryneich, he seems to have taken control of a narrow strip of coastline, probably centred on the rocky outcrop of Bamburgh. He and his men then pushed inland and northwards. They turned Bamburgh into an all-but-impregnable stronghold; took possession of the ancient and strategic site of Yeavering; and went on to overrun an expanse of northern Britain so that, at its greatest extent, Bernicia probably stretched from the River Tees to the Firth of Forth and across to the Solway. Deira evolved out of the British territory with the P-Celtic name of Deywr, which was probably a sub-kingdom of the York-centred kingdom of Ebrauc. Its first Anglian king, Ælle, seems not have been a new arrival in Britain. Anglian mercenaries had been employed in the region in the early 400s, probably to protect the interests of wealthy Britons faced with lawlessness and raiding, and subsequently set up their own communities in the region. When the long-reigning British king of Deywr, whose name we do not know, died in 559 or 560, the leader of the local Angles, Ælle, may simply have taken control and made himself the first king of Anglian Deira. Over the next century, the relationship between Deira and Bernicia was a complicated one. In 588, Ælle died. His son, Edwin, succeeded as king of Deira, but in 590 was expelled by Ida's son, Æthelric. When Æthelric died, his son Æthelfrith succeeded to both kingdoms, but in 616 Edwin returned, supported by King Raedwald of East Anglia. Æthelfrith was killed at the Battle of the River Idle and both kingdoms fell under Edwin's control. They were separated briefly in 633 after Edwin's death, but then reunited under Æthelfrith's son, Oswald. After Oswald's death in 641 they separated again, but in 654 they became provinces of King Oswiu's Kingdom of Northumbria.

Wessex, Mercia, East Anglia, and Northumbria were the four largest and most powerful kingdoms of the Anglo-Saxon period. In the southeast of Britain, there were three others, smaller but still significant. Kent was referred to as a kingdom in the *Anglo-Saxon Chronicle* as early as 459. After that, we know very little beyond the names given in a king list until the reign of Æthelberht (r.c.589–616), in whose territory St Augustine landed in 597. According to tradition, Sussex was founded by a Saxon tribal leader, another Ælle (r.c.477–c.510), who arrived with his three sons in three ships and landed at Selsey Bill in 477. They drove the British who opposed them eastwards to the old Roman fort at Pevensey, massacred the defenders, and set up a new kingdom bordering on Kent and roughly corresponding to today's Sussex. Essex, the third south-eastern kingdom, occupied the lands between the Thames Estuary to the south and the River Stour to the north. The indented coastline with its muddy, shallow inlets was immediately familiar to tribes from the North Sea coasts of the Saxon homelands, and we know of at least eight different groups who settled there. These groups probably came together under the leadership of their first king Æscwine (or Erkenwine) around 527.

The *Anglo-Saxon Chronicle* calls the British fighting against Ælle and his sons 'Welsh', and the term is used frequently to describe Britons who oppose the Anglo-Saxons. The Old English word *Wealh* and its plural *Wēalas* simply means speaker or speakers of Celtic. In practice, this meant speakers of P-Celtic, because the Anglo-Saxons would have had no exposure to the Q-Celtic speakers of Ireland or western Scotland. In time, *Wēalas,* and thus Welsh, came to refer to all Celtic-speaking Britons beyond the borders of the Anglo-Saxon kingdoms; consequently, when Mercia took shape, leaving the Celtic-speaking British in possession of the area we have previously called the Western Uplands, that area became known as the land of the *Wēalas,* or Wales.

Once established, the seven Anglo-Saxon kingdoms spent most of the next three hundred years fighting each other. The smaller kingdoms or polities set up at the very beginning of the settlement period – Lindsey in Lincolnshire; Hwicce in the Severn Valley; Wihtwara in the Isle of Wight; the enclave of the Haestingas – were soon overrun and absorbed into their larger, more powerful neighbours as sub-kingdoms or provinces. The seven kingdoms – Wessex, Mercia, East Anglia, Northumbria, Kent, Sussex, and Essex – are sometimes collectively referred to as the Heptarchy. The term is misleading in so far as it implies a degree of coher-

Map 23   The Kingdoms of the Heptarchy

ence, even coordination, when the reality was one of warfare, raids, shifting alliances, annexation, secession, and general instability – although, despite almost continual warfare, the seven kingdoms did dominate Anglo-Saxon Britain until the arrival of the Danes in the ninth century. They also left a legacy still visible in English administrative and regional boundaries, place names, the words we use for the days of the week, and much else, including the invaluable verb, *to get*.

The difficulties we have understanding the early Anglo-Saxon period are illustrated by Bede's *Ecclesiastical History of the British People*. Bede names those kings who, he says, 'ruled over all the southern provinces that are divided from the northern by the River Humber and the borders contiguous to it.' The list includes Ælle of Sussex (r.c.477–510); Ceawlin of Wessex (r.c.560–c.91); Æthelberht of Kent (r.c.589–616); Raedwald of East Anglia (r.c.599–c.624); Edwin of Northumbria (r.616–632); Oswald of Northumbria (r.633–641); Oswiu of Bernicia and then of Northumbria (r.642–670).[205] Despite Bede's reputation as a reliable source, this is close to nonsense.

The dates for Ælle are uncertain, but we know that he arrived early in the settlement period. While it is possible that he might have pushed the borders of Sussex up to or beyond the Thames Valley, it beggars belief that he could have achieved dominance over all Anglo-Saxons south of the Humber. Similarly, Ceawlin was a powerful figure and a successful war leader, but it is scarcely credible that he could have extended the power of Wessex as far as the Humber. Bede, whose focus was always on the Christian aspects of his story, was eager to promote Æthelberht because it was Æthelberht who received Augustine and his monks in 597, allowed them to settle in Canterbury, and became the first Anglo-Saxon king to convert to Christianity. Æthelberht was able to endow a church in London – dedicated to St Paul and located in a corner of the ruined Roman city – which was part of Essex and ruled by his nephew, Saebert. Bede also suggests that Raedwald of East Anglia deferred to Æthelberht in some way. These events could possibly suggest some kind of overlordship, but Bede states explicitly that 'he had extended his dominions as far as the great river Humber.'[206] Yet we know that Æthelberht lost a battle against Ceawlin of Wessex in 568, so once more Bede's assertion is questionable.

Raedwald of East Anglia is often considered the most likely occupant of the Sutton Hoo ship burial with its array of unique treasures. Many of the books and charters relating to his reign were destroyed by rampaging Danes during the ninth and tenth centuries, but he was certainly a powerful king with a powerful army. He helped restore Edwin to the joint thrones of Bernicia and Deira, and his price may well have been Edwin's pledge of allegiance. Bede's interest in promoting Raedwald's reputation centres on his faith. Early in his reign, apparently during a visit to Æthelberht in Kent, he chose to be baptised. In 616, Æthelberht died. So, too, did his nephew, Saebert of Essex, who was also a Christian. Both were succeeded by aggressive pagans, who expelled Christian missions from their territory. This left Raedwald for some years as the only surviving Christian king in Britain.

The last three of Bede's kings are from Northumbria, the kingdom in which he lived. He was born in or around 673 and was too young to have lived through any of their reigns, but he could have talked to people who had, or heard memories handed down through one or two generations. Once Edwin had been restored to his throne by Raedwald, he and his successors set about building Northumberland into one of the two great Anglo-Saxon powers of the time, so that it is no surprise that Northumbria is presented as powerful, although Bede does make the point that its dominion did not extend as far as Kent.

The other major power was Mercia. For the first hundred years of its existence, Mercia struggled to maintain its borders against pressure from its neighbours, but with the reign of King Penda (r.c.626–55) the kingdom embarked on a period of expansion. Penda defeated Cynegils of Wessex, annexed the territory of the Hwicce, made an alliance with King Cadwallon ap Cadfan of Gwynedd, and in 633 defeated and killed Edwin of Northumbria at the Battle of Hatfield Chase near Doncaster. A few years later, in 642, Oswald attempted to reassert Northumbrian power, but he, too, was defeated and killed, this time at the Battle of Maserfield, usually identified as Oswestry in the Welsh Marches. Northumbria's honour was eventually restored in 655 when Oswald's brother, Oswiu, marched against Penda, defeating him at the Battle of Winwaed, just to the east of Leeds. A by-product of the battle was the Christianisation of Mercia, which effectively sounded the death knell for paganism in Britain. This should have interested Bede, but, as a proud Northumbrian, he saw Mercia as the enemy. His list of kings who had supposedly ruled all the southern provinces includes three Northumbrians (two of whom were killed by Penda), but no Mercians – even though the accession of Penda marks the beginning of the period often referred to as the Mercian Supremacy. All of which shows that, while Bede is probably our most reliable source, he is neither infallible nor unbiased.

The ebb and flow of power between the different Anglo-Saxon kingdoms was a natural, evolutionary process. Angles, Saxons, Jutes, Frisians, and Franks had all brought their culture to southern Britain. Although all were recognisably Germanic, there were cultural and societal differences both between and within them. As they jostled for position, fighting became endemic. Most of the fighting was between bands of warriors perhaps two- or three-hundred strong, capable of travelling long distances to raid a rival's stronghold or force a neighbouring king to swear allegiance to their lord. Battles between forces of this size were intended to gain glory for the victor – most important for an Anglo-Saxon king – and enable him to seize the kind of loot that he could distribute to his followers. They were not strategic battles – two or three hundred men were not enough to seize or hold large swathes of territory – although full scale battles were not unknown. Those between Penda's Mercians and the forces of Northumbria between the 630s and 650s seem to have involved much larger forces, and they did have long-term strategic consequences. Nonetheless, in terms of leaving a still-detectable influence on the political and cultural shape of Britain, the most important conflicts of the time were between the Anglo-Saxons and the British.

It was not until 577, sixty years after Mons Badonicus that Wessex mounted its next major expansion westwards. Under Ceawlin and his son Cuthwine, the forces of Wessex met and defeated the British at Deorham, today's Dyrham, about ten kilometres east of Bristol. It was a major strategic victory. Ceawlin and his men took possession of Cirencester, Gloucester, and Bath – three towns which the archaeological evidence suggests had not declined to the same extent as most other post-Roman towns. At the time of the battle, they were still relatively prosperous, although all three seem to have been abandoned soon afterwards. Victory at Deorham not only opened up the Severn Valley, but also the route to the south-west and the Kingdom of Dumnonia, although in both cases the men of Wessex were slow in following up their victory, perhaps because of internal disagreements.

The economic importance of the South-Western Peninsula had declined from the days when it was a major source of tin. The Romans had done little to exploit or colonise the area, and when Roman administration failed, Dumnonia had been one of the first regions to secure its independence (see Chapter 22). At the turn of the seventh century, it covered Cornwall, Devon, and western Somerset. The Saxons of Wessex gradually pushed the border westwards until, in the early 720s, the Dumnonian British fought back with three victories – Hehil, Garth Maelog, and Pencon – all within a short period of time. In 825 and 838, there was further conflict, and British territory seems to have been gradually whittled away. In 870, the Bishop of Bodmin finally acknowledged the authority of Canterbury, and just a few years later in 875 Donyarth (or Doniert), the last confirmed Cornish king died, apparently by drowning, but the status of the region remains uncertain. In the eleventh century, Cornwall was, notionally at least, part of the estates of Earl Godwin and Harold Godewinson, yet other sources suggest that some kind of Cornish polity continued to exist right up to the Norman Conquest. Like the Romans, the Anglo-Saxons never managed to gain more than a superficial hold on Cornwall. Anglo-Saxon culture never took root as it did even in neighbouring Devon. And the English language took centuries to dislodge Cornish – a version of P-Celtic – which only died out in the eighteenth century. To this day, Cornwall continues to regard itself as part of the Celtic world.

Dumnonia was unique in the British Isles, being the only area that saw a significant level of emigration. From the end of the fourth century right through to the ninth, there were waves of emigration – mainly to Armorica, where the name Brittany recalls the origin of that part of the population, but also to Galicia in north-western Iberia, where the newcomers settled in an area that became known as Britonia. These migrations are very poorly documented, although they were evidently well known at the time. Archaeological finds indicate that Dumnonia continued to trade with distant lands, including Byzantium, where in the sixth century Procopius was able to write about the movement of people from the (to him) semi-legendary Isle of Brittia to the land of the Franks. It has been suggested that the earliest migration, from what was still Roman Britain, may have been a movement of troops and their families ordered by Magnus Maximus, but given how few troops were stationed in the region, this seems unlikely. Later migrations are probably explained by fear of the advancing Anglo-Saxons. Whatever the motivation, the cultural connections between south-western Britain and Armorica, which stretched back to prehistoric times, were still strong enough for P-Celtic-speaking Armorica, rather than Q-Celtic-speaking Ireland, to be seen as the natural destination for migration.

About the same time as Ceawlin and the forces of Wessex fought the British at Dyrham, Urien, King of Rheged decided to move against the Anglo-Saxons encroaching on northern Britain. Rheged was the biggest of the post-Roman kingdoms south of the Antonine Wall, stretching from western Galloway – where the small town of Dunragit derives its name from *Dun Rheged* or 'Fort of Rheged' – to the Ribble Valley in Lancashire. Traditionally supposed to have been based on Carlisle, at least one of its royal strongholds now appears to have been further north, at Trusty's Hill just outside Gatehouse of Fleet in Galloway. Here, as so often, we have to try to separate legend from fact. Urien appears quite suddenly, stepping into the power vacuum left after the Battle of Arfderydd (or Arthuret; c.573) between two lesser British kings. The genealogies make Urien a direct descendant of Coel Hen, and he was clearly a powerful and charismatic leader, celebrated in no fewer than eight of the fifty-six poems in the *Book of Taliesin*. We know little of his early career beyond the names of the battles in which he fought: Gwen Ystrad, against the Angles of Bernicia; the Ford of Alt Clud, about which we know nothing; and the Cells of Berwy, where Urien himself is credited with slaying one of the sons of Ida, Bernicia's first king.

By the beginning of the 580s, he had emerged as the only leader capable of challenging the growing power of the Angles in northern Britain. His personal authority was such that he was able to form a coalition with at least three other kings and their forces from across the Old North: Rhydderch Hael from Alt Clud; Gwallog mab Llaenog, who may have been King of Elmet; and Morgant Bwlch, a prince or sub-king perhaps from the Gododdin. The *Irish Annals* suggest that Fiachna, King of Ulster, also joined. It was probably in 584 that they moved against the Angles of Bernicia, now led by Hussa, Ida's grandson. At first things went well. They drove the Angles from their stronghold in Bamburgh – an impressive feat which the *Annals* credit to the Irish – forcing them to retreat to the island of Metcaud, or Lindisfarne, where they were besieged. It suddenly looked as if the Bernician Angles were on the verge of being expelled from Britain, but, at the crucial moment the British started fighting among themselves. Morgant Bwlch (also Morcant Bulc), apparently driven by jealousy, had Urien murdered – in fact, beheaded. The sixth century was a violent age, but even by the standards of the day this was a shocking act: the chroniclers even recorded the name of the hired assassin, Llofan Llaf Difo. This was a pivotal moment in the shaping of northern Britain. If the British had retaken Bernicia, what might have happened elsewhere? But the coalition broke up; the armies melted away; Hussa and his men not only escaped from their island refuge but reclaimed almost all the lands they had lost.

Urien's son, Owain, had a brief success against the Angles in 593, but he died shortly afterwards, and there followed nothing but defeats for the British. Of these, the Battle of Catraeth, in or around 600, is the best known and undoubtedly the one which had the greatest long-term impact. Much of our knowledge of Catraeth comes from the Old Welsh epic poem *Y Gododdin*, attributed to Aneirin, who had been court bard to both Urien and Owain. The poem was probably written shortly after the battle, and is the longest of several found in a thirteenth-century manuscript named the *Book of Aneirin*. It is very much of its time, a fulsome elegy for those who died. To understand what happened, we have to strip away the heroic trappings.

It seems that another coalition was assembled with the aim of stemming the advancing tide of the Angles of Deira. The instigator this time was Yrfei (or Uruei), king of the northern Gododdin and based in Din Eidyn (Edinburgh). His allies included Cynon ap Clydno of Alt Clud, nobles and warriors from Elmet, Rheged, Gwynedd, and across the Old North, and even some Pictish lords. The poem focusses on the three hundred noble warriors who rode in the vanguard of the expedition, so we have no idea of the size of the army that marched with them. The poem also adds a religious dimension, suggesting that as they rode south they called themselves *Y Bedydd*, 'The Baptised'. This looks like a heroic gloss after the event. The members of the coalition were at least nominally Christian, while the men of Deira were not, but this was not a crusade, so the Gododdin would not have seen themselves as soldiers of Christ. Battle was joined at Catraeth – which is generally identified as Catterick. We know no details of the fighting beyond the fact that it was a slaughter, even by the bloody standards of the day. We do not know how many died or were wounded, but Aneirin tells us that of the three hundred elite warriors, only one survived.

It was another pivotal moment, arguably more significant than the death of Urien on the sands of Metcaud. It marked the beginning of the end for the Old North. In 616 or 617, shortly after Raedwald of East Anglia had restored him to the joint thrones of Deira and Bernicia, Edwin and his men overran Elmet. The Angles of Bernicia overran the lands of the Gododdin. By 632, they had occupied Din Eidyn and Anglo-Saxon had begun to replace P-Celtic along the Firth of Forth. Rheged, so recently so powerful, rapidly faded away. Northern Rheged suffered the same fate as Elmet. Edwin's men swept across the Pennines and burnt its Galloway strongholds of Mote of Mark and Trusty's Hill. The fate of southern Rheged is less certain and may perhaps have been settled by a royal wedding. In 638, there was a marriage between Prince Oswiu – who later, as king, unified Northumbria – and Princess Rhiainfellt (also Rieinmelt and Rieinmelth) of Rheged, who was Urien's great-granddaughter. It is possible that the union of the two royal houses may have led to Rheged being peacefully subsumed into Bernicia. Once again, P-Celtic was soon replaced by Anglo-Saxon, although faint traces of P-Celtic can still be detected in Cumbrian and some Yorkshire dialects, notably in the old oral system of sheep-counting, in which the numbers one to five are pronounced *yan, tan, tethera, methera, pimp*. The Angles were triumphant. Only Alt Clud, the Rock of Dumbarton, still flew the flag of the Old North.

25 Saints and Warriors

Christianity was slow to arrive in south-west Britain. If the first Christians were legionaries or officials posted to the area, they left no inscriptions or other evidence. Instead, we have numerous place names and dedications, particularly in Cornwall, suggesting missionary activity during the fifth and early sixth century, probably from Wales and perhaps also from Brittany. Many of the saints involved – such as St Petroc, St Samson of Dol, and the county's patron saint, St Piran, who is supposed to have died in the village of Perranzabuloe around 480 – originally came from Wales or Ireland. Cornwall's long-standing cultural and linguistic links with Wales and Brittany are evident in the veneration of early saints rarely heard of anywhere else. These include Saint Meriasek, a Breton from a ducal family who became the patron saint of the town of Cambourne; Saint Carantoc who is credited with founding the towns of Llangrannog in Wales, Crantock in Cornwall, and Carantec in Brittany; and Saint Felec or Felix, who was able to communicate with cats. However it came about, by the end of the sixth century, when it began to come under sustained pressure from the forces of Wessex, Dumnonia was a Christian kingdom.

In what became Wales, Christianity was a survival from the Roman period. We saw that two of the first British martyrs, Saints Aaron and Julius, may have come from Caerleon (see Chapter 20). In the sixth century, Gildas is forthright about the shortcomings of the people of Wales but acknowledges that, for all their failings, they were Christians, unlike the pagan Saxon hordes they were fighting. With their eastern border effectively sealed off by the Anglo-Saxons, it was natural that the people of Wales should develop a sense of their own identity. Christianity was an essential part of that identity, expressing itself in the founding of monasteries and in the strict monastic rules that were imposed. This was the age of saints in Wales also, with figures such as St David (c.500–c.89), St Iltud (dates unknown), St Padarn (?–c.550), and St Teilo (c.500–c.60), all of whom were P-Celtic speakers with close links to Brittany. St David, who became the patron saint of Wales, was known for his asceticism. His followers ate no meat, drank only water, and eschewed personal possessions.

Christianity, as it developed in Ireland and then spread across the North Channel to what became Scotland, was a post-Roman phenomenon. The founders and shapers of Irish Christianity had been educated in Rome, France, Wales, and Northern Britain. They applied their knowledge to what was a fluid and complex society at a time when Ireland was to some extent isolated by the turmoil of the Anglo-Saxon wars in Britain. What emerged was a style of Christianity suited to Irish culture and psychology.

We have seen how effective sea travel was in linking the western regions of the British Isles. Monks, abbots, and missionaries travelled up and down the Celtic fringe, sharing their views on matters of doctrine and practice. From the beginning there was a common leaning towards monasticism and asceticism which, during the fifth and sixth centuries, developed into an approach to Christianity that, while not actually heretical, differed in several respects from the practices endorsed by Rome. The method of dating Easter was one area of difference. The nature of a monk's tonsure was another: the Roman version was the familiar shaved circular patch on the top of the head; the Celtic version probably involved shaving the front of the head in an arc from ear to ear. Other differences concerned the practice of penitence and *peregrinatio*. Normally used to describe a brief penitential exile, in Ireland and elsewhere along the Celtic fringe, *peregrinatio* came to mean permanently exiling oneself from one's native land in order to find fulfilment in God, usually by undertaking missionary work. However, the fact that these unorthodox views were widely held in the Celtic provinces should not be taken as suggesting that there was a separate Celtic Church acting in conscious or deliberate opposition to Rome. Throughout the Celtic fringe, clerics communicated and cooperated; certain individuals were listened to with respect because of their spiritual authority; but there was no central authority and no central decision-making. This caused a problem.

The marriage between Æthelberht of Kent and Princess Bertha, daughter of Chabrier, King of the Franks, probably took place about 589, before he came to the throne. It was a marriage full of significance. Under the Merovingian dynasty, the Kingdom of the Franks was the most powerful in Europe. From their point of view, the marriage acknowledged that Kent was a kingdom of some importance. From a Kentish perspective, an alliance with the Franks was a boost in status. It also reduced the likelihood of an invasion from the Continent and allowed Æthelberht to concentrate on expanding Kent's influence within Britain. Beyond the politics, Bertha was a Christian. The marriage agreement stipulated that she should be allowed to practise her religion and bring with her a Frankish bishop named Liudhard. Æthelberht evidently thought this a price worth paying. He restored an old Roman church just outside the walls of Canterbury as her private chapel. It was dedicated to St Martin of Tours and is today recognised as the church with the longest history of continuous worship in the English-speaking world.

It was against this background that Pope Gregory I, or Gregory the Great (r.590–604), sent Augustine (?–604/5) and some forty monks, a mission of unprecedented size, 'to preach the word of God to the English nation.'[207] There has been much speculation about Gregory's motives. Bede, among others, tells the story of Gregory as a young priest seeing boys with white bodies, beautiful faces and fine hair for sale in the slave market. On being told, they were Angles from Deira, he pressed his bishop to send a mission to Britain, and even volunteered to go himself.[208] The story makes awkward reading in the twenty-first century but was clearly intended to emphasise Gregory's sensitivity and purity of heart – as well as to allow Bede to make a pun on 'Angles' and 'angels'. All accounts agree that Gregory was a genuinely pious man, but, having been a papal ambassador to the Imperial Court in Constantinople, he was also politically astute. Italy had been devastated by the Lombard invasions. Gregory needed to rebuild the power and authority of the papacy. Converting the newly-established Anglo-Saxon kingdoms and bringing them under his spiritual authority would be an achievement, and to be seen to be acting in support of powerful Merovingian interests would certainly not hinder his cause. Word would also have reached Rome of developments on the Celtic fringe. Iona had been established for thirty years. Its reputation and influence were spreading. Saints Columba, Donnán, and Moluog were all active in Pictland. They were not heretics, but Christianity as they taught it did not follow Roman practice or look to Rome for leadership. If they took the lead in converting the Anglo-Saxons, the papacy would lose face and authority.

Augustine's mission made a somewhat comic start, with the monks getting cold feet and sending Augustine back to Rome to beg the Pope that they should not have to continue. Tradition has it that when they did arrive, early in 597, it was at Ebbsfleet on Pegwell Bay, where Julius Caesar and Hengist and Horsa are also supposed to have landed. Æthelberht received them, allowed them to use St Martin's Church, and after a short time received baptism himself. There were political motives here, too. Æthelberht's conversion brought him closer into line with his wife's powerful relatives, and the suggestion of Merovingian influence would have been a powerful lever in dealings with other Anglo-Saxon kingdoms. At the same time, he was cautious. He allowed his subjects to convert – and, if Augustine is to be believed, large numbers did so – but he did not compel them.

Augustine was consecrated bishop and founded a monastery in Canterbury dedicated to St Peter and St Paul, which later became St Augustine's Abbey. In 601, he received reinforcements, an additional body of monks bringing with them a pallium from Pope Gregory, signifying that he should now be regarded as an archbishop. In 604, he established a second bishopric in Rochester, and then, following the conversion of Saebert of Essex, a third in London. Æthelberht almost certainly played a role in Saebert's conversion – his sister, Ricula, was Saebert's mother – and in the conversion of Raedwald of East Anglia, who was baptised during a visit to Kent. On returning home Raedwald appears to have hedged his bets, worshipping both Christ and the pagan gods, perhaps because his wife was a pagan, but he eventually become a whole-hearted Christian.

In terms of converting the Anglo-Saxons, Gregory's strategy of using Æthelberht as a point of entry into Britain proved a success, but Augustine's dealings with the British were far less successful. Gregory's commission explicitly gave him authority over 'all the bishops of Britain, we commit them to your care, that the unlearned may be taught, the weak strengthened by persuasion, and the perverse corrected by authority.'[209] Augustine sent messages to the British Christians in the west and met what was probably a delegation of bishops from the British kingdoms in Wales somewhere in the Severn Valley. He urged them to fall in line with Roman practice and help with proselytising the Anglo-Saxons. The British went away to consult, but at their second meeting refused to cooperate. We only have Bede's version of events – which naturally puts the worst possible interpretation on the actions of the British, including accusations that they were guided by the predictions of a hermit – but it is clear that there was a complete breakdown in relations. Religious matters aside, the British would still have seen the Anglo-Saxons as invaders who threatened their way of life. Augustine, protected as he was by Æthelberht, probably appeared as an agent of the Anglo-Saxons.

Augustine's mission was successful in converting three ruling kings to Roman-style Christianity, but its influence did not otherwise spread far beyond the bounds of Kent, and when these royal converts died the fragility of the new religion's hold was revealed. We noted a pagan backlash after the deaths of Æthelberht and Saerbert in 616 (see Chapter 24). In Kent, this was led by Eadbald, Æthelberht's son, but lasted only until Eadbald was persuaded to accept baptism by Laurence, Augustine's successor as Archbishop. In Essex, the resurgence of paganism lasted until the 650s when Sigeberht the Good became king, and there were two further brief outbreaks in the 660s. Raedwald of East Anglia died in 624 to be succeeded by his son Eorpwald. Although not a Christian at the time of his accession, Eorpwald accepted baptism three years later, but was murdered soon afterwards by a pagan called Ricberht, whose origins are unknown. Ricberht seems to have ruled for three years before Sigebehrt, Raedwald's younger son (or possibly stepson), returned from exile, took charge of the kingdom, and restored Christianity. This pattern of a ruler converting and accepting baptism, only for the kingdom to revert to paganism after his death was repeated in all but one of the Anglo-Saxon kingdoms. The exception was Mercia, where King Peada agreed to be baptised in 655 for wholly political reasons. Oswiu of Northumbria had just defeated the Mercian army and killed Peada's father, Penda. He graciously allowed Peada to continue to rule southern Mercia, but only if he converted.

The story of Northumbria's path to Christianity is more complex. Once baptised, Eadbald of Kent seems to have adopted Christianity with enthusiasm, perhaps recognising the political advantages it might offer. When it was suggested that his sister, Æthelburg (also Æthelburh), might marry Edwin of Bernicia and Deira, he agreed on condition that Edwin also converted. In 625, she set off north accompanied by a cleric called Paulinus, who had been in Kent since 601, but had only recently been consecrated bishop. Paulinus revived the bishopric of York, established under the Romans at the beginning of the fourth century but abandoned in the fifth, and set about trying to convert Edwin. Bede turns the story of Edwin's conversion into an epic, playing up the King's indecisiveness. He tells how Edwin allowed his newborn daughter, Eanflaed, to be baptised, but continued to haver himself. He then relates the (improbable) story that, in order to decide which religion to follow, the King called a meeting of his advisers at which Cofi, the leading pagan priest of the kingdom, argued in favour of Christianity and was willing to destroy the pagan idols of his own temple. Edwin was eventually baptised in 627 but seems to have done little to encourage the conversion of his people.

In 633, Edwin was defeated and killed by the allied armies of Penda of Mercia and Cadwallon ap Cadfan, King of Gwynedd. The heir to Deira was his cousin, Osric, while the heir to Bernicia was his nephew, Eanfrith. Both had been baptised but reverted to paganism, and both were almost immediately killed by the unbaptised Cadwallon, who took control of the two kingdoms. Cadwallon ruled for a year before he was himself killed by Eanfrith's brother, Oswald, at the Battle of Heavenfield. Today, a cross by the roadside marks the site of the battle, and a church dedicated to St Oswald, originally Saxon but rebuilt in Victorian times, stands where he is supposed to have raised his standard. The accession of Oswald (r.634–41/2) brought a degree of political and religious stability. A Christian himself, he was determined to bring Christianity to the people of Deira and Bernicia. However, having spent his youth in exile in Dál Riata, he turned not to the Augustinian mission, with its Rome-influenced Christianity –

Paulinus had fled back to Kent when faced with Cadwallon and subsequently become Bishop of Rochester – but to the Celtic Christians of Iona. In the first year of his reign, he gave the island of Lindisfarne to Aidan, a monk from Iona known for asceticism, who founded the monastery there. Bede describes Aidan's work and piety in glowing terms, and it is his account that has led Aidan to be credited with the conversion of Northumbria.

For the Roman or Augustinian Christians of the south to see the Celtic or Ionan Christians of the west entering the Anglo-Saxon world and gaining influence in Northumbria was effectively a defeat. The differences between the two strands of Christianity were not profound: they were issues of practice not doctrine; but they were sufficient to cause problems. After the death of Princess Rhiainfellt of Rheged, Oswiu took Eanflaed, daughter of the late King Edwin, as his second wife. They were both Christians, but he followed the Celtic tradition, while she followed Roman practice, so while he was celebrating Easter, she still had a week of Lent and fasting left. While Aidan lived, his authority was sufficient to prevent serious trouble, but after his death in 651 tensions began to rise. Early in the 660s, Oswiu's son, Alhfrith (also Ealhfrith), who was sub-king of Deira (r.655–64/5) appointed a monk called Wilfrid to the newly-founded monastery of Ripon in what is now Yorkshire. Wilfrid was a Northumbrian by birth. He had studied in Rome and Lyon and would go on to play a leading role in the conversion of Sussex, but he was also a controversial and abrasive figure. He expelled Eata, the abbot of Ripon, and a number of other monks – including one who later became St Cuthbert – for refusing to follow Roman tradition. Complaints multiplied and tensions grew, and so, in 664, in an increasingly polarised situation, Oswiu (r.642–70) called the meeting that has come to be known as the Synod of Whitby.

The Celtic faction at Whitby was led by Bishop Colmán, the third Bishop of Lindisfarne. He claimed that Celtic practice derived from the teachings of Columba, whose holiness was not in doubt. Wilfrid, who led the Roman faction, outmanoeuvred him, claiming that Roman practice was sanctioned by the Pope, the successor of St Peter, and thus by St Peter himself. Oswiu gave his verdict in favour of Wilfrid and Rome and, at the same time, moved the seat of the bishopric of Northumbria from Lindisfarne to York. To some extent Oswiu was pushing at an open door –

Map 24   Saints and Warriors

many Irish monasteries were already adopting Roman practices – and although it took Iona fifty years to fall into line, and the church in Wales nearly a century, his decision was never seriously challenged. There was also an important political dimension to the Synod. Alhfrith had probably espoused the Roman tradition because it brought him the support of Mercia, which he may have wanted in order to mount a rebellion against his father. Bede hints that something of the kind did take place – which may explain why Alhfrith is not mentioned after 664. Equally, Oswiu may well have seen the decision to adopt the Roman tradition as a way of attracting the support of other kingdoms opposed to Mercia. Nor do the political implications end there. Oswiu no doubt saw his decision as bringing Christianity in Northumbria into line with the rest of Britain and with Europe. A later age, however, looked at Whitby through the other end of the telescope. During the Reformation, Protestants from all parts of the British Isles saw the existence of a 'Celtic Church' as evidence that there had existed in Britain 'a pure and uncorrupted faith [that] preceded the rise of Rome.'[210] Whitby thus came to represent the subjugation of native British Christianity to the authority of Rome.

The conversion of Wessex was another long and complicated affair, again closely bound up with political affiliations and alliances. According to Bede, the main agent of conversion was a Frankish monk called Birinus, who landed at Hamwic (modern-day Southampton) in 634. The King of Wessex was Cynegils, who may have been ruling jointly with his son, Cwichelm. Cynegils wanted an alliance with Oswald of Deira and Bernicia in order to resist Mercian aggression, but Oswald refused to ally himself to a pagan. Cynegils allowed Birinus to baptise both himself and Cwichelm, and gave permission for the establishment of an episcopal see at Dorchester-on-Thames. Cwichelm died in 636, but Cynegils lived until 642, and was succeeded by another son, Cenwalh. Wessex was still faced with the problem of Mercian aggression. Cenwalh, a pagan, sought to solve the problem through a dynastic alliance and married the daughter of Penda, Mercia's pagan, warrior king. Unfortunately, the marriage was not a success and Cenwalh seems to have sent his wife back to Mercia. Penda was outraged and invaded Wessex, forcing Cenwalh to flee to East Anglia, where he was sheltered by the Christian King Anna. While he was in exile he accepted baptism, a decision, like his father's, undoubtedly influenced by the desire to secure an alliance against Mercia. Cenwalh returned to

Wessex – perhaps in 655, during a brief period after the death of Penda when Oswiu took control of Mercia – and ruled until 674, latterly in partnership with his second wife, the Wessex-born Queen Seaxburh. Trouble with Mercia, however, continued unabated. Penda's son, Wulfhere, was a Christian, but that did not stop him embarking on a series of campaigns that restored Mercia's dominance and again made deep incursions into Wessex. In 666, he cut a swathe through central Wessex, invaded the Isle of Wight and forcibly converted the entire population, though they reverted to paganism as soon as he left.

What happened next in Wessex is unclear. Cenwalh died in 674. Cetwine, who came to the throne about 676, may have been his brother. Little is known about him beyond the fact that he came to the throne as a pagan but was then baptised and became a patron of the church. He is said to have successfully fought against 'the British', probably meaning the Welsh, although we have no details. Cetwine's death in 685 was followed by the short but eventful reign of Caedwalla. Possibly a usurper of British descent, Caedwalla had not been baptised, but had strong Christian sympathies – although these were not always apparent in his actions. His armies devastated Sussex and swept into Kent where, after much bloodshed, he installed his brother on the throne. When the brother was killed, he ravaged the kingdom for a second time. Wessex did not have the resources to dominate either kingdom for long, but the damage inflicted was such that neither Kent nor Sussex ever re-emerged as regional powers. The Isle of Wight had been overrun more than once, but had somehow managed to retain its status as an independent, pagan kingdom. Caedwalla overran it once again and put an end to its independence. He killed its king, Arwald, in battle, and then executed his two heirs – although he did allow them to be baptised before they were beheaded. Bede, somewhat dubiously, says that 'they joyfully underwent temporal death.'[211] Then, in 688, after less than three years, Caedwalla abdicated and took himself off to Rome, where he was baptised by the Pope and died soon afterwards.

By the end of the 680s, almost all parts of the British Isles – both the Celtic areas and the Anglo-Saxon kingdoms – were at least nominally Christian although, because conversion was led by the rulers and their elites, there would have been great regional variation in the extent to which the new faith had taken root among the wider population. Pope Gregory advocated taking over pagan shrines and festivals and

Christianising them, so that Christian teaching could gradually supersede paganism, thus avoiding abrupt and unsettling change. In the long term, this approach worked. Christianity displaced all rivals, while the old gods dwindled into folklore. At the time, however, pagan rituals and the worship of the old gods often continued after a kingdom had officially converted. It was common practice even among kings – as we saw with Raedwald – to keep a foot in both camps. This may have been a matter of uncertainty, personal choice, or political expediency – not wishing to alienate the unconverted. Despite the praises that Bede and others heap upon missionaries and converts – and without denying Anglo-Saxon monarchs an inner, spiritual life – the conversion of the Anglo-Saxon kingdoms was about politics as much as faith. Conversion did not reduce levels of aggression or violence. Nevertheless, it was part of a maturing process. Roman Christianity with its hierarchy emphasised centralised control over a defined territory. This undoubtedly fed into the process of political centralisation as the Anglo-Saxon kingdoms made their transition from tribal territories carved out of post-Roman Britain to established kingdoms with individual identities whose existence was recognised beyond the confines of Britain.

The 680s also marked the end of Anglo-Saxon expansion in Britain. Cornwall, as we have seen, remained small but stubborn and independent, despite intermittent pressure from Wessex. The British kingdoms of Wales occasionally fought with Mercia, but also allied with Mercia against Northumbria; and the border between them remained broadly stable from 600 onwards. Somewhere at the beginning of the eighth century, the Mercians took control of the area around Wroxeter on the River Severn in Shropshire but were forced onto the defensive by constant problems with the Welsh kingdoms. This led Offa (r.757–96) to build his famous dyke in an attempt to prevent further incursions (see Chapter 28). The one area where expansion was still possible was northwards into Pictland.

Pictland evidently did not have the same degree of political unity as Dál Riata and Alt Clud, but any attempt to reconstruct its political structure is essentially speculation. We have the king lists, taken from the Pictish Chronicle and from various Irish sources, which mix the names of those we know to be real with others who are obviously mythical, and still others who inhabit the shadowlands between mythology and recorded history. We know the names of seven Pictish provinces or kingdoms –

Circinn, Fotla, Fortriu, Fib, Ce, Fidadid, and Cat – named after the seven sons of Cruithne, the legendary father of the Picts. Fortriu and Ce are the best documented, but the extent and, in some cases, the existence of the others is at best vague. We certainly do not have enough information to produce a meaningful map. Attempts have been made but, while the impulse is understandable, they must be regarded as fanciful.

The internal politics of Pictland seem not to have been particularly peaceful, and those Picts whose lands bordered Dál Riata and Alt Clud would have found themselves faced with expansionist neighbours. Throughout the sixth century Dál Riata gradually extended its control over parts of the west coast, while Alt Clud extended its influence up the Clyde Valley and across what is now the Central Belt, in part to compensate for pressure from the Britons of Rheged to the south. These were conflicts among the British: between the Picts of the north, with their unique and elusive culture, speaking their own version of P-Celtic; the Scots of Dál Riata to the west, culturally closer to the Irish, and speaking Q-Celtic; and the Old North, represented by Alt Clud on the Clyde, Rheged to the south, and the Gododdin to the east, culturally similar and speaking a version of P-Celtic that went on to form the basis of Old Welsh. The balance of political and cultural power between these three strands of Britishness had been changing for centuries and the coming of Christianity now played a part in the evolution of their relations. How things would have worked out had they been left alone we can only guess, but when the Anglo-Saxons turned their attention to northern Britain in the latter part of sixth century, they added a new dimension to an already complex situation.

During the mid-seventh century, perhaps during the reign of Oswald, Northumbria appears to have gained suzerainty over at least part of Pictland. This may have resulted from Oswald's conquest of the Gododdin lands in the late 630s and early 640s, or possibly from a later, undocumented campaign by Oswiu in the 650s. From 669 onwards, however, Wilfrid called himself Bishop of the Northumbrians and the Picts, and during the 680s there were Northumbrian missionaries active in Pictland promoting Roman Christianity. Geographical logic suggests that whatever influence Northumbria exerted would have been limited to southern Pictland and perhaps the more accessible areas on the east coast, rather than the whole country. We know that cattle and grain were sent south in tribute, and formal oath-swearing may have been required. In the end, whatever was demanded was too much for the Pictish king, Drest VI (r.663–72) who rose in revolt against the then King of Northumbria, Ecgfrith (r.670–85). Drest's Pictish army was heavily defeated at the Battle of Two Rivers, possibly at Moncreiffe Island in Perth, and the following year Bridei III (r.672–93) seized the Pictish throne.

Bridei was King of Fortriu, centred to the south of the Moray Forth. It is nowhere stated explicitly that he was a Christian, but his parents were – his father was Beli I of Alt Clud, and his mother the daughter of Edwin of Deira and Bernicia – and Bede is critical of Ecgfrith for invading Pictland in a way he would not have been if Pictland had still been under a pagan ruler. Bridei was an aggressive and expansionist king. During his reign, Fortriu established its own overlordship of Pictland, with outlying areas such as Orkney ruled by sub-kings. Bridei's first years in power were uneventful and he may have been consolidating his position, but in the 680s he launched a series of campaigns that would have a lasting impact on the north of Britain. He began in 680–81 by attacking the fortified headland of Dunnottar, just south of Stonehaven. We do not know who held the fortress, but it was probably the stronghold of a rival. In 682, Bridei moved north and attacked Orkney so violently that the Irish *Annals of Tigernach* describes the islands as having been destroyed. The following year, he seems to have been on the receiving end of an attack by the Dál Riata Scots, who besieged his southern capital of Dundurn ('The Fort of the Fist'), situated on a rocky knoll in Strathearn. The Scots failed to take Dundurn and Bridei counterattacked, besieging their capital at Dunadd. No sources tell us the outcome of the siege, but Pictish carvings dating from the period have been found inside Dunadd, suggesting that Bridei's forces were probably victorious.

Ecgfrith of Northumbria saw Bridei's growing power as a direct threat. Like most Anglo-Saxon kings, Ecgfrith was essentially a war leader. He had fought and defeated Wulfhere of Mercia in 674, and subsequently seized the Kingdom of Lindsey. Five years later, in 679, he was defeated by Wulfhere's brother, Æthelstan, at the Battle of the Trent, and Lindsey was returned to Mercia. Undaunted, in 684, Ecgfrith sent what is generally described as a raiding party to Ireland to intervene in the small Kingdom of Brega, part of the Uí Néill lands. There is no record of why he chose to do so, but the result appears to have been bloody, with the capture of large numbers of slaves, and the sacking of churches and monasteries. Ecgfrith's actions attracted strong criticism at the time from the Bishop of Lindisfarne, Ecgberht, and later from Bede. Against this background, despite opposition from his advisers but presumably confident that he had defeated the Picts previously, Ecgfrith decided to move against Bridei.

The Battle of Dun Nechtain (also known as the Battle of Nechtansmere) took place in May 685. The exact location of the battle is disputed. The traditionally favoured site is Dunnichen in Angus, partly on toponymic grounds, and partly because of its proximity to the Aberlemno stone – one of the finest Pictish symbol stones, which features superb carvings of warriors in battle, although there is no certainty that the battle is Dun Nechtain. A more likely site, given the topography – Bede talks of 'inaccessible mountains'[212] – is Dunachton in the district of Badenoch and Strathspey in the Highlands. Bridei's Picts lured the Northumbrians into the mountains until they were trapped between high ground held by the Picts and the marshes of Lake Nechtain. Ecgfrith's men attacked uphill. The Picts feigned retreat and then fell upon the Northumbrians, killing Ecgfrith and a large number of his men, and enslaving many others.

Defeat at Dun Nechtain accelerated the decline of Northumbrian power, which had begun with the Battle of the Trent, leaving the kingdom unable to challenge the supremacy of Mercia. It also drove the Northumbrian missionaries out of Pictland and led the Picts to adopt Celtic practices, again demonstrating how closely interwoven politics and religion had become. Pictland remained Celtic in its religious orientation for the rest of Bridei's reign and during those of his immediate successors, Taran mac Ainftech (r.693–97) and Bridei IV (r.697–706). However, Nechtan mac Der-Ilei (r.706–24 and 728–29) sought to move to Roman practice. The resulting divide between Roman and Celtic factions played a major part in the ten years of internal strife that followed.

In the longer term, Dun Nechtain marked the moment when the Picts established their independence and ended Anglo-Saxon expansion. That does not mean that the Northumbrian Angles, who subsequently became the English, stopped trying to invade and conquer – they would continue to do so for hundreds of years – but the Picts, who subsequently became the Scots, had now established a border and were able to maintain it. One reason for their success in this respect is that Dun Nechtain enabled Bridei and his successors, notably Bridei IV, to establish a single Pictish kingdom – single in that it consisted of a king and numerous subkings, but certainly not unified. The kingdom fractured during the conflicts of Nechtan mac Der-Ilei's reign, but was pulled back together under Óengus son of Fergus (also known as Unust; r.732–61). Óengus was a powerful figure, reigning for thirty years and probably over seventy when he died. In 736, he attacked a weakened and divided Dál Riata, stormed their fortress at Dunadd, and brought the kingdom under Pictish control, a situation that lasted until at least the 760s. Although the *Irish Annals* between 740 and the 760s record no names, the Picts probably ruled Dál Riata through sub-kings – and when names do reappear in the late 760s with Áed Find (Find the White) and his successors, it is not clear whether they are subkings or whether Dál Riata had somehow shaken off Pictish control. In the 740s, Óengus fought campaigns against the Northumbrians and the Britons of Alt Clud. In the 750s, he attacked Alt Clud again, this time in alliance with Eadberht of Northumbria, and forced Alt Clud to submit to his authority. However, the victorious Pictish-Northumbrian army was almost immediately heavily defeated, probably at Newburgh-on-Tyne, by a Mercian army under Æthelbald moving up from the south.

The story of Pictland and Dál Riata in the eighth and early ninth century is a morass of battles and alliances, strange names, and genealogical uncertainties which can be as confusing as they are fascinating. Despite everything, Pictland and Dál Riata retained their separate identities into the ninth century. However, the two royal houses and their aristocratic elites intermingled, probably through marriage alliances, so that some kings of Dál Riata were Pictish, and some kings of Pictland came from aristocratic Dál Riata families. In the end, the achievement of Óengus and his successors in holding together a single Pictish kingdom would become important when a complex interaction between Picts, Dál Riata Scots, and Vikings led to the emergence of a Kingdom of Alba, or Scotland.

26 The Land and the Law

Between 450 and 800, southern Britain was completely transformed in its political and social structures, its religious orientation, and its culture. Our understanding of cultural change rests heavily on the archaeological record, which can be difficult to interpret, but the evidence we have indicates that, in most areas where the Anglo-Saxons exercised political control, the pre-existing British or Romano-British culture was supplanted by Anglo-Saxon cultural norms and practices in a comparatively short period of time. As one might expect, in more remote areas – Cumbria is the best example – the transformation was slower and less complete, leaving behind a substratum of Celtic culture. Nonetheless, in most of what is now England and parts of southern Scotland, by the year 800 Anglo-Saxon dominance was an accepted fact. How the change took place is less clear. It is worth remembering that the term Anglo-Saxon is a generic one and applied retrospectively. The people we call Anglo-Saxons were Saxons, Angles, Jutes, Frisians, and Franks, and that is how they would have thought of themselves. Consequently, to talk of the spread of Anglo-Saxon culture is to describe in general terms a process within which there was much regional variation, for the most part rooted in tribal differences.

Across much of Anglo-Saxon Britain, agricultural land continued to be used – but not administered – in much the same way as during Roman and post-Roman periods. Southern Britain had been farmed since prehistoric times. In many areas, particularly in central and southern England, the Anglo-Saxons adopted unchanged field systems originating in Roman and pre-Roman times. The idea of a rural estate administered from a central residence where produce was collected and animals slaughtered also appears to have carried over, albeit with modifications: the Roman villa became the Anglo-Saxon *tūn*, and later the Saxon manor. At Barton Court in Oxfordshire, Saxon settlers appear to have begun farming on land that had formed a Roman estate in the fifth century. The stone-built Roman villa was demolished – whether before or after the arrival of the Saxons, we do not know – but the extensive complex of yards and paddocks surrounding the villa continued in use, and the Saxons built their own wooden houses and storehouses nearby. Susan Oosthuizen has drawn attention to open-field systems, which she sees as originating in the late- and immediately post-Roman periods. These systems, where a village would hold two or three large fields in common ownership but divide them into strips for cultivation by individual families, placed an obligation on farmers to give a proportion of their produce to the local overlord as payment for his protection – a wise policy in unsettled times. Oosthuizen sees the survival of these open-field systems and the formalisation of their associated obligations as evidence of rural continuity during and beyond the period of Anglo-Saxon settlement.[213] John Blair has pointed to areas of eastern England where large areas of farmland have been carefully laid out on a grid pattern that is apparently Anglo-Saxon in origin.[214] The main point here is that neither the areas displaying continuity, nor those where new land use patterns have been imposed, show any evidence of violence or disruption.

Settlement patterns during the Anglo-Saxon period do show significant divergence from Roman and post-Roman models, but again there is little evidence that the changes were accompanied by violence or disruption. Many Roman towns were abandoned in the wake of the breakdown of Roman government, and those which were not – such as Cirencester, Gloucester and Bath – were abandoned soon after they fell under Anglo-Saxon control. Anglo-Saxon attitudes to deserted towns seem to have varied. In many places – among them Canterbury, London, Southampton, and York – the Anglo-Saxons recognised the strategic importance of the site but built their own settlement at a careful distance from the Roman town. Roman Londinium, which roughly equates to the present-day City of London, was abandoned, and a new Anglo-Saxon settlement, Lundenwic, established early in the seventh century, soon becoming 'a marketplace for many nations who come there by land and sea.'[215] It lay to the west of Londinium, in the area known as Aldwych (*eald-wic* or old settlement), while ships docked on a stretch of riverbank, long-since built over but still known as The Strand. There may have been practical reasons for the Anglo-Saxons choosing to build their own towns. They built in wood – a matter of cultural choice rather than because they did not have the ability to build in stone – and they may well have found it easier to build wooden structures away from ruined and constricted Roman sites. Only churches were built in stone and these – such as Æthelberht's church dedicated to St Paul in London – were often located at the edge of Roman sites. Again, there may have been practical reasons for this – such as the availability of dressed stone – but, particularly in the early stages of settlement, Roman sites seem to have been regarded with suspicion, even fear, perhaps because of their association with alien spiritual beliefs. There are hints of this in the Old English poem 'The Ruin', and it is notable how many Roman buildings were used as cemeteries in the early settlement period. However, Anglo-Saxon practice was not consistent. There were towns – such as Dover, Winchester, and possibly Lincoln – where wooden

Anglo-Saxon buildings were erected within the confines of the deserted Roman settlement.

Urban settlements were fewer and smaller than during the Roman occupation, and villages looked different from their predecessors. The Anglo-Saxons avoided hillforts, some of which had been reoccupied during the fifth century (see Chapter 22). Most of the close-knit, defensible villages in which much of the rural population had lived since long before the Roman occupation soon disappeared. So, too, did the characteristic British roundhouses. They were replaced by looser, more strung-out settlements consisting of square or oblong buildings, bounded by fences or shallow ditches – although in those parts of eastern England where the grid-pattern field systems were created, the pattern is often extended to villages, with houses laid out next to each other on plots of exactly the same size.[216]

Buildings characteristic of Anglo-Saxon settlements included the pit-house, or *Grubenhaus*,[217] and the hall. A pit-house was a rectangular wooden building with a gabled roof, taking its name from a rectangular pit below ground level, perhaps covered by a suspended floor. Pit-houses have been found across north-western Europe, but only appear in Britain with the arrival of the Anglo-Saxons. From the late fifth century onwards, they appear in most areas under Anglo-Saxon control. There is no consensus on what they were used for: dwellings, workshops, and food stores have all been suggested, and all could be correct. The pit itself may have been used to keep food securely and away from light, or as a way of keeping the building warm in winter and cool in summer. The hall was the archetypal Anglo-Saxon building. Some German examples were big enough to accommodate animals as well as people. In Britain, although smaller, they were still substantial buildings – rectangular in plan, anything between six and eleven metres long, and three to five metres wide. There was a single entrance on one side, and possibly a wooden floor.

The choice of wood as a construction material, and the fact that household goods were mostly made of textiles, wood, or leather, means that the archaeological record can be limited, but the number of halls and pit-houses is a reasonable guide to the wealth of a settlement and to the number of families living there. The village of Mucking in Essex had ten halls and fourteen pit-houses. West Stow in Suffolk had fourteen halls and sixty-nine pit-houses. It is always tempting to see Anglo-Saxon halls in terms of the heroic description of Heorot, the hall of King Hrothgar in *Beowulf*, but in Anglo-Saxon Britain even the aristocratic elite lived in smaller, less imposing halls, expressing their wealth through possessions, gifts, and hospitality rather than high-status buildings.

New types of building and new settlement patterns were accompanied by radical changes in land tenure and administration. Those Roman institutions – legal, governmental, and religious – which had survived, albeit in diminished or modified form, were swept aside and replaced with Germanic forms and procedures. This simply did not happen in Gaul or northern Italy, despite widespread Germanic settlement – perhaps because the Roman order had not decayed to the same extent that it had in Britain – and the legacy of this different response underlies many of the legal and social divergences between the United Kingdom and its Continental neighbours that persist into the twenty-first century.

Anglo-Saxon law was very different from Roman law, but no less important or less effective as an instrument of social regulation. Despite differences between tribal groups, the Anglo-Saxons were very conscious of the law, its role, and its social function. Until the beginning of the seventh century, Anglo-Saxon laws were accumulations of long-accepted customs and traditions passed down orally from generation to generation. With his conversion to Christianity, Æthelberht of Kent saw the value of law being enshrined in writing. He commissioned the first Anglo-Saxon law code, datable to between 601 and 604, which – with the exception of the Irish *Senchas Már* (see Chapter 19) – is the earliest legal document in post-Roman Western Europe. Æthelberht's law code provided a model for other kings, notably in Wessex and Mercia. Law codes, sometimes known as 'dooms', increased in importance as the Anglo-Saxon kingdoms matured, and became particularly important during the reigns of Ælfred (r.871–99) and his successors, Edward the Elder (r.899–924), and Æthelstan (r.924–39), when they shaped the peace agreement with the invading Danes and defined the extent and status of the Danelaw.

The basis of Anglo-Saxon law was 'folk-right', the accumulation of precedents, judgements, and rules stretching back into tribal history, and because it was essentially tribal, it could differ significantly between the Angles and Saxons, Jutes and Frisians. Folk-right was administered locally by the *reeve*, the senior magistrate and government official in his region, whose duty was to the king. Once the country was divided into shires, each shire had its own reeve, who eventually became the 'sheriff'. The reeve was supported by a group of *thegns* (or thanes): local landowners, sometimes royal retainers, usually with experience as warriors and leaders of men, broadly analogous to the modern concept of the great and the good. Folk-right could be modified or overridden by 'privilege', and the ultimate source of privilege was the king. The procedure seems to have been that the person or institution seeking change – and it was often the Church – should make a case which would be adjudicated by the king or his nominee, in theory after consultation with the local reeve. In other cases, the king himself may have chosen to override folk-right to reward an individual or a family whose service he valued. Most such decisions were formalised in a charter. Charters were official documents, usually signed by the king and witnessed by a number of churchmen and nobles – the order of whose signatures is often taken as a guide to their relative standing with the king at the time. The importance of charters in the Anglo-Saxon world is evidenced by the number we know to have been issued, and the number which have survived.

Land was of key significance in all Anglo-Saxon law codes – in part because land ownership and its associated duties and obligations were fundamental in defining the position of an individual in the social hierarchy. Land was also important, one suspects, because – even in terms of the genealogies that shaped their sense of their own history – the Anglo-Saxons had not been in Britain long. The process of legalising and formalising land tenure was thus a way for the elite to justify – and reinforce – their position and their authority.

With the caveat that this was a society in the process of evolution, and remembering the likelihood of regional variation, we can reconstruct in broad outline the Anglo-Saxon social hierarchy. At the top, the king spent the revenues of his kingdom and was responsible for its prosperity and its defence, but he did not own it. He was not, in that sense, a feudal monarch. He and his family might own large estates, but for most of the Anglo-Saxon period a king's life was a peripatetic one. He and his court would travel round the kingdom, stopping at centres known as royal *vills* or *tūns*, to administer justice, adjudicate on disputes, and issue charters. Only later did kingdoms adopt fixed capitals: Canterbury for Kent; Winchester for Wessex; and Tamworth for Mercia; while Northumbria had two, Bamburgh in the north and York in the south. Below the king were the *eal-*

dormen, the aristocrats of the Anglo-Saxon world.[218] They were wealthy landowners wielding regional power, who might be charged with leading the militia (or *fyrd*) against enemies in the king's absence. In the early Anglo-Saxon period, kings tended to appoint *ealdormen* in recognition of their personal authority, but the position soon became the most prestigious of royal appointments and often hereditary. Alongside the *ealdormen* were the archbishops and bishops, powerful because of their spiritual authority and because of the Church's extensive landholdings. Like *ealdormen*, their signatures frequently appeared on charters. The next level down comprised the reeves, combining the functions of the civil service and the judiciary, who adjudicated on issues of land tenure and folk-right. Below the reeves came the *thegns*. Originally retainers and/or soldiers in the service of the king, *thegns* evolved into a kind of gentry or lesser nobility, often becoming substantial landowners, but still under an obligation to serve the king when called upon. Most *thegns* inherited their status, but one eleventh-century law code details the level of wealth necessary for a man aspiring to the status of *thegn*. A farmer, for example, needed to own five hides of land, as well as substantial property, such as a church, a kitchen, or a bell-house. (A hide was the standard Anglo-Saxon measurement of land area, used for tax assessment and equivalent to about forty-nine hectares, the amount of land held necessary to support one household.) A merchant had to own his own business and to have travelled overseas at least three times. The lowest and largest social class were the *ceorls* (or churls). Although divided into different degrees according to their wealth and the obligations they owed to their lord, they were all considered free born men. The wealthiest (*geneatas*) owned land, sometimes as much as a *thegn*, but were still required to pay in kind or in service for their lord's protection. Those less wealthy but still owning and farming enough land to feed themselves (*kotsetlas*) were obliged to work on their lord's land for at least a day a week – usually more during the harvest, when they might expect to receive a share of the crop in recognition of their work. The lowest freemen (*geburas*) might own a small parcel of land, but were basically labourers, dependent on their lord for work and food.

The classes and grades of Anglo-Saxon society, their obligations and, most important, their *weregild* – the amount of money the family could expect in compensation if someone were to be killed – were all carefully defined in the law codes. Where the British population fitted into this structure is not altogether clear. When Ine of Wessex (r.689–726) issued a new legal code, probably in 694, he made a separate provision for the Britons living under his rule, even though they were classified as an inferior group: the *weregild* payable for killing a Briton was only half that for a Saxon. It seems probably that, as time went on, the British population simply merged into the Anglo-Saxon scheme of things. Yet there was one other class in Anglo-Saxon society: the slaves.

In the nineteenth century, the ideology of Empire, the presence of Queen Victoria on the throne and Prince Albert in her shadow, led to widespread acceptance of the idea that the Anglo-Saxons were the true progenitors of the English race and English values. Given such a conclusion, it was difficult to draw attention to the issue of slavery which, as a consequence, was largely ignored. True, our main sources say little about the subject. Nennius never mentions it. Gildas says only that the Anglo-Saxons took British prisoners and sold them into slavery.[219] Bede seems to approve of St Wilfrid's actions in baptising and setting free two hundred and fifty slaves in Selsey on the Sussex coast, but he never actually condemns slavery.[220] This is probably because slavery was both normal and accepted in Anglo-Saxon society – as it was in Roman and Celtic society. Estimates vary widely, but slaves may have constituted between 10 and 30 per cent of the total population. Entries in the *Domesday Book* – compiled much later, between 1085 and 1086 – show slaves making up between 20 and 23 per cent of the workforce on most estates.

Most slaves would have been of British or Irish descent. Some may have been Anglo-Saxons, seized when one kingdom raided or overran another. Some free men even sold themselves and their families into slavery to avoid starvation when times were particularly hard. In terms of their function in society, the emphasis – reinforced in the *Domesday Book* – is usually on slaves doing heavy manual labour on the farms and in the fields. Many undoubtedly did so. One unique piece of writing by a tenth century abbot, Ælfric of Eynsham, takes the form of an imaginary dialogue with a slave: "I go out at dawn, driving the oxen to the field... When I have yoked them together, and fastened the ploughshare to the plough, I have to plough a whole acre every day... The work is hard."[221] Life was hard for all classes of society – even *ealdormen* did physical work – but we know that some male slaves became butchers, cooks, millers, carpenters, or weavers. And while women generally acted as domestic servants of various kinds, it is certain that some were kept as concubines for the pleasure of their lord.

Anglo-Saxon law recognised and defined the status of slaves. They had certain (albeit very limited) rights and were subject to specific (often savage) punishments if they transgressed. A slave who raped another slave, for example, could be castrated. It was possible to cease being a slave. Numerous wills have survived granting manumission to individuals or even families; and there are examples of slaves who managed to amass sufficient wealth – through gifts or inheritance: they were not allowed to receive money for their labours – to buy their freedom. Because freedom involved a change of legal status and gave the newly freed individual the right to buy land, it involved a formal ceremony with documentation and witnesses, which was usually performed in a church or, symbolically, at a crossroads.

As we have already noted, when the Roman administration failed, towns declined and many were abandoned, the road network continued to be used but decayed badly for lack of maintenance, and the money economy collapsed. The fighting and the turmoil of the settlement period only made things worse. When the situation stabilised sufficiently for the Anglo-Saxons to build their own towns, they were smaller and fewer in number than their Roman predecessors – and even when they became important markets or ports, they never fulfilled the governmental and administrative functions of Roman towns. Nor were they centres for manufacturing because there was very little manufacturing. The economy of Anglo-Saxon Britain was even more rural and agricultural than that of Roman Britain.

The law codes make it clear that service on the land and the exchange of agricultural produce were fundamental to the social hierarchy. In terms of everyday life, goods and services were exchanged or bartered rather than 'bought'. Daily necessities would have been exchanged between neighbours or at small village markets. In the towns, and fortified locations known as *byrig* (singular *burh*) when they began to appear (see Chapter 28), larger markets carried a wider range of goods, such as farming equipment, weapons, leather goods, and jewellery. Traders with connections to the wider world offered wine from France, bowls and decorated vases from Byzantium, as well as pepper and other spices from Asia.

Barter was the basis of the economy. Coin usage effectively ceased with the end of Roman rule, but by the later decades of the fifth century, gold coins from the Continent – *solidi* and the smaller *tremisses* – were present in Kent, although they were probably available only to the ruling family and leading nobles, and may well have been used as signifiers of wealth and royal favour rather than as money. The use of imported coins, principally *tremisses*, gradually spread until, somewhere around 620, gold coins of the same size known as *thrymsas* began to be minted in one or more of the Anglo-Saxon kingdoms, although we do not know where. These were easy to clip, by shaving gold from the coin's edge, or to debase, by melting and reminting with an admixture of base metal. Small numbers of gold coins continued to circulate but they ceased to be minted and, from the late 600s, almost all the circulating currency consisted of thick silver coins known as *sceattas*. Even though *sceattas* were minted in large quantities and are regularly found in excavations or by metal detectorists, they bear no inscription and cannot be attributed to any particular kingdom or reign with any certainty. Northumbria was still minting *sceattas* in the ninth century, but elsewhere, from the 760s or 770s onwards, new silver coins appeared. Initially associated with Offa, and clearly imitating the reformed coinage of Charlemagne's Empire, these large and thinner coins were known as *pennings* – from which we derive the word *penny* – and featured the name, and often a portrait or bust, of the reigning king, as well as the name of the moneyer or mint. It was during this period, possibly in 775, that a standard weight and equivalence was instituted, so that two hundred and forty silver pennies were the equivalent in weight of one pound of silver metal – the origin of the pound sterling. Offa's pennies were copied by other Anglo-Saxon kings, and by Danish rulers in the later ninth and tenth centuries, and remained the basis of English currency until it was reformed by Henry III in 1247. Coin usage naturally increased as time progressed. It also became common practice for items to be priced in pennies, even though they might be 'bought' through an exchange of goods. In 1066, a sheep cost five silver pennies, a pig ten, and an ox thirty. Nevertheless, even in 1066, the bulk of what was by that time the English economy was conducted on the basis of exchange and barter.

27   Words and Images

The language of the Anglo-Saxons, which spread throughout the areas they colonised and controlled is generally called 'Old English'. This is misleading on two counts. In the first place, it looks nothing like English, and while it is undoubtedly the foundation from which modern English evolved, it is unreadable unless you have studied it. 'Anglo-Saxon' is a more accurate description, and was the term most frequently used when scholars became fascinated by the language and its literature in the sixteenth century. Only in the nineteenth century when, as noted above, the powerful combination of Empire, Queen Victoria, and Prince Albert made it *de rigueur* to emphasise the Germanic roots of England's language and culture, did the term 'Old English' gain wide currency. It is too late to change the accepted terminology but, as with invasion theory, we should be aware how later ages have interpreted the past in a manner which reflected their own contemporary concerns.

Secondly, there was not one Anglo-Saxon language but several. Each tribe had its own language, all of them Germanic, and related to each other much as modern Norwegian, Swedish and Danish relate to each other, but not necessarily mutually intelligible. The pace of linguistic change associated with the coming of the Anglo-Saxons is difficult to assess. We have only a limited corpus of texts to guide us and, as it was Christianity which provided the spur to literacy, none of them date from the early settlement period. The earliest texts are probably the inscriptions on the Ruthwell Cross, in the village of Ruthwell near Dumfries, and on the Franks Casket, a small whalebone chest now in the British Museum. Both probably date from the early eighth century; both use the runic alphabet; and both are in the Northumbrian dialect. The inscription on the Ruthwell Cross consists of twenty-five lines of the Anglo-Saxon poem, 'The Dream of the Rood', in which the narrator dreams he is talking to the Cross on which Christ was crucified. The Franks Casket is more complicated, as some of the runes transcribe Anglo-Saxon and some transcribe Latin. The earliest written Anglo-Saxon may be in what is known as the Épinal manuscript. Possibly originating from the scriptorium of Malmesbury Abbey early in the eighth century, it contains a glossary of Latin and Greek words with their equivalents in the Mercian dialect. The earliest continuous text, again in

Map 25 Anglo-Saxon Law, Language, and Art

the Northumbrian dialect, is the short poem known as 'Caedmon's Hymn'. In terms of composition, it may well be the earliest of all Anglo-Saxon texts. According to Bede, Caedmon 'through God's gift received the art of poetry,' but he gives no date.[222] Working backwards from other events recorded in the *Ecclesiastical History*, we can place composition somewhere between 658 and 680, after which the poem would have been transmitted orally until Bede wrote it down about 725. Most of the surviving documents from the eighth century are in the Mercian dialect, with a handful of charters in Kentish, and just a few in Northumbrian. Some scholars, including David Crystal, are convinced that there was also an East Anglian dialect, and have detected traces of it through detailed textual analysis, but we have no documents in Anglian. Such manuscripts as existed were probably destroyed during the Danish invasions which took their heaviest toll in Anglian areas.[223]

The total surviving corpus of Anglo-Saxon comprises 3,037 texts and some three million words – which, as Crystal points out, is far fewer than the word count of Dickens' collected works.[224] The majority of these documents are written in West Saxon. Although it does not appear before the middle of the ninth century, West Saxon soon became the most widely-used dialect, reflecting the political ascendancy of Wessex at the time. Much of the *Anglo-Saxon Chronicle* is in West Saxon. So, too, are many of the best-known Anglo-Saxon poems, including *Beowulf* (with interpolations that may be Anglian), 'The Battle of Brunanburh', and 'The Battle of Maldon'. Under the influence of King Ælfred (r.871–99), West Saxon became the preferred dialect for important prose works. Ælfred himself translated Pope Gregory's book, *Pastoral Care*, and added an original prologue, part in prose and part in poetry. Ælfred also translated Boethius' *De consolatione philosophiae* (*The Consolation of Philosophy*), and either he or his son, Edward the Elder (r.899–924) probably commissioned the translation by an unknown hand of Orosius' *Historiae Adversus Paganos* (*History against the Pagans*). In the late ninth and early tenth centuries, Wessex expanded to form the basis of what would become a unified English kingdom. West Saxon became the standard Anglo-Saxon dialect – we have charters dealing with land grants in Mercia and Kent written in West Saxon – evolving over time to meet the demands of rapidly changing political and demographic circumstances. During the period of Viking raids and Danish invasions, West Saxon absorbed many Scandinavian loan words, and even some aspects of Old Norse grammar. Whether at court, in a legal context, or in the Church, the other regional dialects appear less frequently and begin to fade away. Kentish and Mercian, being closest to the seat of West Saxon power, probably died out first. Northumbrian, or something very like it, is reported to have continued to be spoken in some areas until the twelfth century.

What then happened to the P-Celtic language or languages previously spoken in those areas of southern Britain now under Anglo-Saxon control? They disappeared, and everything suggests that they disappeared relatively quickly, but exactly how and when is a matter of debate. We might have expected the Anglo-Saxons to adopt the Celtic language. It had been the language of the majority of the British population for two thousand years, and had withstood the impact of Latin during three-and-a-half centuries of Roman occupation. In broadly comparable situations, it was not unusual for the incoming elite to adopt the language of the existing population. In 911, Charles II, King of the West Franks, created a fiefdom in the lower Seine Valley for a group of Scandinavians led by Rollo (also Rolf the Walker, or Ganger Hrólf), which within a few generations took its name from the men who settled there and became the Duchy of Normandy. Rollo and his men probably came from Norway and would have spoken a dialect of Old Norse. A hundred and fifty years later, in 1066, when Rollo's descendant William of Normandy invaded England, he and his Norman elite spoke a version of medieval French, the language of the majority of the population of Normandy. Similarly, when William and his Norman elite conquered England, they made French the language of government and the law, but their descendants ended up speaking English, the language that had evolved from Anglo-Saxon and was spoken by the majority of the population. The process took longer in England – three hundred years as against a hundred and fifty – but England was much bigger and more populous than Normandy. Nonetheless, by the last quarter of the fourteenth century, Chaucer was writing poetry and conducting his business as comptroller of customs for the port of London in English, and in 1399, Henry IV took his oath of accession in English before an English-speaking court. Why then did the Anglo-Saxons not adopt P-Celtic? And why were the P-Celtic-speaking British apparently so willing to adopt Anglo-Saxon?

A related puzzle is the fact that Anglo-Saxon appears to have been almost wholly uninfluenced by the Celtic language or languages it replaced. In parallel circumstances, where two languages have co-existed for several centuries, there is normally a degree of cross-fertilisation, usually visible in loan words. When the Capetian kings took power in France towards the end of the tenth century, Old French replaced Frankish as the language of government, but it was heavily laced with Germanic loan words. When English finally replaced Norman French in England, the lexicon included a large proportion of French loan words. When the British Empire was at its height, English absorbed loan words from several Indian and African languages. But with Anglo-Saxon, this did not happen. The number of Celtic loan words is minimal and, apart from the names of rivers, the number of place names with a Celtic root is also very small.

The writers and historians in the nineteenth and early twentieth century explained the advent of the Anglo-Saxons and the cultural dominance they achieved in terms of invasion theory, often with explicit racial triumphalism. Carlyle, in *On Heroes and Hero Worship* (1841), sees Saxon success as determined by racial superiority. He even tries to turn Robert Burns into a Saxon.[225] For John Mitchell Kemble, it was a matter of destiny: 'Dimly through the twilight in which the sun of Rome was to set for ever, loomed the Colossus of the German race, gigantic, terrible, inexplicable.'[226] By contrast, Professor Meiklejohn's view that, with the landing of Hengist and Horsa, 'English history, as opposed to British history, now begins' sounds the voice of moderation.[227] Following Gildas and Bede, the nineteenth-century view was that Anglo-Saxons killed or enslaved most of the British, driving the remainder westwards into what is now Wales, or northwards to Cumbria or beyond the Forth—Clyde line. An alternative view saw mass migration on a scale that simply swamped the existing population, again pushing the excess west and north. Neither explanation is entirely credible.

That there was fighting between the Anglo-Saxons and the British over an extended period is undeniable. And there were massacres. Ælle and his sons killed all the inhabitants of Pevensey in 477 (see Chapter 24); and, according to Bede, at the Battle of Chester in 616, Æthelfrith of Northumbria was responsible for killing 1,200 monks. Some of the population did flee west and north to areas where they felt safe from the invaders. Yet there is no evidence of violence or killing on the genocidal scale that would have been required to bring about a major population shift. Indeed, there is much evidence to the contrary. Violent changes in land ownership are usually reflected in changes to field systems and the way the land is worked. As noted earlier, this is not the case. Ine of Wessex made provision for the Britons living under his rule in his law code: they were second-class citizens, but they were citizens, and there were enough of them to merit notice. In 536, a massive volcanic eruption in Iceland ushered in a period of reduced temperatures and crop failures. At the beginning of the 540s, bubonic plague struck most of Europe. This was followed by two further Icelandic eruptions.[228] Such events may have killed thousands, but there is no reason to suppose that the British would have suffered disproportionately. Throughout the settlement period, the British population probably continued to live where and how they had always done, gradually becoming accustomed to the new culture.

Accepting that the Anglo-Saxons did not exterminate or swamp the existing population, we need to know how many of them there were during and after the settlement period. Population estimates are notoriously difficult and, on this occasion, DNA analysis, which has proved so valuable in relation to population change – or the lack of it – in the Bronze and Iron Ages, cannot give conclusive answers. As Cunliffe has pointed out, we cannot distinguish the Y chromosomes of the Germanic peoples brought across by the Romans from those belonging to the settlers and invaders in the fifth and sixth centuries. Moreover, many of the Danes who invaded between the ninth and eleventh centuries came from the same regions as their Anglo-Saxon predecessors and will inevitably share certain DNA characteristics. Attempts have been made to interrogate data drawn from settlement and burial archaeology in order to estimate the scale of immigration. Combining DNA and archaeological evidence gives an uncertain estimate that in the south and east of Britain immigrants may have made up 20 per cent of the population, while further north that figure may have dropped to 10 per cent.[229] Estimates for the population of Anglo-Saxon England as a whole vary widely, but if we take a median figure of 1.5 million, we can postulate a total immigrant population of between 175,000 and 225,000 by the year 700. Even if we inflate this figure to 300,000, it is still a small number to have effected such radical cultural change. How did it happen?

Status may be one answer. However many Anglo-Saxons there were, it is clear that they took control of most of what had been Roman Britain in a relatively short space of time. Initially, they exercised power by force of arms, and then as an elite governing class. As Robin Fleming demonstrates in *Britain after Rome*, from the sixth century onwards elite Anglo-Saxon families frequently glorified and re-imagined their past to give themselves greater prestige, and perhaps also to justify their authority in what was still a new land. They elaborated their genealogies, exaggerated the longevity of their dynasties, adopted ancient burial sites as their own, and generally created a heroic, legendary past where one did not necessarily exist.[230] This heroic ideal is reflected in the *Anglo-Saxon Chronicle* and in much Anglo-Saxon poetry. Having achieved power and glorified the process, the new elite would necessarily have looked down upon, and held themselves apart from, the people whose land they had conquered. They would have maintained their position by maintaining their culture. Any recognition of the validity of British culture or the utility of the Celtic language would have been an admission of weakness and would have undermined their newly acquired status.

A related possibility reflects upon the cultural position of the British. Those regions the Anglo-Saxons failed to conquer – and which remained culturally Celtic – were in the difficult and mountainous north and west. The areas where they did take control were geographically easier to access and were those where the Roman presence had had its greatest impact on settlement and on the landscape, and where Roman cultural influence had been strongest. These were areas where many Britons had become integrated in the Roman social and economic order, becoming magistrates, tax collectors, public officials, and members of their local *ordo*. There were also merchants and traders whose businesses had been dependent on the great agricultural estates, or on the presence of the legions. Such people may have lived in stone houses in Roman towns and spoken Latin as well as their native P-Celtic. These were people who saw their world crumble during the first half of the fifth century. The legend of past wealth and past security would have lived on among their children and grandchildren. Such families would have held 'civilised' values no longer shared by much of British society and certainly not by the incoming Anglo-Saxons. They would, to some extent, have become detached from their cultural roots and their confidence would have been at a low ebb.

The other, larger section of the British population lived and worked in the countryside. They worked on the big Roman estates or farmed their own land and lived in villages that were little changed in appearance from pre-Roman times, although they would have begun to benefit from Roman material culture in terms of pots and other basic products. These people were dependent on the Romans, but never part of the Roman world. They were not necessarily badly treated, but they would have been taxed and would have lived according to a foreign legal system that had been imposed upon them. They might not have liked living under the authority of an occupying power, but they would certainly have realised that, since the end of the Roman occupation, they had suffered a significant reduction in prosperity and security.

When the Anglo-Saxons began to arrive in Britain, from the second half of the fifth century onwards, British society had not fully recovered from the collapse of the Roman social and economic order. Nor had it re-established itself culturally. Given this context, it is perhaps not surprising that faced with Anglo-Saxon strength and confidence, the British showed few signs of asserting themselves either politically or culturally. This approach should not be overplayed, but it is noteworthy that there were no rebellions of the kind that were a feature of the early Roman period, and the rapid dominance of the Anglo-Saxon language and Anglo-Saxon culture suggests a willingness on the part of the British to fall into line with the new occupying power.

A third possibility is that the Celtic-speaking population may have found it easier to learn Anglo-Saxon than to try and communicate with their new rulers in P-Celtic. The Romans were used to living in a multi-racial and multilingual Empire. When they invaded Britain, they were experienced in ruling over subject peoples, some of whom spoke Celtic. The Anglo-Saxons had no such experience to guide them, while the British, who were used to a multilingual society, may simply have taken the line of least resistance.

In literature, there were similarities in how and why poetry was composed, in certain recurring themes, even in its delivery, but not in its style or in its character. The Celtic bard and the Anglo-Saxon *scop* (analogous to the Scots *makar* or maker) were both essentially court poets – although there were also unattached or itinerant poets in the Celtic world. They composed for public recitation and depended for their livelihood on their king or lord, whose wisdom and generosity was naturally a frequent subject of praise. Celtic poetry, such as that contained in the *Book of Aneirin* and the *Book of Taliesin*, praises, blames, and satirises in a variety of complex metrical forms. It is mystical, elegiac, and lyrical, but it is rarely, if ever, heroic. The great Celtic epics – the Irish *Táin Bó Cuailnge* (*The Cattle Raid of Cooley*) and the Welsh *Mabinogion* – are in prose, not poetry. Anglo-Saxon poetry, by contrast, is metrically simpler, almost always based on strongly alliterative lines with a marked caesura. It is certainly capable of great subtlety of expression and is often elegiac in tone, but it is powerfully and consistently heroic in character.

The tradition that bards recited their poetry to the accompaniment of a lyre goes back to the eighth century BC. Celtic lyres were known in Latin as *lyra*, in Welsh as *crwth*, and in Old Irish as *crotta*; and they were common throughout Celtic Europe. *Scops* also played the lyre when reciting, although the earliest Anglo-Saxon lyre, found at Abingdon in Oxfordshire, dates only from the fifth century AD. The *Vespasian Psalter*, a superbly illuminated Anglo-Saxon manuscript from the middle of the eighth century, contains an illustration of King David playing the lyre, apparently using a technique known as 'strum and block' that we know was common in Greece and Rome. One complication is that Anglo-Saxon poetry often uses the word *hearpe* for a lyre but, while the triangular harp as we know it today does seem to have evolved from the lyre, it was not in widespread use until the ninth century. There is a Pictish carving of a harp from about 800 on the Dupplin Cross in Strathearn, but the earliest depiction in Ireland is only in the twelfth century. In general, Celtic instruments (see Chapter 11) were more sophisticated than their Anglo-Saxon counterparts, but both cultures used lyres, horns of different kinds, flutes, panpipes, and various forms of percussion, and given that these instruments were common to musical cultures across Europe and beyond, it is not possible to judge the interaction between Celtic and Anglo-Saxon music in any meaningful way.

Only in the visual arts is there is a clear interplay between Celtic and Anglo-Saxon traditions for which Christianity appears to have acted as the catalyst. The manuscript known as the *Lindisfarne Gospels* vies with the *Book of Kells* as one of the great pieces of early medieval art. It contains the gospels of the four evangelists and consists of five hundred and sixteen vellum pages, made from approximately one hundred and fifty calf skins. Sources suggest that the original leather binding, plated with gold and studded with jewels, was looted by Scandinavian raiders during the ninth century. The book itself was saved and remains the most complete manuscript of its kind to survive. It was written, or possibly simply commissioned, by St Eadfrith, who was Bishop of Lindisfarne between 698 and his death in 721. The distinctive script and breath-taking illuminations and illustrations are in what is known as the Insular style – because it originated in the British Isles – or alternatively the Hiberno-Saxon style – because it is a blend of Irish and Anglo-Saxon artistic traditions.

The origins of Insular style lie in the artistic styles and calligraphic techniques developed in Irish monasteries and scriptoria. The Irish monks who, during the conversion period, travelled to Alt Clud, Dál Riata, the Welsh kingdoms, and other parts of Britain, took their skills with them. Once in Britain, Irish art and calligraphy were confronted by the Germanic artistic traditions of the Anglo-Saxons. The result was a hybrid: a colourful, energetic, imaginative, and coherent style that was to remain in vogue until the Norman Conquest. So, for example, the spiral patterns and intricate knotwork characteristic of Celtic art combined with the animal or zoomorphic style found in much Germanic art to produce elaborate, interlaced patterns consisting of the fantastically elongated bodies of stylised animals and birds. There is often a complex relationship of shape and line between the block of text at the centre of a manuscript page and the brightly coloured and illuminated margins. Illustrations that might at first sight seem Celtic in style are frequently enhanced, even subverted by strong, expressive line drawing, as well as by odd, often witty, narrative images – such as the image of the Ascension in which Christ is disappearing into the clouds with only his legs visible – both of which are characteristic of Anglo-Saxon art. The synthesis is enriched by grapes, vines, and acanthus leaves borrowed from the Roman and Byzantine traditions.

Most Insular manuscripts feature what are known as carpet pages. These are pages of abstract or geometrical illustration placed at the beginning of a manuscript, or at the beginning of each section, which in many ways define Anglo-Saxon illustrative art. The oldest known carpet page is found in a seventh-century manuscript of the *Chronicon* of Paulus Orosius, produced in the scriptorium of Bobbio Abbey in Piacenza in Italy, established by the Irish missionary, St Colombanus *c*.612. The oldest complete Insular manuscript, the *Book of Durrow*, written in the late seventh century and named after Durrow Abbey in Ireland's County Offaly, but probably originating in Northumbria, contains several elaborate and richly-coloured carpet pages, including one remarkable depiction of interlaced animals. The testament of each of the evangelists in the *Lindisfarne Gospels* is prefaced by a carpet page of stunning complexity.

Insular style is best seen in manuscripts, but there are also many fine metal items and stone crosses from all parts of the British Isles which display clear Insular characteristics. The Monymusk Reliquary – a small, house-shaped casket from the eighth century unearthed in Aberdeenshire and used to contain the relics of a saint – mixes Celtic and Pictish design with Anglo-Saxon metalworking skills. The Derrynaflan Chalice, from the eighth or ninth century, part of a hoard discovered at Killenaule in Tipperary in 1980, is considered one of the finest examples of Insular metalwork. The Sutton Hoo ship burial contained some spectacular objects in the Insular style, such as a purse lid, some shoulder clasps, and some buckles. The Ruthwell Cross in Dumfriesshire and the Bewcastle Cross in Cumbria, both from the eighth century, show marked Insular features. As do the two ninth-century Sandbach Crosses in Cheshire, and the ninth- or tenth-century Muiredach High Cross at Monasterboice in County Louth. However, Insular influence did not extend to architecture. With the exception of a handful of churches, Anglo-Saxon buildings remained simple, even basic, throughout the period.

The Insular style did not remain insular. Insular script has been identified in manuscripts originating from the court of Charlemagne at the end of the eighth century. The link may well have been the renowned clergyman and scholar Alcuin, a Northumbrian by birth, who studied in York and went on to become head of Charlemagne's court school at Aachen and tutor to both Charlemagne and his sons. Both the script and the illustrations of the *Echternach Gospels*, an early eighth-century manuscript named after a monastery in Luxembourg founded in 698 by a Northumbrian monk named Willibrod, are Insular in style. Some historians have suggested that the manuscript may have begun life in Lindisfarne, but there are sufficient differences from other Northumbrian manuscripts to indicate a Continental origin. Insular influence is also detectable in Continental metalwork: in the richly decorated covers created for manuscripts such as the *Echternach Gospels*, in brooches, clasps, and other items. Between the collapse of the Western Roman Empire in the fifth century and the coronation of Charlemagne in 800, the lands that had once formed part of the Empire underwent sweeping political change; but to a considerable extent they still lived in the cultural shadow of Rome. Insular art allowed the monks, metalworkers, artists, and artisans to move away from a classical and largely naturalistic style, and to adopt a more exciting and exotic mixture of stylisation, geometricity, and colour, even when not using Insular motifs. It was one of those comparatively rare occasions when the tide of influence flowed from the British Isles to the Continent.

28   The Third Wave

The Anglo-Saxon kingdoms became Christian and matured both politically and culturally, but they did not stop fighting each other. After the Battle of the Trent in 679, Mercia and Northumbria agreed a border between them which remained essentially unchanged for nearly two hundred years. This allowed Æthelbald (r.716–57) to extend Mercian power to the south and east. He intervened in a power struggle in Wessex, securing the accession of Æthelheard (r.726–40), but his price was the formal submission of the new king and his kingdom to Mercian overlordship. Æthelheard's reign was thus characterised by Mercia gradually detaching parts of Wessex's territory along the northern border, and exercising ever-greater authority in those areas where Æthelheard notionally still ruled. Æthelheard was succeeded by his brother, Cuthred (r.740–56), who was content to accept Wessex's status as a client kingdom – at least at first. On several occasions, he made common cause with Mercia against Welsh incursions, but in 752 he saw his opportunity. He rebelled, defeated Æthelbald at the Battle of Burford, in what is now Oxfordshire, and secured both Wessex's independence and a major extension of its territories to the north of the Thames.

Mercia's fortunes dipped briefly, but revived in 757, with the accession of Offa, who went on to rule for thirty-nine years – something of an achievement when male life expectancy was less than forty – and took Mercia to the zenith of its power. Essex was already under Mercian domination, which meant that Offa had control of the economically vital port of London. Using Essex as a base, he moved against Kent in 764, gaining the submission of its joint rulers, Eanmund and Heaberht, and allowing them to rule as client kings. Early in the 770s, he took control of Sussex, again ruling through client kings, although in this case his appointees were styled *dux* not *rex*. A lack of documentary sources means that our knowledge of events in East Anglia is limited, but Æthelred I, who probably reigned from the 760s to the late 770s, appears to have submitted to Offa. His son, Æthelred II, seems to have upset Offa badly – possibly by minting coins giving himself the title *Rex*, and thus claiming a greater degree of independence than Offa was prepared to concede. The story goes that, in 794, Æthelred set off for Offa's stronghold of Sutton Walls near Hereford to meet Offa's daughter, Ælfthryth, to whom he was expecting to become betrothed. When he arrived, Offa had him beheaded – a rare incidence of one Anglo-Saxon king directly ordering the death of another – and East Anglia was ruled directly by the kings of Mercia for the next thirty years. Offa also exerted pressure on Wessex. He seems to have intervened in order to help Beorhtric of Wessex (r.786–802) defeat his rival Ecgberht (or Egbert) and gain the throne, an act which would have consequences for his successors. Ecgberht fled to the court of Charlemagne. Offa then arranged for his daughter, Eadburh, to marry Beorhtric, which enabled him to exert considerable influence over his southern neighbour.

Among the Anglo-Saxon kingdoms, Offa sought long-term power and influence. His campaigns against the British kingdoms in Wales were short, punitive raids in response to repeated and destructive cross-border incursions. In the end, the Welsh proved so troublesome that Offa ordered the construction of the enormous, defensive earthwork that bears his name – Offa's Dyke – and stretches for two hundred and forty kilometres from the Estuary in the north to the River Wye in the south. It was a vast undertaking, much of the work probably done by slaves. With a deep ditch on the Welsh side and a massive earthen rampart on the Mercian side – and so positioned in the landscape that it offered clear views into enemy territory – it followed a line close to what is now the border between England and Wales. Only one source – Asser, the Welsh monk and biographer of King Ælfred, writing at the end of the ninth century – actually credits Offa as the originator. However, it is difficult to imagine anyone else having the vision and authority to drive the project.

Offa's dominant position in Britain meant that he was able to establish diplomatic contacts beyond the British Isles, notably with Charlemagne, whose Empire stretched from northern Spain to Germany and Italy. But the nature of those contacts reveals both the limits of his power and his failure to understand them. Charlemagne was happy to discuss trade. In 796, he and Offa agreed the first commercial treaty in the history of the British Isles. He was equally happy to suggest that his second son, Charles the Younger, should marry one of Offa's daughters, probably Ælfflaed. Offa agreed, but wanted a stronger dynastic alliance with his son, Ecgfrith, marrying Charlemagne's daughter, Bertha. Charlemagne was furious. He broke off all contact and prevented British ships landing or trading at Continental ports under his control. What Offa had failed to realise was that, for all his personal success, in the context of Europe Britain remained a comparatively unimportant offshore island. Ælfflaed's marriage to Charles the Younger would have been a gesture of friendship – perhaps a slightly condescending one – to a powerful foreign ruler, but a gesture which involved no obligations; and her children would have strengthened the Carolingian bloodline. Had Bertha married Ecgfrith, it would have suggested that Charlemagne placed a greater value on Offa's friendship than was actually the case, and might also have been taken to imply a commitment on Charlemagne's part to protect both his daughter and Offa's collection of kingdoms. It would also have allowed for the creation of a cadet branch of the Imperial family with all the potential that could entail for dynastic struggle.

As trade prospered, so did the revived money economy. The anonymous silver *sceattas* that circulated in the early part of his reign were replaced by new pennies prominently displaying Offa's name (see Chapter 26). Some coins featured his wife, Cynethryth, the only Anglo-Saxon woman ever to appear on the coinage. Offa evidently intended these changes to keep the Mercian coinage aligned with the Continent where Charlemagne had just ordered sweeping reforms. There were also gold coins in circulation, the most curious being a copy of a dinar minted by the Caliph Al-Mansur (r.754–75), the second Abbasid Caliph and founder of Baghdad. These were probably minted so that Anglo-Saxon merchants could trade with Islamic Spain, but the mint clearly had no knowledge of Arabic so that the words *Offa Rex* on the reverse are surrounded by what may look like Arabic script but is in fact a meaningless scribble.

Offa did issue a law code, but as no copy survives, we do not know what it contained. His domestic policies emphasised the military character of his rule. He may have constructed a small number of *byrig* – fortifications intended to protect a port, a river crossing, or other strategic location

– around the central core of Mercian territory. Hereford, Oxford, Bedford, Northampton, and Stamford are possible locations, although it is difficult to determine which sites were fortified by Offa and which by Ælfred of Wessex a century later. Offa's predecessor, Æthelbald, had exempted all Church lands from tax, but required them to build bridges and such fortifications as were considered necessary for their defence. Offa extended this provision – a way of making the Church contribute to the cost of defending the kingdom – to Kent, and possibly other regions as well. It is tempting to see these defensive measures as designed to prevent Scandinavian raiders attacking prosperous ports or rowing their longships up shallow rivers to undefended areas, but Offa reigned for thirty-nine years and the first known Scandinavian raid was in 789, just seven years before his death. In 792, he did begin putting in place measures to defend Kent, but it is better to see most of his defensive measures as the policies of a shrewd warlord who understood that the need to maintain control of the lands he had conquered.

Like many empires created in a short space of time, Offa's did not long survive his death in 796. He was succeeded by his son, Ecgfrith, who died after just five months and was in turn succeeded by Coenwulf (r.796–821), who came from a distant branch of the Mercian royal house – Offa having eliminated all closer relatives who might have challenged him. At the beginning of his reign, Coenwulf was faced with a rebellion in Kent. He prudently waited for the Pope to excommunicate the leader, Eadberht Praen, before taking action, but then put down the rebellion without mercy, dragging the luckless Eadberht off to Mercia where his eyes were put out and his hands cut off – actions which led Alcuin at Charlemagne's court to condemn Coenwulf as a tyrant. Both Sussex and East Anglia also seem to have attempted to break away from Mercian dominance. We have few details, but it seems that Coenwulf was able to regain control, no doubt in a characteristically uncompromising manner.

The one kingdom which did successfully break away from Mercian hegemony was Wessex. Offa's influence had depended on the fact that his daughter, Eadburh, was married to King Beorhtric. Asser, in his *Life of King Alfred*, describes Eadburh as being tyrannical 'like her father' and given to poisoning those she disliked. According to Asser, she had intended to poison 'a certain young man whom the king loved' when by accident Beorhtric also took the poison and both died.[231] Whether this is true or not – it could well be anti-Mercian propaganda – the new king, Ecgberht (r.802–39) was not going to dance to Mercia's tune. Coenwulf cannot have been surprised – this was the same Ecgberht whom Offa and Beorhtric had forced into exile – but he was already having trouble holding Offa's legacy together and a powerful enemy on his southern border was just what he did not want. Moreover, this was an enemy who had spent the last sixteen years at Charlemagne's court and, in all likelihood, enjoyed the Emperor's support. Coenwulf struck early. Either shortly before Ecgberht returned from the Continent or on the day of his accession (depending which source one favours), he sent an army under Ealdorman Æthelmund to seize control of Wessex. It was a bold stroke, but it failed. Æthelmund was defeated and killed at the Battle of Kempsford in Gloucestershire by a force of Wiltshire militia.

After sixteen years of exile and Mercian dominance in Wessex, Ecgberht spent the early years of his reign strengthening his personal position and rebuilding his kingdom's capabilities. He campaigned against the Dumnonian British in 815 and 825, and it was during this second campaign that the new Mercian king, Beornwulf, decided to invade. Beornwulf was a usurper – Coenwulf had died in 821, to be succeeded by his brother, Ceolwulf, who lasted only two years before Beornwulf seized throne – and probably felt the need to establish himself as a warrior king. It was a disastrous decision. The two armies met at Ellandun, somewhere near Swindon, in September 825. Beornwulf's forces were routed. It was the beginning of the end of Mercian dominance of southern Britain.

In 826, both Sussex and Kent appealed to Wessex for protection against Mercia. Ecgberht sent an army commanded by his son, Æthelwulf, who received the submission of both kingdoms and of King Sigered of Essex. The Kingdom of East Anglia, seeing Mercian power failing rapidly, once again declared itself independent. Beornwulf led an army to try to re-establish Mercian control but was killed in the attempt. The following year his successor, Ludeca (or Ludica) made another attempt to subdue the East Anglians and was also killed. In 829, seeing his enemy's weakness, Ecgberht invaded Mercia itself, putting the new king, Wiglaf (r.827–29 and 830–39) to flight and, shortly afterwards minting coins describing himself as King of Mercia. That same year, the *Anglo-Saxon Chronicle* records that Ecgberht 'led his levies to Dore against the Northumbrians, where they offered him submission and peace.'[232] Dore, on the River Sheaf just south of Sheffield, probably marked the boundary between Mercia and Northumbria. A later chronicler, Roger of Wendover, in the thirteenth century, states that Ecgberht invaded Northumbria and forced the king, Eanred (r.c.810–41), to pay tribute. It seems unlikely that Ecgberht could have conquered both Wessex and Northumbria in one campaigning season, and we should remember that the Chronicle was written in Wessex and is given to boosting the achievements of the rulers of Wessex. The most likely scenario is that the two kings met and Eanred, recognising that Ecgberht had overturned the political status quo which had lasted for more than a century, chose to make a formal submission rather than risk an invasion.

The next year, 830, the *Chronicle* records that 'Wiglaf obtained again the Kingdom of Mercia,' and then that 'Ecgberht led his levies into Wales, and reduced them to humble submission.'[233] No context is given. If Wiglaf had returned at the head of an army, defeated Ecgberht, and re-established an independent Mercia, we might expect the *Chronicle* to downplay the event, and it does. But why would Ecgberht then turn his attention to the Welsh, leaving the Mercians at his back? The relation between the two events remains mysterious, but we can say that in the years between 825 and 830, the face of Anglo-Saxon Britain changed radically. Wessex ruled Mercia only briefly – neither Wiglaf on his return nor his successors acknowledged the overlordship of Wessex – but it was now undeniably the leading Anglo-Saxon power. Mercia may have shaken off Wessex, but it never regained control of Sussex, Kent, Essex or East Anglia. How the long-running rivalry between Mercia and Wessex might have developed is a matter for speculation for, from the 830s onwards, the established Anglo-Saxon order was overturned by the activities of those Scandinavians whom we know today as the Vikings.

Taking the long view, these Scandinavian raiders were simply the third in a series of waves of invaders and settlers that reached the shores of Britain in the first millennium. Many periods of history conjure up mental images, often influenced by Hollywood, and those associated with the Vikings are on view in the 1958 historical epic, *The Vikings*, a full-length feature film starring Kirk Douglas, Tony Curtis, and Janet Leigh. Described by one critic as a 'full-blooded depiction of rape, fire and pillage' (given what the censors would permit in those days), it features dragon-prowed longships, drinking horns, ship cremations, the whole aura of fire and violence that remains the widely accepted view of how the Vikings lived and behaved.[234] (One positive point about the film is that it does not depict the Vikings as wearing horned helmets, an aberration which can be traced back to costume designer Carl Emil Doepler and the 1876 production of Wagner's *Der Ring des Nibelungen* at Bayreuth.) Whether or not there was any connection, in the decades following the release of *The Vikings*, some historians began to question whether the people to whom we attach that name were really as brutal and violent as is usually assumed. They noted that literacy at the time was largely confined to monks, who would have sympathised with their fellow monks who were the principal victims of the early raids, with the result that we might be hearing only one side of the story. They also sought to determine whether the archaeological record confirmed the views expressed in documentary sources. It is the job of every new generation of academics to query the assumptions of their predecessors, but on this occasion little or nothing was discovered to challenge the accepted view. From the later decades of the ninth century onwards, once raiding evolved into settlement, we do get a picture of a much broader-based society, with farmers, merchants, shipwrights, metalworkers, and other artisans. But the first two or three generations of Scandinavian raiders were just that: ruthless and violent raiders intent on amassing wealth through plunder and slaves.

It should be emphasised, however, that there was no single Viking identity. The people we call Vikings came from coastal and rural communities across Scandinavia. In very broad terms, those from Sweden went east. They became known as the *Rus* and gave their name to Russia; they raided the Baltic coasts and made their way down the Volga and the Dnieper; they established trade routes to Byzantium and beyond. The Norwegians were the real seafarers, sailing west to Iceland and across the North Atlantic. In the British Isles, they concentrated their efforts on Shetland, Orkney, the Hebrides, Ireland, and on the western seaways. The Danes looked mainly – although not exclusively – south, to Britain's eastern and southern coasts, eventually despatching fleets and armies across the North Sea and colonising large swathes of eastern England.

Why groups of men from across Scandinavia decided to embark on long-distance voyages and conduct violent raids on communities in other countries still resists explanation, and it is unlikely that there was any single reason. Demographic factors have often been advanced as a possible explanation. Did population growth lead to agricultural shortages and a so-called youth bulge, stimulating an exodus? This might have applied in western Norway where agricultural land was limited, but there is no evidence of significant population growth or food shortages over the region as a whole. And the first Vikings were raiders not settlers. They returned home after their raids. It was fifty years or more before the idea of settling the lands they were raiding gained traction. A related theory argues that Scandinavia was beginning to evolve into a collection of nation states, with rulers centralising power and leaving no room for ambitious young men. Again, this may have been the case in some areas, but Scandinavia was far from politically or socially homogeneous, and there is no evidence that centralisation was a region-wide phenomenon. Another more recent idea is that the earliest raids were a quest for women, stimulated by a shortage of women in societies where polygamy was common and a mark of success and wealth. Tens, perhaps even hundreds of thousands of men and women were abducted during raids on the British Isles and sold into slavery. Even monks were not exempt. Slave-trading was probably a more important economic driver for the Vikings than gold and jewels and more traditional forms of plunder. Those abducted undoubtedly included many young women who became wives or concubines, so again this could be a contributory factor, but it is hard to see it as a primary cause. Yet another possibility is that traditional trade routes had been disrupted by the rise of the Carolingian Empire in Europe and Islam in the Mediterranean, leading the raiders and traders of Scandinavia to seek new sources of wealth. Any or all of these factors could have stimulated the Viking explosion, but it could not have happened without changes in shipbuilding technology which made long-distance raiding possible.

The eighth century saw significant improvements in the technology for cutting and shaping timber, and for producing more durable nails and metal fastenings. This in turn led to changes in ship design and the production of more stable and seaworthy craft. Yet, not surprisingly, just as there was no single Viking identity, so there were many different Viking ships. Perhaps most interesting to the historian is the *knarr*. Like all Scandinavian ships of the period, *knarr* were clinker-built, usually of oak planks, and carried a single, square-rigged sail. They were cargo ships, shorter (about sixteen metres) and broader in the beam than longships, and with a greater draught, capable of carrying up to twenty-five tons of merchandise, supplies or livestock. They would have acted as supply vessels for larger raiding parties, and they would have been familiar as trading vessels in the Baltic and, later, in the Mediterranean. *Knarr* were the vessels that in the tenth and eleventh centuries sailed the North Atlantic to supply Norwegian colonies in the Faeroes, Iceland, Greenland and, presumably, L'Anse aux Meadows in Newfoundland. Now on display in Oslo's Viking Ship Museum, the Gokstad ship, discovered in 1880 near Sandar on the Oslofjord, is the best-known example of a *karvi*. Although impressively sleek and streamlined, up to twenty-three metres long, with places for thirty-two oarsmen, *karv*i were the workhorses of maritime Scandinavia, more often used for fishing or trading than as warships. When the *Anglo-Saxon Chronicle* talks of three hundred ships sailing up the Thames, these would have been *snekkia* (or *snekke*), the craft most commonly used for raiding. Shorter and narrower in the beam than *karvi*, they had places for forty oarsmen and were faster and more manoeuvrable. They were even light enough to be carried or dragged over a short portage. The classic longship of Hollywood and popular imagining was the *skeid* (or *skeið*), which carries the meaning of sliding or slicing, in this case through water. Only a few have been discovered, but they appear to have been about thirty metres long – although one found at Roskilde in Denmark was thirty-seven metres – and carried a crew of sixty or more. Narrow hulls and large square-rigged sails would have allowed both *snekkia* and *skeid* to sail very close to the wind, giving them an immense advantage when manoeuvring in narrow bays and inlets.

The word 'Viking' only entered the vocabulary of English in the eighteenth century – when the Romantic movement saw them as noble savages: brutal perhaps, but courageous and manly – and it meant simply 'someone from Scandinavia'. The meaning evolved and is now applied loosely to anything connected with the Scandinavian attacks and invasions between the eighth and eleventh centuries. *Víkingr* in Old Norse is generally assumed to derive from *vík*, meaning a bay or inlet – with the implication that this was where pirates lay in wait for their prey – although this meaning does not appear in Old Norse or Old Icelandic until the late tenth century. However, *wícing* and *wícingas* both appear in Anglo-Saxon glossaries and poetry in the eighth century, before the beginning of the Viking assault. This has led to the possibly more plausible suggestion that the Old Frisian *wíc*, meaning an encampment, passed into Old

English, and was later applied to the bands of Scandinavian raiders whose visible presence to most people would have been their temporary encampments on the shore. By the time the Icelandic sagas were written down between the twelfth and fifteenth centuries, the verb 'to go viking' had evolved to mean to go raiding; but the men who set off from Norway and Denmark to raid Britain and Ireland in the ninth century did not call themselves Vikings; nor did the British and Irish who were on the receiving end of their attentions call them Vikings.

The first recorded raid on Britain was in 789. The *Anglo-Saxon Chronicle* says that three ships arrived from Hordaland, the area around Bergen in Norway, but goes on to say that they were the first Danish ships to come to Britain. This is not necessarily a contradiction. The *Chronicle* was begun in Wessex during the reign of Ælfred, so the scribe or scribes responsible were describing events that took place a hundred years earlier; and they were doing so in terms of their own time when the Danes were the main enemy. Throughout the *Chronicle* and in many other contemporary sources, 'Dane' is used to describe any Scandinavian. The historian Æthelweard, writing two hundred years after the event, says that the three Danish ships arrived at Portland on the Wessex coast. The crew came ashore, were met by the local reeve, Beaduheard, who assumed they were merchants, and told them they must accompany him to the nearest royal *vill*, which would have been Dorchester, to meet the king. This was apparently what all new and unregistered traders were expected to do. The 'Danes', however, killed Beaduheard and his men on the spot. We have no further detail, but it is clear that to the Anglo-Saxons these new arrivals were essentially alien: an unknown people, ignorant of normal behaviour, and inexplicably violent – which is presumably how the sailors of the *Classis Britannica* saw Saxon pirates in the third century.

In 792, Offa ordered 'the building of bridges, and the defence of forts against the heathen within the confines of Kent.'[235] This suggests that some raids had already taken place, although we know nothing about them. The first significant attack on the British mainland was in 793, when the monastery on Lindisfarne was sacked and burned, probably by a Norwegian raiding party. Lindisfarne was not a large foundation. There were probably some thirty monks, a number of novices awaiting ordination, and a small lay community to serve them. Anything of value was looted, and those who were not murdered were taken away to be sold into slavery. The shock was immense. Lindisfarne was a holy place, the seat of Christianity in Northumbria, the shrine of St Cuthbert, and a place of pilgrimage. The *Anglo-Saxon Chronicle* claimed the attack was presaged by 'terrible portents ... exceptional flashes of lighting and fiery dragons... flying through the air.'[236] Alcuin, writing from Charlemagne's court in Aachen, was outraged that 'the pagans have desecrated God's sanctuary [and] shed the blood of saints around the altar', but warned that such events represented divine judgement on 'the sins of those who live there... It has not happened by chance, but is the sign of some great guilt.'[237] This is exactly how Gildas interpreted the advent of the Anglo-Saxons three hundred years previously. The next year, 794, saw more raiders – again probably Norwegian – sail up the River Wear to attack the monastery at Monkwearmouth, where Bede had lived and worked. The monastery was sacked, but resistance may have been stronger than the attackers envisaged, while at the same time a storm blew up wrecking at least two of their longships, probably on rocks off Tynemouth, and the unnamed leader of the raid was captured and killed. Whether for this or for some other, unknown reason, the Norwegians seem to have shifted their attention to other targets. There were no major attacks on the Anglo-Saxon kingdoms for the next forty years.

In 795, Columba's monastery on Iona was attacked and burned – and once again it was probably Norwegian raiders who were responsible. Across the North Channel, a raid on the island of Rathlin was quickly followed by an attack on Lambay Island, just north of present-day Dublin, where Columba had also founded a religious community. The church was ransacked and burned and seems never to have been rebuilt. In 798, the coast of Brega, a sub-kingdom of Meath, was raided. In 802, Iona was raided again; and in 806 for a third time, when it is said that sixty-eight monks were killed. In 807, the raiders switched to the west coast of Ireland and attacked Connacht. Irish monks recorded these attacks, and some of their descriptions were later incorporated in the *Anglo-Saxon Chronicle*.

Apart from Iona, we know of no other raids on the west of what would soon become Scotland during the first half of the ninth century. This does not mean they did not occur. The Alt Clud-controlled waters of the Firth of Clyde must have been particularly tempting. There were wealthy monastic foundations at Kingarth on Bute and on the nearby island of Inchmarnock, and the Clyde itself was an important destination for merchant vessels trading with Dumbarton Rock and its hinterland. If raids did occur, they either went unrecorded, or perhaps the raiders were driven off by the ships of Alt Clud. Orkney and Shetland were certainly attacked. In 1958, a box containing a spectacular hoard of silver objects dating from the late 700s was discovered under a broken sandstone slab on St Ninian's Isle in southern Shetland. The box and its contents were upside down, and many of the items were tangled up together, suggesting that they were hidden in a hurry, perhaps to keep them safe from raiders. The fact that they were never retrieved may also tell a story.

These early raids were short, sharp and violent. The raiders would appear offshore without warning, sometimes in a single ship, but more usually in three or four. They clearly had good intelligence – presumably from interrogating merchant ships or prisoners taken on previous voyages – for their targets, mainly monasteries and abbeys were evidently chosen in advance. The factor of surprise meant that they rarely encountered opposition, and the raid itself probably lasted no more than two or three days. Descriptions of raids usually dwell on the destruction caused, and on the gold, silver, and artistic treasures that were looted, but the raiders themselves were just as interested in people. Rich or powerful prisoners could be ransomed at once while the young, fit, and good-looking could be taken away and sold as slaves. Slavery was an accepted feature of Celtic and Anglo-Saxon society (see Chapter 26), and Scandinavian society was no different. There are reports of Scandinavian slavers as early as the sixth century, and by the eighth century they were selling into Venetian, Byzantine, and Islamic markets.

Between the Rathlin raid in 795 and 830, the *Irish Annals* record twenty-six major raids, most on the north and east coasts. These, and the raids on Iona, had a profound impact, particularly on the religious community. After the third raid in 806, the monks of Iona – those who survived – packed up, took their few remaining treasures, and moved to the newly-established monastery at Kells in County Meath. Several Irish communities simply took to the sea, sailing south to Brittany or north to the Faeroes and Iceland in search of safety. Other monks fled to Germany and the Carolingian Empire, which could explain how so many manuscripts in the Insular style found their way to Europe.

Beginning about 814, there was a lull of six or seven years in this relentless sequence of attacks. We do not know why, but with hindsight it seems to mark the end of the first wave of largely Norwegian Viking activity. Small-scale raids may have continued, but the next major attack, in 821 (or 819 in some sources), was on the Howth Peninsula, now part of Dublin, where the local chieftain, Éadair or Etar, was killed, and a large number of women were abducted and sold into slavery. This attack seems to have been on a larger scale than before. It is probable that some of the raiders who had been terrorising Ireland and the western seaways had consolidated what were temporary bases in Shetland and Orkney into long-term settlements. About this time, they also occupied the Isle of Man. Permanent settlements such as these suggest larger, long-term ambitions. They not only shortened lines of communication but also marked a turning point in that winter did not necessarily mean a return to Norway. The Vikings may have begun building ships in the islands, using timber brought in from Norway or from Scotland. They certainly began to coordinate the activities of different groups, involving more ships and more men, and targeting inland, as well as coastal, settlements and religious foundations.

In 832, it was a fleet, not just three or four ships, that sailed up the River Liffey to the small town of Clondalkin where they burnt the monastery to the ground. In 836, a fleet of between fifty and a hundred ships sailed into Carlingford Lough and Dundalk Bay, ravaging the lands of the Southern Uí Néill. Given that a longship on a raid might hold forty or fifty men, this was a large-scale operation. According to the *Irish Annals*, large numbers of prisoners were taken and Christians were massacred in County Meath. In 837, a large fleet divided its forces between the Boyne and the Liffey and devastated the lands between the two, while yet another penetrated the River Shannon in the west. In 840, raiders targeted Lough Neagh where, for the first time, they overwintered instead of returning to Norway, or withdrawing to bases in Shetland or the Orkneys. In 841, the Norwegian Vikings built *longphuirt* (singular *longphort*; often anglicised to 'longport') at Dublin, and at Annagassan on the southern shore of Dundalk Bay. *Longphuirt* were large, fortified camps, usually situated on defensible sites on the tributaries of large rivers, but with easy access to the sea. Initially at least, their purpose was to allow the raiders to land, to beach the ships, and leave them in safety while they searched inland for plunder and slaves, or while they overwintered. However, as time went on and the Scandinavian presence grew stronger, *longphuirt* became first trading centres and then towns. Raiding was beginning to evolve into settlement.

The raiders who terrorised the east coast of Ireland were slow in turning their attention to Wales. This may have been due to good intelligence. Wales was a patchwork of nine separate kingdoms, constantly feuding with each other when they were not fighting the Anglo-Saxons beyond Offa's Dyke. The three most powerful kingdoms – Gwynedd in the north; Seisyllwg, occupying present-day Carmarthen and Cardigan; and Dyfed in the south-west – covered all but a small part of the Welsh coastline. The Welsh were not seafaring people, and there is no reason to suppose that they would have been more successful in driving off coastal raids than any other British or Anglo-Saxon kingdom, but they were skilled in turning the difficult mountainous terrain to their advantage. Wales did not offer the raiders the same opportunities as Ireland. It was sparsely populated and not as wealthy. The coastline was rugged with fewer safe harbours, and there were fewer navigable river systems. There were also fewer obvious, coastal targets. A number of the richer monasteries were in narrow river valleys on the edge of the mountains – terrain that would have favoured the Welsh.

The first recorded raid on Wales, apparently conducted by Danish Vikings, took place in 852, but we do not know where – the sources state only that the raiders were opposed by Cyngen ap Cadell of Powys (r.808–54), whose kingdom did not have a sea coast. More raids followed: on Anglesey in 854, and the coast of Gwynedd in 856. This time, resistance was led by Rhodri, King of Gwynedd (also Rhodri Mawr, or Rhodri the Great, r.844–78) and, in 856, Gorn, the leader of the Danes was killed. The Welsh *Brut y Tywysogion* (*Chronicle of the Princes*) credits Rhodri with two further victories, both in Anglesey in 872, by which time he had managed to bring the three kingdoms of Gwynedd, Powys, and Seisyllwg under his control (see Chapter 33). This greatly strengthened his ability to fight off the groups of Danes and Norwegians who were trying to gain a foothold in Wales – and it is certainly true that Wales was never colonised to the same extent as Ireland or Anglo-Saxon Britain. Bringing the kingdoms together was the first of several attempts to bring about a single Welsh kingdom, all of which were frustrated by the complexities of Welsh politics and geography. If any of them had succeeded, the history of the British Isles might have been different.

In 835, a force of (actual) Danes attacked the Isle of Sheppey in the

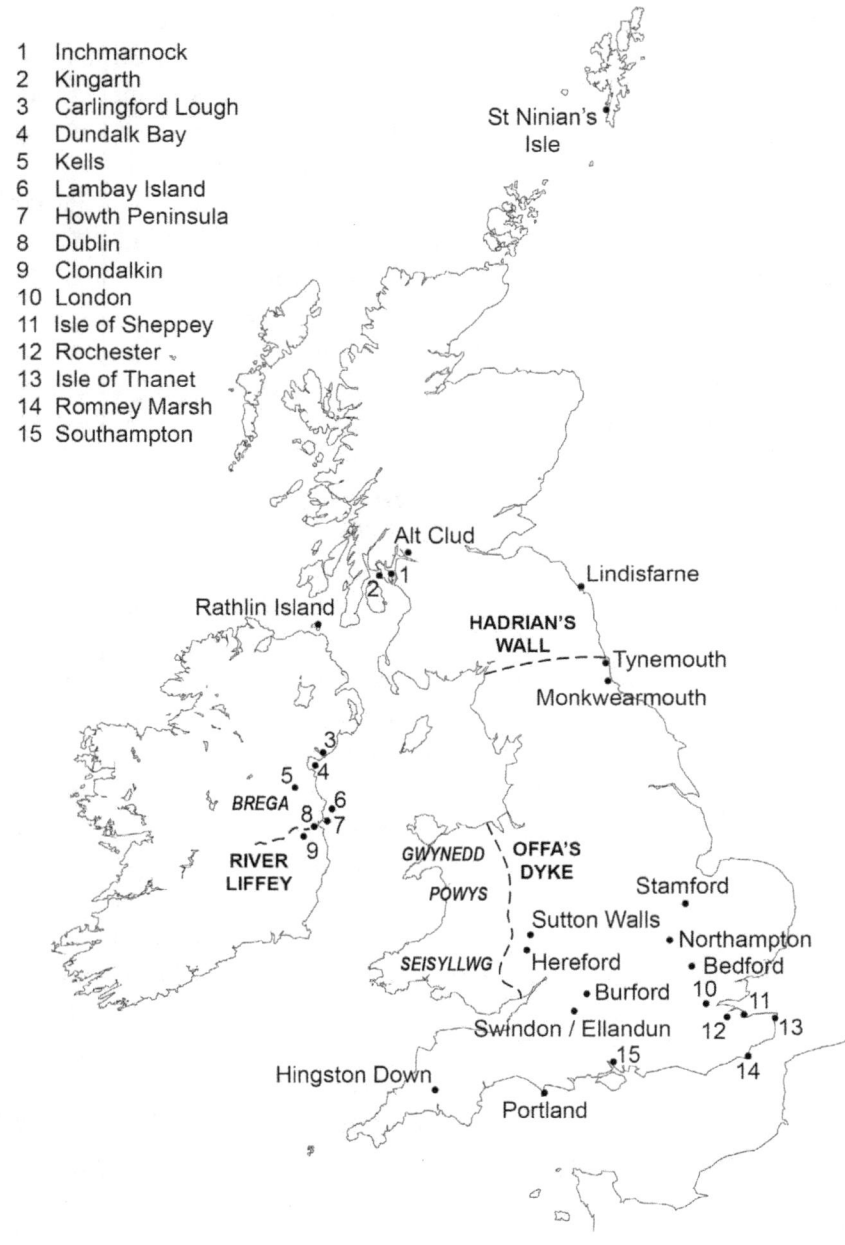

Map 26   The Arrival of the Vikings

north of Kent, where several monasteries situated on low-lying ground close to the coast made easy targets. It was the beginning of a massive onslaught on southern Britain that seems to have taken the Anglo-Saxon kingdoms by surprise. The Anglo-Saxons had nothing as sophisticated as the Roman network of patrols, merchants, and paid informants, but they must have known what was going on in Ireland and elsewhere. Perhaps they were too busy fighting each other to realise that they were facing an existential threat. Perhaps, having had no major raids for forty years, they had become complacent. However it came about, it was soon obvious that they were facing something unprecedented, much more like an invasion than a succession of raids.

According to the *Anglo-Saxon Chronicle*, in 836 thirty-five Danish ships, with a force of perhaps 2,000 men, sailed up the Bristol Channel. Ecgberht of Wessex met them at Carhampton, not far from Minehead on the north Somerset coast, and was defeated. Two years later, an even larger Danish fleet had sailed up the Tamar and joined forces with the Dumnonian British. Ecgberht met them at Hingston Down and this time he won. In 840, the Wessex *ealdorman* Wulfheard was victorious against thirty-three shiploads of Danes at Southampton, while another *ealdorman*, Æthelhem, was defeated and killed by a Danish army at Portland. In 841, one force of Danes landed on Romney Marsh, while another invaded Lindsey in East Anglia. In 842, Anglo-Saxon forces were defeated first outside London and then outside Rochester. In 848, the Danes were defeated in north Somerset. The *Chronicle* tries to make the best of things, talking up Anglo-Saxon victories and minimising their defeats, but cannot disguise that the Danes were making headway. Then, in 851, comes the entry stating that Danes, called 'the heathen' in the *Chronicle*, overwintered on the Isle of Thanet. Although the *Chronicle* is not entirely clear, these Danes probably joined forces with a newly-arrived fleet of over three hundred ships – suggesting a total of between 4,000 and 5,000 men – and drove Beorhtwulf of Mercia and his forces out of Kent and beyond the Thames. As in Ireland, raiding was giving way to invasion and settlement.

29 Kingdoms in the North

One important legacy of the Viking era – albeit indirect and unintended – was the emergence of Scotland as a polity. Shetland was the first place in the British Isles to see any form of Viking settlement. It would have been the first landfall for ships sailing from the north of Norway, and there were probably seasonal camps on the islands by the time the first raids took place on mainland Britain in the 790s. By the 820s, there were settlements in Shetland, Orkney, and the Outer Hebrides. Initially established as bases to which raiding parties could return and where they might overwinter, they quickly became small, permanent communities – mainly Norwegian at first, with the Danish joining later. Although all three archipelagos were culturally Pictish and, notionally at least, part of Pictland, it seems unlikely that the Pictish kings did anything to contest Viking settlement. Sovereignty over such outlying regions was probably notional, and while the Picts certainly had a fleet, their ships could not have matched the speed and manoeuvrability of the Viking craft. Just as the Anglo-Saxons were too busy fighting each other to realise the seriousness of the Viking threat in the south, so the Picts seem to have been preoccupied with the Dál Riata Scots.

Our sources are limited and often contradictory, but we can piece together a broad outline of what happened next. Somewhere in the second half of the eighth century, Dál Riata freed itself from Pictish control and may, for a brief period, even have dominated Pictland. By the 830s, the balance had swung back and, in 834, in a campaign in Galloway, the Picts captured and put to death Alpín MacEchdach, king of the Dál Riata Scots, and many of the Dál Riata aristocracy. The new king, Cináed MacAlpín (r. in Dál Riata 834–58), inherited a much-weakened kingdom with the expectation that it would be subject to Pictish control.

Then in 839, the Picts, led by Eóganan mac Óengusa (also Uun or Wen) found themselves faced with a large-scale Viking attack. The crucial battle took place somewhere on the west coast, but we do not know where. The Picts were comprehensively defeated; Eóganan and his brother, Bran, were killed; and Pictland descended into chaos. The *Pictish Chronicle* lists five kings of Pictland in the next ten years – Uurad, Bridei VI, Ciniod II, Bridei VII, and Drest X – none of them apparently related to the previous ruling family, and, to judge by the brevity of their reigns, all probably deposed or killed. Again, it is not clear what happened, but Cináed MacAlpín scrambled to the top of the pile. His mother was the sister of an earlier Pictish king, Causantín mac Fergusa (or Constantine son of Fergus; r.789–820), so he had a claim of sorts to the Pictish throne. But legitimacy alone was not enough. Ruthlessness was required. One story, a folk tale rather than an entry in the *Annals*, has it that he invited all his rivals to a feast, got them drunk, and then slaughtered them. Whatever his tactics, by 848 Cináed had emerged as the acknowledged king of the Picts and of the Dál Riata Scots.

The traditional view of British history, as narrated by Winston Churchill, and as taught in Scottish schools until the 1970s, anglicises Cináed MacAlpín to Kenneth MacAlpin and makes him the first King of Scotland.[238] This is simply not correct. Bringing the crowns of Pictland and Dál Riata together was a decisive moment, but it was the beginning, not the end, of the process that eventually led to a single Scottish kingdom. In the king lists, Cináed and his successors are recorded as kings of Pictland, not Scotland, and it would be more than forty years before Alba, or Scotland, emerged as a recognisable entity.

Cináed died in 858. He was succeeded first by his brother Domnall mac Ailpín (or Donald I; r.858–62), and then by his son, Causantín mac Cináeda (or Constantine I; r.862–77). Political control of the two kingdoms was one thing, but there remained a cultural gulf between the Scots and the Picts. Domnall tried to address this by applying Dál Riata's legal code, put together by Áed Find in the 770s, to Pictland as well. How successful he was is not known, for both he and Causantín were forced to spend most of their time fighting off renewed Viking attacks. In 866, a large Danish fleet commanded by two brothers, Amlaíb Conung and Auisle, landed in Fortriu, probably around the Moray Firth. The *Irish Annals* say that having devastated the region, the raiders were paid to depart, taking a large number of captives to be sold as slaves: Amlaíb, Auisle, and a third brother called Ímar (or Ívarr in Old Norse) were joint rulers of Viking Dublin during the 850s and 860s, and Dublin was the largest slave market in the British Isles. In 870, Amlaíb switched his attention to the kingdom of Alt Clud, the last remnant of the Old North. He was accompanied by his brother Ímar, a shadowy but powerful figure, founder of the Uí Ímair dynasty of which we shall hear more, and often identified with Ívarr the Boneless, one of the commanders of the Great Heathen Army which swept into the Anglo-Saxon kingdoms in the 860s (see Chapter 30).

We know almost nothing of Alt Clud's internal economy, but the strategic importance of Dumbarton Rock is undeniable. Control of the Clyde estuary and the fertile lands of the Central Belt made the Alt Clud an important focus for trade across the whole of northern Britain. By 870, Dublin was more than just an overwintering base for raiding parties. Originally established by Norwegian raiders, it fell under the control of another Scandinavian group (see Chapter 30), and had since grown into a thriving colony, trading centre, and slave market. Alt Clud was three days' easy sail up the North Channel, and it would hardly be surprising if Amlaíb and his brothers saw it as a commercial rival. They certainly saw it as a target they were prepared to expend considerable effort to subdue. Amlaíb and Ímar besieged Dumbarton Rock for four months – an unprecedented length of time in Viking warfare – and the Britons surrendered only when they ran out of water. The *Annals of Ulster* suggests that among those captured were Picts and Angles, as well as Britons, and that they were all taken to the slave market in Dublin. The king of Alt Clud, Arthgal ap Dyfnwal, may have been among the captives.

Alt Clud only just survived. Dumbarton Rock was abandoned, and a new capital established further up the Clyde at Govan, where the river could be forded. The kingdom ceased to be known as Alt Clud ('the rock of the Clyde') and became *strat clud* ('the valley of the Clyde), or Strathclyde. The first entry in the *Irish Annals* to use the name Strathclyde comes in 872, recording the death of King Arthgal. All sources agree on the date, and the fact that his son, Rhun ap Arthgal (r.872–?76), succeeded him, but the wider context of Arthgal's death is complex and uncertain. Some sources state that he was killed at the instigation of Causantín mac Cináeda, king of the Picts and the Dál Riata Scots. This suggests that he was not among those captured when Dumbarton Rock fell, or, perhaps more likely, that he was ransomed. At the same time, Arthgal's son and successor, Rhun, was married to Causantín's sister, which suggests that Rhun may have conspired in his father's death. Sons killing fathers for the sake of a throne is certainly not unknown, whether in ninth century Scotland or at almost any other time in British history. One scenario is that Arthgal may have chosen another heir, forcing Rhun into exile at the court of Causantín, who then helped him seize power. This would explain indications that for an undefined period during Rhun's reign, he accepted the overlordship of the Picts, while other sources – including the *Prophecy of Berchán*, a late-eleventh or early-twelfth-century Middle Irish poem – suggests conflict between Rhun and Causantín, perhaps implying that at some stage Rhun sought to shake off Pictish overlordship.

Such Byzantine complexities are the norm in early medieval Scotland and were intensified by the speed with which things changed. Amlaíb died in 872: the *Chronicle of the Kings of Alba* says that he was killed by Causantín when he returned to Pictland to collect more tribute. Having achieved overlordship of Strathclyde and personally put an end to the threat posed by Amlaíb, Causantín was at the height of his power, but the moment did not last long. In 875, another massive fleet, probably Danish, sailed up the Firth of Forth and inflicted a bloody defeat on the Picts near Dollar in what is now Clackmannanshire. Two years later in 877, Causantín led his forces against another raiding army, and a battle took place, possibly at Fife Ness, not far from St Andrews. He was captured and, according to some accounts, beheaded on a nearby beach. With his death, the joint kingdom of Pictland and Dál Riata entered a new, even more dramatic phase, which almost proved fatal to the still unborn Kingdom of Alba.

Causantín's death brought his younger brother and Cináed MacAlpín's youngest son, Áed mac Cináeda, to the throne. He had the misfortune to take over the kingdom at its lowest ebb. After killing Causantín, the Danes roamed Pictland and Dál Riata unchecked for two years, stripping the country of wealth, animals, and people. That Áed failed to drive them off and restore order is not surprising. Yet the implication of his nicknames – Áed of the White Flowers, and Aéd the White-Footed – is that he was not up to the task, and just a year after he succeeded his brother, he was murdered at a place called Nrurim, variously identified as Inverurie in Aberdeenshire and Strathallen in Perthshire. The *Annals of Ulster* says only that he was killed by his own companions. A later account, Andrew of Wyntoun's fourteenth-century *Orygynale Cronykil of Scotland*, places responsibility for the murder on Giric mac Dúngail, and it was Giric (r.378–?89) who became king following Aéd's death.

We know little about Giric, save that he was a Dál Riata Scot who entered Aéd's service, perhaps – given his later record – as an army commander, but was not related to the house of mac Alpín. Giric staged a coup and usurped the throne. What he did then was surprising, daring and has left a legacy that still endures. It was, in fact, little short of a cultural revolution. Instead of adapting himself and his regnal style to the majority Pictish culture, he took advantage of the weakness of the Picts following their defeat by the Vikings to impose the culture of the Dál Riata Scots upon Pictland. Later sources, such as the *Chronicle of the Kings of Alba*, Wyntoun's *Orygynale Cronykil of Scotland*, and John of Fordun's *Chronica Gentis Scotorum*, inflate Giric's importance, calling him Giric or Gregory the Great. They portray him as the liberator of the true Scottish church from Pictish oppression, and as a great general who conquered Ireland and most of England. This is largely nonsense and says more about how the writers viewed the troubles of their own time than about ninth century Pictland.

Giric's actions were characteristic of an insecure ruler. He purged the court of Picts who might challenge him, appointing Scots in their place; he seized Pictish estates, distributing them among his supporters; but he did not invade or conquer Ireland, although he may perhaps have raided Bernicia. He did nominate a Scottish bishop as the new head of the church in Pictland. Cellach I imposed Scottish orthodoxy on the Pictish Church, although we do not know what the differences were. They were certainly not significant enough for the Picts to have been deemed heretics. A hundred and fifty years previously, Nechtan mac Der-Ilei's attempt to bring Pictish practice into line with that of the Roman Church caused serious factionalism within Pictland (see Chapter 25), and it may be that Pictish Christians still clung to the Celtic practices disallowed at Whitby. Those writers who call Giric 'the Great' also like to call Cellach the 'first Bishop of the Scots', but this, too, is an exaggeration. Historians in later centuries made heroes of Giric and Cellach so that they could serve as examples of cultural assertiveness at a time when Scotland was under sustained political and cultural pressure from England under the Plantagenet kings.

Terminology is important here. We have used the term Scots to describe the Q-Celtic-speaking tribes whose territory spanned the North Channel, and who, on mainland Britain, established the kingdom of Dál Riata. It follows that we should describe their culture – the culture that Giric sought to impose upon the Picts – as Scottish. It is equally correct to refer to the people as Gaels and their culture as Gaelic. That usage has been avoided here in order to prevent confusion with the use of the terms Gael and Gaelic in relation to Ireland.

The royal houses and the aristocracy of Pictland and Dál Riata had been growing closer together over the previous century, but it is evident from Giric's actions that a significant cultural divide still existed. Knowing so little of the Pictish language, we can only guess at the level of mutual intelligibility between the Q-Celtic-speaking Scots and the P-Celtic-speaking Picts. The upper echelons of society could probably communicate. Further down the social ladder, in the mountainous rural areas and among coastal communities, communication between the two groups was probably limited. Given Giric's other policies, we can assume that he promoted the use of Q-Celtic or Scots Gaelic, at least at court. Over the course of the tenth century, the use of Pictish certainly declined rapidly. The decline may have been faster in political and religious circles where literacy was important – there is no evidence for Pictish as a written language beyond the inscriptions on the symbol stones – and slower among the wider population. There is anecdotal and folkloric evidence that a form of P-Celtic, presumably derived from Pictish, was still in use in isolated rural and coastal parts of Scotland as late as the thirteenth and fourteenth centuries.

Some sources suggest that Eochaid of Strathclyde (r.878–89) ruled Pictland at the same time as Giric. Eochaid was the son of Rhun, and thus the grandson of Cináed MacAlpín, and so may have had a claim on the Pictish throne. But given Giric's character, it is hard to believe that a man of such ruthlessness and drive would have accepted Eochaid as an overlord or even as joint king. Moreover, Strathclyde was not only weak, it was the last remnant of the P-Celtic-speaking Old North, with a culture very different from that of the Dál Riata Scots which Giric was actively imposing upon the Picts. We should probably see them as allies: first and foremost against the seemingly endless threat of the Vikings, but perhaps also, in a much deeper sense, against the Picts who would for both of them have represented the old enemy.

Giric fought off Danish raiders and pushed through his programme of cultural change, but, like so many usurpers, he would have known his position was not secure. Two legitimate heirs to the throne, Causantín's son, Domnall, and Aéd's son, Causantín, were still alive. They had escaped to the Irish kingdom of Ailech, part of the lands of the Northern Uí Néill, where they were given a home by their aunt, Máel Muire. She was not only the daughter of Cináed MacAlpín, but also married to the King of Ailech, Áed Findliath. When Áed Findliath died, about a year after their arrival, the two princes remained in Ireland under the protection of their aunt. She then married Flann Sinna of the Southern Uí Néill, King of Meath and High King of Ireland. Although Scottish Dál Riata had long since broken away from its Irish roots, clan connections and family loyalties were still important, especially in a society where bards were required to learn and recite genealogies to emphasise a king's right to rule. When Domnall and Causantín decided to return to Scotland to claim the kingdom that both their fathers had ruled, they must have received practical support in terms of ships and men from Clan Uí Néill. They had been in Ireland for eleven years. Domnall was in his mid-twenties; Causantín probably in his late teens. We do not know when or where they landed, but they seem to have attracted sufficient support to force Giric to retreat to the hilltop fortress of Dundurn in Perthshire where, in 889, he was besieged and eventually killed.

Domnall mac Causantín, anglicised as Donald II, came to the throne and reigned for eleven years. On his accession he is referred to as King of the Picts, but on his death the *Chronicle of the Kings of Alba* calls him 'King of Alba', using the word in its Latin form *Albanium*. Neil Oliver calls this 'the birth certificate of Scotland'.[239] Domnall was succeeded by his companion in exile Causantín mac Áeda, or Constantine II, who reigned from 900 to 943 and was never called anything but King of Alba. It may well be that some of those who supported him wanted – or even expected – a reversal of Giric's policies and a return to a Pictish kingdom and Pictish culture. If so, they were to be disappointed. Domnall and Causantín were the grandsons of Cináed MacAlpín. Their heritage was Dál Riata Scots; and their years of exile in Irish Gaelic culture, the basis of Dál Riata Scottishness, can only have reinforced their cultural identity.

Throughout both reigns the new kingdom suffered continual raids. Domnall achieved a major victory against Danish raiders at Innisibsolian, an unidentified island on the east coast, but we do not know when. Another major attack took place in 900, which the Icelandic *Heimskringla* saga attributes to Harald Fairhair, often regarded the first King of Norway. Domnall retreated to the Pictish stronghold of Dunnottar where he was killed. The first recorded event of Causantín's reign, in 903, is yet another raid on the east of the kingdom, this time with Dunkeld in Perthshire as its main target. The Vikings responsible were a group who had been driven out of Dublin the previous year (see Chapter 30), led by Ímar, one of the joint kings of Dublin we met earlier. Ímar was killed during a raid the following year somewhere in the north-east, but raiding continued throughout Causantín's reign. In the 930s, however, what had become a traditional pattern of enmities changed, resulting in events that would shape the future of Britain for centuries to come.

Despite the raids and the violence, Domnall was able to reinforce the cultural policies of Giric, while Causantín's long years in power were, in this area at least, a period of consolidation. By the time he abdicated and retired to a monastery, probably St Andrews, in 943, the transformation of Pictland was effectively irreversible. For much of the population, scattered across the country in small communities, the change may have been slow and painful, perhaps even lasting for generations, but there was little they could do. At a political level, and in the Church, the transformation was swift. The chroniclers spoke of Alba, not Pictland, and the Picts themselves simply disappeared from view. Bewildered by this sudden change, historians and conspiracy theorists have come up with a range of explanations including genocide but, in reality, Pictland had simply merged with Dál Riata to become Alba, which would in due course become Scotland. It was a rebranding exercise any modern politician would be proud of.

The late ninth and early tenth centuries were a grim time for the land we can now, without qualification, call Scotland. The low-lying eastern side of the country had been devastated; the fortress of Dumbarton Rock had been overthrown; Viking armies had tramped up and down the Central Belt; Galloway, too, had been attacked and overrun. As far as we can tell, these raids on the mainland – although involving hundreds of ships and thousands of men – were just that: raids in search of loot and captives, not invasions with a view to settlement. By 900, however, different groups of Vikings had established control over a collection of islands and enclaves stretching from Shetland and Orkney to parts of Caithness and Sutherland, and from the Outer Hebrides to Skye and the Isle of Man.[240] Islay, Kintyre and Arran were added during the eleventh century. Between 840 and the 870s, these territories, with the exception of Shetland and Orkney, probably comprised the elusive Viking Kingdom of Lochlann. In the mid-870s, Shetland and Orkney were brought together as the Earldom of Orkney, owing allegiance to the Norwegian crown, while the western territories became known as the Kingdom of the Isles, a territorially and politically unstable entity which nonetheless made its influence felt across Ireland and the northern half of Great Britain.

In Norway, the long process of bringing together some thirty small kingdoms under a single king reached its climactic point in 872 with a huge naval battle at Hafrsfjord in the south-west of the country. Harald Fairhair emerged victorious and, in the wake of his victory, the twelfth-century *Orkneyinga saga* credits him with a mighty voyage of conquest, annexing Shetland and Orkney, and driving his enemies from the Hebrides. The story of the voyage is probably exaggerated to emphasise his heroic status. We know that he created Rognvald Eysteinsson the first Jarl or Earl of Orkney. Rognvald immediately passed both lands and title to his brother Sigurd Eysteinsson (or Sigurd the Mighty; r.c.875–892), who added the territories of Caithness and Sutherland and built the earldom into a powerful political entity. Beyond that, there are doubts about the extent of Harald's conquests. After Hafrsfjord, many of his enemies fled to the Viking lands in the west. Among them was Ketill Björnsson (or Ketill Flatnose), who carved out a domain for himself in the Outer Hebrides and the Isle of Man and is listed among the Kings of the Isles. He would certainly have resisted Harald.

Although Orkney was an earldom owing allegiance to the King of Norway, it was in effect independent. It was arguably politically less unstable than the Kingdom of the Isles, where rulers clawed their way to power and then lost it with bewildering speed. Both depended on the authority and personality of individual rulers – and there were periods, notably in the first half of the eleventh century, when both came under the control of a single individual. At the same time, powerful figures within the islands and archipelagos would undoubtedly have enjoyed significant autonomy. Such internal dynamics are, in the end, less important that the fact that the two polities reflected the Vikings' mastery of maritime technology. They controlled not only territories stretching for over a thousand kilometres, but also a vast arc of sea – from the Moray Firth north to Shetland, round the west of Scotland and south to the Irish Sea.

They reflected Viking culture in other ways, too. For two hundred years, they were both pagan and non-literate. Earl Sigurd Hlodvirsson (Sigurd the Stout; r.991–1014) was apparently converted at sword point by

King Olaf Tryggvason of Norway in 995; Earl Thorfinn Sigurdsson (Thorfinn the Mighty; r.c.1016–65) made a more formal conversion early in his reign; but neither seems to have actively promoted Christianity in his domain. The Earldom and the Isles had both been Christian before the Vikings arrived, and Christianity seems to have revived in the eleventh century – a man named Henry of Lund went to Orkney as a missionary bishop in the 1030s; and there was a Bishop of Mann from about 1079 – perhaps as a result of contact with Christian societies in Ireland and Scotland. Alternatively, Christianity may have continued uninterrupted but hidden, only emerging as the pre-existing Christian population came to terms with their new, pagan overlords. At the same time, pagan practices seem to have persisted into the twelfth and thirteenth centuries, before dwindling to become folk rituals no longer associated with religious belief. Not surprisingly given Viking history, neither the Earldom nor the Isles ever developed the same level of Christian infrastructure, in terms of churches and monasteries, found in the rest of the British Isles. Consequently, documentary sources are scarce, and we hear most about the Earldom, the Isles, and their rulers when they interact with literate, Christian cultures such as Ireland or the Anglo-Saxon kingdoms. Otherwise, we must rely on scrappy, often contradictory references in the *Irish Annals*, or in the Icelandic sagas, such as the *Heimskringla* or the *Orkneyinga saga*, both written two or three centuries after the events they describe and intended as entertainment rather than history.

The early Scandinavian colonies in Wales seem to have had no direct connection with Mann or the Kingdom of the Isles. They were probably just raiding bases that developed into short-term opportunistic settlements. They do not appear in any documentary sources: our knowledge of them comes from place names and, more recently, from archaeology. There were settlements on the coast of Pembrokeshire at St Davids, and on the River Cleddau at Haverfordwest. Swansea is said to derive its name from *Sweyn-ey*, meaning Swein's island, where the Danish king, Swein (or Sweyn) Forkbeard was wrecked in 1016. Whether or not this is true, archaeology tells us that the area at the mouth of the Tawe was already a thriving trading post, and had been for some two hundred years. Headlands such as Worm's Head on the Gower Peninsula, and Great Orme's Head near Llandudno – *ormr* meaning 'dragon' – and islands such as Skomer and Skokholm all attest to a strong Scandinavian presence.

29 Kingdoms in the North

The largest Viking colony in Wales was on Anglesey. Early attempts to create a settlement were beaten off by Rhodri Mawr of Gwynedd (see Chapter 28). Then in 903, a group of Vikings, expelled from Dublin when it was overrun by the Irish, and led by a powerful figure named Ingimund, tried again, but both the *Annals of Ireland* and the *Annales Cambriae* state that they failed to establish a foothold. The same sources say there was another major raid in 918. However, recent archaeological evidence appears to contradict the documentary sources. It suggests that from the late 800s onwards, Penmon in east Anglesey was what has been called a mixed Hiberno-Norse settlement, before being sacked in 971. The coastal fort of Castell Trefadog has been held to demonstrate links between the rulers of Gwynedd and the Vikings, and excavations at Llanbedrgoch indicate that Vikings and local people may have lived alongside each other.[241] Such contradictions are inevitable when we do not have enough information to establish a clear narrative.

Territorial stability was not a characteristic of any of the polities that made up the British Isles in the tenth century. Although the islands of the Inner Hebrides and the north-west coast of Scotland were notionally part of the Kingdom of the Isles, control appears to have been intermittent. There were also periods when the Kingdom of the Isles and the Viking Kingdom of Dublin came under the same ruler or ruling family. Nonetheless, despite factional and family rivalries, despite rebellions and secessions, the Isles retained control of its core territories, the Outer Hebrides and Mann, just as the Earldom, despite its own internal struggles, retained control of Shetland and Orkney. The islands and archipelagos remained under Scandinavian rule for a period longer than the Roman occupation of southern Britain. Only in 1266, after four hundred years, did the Treaty of Perth cede the Outer Hebrides and the Isle of Man to Scotland, while the *Norðreyjar* or Northern Isles – Orkney and Shetland – remained under Norwegian sovereignty until 1470. They were Scandinavian possessions for a period equivalent to that between Chaucer's death in 1400 and the present day.

The legacy of Scandinavian rule varies from place to place. The Vikings stamped their culture firmly on the Isle of Man: there are crosses and stones with runic inscriptions scattered across the island – more, in fact, than anywhere else except Norway, Sweden and Denmark. In the end, however, the Scandinavian population appears to have been absorbed into the existing Irish-influenced Gaelic culture, and Manx, a Q-Celtic relative of Irish and Scottish Gaelic, became the dominant language. As spoken today, Manx contains only seven Old Norse loan words.[242] However, a number of the island's placenames – among them, Ramsey, Jurby, Laxey, Snaefell, Crosby – are of Scandinavian origin; and the Manx parliament is called the Tynwald, deriving from the Old Norse *Þingvǫllr*, originally meaning a field where people assembled. The suggestion that Manx died out during the Viking era and was reintroduced from Ireland later seems unlikely – not least because there is only limited mutual intelligibility between modern Irish and Manx Gaelic.

There are few contemporary or near-contemporary sources relating to the Outer Hebrides – known to the Vikings as *Suðreyar*, the Southern Isles – but those we have, plus archaeology, toponymy and language, give us a picture markedly different from the Isle of Man. There were Viking settlements in the islands by the early ninth century; and settlement was probably preceded by a period of raiding. There were no monasteries or wealthy strongholds to target, so the raids may well have concentrated on taking captives. The Icelandic sagas contain several references to slaves from the Hebrides, which could mean slaves taken directly from the Outer Hebrides, or slaves sold by the *Gall-Ghàidheil*, a gang of pirates and slavers of both Scandinavian and Celtic origin, who used the islands as a base for raids on Ireland and Scotland.[243]

Only two Viking settlements – Barvas (in Scottish Gaelic, Barabhas), and Bosta (Bostadh), both on Lewis – have been securely identified. At the same time, excavations and large-scale surveys show that patterns of settlement and land use remained more or less constant from the Iron Age until the Clearances in the nineteenth century. This implies that Viking occupation took place without disrupting the existing community to any significant degree, and that the practical consequence of continuity has been for later activity to obscure most traces of the Viking presence. The idea that settlement was relatively peaceful is reinforced by the fact that only 9 per cent of the current population show traces of 'Viking' DNA. The linguistic impact of the Scandinavian presence was much stronger in the Hebrides than in Mann. Places names are almost wholly Norse in origin, often suggesting a close, even intimate knowledge of the islands: Papadil, meaning 'valley of the priest'; Leurbost, 'mud farm'; Smerclett, 'butter rock'; Laxdale, 'salmon valley'. Loan words are also extremely common and, as one might expect, many of them are connected with the sea and the coastline, cliffs and harbours.[244]

Unsurprisingly, the nearer to Scandinavia one gets, the higher the percentage of Scandinavian DNA one finds in the present-day population. In Orkney the figure is 18 per cent, in Shetland 20 per cent. Genetically, the two archipelagos are distinct, but they are closer to each other than to any other region on the mainland or in the Hebrides. These figures derive from research published in 2019 which also revealed that it is possible to genetically differentiate islands, or even parishes, that are only a few kilometres distant from each other.[245] Overall, the findings depict a remarkably stable society, and argue strongly against the idea that the Vikings all but wiped out the pre-existing inhabitants of the two archipelagos. No doubt there was violence, and no doubt some islanders were taken as slaves, but the theory that they were the victims of genocide is now effectively disproved.[246]

The lack of pre-Scandinavian names was often cited in support of the genocide version of invasion theory, and pre-Scandinavian names are certainly few and far between. Nonetheless, those that exist are important. The name Orkney is often held to derive from the Old Norse *Orkneyjar*, meaning 'Seal Islands', but this cannot be the case, as centuries before any thought of Scandinavian expansion, both Ptolemy and Tacitus use the name Orcades (see Chapters 11 and 16). In Old Irish *orc* and *erch* mean 'wild pig' and 'salmon' respectively, giving two possible, appropriate, and suitably early roots for the name. Shetland, usually supposed to derive from *Hjaltland*, meaning 'Hiltland', is referred to by Tacitus as the Cat Islands. Old Scandinavian maps give the name as 'Hetland', without the medial 'l', so it is possible that 'Het' may derive from a Pictish tribal name, perhaps for cat. Other Shetland islands – Unst, Yell and Fetlar – also have names of pre-Scandinavian origin.[247]

When the Vikings arrived, the inhabitants of both archipelagos were culturally and linguistically Pictish. Neither their culture nor their language survived, but it is clear that we no longer need to invoke genocide as an explanation. Ties with the Pictish mainland inevitably loosened during the period of Viking and, later, Norwegian rule. On the mainland, during that same period, Scots Gaelic and Scottish culture replaced the language and culture of the Picts. In such circumstances, it would be remarkable if Orkney and Shetland *had* held on to their Pictish culture. With their base

Map 27   The British Isles in the 9th Century

culture weakened, the inhabitants simply did the obvious thing and adopted the language of the political and economically dominant overclass; and, as time went on, perhaps because of their comparative isolation, the Norse spoken in the archipelagos gradually transformed itself into a separate language. Known as Norn, it was spoken in Shetland and Orkney, and also on the northern coast of Sutherland and Caithness. There were differences between Orkney and Shetland, but it was nonetheless the same language. By the time the islands became part of Scotland in 1470, Norn was probably the most widely spoken language, although the ruling elite almost certainly spoke Scots and/or Norwegian. In this context it must be emphasised that Scots, also known as Lowland Scots or Lallans, is a Germanic language, related to English and wholly distinct from Q-Celtic Scots Gaelic. As the islands became more closely integrated with Scotland, so Scots became the language of administration and the Church. Norn declined – more slowly in Shetland than Orkney – becoming the language of older, less educated people, and more isolated communities. The last known true native speaker of Norn was Walter Sutherland, who lived on Unst, Shetland's most northerly island, and died in 1850, just over a thousand years after the first Vikings settled in Shetland.

30   Kingdoms in the South

Viking *longphuirt* – those riverside enclosures where they protected their ships, and where they might overwinter – were crucial to the development of Ireland. They were wooden, palisaded enclosures built on the edge of water, so few archaeological traces remain, but they were positioned on carefully chosen sites at the head of an estuary, or on a tributary, with easy access up the river valley to the interior or, in case of need, to the sea. Although intended as strategic footholds to allow the Vikings to raid freely across Ireland, the wealth that the Vikings amassed meant that they quickly became centres for trade and commerce. Prior to the Viking era, Ireland was a land of small communities and royal strongholds. There were no towns or administrative centres of the kind that the Romans introduced into Britain. Many of Ireland's major cities – Dublin, Wexford, Waterford, Cork, Limerick – formed around *longphuirt* and developed into trading centres, colonies, and towns.

In 841, a group of Norwegian raiders built a *longphort* on the southern bank of the River Liffey near two small settlements. The older of the two was probably *Áth Cliath*, or the Bridge of Hurdles, where travellers could cross the Liffey at low tide on a pathway of osier hurdles. The second, possibly named by monks at a nearby foundation, was next to a pool of black water and named *Dubh linn*. It was where an important east-west route across the island met the north-south coastal route, and it was probably already a centre where goods were traded and exchanged. The Norwegians, led by a man named Thorgest (sometimes Turgesius, its Latin form), moved inland following the river valleys and for several years blazed a trail of destruction across counties Offaly, Laois, and Tipperary. In 845, Thorgest was killed by Máel Sechnaill, the King of Meath (often known as Máel Sechnaill I, or Máel Sechnaill mac Máele Ruanaid to distinguish him from a later, and more important, king of the same name). This was the first in a series of defeats which seemed to threaten the Viking presence in Ireland.

In 847, the new leader of the Dublin Vikings, Hákon, was defeated by Cerball mac Dúnlainge, the King of Ostraige, a small kingdom squeezed between Munster and Leinster. The same year, the *Annals* state that a thousand Vikings were killed, two hundred of them defending the Dublin *longphort*. In 848, the settlement centred on the *longphort* at Cork was overwhelmed and destroyed. In 849, the same Máel Sechnaill I, by this time High King of Ireland, attacked and plundered the settlement in Dublin. Shortly after this, a fleet of a hundred and forty ships arrived in the Liffey. Some sources say they were Danish (although, as we know, 'Dane' was often used to describe any form of Scandinavian raider). An alternative possibility is that King Gofraid of the shadowy kingdom of Lochlann, whose clan may have been of Danish origin, had been watching from the Isle of Man, and sought to take advantage of the weakness of the Dublin Vikings by establishing overlordship of the settlement. That may be more likely for, in 853, Gofraid's son Amlaíb – whom we met besieging Alt Clud – is recorded as king of the Dublin Vikings. The situation stabilised briefly, but in 864, the Irish overran the Viking settlement at Waterford, and in 866, the King of Brega inflicted a defeat on a Viking army north of Dublin. In 866 and 867, the *longphuirt* at Youghal and Cork were overrun, two battles in Leinster were lost, and a defensive position at Clondalkin, just ten kilometres from Dublin, was also destroyed.

Whether it was sheer determination that caused the Vikings to persist when faced with such a string of setbacks, or whether the Irish chroniclers exaggerated the savagery of events to emphasise the heroism of their countrymen is not clear, but the continuing violence did not prevent Dublin growing rapidly into Ireland's leading entrepôt. The slave trade was probably the main driver for Dublin's early growth, and the town soon became the biggest slave market in the British Isles.[248] The *Annals of Ulster* record Amlaíb and Ímar returning from the siege of Alt Clud with two hundred ships full of Angles and Britons and Picts to be sold into slavery. Trade may have been disrupted during times of war but – strange as it may seem to later ages – it did not cease. There was no concept of total war or trading with the enemy. Just because Amlaíb or Ímar went off to raid parts of Pictland or Dál Riata, that did not stop ships setting sail from Dublin to trade with other parts of the same kingdoms.

Dublin's growing prosperity can only have increased the resentment of the Irish natives at the presence of Scandinavian raiders on their soil – not least because that prosperity was based on their continued raiding of other parts of Ireland. Records are patchy but in just two years, 890 and 891, the *Annals of Ulster* record raids on religious foundations in Ardbraccan, Clonard, Donaghpatrick, Dulane, Glendalough and Kildare. Nor did growing prosperity do anything to reduce feuding among the Dublin-based Vikings. Internal divisions became a factor in the colony's inability to resist Irish attacks. Another weakness was that the Dublin colony remained confined to the settlement itself and a small area of rural hinterland. So, when the Kings of Brega and Leinster joined forces in 902 in a concerted effort to oust the Vikings, they could concentrate on a small area. There are no accounts of the battle, but Dublin was quickly overrun, Irish control established, and the Vikings scattered. The king, Ímar ua Ímair – brother of Amlaíb, and besieger of Alt Clud – took his men to Scotland where he died during a raid in 904 (see Chapter 29). Others moved their base to the Isle of Man and continued to raid all parts of Ireland. Still others attempted to settle in Anglesey (see Chapter 29). However, the archaeological record shows that the Irish did not destroy Dublin. What was by that time a small township centred on the port continued to be lived in and to trade. It seems likely that only the Viking rulers and their warriors were expelled.

Probably among those forced out of Dublin were two of Ímar ua Ímair's brothers – Sitric Cáech (also Sitric ua Ímair) and Ragnall ua Ímair. They disappear from the record until 914 when, according to the *Annals*, Ímar won a naval battle against a fellow Scandinavian, Bárid son of Oitir in the waters off the Isle of Man, and subsequently took control in the island. The same year, Ragnall and Sitric mounted a synchronised attack on the Irish coast. Ragnall landed his fleet at Waterford; Sitric landed his at an unidentified location further north. Viking and Irish forces manoeuvred back and forth and fought several inconclusive battles until 917, when Sitric met and defeated the new High King, Niall Glúndub, at the Battle of Confey, on the outskirts of modern-day Dublin. He quickly re-established Scandinavian control over the enclave, with himself as king, but the Irish continued to threaten, and his position was far from secure. Then, in 919, he faced a coalition of Irish forces, again led by Niall Glúndub, at the Battle of Islandbridge (or Áth Cliath) on the River Liffey. Sitric was victorious, and on this occasion the victory was comprehensive: Niall and five other Irish kings were killed. Dublin was secure; Waterford had been re-occupied in 914 when Ragnall landed; and now, in the wake of Islandbridge, the settlements at Wexford, Cork and Limerick were all re-established. The Vikings were back.

Again, Dublin's growth as a port and commercial centre appears to have been unaffected. The web of trade routes that had connected Ireland's east coast with the Atlantic seaboard since Neolithic time was now focussed on Dublin. The port traded with Armorica and other parts of what would soon become France, with the Emirate of Cordoba, even with the Fatimid Caliphate in Morocco. There were also trade links with Chester, Bristol, Strathclyde, the Hebrides, Shetland, and more distant destinations such as Bremen and the Swedish royal centre at Birka. Slaves bought in Dublin might be transported anywhere from North Africa to the Baltic. Other exports included wool and woollen goods, animal hides and furs. Imports included pottery from the Anglo-Saxon kingdoms, wine from France, and oils and dried fruits from the Mediterranean. Among the more exotic imports was walrus ivory from the Arctic, amber from the Baltic, and silver and jewellery from Byzantium and the Middle East. As time went on, despite the damage inflicted by continued raiding, the wealth generated by Dublin – and to a lesser extent by the other Viking ports – began to benefit the Irish kingdoms, and the two became increasingly interdependent.

The Battle of Islandbridge would shape the history of Dublin and Ireland for the next two hundred and fifty years, until the Normans crossed the Irish Sea in the twelfth century, and would also lead to a rebalancing of dynastic power in the rest of the British Isles. When Dublin was retaken, Ragnall was already King of Mann. In 918, he crossed to Britain, where he fought and won a battle at Corbridge, on the Tyne, against a combined force of Anglo-Saxons and Scots, and established himself as King of Jórvik, or York, the southern part of Northumbria. Ragnall died, apparently of natural causes, in 921. Sitric succeeded him in Jórvik, and passed Dublin to yet another brother, Gofraid ua Ímair (sometimes Guthfrith). And when Sitric died in 927, Gofraid took his place in Jórvik, although only briefly. These were the Uí Ímair – descendants of Ímar Ua Ímair, a Scandinavian dynasty who were born, lived, fought, and died outside Scandinavia. During the ninth and tenth centuries, at various times and in various combinations, they ruled Dublin, Waterford, Limerick, Mann, the Isles, Jórvik, and sometimes northern Northumbria or Bernicia as well. Some of them may also have been subkings within the Danelaw, exercising overlordship of East Anglia. The Uí Ímair appear in few history books, probably because their power did not last, but for over a hundred and fifty years they ruled different parts of the British Isles and coordinated their activities in support of their collective interests. The power of the clan is frequently cited as a defining feature of Scottish and Irish society, but it was equally important among the Scandinavian raiders and rulers who, if things had gone only slightly differently, might have taken permanent control of what subsequently became England.

Ecgberht of Wessex died in 839. The accession of his son, Æthelwulf, was the first time that a son had succeeded his father on the throne of Wessex for two hundred years, and Ecgberht's descendants would continue to rule Wessex, and later England, until 1013. Æthelwulf reigned for an impressive twenty years, during which time the struggle against large Danish raids continued. In 851, when Danish forces overwintered on Kentish soil for the first time and subsequently put Beorhtwulf of Mercia to flight (see Chapter 28), it was Æthelwulf and his two eldest sons, Æthelstan and Æthelbald, who rescued the situation, inflicting a defeat upon the raiders that was described in the *Anglo-Saxon Chronicle* as 'the greatest slaughter of a heathen host we have ever heard tell of.'[249] That same year, Æthelstan and an *ealdorman* called Ealhere fought what is usually considered the first recorded naval battle in British history just off Sandwich on the Kent coast. The Danes were again defeated, and Æthelstan's men captured nine longships, although he may well have been killed, for his name does not appear again.

Æthelwulf evidently managed the threat posed by the raiders better than many other leaders, and turned his victories to account by bringing

Kent, Sussex, and Essex under the control of Wessex. The Danes would continue to mount raids, but Æthelwulf was apparently confident that Wessex had the ability to drive them off. In 855, he placed his eldest remaining son, Æthelbald, in charge of Wessex, and his next eldest, Æthelberht, in control of the newly-conquered south-eastern kingdoms, while he set off for Rome. Two previous Anglo-Saxon kings, Caedwalla and Ine, had made pilgrimages to Rome, but they had done so in old age, abdicating in order to make the journey and eventually dying there. Æthelwulf did not abdicate. He clearly intended to pick up the reins of power on his return.

Before he left, Æthelwulf issued the so-called 'decimation charters', by which he freed one tenth of all his lands from tax and tribute and made them over to the Church. Discussion has raged (not too strong a term) among experts about what he really intended, how many of the surviving charters are genuine, and whether he intended them to apply to his personal lands or to the kingdom as a whole. Suffice it to say that there was undoubtedly a genuine religious impulse behind Æthelwulf's trip, but that some of his actions were also designed to have political benefits. Æthelberht of Kent had made a marriage alliance with the Merovingian Franks nearly three hundred years previously, and Offa had indulged in some ham-fisted diplomacy with Charlemagne, but for the most part the Anglo-Saxon kingdoms had lived on the edge of Europe. Diplomatic engagement with Continental kingdoms had been minimal, and any 'international' dimension to the cultural and political life of the kingdoms rested with the Church.

Æthelwulf sought to change this. He understood the importance of establishing cordial relations with European monarchs – an awareness he passed on to his youngest son, Ælfred. In 853, two years before his own trip, Æthelwulf had sent Ælfred on a visit to Rome. The boy was only about four at the time and had travelled surrounded by courtiers, but he was granted an audience with Pope Leo IV, accepted as 'a spiritual son' and given the by-then-purely-ceremonial title of Consul.[250] For a member of a royal house to receive a papal blessing was a useful stamp of spiritual approval, but it is not altogether clear what Æthelwulf wanted to achieve. Ælfred had three older brothers living, so it is unlikely that his father saw him as a potential successor, although if he intended the boy for the Church, a papal blessing would do his career no harm. In the end, it is probable that Æthelwulf was seeking to establish a connection between Wessex and the papacy on which he could build later, one which had the potential to yield political as well as spiritual benefits.

Ælfred returned to Wessex after a short time in Rome, but little more than a year later he set off again, this time accompanying his father. This was a trip of a very different character. They were welcomed at the court of Charles the Bald. Banquets were given and gifts were exchanged. Charles personally escorted them to the border of his territory. In Rome, they went to the Saxon Quarter or Schola Saxonum which had been all but destroyed, first by the Saracens in 846 and then by a major fire the following year. Æthelwulf had made a generous contribution to its rebuilding. They witnessed the ugly power struggle that followed the death of Ælfred's spiritual father, Leo IV, who had died just before their arrival. The Roman clergy had elected Benedict III, but Charlemagne's grandson, Lothair I, who ruled what remained of the Carolingian Empire, tried to get his nominee, Anastasius, appointed instead. Tensions mounted; there were riots in the streets; but rather than risk a wider conflict, Lothair conceded defeat. It is said that he died on the day of Benedict's coronation. Æthelwulf presented the new pope with a collection of magnificent gifts that he had brought from Britain, including a two-kilo golden crown, a golden goblet, an inlaid sword, and a robe coloured with rare and costly purple dye. He also indulged in a public display of wealth by scattering coins to the crowds outside St Peter's.

This display of power politics and diplomacy can only have been an education for Ælfred – and the lesson stayed with him when he eventually and unexpectedly became king. After a full year in Rome, he and his father began their journey home. Returning to the court of Charles the Bald, it was announced that Æthelwulf would marry Charles' twelve- or thirteen-year-old daughter, Judith. She was young, but young women from royal houses were expected to play their part in dynastic politics. Æthelwulf's first wife and Ælfred's mother, Osburh, had probably died a few years earlier, and Æthelwulf had four sons living, so this was a marriage intended to seal an alliance not secure an heir. That did not diminish its importance. Charles was conscious of his status as the inheritor of at least part of Charlemagne's empire, and the wedding of his daughter was solemnized with great pomp and display in his palace at Verberie-sur-Oise. For Æthelwulf, there were risks – not least the fact that Judith was crowned

Queen of Wessex, even though in Wessex itself, such a title was not formally recognised – but he no doubt considered them outweighed by the advantages of an alliance with one of the most powerful royal houses in Europe. No previous Anglo-Saxon king had launched a foreign policy initiative on this scale. Unfortunately, his achievements abroad counted for nothing once he stepped ashore at Dover.

Æthelberht, who had ruled Kent, Sussex and Essex in his father's absence, dutifully allowed Æthelwulf to resume his authority. Æthelbald, having been left in charge of Wessex – and no doubt mindful of the possibility that Judith might produce another male heir – refused to do the same. Civil war of precisely the kind that had engulfed the Carolingian Empire in the years before Judith's birth was avoided by an accommodation which saw Æthelwulf retain the title of King of Wessex and control of the south-eastern kingdoms, while Æthelbald retained the actual power which went with control over Wessex. It was a significant defeat for Æthelwulf, and effectively put an end to his attempts to connect Wessex with the great European polities. It also split the kingdom, although – perhaps fortunately for the future – not for long.

Æthelwulf died in 858, leaving an unambiguous will, bequeathing Wessex to Æthelbald and the south-eastern kingdoms to Æthelberht. Judith married Æthelbald, an act which scandalised some of the clergy – although the practice of a king's widow marrying his heir was not unknown – but that marriage only lasted two years. Æthelbald died, apparently of natural causes, and was succeeded by Æthelberht, who was almost immediately faced with a new Viking incursion. The raiders reached and sacked Winchester – not yet formally the capital of Wessex but certainly among the most important royal *vills* – before being driven off by local militias. Æthelberht reigned for five years, much of which was taken up by struggles against Viking raids. His main achievement, and the culmination of this long sequence of dynastic twists and turns, was to formally annex Kent, Sussex, and Essex, thus creating a larger and unified Wessex. This would prove a source of strength in the difficult years that followed.

Since 835, raids had been more or less constant. Overwintering began in 850–51. Then in 865, the whole character of Viking aggression changed with the arrival of what the *Anglo-Saxon Chronicle* calls 'the Great Heathen Army'.[251] We do not know how big it was. A figure of 3,000 is often quoted but could easily be an underestimate. Early medieval chroniclers use the term 'army' very loosely, often to describe forces of less than a hundred men, but this army was different from any previous Viking force. The aim was not loot or slaves or settlement, but conquest. It was not an army in the modern sense, but it was more than just a horde. Although frequently referred to as Danish, it drew elements from other parts of Scandinavia as well. There were several commanders, each leading warriors from his own region, and these regional bodies were probably broken down into groups loyal to local chiefs or longship owners – men who under other circumstances would have been mounting their own small-scale raids. Service was not obligatory – commanders and their men came and went more or less as they chose – and there appears to have been no overall strategy. Nonetheless, for the next fourteen years, the Great Army moved from place to place, scouring the land, and very nearly extinguishing the Anglo-Saxon kingdoms altogether.

The British Isles were not the sole target of Scandinavian raiders and settlers. In 845, Hamburg was attacked and burnt. The same year, a hundred and twenty ships sailed up the Seine, attacking and looting Paris, and only withdrawing when Charles the Bald paid them 7,000 *livres* (approximately 2,500 kilos) of gold and silver. In the 850s, raiders regularly sailed up the Scheldt, devastating Ghent and the surrounding areas. In 867, Charles the Bald was forced to cede the Cotentin Peninsula to the Breton king, Salomon, to gain help to resist persistent Viking attacks. In 911, Charles II of the Western Franks signed the Treaty of Saint-Clair-sur-Epte which turned Rouen and the lower Seine Valley into a Viking fiefdom (see Chapter 27). The British Isles were not alone, but as an archipelago with long, indented coastlines and easy river access to the interior of both Britain and Ireland, they were particularly attractive to raiders whose strength was the speed and manoeuvrability of their longships.

Whether by accident or design, the Great Heathen Army landed in East Anglia, the weakest of the four remaining Anglo-Saxon kingdoms. Of its king, Edmund, we know little beyond the fact that he came to the throne in 855 at the age of fourteen and died a martyr's death in 869. Realising that he could not fight the invaders, he agreed to provide them with winter quarters and horses. The horses are significant: not only were they expensive and prestigious – used mainly by the ruling elites and their warriors – but the fact that the Vikings wanted them is an indication that they were intent on an extended, land-based campaign. It was the first instance of an Anglo-Saxon kingdom seeking to buy off a Scandinavian force. Edmund probably had no other option, but his decision can only have emphasised the weakness of the Anglo-Saxon kingdoms.

In 866, having overwintered in East Anglia, the Great Army moved north and fell on Northumbria which was already in the grip of a conflict between Osberht, the more-or-less rightful king, and a usurper called Ælle. Once again, the Vikings were able to exploit Anglo-Saxon weakness. They took York – known to the Anglo-Saxons as Eoforwic – and renamed it Jórvik. In March 867, Osberht and Ælle, having made up their differences in the face of the Viking invasion, made a disastrous attempt to retake the city. They were killed, as were many of the Northumbrian aristocracy, and for the next century Jórvik was the Viking centre of power in the north, sometimes ruled by puppet kings, and sometimes directly.

After Northumbria, the Great Army moved against Mercia, overwintering at Nottingham. Burgred, the king of Mercia, appealed to Wessex for help. Æthelberht had died in 865, so the call was answered by Wessex's new king Æthelred, Æthelwulf's fourth son, and his younger brother, Ælfred, the fifth son. The long-standing enmity between Mercia and Wessex was forgotten in the face of such a threat. Kinship may also have played a part, for Burgred's wife was Æthelswith, sister of Æthelred and Ælfred. She was also a warrior queen in her own right, having led an army against the British kingdom of Powys on her husband's behalf. Early in 868, somewhere near Nottingham, the Great Army faced the combined forces of Mercia and Wessex. The Anglo-Saxons seem to have been unwilling to risk a pitched battle, and Burgred decided to pay the Vikings to go away. We do not know the exact terms of the agreement, but it was clearly a humiliation for both Burgred and for the two brothers from Wessex – a humiliation Ælfred's biographer, Asser, neatly glosses over. The Great Army did go away, but only as far as East Anglia, spending the winter of 868–69 at Thetford. King Edmund had taken advantage of their absence to gather his forces. In the spring of 869, he attacked and was decisively beaten. The story of his death that has come down to us tells how Edmund refused to defend himself against Ívarr the Boneless – probably the same Ímar or Ívarr who sired the Uí Ímair clan – was captured, and then given the choice between renouncing his religion and death. Whether this is true or not, his death marks the beginning of his cult as Edmund the Martyr, and the end of East Anglia as an independent kingdom.

The Great Army moved on to Wessex, continuing to campaign through the winter of 879–71, and setting up camp at Reading. When the local *fyrd* scored an unexpected victory against a foraging party, Æthelred and Ælfred followed up with a pre-emptive strike on the main camp, but they were driven off and lucky to escape. At the beginning of January 871, the brothers met the Great Army under its leaders, Bagsecg and Halfdan, at a place called Ashdown, perhaps in Berkshire. The *Anglo-Saxon Chronicle* speaks of a great victory with Bagsecg and no less than five *jarls* among the dead, but this may well be exaggerated, for just two weeks later Æthelred and Ælfred were heavily defeated at Basing in Hampshire. Skirmishes continued, with the Wessex forces gradually being driven back. The next major battle was in March at Meretun, probably somewhere in Wiltshire or Dorset. It was another victory for Halfdan and the Great Army, with many senior Anglo-Saxons figures killed. Less than a month later, Æthelred also died, possibly from wounds sustained during the battle. Æthelred was no more than twenty-five when he died. He had two sons, both far too young to take charge of the kingdom. So, in accordance with an agreement made by the two brothers and the council of the kingdom's leading figures, the *witan*, earlier that year, he was succeeded by Ælfred, his younger brother and the fourth of Æthelwulf's five sons to rule in Wessex.

Just when it seemed that the situation could get no worse, news came that the Great Army was about to receive reinforcements. Another fleet, carrying what the *Chronicle* calls the 'Great Summer Host', had arrived at the Great Army's headquarters in Reading. Ælfred – himself no more than twenty-two – was still at Wimborne in Dorset attending the ceremonies surrounding his brother's funeral when the Vikings again moved on Wessex. Ælfred and what men he could muster faced them at Wilton in Wiltshire. The result was a bloody draw, with the men of Wessex who had fewer resources coming off worse. The *Chronicle* states that there were nine further 'general engagements' and 'innumerable forays' that year.[252] Wessex managed to hold on but, in the end, despite killing one king and nine *jarls*, Ælfred had to buy his way out of trouble – a transaction Asser's biography again glosses over – and the Great Army went to overwinter in London, which was Mercian territory.

In 872, Halfdan and a Dane called Guthrum, who had arrived with the

Summer Army, moved their forces north to put down a revolt against the puppet king who had been installed in Northumbria. They spent the winter of 872–73 at Torksey on the banks of the River Trent in what is now Lincolnshire. By this time, the mere threat of violence was enough to bring Burgred of Mercia to the negotiating table, and he again bought peace with large quantities of gold and silver. The Great Army moved west, camping at Repton over the winter of 873–74. Burgred, under pressure from the Mercian aristocracy who felt humiliated by his actions, decided he had had enough and fled to Rome, where he later died. Halfdan and Guthrum installed a compliant Mercian noble, known as Ceolwulf II, as a puppet king.

In the spring of 874, the Great Army split in two. One part, under Halfdan, headed north. They overwintered on the banks of the River Tyne and spent 875 raiding southern Pictland and Strathclyde. When they returned to Northumbria the following year, Asser says that Halfdan 'shared out the whole province between himself and his men, and together with his army cultivated the land.'[253] It was the first real sign of change.

Guthrum and the other part of the Great Army moved slowly southwards to Cambridge. Then, in the middle of winter, they marched south at speed, right across Wessex to Wareham in Dorset, burning and looting as they went. If he knew what was happening, Ælfred was powerless to stop them. Guthrum's plan was to link up with a fleet of a hundred and twenty ships which was waiting offshore. This would have given him an army capable of conquering the whole of Wessex – or a means of retreat if things went wrong – but he apparently underestimated the difficulties of landing such a fleet at Wareham. Ælfred besieged Wareham, prevented the Great Army and the fleet from joining forces, and was able to negotiate with Guthrum from a position of strength. Hostages were exchanged, and Guthrum agreed to leave Wessex, swearing an oath to that effect on Thor's ring, an oath accepted by Ælfred although he was a Christian. The oath meant nothing. Guthrum slaughtered his Wessex hostages and marched to Exeter, where he might have successfully joined up with the waiting fleet but for the timely intervention of a storm. The fleet was destroyed off Durlston Head, and Guthrum was again forced to negotiate. We do not know whether Ælfred paid him to leave Wessex, but Guthrum and his men marched to Gloucester, which was outside Ælfred's kingdom – but only just.

30 Kingdoms in the South

Ælfred and his court spent New Year 878 at the royal *vill* at Chippenham in Wiltshire, presumably so he could keep an eye on Guthrum who was camped less than fifty kilometres to the north. Ælfred's record against the Great Army up to this point was woeful – Ashdown had been his only victory, and that was seven years earlier during the reign of his brother – and he was apparently facing stiff opposition from his *witan*, some counsellors suggesting that he should submit to Guthrum to avoid paying more Danegeld. Whether some members of the *witan* had been in secret contact with Guthrum, and whether Ælfred was actually facing a coup, is not clear, but on Twelfth Night 878 Guthrum's men mounted a surprise attack on Chippenham. Ælfred was lucky to escape. He and a handful of supporters fled to the Isle of Athelney in the area today known as the Somerset Levels but which was then an expanse of marshland, accessible only to local people who knew the paths. Guthrum seems to have been aided by Wulfhere, the *ealdorman* of Wiltshire, and perhaps other members of the *witan*. He seems to have assumed power with little or no opposition, and rapidly placed an unnamed puppet king on the throne of Wessex. Ælfred and Asser between them made sure that this episode was written out of history.

This was the lowest point in the fortunes of the Anglo-Saxon kingdoms. From uncertain beginnings in the fifth century, the Anglo-Saxons had spread their culture and their language across southern Britain. They had created new political entities and developed their own political culture. The Great Army and its leaders had taken just fourteen years to reach the point where they could overturn the achievements of the previous four hundred. They had forced East Anglia, Northumbria, and Mercia into submission. And they had now conquered Wessex – except for an 8,000 square metre island in the middle of the Somerset swamps where its king still ruled. How had this happened?

The Anglo-Saxon kingdoms undoubtedly failed to realise the seriousness of the threat posed by the Vikings, possibly because they had developed an inward-looking mentality – which is why Æthelwulf's attempt at foreign diplomacy seems so unusual. The rulers of Northumbria and East Anglia must surely have been aware of events such as the sacking of Paris and the occupation of the Scheldt Estuary, but there is no record of any attempt at cross-Channel cooperation. Within Britain, mutual hostility and self-preservation seem to have prevented any common action; and division within individual kingdoms no doubt also played a part. Once they understood that the Great Army was bent on conquest, not just raiding, some among the Anglo-Saxon elite saw collaboration as better than confrontation. Wulfhere at Chippenham may have been an outright traitor; others willing to become puppet rulers or collaborators may have been working out a grievance against the ruling family; still others may have seen cooperation as a route to prosperity, preferable to risking everything by continued opposition.

When it came to navigating Britain's river network, the speed and manoeuvrability of their longships gave the Vikings a significant tactical advantage, allowing them to deliver their forces wherever they were needed. Once on land, the Great Army's main advantage was that it was not a 'national' army. It represented nothing but itself. It had many commanders, but no overall leader. It was fluid – leaders and men came and went – and had no strategic plan or agenda beyond conquest. It depended for its success on men who were there by choice – men whose interest in Britain was limited to what they could get out of it and had, in that sense, nothing to lose. By contrast, the Anglo-Saxon armies, on the defensive from the beginning, had everything to lose. They consisted of shire-based militias, assembled at speed to meet the threat to their lands and livelihoods. If the threat was defeated, or deflected, they were dissolved. If it returned, they reassembled. They were farmers and fishermen and merchants, not full-time soldiers. The distinction, however qualified by the circumstances of the age, was essentially that between professionals and amateurs.

31 England

Ælfred, son of Æthelwulf, is better known to posterity as Alfred the Great. He received the epithet in the sixteenth century, and it was given not for his achievements on the battlefield but for his books – his personal translations of Pope Gregory's *Pastoral Care*, Boethius' *Consolation of Philosophy*, St Augustine's *Soliloquies*, and the first fifty psalms – as well as for his great project to have translated 'certain books which are necessary for all men to know.'[254] The accolade may have been deserved, but it is a further example of the interpretation of history to support a contemporary argument or ideology. Ælfred's works were popular and valued long after his own time. His reputation as a wise and cultured ruler was upheld by medieval historians such as William of Malmesbury, Simeon of Durham, and Geoffrey Gaimar. During the sixteenth century when the English Reformation was in full swing, he emerged as a champion of Englishness and (bizarrely) Protestantism, largely because he advocated English rather than Latin as a medium for education, and because his theological works were not corrupted by the taint of Roman Catholicism. In 1574, Matthew Parker, Archbishop of Canterbury and a proponent of the idea that the English Church had developed independently from Rome, published an edition of Asser's *Life of King Alfred*. Whether this was the primary cause or a reflection of contemporary thinking, Alfred subsequently became 'the Great'. The Church of England still venerates him as a Christian hero on 26 October.

Once established, Alfred's greatness spread into the political sphere. In 1740, Thomas Arne's masque, *Alfred*, was performed before the Prince of Wales. Its finale, with words by the Scottish poet James Thomson, was *Rule Britannia!* In the early nineteenth century, the cult of Alfred – for that is what it became – grew rapidly with the publication of epic poems, historical romances, and five-act dramas, reaching its apogee in the Victorian era. The Anglo-Saxons were seen as the true ancestors of the English (see Chapter 26); Alfred was the greatest Anglo-Saxon; therefore, he was the founder of the English nation and the embodiment of Englishness. The historian, Edward Freeman even called him 'the most perfect character in history,'[255] and in 1899, to celebrate the one thousandth anniversary of his death, a five-metre, bronze statue, designed by the sculptor Hamo Thorneycroft, was erected in Winchester, the town that Ælfred made his capital.

Such an assessment would have been unthinkable in the spring of 878, when Ælfred was hiding on Athelney in the Somerset marshes and another Viking fleet, under Ubba, a brother of Halfdan and Ívarr the Boneless, landed on the North Devon coast. If the plan was for Ubba's force to join with Guthrum's, it failed. An *ealdorman* named Odda mobilised the local *fyrd*, mounted a surprise attack, and killed as many as a thousand of Ubba's men. In the meantime, Ælfred was secretly communicating with those *ealdormen* and *thegns* who were still loyal to him, urging them to gather their local *fyrd* and meet him at Ecgbert's Stone – an unidentified location, probably in Wiltshire, which sounds as if it had some symbolic significance for the men of Wessex. The *fyrd* of Somerset, Wiltshire, and Hampshire, perhaps 4,000 men, all mobilised. With the countryside rising against him, Guthrum could not sit tight in Chippenham and wait as he might have preferred. Battle was joined at Ethandum, probably Edington in Wiltshire. Guthrum's men were outnumbered and heavily defeated. They fled back to Chippenham. Ælfred followed, surrounded the *vill*, and starved them out. After two weeks, Guthrum surrendered and Ælfred was able to impose terms.

Ælfred wanted Guthrum and the remains of the Great Army to leave Wessex but, having been made to look foolish by Guthrum's cavalier breaking of his oath on Thor's ring at Wareham, he had to find a way to ensure the Danes kept their word. His solution was to insist that Guthrum and his men accepted Christian baptism and then to bind them to a Christian oath. This may sound naïve but, like his father, Ælfred's Christian faith was genuine, and he must have believed that it would work – although he was also rubbing salt into Guthrum's wound by insisting that the oath was sworn at Athelney.

It did work. Guthrum and his men withdrew to Cirencester, in Mercia, and negotiations began as to where they should settle. In 879, a new Viking fleet, men driven out of France by Charles the Bald's son, Louis the Stammerer, sailed up the Thames and camped at Fulham. Perhaps they saw themselves as reinforcements for Guthrum's army, but Guthrum saw them as a threat to the new and still fragile peace from which he stood to benefit. In a new role as poacher turned gamekeeper, he moved his army eastwards to contain but not confront them. They took the warning and sailed off to Ghent. Shortly afterwards, Guthrum decided that he and his men would settle in East Anglia. He and Ælfred negotiated a peace treaty and a trade protocol, and agreed the boundaries of their respective kingdoms. Guthrum's new domain would consist of East Anglia, eastern Mercia, and most of Essex – the region which became known as the Danelaw. Ælfred continued to rule Wessex, Kent, and Sussex, and his control of western Mercia was legitimised: he designated a member of the Mercian royal house, Æthelred II, as *ealdorman*, although he was, in effect, a subking. The long story of the Great Heathen Army was effectively over.

From a fugitive in his own kingdom to king of a much-enlarged Wessex, and recognised as such by his former enemy, it was a remarkable turnaround. Would it have happened at any other time? Is it possible that Ælfred was lucky enough to be pushing at a half-open door? Once Halfdan's part of the Great Army had finished devastating Scotland and Strathclyde, they returned to Northumbria, decided their raiding days were over, divided up the land between them, and became farmers. What prompted this apparent change of heart and lifestyle? After years of nomadic violence, could it be that they were tired of raiding and simply wanted to settle down? And if that were true of Halfdan's men, why should it not be true of Guthrum's army? Archaeological evidence suggests that in the years following the peace settlement, East Anglia saw an influx of new settlers – possibly the families and children of Guthrum's followers – and a rapid beating of swords into ploughshares. Perhaps even Vikings could run out of steam.

The Treaty of Ælfred and Guthrum – an original manuscript of which still survives in Corpus Christi College, Cambridge – was probably signed in 880. Ælfred ruled for another nineteen years. It was not exactly a time of peace. In 885, a Danish fleet landed in Kent, and besieged Rochester, but was driven off by Ælfred with assistance from the new East Anglian Danes. Ælfred reciprocated by sending his ships to fight pirates off the mouth of the Stour in Essex. The *Chronicle* entry for the following year, 886, states that Ælfred 'occupied London, and all the English people submitted to him, except those who were in captivity to the Danes.'[256] This raises the question of the status of London before Ælfred occupied it.[257] The old Roman city was still in ruins. Anglo-Saxon Lundenwic (see Chapter 26) was a prosperous port and trading centre. It had belonged to Mercia, but Mercia was now split between Ælfred and Guthrum. Justin Pollard suggests that it may have remained an open city, a kind of freeport.[258] Ælfred had coins minted there in the 870s and early 880s, which shows it was not hostile territory. Whatever its previous status, possession of London undoubtedly strengthened Wessex both strategically and economically.

Ælfred's position was growing stronger when, in 892,[259] another large Danish fleet arrived, dividing its forces between Benfleet in Essex and Appledore in Kent. The Appledore group broke out and rampaged across southern Wessex. Haesten, the leader of the Benfleet group accepted Christian baptism and gifts and agreed to depart, but then broke his word and, with Guthrum now dead, sought to enlist the support of the East Anglian Danes. Ælfred's reorganisation of his army (see below) paid off in what proved to be a complicated campaign. The Vikings suffered a bloody defeat at Buttington in today's Powys, where skulls were still being dug up in the nineteenth century. They were starved out of a camp in the ruins of Roman Chester; chased from east to west and back again; and, eventually, forced to scatter. Most went back to the Viking fiefdom on the Seine where they had come from; some went to East Anglia, and others to Jórvik. The raids and invasions of Ælfred's later years were dangerous, but none was as threatening as the Great Heathen Army in the 870s, and Ælfred was able to pursue the domestic agenda which would form the greater part of his legacy.

The Anglo-Saxon kings were almost continually engaged in military campaigns. At times, their history can seem no more than a catalogue of battles between individuals with strange names, with one group seeking to gain ascendancy over another. This was not a democratic age. Life was cheap. The sensitivity of the rulers towards the ruled was, at best, limited. Particularly during the period of Anglo-Saxon expansion and the Viking era that followed, the ordinary people who farmed the land and made up the *fyrd* had no real voice. The continual march and countermarch of armies probably reduced most people's lives to subsistence level. New social hierarchies were imposed; warriors created new kingdoms; kings issued new law codes; but the mass of the people lived, farmed, ate, and drank much as they had always done. Changes in ship or weapon design, and changes in the style of metalwork, jewellery, or manuscript illustration can help archaeologists date aristocratic graves, buried hoards, and copies of the gospels. When it comes to the villages, farms, and graves of ordinary people, the unchanging nature of their lives makes them less visible, and we have to rely on techniques such as radiocarbon dating, dendrochronology, and isotope analysis. Those who were not members of a ruling family, an aristocratic elite, or the clerical elite had no say in shaping their world or creating a legacy to pass on to later ages, except perhaps as an anonymous crewman on a longship or a member of a *fyrd* serving a victorious king.

It was the wars between the Dál Riata Scots, the Picts, and the Vikings that led to the creation of a unitary Scottish kingdom, the ascendancy of Scots Gaelic language and culture and the demise of Pictish and Pictish culture. It was the sweep of Viking conquest through the Northern and Western Isles which ensured that they are, even today, culturally distinct from the rest of Scotland. It was Ælfred's victory at Ethandum that enabled him to reorganise – even modernise – his kingdom in a way which, for the time, showed a remarkable concern for matters beyond power and wealth, and which still has cultural, psychological, and even ideological echoes in present-day England.

Defence was Ælfred's priority. Having seen how quickly hostile armies could sweep across Wessex, he set up a network of thirty-three fortified *byrig*, all located within thirty kilometres of each other, so that the local *fyrd* could move rapidly between them to confront an enemy. The *byrig* varied in size from whole towns enclosed by walls, such as Winchester, Exeter, and Christchurch, to new ditch-and-bank structures in strategic locations, such as Burpham, and one near Lewes, both in Sussex. Some *byrig* overlooked major rivers. Others protected important bridges (a technique learned from Charles the Bald). The aim was to prevent Viking craft using rivers to move inland. Local landowners and the *fyrd* were responsible for building and maintaining the *byrig*, in accordance with a system formalised in a document known as the *Burghal Hideage* issued by Ælfred's son and successor, Edward the Elder. Depending on the area of a given town or settlement, the *Hideage* calculates what length of wall should be maintained and how many fighting men each *burh* should support. These measures were not always popular, but they allowed for the expansion of the existing, local *fyrd*, and for the establishment of a royal *fyrd* under the king's command. This was the first time in British history that tax was raised to fund a body of men to defend the state – and in that limited sense we may call the royal *fyrd* the first standing army. The impact of Ælfred's *byrig* is shown by the fact that no fewer than twenty-two of the original thirty-three developed into boroughs – an essential administrative designation in post-Conquest England, reflecting the economic value of a town, and conferring privileges and a degree of self-government.

The generations of schoolchildren who were taught that the coming of the Anglo-Saxons marked the true beginning of English history were also taught that Ælfred was the father of the Royal Navy – a title that, later in the syllabus, they discovered was also accorded to Henry VIII. In fact, Wessex had sufficient naval capability for Ælfred's brothers, Æthelstan and Æthelbald, to defeat a Danish fleet off Sandwich in 851 (see Chapter 30). What Ælfred did was to build new and larger ships – perhaps based on classical models – to intercept the Danish ships before they reached the shore. The results were mixed. Where Ælfred's ships managed to come to close quarters and bring the Danes to battle, their weight and the number of men they carried proved decisive. In shallow or confined waters, however, their size and weight told against them: they grounded when the shallower draft Danish ships could still manoeuvre. Nonetheless, as part of Ælfred's overall strategy for the defence of Wessex, they were effective.

When Ælfred put together his law code – often called his *domboc* or book of judgements – in or around 893, it was prefaced by a translation into Anglo-Saxon of the Ten Commandments, and extracts from Exodus and the Acts of the Apostles. It can be difficult for a twenty-first century audience to appreciate the absolute reality of religious belief for men like Ælfred, but Christian belief infuses even the structure of his law code: it is divided into one hundred and twenty chapters – the age at which Moses died, and thus in medieval number symbolism standing for the law. Given Ælfred's experiences with Guthrum and Haesten, the first sentence of the first actual 'law' probably had a personal application: 'We enjoin, what is most lawful, that each man keep carefully his oath and his pledge.'[260] Although it is a somewhat rambling document, the *domboc* undoubtedly represents Ælfred's conception of the relationship between God's law and man's, and – however modified by time, interpretation, and practice – it formed the basis of English Common Law which applies in England and Wales to this day.

Ælfred had a clear – and for the time probably unusual – view of the purpose of education. His own translations, and those he commissioned, were intended 'so that all the youth of free men now in England who have the means to apply themselves to it, be set to learning ... until they know how to read English writing well. One may then instruct in Latin those whom one wishes to teach further and promote to a higher rank.' He followed Charlemagne's example by inviting distinguished scholars and intellectuals to his court, many of them from Europe, and by setting up a court school – for his own children, 'all the children of noble birth from almost the whole region, and a good many of lesser birth also.' Remarkably for the time, 'even before they had the requisite strength for manly skills (such as hunting), they were noted as devoted and intelligent students of the liberal arts.'[261] Equally remarkable was Ælfred's personal attitude to education, summed up in the closing lines of his translation of St Augustine's *Soliloquies*: 'a man who does not seek to increase his understanding while he is in this world strikes me as very foolish and ill-advised.'[262] His concept of learning as a continuous process, not just something revealed by ancient texts, is shown by the way he draws on contemporary issues and on matters germane to his own kingship to illustrate points raised in the works he is translating. The earliest manuscript of *Anglo-Saxon Chronicle* dates from Ælfred's time and is generally assumed to come from Wessex. It is a historical record with a clear Anglo-Saxon/Wessex bias, but it is never simply propaganda. We do not know if it was a royal commission, but it seems to fit with Ælfred's ideas about education.

Ælfred is the first person in British history whose character and attitudes we can reconstruct in such detail. We know that he suffered from an ongoing medical condition which has been diagnosed as Crohn's disease.[263] In one sense, the later cult of Alfred damaged his reputation, engendering a scepticism that can obscure his very real achievements. At the same time, we should be wary of exaggerating what he did achieve. When the *Chronicle* entry for 886 says that 'all the English people submitted to him, except those who were in captivity to the Danes', it could mean just those English who were in London when Ælfred took the city; or it could refer to southern Britain as a whole; but it cannot have meant the Anglo-Saxons of northern Northumbria who freed themselves from Danish rule in the 870s. Coins from the end of his reign describe him as *Rex Anglorum*. Whether translated as 'King of the Angles' or 'King of the English', it is something of an exaggeration. Ælfred pulled Wessex back from the brink. He restructured its defences, reformed its laws, and introduced a new concept of education. But he was not, as the subtitle of Justin Pollard's biography claims, 'The Man Who Made England.' He may have been the man who made England possible, but the making of the new kingdom was the work of his son and grandson, Eadweard and Æthelstan.

Eadweard ruled for twenty-five years, from Ælfred's death in 899 until 924. His name is often anglicised to Edward and given the suffix 'the Elder' to distinguish him from two later Anglo-Saxon Edwards – 'the Martyr' (r.975–78), and 'the Confessor' (r.1045–66). In contrast with his father, he and his achievements are little known. In part, this is because there are fewer documentary sources: he did not have an Asser to record his life and celebrate his victories. In part also, it is because the events of his reign do not fit into the kind of sequential narrative – turning defeat into victory –

that we saw with Ælfred. In fact, Eadweard did turn early weakness into strength, leaving Wessex much stronger on all fronts than at his accession, but the sequence of events was a complex one.

To the north of Wessex proper was Mercia, which had formally recognised Ælfred as king at the time of the peace treaty with Guthrum. It was administered by Æthelred II of Mercia, whom Eadweard recognised as an *ealdorman* but not as a king or sub-king. Æthelred II was married to Æthelflaed, who was Eadweard's sister and the guardian of his son, Æthelstan. To the west of Mercia, beyond Offa's Dyke, were the Welsh kingdoms, for the most part involved in a seemingly endless struggle amongst themselves. Gwynedd and Dyfed were the most powerful; and Gwynedd in particular, under Rhodri Mawr's son, Anarawd ap Rhodri (r.878–916), was always ready to engage in short-term alliances with the Danes or the Northumbrians to raid Mercia. Further north was Strathclyde, still much weakened by the Viking assault of 871, and at times dominated by the new Scottish kings – and the Scottish king in 900 was Causantín mac Áeda, or Constantine II, the first King of Alba (see Chapter 29). To the east was northern Northumbria or Bernicia which had broken free from Danish control and was ruled from Bamburgh Castle as an Anglo-Saxon kingdom. These northern kingdoms were separated from Wessex and Mercia by a great block of Viking- and Danish-controlled territory. On the east coast, it stretched from the Tees to the Thames. On the west, it ran from Barrow-in-Furness to the Dee Estuary, and then followed a line from Chester to London. The northern part of this block was the Kingdom of Jórvik or York. The southern part was the Danelaw, itself divided into the Kingdom of East Anglia; an area known as the Five Boroughs because it contained five Danish strongholds – Derby, Leicester, Lincoln, Nottingham, and Stamford; and a third area based around Northampton, Bedford, Cambridge, and Huntingdon. All these different polities would have a role to play during the complex manoeuvrings of Eadweard's reign.

It was a reign that began badly. When Ælfred came to the throne in 871, the two sons of his brother, Æthelred, were passed over because they were still children. The elder of the two, Æthelhelm, had died some years earlier, but the younger, Æthelwold, now challenged Eadweard's accession. Manoeuvred out of Wessex without a fight, he fled to Jórvik where at least some of the Danes accepted him as their king. This enabled him to bring a fleet south to Essex, where the East Anglian Danes joined him, and they left a trail of destruction across western Mercia and northern Wessex. Eadweard retaliated by raiding and burning East Anglia. He withdrew when he felt he had made his point, but a Kentish force which had made up part of his army decided to continue their campaign of destruction. The Danes met them at Holme, just south of Peterborough. By all accounts it was a bloody battle which the Kentish force lost, but it saw the death of both Æthelwold and the East Anglian king, Eohric.

Now secure on his throne, Eadweard and the rulers of East Anglia and southern and central Danelaw signed the Peace of Tiddingford in 906. Peace lasted for three years until broken by Æthelred II and Æthelflaed of Mercia. They had decided to move their seat of power from Tamworth, on the edge of the Danelaw, to the safer location of Gloucester. This involved rebuilding and rededicating the church, which meant finding the relics of a suitable saint who would attract pilgrims and bring prestige. They mounted a raid on Bardney Abbey, a hundred and fifty kilometres inside the Danelaw, stealing the relics of St Oswald of Northumbria and removing them to Gloucester. Retaliation came the following year. A force of Jórvik Danes swept into Mercia intent on revenge, but they came up against a combined Mercian and Wessex army at Tettenhall near Wolverhampton and were heavily defeated. Eowils and Halfdan, the joint kings of Jórvik, were both killed, as were many other Viking warlords.

We do not know whether Eadweard knew in advance about Æthelred II and Æthelflaed's plans to raid Bardney, but after Tettenhall he seems to have moved on to the offensive. Tettenhall was decisive in that the defeated Jórvik Danes subsequently remained north of the Humber. allowing Eadweard to concentrate his attentions on the southern parts of the Danelaw. Æthelred died in 910 or 911, having been ill or incapacitated for several years, to be succeeded by Æthelflaed, as 'Lady of the Mercians'. Æthelflaed, who had probably been the effective ruler of Mercia for some time, now stepped forward to take a leading role in the campaign against the Danelaw.

When the campaign began, it was relentless. Each time the armies of Wessex and Mercia moved forward, they constructed new *byrig* to secure the area they had overrun. Thirty such fortifications were built over the next ten years. It was a simple but effective process. In 912, Eadweard built a *burh* at Hertford to guard against attack from the north. He then marched east to Maldon on the Essex coast and built a *burh* at Witham just to the north. This effectively cut Essex in half, protected London from attack, and, according to the *Anglo-Saxon Chronicle*, caused large numbers of people who had been under Danish rule to submit to him.

In 914, Eadweard was distracted by a large Viking fleet from Brittany sailing up the Bristol Channel and occupying the Wye Valley. He was forced to pay £40 to ransom Cameleac (Cyfeiliog), the Bishop of Archenfield, but once forces from the *byrig* at Hereford and Gloucester had been mobilised, the Vikings were comprehensively defeated. The survivors mounted a couple of abortive attacks on the Somerset coast, before heading for Ireland. The neighbouring Welsh kingdoms of Gwent and Brycheiniog did not intervene. Both kingdoms had submitted to Ælfred when he had come to their aid in the 890s, and the fact that they did not side with the Vikings suggests that the influence of Wessex remained strong. In the meantime, Æthelflaed had been continuing to build new fortifications – at Stafford, Tamworth, Eddisbury in Cheshire, and Warwick – and the campaign against the southern Danelaw resumed.

Towards the end of 914, Eadweard built a *burh* encompassing the bridge over the Great Ouse at Buckingham. This threatened the position of Thurcytel, the *jarl* in possession of Bedford further downstream. He promptly submitted. Bedford had a symbolic importance as the burial place of Offa, greatest of the Mercian kings, so when Eadweard took possession in 915 it greatly enhanced his prestige. Many of the Danish garrison agreed to serve under him, while Thurcytel and his remaining men sailed for the Continent. In 917, the Danes launched a series of counterattacks, all of which were driven off. Æthelflaed took Derby and Eadweard stormed the Danish fortress of Tempsford, downstream from Bedford, killing Guthrum II, the last king of East Anglia. A final Danish attempt to storm the *burh* at Maldon failed with heavy losses. Suddenly, Danish power collapsed. Northampton submitted. So did Cambridge. So did the now leaderless army of East Anglia. By the turn of the year, only four of the Five Boroughs – Leicester, Stamford, Nottingham, and Lincoln – remained in Danish hands, and these soon gave up the struggle. Leicester surrendered to Æthelflaed early in 918; Stamford and Nottingham to Eadweard a few months later. Lincoln probably submitted to Eadweard at the same time, although it may have used its connection with the Danes in Jórvik to hold out a little longer.

Forty years after his father had been a fugitive on the Isle of Athelney, Eadweard could claim to rule all the lands south of the Humber and east of Offa's Dyke, but the situation was far from static. Æthelflaed died in June 918 and was succeeded by her daughter, Ælfwynn – the only example of woman-to-woman succession in the early history of the British Isles – but her reign lasted only a matter of months. Æthelflaed, as the widow of the Lord of Mercia and a warrior in her own right, enjoyed the support of the Mercian aristocracy. We can only presume that Ælfwynn did not. We do not know what happened, but by the end of the year Eadweard had taken personal control of Mercia and received the submission of all the Mercian nobles. He also received the submission of three important Welsh kings – Hywel and Clydog, joint kings of Dyfed, and Idwal ap Anarawd of Gwynedd (also known as Idwal Foel, or Idwal the Bald) – all of whom had previously pledged loyalty to Æthelflaed. Although Eadweard was now clearly in a powerful position, 918 was the year in which Ragnall ua Ímair crossed from Ireland and installed himself at Jórvik as king of southern Northumbria (see Chapter 30). This was enough to shift the always delicate balance of power in the north and may explain the confusing entry in the *Anglo-Saxon Chronicle* for 924.

> The king of Scots and the whole Scottish nation accepted [Eadweard] as 'father and lord': so did [Ragnall] and the sons of Eadwulf and all the inhabitants of Northumbria, both English and Danish, Norwegians and others; together with the king of the Strathclyde Welsh and all his subjects.[264]

Eadweard never conducted a campaign north of the Humber, so he cannot have imposed his overlordship on northern Britain by military means. It is possible that the northern polities, recognising the strength of Eadweard's position, saw submission as a means of getting him to guarantee the new balance of power that had emerged. Strathclyde, having taken advantage of the same power vacuum that allowed Ragnall to seize Jórvik, now controlled much of Cumbria and wanted to keep it. Ragnall was dead by 924, but neither he nor his successor, Sitric Cáech, had managed to conquer northern Northumbria, ruled by Ealdred I (one of 'the sons of Eadwulf'). A kind of peace had been established, but Ealdred would have wanted Eadweard's protection from Sitric, while Sitric would have wanted to avoid being threatened by an alliance of Ealdred and the Scots. Why Causantín of Scotland should also have submitted to Eadweard (if he did) is a mystery unless he, too, feared a coalition acting against him. The essential point underlying all these complexities is that the power and prestige of Wessex had risen to the point where Eadweard was seen as a potential overlord of, and arbiter among, kingdoms far from Wessex itself. It was a major change.

Eadweard died in 924. He was a soldier, strategist, and commander. He upheld his father's legal code, built a new Minster at Winchester, promoted diocesan reforms across Wessex in cooperation with Archbishop Plegmund, but he took no cultural initiatives and appears to have been little interested in relations with the Continental powers. Nevertheless, his achievements should not be underestimated. What Ælfred had begun, he continued; and what he left behind, Æthelstan turned into something that was recognisably, if still insecurely, England.

Eadweard did not intend Æthelstan to come to the throne. He wanted Ælfweard, his eldest son by his second wife, to be his successor. Unfortunately, Ælfweard died just sixteen days after his father, and the throne passed to Æthelstan, Eadweard's only son by his first wife. Eaweard's choice was not particularly unusual, but it provoked speculation that he had not been married to Æthelstan's mother, or that she had not been from a noble family. A bigger difficulty for Æthelstan was that he had grown up in Mercia, where Æthelflaed had been his guardian. Many of the Wessex nobility and clergy saw him as a Mercian and resented his authority – an indication that, even forty years after Ælfred had brought Mercia and Wessex under the same ruler, suspicion and division still endured. Æthelstan's coronation, in September 925, took place at Kingston-upon-Thames, a significant location on the border between the two polities. Æthelstan evidently wanted it to be the beginning of a new era in other ways, too. The service was specially written for the occasion by Æthelhelm, the Archbishop of Canterbury, and Æthelstan wore a crown not a helmet. Both innovations were influenced by how things were done in the kingdom of the West Franks – where his half-sister, Eadgifu, was married to the king, Charles the Simple – and this was also significant because Æthelstan would prove at least as internationally-minded as Ælfred, if not more so.

Æthelstan began with diplomacy. In 926, he negotiated a non-aggression pact with Sitric of Jórvik, sealing the agreement by arranging that Sitric should marry one of his sisters, whose name we do not know. The peace lasted just a year. In 927, Sitric died and his brother Gofraid sailed from Dublin to assume the kingship. Æthelstan saw and seized his opportunity. He invaded, captured the city of Jórvik, and overran the whole kingdom. Gofraid and his men were driven back to their boats and sailed back to Ireland. Æthelstan received the submission of the whole population, including the resident Danes, and proclaimed himself king. This led directly to a treaty involving all the northern kingdoms signed at Eamont Bridge in Cumbria – a location probably chosen because it was on the border between Strathclyde and Æthelstan's newly-acquired Jórvik. To some extent, Eamont Bridge repeated the terms of Eadweard's agreement in 924 as reported by the *Anglo-Saxon Chronicle*, but his position was much stronger than his father's. The lands under his personal rule now reached the borders of northern Northumbria and Strathclyde. Ealdred of north Northumbria, Causantín of Scotland, Owain ap Dyfnwal of Strathclyde, and Hywel of Dyfed, now King of Deheubarth – a new kingdom comprising Dyfed and Seisyllwg and covering much of South Wales – all accepted him as their overlord. From Eamont, Æthelstan marched south to Hereford where he received the submission of the other Welsh kings – of Gwynedd, Powys, Brycheiniog, and Gwent – and imposed a heavy annual tribute on them. In the years that followed, Æthelstan kept a number of these Welsh kings at his court, presumably to guarantee their good behaviour.

We cannot identify a single moment when England was created, but Eamont Bridge is as good as any – although, of course, this is a retrospective judgement, and neither Æthelstan nor his subjects would suddenly have thought of themselves as 'English'. Of the Anglo-Saxon kingdoms, only north Northumbria was not under Æthelstan's personal rule. From April 928, charters describe him as *Rex Anglorum*. Some coins went even further and described him as *Rex totius Britanniae* (King of the whole of Britain) – although others issued in Mercia used the more modest title *Rex Saxorum* (King of the Saxons), presumably because it was politic to emphasise his Saxon roots to the Mercians. Titles were less important than the way Æthelstan administered his new, expanded kingdom. Not since Roman governors in the third and fourth centuries had one man ruled such a large area of Britain, but Roman governors ruled by *fiat* and force, whereas Æthelstan ruled by managed consent. The new England was no democracy, but without the support of the *witan*, of the *ealdormen*, the reeves, and the *thegns*, the king was powerless. Æthelstan ruled through regional *ealdormen*. They may have been powerful – one who shared the same name came to be known as Æthelstan Half-King – and some were of Danish not Saxon descent, but they were neither subkings nor members of former ruling families, and they were dependent on Æthelstan for their position. This was one aspect of what became a highly centralised administration. Another was the law.

More legal texts survive from Æthelstan's reign than from any other period of the tenth century. Many of them are charters, and many date from the key period between 928 and 935 when he was developing an administrative structure for his new kingdom. They show us the issues he thought important at any given time and, by monitoring the witnesses and the order of their signatures, allow us to trace who was in or out of favour. It seems that all these charters were written by a single individual, known to history as 'Æthelstan A', which suggests that Æthelstan was keeping legal matters under close personal supervision. He issued several law codes in the course of his reign, probably reflecting the advice of, or actually drafted by, Wulfhelm, Archbishop of Canterbury from 926 to 941. These were essentially clarifications or modifications of Ælfred's laws. The earliest concerns the gathering of tithes. The second is a form of Poor Law, obliging reeves to make monies from the revenues from the king's estates available to feed the poor. But such apparent liberality is balanced by the death penalty for anyone guilty of stealing more than eight pence. Æthelstan appears to have been more than usually concerned with social order. He instituted a system known as tithing (which has no connection with tithes), under which groups of ten heads of households from a given area of ten hides were sworn in to help keep the peace. There were severe penalties for reeves who failed to carry out the king's commands in this respect. One key aspect of Æthelstan's reforms, charters, and laws was that they applied across the whole of what we can now call England. Previous administrative and legal differences between the Anglo-Saxon kingdoms were overridden and overwritten. This undoubtedly contributed to the emergence of a unitary kingdom, but it was a gradual, not an immediate, process.

Anglo-Saxon courts had always been peripatetic, moving from one royal *vill* to the next, and from one part of the kingdom to the next, but both Ælfred and Eadweard had shown a preference for Winchester, regarding it as a *de facto* capital. Æthelstan did not share this view, perhaps because of difficulties on his accession when the Bishop of Winchester, Frithestan, was vocal among those who saw him as a Mercian interloper. Æthelstan seems to have spent much time in old Wessex, in the southwest, summoning *ealdormen*, bishops, and subject kings to come to him. One estimate, based on charters, law codes, and other records, suggests that he travelled north of the Thames only a dozen times during his fifteen-year reign. Nonetheless, Æthelstan's court was neither isolated nor lacking in character. Once difficulties with the likes of Frithestan were overcome, he forged a closer relationship with the Church than his predecessors, although this may have been because a much-enlarged kingdom gave him a larger pool of senior clergy to draw into his administration. He took an interest in making appointments to those northern bishoprics, mainly in areas formerly under Danish control, that had been unfilled for some time. He also pressed for the number of northern bishops to be increased. All this gave him additional sources of information, particularly in those areas, such as Northumbria, where his rule was new and untested.

Compared with the courts of his predecessors, Æthelstan's was distinctly cosmopolitan. His three half-sisters all married foreign royalty: Eadgifu had married the Charles the Simple, King of the West Franks; Eadgyth married Otto I, the Holy Roman Emperor; and Eadhild married Hugh, Duke of the Franks. Clerics and scholars from Scandinavia, from the Frankish kingdoms, and from Brittany are all attested at court during his reign. Oda (also Odo, or Odo the Severe), a Dane, perhaps born in East Anglia, who went on to become Archbishop of Canterbury, was an influential figure. Israel the Grammarian, a Breton, and one of the most respected Latin scholars of the period, was another. Cenwald (also Koenwald), the Bishop of Worcester, travelled to the monasteries of St Gall and Reichenau, and brought back ideas that would influence the reform and regeneration of English monasteries. The king himself was known in England and on the Continent as a collector of books and saintly relics. He was also a patron of poets. In her biography, *Æthelstan: The First King of England*, Sarah Foot makes a case – unproven but plausible – for *Beowulf* being written at Æthelstan's court.[265] His patronage of the Church and literature may have extended to commissioning a translation of at least some of the Bible. In 1528, when William Tyndale sought to justify his decision to translate the Bible into English, he claimed to have read that Æthelstan had 'caused' the Bible to be translated into Anglo-Saxon and that the bishops had supported the idea.[266] There is no definite proof of this, but it shows how, in some contexts at least, Æthelstan's reputation echoed down the centuries.

32   War, Peace, and More War

England existed, but there was a long way to go before it became a permanent entity. In the south, Æthelstan had an established system of administration based on his *ealdormen* and reeves, and a working system of defence based on the *fyrd* and the network of *byrig*. In the north, where administrative and military structures existed, they were different, and not necessarily loyal to him. In some newly-conquered territories, he imposed *ealdormen* whom he knew to be loyal; in others, he appears to have recruited local men on the strength of an oath. But these were temporary measures: in the longer term, the plan was to secure his hold on the north by creating a common governmental structure for all parts of his new kingdom. To that end, he embarked on a programme of legal and administrative reforms and, remarkably, the treaty signed at Eamont Bridge in 927 gave him seven years without a major raid or invasion – a long time in pre-Conquest Britain – to get the process under way.

Those years of peace ended in 934 when, according to the *Anglo-Saxon Chronicle*, 'Æthelstan invaded Scotland with both a land and a naval force, and harried much of the country.'[267] If Eamont Bridge was the first recorded diplomatic interaction between England and Scotland, Æthelstan's invasion was the first in a long line of military confrontations which lasted until 1745. The only explanation we have for Æthelstan's action comes from John of Worcester, writing two hundred years after the event. He says that Causantín had 'broken the peace he had made'[268] – which presumably means Eamont Bridge. This is certainly possible. Ealdred I of northern Northumbria had just died, and Causantín may have made a move to occupy the Bamburgh-based kingdom. Alternatively, Æthelstan may have taken pre-emptive action to prevent any such move by Causantín and, in doing so, bring northern Northumbria under his rule – which he did.

The campaign appears to have been short, sharp, and punitive, occupy-

Map 28   England in the 10th and Early 11th Centuries

ing just two months, July and August. Like Agricola and Septimius Severus, Æthelstan marched his army up the east side of the country, while the fleet shadowed his progress offshore. The army included four Welsh kings – of Gwynedd, Deheubarth, Brycheiniog, and Gwent – seven English *ealdormen*, six Danish *jarls*, and no fewer than eighteen bishops.

Æthelstan was showing his power – and making sure that potential troublemakers travelled with him. The Irish *Annals of Clonmacnoise*, probably compiled at the beginning of the fifteenth century, are slightly dismissive, claiming that Æthelstan got no further than Edinburgh and retired without a major battle being fought. Simeon of Durham, writing in the twelfth century, contradicts this, and suggests a successful campaign. He claims that Æthelstan's army ravaged the coastal plain as far north as the ancient fortress of Dunnottar and inland as far as the Grampians, while the fleet sailed north to attack Caithness, which belonged to the Earldom of Orkney. At the end of the campaign when he travelled south, Æthelstan was accompanied by Causantín, Causantín's son, and Owain, the King of Strathclyde, so Simeon's version may be more accurate. A year later, in 935, Causantín was still at Æthelstan's court: his signature, witnessing a charter, makes it clear that he was *subregulus*, a sub-king. Æthelstan was evidently keen to establish himself as *Rex totius Britanniae*.

Just as he had been brought up in the Mercian court with his aunt, Æthelflaed, as his guardian, so Æthelstan acted as host, guardian, and often godfather to members of his half-sisters' families and to the offspring of allied ruling families. One such figure was Hákon (also Haakon), the son of King Harald Fairhair of Norway. Hákon appears to have been a pagan when he arrived at court but converted to Christianity with the king standing godfather. Twelfth-century Norwegian sources suggest that around 934 – presumably after the invasion of Scotland – Æthelstan put a fleet and men at Hákon's disposal so he could return to Norway and remove his reputedly despotic brother, Eirik Blodøks (anglicised as Eric Bloodaxe), from the kingship. A similar story concerns Alain, son of Matuedoi I, Count of Poher in Brittany. In 924, Matuedoi and his family were forced out of their homeland by Viking invasions and fled to the court of Eadweard in Wessex. Matuedoi died in 930, but Æthelstan stood godfather to his son, Alain, and in 936 provided a fleet to allow him and other exiled Bretons to return to Brittany. Alain – later known as Alan Twistedbeard – drove out the Vikings and became Duke of Brittany. In both cases, Æthelstan was supporting his godsons as a godfather should, but there was also an element of self-interest. Both interventions removed a potential threat to England – in one case from a powerful individual (although Eirik Blodøks would return), and in the other from a Viking base of operations. What is striking is Æthelstan's decision to intervene directly in a Continental dispute – something no Anglo-Saxon king had done before – and to take the fight against the Vikings beyond the shores of Britain, a departure that may well have been noted in Dublin.

'Æthelstan the man is elusive,' says his biographer.[269] He was obviously intelligent and politically astute; he was a patron of the Church and the arts; yet there is more than a hint of arrogance about him. We have already noted the coins describing him as *Rex totius Britanniae*. From 931 onwards, the charters go further, describing him as 'king of the English, elevated by the right hand of the Almighty to the throne of the whole kingdom of Britain', while some even call him *basileus*, the term usually reserved for Byzantine emperors.[270] Keeping sub-kings or dependent princes at court was normal practice, but Æthelstan seems to have kept more of them, and kept them for longer than previous kings. And the tribute he demanded from the Welsh kings at Hereford was unprecedented – thirty pounds of gold, three hundred pounds of silver, and 25,000 oxen annually. Whether this arrogance played a part, or whether it was simply that his new-found dominance united all those who opposed him, Æthelstan soon found himself facing an unprecedented coalition.

Both Causantín and Owain of Strathclyde left Æthelstan's court in 935 and returned to their respective kingdoms. Although the Dublin Vikings and the Scots had been enemies for generations, Causantín immediately formed an alliance with Amlaíb mac Gofraid (also Olaf or Anlaf Guthfrithson) of Dublin. And although Strathclyde had frequently suffered at the hands of both, Owain joined them. Causantín and Owain undoubtedly feared further English expansion. Amlaíb probably saw an opportunity to reclaim Jórvik – it was his father, Gofraid, whom Æthelstan had outmanoeuvred to take control of Jórvik in 927. Amlaíb may also have feared that Æthelstan's new forward policy would lead him to cross the Irish Sea to attack Dublin.

All we know of the campaign that followed is its final act, the Battle of Brunanburh, probably in October 937. Amlaíb sailed from Dublin that August, but we have no idea where he landed. This is part of the problem of trying to establish where the battle took place. Sailing directly east across the Irish Sea, he would have landed on the Wirral, and many historians link Brunanburh with Bromorough, just south of Birkenhead. Others, still favouring a west coast landing, suggest the hillfort of Burnswark in Dumfries. However, John of Worcester says that he sailed up the Humber, and an east coast landing is logical if his aim was to re-assert the Uí Ímair claim to Jórvik. Supporters of this view locate the battle at various places in Yorkshire and County Durham. The truth is that we do not know.

Much of Æthelstan's reign has to be pieced together from sources written several hundred years later. Brunanburh, by contrast, is reported in several near-contemporary documents – the *Anglo-Saxon Chronicle*, the *Annals of Ulster*, and Æthelweard's *Chronicon*. It also features in a range of later sources: chronicles and histories from Scotland, Ireland, Wales, England, Normandy, Brittany, and the Frankish kingdoms, as well as the Icelandic sagas. For actual detail, however, we are largely dependent on the poem, *The Battle of Brunanburh*, which is contained within the *Anglo-Saxon Chronicle* entry for 937. The battle lasted all day. It was the greatest slaughter since the arrival of the Anglo-Saxons. Æthelstan and his half-brother, Eadmund, were victorious. Five kings, seven earls, Causantín's son, and a host of Scots and Vikings lay dead on the battlefield. Amlaíb (Anlaf in the poem) and a few survivors sailed back to Dublin. Causantín returned to Scotland. The brothers returned home triumphant and rejoicing. The trouble is that this is a praise-poem, written from the point of view of the victors, and it raises as many questions as it answers. Did the King of Mann fight alongside Causantín and Amlaíb? Owain is not mentioned after Brunanburh. Was he among the kings who died? Who were the others? The Welsh kings seem not to have been involved – which may be an argument against locating the battle at Bromorough on the borders of Wales. There is no reason to doubt the outcome, but the poem says nothing about English casualties. Two hundred years later, William of Malmesbury claimed that two of Æthelstan's cousins, Ælfwine and Æthelwine, were among the dead. Yet surely, if the struggle was long and bloody, there must have been other English dead? How many? And how severely did it affect Æthelstan's ability to defend his kingdom? The poem also emphasises the retrospective nature of our concept of England. It talks of Angles and Saxons. It describes Æthelstan and his brother Eadmund going 'home' to 'the land of the West Saxons'.[271] England had not yet entered the mind of the poet.

The historian Æthelweard, writing in the 970s, says that after Brunanburh 'the lands of Britain [were] consolidated together, on all sides is peace, and plenty of all things.'[272] Eleven hundred years later, in 2011,

Michael Livingston wrote that the battle led all the constituent parts of the British Isles to consolidate the territorial positions which they still occupy today.[273] This is simply not the case. It is true that if Æthelstan had lost at Brunanburh the hegemony of Wessex would almost certainly have been destroyed, and what was in the process of becoming England might well have crumbled. It is also true that Æthelstan was unchallenged while he lived, but he lived only for two more years; and as soon as he died, in October 939, Anglo-Saxon control of the north collapsed. Despite what the poem suggests, Amlaíb mac Gofraid bounced back quickly from defeat. In 938, he carried out a major raid in County Kildare and captured a thousand prisoners. And once Æthelstan's death was known, he left Dublin and returned to Jórvik, where he rapidly and this time successfully established himself as king. Eadmund, who succeeded Æthelstan in 939, seems to have been taken by surprise. He attempted to besiege Amlaíb's forces in Leicester, but Amlaíb escaped. Under a peace deal brokered by Archbishops Oda of Canterbury and Wulfstan of York, Eadmund and Amlaíb agreed to divide England between them. That Eadmund was willing to agree to this suggests that he was in a weak position. In the end, it scarcely mattered because Amlaíb ignored the agreement and reoccupied the Five Boroughs. He then turned northwards, raided Lindisfarne, and in 941 attacked the settlement of Tyninghame, near Dunbar, where he was killed.

Amlaíb mac Gofraid was replaced as King of Jórvik by Amlaíb Cuarán (also Amlaíb mac Sitric and Olaf Sigtryggsson), another of the Uí Ímair dynasty, but his reign did not last long. In 942, Eadmund, having reorganised his army, reconquered the Five Boroughs. Amlaíb Cuarán evidently felt threatened for, in 943, he agreed to a *rapprochement* and accepted Christian baptism with Eadmund as his godfather. Eadmund's view of the role of a godfather evidently differed from Æthelstan's, for the very next year he swept into Jórvik and north Northumbria, re-establishing the control and overlordship of Wessex. His new godson fled to Dublin where, in one of those strange twists that characterise the Uí Ímair dynasty, he was immediately accepted as king. Eadmund continued his campaign. In 945, he devastated Cumbria and other parts of the Kingdom of Strathclyde, apparently ordering the two sons of the king, Domnall mac Eógain, to be blinded. However, having reduced Strathclyde to submission, he made a treaty ceding control of the territory to the new King of Scotland, Malcolm

I, who had succeeded Causantín, in return for Scottish military assistance against England's enemies. In just four years, Eadmund had reclaimed the territory lost after Æthelstan's death, and established a friendly relationship with the Scots. Then, in 946, he was stabbed to death in what may have been a brawl or a political assassination.

The first thing we hear about his successor, his younger brother Eadred, is that he reduced 'all Northumbria to subjection,'[274] suggesting that Jórvik and north Northumbria had rebelled against whatever settlement Eadmund had imposed on them. In 947, the Northumbrians, led by Archbishop Wulfstan, took oaths of loyalty to Eadred, but broke them almost at once by choosing the former King of Norway, Eirik Blodøks, as their king. A year later, in 948, they expelled him, perhaps fearing another invasion by Eadred, and in 949 gave Amlaíb Cuarán a second chance at the kingship. Eadred seems to have tolerated Amlaíb, perhaps because he was Eadmund's godson, but the arrangement only lasted three years. In 952, Eirik returned – it is not clear how, but his career was nothing if not swashbuckling – for his second turn as king, but in 954, he was again driven out and killed at the Battle of Stainmore, high up on the Cumbrian fells. Stainmore finally brought the whole of Northumbria under the rule of the Wessex kings. The leader of the Anglo-Saxon forces was Osulf. Originally the high reeve of Bamburgh, he became an earl and ruled Northumbria from 954 until about 962, remaining loyal to Eadred and his successors throughout. The *Chronicle of the Kings of Alba* says it was during the reign of Indulf, Malcolm I's successor as King of Scotland, that Edinburgh was abandoned to the Scots. This indicates a significant territorial readjustment, for in this context Edinburgh almost certainly means the whole Lothian region. Indulf's regnal dates coincide with Osulf's tenure in Northumbria, so Osulf must have been involved, but we do not know what happened.

Brunanburh confirmed Wessex as the dominant power in the south of Britain but, as this kaleidoscope of names and events demonstrates, it did not decide the mastery or the territorial composition of the north. It was in the years following Brunanburh that two strands of activity which had long affected the north of England were brought to a conclusion. Amlaíb Cuarán's second expulsion from Jórvik marked the end of the Uí Ímair's attempts to unite Dublin and Jórvik into a single kingdom. They subsequently confined their activities to Ireland, the Kingdom of the Isles, and the Isle of Man. Eirik Blodøks' death was the last attempt by a Viking adventurer to carve out a kingdom on British soil. Viking raids did not cease altogether – Indulf was killed fighting raiders at Cullen in Banffshire – but they were smaller and concentrated on Scottish coastal regions.

Between 955 and 980, what was now England enjoyed a quarter of a century of comparative peace, and with peace, the central narrative of the *Anglo-Saxon Chronicle* and other documentary sources switches from the political aspects of the rule by the kings of Wessex to religion and, in particular, to a powerful revival of monasticism. The movement known as the Benedictine Reforms, based on the ideas of St Benedict of Nursia (c.408–c.547), spread across most of western Europe, but manifested itself differently in different countries. Its beginnings can be traced back to the foundation of Cluny Abbey near Mâcon in eastern France in 910, but its origins lay in the Abbey of Fleury, just east of Orléans, where the remains of St Benedict were kept and venerated. From the time of Æthelstan onwards, Fleury had close links with bishops and senior clerics connected with the English court. Monasteries had been among the earliest targets of the Viking raids, and monks had probably suffered disproportionately at the hands of the raiders – although it is possible that the monks who recorded what happened exaggerated the suffering of their fellows (see Chapter 28). Across the British Isles, religious foundations had been destroyed or abandoned. Writing at the beginning of the eleventh century, Byrhtferth of Ramsay claimed that there were no monks left in England by the 940s. Although this is demonstrably untrue, the Anglo-Saxon kingdoms do appear to have been particularly badly affected. Secular clergy – ordinary priests and deacons who were neither monks nor members of a particular religious order – were more effective in ministering to their parishes and to the lay community during the upheavals of the Viking era. Some of them had even taken over the abbeys and other foundations deserted by the monks. However, several sources portray the secular clergy of the English Church at this time as materialistic (owning property privately rather than in common), illiterate, married (often having children), and generally unfit for their office. Some of this was almost certainly true but, again, these accusations were made by literate monks who stood to benefit from reform and had a vested interest in portraying the secular clergy in a poor light.

Ælfred had established a handful of new monasteries – including one at Athelney – but his motive seems to have been personal piety rather than any impulse to reform. It was the cosmopolitan atmosphere of Æthelstan's court that introduced the ideas behind the reform movement to England, although the movement itself did not reach its peak until the reign of Eadgar (r.959–75). In practical terms, reform meant remodelling surviving monasteries along Benedictine lines, founding new ones, refounding abandoned ones – with royal charters granting or regranting the land – and significantly reducing the number and influence of the secular clergy. On the Continent, particularly in Burgundy and northern Italy, the papacy was closely involved. In England, reform was very much a 'national' process, driven by the close relationship between the ruling family and senior churchmen. With the establishment of an English kingdom and a degree of political stability, the Church naturally sought to re-establish the status (and the wealth) it had enjoyed before the years of violence and disruption. During those years, the Church – with the notable exception of Archbishop Wulfstan of York – had loyally supported Wessex and its kings, and it was equally natural that its loyalty should be rewarded. The result was not just a revival of monasticism, but a strengthening of the Church hierarchy and its influence at court.

The central figure in all this was Dunstan (c.909–98), canonised in 1029, and until the canonisation of Thomas Becket in 1173 by far the most popular English saint. He came from an influential Wessex family and was educated by Irish monks at Glastonbury Abbey until, when still a young man, he was summoned to the household of his uncle, Æthelhelm, then Archbishop of Canterbury. Æthelhelm introduced him at court where he quickly became a favourite with Æthelstan, probably because he had a quick and scholarly mind. Being a favourite came at a price. One story has it that jealous enemies accused him of black magic and threw him into a cesspool. He escaped and fled to his other uncle, Ælfheah, who was Bishop of Winchester. It was Ælfheah who persuaded him to take holy orders. Dunstan then returned to Glastonbury where, although living as a hermit, he became a noted illuminator of manuscripts, an expert silversmith, and a skilled harpist.

Dunstan's talents made it impossible for him to keep out of the public sphere. As did his wealth. Æthelflaed of Mercia regularly asked him for advice and, when she died, left him all her money. His father left him both property and money. By the time Eadmund came to the throne and recalled him to court, Dunstan, although still notionally a hermit, was both famous and rich. Eadmund recognised his abilities and made him a minister, but again Dunstan fell foul of court jealousies. He left the court to return to Glastonbury, although this time as abbot. At some stage, Dunstan had come under the influence of the writings of Oda, the Archbishop of Canterbury who had succeeded his uncle. Oda's links with Fleury were one of the channels by which Benedictine ideas reached England. This interest was shared by Æthelwold, another cleric of about the same age who joined Dunstan at Glastonbury and went on to become Bishop of Winchester. Dunstan's priority was to re-establish an enclosed monastic community along Benedictine lines, but he seems also to have embraced the wider responsibilities of the Church. He established a school, and initiated drainage and irrigation projects on the nearby Somerset Levels. Then, in 946, just two years after Dunstan's appointment as abbot, Eadmund was murdered, Eadred became king, and Dunstan was summoned to court for a third time.

Eadred was a warrior king who reconquered and subdued Northumbria, but he was also an astute politician. Perhaps guided by his mother, Eadgifu of Kent, he realised that if the Wessex hegemony was to survive, the Danish regions needed to be integrated into the rest of England. A key aspect of this was Christianity – for paganism remained widespread in parts of the Danelaw – and the authority of the Church. For nine years, Dunstan was one of Eadred's closest advisers, remaining at court even though he was offered the important bishopric of Winchester, and despite opposition from a number of reactionary Wessex nobles – among them some of his own family – who opposed any change that they considered weakened their position.

Eadred died childless in 955. The succession passed to his nephew, Eadwig – the eldest son of his brother and predecessor, Eadmund – who was no more than fifteen when he came to the throne. His short reign nearly proved disastrous for Dunstan and for England. The anonymous eleventh-century *Sancti Dunstani Vita* records how Eadwig disappeared during the great feast staged to celebrate his coronation. Archbishop Oda, who was presiding, regarded this as insulting to the collected nobles present and sent Dunstan and the Bishop of Lichfield to find him. They discovered the new king in a compromising situation with a high-ranking lady called Æthelgifu and her daughter, Ælfgifu. Dunstan dragged Eadwig back to the feast but, in doing so, incurred the enmity of both the king and the two ladies.[275] Eadwig married Ælfgifu shortly afterwards. Her mother intrigued with the Wessex reactionaries who had long opposed Dunstan and persuaded the king to seize all his property. Fearing for his life, Dunstan fled to Flanders where the Count, Arnulf I, lodged him in the Benedictine monastery of St Peter's in Ghent.

Such a story is unlikely to be wholly invented, but it may have been embellished by Eadwig's enemies and Dunstan's friends. What is certain is that Eadwig made a large number of enemies in a short space of time. On the death of Eadred at the end of 955, Wessex, Mercia, and Northumbria had unanimously chosen Eadwig as king. By the second half of 957, Mercia and Northumbria had rescinded their decision and chosen his younger brother, Eadgar, instead. Only Wessex remained loyal to Eadwig, so England was divided along the line of the Thames, and there was every prospect of civil war. Eadwig had also fallen out with the Church. In 958, Archbishop Oda dissolved his marriage to Ælfgifu on grounds of consanguinity – they were probably third cousins – although his decision was, in part at least, an indication of support for Dunstan.

One of Eadgar's first acts as king north of the Thames was to recall Dunstan and appoint him Bishop of Worcester and then, shortly afterwards, Bishop of London as well. That same year, 958, saw the death of Archbishop Oda. Canterbury was south of the Thames, so it was Eadwig who chose his replacement, Ælfsige, then Bishop of Winchester, who was married and had a son, suggesting that Eadwig was hoping for the support of the reactionary faction who opposed Dunstan and the reformers. Ælfsige set off for Rome to receive his pallium from the Pope, but died while crossing the Alps, so Eadwig had to make another choice. This time, in 959, his eye fell on Byrhthelm, the Bishop of Wells, but within months of Byrhthelm's appointment – and perhaps fortunately for the future of England – Eadwig died. Wessex immediately accepted Eadgar as king. England was reunited and Eadgar sent Byrhthelm back to Wells, on the grounds that he was not up to the job of Archbishop of Canterbury, appointing Dunstan in his place. History, as ever written by the victors, may have been unfair to Byrhthelm, but he does seem to have been a nonentity.

Eadgar can have been no more than sixteen when he became King of England in 959. Dubbed Eadgar the Peaceful, this is a characterisation of the reign rather than the man. In or around 960, he married Æthelflaed the Fair, daughter of a Devon *ealdorman*. She gave birth to two sons, Eadweard and Eadmund, but she either died, or was divorced, about 964. What happened next is not clear. Eadgar apparently abducted a woman named Wulfthryth (or Wilfrida) from Wilton Abbey in Wiltshire, where she was probably being educated. She remained with Eadgar for perhaps two years and gave birth to a daughter before returning to Wilton where she became a nun, and later abbess. They were probably not married. Eadgar's second (or possibly third) wife was Ælfthryth (also Alfrida or Elfrida), the widow of Æthelwald, *ealdorman* of East Anglia. She gave him a son, Æthelred, whom we will meet shortly. Unfortunately, it seems that Ælfthryth was only a widow because Eadgar killed her husband. The story goes that Æthelwald had tried to dissuade Eadgar from marrying Æthelfryth but then married her himself, so enraging Eadgar that he murdered him. Such stories are frequently embellished in the telling, but we know that Dunstan made Eadgar undergo serious penance: although king, he was forbidden to wear the crown until his formal coronation, which only took place in 973, thirteen years after his accession.

In contrast to his private life, the policies Eadgar pursued during his reign were largely conciliatory and designed to bind the different parts of England together by more than just the fact of a common ruler. Many of them were probably initiated by Dunstan, who remained the king's closest advisor throughout his reign. In order to push through his monastic reforms, Dunstan created a powerful triumvirate, consisting of himself as Archbishop of Canterbury, his colleague and friend, Æthelwold, as Bishop of Winchester, and another powerful cleric, Oswald, a nephew of the former Archbishop Oda, as Bishop of Worcester. Dunstan and Oswald seem to have taken a gradualist approach, while Æthelwold preferred direct action, including physically ejecting secular clergy from Winchester's New Minister and replacing them with monks. The most important document to come out of the reform process was the *Regularis Concordia*, possibly written by Æthelwold for a meeting between the king and senior clerics in 970. The *Regularis* set out the aims, activities, and daily rituals of monastic culture. It also bound the Crown to support monasteries by formally declaring the king to be the protector of monks and his queen the protector of nuns. Although the reforms may have had less impact in the north where Eadgar did not have the strength the enforce them, the fact that he attempted to introduce them across the whole country strongly suggests that he was thinking in terms of a unified polity.

At the school attached to the New Minster at Winchester, Æthelwold encouraged the standardisation of written Anglo-Saxon. Based on the West Saxon dialect, this form of the language was apparently accepted by scribes in reformed monasteries and soon became the accepted form in which charters and legal documents were drawn up, and in which almost all later Anglo-Saxon literature was written. Eadgar made major efforts to standardise the currency. Every coin was required to be of uniform quality and bear the name of the moneyer and location of the mint. Even more significant was the way in which the former Danish kingdoms were treated. Legislation was introduced to integrate them into the rest of the country. They were allowed to maintain many of their social and legal customs but only, it was clearly stated, within the overall compass of English laws made by the king and his *witan*. In his classic study, *Anglo-Saxon England*, Frank Stenton illustrates how this worked in practice. Eadgar insisted that the laws on trafficking stolen cattle should apply equally in both Anglo-Saxon and Danish parts of England, but he allowed the Danish regions a degree of autonomy in deciding what the actual punishment for an offence should be.[276] Such measures did at least as much to create England as the battlefield conquests and submissions of earlier reigns, and the fact that these conciliatory policies coincided with a period when there were no major raids or invasions meant that the country also prospered economically.

When Eadgar died, suddenly and unexpectedly, in July 975, the unity that he and Dunstan had created was immediately threatened. The kingship passed to Eadweard, his eldest son by his first wife. Eadweard was perhaps thirteen or fourteen at the time, but his succession was immediately challenged by Eadgar's third wife, Æthelfryth, on behalf of her son, Æthelred, who was probably only ten. Groups of nobles formed in support of each candidate. Whether there was violence between them is not clear, but violence did erupt in another context. A number of nobles, led by Ealdorman Ælfhere of Mercia, began sacking and destroying religious foundations in a short but savage reaction against monastic reform. This was sparked not by opposition to monasteries as such, but by the fact that Dunstan's reforms alienated land from powerful families and curtailed the powers of *ealdormen*. There was also a rash of legal cases, challenging the charters that gave the monasteries the right to own their land. Such a sudden upwelling of discontent immediately after Eadgar's death indicates just how much power he exercised. He was a king in his own right and not, as sometimes suggested, merely Dunstan's cipher. He trusted and relied on Dunstan's advice, but it was his authority that ensured the policies and reforms of his reign were carried out. Only once he was gone did those who had always opposed Dunstan's reforms feel free to challenge them publicly.

Dunstan supported Eadweard's accession, even though there were doubts about the boy's suitability. He had an ungovernable temper, and was known to have lashed out verbally and physically at members of his household. Eadweard, or his advisers, made concessions to Æthelred, granting him a number of estates, in order to ease tensions between the two brothers. Relations appeared amicable when, in March 979, Eadweard went to visit his brother at Corfe Castle. According to Byrhtferth's *Vita Sancti Oswaldi*, written some twenty years later, as soon as he arrived, he was dragged from his horse by some of Æthelred's *thegns* and killed. He was then buried quickly and without royal honours at Wareham in Dorset. The consensus among later writers is that Æthelred's mother, Ælfthryth, was behind this not-very-subtle method of making sure her son became king. We do not know whether Æthelred was party to the plan – he was no more than thirteen at the time – but the murder of his brother in broad daylight cast a shadow over his reign from the beginning. Dunstan realised his days of influence at court were over. Having placed the crown on Æthelred's head and issued a stern rebuke for the manner in which he had come to the throne, he retired to Canterbury, emerging only in 980 to move Eadweard's body from an unmarked grave in Wareham to a more suitable tomb in Shaftesbury Abbey. He was probably a leading voice in encouraging people to see Eadweard as a martyr and a saint.

Æthelred is usually known as Æthelred the Unready, although a truer translation of the Anglo-Saxon would be Æthelred the Badly Advised.[277] Whether the king or his advisers were to blame for what followed, history has not judged Æthelred kindly. The *Anglo-Saxon Chronicle* presents his reign as a descent into chaos and ruin, and such judgements have persisted. Writing in 1899 with the conviction of the late Victorian era, Professor Meiklejohn stated that 'the care of this great country was left to a weak and cowardly lad and a few of his unworthy favourites.'[278] Winston Churchill judged him 'a weakling, a vacillator, a faithless, feckless creature.'[279] Recent scholarship has sought to re-examine Æthelred's reign but, while finding some mitigation, has not radically altered the picture of a young monarch presiding over a country sliding into chaos and defeat.

Viking raids on England recommenced in 980. Æthelred was fifteen at most. He had been on the throne just a year. The murder of his brother had not been forgotten. He was regarded with suspicion by the clergy and by many of his nobles and seems to have had little confidence in his own abilities. Whether or not the raiders knew that the country was divided and uncertain, from an English point of view the timing could not have been worse. The first raid of any size saw the sacking of Southampton. It was followed by raids on Cheshire and the Isle of Thanet that same year; on the Devon coast and the monastery of St Petroc in Cornwall in 981; and on Portland in 982. No more raids are reported until 988 when Watchet on the north Somerset coast was attacked, but there may have been others in the years between. The raiders were probably Danes, driven out of their country by the policies of their king, Harald Bluetooth, but all their targets were easily accessible from Normandy, where the ports were open to them and where they seem to have based themselves between raids. We do not know what measures, if any, Æthelred took against the raiders, but at court there was fury towards the Normans for their apparent complicity. Hearing of this, Pope John XV sent an envoy to prevent the dispute escalating into war. He was received by Æthelred, who proposed an agreement under which both parties would refrain from hosting each other's enemies. Duke Richard I of Normandy (also known as Richard the Fearless; r.942–96) formally accepted the terms, and the matter was, in theory, settled[280] – although the agreement proved irrelevant because the next wave of attacks, involving far larger numbers, came directly from the north. Perhaps the most important aspect of this story is that it brought the English and Norman courts into contact with each other for the first time. The relationship was strengthened in 1002, when Emma of Normandy, the daughter of Richard I and sister of the then ruling Duke Richard II (also Richard the Good; r.996–1026), became Æthelred's second wife. Emma was to become a pivotal figure in English history.

In 991, Olaf Tryggvason descended on south-east England with a force of ninety-three ships. Tryggvason, who later became King of Norway (r.995–1000), may have shared command with Swein Forkbeard, the King of Denmark. This was still a raid, not an invasion, but it was a large one. Folkestone and Sandwich were attacked, parts of Essex overrun, and Ipswich plundered. At Maldon on the Essex coast, the raiders were met by an English army led by the local *ealdorman*, Byrhtnoth. As immortalised in the Anglo-Saxon poem of the same name, the Battle of Maldon was a hard-fought yet glorious defeat, with English warriors displaying heroism and loyalty to their lord in the face of certain death. The historical reality was less glamorous. Defeat forced Æthelred to negotiate. On the advice of his new Archbishop of Canterbury, Sigeric, he paid Olaf £10,000 in tribute. We do not know the terms of the agreement. Nor do we know if the agreement was honoured. Olaf and his men evidently overwintered in Essex for, early in 992, Æthelred prepared to attack them. He gathered all his ships in the Thames intending to trap and destroy the Viking fleet while it was still in confined coastal waters. According to the *Anglo-Saxon Chronicle*, the plan was betrayed by Ealdorman Ælfric of Hampshire and all Olaf's ships except one managed to escape. In 994, Olaf and Swein returned, this time with ninety-four ships. They failed to take London but ravaged the length of the south coast from Essex to Hampshire. Æthelred was again forced to agree terms. This time, he provisioned their army and paid £16,000 (some sources say £22,000) in tribute. His one condition, taking a lead from Ælfred and Æthelstan, was to insist that Olaf should be baptised and swear never again to raid England.

This agreement gained Æthelred and England a short breathing space, but in 997 the pattern of raiding and violence was quickly re-established. A fleet arrived in the Severn Estuary, raided parts of South Wales, north Somerset, and the northern coasts of Devon and Cornwall. The raiders then rounded Land's End, sailed up the Tamar Estuary, and went overland to ravage the strategically important town of Lydford. In 998, the south coast was the main target, particularly the Isle of Wight. In 999, it was Kent. In 1001, a new fleet attacked Sussex, Dorset and north Somerset. In 1003, Swein Forkbeard returned, and Ealdorman Ælfric – who despite betraying Æthelred's plans in 992 had somehow managed to reinstate himself in the king's good graces – pretended to be sick in order to avoid leading an army against Swein. The following year, Ealdorman Ulfcetel led a valiant but ultimately unsuccessful campaign against Swein's forces in East Anglia. In 1005, there was a brief respite from violence, but only because famine caused the raiders to withdraw.

No English leader could have successfully resisted this continuing onslaught, but Æthelred was unusually bereft of ideas. His main tactic seems to have been paying tribute – what is usually known as Danegeld – to gain a respite from the raids. The *Anglo-Saxon Chronicle* lists payments of £24,000 in 1002, £36,000 in 1007, £48,000 in 1012, and £21,000 in 1014. Paying tribute was not a new idea. Ælfred and Æthelstan had both done the same but, even allowing for exaggeration in the sums reported in the *Chronicle*, the amount of gold and silver Æthelred handed over was vastly greater. On one level, this shows just how prosperous England had become in the fifteen years of peace leading up to 980. At the same time, there is no doubt that the sums Æthelred was forced to raise caused financial pain for everyone from himself downwards. He issued numerous charters granting lands in return for payment in cash or gold; churchmen had to sell their estates; churches had to be stripped of their wealth; and if the king and the Church suffered, there is little doubt that the ordinary people, the farmers, fishermen and merchants, suffered even more.

In theory, by accepting the money, the Vikings were agreeing not only to stop their attacks but also to protect England from attack by other raiding parties, but there is no evidence that this ever happened. Æthelred's other defensive measures included reinforcing a number of strategic *byrig*, such as Christchurch, Hereford, and Wareham, and moving the country's mints to more defensible locations; but there is no sign of any concerted strategy. Nothing he did seems to have instilled confidence in his leadership. There may well have been other senior figures, apart from the treacherous Ælfric, and especially in the former Danelaw, who saw Swein as preferable to Æthelred. Lacking confidence in himself and unsure of how much domestic support he could rely on, Æthelred resorted to desperate measures. In November 1002, he ordered all Danish men in England to be put to death on the grounds that they were plotting against him. We must presume that this meant Danes who had arrived in connection with the current series of raids: those Danes already settled in East Anglia and Jórvik were surely too well integrated by this time to be a target. We do not know how many were killed in what has become known as the St Brice's Day massacre, but it is generally understood that at least one woman, Swein Forkbeard's sister, Gunhilde, was among the dead, and that this may have motivated his return to Britain in 1003. As with the paying of tribute, violence against civilians was nothing new. It was quite simply part of the armoury available to Anglo-Saxon kings – there are numerous records of torture, murder, and blinding – but Æthelred, whether driven by his own insecurity and paranoia or, just possibly, as Martin Ryan has suggested, by a belief that he could protect his people, took matters to extremes.[281]

33 Beyond England I

The existence of a Kingdom of England inevitably had a profound impact on the British Isles as a whole. It was the most powerful entity in the archipelago. It was the richest in terms of its capacity to produce and distribute food and manufactured goods. It was the most economically advanced in its ability to trade internally and externally, to issue and maintain a reliable coinage, and to raise and collect taxes. It was the most socially advanced, with a legally-defined social hierarchy, numerous urban settlements, and a road network connecting them (albeit largely based on the Roman system). It was the most politically advanced, with an established administrative system, a clear division into shires or counties, and, in the shires, with their reeves and their clerks, the faint foreshadowing of a civil service. It was also the most literate part of the British Isles: certainly, its charters, chronicles, commentaries, prefaces, translations, and poems make it the best-documented.

English dominance can create problems for the historian. Scotland, Wales, Ireland, and the Norse kingdoms all have their own, unique stories to tell, but there is a temptation to tell them in relation to England; to regard English achievements as the norm by which developments in other kingdoms should be judged. This, of course, stems from hindsight, from our knowledge of how relations between England and the other component parts of the British Isles developed in later centuries. It is reinforced by the fact that most of the documentary sources on which we rely are written from an English point of view, and thus often contain innate bias or open prejudice.

This issue is probably most acute in dealing with Scotland, where the relationship with England was for many centuries characterised by violence. As early as the seventh century, it was apparent that, while the Anglo-Saxons might be able to conquer Scotland, the Scots could never overrun the Anglo-Saxon kingdoms. Similarly, in the wake of a victory or a treaty, the English king might claim overlordship of Scotland. Yet no Scottish king, however successful, would ever be in a position to demand the submission of England. The lasting importance of the Anglo-Scottish relationship to both parties can add a further level of distortion by focussing attention on southern Scotland and the Borders, where the struggle was fought out, and distracting from developments elsewhere in the kingdom.

The Scottish dynasty that began with Cináed or Kenneth MacAlpín in the 840s lasted through the reigns of fourteen kings until 1034, although in this case dynastic longevity does not indicate political stability. Only three of them enjoyed extended reigns – Causantín II (r.900–43); Kenneth II (r.971–95); and Malcolm II (r.1005–34). Most of the rest survived less than ten years. As in Ireland, tanistry rather than primogeniture was the accepted method of determining the succession, and not one of the fourteen MacAlpin kings came to the throne as the result of father-son succession. Grandsons and cousins succeeded, while sons who might have succeeded and other potential claimants regularly died violent deaths, sometimes killed by Vikings, but more often by rival members of their own clan.

Disputes over the succession intensified when Causantín retired to a monastery in 943, and again after the death of Indulf in 962. In effect, they became an intermittent civil war which outlasted the MacAlpin dynasty and did not end until the death of Macbeth (r.1040–57) and his stepson, Lulach (r.1057–58). It was a violent and unstable period. The entry for 967 in the *Annals of Ulster* says that Dub, son of Malcolm (r.962–67) 'was killed by the Scots themselves.' The *Annals of Tigernach* record Kenneth II, nicknamed 'The Fratricide', being killed 'by his own subjects', and Constantine III (r.995–97) dying in a 'battle between the Scots.' In 1005, Kenneth III (r.997–1005) was killed in battle at Monzievaird in Strathearn by Malcolm II. Some of this can be blamed on the tanistry system, which readily created rival claimants but, as in England, there were also regions and regional leaders resisting the consolidation of a single Scottish kingdom.

The MacAlpin dynasty faced south. In the 840s, Cináed MacAlpín set up his capital at Forteviot, just west of Perth. Tradition has it that he brought the coronation stone of the Dál Riata kings from the west of the country to Scone, just east of Perth, giving it its modern name – the Stone of Scone – and its symbolic importance for Scottish identity. In 848, he moved St Columba's relics from Iona to Dunkeld, some thirty kilometres north of Forteviot, making it the religious centre of his kingdom. Reorientating his kingdom towards the south was a natural decision. The Central Belt, the Lothians, Fife and the coastal lands of Perthshire and Forfar were the most populous parts of the kingdom, and the richest in both agricultural and economic terms. Consolidating their hold on these areas allowed the MacAlpin kings to expand their territory southwards to the Tweed, and into Cumbria in the west. Such successes brought the rewards that ensured the continuing support of the Scottish lords who could otherwise break a king, but the southward orientation of the MacAlpins also led to outbreaks of trouble in the north. It allowed – or even encouraged – certain powerful families to act in their own interests rather than those of the MacAlpin kings or the new kingdom.

The word 'mormaer' is first recorded in 918 to describe a Scottish aristocrat fighting alongside Causantín II at the Battle of Corbridge. Initially, mormaers may have been men appointed by the king to coordinate military matters in the regions, but in some areas the position appears to have become hereditary. In the tenth and eleventh centuries, the region of Moray stretched from Banff and the Moray Firth the full length of the Great Glen to the west coast. The mormaers of Moray were among the most powerful men in the kingdom. The MacAlpin kings regarded them as sub-kings; Icelandic and Norwegian sources call them *jarls*; while some Irish sources actually call them kings. Just as the English kings found it difficult to enforce their will in Northumbria so, in Scotland, Moray was the focus of resistance to central authority. At least three kings – Donald I, Malcolm I, and Kenneth II – were killed during campaigns involving or supported by Moray. The MacAlpins survived, but the threat posed by Moray, and its frequent recurrence over a period of a hundred and fifty years, clearly shows that they did not exert the same degree of control in the north as they did in the south.

Survival was probably the main achievement of the MacAlpin kings but, despite opposition of the kind encountered in Moray, they did manage to make some progress in defining Scottish kingship. In practice, this meant reducing the formal, rather than the practical powers of regional leaders. The wielders of regional power – whether called mormaers, *jarls*, or lords – were required to recognise and submit to the authority of the Crown; while the Crown for its part tacitly acknowledged that rugged geography and difficulties in communication would continue to allow a significant degree of regional autonomy.

We are used to borders between countries being precisely defined and marked with signs and fences, but for centuries the border between England and Scotland was a zone of disputed territory rather than a line on a map. Giric, the ninth-century usurper who began the process of imposing Dál Riata Scottish culture on the Picts, appears to have controlled Edinburgh and the Lothians. Subsequently, the region came under the rule of northern Northumbria/Bernicia. Then, during the reign of Indulf, Edinburgh and (we assume) the Lothians were 'abandoned to the Scots' (see Chapter 32). In the 970s, Kenneth II invaded northern England, probably in an attempt to gain control of the Merse – that region between the Lammermuir Hills and the River Tweed, comprising modern-day Berwickshire and northern Roxburghshire – but his incursion had no lasting impact. However, in 1018, following the Battle of Carham, Malcolm II did manage to push the border further south to the line of the Tweed. It seems likely that what the MacAlpins really wanted was to reach the Tees, thus recovering the whole of the kingdom/province of Bernicia, but it was something they never achieved. On the western side of the country, the frontier was defined by the status of Strathclyde. Eadmund of England overran much of Strathclyde in 945 and then ceded control of the territory to Malcolm I (see Chapter 32). However, with Strathclyde, as with the Lothians and other territories which are reported as being conquered, ruled or ceded, it is uncertain what level of control is implied. Strathclyde (increasingly referred to as Cumbria) clearly retained a royal family and a king. Dyfnwal ab Owain – the son of the Owain who fought and probably died at Brunanburh – ruled from the late 930s until his death in 975, most of the time presumably as a sub-king, owing allegiance to the King of Scotland as his overlord.

Our understanding of overlordship is complicated by events at Chester in 973. Eadgar of England called a meeting shortly after his much-delayed coronation in Bath. With the exception of the Earl of Orkney, all the leading kings of Britain attended. They accepted Eadgar as their overlord and, as a token of their submission, rowed him in a boat on the River Dee. The *Anglo-Saxon Chronicle* says there were six kings but does not name them. Ælfric of Eynesham, writing around the turn of the eleventh century, says there were eight, and specifically mentions the Cumbrians and Scots. John of Worcester, writing at the beginning of the twelfth century, agrees on eight and names them. They include 'Kynath, King of the Scots, Malcolm King of the Cumbrians,' and further down the list 'Dufnal'.[282] Malcolm is Máel Coluim ap Dyfnwal of Strathclyde (r.?973–97). Dufnal is Dyfnwal, his father, who had probably already abdicated but was evidently still regarded as a powerful figure whose submission Eadgar required. The presence and submission of the king and former king indicates that the English still considered that they were the overlords of Strathclyde; and the fact that the Scottish king also submitted to Eadgar suggests that he exercised rights of overlordship in Strathclyde only because the English permitted him to do so.

Chester marks almost the last appearance of Kingdom of Strathclyde/Cumbria on the British stage. The passing of Dyfnwal in 975 is noted in several sources, as is the passing of Malcolm in 997. Malcolm was succeeded by his brother, Owain ap Dyfnwal (r.997–1015). Æthelred of England devastated Cumbria in 1000, perhaps because the Cumbrians offered shelter to Scandinavian raiders. Owain ap Dyfnwal was succeeded by Owain Foel (r.1015–?18), who was probably Malcolm's son, and is recorded as fighting alongside Malcolm II of Scotland at the Battle of Carham in 1018. After that, Strathclyde/ Cumbria, the last remnant of the Old North, effectively disappears as a political entity, apparently becoming integrated into the Kingdom of Scotland.

Sigurd Eysteinsson (Sigurd the Mighty) built the Earldom of Orkney into a political force, but when he died in 892, it nearly foundered. Danish pirates set up raiding bases in Shetland and Orkney, and neither of his immediate successors – his son, Guthorm, and his nephew, Hallad – could cope with the situation. It was another nephew, Einarr Rognvaldsson (more usually Torf- or Turf-Einarr; r.c.895–c.910), who re-established Norwegian control. According to the sagas, Torf-Einarr was the youngest son of a Norwegian *jarl* by a slave girl and nothing much was expected of him. The story is that he arrived from Norway with a single ship and a band of men, drove out the pirates (whose anglicised names were Thorir Treebeard and Kalf the Scurvy), ruled as *jarl* for fifteen years, and founded a dynasty that lasted for nearly three hundred. And while Torf-Einarr was busy in Orkney and Shetland, his half-brother Rollo or

Rolf was settling those lands in the Seine Valley which would soon become the Duchy of Normandy.

Torf-Einarr had three sons. When he died, in or around 910, they assumed joint rule of the Earldom. The two elder sons – Arnkel and Erlend – accompanied Eirik Blodøks to Jórvik for his second brief period of kingship, and both died with him at the Battle of Stainmore in 918. This left the youngest son, Thorfinn Torf-Einarsson as sole *jarl*. Although known to history as 'Skull-Splitter' – a name that survives as a particularly strong beer brewed by the Orkney Brewery – Thorfinn was probably no more violent than any of his family or peers. He ruled without major upheaval or conflict with Scotland until his death about 965, but the sagas then record a complicated story of betrayal and violence among his offspring. One son, Skuli, apparently pledged allegiance to the King of Scotland in order to fight against his brothers. Another son, Ljot, is said to have defeated and killed Skuli in battle somewhere in Caithness, and then to have defeated a Scottish force led by the Mormaer of Moray at the Battle of Skitten Mire, near Wick *c*.943–45. Having fought heroically, Ljot died of his wounds, and the earldom passed to a third son, Hlodvir Thorfinnson. The sagas revel in family feuds, revenge, and heroic deaths, so we cannot be sure how much is true, but we can believe that the Scots sent an army to try to drive the Scandinavians out of Caithness, and that such an expedition could have been led by a powerful figure like the Mormaer of Moray. Hlodvir also seems to have ruled without major incident until his death, apparently from natural causes in his bed, in 991. His wife, Eithne (also Eðnu and Audna), was a member of the ruling family of Osraige, a small kingdom in south-east Ireland, sandwiched between Leinster and Munster. Their son, Sigurd Hlodvirsson, known as Sigurd the Stout (r.991–1014), adopted a more expansionist policy than his father or grandfather.

In 1004 or 1005, a Scottish army led by Malcolm II defeated a Norwegian force that may have been commanded by Sigurd at the Battle of Mortlach in Moray. Although the Scots won the day, the Norwegians did not incur any major losses. They had a fleet waiting offshore and simply sailed away. Nor did the battle have any territorial consequences, but it does indicate the existence of a frontier zone in north-western Scotland, which was important to both parties. This was the area where the Scottish kings and the Orkney *jarls* were most often in conflict for the next several centuries. For Sigurd, and subsequent *jarls*, his mainland possessions were strategically important because they protected Orkney, the heart of the Earldom, from the Scots. His decision to marry Olith, Malcom II's youngest daughter, and the fact that, according to *Njal's Saga*, one of his sisters married a man described as the 'steward' of Caithness, were clearly diplomatic moves intended to ease the tension, but he was not going to give ground.

Sigurd probably took control of the Hebrides before he became *jarl*: the *Irish Annals* identify a period of violence in 986 and 987, although this could be attributable to Danish raiders. In the west of Scotland and the Irish Sea, Sigurd worked closely with a Scots Gaelic chieftain called Gilli, who may have been a member of the Uí Ímair clan and was probably based on the island of Coll. Gilli collected taxes on Sigurd's behalf and acted as his lieutenant or viceroy. That Sigurd regarded the relationship as important is indicated by the fact that he allowed Gilli to marry his other sister, Hvarfloð.

The Hebrides were part of the Kingdom of the Isles, but the Isles was a flexible and uncertain entity. The title of 'King of the Isles' seems to have denoted a claim to overlordship, which may often not have been enforceable. Amlaíb Cuarán (whom we last met being driven out of Jórvik for a second time by Eirik Blodøks in 952) is recorded in the *Irish Annals* as being King of the Isles from about 941 until 980. During that time, he was twice King of Jórvik, from 941 to 944, and from 949 to 952 (see Chapter 32). He was also twice King of Dublin, from 945 to 947, and from 952 to 980. The terminal date of 980 for his rule in Dublin and the Isles is determined by the fact that he is known to been defeated in battle near Tara that year and to have retired afterwards to Iona, where he died in 981. The *Annals* list Amlaíb's successor in the Isles as Maccus mac Arailt. Yet Maccus, described as 'king of many islands', is listed as one of the eight kings who submitted to Eadgar of England and rowed him on the River Dee in 973.[283] So we cannot be sure when Maccus took the title; nor do we know when he relinquished it; but we do know that his successor was his brother, Gofraid mac Arailt.

Then, in the late 980s, Sigurd the Stout and Gilli overran Mann – and probably much else – with the result that, from 990, Gilli was acknowledged as King of the Isles. In 1004, when Sigurd may have been fighting in Moray on the other side of the country, the Outer Hebrides made a bid to break away from his rule, under Ragnall mac Gofraid, another member of the Uí Ímair, who was briefly King of the Isles. This did not last long. Ragnall died in 1005 – whether in battle or of natural causes, we do not know – and Sigurd immediately regained control of the Outer Hebrides. At this point, the *Annals* list him, not Gilli, as King of Mann and the Isles. Why the situation was reversed in this way we, again, do not know, but it does not appear to have affected their cooperation.

This welter of names and dates raises again the question of the nature of kingship and overlordship among the Norse kingdoms. The fact that kings – usually members of the same clan – could succeed and expel one another, and sometimes return for a second term, with such speed and apparent ease suggests that the making or marring of a king was decided by an elite group, probably clan members and their allies. Violence was endemic, but full-scale, destructive civil wars seem to have been more common among the Anglo-Saxon kingdoms where governmental and administrative structures were more developed. Concepts of submission and overlordship were shared across Europe. The nature of the oaths that went with them no doubt varied, and the oaths themselves were frequently violated or ignored, yet submission and overlordship provided a framework for political relationships that was understood, accepted and, in some cases, maintained for generations. In theory, submission had reciprocal benefits. Eadgar's status as king, as well as his ego, were no doubt boosted by the submission of Chester, but the eight kings who rowed him up the river were entitled to expect protection and to receive help if they were invaded by a third party. That, at least, was the theory. Where problems could, and did, arise was in distinguishing whether the oath of submission was to an individual or to his position. As England and Scotland matured as polities, and as they developed their internal administration, they placed increasing emphasis on 'the Crown' as the recipient of oaths and loyalty. The emphasis placed on the spiritual aspect of early Irish kingship (see Chapter 19) may have been intended to achieve the same end by raising the office of king to a higher status than that of normal individuals. In the Norse kingdoms, by contrast, loyalty and overlordship seem to have been regarded as personal rather than institutional, although the Earldom or Orkney, where Norwegian sovereignty was claimed, usually acknowledged, and occasionally enforced, right up until the thirteenth century is a significant exception.

These issues are illustrated in the career of Sigurd the Stout. By 1005, he was potentially one of the most powerful men in the British Isles, but the lands he ruled did not constitute a single entity. He held Orkney and Shetland as a vassal of the King of Norway and acknowledged the fact. Caithness and Sutherland were subject to the overlordship of the King of Scotland. Given that Maccus submitted to Eadgar in 973, Sigurd, as King of Mann, could theoretically have been subject to the overlordship of Æthelred of England – although Sigurd would surely not have accepted the idea, and Æthelred was in no position to enforce it. Sigurd clearly saw power as personal and used a network of marriage alliances – his own and his sisters' – to protect and expand it. He also exploited kinship networks in the traditional Scandinavian manner. He was himself of mixed Irish and Norwegian parentage and, through the tenth and eleventh centuries, the Hiberno-Norse or Norse-Gaels, as they are called, played an increasingly important part in both the Isles and Ireland. Sigurd was fighting alongside another tough Hiberno-Norse leader, Sigtrygg Silkbeard (also Sihtric or Sigtrygg Olafsson), when he was killed in the Battle of Clontarf, north of Dublin, in 1014.

Apart from the brief interlude between 902 and 917 when the Irish regained control, Dublin had been a Scandinavian-ruled kingdom, controlled by the Uí Ímair family since Amlaíb Conung in the 850s. The Battle of Islandbridge in 919 re-established and secured the Scandinavian presence in Dublin and the rest of Ireland, although that does not mean that there was peace. Historians refer to Viking Dublin as a kingdom but, in reality, it was little more than an enclave. Between 921 and 927, Gofraid ua Ímair – who succeeded Sitric Cáech, the victor of Islandbridge – tried to expand the territory. He conducted several aggressive campaigns in the coastal regions north of Dublin, perhaps hoping to create an Irish version of Jórvik. However, he was defeated in a series of encounters with Muirchertach mac Néill, one of the northern Uí Néills and the son of High King Niall Glúndub who had been killed at Islandbridge. Gofraid was unlucky to come up against Muirchertach, one of the most able commanders of the day, but his failures may also reflect the changing nature of the Scandinavian presence in Ireland. Ireland was still a pre-urban society. There were few stone buildings. The only real towns – Dublin, Waterford, Wexford, Limerick, Cork, Galway – were those which formed the nuclei of the Viking enclaves, and they remained small. The ruthless raiders of the ninth century had become traders and town dwellers. They might still raid other parts of the island, but they were not equipped to rule large rural areas where the Irish – unlike some of their Anglo-Saxon counterparts – were not prepared to accept Scandinavian overlordship.

Dublin was bigger than the other Viking settlements; its slave market and its trading links made it more prosperous; and it was more closely connected with mainland Britain because of the pull that Jórvik exerted on the Uí Ímair kings. In just thirty years, between 921 and 951, no fewer than four of them left Dublin – usually passing control to their offspring – and moved to Jórvik, where they sought to create a larger kingdom, perhaps even linking the two centres.[284] Meanwhile, the other Scandinavian settlements remained separate, independent, powerful in their regions, and ready to exploit each other's weaknesses. Gofraid ua Ímair left Dublin in 927, expecting to succeed his father, Sitric, as King of Jórvik but was outmanoeuvred and driven off by Æthelstan (see Chapter 31). He was away only a matter of months but returned to find that the Limerick Vikings had taken advantage of his absence to seize control of Dublin. He expelled them without difficulty, but internecine feuding between Limerick and Dublin lasted ten years. Only in 937 did Gofraid's son and successor, Amlaíb mac Gofraid, decisively defeat Amlaíb Cenncairech of Limerick and destroy his fleet.

Until the ninth century Ireland's social and political structures – the loose but powerful clans; the allegiance-based regional kingdoms – had developed largely unaffected by invasions or, with the exception of the Church, external influences. When the Vikings arrived, they exposed the weaknesses of the Irish regional kingdoms in much the same way as they did with the Anglo-Saxon kingdoms. They were able to raid at will, destroying monasteries, penetrating the Shannon and other river systems to devastate large areas of the central plain. The Irish had no immediate response. The Vikings overwintered in Ireland ten years before they risked doing so in Britain, and their *longphuirt* quickly developed into settlements and towns. These became enclaves, offering safe havens for raiders and economic benefits for the surrounding region, but they did not develop into anything larger. Given the damage done by the Vikings, Ireland's regional kingdoms proved surprisingly resilient. None of them was overrun and none became subject to Scandinavian rule. In this case, the tanistry system, so often the cause of instability, may have proved a positive factor. When clan chiefs, kings and High Kings were killed, as they frequently were, a suitable replacement could be chosen, passing over sons unfit for kingship or too young to rule without a regency.

Throughout the ninth and tenth centuries, the tribal or sub-kingdoms, the *túatha*, continued to compete and fight with each other as they always had, often weakening the regional kingdom of which they were component parts. In the north, when not fighting the Uí Néill, the Ulaid was consumed by what was effectively a prolonged civil war between two rival but related clans: the Dál nAraidi and the Dál Fiatach. The Ulaid and the Uí Néill did set aside their differences for long enough to expel the Vikings from a string of small settlements on Strangford Lough, Lough Neagh, Carlingford Lough, and at Larne. But by 1003, they were at war again, fighting a particularly bloody battle at Craeb Telcha in County Antrim. The king of the Northern Uí Neill was killed, as were many of the senior Ulaid leaders, which led to a revival of the civil war within the Ulaid.

Airgialla, a confederation of nine sub-kingdoms, was independent, while still falling within the Northern Uí Néill sphere of influence. Its northern half, located between the two great clans of the north, became a testing ground where the Ulaid could challenge the Uí Néill ascendancy. Bréifne was another independent kingdom, although enjoying a close relationship with Connacht. In the eighth century, it was ruled by the Uí Briúin, an offshoot of the ruling family of Connacht. In the late ninth or early tenth century, it passed into the hands of another clan, the Ó Ruairc, who retained a powerful position in the region right up to the seventeenth century. The Ó Ruairc kings fought alongside the kings of Connacht in struggles against the Southern Uí Néill in Meath. During a complicated passage in the later tenth century, four Ó Ruairc kings of Bréifne actually became kings of Connacht at the same time – not by right of conquest but because they were chosen through the tanistry system.

In the first half of the ninth century, Munster was possibly the most aggressive of the Irish kingdoms. Fedelmid mac Crimthainn (r.820–46) was a member of the Eóganachta clan who had ruled all or part of Munster from the Rock of Cashel since the sixth century. Although he was an abbot (and possibly a bishop) as well as a king, Fedelmid conducted a campaign of violence and destruction that reached most parts of Ireland. However, his successors were weakened by the Viking presence in Waterford, Cork, and Limerick, allowing the Southern Uí Néill to extract revenge. By 859,

Munster was forced to acknowledge the independence of the small kingdom of Osraige, of which it had traditionally been the overlord. The Southern Uí Néill kept up the pressure and, in 906, forces led by Flann Sinna, then High King, blazed a trail of devastation right across Munster. Under another bishop-king, St Cormac mac Cuilennáin (r.902–08), Munster fought back, inflicting a series of defeats on Flann Sinna, but it proved a temporary revival. In 908, heavily outnumbered by a coalition of forces drawn from Leinster, Connacht, Osraige and Meath, the army of Munster was shattered at the Battle of Bellaghmoon. Cormac was killed and his severed head presented to Flann Sinna. Under Cormac's successor Flaithbertach mac Inmainén (r.908–44), Munster revived, and in 939 he took the unusual step of making an alliance with the Waterford Vikings against the Southern Uí Néill.

Osraige's western border was the River Suir, and its eastern border the River Barrow. Consequently, it was a natural target for Vikings navigating the river systems to access the interior. Several small *longphuirt* were established along the rivers and there was intermittent conflict over several decades. Unusually, while the Viking threat never went away, Osraige seems to have come out on top. This was largely due to Cerball mac Dúnlainge, who fought against the Vikings of Dublin (see Chapter 30) before he made an alliance with Amlaíb Conung (see Chapter 29). Together, they mounted a series of raids on the lands of High King Máel Sechnaill in Meath, for the most part successfully, although Cerball was sometimes defeated and forced to pay tribute. Cerball's main achievement, in a reign that lasted over forty years, from 843 to 888, was to take Osraige from a being a dependency of Munster to becoming one of Ireland's most influential states; an achievement consolidated by his descendants in the tenth and eleventh centuries.

Leinster also had Viking neighbours – Wexford on its southern border and Dublin to the north – which may have been good for the kingdom's economy, but inevitably weakened the position of the ruling Laigin clan. The Laigin had been driven out of what became Meath by the Southern Uí Néill, probably at the beginning of the sixth century (see Chapter 23). They retreated to Leinster, but in the eighth century underwent their own north-south split, with the northern branch of the clan, the Uí Dúnlainge, emerging as dominant, and remaining so until the eleventh century. Viking Dublin occupied territory that had previously belonged to both Leinster and Meath, and both kingdoms felt the threat of potential Viking expansion, but Leinster, although independent, was too weak to act on its own and most of the time the Uí Dúnlainge followed the lead taken by Southern Uí Néill in Meath. By contrast, Meath was central to the narrative of Irish history during this period in two ways. Although encroached on by Viking Dublin, which was a constant political threat, it had benefited from Dublin's wealth and had a stronger economy than the other regional kingdoms. Politically, it was the centre of Southern Uí Néill power, but because it included the Hill of Tara, the traditional seat of the High Kings of Ireland, it also carried a latent spiritual significance – even though the concept of High Kingship was probably not as fundamental to early Irish history as many medieval sources suggest (see Chapter 19). By the ninth century, it had evolved into an assertion of overlordship, only later, and intermittently, becoming a claim to actual authority and thus an excuse for raiding or invasion. Although Tara was in the lands of the Southern Uí Néill, the Northern and Southern Uí Néill took the High Kingship in alternation (see Chapter 23), using the title to strengthen their claims to antiquity and legitimacy, until that succession was interrupted at the beginning of the eleventh century (see Chapter 35).

Of the four main regions of the British Isles, Wales suffered least from the depredations of the Vikings. There were raids and there were settlements – Anglesey, St Davids, and Swansea appear to have been the largest – but these were overwintering bases or small, commercial colonies. They were smaller and shorter-lived than the settlements in Ireland, and never rose to the status of kingdoms. Consequently, Viking activity did not have the same impact on the economic and political life of the Welsh kingdoms. Rhodri Mawr of Gwynedd was the man credited with driving off attacks on Anglesey in 854 and 856, and again in 872 (see Chapter 28). He was also the first to move towards a unified Wales.

In the early decades of the ninth century, there were nine kingdoms in Wales, most of them with long-established ruling families, often related to each other by marriage, although without the intensity of the Irish clan structure. Primogeniture was not universal among the Welsh kingdoms, but it was more common than in Ireland, and Rhodri succeeded his father, Merfyn Frych, as King of Gwynedd in 844. His mother was the sister of Cyngen ap Cadell, king of neighbouring Powys, and a member of the Gwertherion dynasty, which liked to trace its origins back to Vortigern in the fifth century. In 854, Cyngen went on a pilgrimage to Rome – the first Welsh ruler to do so – apparently hoping to put an end to the still not-fully-healed breach between Celtic and Roman Christianity. He died there in 855, leaving no heir. The throne of Powys passed to Rhodri, and with it also control of the smaller Kingdom of Maelienydd on Powys' southern border.

An even more complex set of circumstances brought Rhodri control of the Kingdom of Seisyllwg, on the southern border of Gwynedd and Powys. The King of Seisyllwg, Meurig ap Dyfnwal, had two children: a son called Gwgon, and a daughter named Angharad, who was married to Rhodri. Meurig died in 870 or 871 and the kingdom passed to Gwgon, who drowned – or perhaps was drowned – within a year of his accession. Rhodri had no claim on the kingship, but his children with Angharad did. The eldest son, Anarawd, was passed over as he was expected to succeed Rhodri in Gwynedd and Powys, but it was agreed that the second son, Cadell, should succeed to Seisyllwg. This gave Rhodri effective control of about two-thirds of what we now regard as Wales and, because Seisyllwg commanded a long stretch of Cardigan Bay's coastline, it greatly increased his ability to counter Viking attacks. Rhodri's achievements were remarkable – news of them even reached the court of the Charles the Bald – but they alarmed the neighbouring kingdoms of Dyfed and Brycheiniog.

Rhodri had only a short time to enjoy the full extent of his power. The border between the Welsh and Anglo-Saxon kingdoms was defined by Offa's Dyke and, while there were raids in both directions, it was generally respected. However, relations between Powys and Mercia were strained because of Mercia's claims to overlordship, which Powys naturally disputed – occasionally sending raiding parties across Offa's Dyke to emphasise the fact. In 878 it was the Mercians, probably led by Ceolwulf II, the puppet King of Mercia installed by Halfdan and Guthrum (see Chapter 30), who raided deep into Wales, perhaps even reaching Anglesey. This may have been a revenge raid, or it may have been stimulated by the kings of Dyfed and Brycheiniog, who feared Rhodri was becoming too powerful. Whatever the case, Rhodri was killed, and although his death was avenged by his son, Anarawd, at the Battle of Conwy in 881 – a decisive victory in that it finally ended Mercian claims to overlordship – by that time Rhodri's kingdoms had been divided among his sons and any impetus towards a unified Wales had been lost.

A complex ballet of shifting allegiances followed. Dyfed, the most powerful of the southern kingdoms, joined its neighbours Brycheiniog and Gwent, in submitting to King Ælfred as way of protecting themselves from the ambitions of the sons of Rhodri. Gwynedd, ruled by Anarawd, and Powys, now ruled by Rhodri's third son, Merfyn, countered by making an alliance with Jórvik as protection from Mercia and the growing power of Ælfred, but then, as the power of Wessex grew, changed their minds. Whatever their relationships with each other, the Welsh kings were conscious of the growing power of the Anglo-Saxon kingdoms, and by the second decade of the tenth century, they were willing to submit, first to Æthelflaed of Mercia and then to Eadweard of Wessex. Later, they submitted to Æthelstan, agreed to pay him heavy tribute, spent time as 'guests' at his court, accompanied him to Scotland, and, most important of all, remained neutral at Brunanburh (see Chapter 28). For the moment, relations between the Welsh kings and the King of England were stable, if one-sided.

The next figure with the potential to unify Wales was Hywel of Dyfed, later known as Hywel Dda or Hywel the Good. Once again, complex ties among the ruling families played an essential part. Hywel was the son of that Cadell whom we saw installed as King of Seisyllwg in 872, and thus Rhodri Mawr's grandson. He married Elen, the daughter and only child of Llywarch ap Hyfaidd, King of Dyfed (r.893–904). When Llywarch died in 904, the kingdom passed to his brother Rhodri ap Hyfaidd, but Rhodri died the following year, leaving no heir. Although there is no evidence, long-standing tradition has it that Hywel ('the Good' notwithstanding) organised Rhodri's death. All one can say is that the timing was convenient. Dyfed passed to Hywel. Soon afterwards, in 909, Cadell died, leaving Hywel and his brother, Clydog, as joint rulers of Seisywllg. When Clydog died in 920, Hywel brought Dyfed and Seisywllg together into a single kingdom with the name of Deheubarth.

Even before the creation of Deheubarth, Hywel had made a formal submission to Eadweard, and he subsequently submitted to Æthelstan at Eamont Bridge. About 928, he made a pilgrimage to Rome, and on his return his name appears as a witness on a number of English charters, indicating his presence at Æthelstan's court. He also accompanied Æthelstan on his invasion of Scotland in 934, and the relationship appears to have been closer than Æthelstan enjoyed with other subject kings. This

Map 29 Ireland, Scotland, Wales, and the Kingdom of the Isles in the 10th and Early 11th Centuries

did not please the anonymous writer of *Armes Prydein*, a poem possibly composed at St Davids around 930, which called for all Celtic-speaking people to unite against the Anglo-Saxon menace. Yet Hywel's pragmatic approach yielded practical results. When he gained control of Brycheiniog in or around 930, Æthelstan raised no objection. His move into Gwynedd and Powys in 942 was conducted in a manner calculated to appear helpful to Eadmund, Æthelstan's successor. That same year, Hywel's cousin, Idwal Foel decided to rebel against English overlordship, perhaps believing that Eadmund was weaker than his predecessor. This was a misjudgement. Eadmund invaded and killed Idwal, which allowed Hywel to force Idwal's sons, Iago and Ieuaf, into exile and assume the kingship of Gwynedd himself. At the same time, he moved against his other uncle, Llywelyn ap Merfyn, King of Powys, who may have supported Idwal's rebellion. These various manoeuvres left him ruler of the whole of Wales with the exception of Morgannwg and Gwent in the far south.

Hywel was essentially a warlord, but he had sound political instincts. Wales remained a wholly agrarian society – there were small settlements and 'capitals' where kings and sub-kings based themselves, but since the demise of Roman Caerwent there had been no towns. Hywel had to find ways of bringing his collection of kingdoms together. One initiative was to introduce coinage and a money economy. His friendship with Æthelstan meant that he was able to use the mint at Chester to produce his own silver pennies, but they do not seem to have been in wide circulation during his lifetime. More important was his law code. Learning from Æthelstan, Hywel saw a common legal framework as a way of unifying the different and disparate kingdoms he now ruled. He organised a meeting of churchmen and other senior figures at Whitland in Dyfed in 930, which resulted in the *Cyfraith Hywel* (*The Laws of Hywel*). It was not a new code, but rather an attempt to bring together and systematise existing laws and customs from different parts of Wales. The legally recognised classes of society were listed – the king (*rhi*) and those lords to whom tribute was payable (*brenin*); the aristocracy and yeomanry (*boneddigion*); the serfs or villeins (*taeogion*) who were bound to a member of *boneddigion* – and their rights spelt out. There was a separate category for people born outside the Welsh kingdoms (*alltudion*). Slaves (*caethion*) had no rights at all. Blood money (*galanas*) was defined, and rights of inheritance and succession set out. Welsh law was generally less favourable to women than Irish Brehon law.

Hywel died in 950. Deheubarth – now including Brycheiniog, and the smaller kingdoms of Maelienydd and Buellt – survived, although ruled jointly by his three sons. Gwynedd reverted to the sons of Idwal Foel, while in the south the Kingdom of Morgannwg, comprising the Glywysing and Gwent, remained independent. Hywel may have simplified the political map of Wales, but the strength of regional dynasties and the complications of inheritance and succession meant that a unified polity remained elusive. Of Hywel's three sons, Owain (r.950–87) lived longest, at some stage regaining control of Powys, and also commissioning the *Annales Cambriae*, an essential source document for the period. It was Owain's son, Maredudd ab Owain, who in 986 conquered Gwynedd and the following year, when his father died, inherited Deheubarth, effectively recreating Hywel's collection of kingdoms.

However, in Wales as in England, the 980s saw a new wave of Viking attacks, effectively preventing any attempt by Maredudd to unify his various kingdoms. The first Viking intervention, in 979, was by invitation. Like so many ruling families, that in Gwynedd was divided. Hywel ap Ieuaf, the grandson of Idwal Foel, enlisted Scandinavian aid, possibly from Mann, to oust his uncle and take control of the kingdom. In 985, he was succeeded by his brother, Cadwallon. In 986, Cadwallon was expelled by Maredudd, but within a year Anglesey suffered its heaviest ever Viking raid with over 2,000 men taken as slaves. In 988, there were raids on monasteries along the Cardigan Bay coast, and in 989, Maredudd was forced to raise a penny poll tax to buy off his attackers. That may have gained him a breathing space but, in 993, Anglesey was raided yet again and, in 999, St Davids was attacked and its bishop killed. Nor did the Vikings limit their attacks to Maredudd's domains. In 988, they attacked sites in the south of Morgannwg and, in 997, sailed up the Severn Valley, raiding as they went. Anglesey may well have acted as a buffer zone, nominally under Maredudd's control, but with parts used by the raiders as a temporary camp. In the end, whether because of the strength of the opposition, or, more likely, because they did not think it worth their while, the Vikings did not establish any long-term colonies in Wales. Maredudd died in 999. Gwynedd returned for a third time to the descendants of Idwal Foel, and another attempt to bring all parts of Wales together into a single kingdom failed."

34   Dynasties and Directions

The story of England in the eleventh century is traditionally told with the full benefit of hindsight, as if the Norman Conquest was somehow inevitable, and the events leading up to it merely a preparation. Winston Churchill's *History of the English-Speaking Peoples* typifies this approach. His chapter 'The Saxon Dusk' suggests that Anglo-Saxon England was suffering from a moral decay that made invasion not only inevitable but necessary.[285] It is a view which is not borne out by the facts. For the first half of the century, the greatest external threat was not the Normans, but the Danes – indeed, Æthelred looked to Normandy for support in his struggle against the Danes – and the greatest internal threat was not moral decay, but cultural and political division.

While still in his teens, possibly in 985, Æthelred married Ælfgifu (or Elgiva), probably the daughter of Thored, the *ealdorman* of York. They had ten children, six sons and four daughters, all of whom were still alive when she died in 1002. Shortly after her death, Æthelred married Emma of Normandy. It was the first time an English king had not taken an English wife. Emma was some twenty years younger than her new husband and, as he had six sons still living, she would not have been expected to provide an heir. It was a political marriage, perhaps intended to seal some treaty or agreement between the Norman and English courts, but Emma did give Æthelred three more children – two sons and a daughter – and, by doing so, changed the course of English history.

Æthelred struggled to contain wave after wave of Danish raiders and was forced to buy them off at great cost both financially and in terms of prestige (see Chapter 32). In 1009, the situation deteriorated still further. Æthelred imposed a special tax in order to build and man a hundred ships but, in one of those episodes that seem to have dogged his reign, everything went wrong. The commander of one of the ships, Brihtric – brother of Eadric Streona, *ealdorman* of Mercia, of whom we shall hear more – denounced another, a South Saxon *thegn* called Wulfnoth, for some kind of criminal activity.[286] Æthelred banished Wulfnoth, who immediately took off with twenty of the new ships and began ravaging the south coast. Æthelred sent the rest of the ships after him, but they were caught in bad weather and driven ashore, where Wulfnoth succeeded in burning a number of them. Æthelred ordered the remaining ships to withdraw to London, which meant that when a new and extremely powerful Danish force under the command of Thorkell the Tall arrived in Kent, it was able to land unopposed.

Once ashore, Thorkell and his men swept across southern England, looting and burning at will, still apparently unopposed. The *Anglo-Saxon Chronicle* claims that this was because Eadric Streona advised Æthelred against direct confrontation and prevented the county *fyrd* from coming to grips with the enemy. It was bad advice. By 1011, less than two years after he had landed, Thorkell controlled all of England east of a line between the Wash and Weymouth except London. Æthelred was forced to negotiate and managed to raise the enormous sum of £48,000 to meet Thorkell's demands. Part of this sum was intended to ransom the Archbishop of Canterbury, Alphege (or Alfheah), but when he refused to be ransomed, Thorkell's men pelted him 'with bones and the heads of cattle' before despatching him with an axe.[287] The *Chronicle* suggests that Thorkell, who seems to have been a Christian, was so disgusted that he suddenly switched sides, bringing forty-five ships and their crews to enter Æthelred's service.

Thorkell's defection did little to relieve the pressure on Æthelred for, in 1013, Swein Forkbeard returned with a new army, and this time he intended conquest. Already King of Denmark and overlord of much of Norway, he wanted to be King of England as well. He entered the Humber Estuary and sailed up the River Trent, beaching his ships at Gainsborough in Lincolnshire in the heart of the Danelaw. Within days, East Anglia, the Five Boroughs, Eastern Mercia, and what had been Jórvik had all acclaimed him as king. Swein drove south, forcing Oxford and Winchester to surrender, before circling back to besiege London. Defended by Æthelred and Thorkell, London resisted, so Swein turned west and overran those parts of Wessex that had not already submitted to him, before advancing on London again. Æthelred withdrew to Greenwich where his fleet – or what was left of it – was based. He sent Emma and his younger children to the court of her brother, Duke Richard II, in Normandy. Fearing what Swein might do if he was held at bay any longer, London surrendered, leaving Æthelred powerless. He followed his wife into exile and, on Christmas Day 1013, the *witan* formally proclaimed Swein King of England. The country had undoubtedly been weakened by Thorkell's rampaging over the previous four years, but Swein's tactical skill had brought him the crown in a campaign lasting barely six months. His reign, however, lasted barely six weeks. Returning to his military headquarters at Gainsborough, where his son was guarding both the fleet and the many hostages taken during the campaign, he fell from his horse and died.

The son in question was Cnut, later known as Cnut the Great. The English Danes immediately declared him King of England in succession to his father. Cnut's elder brother, Harald, had remained in Denmark, looking after the kingdom in Swein's absence, and the Danish Danes unsurprisingly chose him to succeed his father as Harald II of Denmark. To divide inherited kingdoms in this way was not unusual – the Welsh kingdoms were shared out among the sons of Rhodri the Great and Hywel Da – but in this case there were complications. When the members of the *witan*, who were overwhelmingly Anglo-Saxon, gathered to choose a king, as was their traditional right, they called for the return of Æthelred – although it was a qualified call: 'no lord was dearer to them than their rightful lord, if only he would govern the kingdom more justly than he had done in the past.'[288] Æthelred gave fulsome assurances that 'everything should be forgiven', returned to England, raised the *fyrd*, and advanced on Gainsborough. Cnut realised he did not have the strength to meet Æthelred's army and immediately put to sea. However, before returning to Denmark, he mutilated the hostages taken by his father – cutting off hands, ears, and noses – and landed them at Sandwich.

England was deeply divided – politically, culturally, and linguistically. Eadgar had attempted to build bridges between the Anglo-Saxon and Danish communities, but his laws and his initiatives lay buried under years of raids and invasions. This was a pivotal moment. Having forced Cnut to flee and regained his throne, and with the added advantage that the Danish community felt abandoned following Cnut's hasty departure, Æthelred had a unique opportunity to make a gesture of peace and conciliation. With his unerring instinct for doing the wrong thing, he did the opposite. He moved into the Danelaw, looting and burning, and putting to death anyone suspected of supporting Swein or Cnut. Everything was clearly not forgiven. The immediate impact was to alienate Thorkell – some of whose men may have been mistakenly, or even treacherously, killed in the reprisals – who now changed sides again, deserting Æthelred and offering his services to Cnut.

The English-Danish divide became even more complicated in 1015, when Æthelred called 'a great council' at Oxford. Among those attending were two *thegns* from the Danelaw, Siferth and Morcar. They had intended to beg the king's forgiveness for supporting Cnut but were murdered by Eadric Streona – whether on Æthelred's orders or not we do not know. Æthelred moved to confiscate their estates, but was forestalled by his son, Edmund, who not only took possession of their estates, but also of Siferth's widow, Edith, whom he married. Having established himself as a landowner and figurehead, he sought the backing of the English Danes, who declared him overlord of the whole of the Danelaw. By this time, four of Æthelred's sons by his first marriage were dead and Edmund was his heir apparent, so the rift was serious. How it would have developed, and whether it would have led to civil war, we can only guess, for in September 1015 Cnut returned.

We know little of Cnut's early life beyond the fact that he was the younger of Swein Forkbeard's two sons and that he was a Christian from birth – although this is not always evident from his conduct. He was born somewhere between 980 and the mid-990s. The German chronicler, Thietmar of Merseburg, identifies his mother as the unnamed sister of the Polish king, Bolesław I, but this is not certain. All we know of his education is a single sentence in the thirteenth-century Icelandic *Flateyjarbók* making the strange claim that he was taught by Thorkell the Tall. However, once Cnut appears in the historical record, we can watch him developing from an inexperienced prince into a powerful warrior king, ruthless when necessary, but also with statesmanlike qualities and a broader vision of the world than his Anglo-Saxon predecessors.

Cnut's rapid retreat in 1013 had laid the English Danes open to Æthelred's savage retributions, and he realised that he could not rely on their support this time. In a bold and unexpected move, he landed more than two hundred longships and perhaps ten thousand men at Poole Harbour, in the heart of Wessex, the homeland of the Anglo-Saxon kings. Among his commanders were Thorkell and a man called Eirik Hákonarson, who had been a Danish viceroy in Norway and had travelled the Russian river systems to Kiev and beyond. Faced with the threat of Cnut, Edmund and Æthelred were quickly reconciled. Edmund raised an army from the London region. Eadric Streona raised another army in Mercia, but as soon as conflict threatened, Eadric and his army defected to

Cnut, forcing Edmund to withdraw. By the end of 1015, Cnut had secured the submission of Wessex, apparently without any pitched battles. At the beginning of 1016, he moved north of the Thames and blazed a trail across Warwickshire. Edmund was reduced to desperate measures. Together with Uhtred, the Earl of Northumbria, he ravaged all those parts of western Mercia owing allegiance to Eadric, partly to deny Cnut any advantage from Eadric's defection, and partly as a matter of revenge. Cnut was undeterred. He bypassed Mercia and the Danelaw, and drove northwards into Northumbria, where he forced the submission of Uhtred – who was then killed by his own people – before rejoining his fleet and sailing south to Greenwich.

Edmund reached London before Cnut, but as soon as he arrived Æthelred died after a reign which – ignoring Swein's brief interruption – had lasted thirty-eight years. During that time England had gone from the stability and prosperity of Eadgar's reign to being a failed and conquered state. In large measure, this was due to the revival of Viking raids and the subsequent Danish invasions, but Æthelred's indecisive and ineffectual character – and also a certain amount of plain bad luck – undoubtedly contributed to the disaster. On Æthelred's death, London and the southeast, the only areas that had not submitted to Cnut, naturally declared for Edmund. A version of the *witan* representing the rest of the country met at Southampton and declared for Cnut. The size of Cnut's army is indicated by the fact that he was able to besiege London by building an earthwork that encircled the town. Edmund somehow managed to slip away to gather support in Wessex. Cnut followed with part of his army. Edmund evaded him and managed to raise the siege of London but suffered so many casualties that he had to return to Wessex to regroup. Cnut launched another attempt to take London. It failed, and he, too, suffered significant casualties and was forced to withdraw to Suffolk. Eadric Streona suddenly redefected to the English side – or appeared to do so. Edmund can only have accepted him out of desperation, for in the battle that followed – variously known as Ashington, Assandun, or Essendune, and located sometimes in Essex and sometimes in the Forest of Dean – Eadric betrayed the English once again, leaving the field at a crucial moment and allowing Cnut's men to win a decisive victory. Edmund was wounded but escaped to Wessex. Cnut pursued him and in October 1016, after several skirmishes, they met on an island in the River Severn, to sign the Treaty of

Deerhurst. From an English point of view, this turned the clock back a hundred and forty years to the time when Ælfred and Guthrum divided England between them. On this occasion, it was agreed that Cnut should rule north of the Thames, and Edmund to the south. Deerhurst is noteworthy as the last time that the territory we know as England was formally divided into separate kingdoms.

Within a month Edmund died, probably from the wounds he suffered at Ashington, although there were rumours that he was murdered. He was buried at Glastonbury Abbey and given the sobriquet 'Ironside' to reflect his unwavering resistance to the Danes in what was probably an unwinnable war. Cnut called a meeting of the *witan*, which unanimously declared him King of England. They had no real alternative. Edmund had two sons, but they were both infants. Cnut sent them to Sweden, probably with instructions that they should disappear. In the end, and no doubt with help, they made their way to the court of Iaroslav (or Yaroslav) I in Kiev. Their survival would have an impact in years to come. Edmund also had a brother, Eadwig, who had taken little or no part in the fighting. Cnut initially banished and outlawed him, then later had him killed, probably for stirring up trouble in the west country. Emma's two sons by Æthelred – Edward and Ælfred – had no following and joined the rest of the family at the ducal court in Normandy. They, too, would reappear.

Cnut's coronation took place at St Paul's in London in January 1017. England had a Danish king for the second time in three years. He was probably in his late twenties and there was every possibility that he would establish a Danish dynasty which would last for the foreseeable future. He already had two sons by Ælfgifu of Northampton, the daughter of the *ealdorman* of Northumbria, whom he had married in 1013, and he had no obvious political challengers. It was only a series of unforeseen events affecting a handful of individuals that caused the Danish line to fail and, ultimately, open the way for the Norman invasion. Had it been otherwise, England could have become politically and culturally bound to Denmark and Scandinavia rather than Normandy and France.

By the end of the seventh century, the Germanic immigrants we have been calling Anglo-Saxons had established cultural and political dominance in what was to become England. Externally, they were challenged by 'Celtic' incursions from Scotland, Wales, and even Cornwall. Internally, there was almost continual warfare and raiding of a political rather than cultural or racial character. In the wake of the Great Heathen Army and the treaty agreed between Ælfred and Guthrum, there was considerable Danish settlement, mainly in those areas where Danish migrants had established themselves in earlier centuries. The new inhabitants of these areas, the Danelaw, proved slow to integrate and often manifested separatist tendencies. To some extent, this may have been culturally and linguistically based, but it was certainly the cause of much bitterness and division. Swein Forkbeard took advantage of this situation when he used the Danelaw to launch his invasion. Cnut did not, and there were sound practical reasons for his not doing so, but his decision gives us a clue to the nature of his kingship. Cnut and his father were Danes and conquerors, but they did not represent a new wave of migration. The great age of migrations was over. It is possible to argue that the next mass movement of people with the potential to alter the balance of the population of Britain did not occur until the post-Imperial migrations of the mid-twentieth century. Cnut's aim was to establish personal and dynastic rule over the English. In that sense, he may appear similar to the Viking rulers of Jórvik or Dublin, although their interests centred on power and wealth: they had little interest in governing. Cnut did. His ambitions were on a grand scale, and he very nearly achieved them.

Winston Churchill, patriotically English to the last, states that 'Edmund Ironside died, and the whole realm abandoned itself to despair.'[289] At this distance, we can have no idea what people's expectations were, but we can guess that they did not want more violence. Cnut's immediate concern was security. He did what was necessary to secure his position, while trying to assure the wider population of his *bona fides*. During the first year of his reign, he ordered the deaths of several senior regional figures whom he feared might stir up trouble or favour the House of Wessex, but he did not order the kind of general retribution that Æthelred had visited upon the Danelaw. He divided England into four administrative regions. He gave Northumbria to Eirik Hákonarson; East Anglia to Thorkell; and Mercia to Eadric Streona. Initially, he kept Wessex, where trouble was most likely to arise, under his personal rule, but then divided it into two. The eastern part was administered by a man named Æthelweard; the western part by Godwine, a South Saxon *thegn* – who may have been the son of that Wulfnoth who had made off with twenty of Æthelred's ships. This may reasonably be termed a fateful appointment.

Within six months of his coronation, Cnut had married Æthelred's widow, Emma. Ælfgifu, his first wife, was not put aside or forced into a nunnery: at a later stage, Cnut appointed her regent of Norway. It seems that he simply ignored his existing marriage and took a second wife who would be politically and dynastically more useful. Such events may have been more common than we realise. Marriage to Emma was clearly intended to signal a wish to maintain stability and continuity at court and in the country. It also effectively neutralised any threat from Normandy which might champion her sons by Æthelred. Emma was a powerful figure in her own right, proud of her own Danish heritage, and she may have found a warrior king some years younger than herself preferable to the ineffectual Æthelred. All sources suggest that it was a happy marriage, and it produced a son, Harthacnut, and a daughter, Gunhilda. In 1017, Cnut made a further move to secure his position by dealing with Eadric Streona. Some years later, about 1042, Emma commissioned the *Encomium Emmae Reginae*, a chronicle of the events of her life. It naturally portrays her and her offspring in a positive light and is often unreliable. It does, however, include some good stories, one of which tells how Cnut one day was speaking to Eirik Hákonarson and Eadric Streona. He told Eirik to pay 'this man what we owe him'. Eirik picked up an axe and decapitated Eadric on the spot.[290] Cnut also outlawed and then executed Æthelweard, his representative in eastern Wessex who may have been Eadric's brother, presumably for trying to organise some kind of uprising.

The leading clerical figure in England was Archbishop Wulfstan of York – sometimes called Wulfstan II to distinguish him from the earlier Wulfstan of York, who championed Eirik Blodøks in the 940s. Wulfstan II was strongly influenced by the Benedictine Reforms, believing that the promotion of Christianity, the protection of the Church, and the promulgation of just laws were essential duties for a king. He was also a master of Anglo-Saxon prose. He had written several law codes for Æthelred and wrote several more for Cnut – even if Cnut was literate, he may not have been able to read and write Anglo-Saxon. Cnut's codes, no doubt influenced by Wulfstan, revived many of the articles, and the conciliatory spirit, of those issued by Eadgar nearly fifty years before. The earliest focussed on preventing the abuse of power by lords and landowners, suggesting that Cnut was actively seeking to reassure the population of his benevolence. Wulfstan's acuity is shown by the fact that the laws he drafted lasted into the post-Conquest era, many of them remaining current in the reign of Henry I (r.1100–135).

In 1018, Cnut raised the immense sum of £82,500 in taxes, an indication of the economic strength of the kingdom. This was undoubtedly unpopular, but there was no active resistance, and the fact that he used the money to pay off the fleet and the fighting men who had helped him to power demonstrates the strength of his position. He kept only forty ships and their crews as a standing defence force, a much smaller number than Æthelred had maintained. By late 1019, he felt secure enough to leave Emma in control, while he returned to Denmark to claim the Danish throne following the unexpected death of his brother, Harald. He took only nine ships, suggesting that he had been invited by the Danish nobility and did not anticipate any opposition. It seems to have been a trouble-free accession. Among those accompanying Cnut was Godwine, whose abilities impressed the king so much that, once the formalities were over and they returned to England in 1020, he was made Earl of Wessex.

Denmark did, however, create problems in the years that followed. Possibly in 1021, Cnut came to suspect Thorkell of fomenting trouble among the English Danes and exiled him to Denmark. Predictably, Thorkell began stirring up trouble there. Cnut sailed to Denmark to confront him, quite unusually taking English forces with him, and fought a series of battles, in which Godwine again distinguished himself. Eventually, in 1023, Cnut and Thorkell reached a negotiated settlement, after which Thorkell simply disappears from the historical record. Cnut sent his son by Emma, Harthacnut, who can have been no more than five, to be Crown Prince in Denmark, and appointed his sister's husband, a Danish noble called Ulf Jarl, as regent. In 1025, using a joint Swedish and Norwegian attack as an excuse, Ulf proclaimed Harthacnut as King of Denmark, which left him a still more powerful regent. Cnut again sailed his English fleet to Denmark and joined with the Danes under Ulf to face the Swedes and Norwegians at the Battle of Helgeaa (or Holy River) in southern Sweden. Neither side was a clear victor, but Cnut drove the Swedish and Norwegian ships eastwards into the Baltic and blockaded them there. The Swedes simply gave up and went home; the Norwegians were forced to abandon their ships and trudge through forests and over mountains to their homeland. Many of them died on the way. Cnut emerged from the conflict as the most powerful ruler in Scandinavia; and in his native Denmark, his position was not only re-established but strengthened – which allowed him to have Ulf killed.

As King of England, Cnut ruled a country that was richer and more powerful than Denmark. Yet he was a Dane, Denmark was important to him, and he was prepared to expend time, effort, and English resources to maintain his position there. This could have made him unpopular, but it was done in a clever and calculated way. In 1021, Cnut's decision to exile Thorkell rather than challenge him directly avoided any confrontation on English soil that might have allowed Thorkell to exploit the English-Danish divide. Then Cnut used English soldiery and the English fleet to secure his position in Denmark. Instead of making him unpopular, the fact that the familiar roles were now reversed and English forces were winning victories in Scandinavia seems to have gained him prestige.

In 1028, Cnut invaded Norway. He set sail for Trondheim, leaving Godwine, who had rapidly become his most powerful and influential adviser, in effective control of England. The King of Norway, Olaf II Haraldsson (later St Olaf or St Olave) put up little resistance and fled. Cnut now ruled England and most of Scandinavia. He had intended Hákon Eiríksson, the son of Eirik Hákonarson to whom Cnut had entrusted Northumbria, to be his viceroy in Norway, but Hákon drowned before he could play his part in Cnut's great design. In his place, Cnut installed his eldest son, Sweyn Knutsson, who was probably thirteen or fourteen, together with his first wife, Ælfgifu of Northampton. It was probably his greatest strategic mistake. Sweyn and Ælfgifu instituted a regime of high taxes and oppressive laws, alienating the Norwegian nobles, who united against them and, in 1034, forced them to flee to Denmark. But the resurgent Norwegians, led by Magnus Olafsson (also Magnus I, or Magnus the Good) were not going to give up and, in 1035, launched an invasion of Denmark, at which point the news of Cnut's death arrived.

Cnut had arrived as a conqueror, and there had been plenty of bloodletting during the early years of his rule, but while ruthless where his personal political survival was concerned, he proved to be a king who brought a degree of peace and stability. There was an unusual duality about his character. Faced with a potential insurrection in Wessex or East Anglia, he would order the leaders killed, but then choose to defuse the situation by settling his own followers in the region rather than taking revenge on the population as a whole. He could be a statesman, travelling to Rome for the coronation of Conrad II as Holy Roman Emperor in 1027, gaining the friendship of the Emperor and the King of Burgundy, and negotiating privileges for English pilgrims. Then, on his return, he could revert to his warrior persona and invade Norway. For a brief period, England was politically part of Europe, the hub of a Scandinavian Empire. Nor was Cnut's empire a collection of territories held under different allegiances like those of Sigurd the Stout. Cnut owed allegiance to no one. He was a ruler of European significance. But, like other empire builders, he was not able to secure the future of his creation.

When Cnut died in 1035, there were five potential claimants to succeed him: Harthacnut, his son by Emma; Sweyn Knutsson and Harald Harefoot,[291] his sons by Ælfgifu; and, with a less immediate claim, Edward and Ælfred, Emma's sons by Æthelred. When they married, Cnut and Emma had agreed that any sons they had together would take precedence over his sons with Ælfgifu. This meant that the English throne should have passed to Harthacnut, which is what would almost certainly have happened had he been in England. Unfortunately, he was in Denmark facing the Norwegian invasion that followed Sweyn and Ælfgifu's expulsion from Norway. Sweyn, having been given and then lost Norway, does not seem to have been considered as a potential king; nor at this stage were Edward and Ælfred. But Harald Harefoot was in England and when the *witan* met at Oxford, they had a choice between him and Harthacnut. The *witan* and the country split along the now traditional dividing line of the Thames. To the south, one faction, led by Emma and Godwine, declared for Harthacnut. The rest of the country, led by Leofric, Earl of Mercia – Ælfgifu's home region – declared for Harald. A compromise was reached: Harald and Harthacnut would rule jointly. Joint rule was not unusual in Scandinavian kingdoms, but it was an innovation for England. The fact that Harald was in England, while Harthacnut was not, obviously put him in a stronger position – a position he reinforced by raiding the royal treasury at Winchester and moving its contents to London.

Shortly after this, in 1036, Edward and Ælfred, who were still living at their uncle's court in Normandy, received a letter. Ostensibly from Emma, but probably forged by Harald, it suggested that most of the English would prefer them as rulers of the kingdom. The brothers appear to have trusted the contents of the letter sufficiently to make a test, but they remained cautious and chose to make separate landings. Edward sailed directly from

Normandy to Southampton, perhaps intending to meet up with Emma in Winchester, but he had only a small force with him, and as soon as he encountered resistance, he returned to Normandy. Ælfred sailed to Boulogne before crossing to Kent, where he was immediately captured by Godwine's men. Godwine was notionally a supporter of Harthacnut rather than Harald, but the return of the House of Wessex was the last thing he wanted to see: it would have put at risk the position and the wealth he had acquired under Cnut. So, having captured Ælfred, he took him to London and handed him over to Harald, who immediately had his stepbrother blinded so severely that he died of his injuries. Although ambitious and ruthless, Godwine always denied knowing what Harald intended. Nonetheless, his actions would not be forgotten.

A few weeks later, Harald I was crowned at Oxford, and ruled as sole monarch for just over four years. Emma fled to Flanders, where she continued to intrigue on Harthacnut's behalf. Harald had gained the crown through intrigue and kept it by force, but he appears a somewhat colourless figure. Godwine and Leofric were among his chief advisers, but Stenton considers that his mother, Ælfgifu, was the effective ruler of the country during his reign.[295] Early in 1040, Harthacnut, anxious to pursue his claim to the English throne, negotiated an agreement with Magnus Olafsson of Norway to the effect that whoever died first would pass their lands to the other – something else that would not be forgotten. This freed him to sail south to Bruges, where he met his mother. They were planning an invasion when news reached them that Harald was ill. He died in March 1040. The *witan* declared for Harthacnut, who landed at Sandwich that June without opposition, and was crowned in Canterbury Cathedral. He was twenty-two and already an experienced warrior and ruler. It looked as if England could expect a continuation of the line of *Knýtlinga*, the descendants of Cnut, and a consolidation of the Danish monarchy.

It did not happen that way. In June 1042, the daughter of Tovi (or Tofig) the Proud, a landowner in both Denmark and England, who had been among the most powerful men at Cnut's court, was getting married in Lambeth. Harthacnut stood up to drink the health of the bride, collapsed, and died. It is usually assumed that he died of a stroke brought on by drink, but he could have been poisoned. His reign had lasted just two years and two months, yet his actions had not been calculated to make friends. He had disinterred the body of Harald Harefoot and thrown it into a marsh. He had quadrupled taxes in order to double the size of his fleet, and when rioters in Worcester killed two of his tax collectors, he had had the town burned and several of the inhabitants killed. He had promised Eadwulf, the ruler of North Northumbria, safe conduct and then ordered his murder. The verdict of the *Anglo-Saxon Chronicle* was that 'he never did anything worthy of a king while he reigned.'[293] On the other hand, his actions were not unprecedented for an early medieval monarch, and he is recorded as behaving generously to the Church and to his retainers. Cnut's reign did not start well, but he developed into a respected and statesman-like figure. Harthacnut might have done the same had he lived long enough.[294] And had there been a strong Danish king on the throne of England for twenty years or more, it is likely that neither the excuse, nor the opportunity, for a Norman invasion would have arisen.

Harthacnut's main achievement was probably securing a peaceful succession by inviting his stepbrother, Edward, to return to England from Normandy. We can discount the suggestion in Emma's unreliable *Encomium* that Harthacnut's invitation to Edward was a matter of brotherly affection. They can barely have known each other, and Harthacnut was not a man to be driven by sentiment. There have been suggestions that he knew he was ill and recalled Edward to England to ensure a peaceful succession. This is possible, but more plausible is the idea that he wanted to return to Denmark to fight his Scandinavian wars, while maintaining his hold on England, his main source of men and money. To invite Edward to England and leave him in charge, no doubt closely watched by their mother, Emma, would have been a clever way of achieving this and defusing the possibility of Edward obtaining Norman support for an invasion in his absence.

Edward was something of a forgotten man. Born in Islip near Oxford, he had been in exile at the court of his uncle, Duke Richard II of Normandy, since 1016, when he was eleven or twelve. There were nine male heirs ahead of him – Æthelred's six sons by Ælfgifu, and Cnut's three sons, Sweyn and Harald by Ælfgifu of Northampton, and Harthacnut with Emma – so he can never have expected to inherit the English throne. Perhaps because of this, Edward developed into an intelligent and pious character, although his later apologists no doubt emphasised these characteristics. At the same time, he was not lacking in ambition, and clearly understood the strength of his claim to the English throne, but it was not until the 1030s, by which time he was the only one of Æthelred's six sons by Ælfgifu still surviving, that he began to take his first steps in that direction.

Duke Richard died in 1026. His son, Richard III, ruled for only a year before being succeeded by his younger brother, Robert. He was just four years older than Edward, and the two of them had known each other since Edward arrived in Normandy ten years previously. Somewhere around 1033 or 1034, Robert agreed to allow Edward to call himself 'King' and committed to sending a fleet to allow him to invade England. However, by the time Edward attempted an invasion, in 1036, Robert was dead, and the new duke, William I, a boy of no more than eight or nine, was struggling to maintain control of his Duchy. Wholly dependent on a handful of supporters who saw their interests best served by keeping him in power, William could offer no help to a long-term exile making a bid for the English throne. Consequently, Edward's landing in 1036 was a curiously half-hearted affair, consisting of men and ships he had managed to gather together himself. And it was over almost as soon as it had begun.

Whatever the motive for Harthacnut's invitation, when Edward received it – in 1041, just five years after his abortive landing at Southampton – he was wisely cautious. He arrived with a small fleet and met Godwine and Bishop Ælfwine of Winchester on Hurst Spit, a two-kilometre shingle bank jutting out into the Solent. There, they negotiated the terms of his return, the most important of which was that he should be recognised as next in line to the throne. It is possible that Godwine and Ælfwine were acting behind Harthacnut's back, but they were certainly doing Emma's bidding. She remained a powerful figure. By now in her late fifties, she had been married to the last two kings of any stature. She had had sons by both and was determined to secure the English throne for her descendants. This was another pivotal moment. Had Harthacnut's promise that his kingdoms would pass to Magnus Olafsson been honoured, England would have remained attached to Scandinavia and English history might have taken a very different course. Edward, by contrast, had a strong claim to England, but none to the Scandinavian kingdoms. The moment he was proclaimed king – 'as was his right by birth'[295] – England became decoupled from Scandinavia. It remained agriculturally and economically strong, but it lost the political and military leverage offered by the Danish connection. The consequences of that decisive change still reverberate.

35 Beyond England II

Malcolm II of Scotland died in 1034. He had fought off challenges from the Norwegians and the troublesome Mormaers of Moray; he had pushed the border southward when he could get away with it; he had submitted to Cnut when it was prudent to do so; and he had arranged dynastic marriages for his three daughters. The *Annals of Tigernach* calls him 'the honour of all the west of Europe.' The *Prophecy of Berchán* calls him 'the Aggressor',[296] and at times his behaviour could match the violent age in which he lived, but he survived, and so did the Kingdom of Scotland.

Had he followed tradition, Malcolm would have selected his successor from among the male descendants of his ancestor, Cináed MacAlpín. Instead, he chose his grandson, Duncan, the son of his eldest daughter and Crinán, Abbott of Dunkeld and (probably) Mormaer of Athol. Thus, in genealogical terms, the accession of Duncan I (r.1034–40) marked the end of the line of MacAlpin kings and beginning of the House of Dunkeld. Malcolm may have appointed Duncan as his viceroy in Strathclyde/Cumbria in preparation for the kingship. If true, this might explain Duncan's angry reaction when, in 1038, Eadulf (or Eadwulf) of Bamburgh mounted a raid into Cumbria. Duncan retaliated in 1039 by leading his army south to besiege Durham, a much bigger undertaking than a mere cross-border raid. It ended in disaster. His forces were routed; the heads of his foot soldiers were hung on posts in the market square; and he returned, much weakened, to Scotland, to be faced with a rebellion in the ever-troublesome region of Moray, led by Macbeth.

The point has been made many times, but it bears repeating, that the real story of Duncan and Macbeth has little or nothing in common with Shakespeare's play. Duncan was a comparatively young man, perhaps thirty-eight or thirty-nine when he moved against Macbeth in 1040. Macbeth (Mac Bethad mac Findlaích) was three or four years younger, and they were cousins. Macbeth's mother, Donalda, was Malcolm II's second daughter, and she had married Findlaích, Mormaer of Moray – so Macbeth was also Malcolm II's grandson, with a claim to the throne that was only marginally weaker than Duncan's. Macbeth makes an appearance in the *Anglo-Saxon Chronicle* in 1031 when Cnut travelled north to receive the submission of Malcolm II and 'two other kings, Maelbeth and Iehmarc.'[297] This is confusing. Iehmarc is almost certainly Echmarcach mac Ragnaill, whom we have seen as King of Dublin and of Mann, but Macbeth was not a king. He was Mormaer of Moray and in theory subject to the overlordship of Malcolm – he may even have been one of Malcolm's army commanders – but his inclusion alongside Malcolm as someone whose submission Cnut required makes it clear that he was already a powerful figure. Macbeth evidently saw Duncan as a weaker figure than Malcolm II, but whether his rebellion in 1040 was an assertion of regional independence or a bid for the throne we do not know. In the event, Duncan's punitive expedition was another disaster. He was killed somewhere near Elgin and Macbeth took the Scottish throne with little or no opposition.

By the standards of the time, Macbeth's seventeen-year reign was comparatively peaceful. In 1045, he saw off a revolt by Crinán of Dunkeld on behalf of Duncan's sons, Malcolm and Donald (who would later return and became Malcolm III and Donald III). Crinán was killed, and Duncan's sons fled to Northumberland. By 1050, Macbeth felt secure enough to make a pilgrimage to Rome, where he is reported to have made generous donations to the poor. In 1052, when Edward the Confessor was forced to restore the Godwine family to their positions of power (see Chapter 36), a number of his Norman advisers fled north to Scotland. Macbeth allowed them to remain but does not appear to have offered support to either party in the English power struggle. Only in 1054 did he begin to lose his grip.

After Duncan's disastrous siege of Durham in 1039, Earl Siward of Northumbria had taken advantage of the situation to kill Eadulf of Bamburgh and make secure his hold on north as well as south Northumbria. Duncan I had married Siward's niece, Suthen Bjornsdottir (also Suthen Sibylla), and after the failure of Crinán's revolt, Siward had offered a home to Suthen and her sons, Malcolm and Donald. He waited another nine years, until 1054, before making a serious move against Macbeth. He may have been waiting until he considered Malcolm was old enough to rule, or he may have been waiting for the convulsions in England, in which he was involved, to settle down, but, when it came, Siward's invasion spelt the beginning of the end for Macbeth. In time-honoured fashion, his army pushed north of the Firth of the Forth, shadowed offshore by his fleet. When Macbeth eventually chose or was forced to engage, the conflict was long and bloody. The Battle of the Seven Sleepers – some later writers chose to call it the Battle of Dunsinane – left many dead, including Siward's son, Osbjorn (or Osbeorn), but the Scots were soundly defeated, and when the dust had cleared, Siward, acting on Malcolm's behalf, had secured control of most of southern Scotland.[298] Siward died the following year, but by that time Malcolm was sufficiently established to continue the campaign with his own resources. He consolidated his position and then, in 1057, pushed north. Macbeth was defeated and wounded in a battle at an unidentified location north of the Mounth. He retreated over the Cairn O'Mount Pass to Lumphanan in modern-day Aberdeenshire, where he made a last stand. According to some sources, he was killed by Malcolm himself. It is worth noting that no contemporary or near-contemporary source describes Macbeth as a usurper or as tyrannical, and that he was buried on Iona in the graveyard traditionally reserved for Scottish kings. He was succeeded by his stepson, Lulach, but Lulach had little more than the title and his reign lasted just four months. Described in the *Chronicle of the Kings of Scotland* as a 'simpleton', and in the *Chronicle of Melrose* as 'unfortunate' and 'hapless',[299] he walked into an ambush organised by Malcolm at Strathbogie.

Malcolm III, later nicknamed 'Canmore' – meaning 'big head' or 'great chieftain', depending on one's point of view – ruled for thirty-five years from 1058 and to 1093. Lulach's death meant that the threat posed by Moray diminished but did not disappear. Lulach's son, Máel Snechtai, then became Mormaer, although some chroniclers, perhaps for their own political reasons, call him 'king'. In 1078, there was a confrontation with Malcolm, who drove through Moray capturing Máel Snechtai's mother, seizing his property, and forcing him to flee. Máel Snechtai evidently survived but was killed in another confrontation with Malcolm in 1085. If Moray was one long-term threat to Malcolm III's emergent Scotland, the Scandinavian north was another. Malcolm sought to neutralise it by marrying Ingibjorg, who was the widow of Thorfinn the Mighty, and may have been the niece of the Norwegian king, Harald Sigurdsson, better known as Harald Hardrada. In 1065, Malcolm may also have played a part in encouraging the alliance between Harald Hardrada and Earl Godwine's third son, Tostig, which would have a long-lasting impact on English history (see Chapter 36).

Most of our information about the Kingdom of the Isles and the Earldom of Orkney comes from the sagas, notably the *Heimskringla* and the *Orkneyinga Saga*, or from Irish sources, such as the *Annals of Ulster*, the *Annals of Tigernach*, the later *Annals of the Four Masters*, or poems such as the *Prophecy of Berchán*. Pieces of the jigsaw are also found in the Scottish chronicles and king lists, such as those preserved in the fourteenth-century Poppleton manuscript, and in odd Welsh sources, such as the *Historia Gruffudd vab Keenan*. Even when it is accurate – and the sagas are frequently imaginative – the picture we get is at best impressionistic, consisting of a handful of verifiable events, often those which also affected Ireland and Scotland, set against a blurred background of probabilities and possibilities.

Sigurd the Stout appears in at least eight sagas and Old Norse tales. Much of what is said about him is wildly exaggerated, if not complete fiction, but the frequency with which his name crops up is an indication of what a dominant figure he was. Following his death at the Battle of Clontarf in 1014, his lands and his titles were divided among his five sons, and, as so often, the inheritors fought among themselves, quickly dissipating the power and the influence he had exerted. By 1016, the connection between the Isles and Orkney had been severed, and the Isles had reverted to their usual instability, with local rulers asserting their autonomy over their islands and archipelagos while ordinary people farmed and fished as best they could. Hákon Eiríksson held the kingship from 1016 to 1030, along with a confusing array of other titles, although not Earl of Orkney. Hákon was another Scandinavian with a more than usually varied career. The son of Eirik Hákonarson, one of Cnut's commanders and, later, Earl of Northumbria (see Chapter 34), he succeeded his father as Jarl of Hlaðir in Norway in 995, and was appointed Regent of Norway in 1015, holding both titles as a vassal of the King of Denmark. Forced to flee by the resurgent Norwegians under Olaf II in 1016, Hákon arrived in England, where Cnut made him both Earl of Worcester and King of the Isles. His interest and authority in the Isles seem to have been notional, and when he drowned in a shipwreck in the Pentland Firth in 1030, he was on his way back to Norway to act as viceroy in the aftermath of Cnut's conquest.

With Hákon's death, the title of 'King of the Isles' passed back to the Uí Ímair, in the person of Olaf Sigtryggsson (Amlaíb mac Sitriuc), the son of Sigtrygg Silkbeard – then ruling King of Dublin – and grandson of

Brian Boru, whose career we will consider shortly. All we know of Olaf is that, in 1034, he set off on a pilgrimage to Rome, but got no further than England where, according to the *Annals of the Kingdom of Ireland*, he was 'slain by the Saxons.'[300] However, he was survived by his daughter, Ragnhild (or Ragnailt), who married Cynan ab Iago, a member of the House of Aberffraw and thus a descendant of Rhodri the Great – an indication that Hiberno-Norse families were spreading beyond Ireland and the Isles. Ragnhild became the mother of Gruffudd ap Cynan, who, after a very rocky start, was King of Gwynedd for more than fifty years (r.1081–1137).

It was Thorfinn Sigurdsson (more usually Thorfinn the Mighty) who again united the Kingdom of the Isles and the Earldom of Orkney in a single individual – and he was only able to do so after a prolonged, fascinating, but ultimately unedifying power struggle. Sigurd the Stout married Olith, daughter of Malcolm II of Scotland (see Chapter 33). He was over forty by that time and already had four sons. Olith gave him a fifth, Thorfinn, who was considerably younger than the others. When Sigurd died, Thorfinn was no more than five of six, and his inheritance was limited to the mormaership of Caithness, a title held as a vassal of his grandfather, the King of Scotland. His three surviving brothers – Brusi, Sumarlidi and Einar – divided Orkney and Shetland between them, and the trouble began.

Sumarlidi died. Einar seized his share of the Earldom, raised taxes, forced men to join his raiding expeditions, failed to reward them properly, and generated a wave of opposition among the islanders led by a man named Thorkel Amundason. Einar forced Thorkel to flee to Caithness, where he established a close and protective relationship with the young Thorfinn, earning the nickname Fóstri, or foster-father. Probably encouraged by Thorkel and Malcolm II, Thorfinn claimed Sumarlidi's share of the Earldom. Einar refused. Brusi mediated; violence was avoided; and Thorfinn received his third of the earldom, but undiplomatically installed Thorkel as his representative. Einar again obliged Thorkel to flee. Thorfinn appealed to Olaf II (Olaf Haraldsson), the King of Norway, who was, in theory, the Earldom's overlord. Olaf supported Thorfinn. Einar again threatened violence. Brusi again acted as peacemaker. Einar appeared to back down, but laid a trap for Thorkel, who saw through it and killed Einar. Brusi now claimed Einar's third of the Earldom, while Thorfinn insisted that it should be divided equally. This time Brusi appealed to King Olaf, who decreed that the brothers should have a third each and surrender the remaining third to him. Olaf allowed Brusi to administer his third but kept Brusi's son, Rognvald, in Norway as a hostage to make sure that he did so honestly.

Thorfinn and Brusi ruled jointly until 1030, when Olaf II was ousted by Cnut, and Orkney and Shetland became the target of Danish raids. Brusi seems to have retired. At any rate, Thorfinn had sole charge of the defence of the Earldom for the next five years. In Caithness, he fought off a challenge from the shadowy figure of Karl Hundason, whom the *Orkneyinga Saga* misleadingly calls King of the Scots and, with his position apparently secure, began to look further afield. He conquered the Hebrides, probably in 1034, and the following year established himself as King of the Isles. Brusi died, probably in 1036, and for the next ten years Thorfinn ruled jointly with his son, Rognvald. They raided widely and extended their authority along the coasts of western Scotland and the Irish Sea. They may even have raided parts of western England. Eventually – and probably inevitably – they fell out. Rognvald enlisted Norwegian support and the struggle seemed to be going in Rognvald's favour. Thorfinn was forced to flee to Caithness. However, in 1046, Rognvald attempted a surprise attack on the island of Papa Stronsay, was given away by a barking dog, and killed by Thorkel Fóstri. King Magnus Olafsson of Norway threatened to avenge the young man he had supported, but was distracted by more Danish wars, and then died the following year. The new king, Harald Hardrada, had other interests and was content to accept gifts from Thorfinn and make peace, so Thorfinn remained sole ruler of the Earldom, the Isles, and Caithness until his death, probably in 1065, although it may have been earlier.

The Welsh text, *Historia Gruffudd vab Keenan*, states that the rule of Olaf Sigtryggsson, Thorfinn's predecessor in the Isles, extended beyond Mann and the Hebrides to include Galloway and the Rhinns, and even Anglesey. We do not know how much of this passed to Thorfinn. Although he remained King of the Isles until his death, the territories he controlled may well have been eroded in later years by the resurgence of Dublin. Some sources name Echmarcach mac Ragnaill, who had two spells as King of Dublin (r.1036–38, and 1046–52), as King of Mann between 1052 and 1061. Echmarcach's successor in Dublin, Murchad mac Diarmata (r.1052–70), is sometimes listed as King of Mann between 1061 and 1070. We do not know whether they were sub-kings under Thorfinn, or whether Mann was detached from the rest of the Isles, but such uncertainty is characteristic of Mann, and of the Isles as a whole. The Isles had no institutions. There was no *witan* to confer kingship, and titular authority, even when accepted, could easily be overturned by the fleet of the next ambitious young upstart.

That said, the territories held by Thorfinn at the height of his power – Caithness, Orkney, Shetland, the Hebrides, islands and enclaves around the Firth of Clyde, the Isle of Man – constitute a remarkable and potentially powerful realm. They allowed for control of the Irish Sea, and of the seaways around most of Scotland and between Britain and Norway. They were held together by the sea which, as we have seen so often, offered quicker and more efficient transport than land. They were conveniently separated from England, the most powerful polity in the British Isles, and archaeological data suggest that agriculture and fishing allowed the population to live above subsistence level. Scandinavian settlers left a linguistic legacy among the islands (see Chapter 29); and the interaction between Scandinavians, Scots, Irish, and Hiberno-Norse left a fragmented but still detectable cultural legacy; but beyond the fact that the Isle of Man's parliament, which claims to be the oldest continuous parliament in the world, is called the Tynwald, and that its laws are read aloud in public once a year, as they were in medieval Iceland, there is no corresponding political legacy.

The reason the sea kingdoms did not exert a greater influence on the political history and structure of the British Isles is due to their failure to evolve a workable system of inheritance and to develop institutions. In the Anglo-Saxon world, an inheritance might be divided among two or more sons, but joint rule of an earldom or a kingdom was rare – and usually a last resort to avoid conflict. By contrast, Scandinavian rulers routinely divided their earldoms and kingdoms between their offspring. This inevitably meant that the many different territories amassed by men like Sigurd the Stout and Thorfinn were divided before they could begin to cohere into a single polity. This in turn prevented the development of institutions and administrative units, such as counties, that could create stability. Nor was there an ecclesiastical organisation to complement, or even oppose, the political power structure. The *Orkneyinga saga* claims that Thorfinn instigated the appointment of the first Bishop of Orkney somewhere around 1050. And the overlordship structure which allowed Sigurd and Thorfinn to hold one territory from the King of Scotland and another from the King of Norway militated against the establishment of a single polity.

After Thorfinn's death, division and disunity returned. The Isles were again detached from Orkney. Mann grew closer to Dublin, with several rulers combining the kingship of both. Elsewhere in the Isles, local rulers asserted their independence, Orkney was split between Thorfinn's two sons, Paul and Erlend, who appear to have cooperated until a dispute arose between their two sons. However, that story, and the story of the unique attempt, at the end of the eleventh century, by the rulers of Norway to exert real control over Orkney and the Isles, need to be seen in the context of the aftermath of the momentous changes of 1066.

Like the Battle of Brunanburh in the context of English history, the significance of the Battle of Clontarf, which took place on the north side of Dublin Bay in 1014, has been exaggerated and misrepresented. It has been presented as a struggle between righteous Christians and savage pagans; as the apotheosis of the career of High King, Brian Boru; and as the moment when the Irish expelled the Vikings from their soil. None of these interpretations will stand examination, but the last was adopted with great enthusiasm by nationalist groups opposed to British rule in the nineteenth and early twentieth centuries. In 1843, the nationalist leader Daniel O'Connell sought to exploit the power of the name 'Clontarf' and rally support by holding a meeting on the supposed site of the battle. The Prime Minister, Robert Peel, personally banned the event for fear of the consequences. Clontarf was unusual in that all of those with significant political ambitions in Ireland were involved and can best be understood as the climactic point in a conflict which had been building for some years. It did not radically change the course of Irish history, but it did set the direction of travel for the next century and a half.

Brian mac Cennétig (*c.*941–1014), better known as Brian Boru, was the son of Cennétig mac Lorcáin, leader of the Dál gCais or Dalcassian clan, and King of Tuadmumu, or Thomond, a sub-kingdom of Munster roughly equivalent to County Clare. 'Boru' is an Anglicisation of the Irish *Bóruma*, probably deriving from the ringfort in County Clare where he may have been born. As the youngest of twelve sons, he was not expected to inherit the kingdom and was sent to be educated by the monks of the island of Inisfallen. Somewhere around 951, his life was transformed. Viking raiders sailed up the River Shannon from Limerick and attacked the Dál gCais capital, killing his father, his mother, and most of his brothers. Tales of the youthful exploits of early medieval kings need to be treated with caution, but revenge does seem to have been a driving force in his early years. His brother, Mathgamain, assumed the kingship of Thomond, and the two of them fought alongside each other in several campaigns. In 964, they conquered the Rock of Cashel, the capital of the Eóganachta clan, and Mathgamain declared himself King of Munster. Four years later, the brothers inflicted a major defeat on the Limerick Vikings at the Battle of Sulcoit, burning the town, and slaughtering or enslaving much of the population, but failing to capture the Viking leader, Ivar.

As ever, Irish alliances were complex and shifting. For a time, Mathgamain joined with Máel Murda, heir of the Eóganachta he had displaced, and other sub-kings in an effort to drive the Vikings from Munster. But in 976, Mathgamain was betrayed and captured by Donnabán mac Cathail, the king of the Uí Fidgenti, a small clan in northern Munster. Donnabán handed Mathgamain over to Máel Murda, who promptly murdered him and took back the kingship of Munster. Brian was crowned King of Thomond under the sacred tree of Adair, the traditional site of Dál gCais coronations, and embarked on a campaign of violence and revenge. He attacked and killed Ivar of Limerick. He pursued Ivar's successor, Imar, to the monastery on Inis Cathaigh (Scattery Island), where he broke the rules of sanctuary and slaughtered Imar and his men on consecrated ground. He moved against Máel Murda, killing him at the Battle of Belach Lechta in 978, and taking the kingship of Munster for himself. He also took a bloody revenge on Donnabán mac Cathail, who had allied himself with some of the last remaining Limerick Vikings, at the Battle of Cathair Cuan.

It may have been at this point, with Munster under his control, that Brian decided that he wanted to impose his authority of the whole of Ireland. Certainly, he prepared his next steps with care. His attitude towards Munster's three Viking settlements – Cork, Wexford, and Waterford – changed. As long as they accepted his authority, he was prepared to tolerate and use them. They had brought wealth into the kingdom, and they had ships. He had learnt from his enemy and, although his tactics developed over the years, his preferred approach was to deploy a fleet of anything up to three hundred ships along the nearest navigable river, while at the same time attacking with land-based troops. It was a tactic that would serve him well. In tenth- and eleventh-century Ireland, with its myriad of small territories and constantly shifting allegiances, defeats and setbacks were inevitable. Brian suffered his share, but tactical skill, persistence and determination made him the only man ever to receive the submission of all the Irish kingdoms.

In 982 he invaded Osraige. This brought him into conflict with the Máel Sechnaill mac Domnaill (or Máel Sechnaill II), King of Meath, leader of the Southern Uí Neill, and the new High King of Ireland. They were to be rivals, and occasional allies, for the next thirty years. Having been elected High King in 980, Máel Sechnaill went on to bring the long reign of Amlaíb Cuarán as King of Dublin to an end at the Battle of Tara, before besieging and sacking Dublin itself. The new High King did not want Brian Boru as an assertive King of Munster threatening his southern border. Osraige was not formally Uí Néill territory, but Brian's invasion was sufficient excuse for Máel Sechnaill to raid Munster while it was undefended, attacking Brian's home region and burning the sacred tree of the Dál gCais. Reciprocal raids followed until Brian apparently realised that he was not yet strong enough to defeat Máel Sechnaill and turned his attention towards Leinster.

In 993, having brought much of Leinster under his control, he made a bold strategic move. Drawing on what he had learned from the Vikings, he sailed his fleet from Limerick more than a hundred and fifty kilometres up the River Shannon to attack the Kingdom of Bréifne. He now had the ability to threaten Máel Sechnaill from Leinster in the south and from Bréifne in the north. In 996, the King of Leinster, Donnchad mac Dómnaill Clóen, finally submitted, which forced Máel Sechnaill to come to terms. He and Brian met on the banks of Lough Ree, one of the great lakes of the Shannon, and at the time on the border between Connacht and Meath. Máel Sechnaill recognised Brian's authority over the southern half of Ireland – Munster, Leinster, and Ostraige. Brian acknowledged that the north of Ireland – Meath, Connacht, Bréifne, and Ulster – owed allegiance to Máel Sechnaill. The difference was that whereas in parts of the north, notably Ulster, Máel Sechnaill's authority was notional, Brian exercised real power in all parts of his expanded domain.

Donnchad's submission to Brian was seen as shameful in Munster and provoked a revolt led by Máel Mórda mac Murchada, whose lands were in what is now County Kildare. Máel Mórda allied himself with his nephew, Sigtrygg Silkbeard, the Hiberno-Norse and Uí Ímair, King of Dublin. Acting together, they overcame Donnchad and imprisoned him in Dublin, thus making Máel Mórda the effective ruler of Leinster. The new situation posed risks for both Brian and Máel Sechnaill, so they set aside their differences and, in 999, the combined armies of Munster and Meath faced those of Leinster and Dublin at Glenmama, just south of Dublin. The result was a victory for Brian and Máel Sechnaill and – given that it would be fourteen years before Brian faced another such revolt – probably justifies the term decisive. Máel Mórda submitted to Brian immediately. Brian sacked Dublin – and presumably freed Donnchad, whom the *Annals* list as King of Leinster until 1003. Sigtrygg Silkbeard fled north, first to the Ulaid and then to the Northern Uí Néill in search of sanctuary and support. Neither clan would help, and he was forced to return to Dublin where he, too, submitted to Brian. Glenmama and its aftermath greatly strengthened Brian's position, and it was inevitable that he would soon turn on his new ally. He waited only until the next year, 1000. Brian was now able to draw on the combined resources of Munster and Leinster. Máel Sechnaill allied his kingdom of Meath with Connacht. Brian sailed his fleet up the Shannon which divided Meath from Connacht and was thus able to divide his enemies. We know nothing of the campaign, but the result is undisputed: in 1002, Máel Sechnaill ceded the title of High King to Brian. Only Ulster – the Northern Uí Néill and the Ulaid – now resisted him.

Brian waited until 1005 before making his next move. Both the Uí Néill and the Ulaid had been weakened by the battle at Craeb Telcha in 1003, which had seen the deaths of many of their leaders (see Chapter 33), and he was now supported by the ships of his former enemy, Sigtrygg Silkbeard, who appears to have wanted to punish the two northern clans for their failure to help him after Glenmama. Within a year, he forced Flaithbertach Ua Néill, King of the Northern Uí Néill, into submission. He then brought many of the leaders of the fragmented Ulaid clan to their sacred site of Emain Macha where they, too, were obliged to submit. He might have been forgiven for thinking he had achieved his goal, when Flaithbertach broke his oath and attacked the Ulaid, slaughtering many of their remaining leaders and taking others hostage. Brian lived by the rules of his age, which meant that as an overlord you were obliged to defend those who had submitted to you. So in 1006 and 1007, he campaigned in the north of Ireland on behalf of the Ulaid, freeing the hostages, bringing Flaithbertach to submission again, and arranging a marriage between Flaithbertach and his own daughter to seal the relationship. Even that was not enough. In 1009, Flaithbertach broke out again, killing the king of the Cenél Conaill, a rival faction of the Uí Néill, which ruled the area later known as Tyrconnell and now County Donegal. For a third time, Brian forced Flaithbertach to submit; and with yet another rapid change of allegiance, in 1011 Flaithbertach campaigned first alongside Brian's sons, Murchad and Domnall, and then alongside Brian himself, in naval and land operations which eventually forced the Cenél Conaill into submission.

Brian understood power, both on and off the battlefield. He had a strong sense of political theatre and liked to stage ceremonial events that emphasised his power and the weakness of others. One such was to insist that the submission of the Ulaid should take place on the sacred hill of Emain Macha. Another, which perhaps took place about the same time, was to bring those kings who had submitted to him to Armagh Cathedral to witness him placing twenty-two ounces (630 grams) of gold on the altar. This may have been the occasion for Brian's amanuensis, Máel Suthain, to write a fourteen-line insertion in the *Book of Armagh*, confirming the primacy of Armagh as the religious capital of Ireland, and referring to his master as *Imperator Scottorum* (The Emperor of the Irish), a title never used before or since, and one that implies authority over the Viking settlements as well as the Irish kingdoms. Whenever these lines were written, it was only in 1011 that Brian could truly claim to be the acknowledged ruler of all Ireland. And in 1012, it all began to fall apart.

Máel Mórda declared himself free of Brian's authority and invaded Meath. In 1013, whether in concert with Máel Mórda or independently, Flaithbertach of the northern Uí Néill broke his oaths yet again and also attacked Meath. Brian responded by ravaging Leinster. Eventually, in April 1014, after much toing and froing, the armies faced each other at Clontarf. Those opposing Brian were led by Máel Mórda, and included forces from Ulster sent by Flaithbertach, as well as the Dublin Vikings led by Sigtrygg – who had not only changed sides once more, but recruited Sigurd the Stout from Orkney, and forces from Mann led by a Dane named Bródir, probably as mercenaries. It is even possible that Máel Mórda's army may have included men from Cornwall. Brian and his son, Murchad, led the forces of Munster. With them were the men of Meath, in theory under Máel Sechnaill – although what role, if any, he played in the battle is uncertain – the forces of Connacht, and Viking contingents from Waterford, Wexford and Cork, as well as some more Vikings from Mann led by Óspak, brother of Bródir, who was fighting on the other side. Brian was supported by Domnall mac Eimín, the Mormaer of Mar in Scotland, although we do not know how many men he had brought with him. Apart from those forces sent by Flaithbertach, Ulster appears to have remained neutral.

A handful of the Vikings may still have been pagan, but the vast majority of participants were Christian, and the battle cannot be accorded any particular religious significance. There were Vikings on both sides supporting Irish leaders who they thought would support their interests. Their involvement was natural and inevitable: they had been settled in Ireland for over a hundred and fifty years and were a part of the Irish social and political order. They did not seek to conquer Ireland, nor were the Irish fighting to expel them. Brian had disrupted the age-old order – or disorder – which constantly flexed and rebalanced itself so that no one kingdom or individual became dominant. Clontarf was the climactic point in the old order's fightback.

The fighting was long and bloody. Brian was killed – possibly by Bródir – while praying in his tent. His son, Murchad, and grandson, Toirdelbach, were also killed. So too was Domnall, the Scottish mormaer. Óspak was wounded and two of his sons were killed. Máel Mórda was killed. So was Bródir. So was Sigurd the Stout. Brian's forces won the battle. They probably outnumbered those of Leinster and Dublin, and on the battlefield their use of the short, throwing spear gave them an advantage. But they lost the war. With Brian's death, his collection of kingdoms and territories – his empire – simply fell apart. The Irish clans and Irish regional identities had proved too strong for him. Almost at once, his two surviving sons, Donnchad mac Briain – who was probably the hero of Clontarf, rallying the forces of Munster towards the end of the battle – and the younger Tadc mac Briain, found themselves fighting their traditional enemies, the Eóganachta, who, in the wake of Clontarf, had clawed back the kingship of Munster. It took Donnchad until 1025 to regain Munster for the Uí Briain – having killed off Tadc as a potential rival for the throne in the process. He ruled until he was deposed in 1063.

Whatever Máel Sechnaill's contribution to the battle – he may have held back the army of Meath until Brian's men had borne the brunt of the fighting – he was certainly the main beneficiary. He regained the title of High King and retained it until his death in 1022, but the mystique had gone. The line of High Kings continued into the twelfth century – most of them descendants of Brian, and including Donnchad – but the fact that Brian had been able to wrest the title by force removed any remaining sense of continuity or spiritual authority. Sygtrygg survived the battle and remained King of Dublin until 1036. He went on a pilgrimage to Rome in 1028 and may have been involved in founding Dublin's Christ Church Cathedral in or around 1030. Dublin continued to prosper but, like all Ireland's Scandinavian settlements, it had been drawn into essentially Irish political quarrels and politically weakened as a result. In 1052, it was forced to acknowledge the overlordship of the Mac Murchada (or Uí Cheinnselaig), the royal house of Leinster. Over the course of the next hundred years, it was controlled by Leinster, by the Uí Briain of Munster, by the tail end of the Uí Ímair dynasty, by Connacht and, on one occasion, by a King of Norway.

The fifty-year career of Brian Boru showed what could and could not be done in Ireland. He conquered. He shifted the balance of power between Ireland's kingdoms. He briefly brought all of Ireland under his authority, but he could not unify it. He was a warlord, perhaps an emperor, but not a ruler. After his death, Ireland reverted to its traditional pattern of inter-kingdom and inter-clan raiding. In Munster, the Uí Briain ruled until the end of the twelfth century – despite family feuds and a short interlude when the Eóganachta again seized power. Osraige had a brief period of glory under King Donnchadh (*sic*) mac Gilla Pátraic who conquered Leinster in 1033, but by the early twelfth century, feuding within the clan meant that it broke up into three separate kingdoms, all of which fell under the domination of Leinster in the 1150s. The titular kings of Connacht were the Ó Conchobair, but their control was contested from within by the powerful sub-kingdom of Uí Máine, and from without by the Ó Ruairc kings of neighbouring Bréifne. In the first half of the twelfth century, Tairrdelbach Ua Conchobair (r.1106–1156) made Connacht possibly the most powerful of the Irish kingdoms. He built the first stone castles on the island – notably at Galway and Sligo – forced the partition of Munster, conquered Meath, and became King of Dublin. In Ulster, the

Ulaid and the Northern Uí Néill continued to suffer from complex internal factionalism, while at the same time maintaining their long-standing hostility to each other.

Between the ninth and eleventh centuries, the political and social structures of England and Scotland underwent radical change. In Ireland this did not happen. Despite raids, incursions, battles, power struggles, and constantly shifting allegiances, a map of the Irish kingdoms and clan territories would have looked much the same in the 1050s as it did in the 850s. The main differences would have been the presence of the Viking kingdoms – Dublin, Wexford, Waterford, Cork, and Limerick. Yet, as we have already seen, these never developed beyond enclaves and, while they did not disappear until the Anglo-Norman invasion in the twelfth century, they became increasingly integrated into existing social and political structures. The Brehon law codes, first written down in the seventh century, may have been modified, but were not significantly redrawn. In those areas where Gaelic culture remained strongest, they were in daily use until English common law was imposed in the seventeenth century. Christian property may have been plundered and Christians taken as slaves, but the Church itself remained unchallenged, and emerged triumphant. The conversion of the Scandinavian population is largely undocumented, but as early as 921 Gofraid ua Ímair is said to have spared churches when raiding; and in 926, shortly after leaving Dublin for Jórvik, Sitric Cáech married Æthelstan's sister, something that Æthelstan would surely not have allowed had Sitric remained a pagan.

The Uí Ímair were among the first Scandinavian families to seal alliances with marriage agreements and begin the process of integrating themselves into Irish society. By the eleventh century, many of the Irish and Viking kingdoms were ruled by families which were, in effect, Hiberno-Norse or Norse-Gael. In the aftermath of Clontarf, when so many ruling families suffered losses, the two communities became increasingly integrated. The complexities of the relationships that arose are illustrated by the life and career of Gormlaith ingen Murchada (960–1030). She was the daughter of King Murchad mac Finn of Leinster and sister of Máel Mórda. It is possible, though not certain, that she married Máel Sechnaill of Meath but, if so, the marriage lasted only a short time. She then married Amlaíb Cuarán, whom we have seen as twice king of both Jórvik and Dublin, becoming the mother of his son, Sygtrygg

Silkbeard. Meanwhile, her first husband, Máel Sechnaill, seems to have taken a daughter of Amlaíb Cuarán by an earlier marriage as his second wife. In 999, at the battle of Glenmama, Gormlaith's brother Máel Mórda and her son Sigtrygg were defeated by the forces of Máel Sechnaill and Brian Boru. Gormlaith then married Brian, later becoming the mother of his son, Donnchad, while Brian's daughter by his first marriage, Sláine, married Sygtrygg. Donnchad later married Cacht ingen Ragnaill from the Uí Ímair dynasty. Their daughter, Derbforgaill, married back into the royal house of Leinster, and her son, Murchad mac Diarmata (c.1025–70), with his Hiberno-Norse ancestry, was able to be King of Leinster, as well as King of Dublin and King of the Isles. Such family and dynastic relationships are not easy to follow, but they constitute the essential background to the interactions and shifting allegiances between the Irish kingdoms in the three centuries leading up to the Norman invasion. The Hiberno-Norse had a significant cultural influence which would endure for generations, but they did not succeed in altering the political structure of the island.

Across the Irish Sea, there are indications that from about 950 to 1100, the cultural life of Wales enjoyed a period of revival. John Davies draws attention to a number of elaborate stone crosses, to religious works, such as *The Life of St Cadog*, *The Life of St Telio*, *The Life of St David*, and above all to the remarkable *Pedair Cainnc y Mabinogi* (*Four Branches of the Mabinogion*), the earliest-known prose stories from the British Isles and a treasury of Celtic mythology and romance.[301] For all that, political life in Wales seems to have remained violent and brutal. Much of our knowledge comes from *Brut y Tywysogyon* (*The Chronicle of the Princes*), a Welsh translation of a lost Latin text, which is a catalogue of murders, mutilations, blindings, and other horrors.

Nowhere is this more clearly demonstrated than in the career of Gruffudd ap Llywelyn, the grandson of Maredudd (see Chapter 33). Gruffudd was the one man who did manage to unite all the kingdoms of Wales, albeit briefly. He was born about 1010. His father, Llywelyn ap Seisyll was King of Powys and Gwynedd, but on his death, in 1023, he was succeeded not by Gruffudd, who was probably considered too young, but by Iago ap Idwal, a member of the House of Aberffraw, and a great-grandson of Idwal Foel.

Gruffudd's career began in 1039, when he seized control of Powys. Having established himself there, he moved on Gwynedd. At some stage,

Iago seems to have submitted to Earl Leofric of Mercia, because when he was killed – either by Gruffud himself or at his instigation – a Mercian army under Leofric's brother, Edwin, crossed into Powys and began raiding. Gruffudd mounted a surprise attack, killing Edwin, and driving the Mercians back across the border. This left him free to move south and attack Dyfed. He drove out its ruler, Hywel ab Edwin, carried off Hywel's wife, and married her – whether she was willing or not, the sources do not say. In 1044, Hywel tried to reclaim his kingdom, but Gruffudd killed him. In 1047, Gruffudd attacked Deheubarth. He was successful at first, but the King of Gwent – another Gruffudd, Gruffudd ap Rhydderch – fought back and drove him off, perhaps with Viking assistance. Gruffudd ap Llywelyn's advance was stalled, but in 1055 he changed tactics, and allied himself with Earl Leofric's son, Ælfgar, who had been exiled by Edward the Confessor at the instigation of Earl Godwine's sons, Harold and Tostig. Together, they raided the borderlands, attacking and burning Hereford. Gruffudd then contrived to have Gruffudd ap Rhydderch killed, took possession of Deheubarth, and drove south into Morgannwg and Gwent. In 1056, Edward the Confessor sent an army against him, but it was defeated at Glasbury near Hay-on-Wye. By 1057 Gruffudd was master of the whole of Wales, but it had been a bloody progress, and he had made few friends, either at home or abroad.

In 1062, Gruffudd reached some kind of peace agreement with Edward the Confessor and retired to his castle at Rhuddlan in Denbighshire. That Christmas, Harold and Tostig, probably aided by some of Gruffudd's many domestic enemies, mounted their own surprise attack. Gruffudd escaped into the mountains of Snowdonia, but his days were numbered. How Harold and Tostig brought about his death is not recorded, but early in 1063 they were able to send his severed head back to London and, to mark their victory, arranged for triumphal monuments to be erected across Wales. The kingdoms of Wales quickly resumed their customary disunity. Gruffudd's half-brothers Bleddyn and Rhiwallon became joint kings of Gwynedd and Powys. The descendants of Hywel Dda, in the person of Maredudd ab Owain, took back control of Deheubarth. Caradog, the son of Gruffudd ap Rhydderch became ruler of Gwent and most of Morgannwg. What part the English victors played in breaking up Gruffudd's brief empire we do not know, but Harold and Tostig's actions made it clear that, while the English did not necessarily wish to conquer Wales, they would not tolerate an aggressive and unified Welsh state on their western border. Rhodri Mawr, Hywel Dda, Maredudd, and Gruffudd ap Llywelyn all presided over territorial acquisitions and conquests which looked towards, and in one case achieved, unity. All four foundered because of external intervention – from the Vikings or the English – or dynastic power struggles, or both. Yet there was another, deeper factor working against unity.

In Scotland, there was one extended region – the Central Belt, with the contiguous low-lying parts of Fife, Perthshire and Angus – which had the agricultural wealth, the ports, and the trade routes to allow whoever controlled it to achieve political and economic dominance. In England, the area that we have called the Lowland Zone fulfilled much the same function. It was, of course, on a much larger scale and achieving dominance took much longer. Nonetheless, control of the Lowland Zone was a determining factor in establishing a single English kingdom. Neither Ireland nor Wales had a single region that would allow such dominance. Ireland presented a series of river valleys running to the coast, none of which was notably wealthier than the others; and while Dublin's location and its easy access to ports in Britain meant that it became wealthier than the other Viking-founded towns, it was never powerful enough to exert wider control. Wales had three main agricultural zones – Anglesey, the Dyfed Peninsula, and the coastal lands along the Bristol Channel – all more or less in balance, and thus effectively preventing a single region from gaining overall dominance. Whatever the underlying reasons, the failure to achieve unity in Ireland and Wales would have a significant impact later when the two regions were faced with the concentrated power of the Anglo-Norman kings.

36 Power Struggle

The man who acceded to the English throne in June 1042, and was crowned in Winchester Cathedral the following April, is usually known as Edward the Confessor. As ever, the sobriquet was added later – in 1161, when he was canonised by Pope Alexander III. The term 'Confessor' denotes a man whose life testifies to his Christian faith but who was not martyr. It also serves to distinguish him from the earlier King Edward, his uncle, who following his murder was proclaimed a martyr. At the time, the new king was simply Edward, the last surviving son of the long-deceased King Æthelred, who had returned to England after more than a quarter of a century of exile in Normandy to reclaim the throne for the House of Wessex.

All sources agree that Edward was genuinely pious. He was renowned for giving alms to the poor; he was generous in his gifts to monasteries and religious foundations – among them Bury, Ely, Christ Church in Canterbury, Ramsey Abbey, and Lakenhurst in Suffolk – and there are suggestions that he may have taken an oath of chastity. Such accounts have played a part in the traditional – and, in many cases, still current – estimation of Edward as a weak and unworldly king, but they had their origins in the suspicion, uncertainty, and self-justification that followed his death; and they were perpetuated under later monarchs whose interests were served by portraying the last legitimate Anglo-Saxon king as ineffectual. They also succeeded in establishing Edward as one of England's national saints, imagined by writers and illustrators as aged, frail, and otherworldly. In reality, when circumstances allowed, Edward could display an effective, even robust, balance between piety and an astute awareness of secular issues.

An example of this was his decision to make Westminster the centre of political power in England – which it remains to this day. When the kings of Wessex became kings of England, their traditional seat, Winchester, became the effective capital of England. Yet England remained deeply divided, and to many of those north of the Thames – which, in the past, had constituted the border when England threatened to fall apart – Winchester represented the dominance of Wessex. The city that spanned the divide was London – which by the late tenth century had re-established the position it held under the Romans as the country's largest and richest city, and leading port. Just four kilometres upriver from London, was the West Minster, home to a small, poor, and undistinguished community of monks. During his short reign, King Harald I may have identified the area as suitable for a new royal palace, but it was Edward who, on his accession, became the community's patron and completely rebuilt their church. This first Westminster Abbey – an image can be seen on the Bayeux Tapestry – was both the largest church in the British Isles and the first to be built in the Romanesque style. At the same time, a stone's throw from the abbey, Edward built a new royal palace of equal size and splendour, which remained the principal residence of English kings until Henry VIII. With these two buildings, Edward was demonstrating the indivisibility, as he saw it, of the spiritual and the secular, and also making a gesture of unity, moving his capital away from the traditional seat of the Wessex kings to the one city which did not 'belong' to either faction in his divided land.

England had long been divided into English and Danish regions and factions. If the nature of that division changed during Edward's reign, the fact of division did not, and it was his failure to overcome the problems it caused that led, ultimately, to Duke William's invasion in 1066. Edward represented the House of Wessex. He was a descendant of Ælfred and Æthelstan, the men who laid the foundations of England. In theory, this should have given him a power base in Wessex, but during his twenty-five years of exile loyalties had changed. Godwine, who owed his position entirely to Cnut, had been Earl of Wessex for more than twenty years. He was rich; he was the most powerful man in the kingdom; and he was a patron to many. Edward, by contrast, was an unknown quantity. Despite his lineage, he knew more about Normandy than England. He needed Godwine, and Godwine undoubtedly let him know it.

The two men were publicly reconciled. Godwine swore all kinds of oaths and presented Edward with a gilded warship. Edward promoted Godwine's family to positions of power. Probably in 1043, he made Godwine's eldest son, Sweyn (or Swegn), an earl responsible for the South-West Midlands. In 1045, Godwine's second son, Harold, became Earl of East Anglia, while his nephew, Beorn Estrithsson, the brother of the King of Denmark, received an earldom in the East Midlands. There were sound reasons for these choices: the aggressive Sweyn could deal with the Welsh; Harold's background made him the ideal candidate to win the confidence of the Anglo-Danish population of East Anglia; the appointment of Beorn would smooth relations with the Danes. Also in 1045, Edward married Godwine's daughter, Edith (or Ealdgyth), who was described as pious, well mannered, and able to speak Latin, French, Danish, and Irish, as well as English. Edward was content, at least for the present, to allow the Godwine family to maintain their dominant position, and the marriage set the seal upon the alliance. However, Edward had not forgotten Godwine's role in the blinding and death of his brother, Ælfred.

England would soon be divided into pro-Edward and pro-Godwine factions, and this is reflected in our principal sources for the reign. Of the three relevant versions of the *Anglo-Saxon Chronicle* – known as the C, D, and E texts – C and D are broadly pro-Edward, while E is pro-Godwine and the *Vita Edwardi regis* (*The Life of King Edward*), commissioned by Queen Edith after Edward's death, closely follows the Godwine version of events.

The problem with Edward's strategy was that it maintained the divisions and tensions that continued to simmer beneath the surface. Godwine's main rival was Leofric, Earl of Mercia, son of one of Æthelred's *ealdormen*, and a member of the only old Anglo-Saxon family in the south not to have been purged by Cnut. Mercia had traditionally opposed not only the dominance of Wessex, but also Danish influence, both of which were in the ascendant while Godwine – whom Leofric saw as an upstart – exercised so much influence over the king. Further north, Earl Siward of Northumbria, himself of Scandinavian origin and, like Godwine, a protégé of Cnut, exercised a degree of autonomy. Although loyal to Edward and ready to take up arms against the Godwine faction if an advantageous opportunity arose, Siward was much preoccupied with the Scots – and with his own interests (see Chapter 35). Having grown to maturity in Normandy, where Duke Richard II had established a unified and largely peaceful polity, Edward no doubt hoped to create something similar in England. To do so, he needed to establish and assert his authority, but many of his policies and actions actually deepened long-standing divisions and exacerbated existing tensions.

He began well. In 1043, he moved to break the power of his mother, Queen Emma. She had done little to support him over the years, naturally preferring to promote the interests of her other children. Edward gathered his leading earls – Godwine, Leofric, and Siward – and they rode to Winchester, where he relieved her of most of her property. She was probably holding on to treasure, relics, and other valuables that properly belonged to the royal household. He also removed her closest adviser, Bishop Stigand of Elmham from his see. It was a demonstration that he was his own man and that she was now the dowager queen, no longer the power behind the throne. In 1044 and 1045, he showed leadership and an understanding of naval defence, gathering ships at Sandwich to fight off an anticipated attack from King Magnus Olafsson of Norway, who needed money to continue his war with Denmark. Such instances of assertiveness succeeded because they did not conflict with the interests of Earl Godwine and his family.

Edward wanted to be a just king, guided by God: he chose Easter Day for his coronation, and his first coins had 'PAX' and the cross on the reverse. He also had a strong sense of his royal bloodline and his right to rule. Godwine came to power as Cnut's henchman. He was ambitious, ruthless, and hungry for power for himself and his family. With hindsight, a clash was inevitable. When it came, it stemmed not so much from differences over policy as from their backgrounds and their cultural orientation. The first sign of trouble came in 1047 when Sweyn Estrithsson (or Estridsson), the new King of Denmark, asked for fifty English ships to help him resist the attacks of Norway's King Magnus. Godwine was in favour, not least because Sweyn was connected to his wife's family. Edward was not; nor was Earl Leofric; nor were the rest of the *witan*. Godwine was in a weak position at the time because his son, Sweyn, had followed a successful, if brutal, defence of the Welsh marches, by abducting and raping the Abbess of Leominster. Sweyn was duly exiled, and Edward divided his lands between his brother, Harold, and Beorn Estrithsson. Consequently, Godwine was forced to swallow this small defeat, but it was an indication of things to come.

Two years later, however, Edward was willing to deploy his ships in support of the Holy Roman Emperor, Henry III (r.1046–56). The key players were Baldwin V of Flanders (r.1035–67), and Eustace II, Count of Boulogne (r.1049–87). Between them, they controlled those stretches of the European coast which gave easiest access to London, the south-east, and the prosperous ports of East Anglia. In 1049, both were persuaded to support Duke Godfrey of Upper Lorraine in what was his second rebellion against his overlord, Emperor Henry III. Baldwin had hitherto been on good terms with Edward. So had Eustace, who had married Edward's sister, Godgifu, although he seized this opportunity to put her aside because she had not given him the male heir he wanted. These were politics – unlike those of Scandinavia – that Edward understood. He had a traditional view of overlordship, a natural inclination to support the Pope, who supported the Emperor, and to maintain family honour. He blockaded the coast of Flanders, and the Emperor quickly brought the rebels to heel.

At the same time, Sweyn Godwineson, who had been in exile in

Flanders, returned to England to seek reconciliation. The different versions of the *Chronicle* disagree on whether Edward was prepared to forgive him, but they agree that neither Harold nor Beorn were prepared to give back the lands they had received following his disgrace. Sweyn reacted by tricking Beorn into coming on board his ship, murdering him, and fleeing back to Flanders. Edward outlawed him as soon as he found out what had happened.

For all Sweyn's savagery, he had been highly effective in controlling the Welsh marches. In his absence, Edward built the first stone castles in England and installed Norman castellans and Norman troops who, unlike local levies, could be relied on not to have personal sympathies with those they were called upon to fight. Some sources, following the Godwine version of events, claim that Edward brought a large Norman entourage with him when he returned from exile in 1041. This does not seem to have been the case, but by the end of the 1040s, perhaps understanding that good relations with the Godwine family could not last, he began to appoint Normans to a number of influential positions as a way of shoring up his own. His nephew, Ralph of Vexin (sometimes of Mantes) – Godgifu's son by her first marriage – was given Beorn's vacant earldom. An Anglo-Breton named Ralph and the Frenchman Robert fitz Wimarc were appointed to administrative posts in East Anglia and Wessex respectively. French and Norman priests took up positions in the royal chapel and the royal household. Such appointments made Godwine suspicious, but Edward was careful to make conciliatory gestures in his direction. Perhaps surprisingly, he restored Sweyn to his position in the Welsh marches, placing him in command of the Norman castellans and their troops. He gave his approval to the marriage of Godwine's third son, Tostig, to Baldwin V's half-sister, Judith, in the hope of improving relations with Flanders and preventing any future disruptions of trade, something that was in both Edward's and Godwine's interest.

However, the appointment which caused most trouble, and eventually led to a breakdown in relations, was that of Robert of Jumièges to the Archdiocese of Canterbury in 1051. Robert, who had been Abbot of St Ouen and then Jumièges, had known Edward during his exile. He was appointed Bishop of London in 1044, and rapidly became one of Edward's closest advisers. That may have been enough to arouse Godwine's hostility but, however it happened, Robert was soon seen as one of Godwine's main opponents. When Archbishop Eadsige of Canterbury died in 1050, the cathedral chapter elected a monk called Æthelric, who had not previously been a bishop, although he was a connection of the Godwine family and Godwine had lobbied for his appointment. Edward overruled the chapter and chose Robert instead. He had good reasons for doing so. Robert was an experienced churchman and a supporter of the reform agenda promoted by Pope Leo IX, later known as the Gregorian Reforms, which focussed on the moral status and the independence of the clergy. This again put him at odds with Godwine, who appears to have opposed the reform movement, perhaps fearing he would lose the influence and patronage he enjoyed over the clergy within his lands. Nor did Robert improve the situation when he attempted to recover estates and revenues that were in Godwine's hands but which he considered belonged to the see of Canterbury. For all his opposition to Godwine, Robert was not Edward's lackey. He opposed Edward on several important issues, most notably by refusing to consecrate Edward's nominee for the see of London – a monk, illuminator, and goldsmith, known as Spearhafoc, who later ran off with the gold and precious stones from which he was supposed to fashion a new crown.

Robert was not directly involved in the event that led to open hostility between Edward and Godwine, although he may have conditioned Edward's reaction by warning that Godwine was plotting against him. In September 1051, Eustace of Boulogne visited Edward to rebuild the relationship that had been damaged by the events of 1049. All went well until, on their way home, Eustace and his men stopped at Dover, where they became involved in a dispute over their lodgings. The dispute escalated into a major confrontation leaving twenty dead. Dover was in Godwine's territory and Edward ordered him to ravage the town as punishment. This was not an unusual way of exacting retribution for bad behaviour – Eadred, Eadgar, and Harthacnut had all done the same in response to the murder of guests or visitors. Godwine was trapped. If he ravaged Dover, he would lose the allegiance of his people. If he did not, he would be guilty of disobeying the king. He chose to disobey, called on Sweyn and Harold for help, and began assembling an army. Edward responded by calling on Leofric and Siward. Neither side wanted open war. Edward summoned Godwine to account for himself, but in the middle of negotiations the long-buried issue of Godwine's role in the death of Edward's brother

Ælfred resurfaced. The *Anglo-Saxon Chronicle* claims that Stigand, now Bishop of Winchester and acting as intermediary, told Godwine that the King would grant him peace if he restored Ælfred alive, but Stigand would scarcely have said such a thing without a direct order. This was too much for Godwine. He, his wife, and three of his sons – Sweyn, Tostig, and Gyrth – fled to Bruges. Harold and Leofwine fled to Ireland. Under Anglo-Saxon law, by refusing to face the king and justify himself, Godwine had admitted his guilt. The *witan* outlawed the whole family and confiscated their estates, while Edward sent his wife, Edith, to a nunnery – an act of some significance which we will consider in due course. It seemed that Edward had risen to the challenge and freed himself from the Godwines. He took immediate steps to strengthen his position by redistributing the Godwine earldoms: Harold's East Anglian lands went to Leofric's son, Ælfgar; the western part of Godwine's Wessex earldom went to Edward's kinsman, Odda; the eastern part – where Godwine's power had been greatest – remained under the direct control of the King and his advisers. He also invited Duke William of Normandy to visit, receiving him – according to the *Chronicle* – as a vassal. We do not know what they discussed, but Edward needed allies and this was clearly an attempt to strengthen the relationship with the Duchy which had given him sanctuary in his youth.

In June 1052, Godwine made his first attempt to come back. He sailed to Dungeness and Pevensey. Perhaps it was a reconnaissance to determine how much support he retained, but a combination of bad weather and a fleet raised by Edward's newly-promoted earls chased him off. He returned that August at what proved to be the worst possible time for Edward. The fleet raised by the earls had disbanded, and there was no permanent naval defence. Edward had abolished the permanent fleet – and the tax used to maintain it – possibly to gain public favour, but probably also because the ships were crewed by Scandinavians, whose loyalty he could not necessarily rely on. Godwine joined forces with his sons, Harold and Leofwine, who had sailed from Ireland, off the south coast – the psychopathic Sweyn having (somewhat surprisingly) gone on a pilgrimage to Jerusalem and died in Constantinople on the way back. They sailed up the Thames while at the same time an army raised by Godwine's supporters marched on London from the south. Edward was now trapped. Whatever Leofric and Siward might think of Godwine, whatever commitments

Duke William may have made, everything had happened too quickly for them to come to his aid. His capitulation was dressed up as a reconciliation, but the reality was an abject defeat. The Godwines were restored to their earldoms; Edith was rescued from her nunnery and restored to her position as Queen Robert of Jumièges fled to Normandy; and Edward's other Norman advisers scattered, some to Normandy, some to Flanders, some to Scotland. Having briefly tasted freedom from Godwine's influence, Edward was now reduced to a figurehead instituting Godwine policies. He spent his time hunting and hawking; he focussed on building the Palace of Westminster and Westminster Abbey; he became ever more devout, although he was allowed no say in important ecclesiastical appointments. The now absent Robert of Jumièges was replaced as Archbishop of Canterbury by Stigand, a secular priest rather than a monk, and a member of the Anglo-Danish faction whose views and sympathies were in complete contrast to those of Robert and Edward.

The next few years saw a series of deaths and a consequent redistribution of earldoms. Godwine himself died in 1053, struck down by a seizure a matter of months after his triumphal return. The vast earldom of Wessex passed to Harold, Godwine's heir since the death of Sweyn. Harold's earldom in East Anglia passed to Leofric's son Ælfgar, who had held it briefly during the Godwines' exile. In 1055, Siward of Northumberland died, and his position was taken by Tostig. In 1057, Leofric died. Ælfgar inherited Mercia, leaving East Anglia to the command of Gyrth Godwineson. In 1058, a new earldom was created in south-east England for the fifth Godwine brother, Leofwine. Edward had lost his two most powerful and reliable allies, and the position of the Godwine family was strengthened even further.

History has tended to see Godwine himself as a villain, ruthless and hungry for power. While this is true, it can also be argued that, having risen to power and influence under Cnut, and wishing to retain the benefits of the status quo, he acted as a force for stability during the uncertain reigns of Harald I and Harthacnut, and during Edward's early years. The roles are not mutually exclusive. By the later 1040s, however, the focus of Godwine's ambition had changed. The subtext of his feud with the King, and of the years that followed, was not simply power but the succession.

In theory at least, English kingship was not a matter of primogeniture: it was in the gift of the king's council, the *witan*. In the case of Swein

Forkbeard and Cnut, the *witan* had bowed to the political realities of the day. However, as Edward's accession made clear, where possible the *witan* would show a preference for members of the House of Wessex – partly because most of the *witan* had themselves been connected with the family of the Wessex kings at some time. Godwine understood this, and when his daughter married Edward in 1045, he had every prospect of seeing a grandson on the throne. By the end of the decade, when there was no sign of a royal heir, both the King and Godwine began to consider who might succeed. The suggestion that Edward had taken a vow of chastity needs to be treated with caution. It comes from the *Vita Edwardi regis*, commissioned by Edith, and fits a little too well with the air of ineffectual saintliness, which was how the Godwines later sought to characterise Edward. It is also at odds with the fact that, once the Godwines had been exiled and Edith shipped off to a nunnery, Edward tasked Robert of Jumièges with securing him a divorce – which he suggests he intended to remarry and produce an heir.

Then there is the oft-repeated assertion that Edward promised the kingship to William of Normandy during William's visit to England in 1051. Even recent scholars, such as Marc Morris, treat this as fact.[302] Again, it seems unlikely that Edward would make such an offer if he was seeking a divorce. Moreover, none of the Norman chroniclers reports such an offer until after 1066, when William was seeking to justify his invasion. The chronicler William of Poitiers claims that during the visit Godwine, Leofric, Siward and Bishop Stigand all swore that they would accept William as king – but his *Gesta Guillelmi* (*The Deeds of William*) is a panegyric on William's life, written many years after the events it describes when all the actors were dead. More significantly, Edward's whole life and his eventual accession demonstrate his belief in the importance of royal blood, and his later actions show him actively seeking an heir of the blood. In 1017, Edmund Ironside's two sons were sent by Cnut to Sweden and eventually made their way to Kiev (see Chapter 34). One of those sons – known as Edward the Exile to distinguish him from the other Edwards in this story – was still alive, married to the daughter of Iaroslav I of Kiev and living in Hungary. In 1054, the King sent Bishop Ealdred of Worcester to persuade him to return to England, which he did, although he died shortly after his arrival. Whether or not he was poisoned by the Godwine faction we cannot know, but he left a son, Edgar, who was brought up at Edward's court. So, too, was another child of royal blood: another Harold, the son of Ralph of Vexin, and thus Edward's great-nephew. Again, the evidence suggests that Edward wanted an heir of the blood.

Meanwhile, Godwine fortunes continued to prosper. In 1060, Bishop Ealdred became Archbishop of York, so that both archbishoprics were now in the hands of men who were close to the Godwines. Harold and Tostig gained glory for their successful attack on Gruffydd ap Llywelyn, forestalling his attempt to create a single Welsh kingdom (see Chapter 35). In theory, Harold was representing Edward. In practice, he was acting as if he was already king, and the pro-Godwine sources portray him as everything a king should be: tall, handsome, just, generous, kind, and – of course – fearless.

In 1064 came Harold's critical voyage to Normandy. There is no consensus on why he made the trip. The most likely explanation is that he went to try to arrange the release of his younger brother, the sixth Godwine son, Wulfnoth, and his nephew, Sweyn's son, Hakon, both of whom were being held hostage by Duke William – although we do not know how they came to be there. Harold set off from Bosham in Sussex but was blown off course in a storm and shipwrecked on the coast of Ponthieu. He was captured by the Count of Ponthieu, Guy I, and taken to his castle at Beaurains, just south of Valenciennes. Crucially, in view of what was to come, he was freed through the intervention of Duke William and taken to Normandy. Harold subsequently fought alongside William in a campaign in Brittany. The Bayeux Tapestry shows him rescuing two Norman soldiers who were sinking in quicksand, and later, after taking the town of Dinan, receiving armour from William on the battlefield. What is implied by this – simple gratitude, a pact of friendship, or Harold's agreement to accept William as his overlord – is uncertain. Both documentary sources and the Tapestry tell us that Harold swore an oath to the effect that he would support William as successor to Edward, but these sources are all Norman, and all date from after the Conquest. The *Anglo-Saxon Chronicle* does not mention Harold visiting Normandy at all. Given the number and the broad coherence of Norman sources, we must assume that the writers of the *Chronicle* chose – or were told – to omit the story. We will never know exactly what happened, but it seems likely that Harold swore an oath, probably on holy relics, committing himself to offering some kind of support to William. William, to emphasise the balance of power between them, allowed Harold to take Hakon Sweynson back to England, but kept Wulfnoth in Normandy.

Neither man was trustworthy. Harold, for all the adulatory Godwine propaganda, was a proud, domineering figure, used to getting his own way: a man whose word might only temporarily be his bond. William had endured a long, hard road from being an illegitimate child ruler to being the feared and undisputed Duke of Normandy. He, too, was capable of distorting the facts if it was in his interest to do so. Nonetheless, what happened between them and their subsequent relationship is of critical importance, for it determined the political and social future of most of the British Isles.

Meanwhile, Edward appears to have made his decision. About the time that Harold was in Normandy, an entry appears in the *Liber Vitae* (*Book of Life*) in Winchester's New Minster, referring to Edgar as 'Ætheling', a title usually reserved for the king's eldest son. This is an isolated reference, but, as Tom Licence observes in his *Edward the Confessor*, the majority of sources were written after 1066 by 'supporters of Harold or William [who] can be guaranteed to have done the job of airbrushing Edgar from the record.'[303] If Edward did make a decision in favour of Edgar, he is unlikely to have done so in private, and this chimes with the story reported by the chronicler Hariolf (also Hariulf and Eriolf) of the Abbey of Saint-Riquier in Ponthieu, writing in the 1080s. Hariolf claims that when Edward died, Harold seized the throne despite having sworn he would uphold Edgar's claim.

There was a fourth figure with a claim to the English throne – albeit a tenuous one: Harald Hardrada, the King of Norway, who would also play a part in determining Britain's political future. The sobriquet Hardrada means 'hard counsel' or 'tough advice', and there is no doubt that he was a tough individual. He had seen service under Iaroslav I in Kiev, joined the Varangian Guard and fought everywhere from Sicily to Mesopotamia in the service of the Byzantine Emperor, before returning to Scandinavia and, in 1047, becoming sole ruler of Norway. In 1040, his predecessor, Magnus Olafsson, had agreed with Harthacnut that whoever died first would allow their lands to pass to the other (see Chapter 34). When Harthacnut died in 1042, Edward became King of England. Magnus threatened to invade in support of his claim but was distracted by events in Denmark. Harald Hardrada considered that he had inherited Magnus' claim to the English throne but did nothing about it until drawn into English affairs in 1065 by Tostig Godwineson.

Tostig's appointment as Earl of Northumbria was unpopular from the start. The Northumbrians felt he had been imposed on them, and he compounded his unpopularity by raising taxes and instituting what amounted to a reign of terror, killing anyone who opposed him and confiscating their lands. In the autumn of 1065, when Tostig was with Edward and Edith at the rededication of Wilton Abby in Wiltshire, two hundred Northumbrian *thegns* broke into his headquarters in York, killed his retainers, broke open the treasury and took gold, silver, and weapons. The rebellion spread rapidly. Men came from Mercia and even from Wales. They called for Morcar, son of Ælfgar of Mercia, to replace Tostig. Harold met them at Northampton with a message that the King would address their grievances if they returned home. They replied that they would only do so if Tostig were banished. Edward wanted to confront the rebels, but no one else wanted civil war. Harold would not fight against his brother. Winter was coming on. It was difficult to raise troops. Edward was furious but forced to capitulate. Tostig, equally furious, accused Harold of conspiring against him and fled to Flanders, where he was welcomed by Count Baldwin.

That was October. By December, it was obvious that Edward did not have long to live. The dedication of his new abbey at Westminster was brought forward, but he was too ill to attend. He died on 5 January 1066. The Godwines claimed that with his dying breath Edward committed England to Harold's care. The *witan* bowed to political reality. Edgar the Ætheling was an untried teenager. Harold was a proven warrior and administrator, as well as the richest and most powerful man in the kingdom. The two archbishops were behind him, and he had done a deal with the two non-Godwine earls, the newly-appointed Morcar in Northumbria and his brother, Eadwine, in Mercia. They would support his kingship if he set aside his long-time partner or common-law wife, the remarkably-named Edith Swan-Neck, and married their sister Eadgyth (or Edith). It was swift and bloodless. Harold – technically Harold II – was crowned the very next day, 6 January. But rapid coronations are often an indication of insecurity.

At home, Harold was politically secure, despite many whisperings and suspicions surrounding the manner of his accession. The Godwine propaganda machine endeavoured to give the new reign an aura of respectability by praising Edward's holiness and wisdom. A poem written during Harold's brief reign states that Edward was carried up to heaven by angels. The *Vita Edwardi regis* links Edward's moral righteousness to his wisdom in entrusting the realm to Harold. In the end, the legend of Edward's saintliness endured a great deal longer than Harold's kingship.

Whatever his position at home, abroad Harold suddenly found himself ringed by hostile powers. From Normandy, he could expect nothing but hostility. He must have hoped that Duke William would not risk an invasion, but within weeks of Harold's accession, it was known that an invasion fleet was under construction. Baldwin V of Flanders was also hostile. He had given refuge to Tostig, but he was also William's father-in-law. Unable to back both horses, he expelled Tostig. Eustace II of Boulogne was sandwiched between Normandy and Flanders. Whatever his relations with Edward, he had no love for Harold and the Godwines, and it was clearly in his interest to support William.

On being driven out of Flanders, Tostig embarked on a search for someone who would help restore him to what he saw as his rightful place in England. He sailed down the Channel and approached Duke William, who was presumably maturing his own plans. He made his way north to Scotland where Malcolm III gave him a warm welcome but no practical or material support. He crossed to Denmark where his cousin, Sweyn II Estridsen, offered an earldom if he wished to settle there, but Tostig was not interested. Then, according to *King Harald's Saga,* he visited Norway and persuaded Harald Hardrada that King Harold was deeply unpopular and if Hardrada invaded he would attract widespread support. *King Harald's Saga* is not always reliable, but whatever did happen – whether they met face to face or corresponded through intermediaries – they agreed to launch an invasion later that year. The two men had very different aims. Hardrada clearly wanted the English throne for himself. Tostig is unlikely to have seen himself as a candidate for the throne, but he certainly wanted revenge, and may also have seen his future as Hardrada's viceroy in England. Malcolm III, watching from the sidelines, had no interest in the English throne and was too politically astute to commit himself to the alliance, but he was happy to encourage any instability that might reduce the potential for an English invasion of Scotland. As Licence suggests, the fact that the rulers of all England's neighbours should suddenly have turned against Harold indicates that they did not regard his kingship as legitimate.[304]

37 Conquest

> Harold was not destined to gain quiet possession of a throne the work of which he had done – and done well – for the last twelve years. He had to reckon with the most terrible and determined foe in Europe. William [was] ... descended from the fierce Scandinavian pirates, a giant in height, of enormous strength, savage in numbers, furious in anger, and remorseless in revenge. — Professor J.M.D. Meikeljohn[305]

> Although here the English once again accepted conquest and bowed in a new destiny, yet ever must the name of Harold be honoured in the Island for which he and his famous house-carls fought indomitably to the end. — Winston Churchill[306]

Ten sixty-six is said to be the one date in English history that everyone knows. With the benefit of hindsight, we can see that by the spring of that year the stage was set for momentous events, but we should remind ourselves that nothing that happened was inevitable. It was determined by circumstances, by resources, and by personalities. There were three great battles: Fulford, Stamford Bridge, and Hastings. The first is usually overlooked, but it had important consequences for the other two. Unlike Brunanburh and Clontarf, the significance of these battles has not been inflated or distorted by historians or commentators with an axe to grind. It would be difficult to overstate the importance of the events of the second half of the year, but that does not make interpretation easier. The events themselves are so well known (as opposed to understood), that the issues involved are often massively over-simplified. This is summed up on a BBC educational website as 'plucky English underdogs against the nasty Normans'.[307] The not-entirely-logical idea that the wrong side won at Hastings was particularly prevalent in England in the nineteenth and early twentieth centuries and was closely related to the conviction that the English were essentially a Germanic race, descended from the Anglo-Saxons (see Chapter 26). This in turn led to historians taking an idealised view of Harold's character and seeing him as the embodiment of noble English virtues. The reality, of course, was more complex and more nuanced. Neither Harold nor William was a model of virtue. Nor were Harald Hardrada and Tostig. But their actions, and the wars their actions engendered, need to be seen in the context of the *realpolitik* of their age. Harold was at the centre of events. Whatever the rights or wrongs of his position, he was in possession of the English crown, and a desire to overthrow him was possibly the only thing that Duke William, Harald Hardrada, and Tostig had in common.

In the first months of his reign, Harold seems to have made two assumptions. The first was that Tostig would not cause any further problems. If news ever came to Harold of Tostig's meeting with Harald Hardrada, he presumably decided that nothing would come of it. That summer, Tostig made a nuisance raid on the Isle of Wight and an abortive landing on the coast of Yorkshire, but had subsequently been deserted by some of his crews, leaving him with only twelve of his original sixty ships. The second assumption was that he could face down William of Normandy. A contemporary Norman chronicler, William of Jumièges, describes William as apoplectic with fury on hearing of Harold's coronation. He sent a protest, demanding that Harold honour his oath and step aside. Harold replied that the kingdom was not his to promise, and that he had been chosen by the *witan*. Angles, Saxons, Jutes, Danes, and Norwegians had all arrived in the British Isles by sea in previous centuries. Nonetheless, a seaborne invasion of England was a huge undertaking. Harold was gambling that William would not take the risk. And it was a risk. Normandy under William was an up-and-coming power, heavily dependent on the personal qualities of its still-young Duke, but England was rich and powerful, with well-established arrangements for mobilising the *fyrd* and defending itself. Yet written sources and the Bayeux Tapestry confirm that as soon as he received Harold's reply, William ordered the construction of an invasion fleet.

There was also a strong religious dimension to the situation, the full significance of which can be difficult for a twenty-first century audience to grasp. These were violent men, but they lived in a religious age. During his reign in Norway, Harald Hardrada built and repaired many churches and, influenced by his earlier travels, brought in clerics from Kiev and Byzantium. Tostig was chosen by Edward the Confessor as a suitable companion to travel to Rome with Archbishop Ealdred of York. Duke William was a generous supporter of the Church, employing clerics as some of his closest advisers and establishing at least twenty new monasteries in Normandy before 1066. Harold Godwineson was a major benefactor of Waltham Church – later Waltham Abbey – where he is supposed to have been buried. All four understood that the Church was the arbiter of right and wrong. It made judgements that influenced the behaviour of ordinary people, and, in doing so, exercised enormous influence in the secular as well as the spiritual world. This was an area where Harold began at a disadvantage and was then completely outmanoeuvred by William.

When the Godwines returned from exile in 1052, Robert of Jumièges fled to Normandy and was replaced as Archbishop of Canterbury by Stigand (see Chapter 36). The Pope at the time, Leo IX, and his successors all condemned the circumstances that forced Robert to flee. They continued to regard him as the legitimate Archbishop and, to emphasise the point, excommunicated Stigand. Consequently, it was Ealdred, not Stigand, who officiated at Harold's coronation. Unfortunately for Harold, Ealdred was also the subject of controversy. When appointed Archbishop of York, he had tried to retain the see of Worcester at the same time (a practice known as pluralism) and papal approval was delayed until he surrendered it. Such disputes were not unusual – there was even a series of alternative popes at the time – but William and his adviser, Abbott Lanfranc of Caen, skilfully exploited these two high-profile cases.

Both Stigand and Ealdred had been appointed by Edward the Confessor while under the influence of the Godwines. This allowed William to exploit the long-standing controversy over whether secular rulers or the Church should appoint bishops. He sided with the Pope, Alexander II, and promised to reform the English Church. He accused the Godwines of plundering church lands and stealing church property. Whether this was true or not barely mattered. He had the Pope's ear. Then there was Harold. We know that oath-breaking was not unusual, but that Harold had broken an oath sworn on holy relics could, when presented to the Pope, be seen as clear evidence that he was not fit to rule. William asked for papal blessing for his invasion of England, and received it, together with a banner and a ring as a gift of the Pope.

The Pope's blessing turned out to be crucial, not to the success of the invasion, but to it happening at all. Normandy was a feudal state to a degree that England, at this stage, was not. What constitutes feudalism, and the impact of Norman feudalism as imposed on England by William after the Conquest is something we shall consider in due course (see Chapter 38). At this point, it is sufficient to note that – in theory at least – William enjoyed more authority over his subjects in his duchy than Harold did in his kingdom. Nonetheless, when he ordered his nobles to raise an army to invade England, they pointed out – no doubt politely – that their feudal obligations ceased at the Channel coast. Their attitude only changed because of Pope Alexander's blessing which, in Simon Schama's words, 'managed to convert a personal and dynastic feud into a holy war.'[308] It was not only Norman attitudes that changed. William's army was swelled by volunteers from Brittany and Flanders, possibly lured by the prospect of being rewarded with land in England.

Harold must have realised what was coming. No doubt he received intelligence of William's preparations and was able to time his own preparations and the mobilisation of the *fyrd* accordingly. Establishing the numbers on each side at this stage is a matter of educated guesswork, as most of the figures in contemporary sources are exaggerated. Harold had perhaps 2,000 or 3,000 professional soldiers, his housecarls – those axemen with kite shields and helmets with nose-guards who appear in the Bayeux Tapestry and have become the accepted image of Anglo-Saxon soldiery. The *fyrd*, consisting of the *thegns* and other classes of freemen mobilised to defend the country at a time of need, may have amounted to another 10,000 to 15,000. In addition, Harold requisitioned ships of all kinds, and their crews, from the ports of Kent and Sussex. He based himself at Bosham in West Sussex, knowing that William would have to land somewhere along that stretch of coast. This was Godwine territory – the region that had supported his father when he returned from exile in 1052 – and he believed it would now fight for him.

William's army was camped on the banks of the River Dives, about twelve kilometres from his capital at Caen, and his ships were moored in the sheltered waters of the estuary. He had between 1,000 and 2,000 knights, each with a squire and up to five horses, and perhaps 7,000 or 8,000 foot soldiers. When the moment came, they would be packed into his ships, together with all their equipment and stores – and three prefabricated wooden castles. Chroniclers and commentators have put the size of William's fleet at anything between 400 and 3,000 ships. More recent estimates, based on the weight and volume of the men, horses and materiel that required transporting, suggest a more plausible figure of between seven hundred and seven hundred and fifty. The ships themselves, depicted in the Bayeux Tapestry, were high-prowed and high-sterned, with a single sail, probably like Viking *snekkia*, but with higher sides, more freeboard, and thus capable of carrying a greater load.

By the second week in August, the two forces were drawn up on opposite sides of the Channel. Harold was waiting for an invasion. William was waiting for a wind. It had to be southerly: his ships, crammed with men and horses, needed a following wind to avoid potentially dangerous manoeuvres. They waited throughout August. Then, at the beginning of September, it was Harold who discovered that his authority had limits. The king could summon the *fyrd*; he could demand service from the crews of the ships he requisitioned; but only for forty days. It was harvest time and they wanted to go home. On 8 September, he gave in and disbanded his forces. A few days later, he returned to London. About the same time, William made his move. He ordered his ships to sea, but a gale drove them up the Channel to St Valéry at the mouth of the Somme, where the waiting continued.

In the meantime, Harald Hardrada had sailed from the Songefjord on Norway's west coast to Orkney, where he gathered supplies and reinforcements. On his way south, he may have visited Malcolm III at Dunfermline, although this is uncertain. He met Tostig at Tynemouth. Although Tostig had only twelve ships to Hardrada's three hundred, he was a Godwine and his presence was of paramount importance. Their army may have numbered between 9,000 and 10,000 men. From Tynemouth, they sailed south, raiding the coast of Yorkshire – part of Tostig's former Earldom of Northumbria – before making their way up the Humber and the Ouse to land at Riccall, just twenty kilometres south of York. Messengers were despatched to London to warn Harold, but that took time. Harold is supposed to have received the news on 19 September – although it may have been three or four days earlier. By that time, Morcar, who had replaced Tostig as Earl of Northumbria, and his brother, Edwin, Earl of Mercia, had mobilised their forces and positioned themselves to the south of York, hoping to deny the invaders access to the most important city in northern England.

The Battle of Fulford took place on 20 September. Estimates suggest that some 11,000 men took part, with the Norwegians having a slight numerical advantage. Morcar and Edwin were young – probably still in their teens – and the men they were leading were not experienced soldiers. They began well, pushing the Norwegian line back, but Hardrada led a counterattack, forcing the English into marshy ground. The young earls escaped, but their forces were routed, and many were killed. York was theirs for the taking, but Tostig and Hardrada did not allow their men to loot and burn. Their aim was conquest, and they could not afford to alienate the Northumbrians. At a meeting outside the city walls on 24 September, they offered peace and encouraged the Northumbrians to join them in their march south. The Northumbrians agreed, but Tostig and Hardrada's price was five hundred hostages drawn from the leading local families – who would have been known to Tostig from his time as Earl – to ensure that the agreement was honoured. It was agreed that the hostages were to be handed over the following day at Stamford Bridge, some ten kilometres east of the city.

What Tostig and Hardrada did not know is that, on the evening of 24 September, the gates of York had quietly opened to admit Harold Godwineson and his army. Even with the benefit of hindsight, it is difficult to understand how Harold managed to reassemble so much of the *fyrd* he had sent home two weeks previously, and march both the *fyrd* and his housecarls over fifty kilometres a day along what were still essentially Roman roads to reach York in just five days. Even if he received news of the invasion earlier than usually supposed, to arrive in York by 24 September was still a remarkable feat. The next morning, 25 September, Harold and his men marched out to confront Tostig and Hardrada. The surprise was complete. We have no contemporary accounts of what happened, but it appears that only about two-thirds of the Scandinavian army was there, and that because it was hot and they were not expecting to fight they had left some of their armour behind. *King Harald's Saga* tells how Harold rode out from the English lines to banter with Tostig and offer Hardrada seven, rather than six, feet of English soil because he was taller than most men. A twelfth-century interpolation in the *Anglo-Saxon Chronicle* claims that the crucial bridge over the River Derwent was held by a single Norwegian axeman until an English soldier managed to float underneath him in a barrel and stab him from below. Such colourful incidents are probably later inventions, but Harold and his men undoubtedly won a major victory. It was carnage. Tostig and Harald Hardrada were killed. Hardrada's son, Olaf, was spared; so, too, were the young Earls of Orkney, Paul and Erland Thorfinnsson, who had been left guarding the ships; but so many of the invaders were killed that only twenty-four of the three hundred ships that had arrived were needed to convey the survivors home. Harold had managed to gather his scattered army, bring it to York, fight and win a battle. He had also seized Hardrada's extremely valuable store of loot and treasure. The battle had not been completely one-sided – English losses were significant – but he had completely destroyed the Scandinavian threat to his throne. It was a remarkable achievement, and he and his men retired to York to rest.

The rest, and whatever relief or satisfaction he may have felt, lasted only a few days. On 1 October, he received the news that William's fleet had landed on the Sussex coast. Tradition reports that William's luck changed when he attempted to maintain morale by exhibiting the relics of St Valéry to his troops. The wind changed, and the next day, 27 September, the armada set off on the afternoon tide. A southerly wind and the strong tidal currents would have kept them on a north-westerly course throughout the night. The English coast would have come into view at first light, and the armada was able to come ashore with the rising tide that morning. Scholarly tradition says that William came ashore at Pevensey. Sussex tradition says it was Bulverhythe, ten kilometres further east. Both could be right. Crossing the Channel at night in late September with no means of communication beyond lanterns and shouting, it would have been impossible to keep seven hundred ships together. Even if they had arrived in perfect order, they would have had to be beached along six or seven kilometres of shoreline. From William's point of view, this was the most dangerous moment of the invasion. Had Harold's forces been at hand, they could have picked off the Norman ships as they landed, but they were in the north recovering from Fulford and Stamford Bridge. As it was, if the Normans faced any opposition, it was negligible.

Once ashore, William erected one of his prefabricated castles within the walls of Roman Pevensey, while his troops foraged and pillaged. One panel of the Bayeux Tapestry shows a mother and child apparently fleeing their burning home. Schama notes that this is 'the very first image in European art that makes space for the ruin of its victims.'[309] William's campaigns in Brittany had been rapid and aggressive. His men would ravage the countryside across a wide front, burn towns, set up castles, and move forward once again. In England, he was uncharacteristically cautious. This may have been because he was unfamiliar with the geography of the region, because he lacked intelligence on Harold's movements, or perhaps because Robert fitz Wimarc was feeding him warnings about the strength of Harold's army. For two weeks following the landing, the Norman army remained close to the coast, moving slowly east to the area around Hastings, which was better suited to concentrating their forces and offered access to a road leading north.

Meanwhile, Harold and his housecarls had made another exhausting march southwards, calling out those elements of the *fyrd* that had not already been mobilised, before pausing for a few days in London. Harold ordered a fleet into the Channel to intercept any vessels trying to supply or reinforce William from the Continent, then moved towards the south coast. The timing of the Battle of Hastings was probably Harold's greatest error. His forces had been victorious in the north, but they had been badly weakened. Some of the *fyrd* marched with him, but much of it was still mobilising. The longer Harold delayed, the stronger he became. By contrast, William needed a battle as soon as possible. While he remained inactive at Hastings, he was using up supplies, and his men – who had already waited for weeks on the other side of the Channel – were losing patience. Harold had no chance of surprising William, so why did he set off with a force smaller than it would have been if he had waited an extra week? Was he overconfident? Was it because the area where William's troops were foraging and burning included some of his personal estates? Or perhaps he did not intend to bring William to battle immediately. He may have intended to contain him around Hastings while his supplies diminished – which would fit with the tactic of sending a blockading fleet into the Channel – but was himself surprised by the sudden proximity of the enemy.

However it came about, on the morning of 14 October, the two armies were finally in sight of one another. The traditional view, based on the near-contemporary account of Orderic Vitalis, an English monk living in Normandy, is that the English forces were drawn up on the ridge of Senlac Hill, where Battle Abbey now stands, while the Normans occupied the lower, softer ground to the south. More recently, it has been suggested that the battle may have been fought on Caldbec Hill, a little to the north, or between Telham and Crowhurst, four kilometres to the south, but there is no substantive evidence to change the accepted view.[310] Again, we can only estimate the size of the armies. The Normans may have had about 8,000 men in all, while the English held a slight numerical advantage with perhaps 9,000. The key difference – which probably proved decisive in the later stages of the battle – was that the Normans had cavalry whereas the English all fought on foot.

The story of the Battle of Hastings has been told too often to need repeating here in any detail. It was one of the longest medieval battles on record, lasting the whole day. Whether the story of a feigned retreat by the Normans is true or not, and however valiantly Harold's housecarls fought, once the English ceased to stand behind their shieldwall the Norman cavalry were able to hunt them down across open ground. The result was a complete Norman victory. Not only was Harold killed, but so, too, were his brothers Leofwine and Gyrth. His sons survived, but the power of the Godwine family was ended. The Bayeux Tapestry shows Harold dying after being struck in the eye by an arrow. The twelfth-century Norman chronicler, Wace, says that he cannot confirm the story of the arrow. Another tradition has it that his body was so mutilated that only Edith Swan-Neck was able to identify it. Harold's mother, Gytha, is said to have offered William her son's bodyweight in gold if she could take him away for burial. William apparently refused and had the body buried secretly on the seashore. Not even Cnut treated his defeated rivals in such a contemptuous way. Was William punishing Harold for breaking his oath even after death? Or did he want to avoid creating another English martyr?

Yet another story has it that Harold did not die at Hastings but became a pilgrim on the Continent and a hermit at Chester and elsewhere. Such stories have their fascination, and the claims made in two manuscripts originating in Waltham Abbey are fully examined in Teresa Cole's *The Norman Conquest*.[311] To the historian looking at the impact of William's victory on the political and social evolution of England and the British Isles, the sad fact is that it does not really matter. What matters is that everyone believed him to have died, and that he did not re-emerge as a focus for opposition to the new order.

Hastings was decisive, but it was not the end of the story. Harold was dead, but William was not yet king and not yet a conqueror. The dead were buried, and he sent to Normandy for reinforcements. He waited a few days at Hastings, then moved on to Dover, which opened its gates to him, as did Canterbury. Local landowners submitted to him, but the English nobility remained in London, uncertain what to do. The *Anglo-Saxon Chronicle* records that Archbishop Ealdred and the citizens of London proclaimed Edgar the Ætheling their new king. It was a gesture of faith in the old order, but it was misplaced. Edgar was no more than fourteen, and the two earls who promised to fight for him, Edwin and Morcar, were not yet twenty. Events hung fire for several weeks while William and much of his army endured an outbreak of dysentery. Had the young earls seized the opportunity and made a rapid attack, they might have altered the situation, but they remained in London, waiting for William to make the next move.

William moved his forces up to the south bank of the Thames. He sent his cavalry to try to force London Bridge, but they were repulsed, and William contented himself with burning Southwark. Unwilling to waste resources attacking what was probably the best-defended city in the kingdom, he moved towards the old capital of Winchester. Edith of Wessex, Edward the Confessor's widow, chose to surrender without bloodshed, and William took control of both the town and the royal treasury. Reinforcements arrived. He crossed the Thames at Wallingford, where Archbishop Stigand became the first member of the old regime to pay homage and become his man. Edwin and Morcar withdrew northwards. William followed them, giving his men increased licence to pillage and burn as they went. By the beginning of December, he had turned south again and reached Berkhamsted in Hertfordshire, forty kilometres northwest of London, which he burned. At this point, support for the old order finally collapsed. Edgar, Archbishop Ealdred, Edwin, Morcar, and 'all the best men of London ... submitted to the force of circumstances ... gave him hostages and swore oaths of loyalty.'[312]

William was crowned King of England on Christmas Day 1066 in Edward the Confessor's new Romanesque abbey at Westminster. Archbishop Ealdred presided, pronouncing the words of St Dunstan, written for the coronation of King Eadgar in 973 in English, while the Bishop of Coutances gave a French translation. The coronation rite contained a promise to rule 'in accordance with the laws and customs of ancient kings, and with rights and privileges granted to the English people.' William added the *caveat* that he would do so provided his subjects remained loyal. When the moment came for the new king to be acclaimed by the congregation, the day descended into chaos. Hearing the noise, William's knights assumed it was an attack and set the neighbourhood on fire. William was furious; the English suspected a trick and lost what little trust they may have had in the new regime; and William gave orders for the construction of the massive stone-built stronghold we now know as the Tower of London.

A period of calm followed – perhaps born of shock as far as the English were concerned. William received repeated assertions of loyalty from Edwin and Morcar who were allowed to retain their titles and most of their lands – although northern Northumbria passed to a man called Copsig (or Copsi). He had been a close ally of Tostig, but early in 1067 came to William's camp at Barking, close to the site where the Tower of London was being built, to throw himself on William's mercy. Waltheof, the son of Siward of Northumbria, was allowed to keep his lands in Northampton and Huntingdon. Leofwine's Earldom of East Anglia passed to William's half-brother, Odo of Bayeux, while William Fitzosbern, possibly William's closest adviser, became Earl of Wessex and Earl of Hereford.

In March 1067, having satisfactorily begun to re-order his new kingdom, William left Odo and Fitzosbern as co-regents, and returned to Normandy. Following in his train were the two archbishops, Ealdred and Stigand, and three earls, Edwin, Morcar, and Waltheof. Officially guests, in reality they were hostages, their presence demonstrating William's power and preventing them stirring up trouble in England. William stayed in Normandy for most of 1067. In his absence, there were rumblings of discontent. Odo and Fitzosbern appear to have turned a blind eye to their soldiers robbing and raping, while some of the English leaders had recovered from their shock and were beginning to regroup. A Herefordshire *thegn*, Edric (or Eadric) the Wild, attacked the castles that Edward the Confessor had built along the Welsh marches. He then allied himself with Bleddyn and Rhiwallon ap Cynfyn, two princes of Gwynedd, and they mounted raids into England. The men of Kent involved Eustace of Boulogne in a plot to seize Dover from Odo of Bayeux. Copsig, who was hated by the Northumbrians because of his connection with Tostig, was murdered.

More serious than such acts of local resistance were the attempts by the Godwine family to stage a comeback. Harold's mother, Gytha, his common-law wife, Edith Swan-Neck, and her sons, Edmund and Magnus, gathered in Exeter and began canvassing support for a rebellion. In the last days of 1067, William demanded that the citizens of Exeter should swear formal oaths of submission and loyalty. They refused. Having tried negotiation, William resorted to force. This was the first occasion when he sought to raise an army from among the English, and he may have regarded it as a test of his new subjects' loyalty. In the event, Exeter was besieged for eighteen days before the Godwines fled – Edmund and Magnus to Ireland; Gytha and Edith to an island in the Bristol Channel, and from there, possibly, to Scandinavia. Exeter sued for peace, and William, still in conciliatory mood, accepted the surrender without burning or looting the city.

As if to demonstrate his confidence, William brought his wife, Matilda, to England, and she was crowned Queen in Westminster Abbey. Edgar the Ætheling may have been present at the ceremony, but shortly afterwards he fled to Scotland with his sister, Margaret (see Chapter 39). About the same time, William appointed a man named Gospatric to replace Copsig in northern Northumbria, apparently in exchange for a large sum of money. Almost immediately, he was faced with a rebellion, probably instigated by Edwin and Morcar, but ostensibly led by Edgar the Ætheling, Maerleswein – William's lieutenant in York – and the newly-appointed Gospatric. William was no longer in conciliatory mood. He made a slow progress north, allowing his men to burn, pillage, and sow fear among the population. He raised motte-and-bailey castles at Warwick and Nottingham, moved on to York which surrendered without a fight, and built another castle there. Edwin and Morcar appear to have submitted to William at an early stage, while the other leaders fled to Scotland. William made his way south, setting up more castles at Lincoln and Cambridge.

Within months, the rebellion flared up again, and the pace of events accelerated. Rebel Northumbrians entered Durham, killing the new Earl of Northumbria, Robert of Comines, and as many as nine hundred of his men. The rebel leaders marched south from Scotland, once again heading for York. William arrived with a large army and drove them off, but much of York was burned in the fighting. Harold's sons raided Barnstaple and the Taw Estuary from their base in Ireland, but they, too, were driven off. Then came an even bigger threat. Tostig's cousin, Sweyn II of Denmark (also Sweyn Estridsen) sent a fleet of some three hundred ships under the

Map 30   England Conquered and Transformed

command of his brother, Osbeorn. They raided the southern and eastern coasts before sailing up the Humber and making for York, where they were joined by Edgar the Ætheling, Gospatric, and Maerleswin, with the addition of the young Earl Waltheof. Beyond unseating William, their aims are uncertain. Edgar could claim to be the legitimate heir of the last Anglo-Saxon king, while Sweyn's involvement seems to have been based on the fact that his grandfather, Swein Forkbeard, had been king fifty years previously. We do not know what agreement, if any, the two may have reached but, as Teresa Cole points out, many people in the north of England would have preferred a Danish king to a Norman one.[313]

The Danish and rebel army reached York, killing most of the Norman garrison and taking large numbers of prisoners, while the city burned yet again. By the time William arrived with an army of mercenaries, the Danes had retired to Axholme, now a small town in Lincolnshire, but at the time an island amid the marshy ground south of the Humber and impossible for him to approach. Suddenly, everything was happening at once. A castle at Montacute in Somerset was attacked. Exeter was attacked again. Edric the Wild and his Welsh allies burned Shrewsbury. The Danes and Earl Waltheof attacked York yet again but were gone by the time William returned. He brazened out Christmas 1069 in York, celebrating with full regal splendour despite his difficulties, before embarking on a policy of divide and rule. He would leave the Danes alone, and they could keep the loot they had amassed, if they departed peacefully in the spring. Some sources say he offered a substantial sum of money as an added incentive. Osbeorn agreed, leaving William free to suppress the English rebels in other parts of the country with as much savagery as possible.

What followed has become known as the 'Harrying of the North'. Gospatric and Waltheof submitted to William and were spared but allowed no lands and no authority. Edgar and Maerleswin fled back to Scotland; but this was not enough for William. Determined to prevent any recurrence of trouble, he let his army loose. Right across the northern shires, towns and villages were razed, crops burned, livestock slaughtered, and local people killed. Many of those who were not killed at the time died of starvation in the aftermath. The *Domesday Book* indicates that more than 75 per cent of the original inhabitants never returned to their homes. Orderic Vitalis puts the number of dead at 100,000. Some have questioned whether William had enough men to wreak such devastation, but archaeological evidence supports the picture of widespread destruction and displacement of population. One American scholar has even accused

William of genocide.[314] With the northern counties devastated, William marched his men over the Pennines to retake Chester and relieve Shrewsbury, before paying them off at Salisbury in March 1070.

In the meantime, the Danes had not gone home as they promised, but colonised the (then) Isle of Ely. They attracted many of those Englishmen who were still prepared to oppose William, the most famous of whom was a man called Hereward, later known as 'the Wake', which probably meant 'keen-eyed' or 'vigilant'. Ely was never really a threat to William, but it was a challenge to his pride. The Danes departed in the summer of 1070, but Hereward and his band of rebels continued to occupy the island, and were joined by Earl Morcar and Æthelwine, a former Bishop of Durham. William decided to act. He persuaded (or bribed) someone to show him the way through the marshes. Many were killed; Morcar was locked up for the rest of his life; but Hereward and his followers escaped. We do not know what happened to them, but the twelfth-century *Gesta Herewardi* and Charles Kingsley's nineteenth-century novel *Hereward the Wake: Last of the English* elevated Hereward to the status of a great English hero.

William began his reign in a spirit of conciliation, even when provoked, but from the middle of 1068, when those who had sworn allegiance to him began to organise large-scale rebellions, his attitude changed. The physical manifestation of the change was the Norman castle. Stone castles were essentially a Continental idea, necessary to mark and defend land frontiers. The English equivalents were the forts and harbours used for shore defence. Edward the Confessor authorised the building of a handful of castles along the land border with Wales, but the absence of castles across the rest of the country made it easier for the Normans to impose their authority. At the beginning of his reign – in some cases even before his coronation – William ordered the construction of castles in key locations, among them Hastings, Dover, the Tower of London, Colchester, and Norwich. From 1068 onwards, castles became central to his strategy of repression. Wherever he faced or expected resistance, he would order the construction of a motte-and-bailey castle, partly as a base for operations, and partly to awe the local population. Many were subsequently replaced by stone-built strongholds with their characteristic square keeps. Thirty-eight stone castles can be dated to the twenty years of William's reign, together with as many as four hundred motte-and-bailey structures – and it is clear that the Normans did not do the digging and the heavy lifting themselves. For the Normans, castles were instruments of control. For the Saxons, they were symbols of occupation: the Normans 'filled the whole land with these castles ... burdened the unhappy people ... with forced labour ... and when the castles were built, they filled them with devils and wicked men.'[315]

38 Transformation

Luck and circumstance favoured William at Hastings. The quarrel between Harold and Tostig played a major part in their downfall and that of Anglo-Saxon England. It led to the Tostig and Hardrada's invasion, which led to Edwin and Morcar's forces being badly mauled at Fulford, which in turn caused Harold to race north and expend the lives of many of his housecarls and members of the *fyrd* at Stamford Bridge, men who were not in the ranks at Hastings. Without that sequence of events, William might well have faced a far tougher challenge when he arrived on the Sussex coast. To conquer England, William was always going to have to defeat Harold on the battlefield, but in his mind the submission of the English nobles at Berkhamsted was probably of greater significance. It marked the moment when the stalwarts of the old regime accepted defeat. In the more remote areas of the kingdom, his authority might still be theoretical rather than actual; there would be resistance and rebellions; nonetheless, after Berkhamsted, he was king, and his coronation marked the end of Anglo-Saxon England.

The *witan* chose William as king, just as they had chosen Cnut in 1016, because there was no alternative. They bowed to political reality and hoped for the best. Cnut had married Emma, the widow of a former English king, had chosen an English archbishop, Wulfstan II, as one of his closest advisers, and had been able to rely on both his army and, once he had achieved power, on the English Danes, who made up a significant proportion of the population. For the most part, he had accepted and worked within the social and political structures that had evolved as the English polity evolved. William's position was different. He had his army and – if they remained loyal – the support of those who had sworn allegiance when they realised they could no longer resist him, but there was no Norman population to look to for support. The twenty years of his reign saw more changes to the way England was organised and governed than the previous two hundred. It was his way of embedding his regime. Cnut's soldiers conquered, then settled down to become farmers or merchants. William's Normans rapidly formed themselves into a controlling overclass.

The political and administrative divisions of Anglo-Saxon England were clearer and better defined than those of the Duchy of Normandy, and the legal procedures were better established. By 1000, England was divided into thirty-two counties, each divided into 'hundreds'.[316] Each county or shire had a sheriff (from 'shire-reeve'), and both counties and hundreds had courts which usually met twice a year. William changed none of this. Indeed, it is a remarkable fact that, although some counties were sub-divided, and some new ones were added, most county boundaries remained unchanged until the local government reorganisation of 1974. William did not change how the land was divided: he changed who owned it, and how it was owned. 'Feudal' is a loose term, invented in the sixteenth century to describe aspects of medieval society that had survived into the post-medieval world. Some of the duties and obligations owed by Anglo-Saxons to their overlords were undoubtedly what we would call feudal. The Continental system imposed by William was more developed and more centralised. Its central tenet was that, as king, all the land in England belonged to him. He kept about 20 per cent as his personal estates; granted 25 per cent to the Church, with the bishop of each diocese acting as tenant-in-chief; and gave most of the remaining 55 per cent to the barons, those men he wished to reward for their service during the invasion. There were probably about two hundred such individuals, and the estates they were granted were often scattered across several counties to prevent them being able to consolidate a power base. He did allow a few of those English nobles who had sworn allegiance to keep their lands, but they had to pay for the privilege.

The second key element of William's feudalism was that every tenant-in-chief – anyone accepting land from him – had to swear an uncompromising oath of allegiance on the Bible to 'become his man'. Tenants-in-chief had to promise to pay their taxes and to provide a given number of knights, depending on the size and wealth of their manor, to fight for the king when required. These conditions applied to bishops as well as barons, and both replicated these terms when granting land to their under-tenants. Under-tenants, in turn, granted some of their land to free peasants in return for rent, and some to bonded peasants or serfs in return for labour. Anglo-Saxon society had been structured in a broadly similar way, but William defined the conditions and obligations of landholders with more precision, applied them more systematically, and enforced them more strictly.

His aim was to consolidate Norman control over all aspects of English society. The implementation was ruthless and rapid. By the 1070s, all England's earldoms were held by Normans, and most sheriffs were Norman. The courts were not only more active, hearing a much larger number of cases, but also more of an instrument of the royal will. The *thegns* who had formed the basis of the landholding system under the Anglo-Saxon kings were swept aside. The full extent of the redistribution of land is revealed in the *Domesday Book*, an initiative William undertook towards the end of his reign. The *Anglo-Saxon Chronicle* tells how

> he sent his men all over England ... to find out how many hundred of hides there were in each shire, how much land and what livestock the king actually owned ... what annual dues were lawfully his ... how much land his archbishops had, his abbots and his earls ... how much each landholder had ...and how much money it was worth.'[317]

Completed in 1086, the two massive volumes that resulted reveal that there were some 6,000 manors across England, most of them held by Normans. South of the Tees, only 5 per cent of the land remained in English hands; south of the Thames it may well have been none at all.

Modern historians like to see the *Domesday Book* as an early exercise in data collection. It was, but context is everything. The name was coined in the twelfth century and intended ironically, suggesting that judgements based on the contents of the William's great volumes were as immutable as those Christians would face on the Day of Judgement. William wanted detailed knowledge about everything in his new kingdom – names, numbers, values, areas, the potential for raising revenue – for he understood that such knowledge was power. Whatever else it was, the *Domesday Book* was an instrument of control.

In 1070, having put down what was probably the most serious challenge to his rule, William fulfilled his promise to Pope Alexander II and asked for a papal legate to investigate the state of the English Church. The visit, unsurprisingly, resulted in precisely those changes William wanted to see. Archbishop Ealdred of York, who had died a year earlier, was replaced by Thomas of Bayeux. Stigand was deposed and replaced as Archbishop of Canterbury by William's long-term ally and adviser, Lanfranc. The Bishops of Elham and Selsey were also deposed, probably because William suspected them of supporting the Godwines. A dispute over precedence between Thomas in York and Lanfranc in Canterbury was settled at a synod in Winchester in 1072, which recognised the primacy of Canterbury – something which remains the case to this day – and Lanfranc, armed with this authority, proceeded with his own process of Normanisation.

By making bishops tenants-in-chief and requiring them to provide knights to fight on his behalf, William had drawn the Church into the secular hierarchy. Lanfranc went further, making the Church reflect the Norman state in its culture and its physical appearance. The result increased the interdependence of the secular and religious authorities and benefitted both. Church discipline was a particular concern. Among England's monks, and among the clergy everywhere from cathedrals to parish churches, the rules governing pluralism, simony – the selling of offices – and celibacy were at best intermittently observed. Lanfranc enforced them strictly. Monasticism was revived along strict Benedictine lines. New Benedictine monasteries were established at Canterbury, York, Battle, and Selby, and an old one at Whitby revived. The even stricter Cluniac order entered England in 1077 when William of Warenne founded a priory at Lewes in Sussex. Several important monasteries, such as Glastonbury and Westminster, saw their English abbots replaced by Normans. Among the episcopate, the substitution of Norman for English clergy reached the proportions of a cultural revolution: between 1070 and 1140 – over fifty years after William's death – only one English-born bishop was appointed.

The career of Osmund – canonised as St Osmund in 1457 – illustrates the new relationship between Church and state. Osmund was both a cleric and Count of Sées in Normandy. He came to England with William and in 1070 was appointed Chancellor. Much of William's administration was modelled along broadly Carolingian lines, and the office of Chancellor had its origin at the court of the Carolingian kings. It may have existed under the later Anglo-Saxon kings but under William it came to the fore, principally as the office responsible for issuing and keeping a record of all charters, writs, and other legal documents. Osmund was an influential figure at court and one of those charged with overseeing the collection of information for the *Domesday Book*.

Between his abortive attempt on London Bridge and his entry into Winchester, William's forces may have camped in the massive hillfort of Old Sarum, just outside modern-day Salisbury. He certainly recognised the potential of the site. In 1069, a motte-and-bailey castle was erected there and, in 1075, work began on the construction of a cathedral. In 1078, Osmund was appointed Bishop of Salisbury or Old Sarum – the names remained interchangeable for many years – and continued in office, overseeing the completion and consecration on the cathedral, until his death in 1099. The still unfinished cathedral was the setting for an important ceremony in 1086, when William formally accepted the *Domesday Book* – and at the same time obliged all the leading bishops and landowners to renew their oaths of loyalty. Osmund was also responsible for another influential innovation. He introduced the Sarum Rite, or Use of Salisbury, which standardised the order and form of Christian worship throughout England and remained current until the Reformation.

Cathedrals were a Norman speciality, matching in scale the massive stone castles that were being constructed up and down the kingdom. During William's reign new cathedrals were begun in Salisbury, Canterbury, Lincoln, Chichester, Winchester, York, Rochester, Ely, Hereford, Worcester, Leicester and at St Paul's in London. Most Anglo-Saxon churches were small and built of wood. Even larger towns had several small places of worship, rather than a big, central church. Winchester's New Minster and Westminster Abbey were exceptions. The Normans built in stone and on a monumental scale. Their cathedrals were statements of power as much as faith. They were designed to impress, to awe, even to intimidate – and they concentrated ecclesiastical power in the same way that castles concentrated political power. The carved stonework, the elaborately painted ceilings, the sound of a choir echoing through the volume of the nave, all reflected architectural developments elsewhere in Europe, but also served to emphasise the difference between the way the Normans proclaimed their Christianity and what had gone before. And cathedrals were organised on strict, hierarchical lines with a dean, precentor, chancellor, treasurer, and a number of canons – another innovation pioneered by Osmund.

Also fundamental in driving a wedge between the small group of conquerors and the great mass of the conquered was language. The conquerors spoke Norman French, which was from the beginning the language of the court, and rapidly became the spoken language of administration. Some documents were written in French, but the written language of administration was predominantly Latin. The *Domesday Book* was written in Latin, with occasional words of Anglo-Saxon, with or without glosses. Latin remained the language of religious expression and of the Church which, at a senior level, rapidly became a Norman preserve. By contrast, the majority – though not all – of the conquered spoke Anglo-Saxon. There were other languages, the speakers of which had themselves been conquered or overborne by the speakers of Anglo-Saxon as England evolved. Cornish, a version of P-Celtic, was still spoken in the south-west. It never spread beyond Cornwall and parts of Devon, but it was a written language from at least the tenth century, and outlasted Norman French by several centuries, only becoming extinct in the eighteenth century. In the east, from East Anglia right up to the Scottish border, there were people of Danish extraction who spoke or had some understanding of Scandinavian languages. And in Cumbria and the north-west, traces of the P-Celtic language of the Old North probably survived into the twelfth century. The isolation and alienation of those who spoke these languages could only have been intensified by the advent of Norman French.

As with Latin during the Roman occupation, following the Norman takeover and the redistribution of lands and manors, some Normans will have learnt sufficient Anglo-Saxon to communicate with their clerks and those they depended upon to run their estates. And there will have been some among the English population – clerks in holy orders; former reeves, *thegns*, and royal retainers; ambitious traders and merchants – who will have learnt enough Norman French to be of use to the new ruling class. The situation was possibly less acute than under the Romans because by the eleventh century it was assumed that all priests and most educated people would know Latin. On the other hand, the dominance of Norman French and Latin among the upper echelons of society left the less educated, the peasants and serfs, at an even greater disadvantage than before, particularly when it came to legal and administrative matters. Language rapidly became an indicator of social status, with Anglo-Saxon being seen as the language of the lower orders. The thirteenth-century Middle

English chronicler, Robert of Gloucester, states explicitly that 'unless a man knows French, he is held of no account.' The Normans 'could speak nothing but their own language' but were nonetheless the 'heyemen ... of engelonde,' while the Saxons were 'lowemen' because they spoke only English.[318] Except within the Church, where some vernacular manuscripts continued to be produced, Anglo-Saxon all but ceased to be a written language, while P-Celtic and Danish speakers were at an even greater disadvantage, even further distanced from the structures of power. Eventually these social divisions would erode. Anglo-Saxon and Norman French would meld and mutate into Middle English, but it would be a long process. Only when Henry IV came to the throne in 1399 would England have a king whose mother tongue was English.

Castles, cathedrals, the courts, land ownership, and language all became instruments of control. Early Norman rule was undeniably harsh, but, from a Norman point of view, strict control was essential if that rule was to continue. The population of England during the mid-1080s when the *Domesday Book* was compiled was probably about two million. The size of the Norman population is difficult to estimate, but it was not large. As noted earlier there were some 6,000 manors. Manors could be divided, so this may translate into perhaps 8,000 Normans holding the land from the king and accepting the obligations that entailed. Landholders would have had families, and quite possibly extended families, managing their estates. The barons, who were their overlords would themselves have had families, and as well as Norman clerks and overseers. There was the king and the court. There were Norman bishops and clergy. There were merchants and traders. But there was no significant influx of Norman peasantry. Even the most generous estimate must struggle to raise the Norman population much above 150,000, or 7.5 per cent of the total. The risk was that, if not cowed and controlled, the English could overwhelm them.

Strict control of England was all the more necessary for William because, like Cnut before him, he was attempting to rule two political entities, separated by sea and distinct in character – although in William's case the difficulties in communication were significantly less. All the Norman aristocracy, including William himself, had important landholdings in Normandy which contributed to their wealth and required attention and management. It became normal for them to divide their time between their new possessions in England and their old ones in

Normandy. After devastating England's northern counties in 1070 and eliminating the threat from Edgar the Ætheling and Malcolm III of Scotland (see Chapter 39), William felt secure enough to spend most of his time in Normandy. Almost eleven of his last fifteen years were spent there. Nonetheless, he continued to face threats caused – or exacerbated – by the divided nature of his domains. The Earls' Rebellion of 1075 saw Ralph de Gael of Norfolk, Roger de Breteuil of Hereford, and Waltheof of Northumbria – the last surviving Anglo-Saxon earl – join together in an attempt to overthrow him. They were supported by several Breton nobles whose lands William had conquered before he invaded England, and by the brother of the Danish king, another Cnut. William stayed in Normandy overseeing operations against the rebels there, while his half-brother Odo of Bayeux and various tenants-in-chief – including the Bishop of Worcester and the Abbot of Evesham – squeezed the life out of what was not a particularly well-organised revolt. Their success was a vindication of the system William had put in place to manage the defence of England. He waited until the following year before returning to England to deal with the Danish threat and order the execution of Waltheof, the only earl to be executed during his reign. On the Continent, things did not go as smoothly. Ralph de Gael fled to Brittany and seized the castle at Dol. William besieged him there but Ralph attracted the support of William's enemies, among them Philip I of France. William was defeated at the Battle of Dol and forced to lift the siege. Although no more than a temporary setback, it was his first ever military defeat. Hostilities continued sporadically until 1077 when all the parties agreed an indefinite truce.

More serious for William was the problem posed by his eldest son, Robert, nicknamed Curthose or 'short-socks', who was evidently something of a tearaway. Probably early in 1078, Robert – at that time twenty-six or twenty-seven – became the leader of a group of young nobles, mainly the sons of barons to whom William had given land in England. Based in the castle of Rémalard on the south-eastern edge of Normandy, they began to mount raids into the heart of the Duchy. William, naturally furious, drove them out of Rémalard, but Philip I – who was always seeking ways to weaken William – gave them the castle at Gerberoi, on the eastern border of the Duchy. William attacked Gerberoi but was unhorsed during the fighting. One version of events states that he was saved by the intervention of one Toki (or Toking) – the son of Wigod, an English *thegn* who had helped William in 1066 and been rewarded with land in Oxfordshire – who was then killed in the fracas. Another version has it that William was only spared because Robert recognised his voice.

Queen Matilda intervened and in 1080 William and Robert made peace, on the renewed understanding that Robert would inherit Normandy when William died. Meanwhile, news that William – up to that point a seemingly invincible warrior – had suffered a defeat at the hands of his son had travelled far and wide and may have contributed to a renewed wave of trouble in Northumbria, which at once caused Malcolm III to mount a cross-border raid. William, presumably glad to find an occupation for his troublesome offspring, sent Robert to pacify Northumberland and deal with the Scots, which he did with some success (see Chapter 39).

Robert, like other rogue individuals such as Sweyn Godwineson, continued to cause problems. His story illustrates how the tensions and conflicts which swirled around the ruling family after William's death were complicated by the possession of two separate polities. Queen Matilda, who had always supported Robert, died in 1083. The following year, Robert seems to have left his father's court, suggesting that the relationship between father and son continued to be difficult at best. He wandered around Europe, apparently searching for a wealthy bride, and fathering at least two illegitimate children. When William died in September 1087, following a horse-riding accident, Robert, as promised, inherited Normandy. His younger brother, William – known as William Rufus, because of his red hair and in order to distinguish him from his father – inherited England, while the third surviving brother, Henry Beauclerc, later Henry I, was given a large sum of money to buy land. Why did William leave Normandy to Robert? It was not as wealthy as England, but he was the eldest son and William may well have seen it as their dynastic homeland – an idea supported by the fact that he spent so many of his later years there. Alternatively, he may have feared that Robert's apparently unstable character would not be able to manage the complexities of governing England. Or he might simply have been punishing his eldest son by preferring to see William Rufus as King of England. On William's death, Robert and William Rufus agreed that they should be each other's heir. However, this arrangement and the terms of William's will lasted barely six months.

The barons' rebellion of 1088 had its origins in the centralised and personal feudalism that William had imposed upon England – as well as in the ambition and greed of the barons themselves. In the Kingdom of the Isles, the Earldom of Orkney, and parts of Scotland, it was possible – even normal – to hold lands and titles from two or more different overlords. However, to those barons who held lands in both England and Normandy, it was already apparent that Robert and William Rufus were very different characters. According to Orderic Vitalis, they feared that they could not properly serve two such masters without the risk of offending one or other and having their lands and revenues seized as a result. The revolt was masterminded by Odo of Bayeux, though his motivation is not entirely clear. Six of the largest landowners in England were recruited. The plan was for them to rise up against William Rufus and distract him while Robert brought an army across from Normandy. Robert, whom the barons saw as more malleable, would then rule both England and Normandy.

Odo's plan proved optimistic. The rising took place in Kent, Northumberland, Norfolk, and Shropshire, but William Rufus was able to call on a number of loyal barons for support, and to rally many of the English to his cause. Across the Channel, Robert was slow to raise an army because, characteristically, he had run out of money. He turned to his brother, Henry Beauclerc, who refused him a loan, but agreed to buy Robert's estates in Cotentin, Avranches, and Mont-Saint-Michel. Robert hurriedly assembled an army and a fleet, but on setting sail, his ships ran into a storm and were forced back to the French coast. By that time, however, it was probably too late. William Rufus had penned Odo, Robert de Mortain, and some of the other leaders in Pevensey Castle. A six-week siege saw them forced to surrender. William Rufus then turned his attention to Rochester Castle, where Eustace of Boulogne and Robert of Bellême continued to hold out, but when Rochester fell, the rebellion was over. Paradoxically, the rebellion strengthened William Rufus' position, so that he felt able to pardon most of the rebels – Odo he stripped of his lands and exiled.

Robert continued to rule Normandy, although with a much-reduced income, having sold many of his estates to his brother, Henry, and plagued by raids and rebellions – Robert of Bellême appears to have been a serial offender. His next project, in 1096, was to raise an army to fight in the First Crusade. In order to do so he was forced to mortgage his Duchy to William

Rufus for 10,000 marks. Unlike many others who served in the Holy Land, he not only survived, but returned with the prestige and reputation – whether deserved or not – of one who had fought in the cause of the Christian faith. This may have been how, on his return journey, he was able to marry Sybilla of Conversano, a Norman Italian heiress sufficiently wealthy to enable him to redeem his Duchy.

William Rufus died, his lung pierced by an arrow, while out hunting in the New Forest. Whether his death was an accident or murder has been much debated, but his younger brother, Henry Beauclerc, who was on the same hunting trip, left immediately for Winchester where he secured the royal treasury and moved swiftly on to London. We have noted already that rapid coronations suggest insecurity on the part of the newly-crowned monarch. Henry Beauclerc was crowned Henry I just three days after his brother's death. The Bishop of London officiated because the Archbishop of Canterbury had been exiled by William Rufus and the Archbishop of York was in York, and thus several days away. William Rufus never married and had no children – whether or not he was homosexual is another topic that has been much debated – so the succession would naturally have fallen to one of his brothers, but neither had an incontrovertible claim. Henry was younger, but he was in the right place at the right time – and may conceivably have engineered William Rufus' death. Robert was still in Italy and was predictably furious at being outmanoeuvred. All he could do was cite the 1087 agreement by which he and William Rufus agreed to be each other's heirs – an agreement he himself had broken within six months of making it.

During his thirteen years on the throne, William Rufus had managed to upset the barons, the Church, and the native English, but that did not mean that Henry could rely on their support. In an attempt to persuade them – largely successfully as it turned out – he issued a Coronation Charter, or Charter of Liberties, a kind of post-coronation manifesto, which promised concessions to the barons, reconciliation with the Church, and fairer treatment for the English. His also married the daughter of Malcolm III of Scotland, whose lineage combined the royal houses of Scotland and of Wessex, another move which proved popular with the English. All this proved effective in so far as, in 1101, when Robert invaded to try and overthrow Henry, he received little or no popular support. Landing at Portsmouth, he headed for London but was intercepted by

Henry at Alton in Hampshire. With no prospect of a military victory, Robert was forced to negotiate. The result was the Treaty of Alton, by which he gave up his claim to the English throne in exchange for 3,000 marks a year to ease his chronic shortage of cash, while Henry gave up any claim to Normandy. But Alton was not the end of the matter. There was clearly no trust between the brothers. Robert encouraged landowners with estates on both sides of the Channel to stir up trouble in England, while Henry built up alliances by marrying his illegitimate daughters to powerful Norman landowners. He also looked for – and found – excuses to withhold Robert's 3000 marks. In Normandy, Robert's instability and Henry's manoeuvring led to a breakdown of law and order. Eventually, in 1105, this gave Henry the excuse to invade. In 1106, the decisive battle took place at Tinchebrai (or Tinchebray). Robert was captured and spent the rest of his life in prison, and Normandy was once again attached to the English crown – although Henry only ever claimed to be a caretaker ruler. He never used the title Duke of Normandy.

England under Cnut became, albeit briefly, the hub of a Scandinavian empire. With William I's coronation on Christmas Day 1066, England was again connected to the Continent. William's Continental possessions were small compared with Cnut's, and the connection was never stable and never peaceful, but it endured for very nearly five hundred years. Henry II (r.1154–89), the first of the long line of Plantagenet kings, took advantage of French weakness to extend English rule to cover most of western France. His reign marked the high watermark of English power on the Continent. The two reigns which followed – Richard I (r.1189–99) and King John (r.1199–1216) – saw much of this territory lost to the French. Normandy, where it all started, was seized by Philip II of France in 1204, and those families still holding lands in both England and the Duchy found themselves forced to choose between two overlords who were at war with each other. In 1216, the last year of John's reign, the French, encouraged by a number of those English barons who were outraged at the loss of Normandy and, led by Prince Louis, tried to extend their run of military successes by invading England. When John died, his son and successor, Henry III (r.1216–72), was only nine, so it was left to his captain, William Marshal, to defeat the French and English rebels, and to restore royal authority in England. However, in 1230, just three years after he had assumed formal control of his kingdom, Henry launched his own invasion of France, apparently convinced that he could reclaim Normandy and all the other provinces that had once belonged to the English Crown. The whole affair was a costly failure. Only in 1259 with the Treaty of Paris, almost half a century after the French had taken control of Normandy, did the English formally recognise the fact. The treaty is still relevant because, while the English gave up their claim to Normandy, the French agreed to cede the Channel Islands – still known in French as *Les Îles Anglo-Normandes* – to the English Crown. And today they remain Crown Dependencies: self-governing territories which are not part of the United Kingdom, but possessions of the Crown in the person of the English monarch.

Edward I (r.1272–1307) lost the Duchy of Gascony to Philip IV of France and then fought successfully to regain it. In 1324, the War of Saint-Sardos saw Charles de Valois comprehensively outmanoeuvre the forces of Edward II (r.1307–27), commanded by Hugh le Despenser, so that the English were compelled to give up most of the Duchy of Aquitaine. Then, in the middle of the fourteenth century, came what is known as the Hundred Years War. From 1337 to 1453, England and France were more or less constantly at war, with the pendulum of advantage swinging back and forth. The one battle from this period that everyone knows about is Agincourt, largely because of Shakespeare. The forces of Henry V (r.1413–22) cut down swathes of the French nobility, and for a brief period, it looked as if England might achieve lasting dominance in France. Under the terms of the Treaty of Troyes in 1420, Henry V would marry Catherine de Valois, the daughter of the French king, Charles VI, and their offspring would inherit the thrones of both England and France. In 1431, Henry V's nine-year-old son, Henry VI of England (r.1422–61 and 1470–71), was actually crowned King Henry II of France, but by that time the tide was already on the turn. The visions of Jeanne d'Arc, the battlefield successes of the Dauphin – shortly to be Charles VII – and the defection of the Duke of Burgundy all gave the French resurgence an irresistible momentum. By 1453 only the so-called Pale de Calais – some fifty-two square kilometres, comprising the port and its hinterland – remained in English hands. Calais remained English for another century. It was politically important, and as a major entrepôt it was also the source of valuable customs revenues. As late as 1532, Henry VIII reformed its governmental standing and organisation, allowing it to send representatives to the House of Commons. The

French naturally regarded the continued English presence in Calais as a thorn in their flesh and, whenever relations between the two countries were at a low ebb, would attempt to retake the city. In January 1558, with the French threatening a siege, the English Governor, Lord Wentworth, was too late asking for reinforcements from England and then failed to order the opening of the defensive sluices, which could have flooded the hinterland, in time. The end came swiftly, and it fell to him to hand to the French the keys of the last English possession on the Continent. So, it could be said, ended the story of William the Conqueror's Continental legacy.

It was a legacy of which the *Britannica* website says:

Perhaps one of his greatest contributions to England's future was the linking up of England with continental affairs. If the country had been conquered again by the Danes, as seemed possible, it might have remained in a backwater of European development. In the event, England was linked, economically and culturally, to France and continental Europe.[319]

This is a curious, after-the-fact judgement, which suggests that England over the five centuries following the arrival of the Normans was simply a receiver of influence. There is no doubt that William I set in motion a radical transformation of English political and social life, and that, for many years, Englishness was the culture of *lowemen*, with little social and political influence. Yet the Norman-Angevin-Plantagenet kings who ruled for more than four hundred years after 1066 were constantly active, and usually at war, in France. The resources demanded were a continual drain on England – which was, by European standards of the time, a prosperous country – and while the English, of all social levels from nobles to servants and fighting men, no doubt absorbed much that was French in terms of culture, religion, and society, they influenced France and the French in equal measure. The fifteenth century saw England weakened by civil war, as well as by frequent outbreaks of the plague, and by the time the first Tudor King, Henry VII, came to the throne in 1485, the country was undoubtedly a European backwater. Henry VIII's famous meeting with Francis I of France at the Field of the Cloth of Gold in the Pale of Calais in 1521 was an expensive and vainglorious attempt to relaunch England as a Continental power, and the Reformation – in England a political as much as a religious movement – left the country even more isolated and reduced still further its influence with France, Spain, and the other European powers.

To speculate on what would have happened had England been conquered by the Danes rather than the Normans is to play what-if games. Nonetheless, if Britain had been conquered by the Danes and remained connected to Denmark, both countries would have been profoundly different, and each would have played a different historical role from the one they did. If the English resources poured into France over four or more centuries had been poured into Denmark, the whole balance of the western European seaboard might have been altered. An English-Danish kingdom might not have been a backwater. These are guessing games, but what emerges from such speculations is that even in these early medieval times, England was never going to stand alone. Æthelstan, in the tenth century, recognised the need to engage with the Continental powers. As it happened, William of Normandy became William I of England and English history as we know it today developed from there. Yet whether actively and aggressively engaged on the Continent, as were Henry II and Henry V, or standing aloof, perhaps somewhat nervously, as was the case with Elizabeth I, England's connection with the Continent of Europe was visceral and inescapable. It was also – whether in engagement or separation – a yardstick by which the English judged themselves.

39 Scotland and the Isles

Malcolm III of Scotland avoided active participation in the great events of 1066. He undoubtedly knew about and encouraged the alliance between Tostig and Harald Hardrada, but he neither joined their invasion, nor committed Scottish warriors to their army.[320] His concern was to maintain and strengthen Scotland, and that explains the apparent contradictions and policy reversals of his thirty-five-year reign. In the north, the Earls of Orkney and the Mormaers of Moray – who were in theory vassals of the Scottish kings – had long posed a threat to the unity of Scotland. In the early years of his reign, Malcolm did his best to neutralise this threat by marrying the widow of Thorfinn the Mighty and suppressing the ambitions of Macbeth's descendants in Moray (see Chapter 35). He did so because, like all Scottish monarchs, he feared an English invasion. Even before the events of 1066, while Edward the Confessor was still on the throne, Malcolm evidently realised the danger posed by his increasingly wealthy and powerful southern neighbour under the leadership of Harold Godwineson.

Malcolm came to the throne with the help of Earl Siward of Northumbria, an old-fashioned regional warlord who had risen to power under Cnut and exercised a significant degree of autonomy, thereby shielding Scotland from threats from the south. When Siward died in 1055, to be replaced by Tostig, it appeared that Northumbria might become more closely integrated with the rest of England. Tostig was powerful, but unpopular among those Northumbrians who had supported Siward, so in 1061 when Malcolm launched a cross-border raid – the first of five during his long reign – his aim was to exploit Tostig's unpopularity. As far as the English were concerned, the raid was probably no more than a nuisance, but for Malcolm, who had been king for just three years, it was a statement of intent. Four years later, stripped of his earldom and forced into exile, Tostig was a welcome guest at Malcolm's court. This sudden reversal may emphasise the fluidity of the political situation and the degree to which it depended on individual relationships, but it did not signal a change of heart or policy. A disgraced Tostig represented a useful tool to inflame and aggravate the divisions that had now surfaced in England. The border between Scotland and England was still ill-defined, with the status of Cumbria and the Lothians a matter of constant dispute. Whether Malcolm's aim in subsequent raids and invasions was permanent territorial expansion or just the creation of a buffer zone against the English is difficult to judge, but he certainly welcomed any opportunity to exploit divisions and stir up trouble south of the border.

Malcolm's second raid took place under very different circumstances and had lasting consequences. Edgar the Ætheling submitted to William at Berkhamsted, but William realised he could be a focus for opposition and kept him close to the court, even taking him to Normandy in 1067. The following year, Edgar and his sister, Margaret of Wessex, escaped and fled to Scotland, where they were welcomed by Malcolm. Edgar immediately became involved in the 1068 rebellion in the north of England. Malcolm again avoided active involvement but did nothing to hinder the rebels – he continued to see instability south of the border as the best way to prevent an English invasion – and he allowed Edgar and the other leaders to return to Scotland when it failed. William's response was the savage, scorched-earth campaign known as the Harrying of the North (see Chapter 37). This provoked Malcolm's second incursion in 1070.

What he was trying to achieve is something of a mystery. Was he expecting to be welcomed by those who had suffered from William's savage tactics? Was he acting in support of Edgar the Ætheling? He had not done so in 1068 but had recently married Margaret of Wessex and may have felt the need to demonstrate his commitment to Edgar's cause. Or was he simply showing William – and his own supporters in Scotland – that he was not cowed by the Harrying of the North? Unusually, this raid began in the west. Malcolm's forces were made up predominantly of men from Galloway. They moved into Cumbria, crossed the Stainmore Gap into Northumbria, but the raid came to grief when they were surprised in an engagement outside the walls of Durham, and they returned home having gained little or nothing.

William, however, had been provoked and was not content to let Malcolm go unpunished. In 1072, he launched his invasion of Scotland. Using tactics first employed by Agricola nearly a thousand years before, he moved his army – consisting mainly of cavalry – up the east coast, while his fleet shadowed its progress offshore. He crossed the Forth near Stirling and moved north-east towards Perth, meeting up with the fleet which had entered the Tay Estuary. It was a bold strategy but frustrated by Malcolm who, like the tribal leaders of the distant past, refused to commit his forces to a pitched battle. Malcolm was in the weaker position, but it was late in the campaigning season and William's supply line was subject to guerrilla attacks, so they agreed to negotiate. By the Treaty of Abernethy, Malcolm accepted William as his overlord – in Norman terms, became his man – and gave his eldest son, Duncan, as a hostage. He also agreed to expel Edgar the Ætheling from Scotland. William withdrew his forces to York. The problem with Abernethy was what it meant to the signatories. For Malcolm, aware that he was not the first Scottish king to accept English overlordship, it meant very little. To William, who took such matters seriously – witness his reaction to Harold Godwineson's oath-breaking – it was a binding and permanent commitment. William's view of the matter was repeated by English chroniclers right up until the Acts of Union in 1707.

In 1079, perhaps influenced by news of William's defeat at Gerberoi,

Malcolm again crossed the border and ravaged Northumbria for three weeks. William Walcher, the first of the famous Prince-Bishops – he had become Bishop of Durham in 1071 and Earl of Northumberland in 1075 – failed to deal effectively with the raid and was criticised by one of his councillors, Ligulf, a descendant of Earl Siward. Ligulf was murdered – probably at Walcher's instigation – and there was an explosion of unrest in which Walcher and many of his followers were burnt or butchered. This kind of instability was just what Malcolm's raid was designed to provoke. William sent Odo of Bayeux to pacify the Northumbrians and Robert Curthose to punish the Scots. Robert pursued Malcolm as far north as Falkirk, but Malcolm again avoided any direct confrontation, and again the two sides agreed to negotiate. The conditions of Abernethy were reaffirmed, but a new border was agreed, stretching from the Tyne across the Stainmore Gap, and seeming to indicate that Cumbria was part of Scotland. This reflected the fact that Malcolm's position was stronger than in 1072, and the existence of the new frontier was confirmed by Robert's construction of a new castle at what became Newcastle-upon-Tyne. In political-territorial terms, this marked the high point of Malcolm's reign.

It was not until 1091, ten years later, that Malcolm again crossed the border and again besieged Durham, perhaps sending a message to William Rufus, who had been king for just three years. William Rufus marched north. Malcolm retreated into Lothian, yet again refusing to give battle. Yet again, the two sides negotiated, and the terms of the Abernethy treaty were restated and reaffirmed, but the balance of advantage was now with the English. They reclaimed Cumbria, and in 1092 William Rufus consolidated the new frontier by ordering the construction of a major new castle at Carlisle. Malcolm seems to have regarded this as a breach on the 1091 agreement and travelled south to Gloucester to talk to the English king, but William Rufus refused to meet him. This snub may well have provoked his fifth – and final – incursion in November 1093. He got as far as Alnwick, when he was ambushed by Robert de Mowbray, the Earl of Northumbria, whose domains he had so often raided. Both Malcolm and Edward, his eldest son by his second wife, were killed.

Malcolm's raids and incursions show the Scots as aggressors, intent on destabilising the areas immediately south of the border. They show that the border itself was liable to move north or south depending on whether England or Scotland held the advantage. And they show that

Malcolm regarded submission to the King of England was a matter of form rather than substance: a concession he was prepared to make in order to avoid a battle and to allow the Anglo-Norman forces to claim a positive outcome from their campaign. Yet it would be wrong to see Scotland at this time as defined wholly by border struggles with the Norman kings. It is during Malcolm III's reign that we see the first signs of a complex pattern of cultural influence and opposition that is still visible in Scotland in the twenty-first century.

Following the death of his grandfather, Duncan I, and father, Crinán, at the hands of Macbeth, Malcolm went into exile: first to Northumberland under the protection of Siward, then to the court of Edward the Confessor, and possibly also to Orkney under Thorfinn the Mighty. His first marriage, to Ingibjorg, Thorfinn's widow, was evidently a political one, although it produced two sons – Duncan (who reigned briefly as Duncan II) and Donald. His second marriage, in 1070 to Margaret of Wessex, has been much romanticised, but seems to have been based on genuine affection. Canonised by Pope Innocent IV in 1250 as St Margaret of Scotland, her piety – perhaps stemming from her upbringing at the notably religious Hungarian court – is not in doubt. She is known to have instigated a number of religious reforms relating to the celebration of the Mass, the observance of fasting, and the prohibitions of kinship marriage – bringing Scotland closer to the norms of the Roman Church – and to have helped orphans and the poor.

However, her influence went beyond religion. She was Queen of Scotland, but also one of the last representatives of the House of Wessex, and sister of a man who – albeit very briefly – had been King of England. Her husband had spent his formative teenage years at the English court, so much richer and more sophisticated than the one over which he now presided. And the Scottish court was home to a group of Anglo-Saxon exiles who had fled north beyond the reach of William I. Yet, ironically, the Anglo-Saxon culture that they brought with them, making the Scottish court more cosmopolitan, was changing, even disappearing, under Norman influence south of the border. It is doubtful whether this Anglo-Saxon influence spread far beyond the court. Malcolm was bilingual, but Margaret is reported to have spoken no Gaelic, and it is unlikely that the exiles spoke more than basic Gaelic. Nonetheless, it had the potential to create resentment among the Scottish nobility, and when the King and

Queen chose to give their eight children Anglo-Saxon rather than Scottish names – Edward, Edmund, Ethelred, Edgar, Alexander, Matilda, Mary, David – it would not have gone unnoticed.

Malcolm III was the second Dunkeld king. He reclaimed the throne for his family after the intrusion of Macbeth and Lulach and held on to it for thirty-five years without serious domestic opposition. The southern border moved back and forward, but the rest of the kingdom remained intact. Although he was followed by nine further Dunkeld kings, who ruled for nearly two hundred years until 1286, his death in 1093 was the cue for an extended power struggle and civil war.

Malcolm's successor was his brother, Donald – reigning as Donald III, but widely referred to as Donald Bán or Donald the Fair. Like Malcolm, he had spent his youth in exile, but in his case this meant Ireland and (probably) the Western Isles, and his cultural orientation was more traditionally Celtic than Malcolm's. Primogeniture was still not the norm in Scotland, and the *Anglo-Saxon Chronicle* states clearly that the Scots – meaning the aristocracy and the regional lords – 'chose' or 'elected' Donald, and 'drove out the English who were with Malcolm before.'[321] This suggests a reaction by an assertive Scottish aristocracy against the Anglo-Saxon influences prevailing under Malcolm and Margaret (who had died just days after her husband). It could also indicate that the new king was keen to remove anyone who might support one of Margaret's children should they mount a challenge for the throne.

As it was, the challenge to Donald Bán came not from Margaret's children, but from Duncan, the son of Malcolm's first marriage to Thorfinn the Mighty's widow, Ingibjorg. Given as a hostage to William I under the Treaty of Abernethy in 1072, he was allowed to return to Scotland as a goodwill gesture in 1087 on the accession of William Rufus. In those crucial fifteen years, between the ages of twelve and twenty-seven, he had lived at the court of William I in England and in Normandy and trained as a Norman knight. Michael Lynch notes that his seal shows him on horseback wearing the characteristic Norman conical helmet.[322] Duncan's invasion and brief reign are a study in contradictions. He swore allegiance to William Rufus, who clearly saw him as a potential client king. This gained him the 'English and French assistance' he needed. Early in 1094, he crossed the border, forced Donald Bán to withdraw to the Highlands, and was able to get himself crowned as Duncan II at Scone. However, in order to overcome opposition from the aristocracy and the local population who saw him as a usurper, he was forced to swear that he would 'never again [introduce] Englishmen or Frenchmen into that country.'[323] This meant dismissing the troops that had brought him to power, which in turn allowed Donald Bán, who had spent the intervening time rebuilding his support, to sweep down from the Highlands. The end came quickly. In November 1094 at Monthechin near Kincardine, Duncan II, who was culturally Norman and came to power with Norman support, was defeated and killed by the combined forces of the culturally Celtic Donald Bán and the Anglo-Saxon-orientated Edmund, Malcolm and Margaret's second son. He had reigned just over six months.

The struggle between Donald and Duncan has been seen as a conflict between tanistry, as practised by the Scots and (with qualifications) the Anglo-Saxons, under which system Donald Bán was the legitimate ruler of the kingdom, and primogeniture, as practised by the Normans, which made Duncan the legitimate king.[324] In reality, the differing systems of succession were part of a much more complex struggle that had both its roots and its expression in differing – if not always clearly defined – views on the cultural and political future of Scotland.

Donald Bán, receiving strong support from the northern clans, resumed his reign, while Edmund, having thrown his lot in with Celtic Scotland, appears to have been nominated as his successor. However, immediately after Duncan's death, the kingship was claimed by the fourth son of Malcolm III and Queen Margaret, Edgar, but he had no hope of displacing Donald without help from William Rufus, who was preoccupied with a revolt by Robert de Mowbray in Northumbria. Given that de Mowbray had killed Malcolm III, it may seem strange that Donald Bán and Edmund appear to have supported his revolt, but, like Malcolm, their principal concern was to promote instability south of the border. Only in 1097, with de Mowbray captured and locked up, did William Rufus turn his attention to Scotland and make an army available to Edgar. Another strange twist of fate meant that Edgar's army was commanded by his uncle, Edgar the Ætheling. Thirty years earlier, he had been King of England for six weeks. He had led the resistance against the Normans in northern England before submitting to William. He had been sent off to conquer Apulia in southern Italy, and on his return become involved in the struggle between William Rufus and Robert Curthose. He had conducted negotiations between William Rufus and Malcolm III and was now sufficiently trusted to be appointed commander of an English army.

Donald Bán's forces do not seem to have put up much resistance. Donald himself fled into the Highlands and Edgar was crowned at Dunfermline. A charter issued at the time states that he possessed 'the whole land of Lothian and the kingship of the Scots by the gift of my lord William, king of the English, and by paternal heritage,'[325] neatly acknowledging his vassalage to William Rufus and claiming the crown by right of primogeniture. The implication that Lothian and Scotland were somehow separate is reflected in the fact that he had one royal residence in Edinburgh, and a second at Invergowrie, north of the River Tay – although his seal carried the unifying if inflated claim, *'Edgari Scottorum Basilei'*. During his ten-year reign, Latin began to feature in certain court documents, and his charters address his subjects as 'Scots and English.'[326] Norman settlement in southern Scotland appears to have increased, bringing Norman-style feudalism and land management practices. The nature of Edgar's relationship with William Rufus is shown by the fact that he travelled to London in 1099 to serve as William's sword-bearer at a ceremony inaugurating Westminster Hall. While he was away, Donald Bán attempted to return to power, but he was captured, blinded, and immured in Rescobie Castle in Angus where he died shortly afterwards.

Although both Norman influence and the Norman population were increasing, Edgar, unlike Duncan II, was never forced to promise to limit foreign influence; nor was there any significant uprising against him; but it is not certain how far his control extended. Southern Scotland and the lower-lying lands in the east of the country were more populous, more prosperous, and easier to control. They usually accepted political change with little resistance. The status of Moray is uncertain; and in the more remote areas and the Highlands, where Celtic culture had been less subject to Anglo-Norman influences, royal authority was probably notional. Moreover, in 1098, Edgar was forced to acknowledge that the west coast was beyond the reach of royal power. He agreed a treaty with the King of Norway, Magnus III or Magnus Barelegs (also Magnus Barefoot or Magnus Olafsson; r.1093–1103), who was re-establishing Norwegian authority in the west of Scotland and the Irish Sea. Edgar formally ceded the Hebrides – including Iona, the traditional resting place of Scottish kings – and Kintyre to the Norwegians. It was not until 1266 that the west coast returned to Scottish rule.

Under Edgar's successor, his younger brother, Alexander I (r.1107–24), Anglo-Norman influence continued to grow. He, too, had been brought up in England. Scotland was foreign to him. He accepted that his rule was dependent on English support and did what was necessary to maintain the relationship. He probably paid homage to Henry I of England; he certainly married Henry's illegitimate daughter, Sybilla of Normandy; and he fought alongside Henry against the King of Gwynedd, Gruffudd ap Cynan, in 1114. In Scotland, he began building Norman-style castles, including the first major structure on the great crag at Stirling – a castle that was to play a pivotal role in Scottish history. Alexander also encouraged the religious orders that were active in England and France to enter Scotland, beginning the close relationship between the House of Dunkeld and the Augustinian order and suggesting that they found a priory at Scone.

Edgar, Alexander, and Alexander's successor, David I, had all been brought up at the English court and the spread of Anglo-Norman influence in Scotland was only to be expected. Naturally enough, it was also encouraged by Henry I of England. During Alexander's reign, he pressed for David – Malcolm III and Margaret's youngest son – to be given authority in southern Scotland. For some ten years before his accession, David thus became Henry's agent in the north, overseeing Norman settlement in Northumbria, Cumbria, and southern Scotland. By the time he succeeded Alexander in 1124, he was about forty, and he ruled Scotland for twenty-nine years until 1153. The events of his reign are often referred to as the 'Davidian Revolution', a misleading label in so far as, while the pace of change accelerated, the changes themselves largely developed what had begun under Edgar and Alexander. Castle building continued. David also continued Alexander's practice of granting lands to religious orders, notably to the Augustinians – who established new foundations at centres of royal power such as Holyrood, Stirling, and Jedburgh – as well as to Benedictines, Cistercians, Premonstratensians, and Tironensians. The number of small churches built by landowners on their estates to serve the local community increased considerably during the twelfth century. David's innovation was to enact a law that made the payment of the tithe (in Scotland, known as the *teind*) compulsory, thus delineating the catchment areas of individual churches and leading to the creation of parishes. Another innovation was the creation of royal burghs. We do not know how or when new towns were established in the eleventh and early twelfth centuries, but by the end of David's reign there were at least fifteen of sufficient importance to have been granted royal status. They reflected the importance of wool and the general increase in trade which characterised the twelfth century, and which grew to even greater heights in the thirteenth. Most of the royal burghs – including Berwick-upon-Tweed, Roxburgh, Edinburgh, Stirling, Perth, Dundee, and Aberdeen – were in the south and east. However, the inclusion of Elgin and Forres emphasised the growing economic importance of the Moray Firth, while Tain, on the northern border of what is now Ross-shire, cannot have been far from the border of the lands held by the Earldom of Orkney. All these various measures served to bring Scottish political and religious governance closer to the systems operating south of the border, and all had at their heart the extension of feudal obligation and thus royal control.

Edgar projected an image of himself as a *basileus*, an emperor. David liked to present himself as a patriarch, wise, grey-haired and long-bearded, holding a sword and an orb as symbols of authority, but this did not convince the Scottish nobles who resented his attempts to centralise power on the person of the king. He faced four rebellions during his reign – in 1124, 1130, 1134, and 1151 – all of which he survived. Perhaps the most significant was that in 1130, led by Óengus, the Mormaer of Moray, whose defeat at the Battle of Stracathro marked the end of Moray's power to resist royal authority.

David was also responsible for the last Scottish incursion into England to result in a significant and (comparatively) long-lasting repositioning of the border. Henry I died in 1135, intending that his daughter, Matilda, should inherit the throne. Unfortunately, she was not in England at the time. In her absence, the rich and popular Stephen of Blois was proclaimed King by the citizens of London, receiving the support of the Church and many leading nobles. In the extended civil war that followed – often known as 'The Anarchy' – David, whether out of loyalty to his mentor, Henry I, or out of opportunism, supported Matilda. In 1138, he led a large Scottish force across the border, occupied most of Northumberland, and marched south towards York. He met the English forces, which consisted mainly of militia and baronial levies from Yorkshire, near Northallerton. The Battle of the Standard (sometimes the Battle of Northallerton) was a major defeat for the Scots. King David and his son, Henry of Scotland, withdrew to Carlisle, but instead of pursuing the Scots, the English forces simply disbanded and went home. Protracted negotiations led to an agreement that David should retain Cumberland and Carlisle, while Henry of Scotland should be established as Earl of Northumberland. This left northern England under Scottish rule, and at one time it looked as if the situation might become permanent. In 1149, Matilda's son, another Henry – later Henry II of England – was still looking for help to fight Stephen. Having taken refuge in David's court, he swore that, should he become King of England, he would cede to David and his heirs all the lands between the Tweed and the Tyne.[327]

A series of deaths changed all this. Henry of Scotland died in 1152, leaving David without a mature heir; David himself died in 1153, bringing his young grandson, Malcolm IV (r.1153–65), to the throne; and King Stephen died in 1154, leaving the way open for Henry II to ascend the English throne. Henry was already Duke of Normandy and Count of Anjou and had vast resources at his disposal. Faced with such a powerful figure, Malcolm IV, only twelve at the time of his accession, had no chance. They met at Chester in 1157, and according to the English chroniclers, Malcolm stated that 'the King of England ought not to be defrauded of so great a part of his kingdom.' He 'restored … in their entirety' the territories David had acquired in 1138,[328] and in return received the Earldom of Huntingdon, which had previously belonged to Henry of Scotland. Malcolm's decision may not have been as spontaneous as the chroniclers suggest – an impression confirmed by the fact that he remained at Henry II's court for some time, accompanying Henry's army to France and being present at the siege of Toulouse in 1159.

Malcolm IV ruled for twelve years and died at the age of twenty-four. His brother and successor, William I, ruled for forty-nine years, from 1165 to 1214, and died at the age of seventy-two. He has gone down in history as William the Lion, but the sobriquet is evidently a product of later mythmaking. Entries in the *Irish Annals* for the year of his death prefer the name Uilleam Garbh (William the Rough). The year after his accession, he travelled to Normandy to do homage to Henry II, but the two did not see eye to eye and, in 1168, William negotiated the first alliance between Scotland and France. In 1174, when Henry II's sons – the eldest, yet another Henry; Richard, later Richard I of England; and Geoffrey, Duke of Anjou and later of Brittany – staged an orchestrated revolt against their father, William was persuaded to join them. It was a disastrous decision. He was captured under the walls of Alnwick, imprisoned in Newcastle, in Northampton, and then in Falaise in Normandy. To regain his freedom, William was forced to do homage to Henry II for his kingdom; to agree that all the Scottish clergy would do likewise; to pay the costs of an English army of occupation in Scotland; and to surrender the castles at Roxburgh, Berwick, Jedburgh, Edinburgh, and Stirling to the English. It was a serious humiliation, and it provoked a revolt in Galloway that smouldered for over ten years.

Restored to his kingdom, William concentrated on domestic issues, continuing to build Norman-style castles and impose Anglo-Norman institutions, such as sheriffs. He faced repeated challenges to his authority in the north but made no further incursions into England. He did, however, manage to regain Scotland's formal independence, although it came about through external circumstances rather than his own efforts. Richard I of England, who came to power in 1189, was a complicated character, keen to be a valiant knight and leader of men, courageous, generous, and Christian. He may well have been all these things, but he was also proud, greedy, and cruel, and he lacked political acuity and economic understanding. Within months of his accession, he had emptied the healthy treasury that he had inherited. Yet he remained determined to play a role on the European stage and fight alongside Philip II of France in the Third Crusade. Among the measures he took to raise money was to offer William the opportunity to buy Scotland's freedom for 10,000 marks. The price was paid, and under the terms of the Quitclaim of Canterbury of December 1189, Scotland was released from the feudal overlordship of England.

In 1194, William tried to buy Northumbria, offering Richard 15,000 marks, but nothing came of it. He conducted several campaigns in northern Scotland but no further raids into England, although relations between the two countries remained tense. When Richard I was succeeded by King John (r.1199–1216), William refused to meet John in England until he received 'royal letters patent of safe-conduct.' The chroniclers differ in their accounts of the meeting, which took place in Lincoln in 1200. Some suggest that William did homage 'for his right', meaning his possessions in England, while others claim that he did homage for all his lands. In 1209, King John seemed to threaten invasion when he marched his army up to Norham on the south bank of the Tweed, but he was bought off with cash and marriage alliances.

In 1215, a group of leading English magnates, incensed by John's failure to hold on to English possessions in France and by his refusal to accept Magna Carta, staged a full-scale rebellion, known at the First Barons' War, and invited Prince Louis of France to become king. The new Scottish king, Alexander II (r.1214–49) sent troops to occupy Northumbria and travelled to Dover to do homage to Louis as King of England, but John's death in 1216 changed everything. His son, Henry III (r.1216–72), came to the throne and negotiated the 1217 Treaty of Lambeth. Prince Louis returned to France, and the Scots withdrew from Northumbria. Despite the fact that Alexander did not do homage to Henry and refused to accept English overlordship of Scotland, the two kings established a strong personal relationship, marked by a sense of realism on both sides, which led to the Treaty of York in 1237, a key event in Anglo-Scottish relations. Alexander gave up all claims to Northumbria, Cumberland, and Westmorland – although retaining certain estates within these counties, for which he paid feudal homage to English king. More important was the fact that the border between the two countries – the Solway–Tweed line – was legally defined for the first time. The agreement did not mark the end of cross-border troubles. The so-called Wars of Independence (1296–1328 and 1332–57) were as violent and as long-lasting as any previous conflict between the two nations, and in 1334, Scotland was briefly obliged to cede Kirkcudbrightshire, Dumfriesshire, and the entire Border region south of the Lothians to England. More remarkable, however, is that with minor modifications – such as the division of the Debatable Lands, and Berwick-on-Tweed changing hands at least a dozen times – the Solway–Tweed line has endured to this day, and the Treaty of York thus marks the point where we can say that Scotland's southern territorial limits were finally defined.

To Scottish kings of the medieval period, England was a challenge: often a threat, sometimes an opportunity, sometimes their ruin. The twists and turns of Anglo-Scottish relations – from marriages and troop movements to treaties and arguments over feudal overlordship – are so well documented that it is natural that they should loom large in the assessments and judgements of historians. However, in terms of Scotland as a whole, events in the islands and on the rugged coasts of the west and north were at least as important. Relations with England were the dominant, but far from the only, factor in determining Scotland's political future. The Norse-Gaelic synthesis which characterised the Kingdom of the Isles, and the Scandinavian presence in Orkney and Shetland, were equally crucial in moulding Scotland's cultural and linguistic balance and in shaping Scotland's subsequent identity.

With the death of Thorfinn the Mighty, somewhere around 1065, the Earldom of Orkney passed to his sons, Paul and Erlend, while the other parts of his loose empire relapsed into their immemorial practice of raiding and feuding (see Chapter 35). Only in the last decade of the eleventh century did another Scandinavian strongman appear. Magnus Barelegs became King of Norway in 1093 on the death of his father, Olaf III or Olaf Kyrre (the Peaceful), but in character he seems to have taken after his grandfather, Harald Hardrada. The first years of his reign were spent establishing himself in Norway, particularly countering the challenge posed by his cousin, Haakon Magnusson, but from the beginning he appears to have been looking westwards. Before he became king, he may have fought alongside Donald Bán during Donald's successful bid for the Scottish kingship, but his first major campaign was in 1097 in the Scottish archipelagos and the Irish Sea.

The previous King of the Isles, Godred Crovan (also Gofraid Crobán and Guðrøðr Crovan), had died in 1095, leaving a power vacuum in which local chiefs asserted themselves and fought each other. Magnus initially sought to re-establish Norwegian control by installing a client king, Ingimund, who was based in Lewis. He then sailed back to Orkney – of which, as King of Norway, he was technically the overlord – where he removed the ruling joint Earls, Paul and Erlend Thorfinnson, and installed his own son, Sigurd. In 1098, hearing that Ingimund had been killed, Magnus returned to the west. Beginning in Lewis, he worked his way south, through the Uists to Skye, Islay and Kintyre. He took possession of the Isle of Man, killing the ruler, Earl Óttar, and making the island his base, encouraging Norwegian settlement and importing timber from Galloway, parts of which he may also have controlled.

It was at this point that he and King Edgar of Scotland negotiated the treaty which confirmed Norwegian possession of the Hebrides and Kintyre. From Edgar's point of view, this bought peace in the west at a time when he was trying to stamp his authority on the rest of Scotland, while Magnus would no longer have to reckon the Scots as potential enemies and could concentrate on reducing opposition in the Isles. He also met

Gruffudd ap Cynan, the King of Gwynedd, who had just been expelled from his kingdom by a Norman army led by Hugh d'Avranches, the Earl of Chester, and Hugh of Montgomery. Magnus sailed his fleet to Anglesey, taking the Normans by surprise. The Battle of Anglesey Sound (another name for the Menai Straits) saw the Normans put to flight and Hugh of Montgomery killed by an arrow shot by Magnus himself. Magnus apparently took control of Anglesey, while Gruffudd returned to Gwynedd, which he continued to rule until 1137. By the winter of 1098–99, Magnus was the ruler of a collection of territories stretching from Norway to the north of Scotland, and from the Western Isles to Mann and Anglesey. In many of the islands, his control may only have been nominal, but the extent of his possessions gave him control over many important seaways. It is unlikely that he could or would have wanted to invade England, but defeat in Gwynedd and the death of Hugh of Montgomery will have alerted the Normans to the rise of a new and potentially powerful force in the north and west.

In the event, there were no further confrontations with the Normans. Magnus returned to Norway in the summer of 1099 and spent the next two years fighting the Swedes. His second western campaign began in 1102 and was directed at Ireland. He seized Dublin without difficulty, and declared himself king, but was then sucked into the long, unedifying struggle for power between Muirchertach Ua Briain, King of Munster and High King of Ireland, and Domnall Ua Lochlain, a leader of the northern Uí Néill, who also claimed to be High King. Magnus and Muirchertach agreed a treaty which recognised Magnus as King of Dublin and arranged for his son, Sigurd, to marry Muirchartach's daughter. Sigurd was made joint king with his father, and their men fought alongside Muirchertach in the struggle against Domnall. But Magnus and Muirchertach never really trusted each other, not least because Muirchertach feared, probably correctly, that Magnus wanted the Irish High Kingship for himself.

Magnus was ambushed and killed in the summer of 1103. Did Muirchertach arrange it to safeguard his own position? Did the Uí Néill decide to remove what they saw as a dangerous ally of Muirchertach? Was he betrayed by his own men? In Ireland and in Wales, we have seen how warlords such as Brian Boru, or Gruffudd ap Llywelyn were able to bring any number of territories under their control in a short time, but with their deaths there was nothing to hold their new empires together. The same was true of Magnus Barelegs. Sigurd retired to Norway where he ruled, at first with his half-brother, and then alone until 1130. The title of King of the Isles reverted to the sons of Godred Crovan, while the Isles themselves went back to raiding and feuding as before. And the Earldom of Orkney reverted to the descendants of Thorfinn the Mighty. Magnus Barelegs' great adventure had lasted just six years.

In theory, the Isles remained subject to the authority of the Norwegian Crown, but it would be a century-and-a-half before any Norwegian king tried to exert direct control in the region. Godred Crovan's son, Olave the Red (also Óláfr Guðrøðarson) was King of the Isles from 1112 to 1152. In a time of comparative peace, he introduced elements of feudalism into the governance of Mann and some of the larger islands – although, as ever, it is not clear how far his authority really extended. His death, and the accession of his son, Godred the Black (also Guðrøðr Óláfsson), paved the way for the rise of the much-mythologised figure of Somerled, Lord of Argyll and Lord of the Isles. During the Celtic Revival in the nineteenth and early twentieth centuries, Somerled came to be seen as a champion of the Celtic people and Celtic values resisting Scandinavian colonisation. Such a view was very much a product of its time. Somerled was clearly a charismatic figure, but he was essentially a Norse-Gael warlord. Our first knowledge of him is when he sacked Glasgow in 1153, either joining a rebellion against the new Scottish king, Malcolm IV, or opportunistically taking advantage of the chaotic situation which followed Malcolm's accession. Between 1156 and 1160, Somerled exploited both the unpopularity of Godred the Black and the Isles' patchwork of feuds and kinship alliances to establish himself as the controlling figure in the long chain of islands from Lewis to Mann. In 1164, he launched an invasion of mainland Scotland. He sailed one hundred and sixty galleys up the Clyde and landed at Renfrew. What lay behind his decision remains unclear. Powerful as he was, and although Malcolm IV was known to be ill, Somerled had no chance of seizing the Scottish crown. In the event, he was killed at the Battle of Renfrew soon after landing, and his rapidly constructed empire, like others before it, simply fell apart.

The Isles were finally absorbed into Scotland in 1266, a hundred years later. Haakon IV (or Haakon Haakonsson; r.1217–63) of Norway created a northern empire: he brought Iceland and Greenland under Norwegian rule, and sought to strengthen control over the Faeroes, Orkney, and the

Isles. Having defined Scotland's southern border by the Treaty of York in 1237, Alexander II offered to buy the Hebrides, but was rebuffed and decided to pursue his objective by force. He assembled a fleet with the intention of forcing Haakon's appointee as King of the Isles, Eóghan (Ewen) of Argyll, to acknowledge Scottish overlordship. Before anything could happen, he was struck down by a fever and died. The fact that his son and successor, Alexander III (r.1249–86), was only eight precluded any further action, but when Alexander came of age in 1262, he determined to fulfil his father's wish and bring the Isles under Scottish control. Responding to the challenge in 1263, Haakon brought a fleet to the west coast. In the battle that followed, near Largs on the North Ayrshire coast, neither side could claim a comprehensive victory, although the Norwegians came off worse. Haakon withdrew to Orkney, intending to overwinter there before renewing his attack, but died that December. His son, Magnus VI (r.1263–80), realised that, even if he defeated Alexander, he could not make the Isles defensible against an increasingly powerful Scotland. The Treaty of Perth was signed in July 1266. Norway recognised Scottish sovereignty over Mann and the Hebrides in return for an annual payment and confirmation of Norwegian sovereignty over Orkney and the Shetlands. The cultural heritage of Norse and Norse-Gael rule would endure – it remains an essential part of cultural identity in the islands – but politically the Isles became part of the emerging Scottish nation state. It was not a fairy-tale ending. The title Lord of the Isles continued to be used. Those who bore it frequently had interests that diverged from mainland Scotland. There was disobedience, dissent, even armed insurrection, but for all that the Isles had become, and would remain, an integral part of Scotland.

It took longer to bring Orkney and Shetland under Scottish rule, but the process was, in the end, less complicated. In the 1130s and 1140s, David I of Scotland gradually took control of those areas of the mainland, in Caithness and Sutherland, that were formally part of the Earldom of Orkney. In 1138, he installed his five-year-old cousin, Harald Maddadsson, as joint ruler of Orkney. The other joint ruler was Rognvald, who had been appointed some twenty years earlier by Sigurd of Norway, the son of Magnus Barelegs. The intention was that Rognvald would die first, and the succession would then be determined by Scotland. However, this plan was forestalled by King Eystein II of Norway, who in 1151 sailed a fleet through the Pentland Firth and captured Harald Maddadsson. To secure his release, Harald was forced to swear an oath acknowledging that he owed his earldom to the Norwegian Crown. It was an unpromising start, but Harald went on to be one of the most powerful Earls of Orkney, outliving those who sought to control him, maintaining the integrity of his territories, and ruling for sixty-seven years until his death in 1206 at the age of seventy-two. Yet for all his power in Orkney and Shetland, Harald Maddadsson never sought, and was never in a position, to threaten the Scottish kings. The days of Viking adventurers were over. Scotland was an established polity, not necessarily internally stable, and often under pressure from the English, but — and this is the lesson of Haakon IV's attempt to invade mainland Scotland in 1263 — too well established to be destabilised by a fleet of longships.

In 1231, Earl Jon Haraldsson died, either lost at sea or burnt to death in his hall in Thurso, depending on which source one believes. He was the youngest son of Harald Maddadsson and with him, the long line of Norwegian earls died out. The earldom remained vacant for five years before the Norwegian king appointed a Scottish earl, Magnus II, son of the Earl of Angus. The Angus line held the title until 1320, when the Norwegians appointed a second line of Scottish earls. At the time, Norwegian commercial, if not political, power was expanding, but then between 1349 and 1400 the Black Death wiped out up to half the country's population, with a commensurate effect on trade and the economy. In 1380, as a result of inheritance rather than war, Olaf Haakonsson became king of both Norway and Denmark. His successor, Margaret I brought about the Kalmar Union, which unified Norway, Denmark, and Sweden. These changes naturally led Norway to look towards the rest of Scandinavia rather than westwards to the Atlantic. As a result, the Earldom of Orkney became more and more of a backwater.

In the end, Orkney and Shetland were united with the rest of Scotland not as a result of a war, but because of an unpaid debt. In July 1469, the thirteen-year-old daughter of King Christian of Norway, Sweden, and Denmark was married at Holyrood Abbey to the seventeen-year-old King James III of Scotland. It was a political marriage, intended in part to end a long-running dispute between the two countries over the payments due to the Norwegian Crown under the terms of the Treaty of Perth. Margaret of Denmark, as she is known, was popular with the Scottish people, though the marriage is reported to have been an unhappy one. The marriage agreement remitted all Scotland's accumulated debts under the Treaty of Perth, and in addition promised the sum of 60,000 Rhenish francs – 10,000 to be paid immediately, with Orkney and Shetland temporarily placed under Scottish control as surety for the remaining 50,000. The agreement gave King Christian the right to redeem the islands against payment of the balance, but the balance was never paid, and in 1472 Orkney and Shetland formally became part of the Kingdom of Scotland. It may be that Christian had never intended to pay his daughter's dowry in full, but the Scots certainly valued the two archipelagos more than 50,000 Rhenish francs.[329]

40 Wales

William of Normandy invaded England in 1066 because he believed Harold Godwineson had sworn a binding oath to support his claim to be the next King of England. When Harold reneged on that oath and took the crown for himself, William believed he had a legal – and moral – right to invade. His decision to invade Scotland when Malcolm III cavalierly disregarded the oath of submission that formed the basis of the Treaty of Abernethy had the same origin: a concern for legality and the swearing of oaths. Given this attitude – which sits uneasily with the ruthlessness he could display in other contexts – it is possible that William would have avoided confrontation with the Scots and the Welsh had he not been provoked. But when England was thrown into turmoil in 1066, it was natural for the Scots and the Welsh to exploit the situation. For the Scots, instability south of the border represented a form of defence. For the Welsh, cross-border raiding was a time-honoured habit, and on both sides of the ill-defined Anglo-Welsh border there were areas of wasteland attesting to the devastation it had caused.

This concern for, and understanding of, the legal basis of his actions is demonstrated by the way William treated Scotland and Wales differently. Malcolm III offered passive support to Edgar the Ætheling and the English rebels in 1068 and launched his own incursion in 1070. William responded by invading Scotland to put Malcolm in his place, and the matter was concluded with the Treaty of Abernethy. In Wales, Edric

Map 31 The British Isles in the 12th and 13th Centuries

the Wild together with Bleddyn and Rhiwallon ap Cynfyn of Gwynedd attacked the border garrisons and burnt Shrewsbury before being defeated by William in battle outside Stafford. Edric submitted and became William's man, but there was no treaty, nothing but rough justice. Scotland was an established polity with a king that could be invaded, negotiated with, and brought to heel in legal form. Wales was different. The term referred to the area west of Offa's Dyke, perhaps indicating the area occupied by P-Celtic Welsh speakers, but in no sense signifying political or social unity. To William and his Normans, Wales was a collection of unstable kingdoms inhabited by savages – and the 1070s, when the rulers of Gwynedd, Deheubarth, and Morgannwg murdered each other in turn, can only have confirmed that opinion.

Because Wales offered no central or dominant entity with which to deal, William chose to fortify the frontier. In 1067, he revived the Earldom of Hereford, which had formerly belonged to Harold Godwineson, and created two new earldoms at Shrewsbury and Chester. Hereford went to William Fitzosbern; Shrewsbury to Roger of Montgomery, one of William's principal commanders at Hastings; while Chester went initially to Gerbod the Fleming, who had also fought at Hastings, and then to Hugh d'Avranches, who may have been related to William. These were the first Marcher Lords, powerful landowners who could command men and resources. Over the next three decades, they and their successors built some five hundred motte-and-bailey castles along the borderlands, many of them later rebuilt in stone.

Neither William I nor William Rufus sought the conquest or annexation of Wales, but the earls, whose job it was to defend the border, found the best form of defence was to push the Welsh back, so the first phase of the conquest of Wales began in a piecemeal manner. After two or three years of pressure from William Fitzosbern, the kingdom of Gwent, having existed for seven hundred years, simply disappeared from the map.[330] Roger of Montgomery pushed into Powys, building a castle on the Severn which he named Montgomery after himself, and which rapidly became first a town and later the administrative centre of Montgomeryshire. In 1088, a minor Norman nobleman, Bernard de Neufmarché, swept into Deheubarth and began building a castle at Brecon, which became the centre of the Anglo-Norman lordship of Brecknock. In 1093, the King of Deheubarth, Rhys ap Tewdwr, was killed. He seemed the last figure capable of galvanising Welsh resistance, and Roger of Montgomery's forces drove through Ceredigion into Dyfed where, on a rocky outcrop overlooking the Pembroke River, Roger's son, Arnulf, began the construction of the massive stronghold that is Pembroke Castle. At the same time, Morgannwg fell to Robert Fitzhammo (or Fitzhamon), the first Norman baron of Gloucester. In the north, Hugh d'Avranches, acting in concert with Roger of Montgomery, pushed into Gwynedd. In 1081, when Gruffudd ap Cynan became King of Gwynedd, they invited him for a meeting, captured him, and kept him prisoner for twelve years. In 1093, he escaped and fought a losing battle against the Normans until he met Magnus Barelegs, who helped him recover his kingdom (see Chapter 39).

The Battle of Anglesey Sound and the subsequent expulsion of the Normans from Gwynedd was the first of a series of reverses suffered by the Normans in the 1090s. It had looked as if the whole of Wales would quickly fall under Norman rule. They had forced their way up the river valleys, toppled ruling families, and built impressive castles in strategic locations, but there remained many remote and mountainous areas from which the Welsh could and did counterattack. The Welsh fightback was not an orchestrated or coordinated rising: it was a spontaneous and simultaneous reaction across Wales to the death, destruction, and cruelty brought by the invaders. The actions of the Marcher Lords and the lesser Norman adventurers who followed in their wake provoked such furious resistance that, in 1095 and 1097, William Rufus was forced to send reinforcements from his English army to prevent them from being driven back to the border. By the turn of the century, the lands retained by the Normans were limited to what is now Pembrokeshire in southern Dyfed, Brecon, Gwent, and the borderlands of Powys and Gwynedd. These areas, modified by occasional gains and equally frequent losses, became known as *Marchia Walliae* (the Welsh Marches), while the rest of the country, once again ruled by the Welsh, became known as *Pura Wallia* (Independent Wales). The position of *Marchia Walliae* was anomalous. Although ruled by the Marcher Lords, who were subjects of the King of England, it was not part of England. English law did not apply, and the Marcher Lords were free to fortify their lands and employ private armies in a way that the English barons were not. For all that, in the first decade of the twelfth century, the Welsh continued to press and menace and threaten.

Henry I saw instability in Wales and the Marches as a genuine threat. Once he had sorted the problem of Normandy by defeating and imprisoning his brother Robert after the Battle of Tinchebrai in 1106, he turned his attention to Wales. In 1108, he drove his forces across South Wales, founding a castle at Carmarthen, a strategic crossing place on the River Tywi, and strengthening the Norman enclave around Pembroke by encouraging Flemish and, later, English settlers, so that it became one of the first places in Wales where Welsh ceased to be spoken. At this point, Owain ap Cadwgan enters the story. His father, Cadwgan, had been one of the leaders of the Welsh fightback in the 1090s, and still ruled Ceredigion and part of Powys. In 1109, Owain abducted and seduced a woman of great beauty called Nest (or Nesta) ferch Rhys, who had previously been King Henry's mistress – and had probably borne him a son – but was now the wife of Gerald of Windsor, the Constable of Pembroke Castle. Henry was furious. He ordered Richard de Belmeis, his chief agent in the Marches (and also Bishop of London), to invade Cadwgan's territory. Cadwgan immediately sued for peace and was deprived of almost all his lands, while his son, the cause of the trouble, fled to Ireland. Nest later married Étienne, the Constable of Cardigan.

For the next three or four years, Henry was distracted by events on the Continent, but his occasional interventions in Wales did little to ease the ever more convoluted situation. He allowed Cadwgan to return to Ceredigion in return for a fine and a promise to exile and disinherit his son. Nonetheless – with or without his father's blessing – Owain returned to Wales and allied himself with Madog ap Rhiryd, a member of the ruling house of Powys. Henry countered by releasing from prison Iorwerth, Cadwgan's brother, another Welsh leader from the 1090s. At Henry's bidding, Iorwerth led a force against Owain and Madog. Owain took refuge in his father's territory of Ceredigion, but then raided the Norman-controlled area around Pembroke in Dyfed, taking prisoners and selling them as slaves, and also killing William of Brabant, one of the Flemish barons installed by Henry. Cadwgan was stripped of his lands for a second time, and Owain again fled to Ireland. In 1111, Madog – having apparently fallen out with Owain – killed Iorwerth. Faced with a power vacuum and more instability, Henry was forced to restore Cadwgan to authority in Powys. But Madog then killed Cadwgan, which meant that Owain became ruler of most of Powys, and in revenge for his father's death had Madog blinded. And while these events were unfolding in South and Mid-Wales, in the north in Gwynedd Gruffudd ap Cynan had consolidated his position to the point where he appeared as a potential threat to Chester.

By 1114, King Henry had had enough. Three armies crossed the

Marches into Wales. The northern army was commanded by Alexander I of Scotland; the southern by Gilbert de Clare (also Gilbert de Tonbridge and Gilbert fitz Richard); while Henry took command in Mid-Wales. The campaign was uneventful. Faced with overwhelming force, both Owain and Gruffudd ap Cynan sued for peace and paid tribute. Owain, accepting the reality of the situation, switched sides completely. He accompanied Henry to Normandy and was knighted. In 1116, he took Henry's side against Gruffudd ap Rhys, who returned from exile in Ireland in an attempt to recover his father's kingdom of Deheubarth. This Gruffudd was the brother of Nest, whom Owain had abducted, and among those opposing him was Nest's former husband, Gerald of Windsor. That he and Owain were now allies against Gruffudd did not prevent Gerald from ambushing and killing Owain in revenge for his earlier humiliation.

Henry I never managed to subdue Wales, but, through a mixture of force, diplomacy, and marriage, he managed to exert a significant degree of control, particularly in the south. Probably in 1122, he made peace with Gruffudd ap Rhys, restoring him to part of Deheubarth. Miles of Gloucester, a trusted adviser and the first incumbent of the revived Earldom of Hereford, was married to the heiress of Brecon. Henry's illegitimate son, Robert, married the heiress of Glamorgan and was created Earl of Gloucester. The two sons of Gilbert de Clare were also important figures: Richard de Clare held Ceredigion, while his brother Gilbert controlled much of Gwent and Monmouth. In Gwynedd, Gruffudd ap Cynan was not perhaps an ideal neighbour, but his long reign did provide a degree of stability in the region. However, little of this survived Henry's death in 1135 and the beginning of 'The Anarchy'.

When Stephen of Blois seized the throne in December 1136, in defiance of Henry I's known wishes, many English barons refused to accept his kingship. As in Scotland, so in Wales, instability across the border was viewed as an opportunity. In April 1136, Richard de Clare was ambushed and murdered, and a general rising ensued. The sons of Gruffudd ap Cynan attacked Ceredigion from the north, while the sons of Gruffudd ap Rhys attacked from the south. Ceredigion, until then among the most secure parts of Norman Wales, was overrun. So was much of Dyfed. Carmarthen Castle was seized and burnt. Pembroke was cut off. Only Brecon and parts of Gwent and Monmouth remained under Norman control. Matilda landed on the Sussex coast near Arundel in 1139. Her half-brother, Robert of Gloucester, and the Earl of Chester both declared their support. Scottish forces swept south across the border, and most of the north of England was in revolt. Wales was not among Stephen's priorities, and from 1139 onwards, the Welsh rulers were able to consolidate their grip on the territories they had recovered and gradually extend their power. By the time Henry II came to the throne in 1154, there were three dominant figures. In Gwynedd, Owain ap Gruffudd had made inroads into the lands of the Earl of Chester by seizing Rhuddlan Castle. In Powys, Madog ap Maredudd had pushed beyond the border of Shropshire and established a castle at Oswestry. And in Deheubarth, Rhys ap Gruffudd (the son of a different Gruffudd) had beaten off a challenge from Gilbert de Clare and strengthened his hold over Ceredigion.

Henry II was more than just King of England. He ruled an empire which stretched from Scotland to Spain, and later added Ireland to it, but even he had problems with Wales. If his first priority on acceding to the English throne was to restore royal authority after nearly two decades of civil war, his second was Wales. He clearly saw Owain of Gwynedd as a significant threat. So, too, did Madog of Powys, who saw in Henry a potential ally and protector. In 1157, Henry and Madog joined forces and crossed Gwynedd's eastern border. Henry had intended a two-pronged attack, with his fleet landing on Anglesey at the same time, but the campaign did not go according to plan. The Battle of Ewloe (or Coleshill) saw Henry and Madog's army ambushed, Henry himself very nearly killed, and the invaders forced to retreat. At the same time, most of the fleet was destroyed attempting to establish a bridgehead on Anglesey. Henry persisted and in the end Owain, while not defeated, was brought to terms, although he was only obliged to surrender the *cantref* (or county) of Tegeingl, that area bounded by the Dee Estuary and the River Clwyd, which included Rhuddlan. After this experience, Henry chose not to involve himself in invading Deheubarth but he made troops available to the Marcher Lords who, over the next five or six years, reclaimed most of the kingdom, despite stubborn resistance from Rhys ap Gruffudd.

In 1163, the Welsh rulers agreed to unite under the leadership of Owain of Gwynedd in an attempt to recover the lands they had lost over the previous decade. In 1165, Henry tried to forestall their efforts by leading a large army, much of it mounted, from Oswestry through the Berwyn Mountains, with the aim of attacking Gwynnedd from the south. A skirmish in the Ceiriog Valley saw the Welsh inflict casualties on his forces, but it was days of rain that defeated Henry's army. Horses found no footing on roads that had turned to mud. Soldiers could not march. Henry was forced into an ignominious retreat and never again invaded Wales. Owain recaptured Tegeingl. Rhys ap Gruffudd took control of Ceredigion and drove south into Dyfed, with momentous consequences for Ireland that we shall examine shortly.

Henry II was a realist. If Wales could not be conquered, it must be controlled. Circumstances helped him in that Madog died in 1160 and Owain in 1170, so both Gwynedd and Powys turned inwards, consumed by struggles over the succession. However, the one remaining Welsh strongman, Rhys ap Gruffudd, controlled territories in South Wales that allowed him to threaten the route between Gloucester and Pembroke. This was important to Henry because, from 1171, he was involved in Ireland. The Gloucester–Pembroke road was his main supply line, and he could not risk it being disrupted. His solution was not just to make peace with Rhys, but to make him responsible for maintaining order in the region. According to *Brut y Tywysogion* (*Chronicle of the Princes*), Rhys was appointed Henry's 'justice over the whole of South Wales.'[331] In practice, he became the King's representative with the power to challenge anyone, Welsh or Norman, who threatened Henry's interests – and, despite his history, Rhys proved surprisingly loyal. He could easily have turned the so-called Great Revolt of 1173, when Henry's three eldest sons rose against him, to his advantage, but he remained Henry's man. In Gwynedd, in 1174, the much-weakened ruler, Dafydd ap Owain, married Henry's half-sister, Emma, and in 1177 was induced to swear loyalty to the English king. Powys offered no threat, remaining divided and powerless. The potentially explosive forces of *Pura Wallia* were thus contained. At the same time, Henry also strengthened the position of the Marcher Lords, so that for the last decade of his reign he had achieved, if not peace – there were always raids and feuds – at least a degree of stability.

With Henry's death in 1189, everything changed. Despite his powerful and apparently secure position, Rhys decided that his agreement to serve as 'justice' terminated with the King's death. He immediately attacked and overran Norman territories in Gower, Carmarthen, and Pembroke and, by the time he died, unexpectedly, in 1197, he controlled most of Deheubarth. With his death, as so often, his sons embarked on a destructive power struggle. King Richard (r.1189–99) took little interest in Wales, but his brother, Prince John, had married Isabella, Countess of Gloucester, and the estates that she brought to the marriage made him the most powerful of the Marcher Lords. The Archbishop of Canterbury annulled the marriage because of consanguinity – they were half-second cousins – but John kept her lands and, once he became King in 1199, intervened directly in Wales. He effectively partitioned Deheubarth, ensuring that it could not again exercise the power it had under Rhys. Resistance seemed to centre on the figure of Gwenwynwyn in Powys, but he did not have the resources to challenge John, and it was again Gwynedd where the next challenge to English power in Wales arose.

Llywelyn the Great (or Llywelyn mab Iorwerth) was the grandson of Owain of Gwynedd. He began his rise to power early. By 1195, at the age of about twenty-two, he was the recognised ruler of eastern Gwynedd, and by 1200 he was sole ruler of the kingdom. In 1201, he swore an oath of allegiance to King John, and four years later married John's illegitimate daughter, Joan (or Siwan) of Wales. In 1208, John stripped Gwenwynwyn of Powys of his lands and titles, and Llywelyn seized the opportunity to take control of much of Powys and northern Ceredigion. He seems to have fulfilled his feudal duties – when John mobilised his forces to threaten Scotland in 1209, Llywelyn was by his side – but John was an unstable character, not given to trusting people. He convinced himself, perhaps not without reason, that Llywelyn intended to establish himself as the leader of the whole of *Pura Wallia*, and so, in 1210, he invaded Gwynedd. His forces swept rapidly across the kingdom, reaching the Menai Straits and forcing Llywelyn to surrender much of his territory. Most of the other Welsh rulers, who had seen Llywelyn as a potential leader against the English, abandoned him and swore oaths of loyalty to John, perhaps believing he would constitute less of a threat to their autonomy than Llywelyn. They were wrong.

It took less than two years for the Welsh rulers to realise that John was intent on their subjugation. The inevitable uprising began in 1211, with Llywelyn at its head. John's string of new castles in Gwynedd were seized and destroyed. The new castle at Aberystwyth was demolished. Llywelyn seized Shrewsbury and threatened John's lands in the Marches. In doing so, he aided the English barons who were actively opposing John following the loss of Normandy and other territories in France and trying to force him to sign the *Magna Carta*. As a result, when the *Magna Carta* was signed in June 1215, it contained two important provisions which distanced Wales from English law: land rights in *Pura Wallia* should be subject to the Laws of Wales, while land rights in the Marches should be subject to the Laws of the Marches. Another Welsh offensive that December saw the castles of Cardigan, Carmarthen and Kidwelly all falling to Llywelyn's forces. All the time, he was gaining authority, influencing the choice of new bishops at St Davids and Bangor, and in 1216 calling the Council of Aberdyfi, where all the Welsh princes took oaths of loyalty to him. When Gwenwynwyn reneged on his oath, he was forced into exile in England, and when his son-in-law Reginald de Braose, who held Brecon and Abergavenny, also reneged, he was forced to submit, heavily fined, and obliged to give hostages for good behaviour.

John died in 1216. His son and successor, Henry III, was only nine, so until his majority power was in the hands of a council of loyalist nobles. They brought an end to the long-running struggle between the Crown and the barons and negotiated the 1218 Treaty of Worcester with Llywelyn. At first sight, the treaty appears to place significant limitations on Llywelyn's power. He agreed that he and all the other Welsh rulers would swear fealty to the English Crown. However, the Crown explicitly recognised the legitimacy of the oaths sworn at Aberdyfi. This meant that while Llywelyn enjoyed absolute power over none of the Welsh rulers, he enjoyed *some* authority over all of them, and that authority derived from the King. He surrendered Cardigan and Carmarthen, only to be appointed the King's bailiff in both. He kept all his other territorial gains. Llywelyn was a realist, and the Crown was weak: he preferred power to constitutional forms, even if that made him the King's justiciar rather than the acknowledged ruler of Wales.[332]

Llywelyn the Great died in 1240. The intervening years were anything but peaceful. Castles and territories changed hands. Alliances came and went. The Marcher Lords, led by William Marshal, Second Earl of Pembroke, brought troops from Ireland to try to dispossess him. He fought back, but at the same time did homage to the King to emphasise his loyalty. A few years later, he allied himself to the Marshal family against Henry III. Llywelyn played many often-contradictory roles – the conqueror who sought to establish cohesive government; the warrior who encouraged the development of small, urban centres to boost trade – but whatever his title, and whatever lands he controlled, for the last thirty years of his life, there was no more powerful figure in Wales.

Henry III recognised this and made it clear to Llywelyn's son, Dafydd, that he could not expect to enjoy the power and status of his father. Cardigan and Carmarthen returned to the King. Powys returned to the descendants of Gwenwynwyn. Dafydd was left with Gwynedd and little else. Nonetheless, he began calling himself Prince of Wales, and made diplomatic overtures to Pope Innocent IV and Louis IX of France. Henry was not amused. In 1241, he mounted a rapid, savage, and effective invasion which ended in the Treaty of Gwerneigron. Dafydd was reduced to ruling western Gwynedd only, and forced to promise that, if he died childless, the whole of Gwynedd would pass to Henry. In 1246, Dafydd did die childless, but the men of Gwynedd refused to enact the provisions of the treaty. They proclaimed Dafydd's nephews, Owain and Llywelyn ap Gruffudd (also Llywelyn II or Llywelyn the Last), as rulers. Henry invaded again and, by the Treaty of Woodstock in 1247, effectively reduced Gwynedd to the status of an English lordship and its rulers to tenants-in-chief. The Marcher Lords watched from the sidelines, equally suspicious of both sides. Established as an English barrier against Welsh incursions, they now controlled most of South Wales as well, and increasingly saw themselves as an autonomous polity. They knew that, given the opportunity, Henry III would curb their powers. At the same time, they feared the emergence of a leader who might unite the Welsh against them.

In 1255, Llywelyn II threw off the terms of Woodstock, imprisoned his two brothers – Owain and (another) Dafydd – and having thus removed the possibility of a palace coup, led his army southwards. By 1258, the rulers of Powys, Deheubarth and Glamorgan had paid homage to him as their overlord, presumably persuaded that he would be a more acceptable overlord than Henry III. Llywelyn II also established contact with Alexander III of Scotland, styling himself 'Prince of Wales' and making it clear that he regarded Wales as a single, independent polity. Between 1258 and 1262, he tried to gain recognition for himself and for Wales from Henry III, but Henry, distracted by a revolt among the English barons led by Simon de Montfort, refused to negotiate. Llywelyn lost patience and attacked Brecon, Abergavenny, and parts of the Marches. At the beginning of 1264, he allied himself with Simon de Montfort, and that May, de Montfort defeated and captured Henry at the Battle of Lewes. This allowed

Llywelyn to negotiate the Treaty of Picton of 1265, which recognised Wales as a principality with Llywelyn as its Prince and as overlord of *magnates Wallie*, the great magnates of Wales. The price was that he should hold the principality as a vassal of the English king – thus according the new Prince of Wales the same status (in English eyes) as the King of Scotland – and that he should pay the sum of £20,000.[333] Six weeks later, de Montfort was dead. Llywelyn quickly launched another campaign to press home his advantage while Henry was still weak. It concluded in 1267 with the Treaty of Montgomery which, with minor amendments, confirmed Llywelyn's status as Prince of Wales under the English Crown.

Given where Llywelyn II and Wales had been twenty years earlier, this was a heroic achievement. Wales appeared on the verge of nationhood, but the cracks were beginning to show, and the next twenty years would see everything he had achieved swept away. One brother, Owain, was still in prison, but the other, Dafydd, had escaped and defected to the English. Llywelyn had promised to pay Henry III a sum that was probably about six times his annual income. The ruling families of Powys and Deheubarth were happy to have Llywelyn as an ally, but less happy to have to pay homage to him. It was in 1272, when Henry died and Edward I came to the English throne, that the tide turned decisively against Llywelyn. Among his enemies were Roger Mortimer, whose stronghold was Wigmore Castle in Herefordshire, and Gilbert de Clare, Lord of Glamorgan and possibly the richest of all the English barons. Both had been attacked by Llywelyn, and both had the ear of the new king, who resented Llywelyn's loyalty to the de Montfort family, which had captured and humiliated his father. In 1275, Llywelyn made a proxy marriage to Simon de Montfort's daughter, Eleanor, who was living in France. Sailing to North Wales to join her new husband, her ship was intercepted, and she was imprisoned for three years.

In 1276, Edward I declared Llywelyn II an outlaw, and in 1277 crossed the frontier into Gwynedd with a 15,000-strong army, supported by a fleet which had sailed round from the Cinque Ports. There was no real contest. Faced with such overwhelming force, the Welsh princes who had supported Llywelyn simply melted away. Edward's army drove westward from Chester. His fleet landed on Anglesey and seized or destroyed the harvest. Llywelyn had no choice but to sue for peace. The Treaty of Aberconwy released his wife from prison, but his rule was reduced to western

Gwynedd, while his brother Dafydd was given control of the east. He retained the title Prince of Wales, but it had little meaning now.

South Wales was firmly under the control of the Marcher Lords. In Mid-Wales Edward now increased the proportion of royal land and made sure that the rest was in loyal hands. Only Gwynedd in the north remained under Welsh rule, and in 1282 Dafydd played into Edward's hands by mounting a rebellion. Llewelyn gave his support. Edward launched another attack, and this time faced stronger resistance. The Earl of Gloucester was defeated at the Battle of Llandeilo Fawr. Luke de Tany captured Anglesey, but was ambushed and defeated at Moel-y-don as soon as he set foot on the mainland. However, that December, Llywelyn misread or was deceived about the situation in Mid-Wales. He marched south from Gwynedd and straight into a trap. The Battle of Orewin Bridge, where he was killed, marked the end of Wales' bid for nationhood. Dafydd fought on, but was captured in June 1283, brought before Edward, and taken to Shrewsbury where he was hanged, drawn, and quartered.

The following year, 1284, saw the Statute of Rhuddlan. Wales became, to all intents and purposes, part of England. The former principality was divided into counties, administered by sheriffs, with English-style courts enforcing English laws – only where property was involved did Welsh law still apply. English settlers were encouraged. New castles were built to keep Gwynedd obedient – at Beaumaris, Caernarfon, Conwy, and Harlech. In the shadow of existing castles such as Flint and Aberystwyth, small towns sprang up, and increased trade, mainly in agricultural products and timber, began to bind Wales closer to England. There were rebellions – in the 1280s, the 1290s, the 1310s, and the 1370s – the biggest and most nearly successful of them led by Owain Glyndŵr (Owen Glendower) at the beginning of the fifteenth century. However, taking the long view, the integration of Wales and England was a comparatively smooth process. Wales retained, and retains, its distinct culture and its language. Politically it has been less assertive than Scotland or Ireland, and even today Plaid Cymru shows less potential for disturbing the status quo in the United Kingdom than the Scottish National Party or Sinn Fein. It is ironic, therefore, to realise that the long, unhappy – even disastrous – involvement of the English in Ireland has its origins in Wales.

41   Ireland

The *Anglo-Saxon Chronicle* says that, had William the Conqueror lived a couple of years longer, 'he would have conquered Ireland by his astuteness and without any display of force.'[334] William Rufus is supposed to have said that he would make a bridge of ships across the Irish Sea in order to invade.[335] Such boasting was part of medieval kingship, but faced with uncertain loyalties among the barons in England and Normandy, incursions by the Scots, and raids by the Welsh, the early Norman kings had no reason to invade Ireland. Political fugitives regularly took refuge there – Harold Godwineson had done so when exiled by Edward the Confessor, and his sons Edmund and Magnus followed his example after 1066 – but that was a minor irritant. In 1102, Arnulf de Montgomery, Lord of Pembroke, was accused of treachery by Henry I, and in an unprecedented move, he appealed to the King of Munster, Muirchertach Ua Briain, for miliary assistance. He even married Muirchertach's daughter, but his rebellion was quickly quashed and he, too, fled to Ireland. Shortly after becoming king in 1154, Henry II appears to have considered invading Ireland, probably encouraged by the Archbishop of Canterbury, Theodore de Bec, who had ambitions to control the Irish church. Nothing happened, but Henry did break new ground by making an alliance – directed against Malcolm IV of Scotland – with both Muirchertach Mac Lochlainn of the northern Uí Néill, also high King of Ireland, and Somerled, Lord of the Isles. Ireland was perhaps growing in importance in the eyes of the English kings, but such contacts as there were remained distinctly low key.

Any assessment of Anglo-Irish relations, even when it concerns the twelfth century, is necessarily coloured by the hostility engendered by centuries of war, persecution, and famine. Some historians have chosen to see the first invaders as 'English' and the invasion itself as containing the seeds of later Anglo-Irish conflicts.[336] The issue is complicated by the terminology employed by the chroniclers of the period. Before 1066, the Welsh chroniclers call their neighbours 'Saxons', but they call their later, Plantagenet invaders 'French' – whether referring to their language or their origin is unclear. The Irish chroniclers do not make the same distinction. The *Annals of Ulster* entry for 1171 states that 'There came into Ireland Henry ... most puissant king of England and also Duke of Normandy and

Aquitaine and Count of Anjou and Lord of many other lands, with 240 ships. (So that was the first advent of the Saxons into Ireland.)'[337] Similarly, the *Annals of the Four Masters*, while distinguishing carefully between 'Leinstermen' and 'the men of Bréifne and Airghialla', refers to their enemy as 'Saxons' (*saxain*) or 'foreigners' (*gaill*).[338] This may be simply a matter of common usage – although the terms *engleis* and *angli* did exist – or perhaps the words were being used pejoratively.

The men who invaded Ireland in the later twelfth century were not English in any simplistic sense. The traditional description, 'Anglo-Norman', remains the most accurate. They were of Norman heritage and most probably had more Welsh than Anglo-Saxon blood. They or their families held estates in Normandy as well as in England and Wales, and their sense of collective identity stretched beyond the Channel to include the lands of their origin. After the loss of Normandy and their Continental estates, the Norman aristocracy would identify more closely with England, and English would become their vernacular – although French remained the language of the law and formal documentation right up until the fourteenth century – and at this stage they still spoke Norman French.

Invasion and conquest led to a political structure based on control and oppression that was continued by the descendants of the invaders – descendants who became English over the next two or three centuries. Nor were the Anglo-Norman invaders anything less than brutal: when Raymond Fitzgerald broke out of Waterford and put a besieging Irish and Norse-Gael army to flight, he ordered seventy prisoners to have their legs broken and their heads cut off before their bodies were thrown into the sea. Yet it is important to realise that what we are seeing is a typical medieval conflict, with conquest and wealth as its principal objectives. The combination of prejudice and oppression that was subsequently to characterise Anglo-Irish relations – a blend of religious bigotry and medieval brutality surviving into what should have been a more enlightened age – developed later and had little or no cultural or ideological connection with the invasion of the 1170s.

It is difficult to judge how far the Normans understood Ireland and the Irish, and *vice versa*. The transformation of Rollo's colony of Viking raiders into a Continental duchy with a developed feudal system was remarkably rapid. To a significant extent this was due to the proximity of a politically sophisticated – if not always stable – and culturally powerful Frankish kingdom, descended from Charlemagne's empire. Those Vikings who had settled in Ireland gradually became integrated, but it was a long, slow process, and the main actor was time, for Ireland – although its art and religious learning had enriched the whole of Europe – offered little or nothing to those seeking to create a workable polity to suit changing circumstances. The Normans and the Irish Vikings may have had common roots, but they had little in common. Nor was there common ground between the Normans and the native Irish. The Normans made a distinction between established polities, such as Scotland, and the inchoate patchwork of Welsh territories. Ireland, with its clan-based kingdoms, blood feuds, and constant round of raids and alliances, conquests and reversals must have seemed at least as dysfunctional as Wales. Trade between Ireland and England – mainly in food, cloth, and slaves – was well established and profitable. Dublin was a major slave market, and the *Domesday Book* suggests that at least ten per cent of the English population were slaves. Contacts between Ireland and England were not lacking, but they were not, for the most part, contacts between rulers or the aristocracy. Both the Anglo-Saxon kings and the Normans sought to manage their problems with Scotland through a combination of force, diplomacy, and dynastic marriages. A similar approach was tried in Wales, although the inherent instability of the region meant that it was less successful. In Ireland, force was paramount, diplomacy was non-existent, and political or dynastic marriages only began once Anglo-Norman barons and their men were on Irish soil and the process of conquest had begun.

Anglo-Norman interest in Ireland began in 1165 after Henry II's army had been reduced to a bedraggled rout in the Berwyn Mountains. With Henry no longer a threat, Rhys ap Gruffudd drove southwards towards Pembroke. The Marcher Lords of South Wales knew they could expect no further help from the English king. Negotiations took place in 1166. No one wanted a direct confrontation, and Rhys suggested that, rather than remaining a source of tension in Wales, the Marcher Lords and their men might cross to Ireland to support Diarmait MacMurchada (Dermot MacMurrough), the King of Leinster. Diarmait had been expelled from his kingdom by the combined forces of Tigernán Ua Ruairc (Tiernan O'Rourke), King of Bréifne, and Ruaidrí Ua Conchobair (Rory O'Conor), King of Connacht, the new but, as it turned out, last High King of Ireland – although, as ever in Ireland. the story was not that simple: some years earlier, Diarmait had abducted Tigernán's wife, Devorgilla, so hostilities were not unprovoked. Diarmait had petitioned Henry II for help, but Henry was fully involved in fighting Louis VII of France and unwilling to intervene, although he did give Diarmait permission to recruit troops from within the Angevin domains. To the Marcher Lords, Rhys ap Gruffudd's proposal seemed like an ideal solution. Wales was proving a constant source of trouble, and their estates were not as profitable as they had hoped or been led to believe. In Ireland, they were needed, although as Simon Schama points out, at this stage they were – in principle at least – mercenaries not conquerors.[339]

The first contingent sailed with Diarmait when he returned to Ireland in 1167. At first driven back by the forces of Tigernán Ua Ruairc, they were reinforced in 1169 by a larger Anglo-Norman expedition comprising mounted knights and archers under the leadership of Gerald de Barry. The new army took Wexford, at which point Tigernán Ua Ruairc and Ruaidrí Ua Conchobair, realising the danger, agreed to recognise Diarmait as King of Leinster if he dispensed with his foreign help. Instead, Diarmait called for increased Anglo-Norman support and, in August 1170, Richard de Clare, Second Earl of Pembroke, arrived. The presence of de Clare (1130–76), better known as Strongbow, changed the nature of the campaign. His terms were that he should marry Diarmait's daughter and, in the event of Diarmait's death, become King of Leinster. When these were agreed, he attacked Waterford with two hundred knights and 1,000 foot soldiers. The Irish cavalry were no match for armoured knights, and the Irish army was crushed by the superior discipline and equipment of the Anglo-Normans. The city fell with great brutality and loss of life. Strongbow married Diarmait's daughter, Aoife, in Christ Church Cathedral, and the combined forces of Strongbow and Diarmait pushed on northwards. They outflanked the defences of Dublin and in late September broke into the city. Askulf (also Ascall or Asgall), the last Norse-Gael King of Dublin, fled either to Mann or to the Hebrides. The Irish *Annals of the Four Masters* says that the inhabitants of the city were slaughtered, and their cattle and belongings seized. The Anglo-Norman *Expugnatio Hibernica* claims that a massacre and looting were avoided. What is certain is that, in May 1171, Diarmait died and, in accordance with their agreement, Strongbow became King of Leinster. Predictably, Tigernán Ua Ruairc, Ruaidrí Ua Conchobair, and Askulf refused to accept an Anglo-Norman king and mounted repeated and furious attacks on Dublin, all of which were repelled by Strongbow's forces.

At this point, Henry II, although still preoccupied with Louis VII, and mired in the furore following the death of Thomas Beckett, woke up to the fact that one of his most powerful – and frequently most troublesome – subjects had become ruler of a large polity beyond the feudal reach of the English Crown and was calling himself a king. If Henry was going to exert royal authority in Ireland, he needed to change his policy in Wales. And he did. He made peace with Rhys ap Gruffudd, appointing him justiciar in South Wales, thereby securing the English supply line to Pembroke (see Chapter 40). It is an indication of his determination and the resources at his command that in October 1171, just five months after Diarmait's death, he landed near Waterford, with an army of five hundred knights and 4,000 soldiers. Thomas Bartlett notes that he also brought large numbers of crane, which he liked for his Christmas feast, and sacks of almonds.[340]

Henry's invasion of Ireland was a matter of political realism, although, if challenged, he could claim that he had papal approval, albeit from a decade earlier. Adrian IV, the only Englishman ever to become Pope, was elected in 1154. The Archbishop of Canterbury's secretary at this time, the philosopher and diplomat, John of Salisbury, was a long-standing friend. He made skilful use of the *Life of Malachy*, written about 1150 by the mystic and traditionalist St Bernard of Clairvaux (*c*.1090–1153), which portrayed life in Ireland as barbaric and lacking any sense of sexual morality. St Bernard's aim was to make Malachy shine with saintly brilliance against the wayward and iniquitous background of his native land, but John of Salisbury used his words to persuade Pope Adrian that Ireland was a sink of chaos and depravity that required reform and rehabilitation. Adrian issued a papal bull – or possibly a papal letter – entitled *Laudabiliter*. No copy survives, but it evidently gave Henry II the papal backing he felt he needed in order to invade and govern Ireland. The only proviso was that he should enforce Gregorian Reform on the Irish Church.

Faced with Henry's impressively large army, the Anglo-Norman barons in Ireland took no chances. They did homage to the king, and he divided the territories they had conquered between them. He kept Dublin, Waterford, and Wexford for himself as royal territory. He confirmed Strongbow as Lord – not King – of Leinster, but balanced Strongbow's power by making Hugh de Lacy, his friend and ally, Lord of Meath. Over the next few years, De Lacy dropped in and out of royal favour at least twice, but nonetheless acted as justiciar, with powers equivalent to those given to Rhys ap Gruffudd in South Wales. At least fifteen Irish kings, together with archbishops and bishops also paid homage to Henry, apparently believing that he would protect them from the brutality of the Anglo-Norman barons. However, three of the most powerful kings – of Meath, Connacht, and Ulster – stood apart. Henry marked them down as targets for a campaign in the summer of 1172.

Had that campaign taken place and the three kingdoms been brought to acknowledge Henry's authority, it is at least arguable that the history of Ireland might have been different. As it was, he returned to France and the Anglo-Norman barons were quickly sucked into the seemingly endless Irish round of violence and instability. In 1174, while Henry was struggling to put down a rebellion by his sons, the Irish – by now disabused of the idea that he might protect them – took the opportunity to stage a massive uprising, centred on Meath where Hugh de Lacy was trying to establish himself, and led by Ruaidrí Ua Conchobair of Connacht. This led to the Treaty of Windsor the following year by which Henry recognised Ruaidrí as High King with authority over all those areas not held by Henry and his barons. Given the aggression of the barons and the resentment of the Irish, the agreement was never going to work and within less than two years it had broken down. Robert FitzStephen and Miles de Cogan were then granted the fiefdom of Cork, while Philip de Braose received that of Limerick, thus bringing to an end the last vestige of Scandinavian rule in Ireland. At the same time, Henry awarded John de Courcy, a loyal but, up to that point, not particularly distinguished knight, whose family held estates in Somerset, the right to hold Ulster as a fief – with the proviso that he had to conquer it first. He did. In January 1177, he marched north with just twenty-two knights and three hundred men and took Downpatrick by surprise. After that it took just two battles, hard fought though they were, to bring down the ancient kingdom of Ulaid. Within six months, De Courcy was the effective ruler of Ulster. He built a massive stone castle at Carrickfergus, which became his capital and rapidly developed into a trading centre and one of the first urban settlements of any size in the region.

In 1185, Henry II created his son, Prince John, Lord of Ireland. It was John who ordered the construction of Dublin Castle, the great stone fortress that was to be the symbol of English colonial rule until the 1920s. He also recruited and granted lands to families such as the Brughs, the Verduns, and the Butlers who were to play an important part in colonial administration over the centuries. Yet John was not popular in Ireland. He mocked the native Irish – Gerald de Barry says that he allowed members of his entourage to pull their shaggy beards – and offended the Anglo-Normans. He returned to England in 1187, but retained the title Lord of Ireland, so that when he became King in 1199, Ireland became a part of the Angevin lands, ruled directly by the King of England.

The Anglo-Norman invasion pitted two fundamentally different political, social, and economic systems against each other. Irish political and social structures had evolved only slowly, partly due to their isolation from external influences – other than the Church and the Vikings – and there was much that would have been recognisable to an observer from a thousand years earlier. By contrast, in their political and social structures, in the complex net of their feudal duties and obligations, in the organisation of their taxation and legal systems, the Anglo-Normans were modern, which is to say medieval. They could deploy medieval technologies – stone-built castles, mounted knights, hauberks for protection, stirrups for greater manoeuvrability on horseback – so they won. What went wrong was that Henry II, for all his medieval modernity, could not manage the addition of Ireland to his already vast domains. He went to Ireland in 1171 to forestall a potential challenge from Strongbow or any of the other barons who had been successful in Ireland. He achieved that objective without difficulty, but as far as Ireland itself was concerned, he did not finish the job. And in this he was setting a pattern that would be repeated. By 1177, most of Ireland was ruled by the King and his Anglo-Norman barons – although there were still Irish-ruled enclaves. The biggest of these comprised most of what is now Donegal, Londonderry, Tyrone and Fermanagh, but there were others in western Galway, in Clare, in Cork and Kerry, in parts of Offaly and Laois, and parts of Kildare and Carlow. This meant that Ireland was divided into three: those areas belonging to the Crown but ruled by a governor or viceroy; those areas held by the great nobles as fiefs from the Crown; and the remaining, somewhat fragmented, native kingdoms.

In the thirteenth century, the Anglo-Norman lords introduced a form of feudalism into Ireland: not feudalism as we usually understand it in

England and elsewhere, but a version adapted to a society where feuding and warfare were largely endemic and specific arrangements were required to suit particular localities – and where, if you were a baron or a native Irish ruler, a private army was essential for survival. Attempts were made to divide the land into shires on the Anglo-Saxon/English model. *Magna Carta* was extended to Ireland in the Great Charter of 1217. The Magnum Concilium, set up to advise the King on Irish matters, evolved into an Irish Parliament which, from 1297 onwards, had elected members – although the franchise was extremely limited. Yet none of this was enough to make a cohesive or a peaceful whole. As early as 1261, Anglo-Norman power in Ireland was already weakening, and over the next two centuries, the Irish won back many of the kingdoms and much of the land they had lost in the period after the invasion. By the fourteenth century, the Anglo-Normans were well on their journey to becoming English. In social terms they remained separate from the native Irish, concentrated in the port settlements that had once been Viking or in the new market towns that had sprung up around the great stone castles which, in Ireland as elsewhere, were characteristic features of Norman conquest and control. Consequently, when the Black Death – which had a greater impact on urban as opposed to rural populations – spread to Ireland in 1348, the Anglo-Norman/English population suffered disproportionately, and their position was correspondingly weakened. By 1450, the King of England's authority was limited to an area known as the Pale: an enclave based on Dublin, stretching from Dalkey to Dundalk on the coast and inland as far as Trim. It was from the Pale that Henry VIII launched a second, and genuinely English, invasion in 1536.

In 1542, Henry VIII declared himself King of Ireland. The title was not immediately recognised by the Pope – an important factor given the numerical dominance of Roman Catholics – but after the reign of Mary Tudor (r.1553–58), it became accepted as one of the many titles attached to the English Crown, so that in 1603 when the Union of Crowns made James VI of Scotland James I of England, it also made him James I of Ireland. In 1707, when the English and Scottish Parliaments passed their respective Acts of Union, the Irish Parliament formally congratulated Queen Anne, adding the hope that 'May God put it in your royal heart to add greater strength and lustre to your Crown, by a still more comprehensive Union.'[341] The heavy hint was not taken, and it was only in 1801 that

Ireland formally became part of the United Kingdom of Great Britain and Ireland.

From the time of Henry II until the Partition of Ireland and the establishment of the Irish Free State in the aftermath of the First World War, Irish society was deeply divided along lines which shifted only a little. Real power lay with the English Crown and the Westminster Government. The Anglo-Normans became the Anglo-Irish, landowners and professional men, who benefitted from the status quo. The native Irish remained the native Irish, poor, and too often hungry and dispossessed. But from the sixteenth century onwards, those divisions were overlaid and exacerbated by religious schism, by the sectarian brutalities of Cromwell and William III, and by the fact that until 1829 Catholics were not allowed to sit in Parliament or accept public positions, despite the fact that they constituted the overwhelming majority of the population. Ireland was ruled by Protestants: by a small, close-knit ruling class known as the Protestant Ascendancy, consisting of landowners, members of the financial, legal, and medical professions, wealthy traders, and the Anglican clergy. It was these men who initiated the measures designed to bring England and Ireland closer together: measures which may have been written into law, but which did not have the support of the majority of the population, and thus served to maintain the divisions in society.

Partition and the separation of the six Protestant counties of Northern Ireland from the rest of Ireland in 1921 only compounded the politico-religious divide. With England, Scotland, and Wales, we have been able to identify the emergence of elements or institutions that point to the realisation of the nation we recognise today. Borders were defined – even if disputed later; governmental structures were established; assumptions of nationhood or statehood were written into law. With Ireland, it is different. Sadly, it is easier to identify the factors – religious schism, bigotry, plantation, exploitation, and much else – that gave rise to later conflicts rather than elements that shaped a nation. For all that the Scottish National Party and Plaid Cymru wish to redraw the political map of Great Britain; for all that there are significant cultural divisions both between and within England, Scotland, and Wales; all one can say is that Ireland remains divided on a deeper and more fundamental level.

Closing the Dig

I

As far back as archaeology can take us, the British Archipelago has been inextricably bound to Continental Europe. It has followed the same sequence and the same pattern of development; and perhaps the only generalisation one can safely make across the 850,000 years covered by this study is that the overwhelming majority of the innovations, changes, and influences that reached the British Isles during that time came from the Continent. Of course, once they arrived, they evolved to suit local conditions and took on a 'British' identity. And it is equally true that the British Isles produced its own innovations. The Ness of Brodgar 'despite its seemingly remote location ... was at the centre of Neolithic Europe.'[342] Stone circles appear to have originated in the Archipelago. So, quite possibly, did druidism. Nonetheless, the relationship with the Continent has frequently been a determining factor in the evolution of the Archipelago.

Historians inevitably see incidents or phases in history in the context of their broader 'significance'. Whether we are talking about the arrival of the Beaker People or the construction of the first Westminster Abbey, the events described in this study are components of a greater narrative. Whatever their individual importance, whatever their long-term impact, these events are part of the maelstrom of peoples and cultures that eventually coalesced into what we would today call European civilisation and European culture. It is equally inevitable that historians should seek to explain the emergence and spread of far-reaching changes in terms of collective movements, visualising them as arrows sweeping from east to west or south to north across a map of the Continent. It is a natural and useful simplification, but we should remember that such movements represent real people: tribes and individuals seeking to explore, to trade, to settle, or simply to satisfy their curiosity about what lay further up the river.

Throughout our 850,000 years, the salient characteristic of man has been his mobility. The Happisburgh group were walking along the bank of a river. Neolithic and Bronze Age man braved the Atlantic seaboard in hide-covered boats. The Vikings conquered the northern oceans in their *snekkia* and *skeid*. The Romans could transfer legions from Britain to the

Balkans without difficulty. They could even transport oysters to Rome. The Church would happily send missionaries or bishops half way across Europe. Pilgrimages to Rome became if not commonplace, at least unremarkable. People moved. People travelled. Movement might lead to settlement, to marriage, to trade, or to war; but whatever the motivation, constant movement brought individuals and groups into contact with each other. It led to exchanges – whether political, cultural, economic, or violent – and those exchanges are the bedrock of cultural and societal change and of the historical narrative.

II

A central aim of this study has been to give greater weight and space to Scotland, Wales, Ireland, and the Kingdom of the Isles. The tradition of historical writing about the British Isles over the past several centuries has been firmly Anglocentric. The same is true of history syllabuses in schools and universities. The social and political evolution of the other regions or nations of the British Isles has not been ignored so much as distorted: considered and examined only in so far as it impacts on England and English affairs. This is not wholly surprising. By the high medieval period where this study ends, England had become the richest and most powerful polity in the British Isles, a position it has retained ever since. It went on to be the dominant force in the British Empire, a role which, although the days of Empire are past, continues to hover in the background of many social and political attitudes. Consciousness of England's dominance and the ideology that sprang out of it naturally influenced the way generations of historians approached the history of the British Isles, and, as we have noted more than once, it is difficult to stand aside from the orthodoxies of one's own age.

The result has been to confuse not just the role played by England and that played by the other regions and nations of the British Isles, but also their respective identities. This is illustrated by fact that, as Norman Davies has pointed out on more than one occasion, we do not quite know what to call ourselves.[343] Nor do other people. From 1800 until 1922, the British Isles were coterminous with the United Kingdom of Great Britain and Ireland. Since 1922, they have been divided between the Republic of

Ireland and the United Kingdom of Great Britain and Northern Ireland. The full United Kingdom is such a mouthful that it is frequently shortened to 'Britain' and used in connection with the adjective 'British'. This only makes things worse because of the potential confusion between Britain and Great Britain, the island which is home to England, Scotland, and Wales, but does not include Ireland. During the Peninsula Wars, the Duke of Wellington would talk of British soldiers and the English Army. A hundred years later, Kaiser Wilhelm would talk of England when he meant the United Kingdom or the British Empire. Hitler made speeches threatening Great Britain, not the United Kingdom. When we compete in the Olympics, we do so as 'Team GB', which in theory means there are no athletes from Northern Ireland participating.

This may seem a minor point, but it illustrates a deeper problem, and I should emphasise here that my argument here is historical, not political.

In the introductory chapter to this volume, we noted how the serious study of prehistory coincided with the development of archaeology, and that both occurred at a time when the British Empire was expanding rapidly, and theoretical explanations were being sought for its success. Enough was known of the Archipelago's past to render any idea of racial purity untenable, so the concept of the British as an Imperial race of super-mongrels, beneficiaries of the positive characteristics of wave after wave of Continental invaders, was born (see Groundwork). The rulers of the Empire could thus claim an exceptionalism with a basis in a form of social Darwinism.

But to whom did this apply? Was it British or English exceptionalism? Invasion theory was broad enough to be applied in ways that reflected changes in fashion and cultural orientation. During the nineteenth century, it became increasingly identified with English exceptionalism. This was due in large measure to the rediscovery – or creation – of a sense of Celtic identity, which soon sparked nationalist feeling among the nations of the Celtic fringe, and thus set itself in opposition to Englishness. In Ireland, the new Celtic identity gave the long tradition of resistance to English rule an ideological and racial basis. Scotland, often known during the seventeenth and eighteenth centuries as 'North Britain', recovered its name and took a new interest in its cultural heritage. By the mid-nineteenth century, there were demands in Wales for bilingual education, and by the end of the century, even Cornwall had a nationalist movement.

However, in one of the great ironies of history, the different strands of Celtic identity were held together by the fact that their common language was English.

Yet at the same time as the Celtic revival was strengthening the Celtic nations' sense of identity, the marriage of Queen Victoria and Prince Albert led to a shift in English cultural awareness, emphasising the Germanic component of English identity. This situation produced some odd contradictions – such as the appropriation of Celtic Arthur as an English hero; or the perplexed response to the uncivilised but British Boudicca (identified with Queen Victoria, whose heredity was German) in her struggle against the civilised but foreign Romans. It also saw certain characters reassessed and reputations inflated in the service of Englishness: Alfred the Great and Harold Godwineson were among the beneficiaries. Both the Celtic Revival and the emphasis placed on the Germanic roots of the English increased the sense that there was a cultural and racial difference between the English and the other inhabitants of the British Isles. That perception contrasted charming-but-primitive Celtic culture with the flattering self-image of England's political and economic dominance, which strengthened the Anglocentric approach not just to the interpretation of history, but also to many other facets of British life and society.

Scotland, Wales, Ireland and what was once the Kingdom of the Isles all have fascinating histories in their own right – histories which are rarely taught in detail in schools in the countries concerned and not at all in England. In Ireland, possibly because the divisions in society have historical roots which are still visible and still celebrated as badges of communal identity, there is often a degree of knowledge, albeit frequently partisan, of the island's past. In Scotland and Wales, it is alarming how few people can give a coherent account of their nation's history. All four regions played and – with the exception of the Kingdom of the Isles – continue to play an essential part in shaping all aspects of life in the British Isles from the arts to economic policy and from fashion to scientific research. Their contribution comes not just through their interaction with England and the Westminster-based government of the United Kingdom, but also through their interactions with each other and with countries beyond the British Isles. The relations that have developed between Ireland and North America, Scotland and Scandinavia, or Wales and Brittany, acknowledge their distinctiveness and also add to the sum of the cultural and social wealth of the British Isles. By giving the Celtic regions more space, it has been possible to give a fuller picture of their contribution to the history of the British Isles and a more balanced account of that history as a whole. If this has resulted in several chapters giving accounts of places and characters that will be unfamiliar to many – if not most – readers, that is a reflection of the underlying situation.

England's dominance within the British Isles has lasted over a thousand years and may seem permanent, but we saw that the Neolithic era lasted for millennia before it was overtaken by new people with a new culture and new technologies. We saw Roman Britain as prosperous and secure before it was swept aside by tribes from the north. Nothing is permanent. Change is accelerating. On-line commerce is eroding the role of the local shop and the High Street. Communication technologies have made 'working from home' a realistic option. As a consequence, cities and towns are losing the centrality they have traditionally enjoyed in economic life. The ethnic composition of Britain is changing. Islamic, South Asian, and West Indian communities are growing as a percentage of the population and exerting increasing influence. For good or ill, the United Kingdom has left the European Union and its relationship with Europe has changed. Its political future is being questioned, some might say threatened, by growing demands for Scottish independence, by post-Brexit complications in Northern Ireland, and above all by demographic change.

This is not prophecy. How these issues develop and evolve remains to be seen and will be for historians of the future to assess. But any or all of them have the potential to challenge assumptions of permanence and have a significant impact on the cultural and political future of the British Isles. In such a context, there seems every prospect of the Celtic nations exerting more political and cultural influence in the future, and this study has attempted to reflect their present importance in its treatment of their past. More significant, however, is the possibility that the climate of change – political, social, economic, demographic, even climatic – will finally force the United Kingdom and its constituent nations to throw off the legacy of Empire and redefine their role in the world.

Notes

1. Sir John Lubbock, *Pre-Historic Times, As Illustrated by Ancient Remains, and the Manners and Customs of Modern Savages*, Williams & Norgate, London, 1865, pp.2–3.
2. Oxford University Museum of Natural History. http://www.oum.ox.ac.uk/learning/pdfs/buckland.pdf. Consulted 1 January 2019.
3. J.M.D. Meiklejohn, *A New History of England, Part I: B.C. 55–A.D. 1509*, Alfred M. Holden, 1899, p.3.
4. See Norman Davies, *The Isles,* Macmillan, 1999, pp.8–11; and Alistair Moffat, *The Borders,* Birlinn, 2007, pp.16–24.

1 A Sense of Perspective

5. There is no scientific consensus as to whether Neanderthal man was a separate species or a subspecies of humankind. They are referred to here as a species because current scientific opinion appears to be moving in that direction.
6. Dan Jones, 'Neanderthals wore make-up and liked to chat', New Scientist, 27 March 2008 https://www.newscientist.com/article/dn13536-neanderthals-wore-make-up-and-liked-to-chat/. Consulted 30 March 2018.
7. Ronald Hutton, *Pagan Britain,* Yale, 2013, p.8.
8. John Pickrell, 'Unprecedented Ice Age Cave Art Discovered in U.K.', National Geographic News, 18 August 2004, https://news.nationalgeographic.com/news/2004/08/0818_040818_ice_age_caveart.htm Consulted 30 March 2018.
9. These tribes are known to archaeologists as representatives of Ahrensburg culture, named after the village near Hamburg where their remains were first excavated.

2 Settling the Archipelago

10. http://www.maritimearchaeologytrust.org/bouldnor. Consulted 2 April 2018.
    Quirin Schiermeier, 'Ancient DNA reveals how wheat came to prehistoric Britain', *Nature*, 26 February 2015. https://www.nature.com/news/ancient-dna-reveals-how-wheat-came-to-prehistoric-britain-1.17010. Consulted 7 April 2018.

11　The Wikipedia page https://en.wikipedia.org/wiki/Bouldnor_Cliff perpetrates an anachronistic howler by discussing the wheat grains under a subheading 'International Trade'. Consulted 9 April 2018.
12　'Mesolithic Timelords: A monumental hunter-gatherer 'calendar' at Warren Field, Scotland', *Current Archaeology*, 283, 5 September 2013. https://www.archaeology.co.uk/issues/ca-283-out-now.htm. Consulted 12 November 2018.
13　Matriarchal religion was identified as a second stage in the cultural evolution of early societies by the Swiss antiquarian and anthropologist, Johann Jakob Bachofen (1815–87).
14　Douglas Adams, *The Hitchhiker's Guide to the Galaxy*, 'Fit the Second', BBC Radio 4, 15 March 1978.

3　Paths across the Sea

15　Selina Brace, Yoan Diekmann, Thomas J. Booth *et al.*, 'Ancient genomes indicate population replacement in Early Neolithic Britain', *Nature, Ecology & Evolution*, 3, 2019, pp.765–77.
16　Francis Pryor, *Britain B.C.*, Harper Collins, 2003, p.124.
17　Barry Cunliffe, *Britain Begins*, OUP, 2012, p.65.
18　Peter Fletcher, 'Discussions of the Possible Origin of Europe's First Boats – 11,500 BP', http://www-labs.iro.umontreal.ca/~vaucher/History/Prehistoric_Craft/1031-3451-1-PB.pdf. Consulted 5 May 2018.
19　Caesar, *Commentaries on the Civil War*, Book I, Chapter 54.
20　Barry Cunliffe, *Britain Begins*, p.75.
21　http://rspb.royalsocietypublishing.org/content/283/1828/20160095. David W. G. Stanton, Jacqueline A. Mulville, Michael W. Bruford, 'Colonization of the Scottish islands via long-distance Neolithic transport of red deer (Cervus elaphus)' *Proceedings of the Royal Society*, Series B, 6, April 2016, Consulted 12 May 2018.

4　Marks upon the Land

22　McClatchie, M., Bogaard, A., Colledge, S., Whitehouse, N. J., Schulting, r.J., Barratt, P., & McLaughlin, T. R., 'Neolithic farming in north-western Europe: archaeobotanical evidence from Ireland', *Journal of Archaeological Science*, 51, 2014, pp.206–15.
23　Barry Cunliffe, *Britain Begins*, pp.147–48.
24　Timothy A. Kohler *et al.*, 'Greater post-Neolithic wealth disparities in

Eurasia than in North America and Mesoamerica', *Nature,* Vol.551, 30, November 2017, pp.619–23.
25 Barry Cunliffe, *Britain Begins,* p.145.
26 Jessica Smyth, 'The house and group identity in the Irish Neolithic', *Proceedings of the Royal Irish Academy: Archaeology, Culture, History, Literature,* Vol. 111C, 2011, pp.1–31.
27 Graham Taylor, http://pottedhistory.blogspot.com/2015/05/neolithic-carinated-bowl-complex.html; http://www.pottedhistory.co.uk/Prehistoric_Pottery.html. Consulted 30 November 2018.
28 Orkney Pottery, http://orkneypottery.co.uk/prehistoric-pottery/neolithic-pottery-firings/. Consulted 3 December 2018.
29 https://finds.org.uk/database/artefacts/record/id/512552. Consulted 1 December 2018.
30 Neil Oliver, *A History of Scotland,* Weidenfield & Nicolson, 2009, p.14.
31 Wes Forsythe and Niall Gregory, 'A Neolithic Logboat from Greyabbey Bay', *Ulster Journal of Archaeology.* Third Series, Vol.66, 2007, pp.6–13.
32 Finbar McCormick, 'The Horse in Early Ireland', *Anthropozoologica* 42, 1, pp.85–104 (p.86).
33 *Civilisations Disparues.* http://www.civilisationsdisparues.com/pages/articles/les-plus-vieilles-roues-du-monde.html. Consulted 14 August 2018.
34 Science Daily. https://www.sciencedaily.com/releases/2009/08/090812104141.htm. Consulted 8 August 2018.
35 Archaeology News Network. https://archaeologynewsnetwork.blogspot.com/2018/06/neolithic-henge-site-unearthed-in.html#K5h9ZvAt0tR7PkBe.97. Consulted 8 August 2018.
36 Susan Foster McCarter, *Neolithic,* Routledge, 2007, pp.132–35.

5 Structures upon the Ground

37 Niels H. Andersen, 'Causewayed Enclosures in Northern and Western Europa', https://www.academia.edu/20105549/Causewayed_enclosures_in_Northern_and_Western_Europa. Consulted 24 August 2018.
38 Michael Macdonagh, 'Valley bottom and hilltop: 6,000 years of settlement along the route of the N4 Sligo Inner Relief Road'. http://www.tii.ie/technical-services/archaeology/publications/archaeol-

ogymonographseries/Ch-2-MacDonagh.pdf. Consulted 23 August 2018.
39 Barry Cunliffe, *Britain Begins*, p.165.
40 Isobel Smith, *Windmill Hill and Avebury. Excavations by Alexander Keiller 1925–1939*. OUP, 1965, pp.19–20.
41 Francis Pryor, *Britain B.C.*, pp.170–72.
42 Alice Roberts, *The Celts: Search for a Civilization*, Heron Books, 2016, p.188.

6   Ritual in the Landscape

43 There are also a few stone circles in the Basque country of northern Spain, but these appear to date from the late Bronze Age.
44 Parker Pearson, M., Pollard, J., Richards, C. and Welham, K., 'The origins of Stonehenge: on the track of the bluestones', *Archaeology International*, 20, 2017, pp.52–57. http://doi.org/10.5334/ai.353 Consulted 20.01.2019.
45 Parker Pearson *et al.*, 'The original Stonehenge? A dismantled stone circle in the Preseli Hills of west Wales', *Antiquity*, Vol. 95, No. 379. https://www.cambridge.org/core/journals/antiquity/article/original-stonehenge-a-dismantled-stone-circle-in-the-preseli-hills-of-west-wales/B7DAA4A7792B4DAB57DDE0E3136FBC33. Consulted 22.01.2022.
46 Julian Richards, *Stonehenge: The Story So Far*, Historic England, 2017, p.229.
47 Julian Richards, *Stonehenge: The Story So Far*, p.213.
48 Alexander Thom, 'The megalithic unit of length', *Journal of the Royal Statistical Society*, Series A 125, 1962, pp.243–51.
49 Barry Cunliffe, *Britain Begins*, p.191.
50 Bend in the Boyne is the usual English name, but it is not a translation of Brú na Bóinne, which means Palace on the Boyne.
51 Gerald S. Hawkins and John B. White, *Stonehenge Decoded*, Doubleday, 1965
52 https://www.newscientist.com/article/2209691-hear-what-music-would-have-sounded-like-at-stonehenge-4000-years-ago/ Consulted 12 July 2019.

7   Beakers and Bronze

53 Maev Kennedy, 'Arrival of Beaker folk changed Britain for ever, ancient DNA shows', *The Guardian*, 22 February 2018.
54 This is also called Egyptian faience to distinguish it from English tin-glazed pottery of the same name.
55 Iñigo Olalde *et al.*, 'The Beaker Phenomenon and the Genomic Transformation of Northwest Europe', https://www.biorxiv.org/content/biorxiv/

early/2017/05/09/135962.full.pdf. Consulted 27 February 2019.
56 Richard Tipping *et al.*, 'Moments of crisis: climate change in Scottish prehistory', Proceedings of the Society of Antiquaries of Scotland, Vol. 142, 2012, pp.9–25.

8 Walls and Weapons

57 Barry Cunliffe, *Britain Begins*, p.260.
58 https://www.irishtimes.com/news/call-for-1200-bc-hill-fort-to-be-secured-as-national-monument-1.957169. Consulted 22 March 2019.
59 https://www.irishtimes.com/news/call-for-1200-bc-hill-fort-to-be-secured-as-national-monument-1.957169. Consulted 22 March 2019.
60 https://finds.org.uk/guides/bronzeage/objects/swords. Consulted 23 March 2019
61 Nipperwiese shields are named after the village in Western Pomerania where the first example was found. Today it is in Poland and called Ognica.

9 Hoards and Water

62 Barry Cunliffe, *Britain Begins*, pp.271–73.
63 Andrea Pinter, 'Rivers Keep Many Secrets: Bronze Age Depositions of Human Remains in River and Settlement Contexts,' M.A. thesis, University of Amsterdam / VU University, 2016, p.27.
64 Kristina Krawiec, *The Mesolithic to Bronze Age Landscape Development of the Trent-Derwent Confluence Zone at Shardlow Quarry*, Ph.D. thesis, University of Birmingham, 2012, p.70.

10 Iron and Settlement

65 Harald the Smith, https://www.haraldthesmith.com/iron-smelting-part-iv-furnace-design/. Consulted 1 June 2019.
66 Barry Cunliffe, *Britain Begins*, p.304.
67 https://hillforts.arch.ox.ac.uk/. 13 July 2019.
68 Barry Cunliffe, *Danebury Hillfort*, The History Press, 2011, pp.91–93.

11 Sounds and Speech

69 Avienus, *Ora Maritima*, lines 107–13.
70 George Broderick, 'The Names for Britain and Ireland Revisited', *Sonderdruck aus Beitrage zur Namenforschung*, Vol.44, Notebook 2, Universität Mannheim, 2009, pp.151–72.

71 Herodotus, *Histories,* Book 3, Chapter 115.
72 Diodorus Siculus, *Bibliotheca Historica,* Book V, Chapters 21–22.
73 Pliny, *Natural History,* Book IV, Chapter 37. The distinction between Ictis and Mictis looks like a scribal error, but six day's sail inwards (that is, presumably, towards the Continent) puts Diodorus' 'nearby island' a long way from the Cornish shore.
74 George Broderick, 'The Names for Britain and Ireland Revisited', p.160.
75 Proto-Indo-European Roots. https://tied.verbix.com/project/phonetics/word11.html. Consulted 20 October 2019.
76 George Broderick, 'The Names for Britain and Ireland Revisited', p.161.
77 George Broderick, 'The Names for Britain and Ireland Revisited', p.163.
78 Norman Davies, *The Isles,* p.57.

12 A Question of Identity

72 Cassius Dio, *Historia Roma,* Book LXXVII, Chapter 12.
80 Procopius, *De Belli,* Book VII, Chapter 20.
81 Julius Caesar, *Commentaries on the Gallic Wars,* Book V, Chapters 12 & 14
82 Tacitus, *Agricola,* Chapter 11.
83 Timothy P. Bridgman, 'Keltoi, Galatai, Galli: Were They All One People?', *Proceedings of the Harvard Celtic Colloquium,* Vol. 24/25, Harvard University, 2005, pp. 155–62.
84 Barry Cunliffe, *The Extraordinary Voyage of Pytheas the Greek,* Penguin Books, 2002, p.98.
85 'The Genetic Landscape of Scotland and the Isles', *Proceedings of the National Academy of Sciences,* Vol.116, pp.19604-19070, 17 September 2019. It is noteworthy that this paper makes it clear that previous studies have undersampled Scotland compared with the rest of the British Isles. Consulted 20 October 2019
86 'Scottish people's DNA study could 'rewrite nation's history'.' https://www.theguardian.com/uk/2012/aug/15/scotland-dna-study-project. Consulted 20 October 2019.
87 'Insular Celtic population structure and genomic footprints of migration'. https://journals.plos.org/plosgenetics/article?id=10.1371/journal.pgen.1007152. Consulted 20 October 2019.
88 Leslie, S., Winney, B., Hellenthal, G. *et al.,* 'The fine-scale genetic structure of the British population', *Nature,* 519, 2015, pp.309–14.

13 Culture and Language

89 Full title: *Archaeologia Britannica: an Account of the Languages, Histories and Customs of Great Britain, from Travels through Wales, Cornwall, Bas-Bretagne, Ireland and Scotland.*
90 Caoimhín De Barran, 'Opinion: Our Celtic identity might not be what we think it is', *thejournal.ie*. https://www.thejournal.ie/readme/celts-ireland-4199945-Aug2018/. Consulted 25 October 2019.
91 Herodotus, *Histories*, Book IV.
92 Barry Cunliffe, *Britain Begins*, p.316.
93 Herodotus, *History*, Book II.
94 Strabo, *Geography*, Book III.
95 Strabo, *Geography*, Book IV.
96 Barry Cunliffe, *Britain Begins*, p.244.
97 Barry Cunliffe, *Britain Begins*, pp.246–48.

14 Belief and Ritual

98 James Morris, 'Animal Ritual Killing: from Remains to Meanings'. https://www.academia.edu/226219/Animal_ritual_killing_from_remains_to_meanings. Consulted 27 December 2019.
99 'World's oldest bog body hints at violent past' https://www.bbc.co.uk/news/science-environment-24053119. Consulted 27 December 2019.
100 Ronald Hutton, *Pagan Britain*, Yale University Press, 2014, pp.205–6.
101 Caesar, *Commentaries on the Gallic Wars*, Book VI, Chapters 13–18.
102 Diodorus Siculus, *Bibliotheca Historica*, Book II, Chapter 47.
103 Not to be confused with Hecateus of Miletus, who lived at least a century earlier.
104 Barry Cunliffe, *The Extraordinary Voyage of Pytheas the Greek*, pp.123–4.
105 Tacitus, *Annals*, Book 14, Chapters 29–30.
106 Strabo, *Geography*, Book 4 Chapter 4.
107 Dio Chrysostom, *Discourse 49*, Chapter 7.
108 Pliny, *Natural History*, Book 16, Chapter 95.
109 Pliny, *Natural History*, Book 29, Chapter 12.
110 Pliny, *Natural History*, Book 24, Chapter 62.
111 Pliny, *Natural History*, Book 24, Chapter 63.
112 Pliny, *Natural History*, Book 30, Chapter 4.
113 Pomponius Mela, *De Situ Orbis*, Book 3, Chapter 2.

114 Suetonius, *Life of Claudius*, Chapter 25.
115 Tacitus, *Annals*, Book 14, Chapter 30.
116 Barry Cunliffe, *Druids: A Very Short Introduction*, OUP, 2010, pp.81–83.
117 William Camden, *Britannia*, 1607, p.35.
118 Henry Rowlands, *Mona Antiqua Restaurata: An Archaeological Discourse on the Antiquities, Natural and Historical, of the Isle of Anglesey, the Antient Seat of the British Druids*, 1723.
119 *The Monthly Register*, 3, January 1793, p.19.

15   Invasion and Influence
120 Appian, *The Civil Wars*, Book 2, Chapter 9.
121 David Woods, 'Caligula's Seashells', *Greece & Rome*, Vol.47, No.1, pp.80–87.
122 Strabo, *Geography*, Book 4, Chapter 5.

16   Invasion and Conquest
123 Flavius Eutropius, *A Brief History of Rome*, Book VII, Chapter 13.
124 Cassius Dio, *Roman History*, Book LXI, Chapter 33.
125 Cassius Dio, *Roman History*, Book LX, Chapter 21.
126 Tacitus, *Annals*, Book XIV, Chapter 33.
127 Cassius Dio, *Roman History*, Book LXI, Chapter 12.
128 Tacitus, *Annals*, Book XIV, Chapter 37.
129 Kenneth Jackson, 'Queen Boudicca?', *Britannia*, 10, 1979, p.255.
130 Gildas, *De Excidio et Conquestu Britanniae*, Part II, Chapter 6.
131 Reverend J.A. Giles, *Six Old English Chronicles, of Which Two Are Now First Translated from the Monkish Latin Originals*, Bell and Daldy, 1848.
132 Diodorus Siculus, *Bibliotheca Historica*, Book V, Chapter 31.
133 Diodorus Siculus, *Bibliotheca Historica*, Book V, Chapter 29.
134 Polybius, *Histories*, Book II, Chapter 28; Diodorus Siculus, Bibliotheca Historica, Book V, Chapter 30; Dionysius of Halicarnassus, *Roman Antiquities*, Book XIV, Chapter 9.
135 Julius Caesar, *Commentaries on the Gallic Wars*, Book IV, Chapter 1.

17   Romans in the North
136 Tacitus, *Agricola*, Chapter 30.
137 Tacitus, *Agricola*, Chapter 33.
138 Tacitus, *Histories*, Book I, Chapter 2.
139 Cassius Dio, *Roman History*, Book LXXII, Chapter 8.

140 Cassius Dio, *Roman History,* Book LXXVI, Chapter 6.
141 Cassius Dio, *Roman History,* Book LXXVII, Chapter 12.
142 Cassius Dio, *Roman History,* Book LXXVI, Chapter 5.
143 Cassius Dio, *Roman History,* Book LXXVII, Chapter 11.
144 Herodian, *History,* Book III, Chapter 3.
145 Cassius Dio, *Roman History,* Book LXXVII, Chapter 13.
146 Cassius Dio, *Roman History,* Book LXXVII, Chapter 13.

18   Romans in the South

147 Strabo, *Geography,* Book IV, Chapter 5.
148 Cassius Dio metathesises the name to Bodunni.
149 Strabo, *Geography,* Book IV, Chapter 5.

19   Over the Wall and across the Sea

150 Tacitus, *Agricola,* Chapter 24.
151 Katharine Simms, *From Kings to Warlords: The Changing Political Structure of Gaelic Ireland in the Later Middle Ages,* Boydell Press, 2000, p.11.
152 Cassius Dio, *Roman History,* Book LXXVII, Chapter 16.
153 Eumenius, *Panegyric VI,* Chapter 6. https://open.uct.ac.za/bitstream/handle/11427/22167/thesis_hum_1979_sang_john_campbell.pdf. Consulted 5 May 2022.
154 Alistair Moffat, *Before Scotland,* Thames and Hudson, 2005, pp.286–87.
155 Stuart McHardy, *A New History of the Picts,* Luath Press, 2010, pp.36–37.
156 Cambridge Core. https://www.cambridge.org/core/journals/antiquity/article/development-of-the-pictish-symbol-system-inscribing-identity-beyond-the-edges-of-empire/4F09B9C943A1C29F226591A20BEC5248/core-reader. Consulted 12 June 2020.

20   God and the Gods

157 Ronald Hutton, *Pagan Britain,* Yale, 2014, p.233.
158 Tertullian, *Adversus Judaeos,* Chapter 7.
159 Origen, *Homilies on Ezekiel IV,* Chapter 1.
160 Bede, *An Ecclesiastical History of the English People,* Book I, Chapter 4.
161 Quoted in James Bentham, *The History and Antiquities of the Conventual & Cathedral Church of Ely,* Vol. 3, Stevenson, 1817, pp.145–46.

162 John Morris, 'The Date of St Alban', *Hertfordshire Archaeology*, 1, 1968, pp.1–7
163 Alastair Moffat, *The Wall*, Birlinn, 2009, p.223.
164 R.G. Collingwood, *The Archaeology of Roman Britain*, Methuen & Co., 1930, p.145.
165 J.M.C. Toynbee, 'Christianity in Roman Britain', *Journal of the British Archaeological Association*, Vol. 16, No.1, 1953, pp.1–24.
166 Ronald Hutton, *Pagan Britain*, Yale, 2014, p.276.
167 Ronald Hutton, *Pagan Britain*, p.281.
168 A.Woodward and P. Leach, The Uley Shrines: Excavation of a Ritual Complex on West Hill, Uley: Gloucestershire, 1977–9, *English Heritage Archaeological Report*, 17, English Heritage, 1993.
169 Ronald Hutton, *Pagan Britain*, p.281.
170 Dorothy Watts, *Religion in Late Roman Britain*, Taylor & Francis, 2002, pp.74–95.
171 Michelle Brown, *How Christianity Came to Britain and Ireland*, Lion Hudson, 2006, pp.43–47.
172 David Calderwood, *The History of the Kirk of Scotland*, Volume 1, Wodrow Society, Edinburgh, 1843. p. 37. An abridged version was published in 1646. The full version did not appear until 1843.
173 John Spotiswoode, *The History of the Church of Scotland: Beginning the Year of our Lord 203, and Continued to the end of the Reign of King James VI of Ever Blessed Memory*, Book 1, 1639, pp.3–4.
174 Bede, *An Ecclesiastical History of the English People*, Book III, Chapter 4
175 *Chronicle of Prosper of Aquitaine*, entry for 431 AD.

21   The Crumbling Façade

176 J.M.D. Meiklejohn, *A New History of England*, Part I: *B.C. 55–A.D.1509*, p.3.
177 Winston Churchill, *A History of the English-Speaking Peoples*, Vol.I: *The Island Race*, Cassell, 1956, p.42.
178 Simon Schama, *A History of Britain*, 1, *At the Edge of the World?*, BBC, 2003, p.42
179 Zosimus, *Historia Nova*, Book VI, Chapter 10.
180 David Woods, 'On the Alleged Letters of Honorius to the Cities of Britain', *Latomus*, Vol.71, 2012, pp.818–26.
181 E.A. Thompson, 'Zosimus 6.10.2 and the Letters of Honorius', *The Classical Quarterly*, Vol.32, No.2, 1982, pp.445–62.

182 Eumenius, *Panegyric VI*, Chapter 7.
183 Ammianus Marcellinus, *Rerum gestarum libri (The Chronicles of Events)*, Book XIV, Chapter 5.
184 Ammianus Marcellinus, *Rerum gestarum libri (The Chronicles of Events)*, Book XX, Chapter 1.
185 Zosimus, *Historia Nova*, Book VI, Chapter 5.

22 Chasing Shadows

186 Bede, *An Ecclesiastical History of the English People*, Preface.
187 Patricia Southern, *Roman Britain*, Amberley, 2013, p.335.
188 Robin Fleming, *Britain after Rome*, Allen Lane, 2010, pp.32–38.
189 Gildas, *De Excidio et Conquestu Britanniae*, Part II, Chapters 22 and 23.
190 Bede, *An Ecclesiastical History of the English People*, Book I, Chapter 15.
191 Gildas, *De Excidio et Conquestu Britanniae*, Part II, Chapter 25.
192 Gildas, *De Excidio et Conquestu Britanniae*, Part II, Chapter 265.
193 Nennius, *Historia Brittonum*, Chapters 31, 48, 66.
194 Nennius, *Historia Brittonum*, Chapter 50.
195 *Annales Cambriae*, entries for years 516 and 537.
196 Alistair Moffat, *Arthur and the Lost Kingdoms*, Weidenfeld & Nicolson, 1999.
197 Nicholas Higham and Martin Ryan, *The Anglo-Saxon World*, Yale, 2015, pp.65–66.

23 Spreading the Word

198 Michael Richter, *Medieval Ireland*, Gill & Macmillan, 2005, p.31.
199 Michael Richter, *Medieval Ireland*, p.35.
200 Sir Kenneth Clark, *Civilisation: A Personal View*, BBC, 1969, Episode 1 'The Skin of our Teeth'.
201 The nineteenth century Glaswegian writer, Aonghas MacCoinnich, suggested that *Scotti* derived from the Gaelic *sgaoth* meaning 'swarm', but his Gaelic derivations have been described as 'fanciful'.
202 Bede, *An Ecclesiastical History of the English People*, Book III, Chapter 4.
203 Norman Davies, *Vanished Kingdoms*, Allen Lane, 2011, pp.51–2.

24 Building Kingdoms

204 Gildas, *De Excidio et Conquestu Britanniae*, Part II, Chapter 265.
205 Bede, *An Ecclesiastical History of the English People*, Book II, Chapter 5. These kings are sometimes described as *Bretwalda*, meaning 'Britain ruler' or

possibly 'broad ruler'. Bede does not use the term. It is applied retrospectively from a late ninth-century text of the *Anglo-Saxon Chronicle*. What is implied is uncertain. There has been speculation that it might denote a position analogous to the Irish high King, but there is no evidence for this.
206 Bede, *An Ecclesiastical History of the English People*, Book II, Chapter 25.

25   Saints and Warriors
207 Bede, *An Ecclesiastical History of the English People*, Book I, Chapter 23.
208 Bede, *An Ecclesiastical History of the English People*, Book II, Chapter 1.
209 Bede, *An Ecclesiastical History of the English People*, Book I, Chapter 27.
210 Donald E. Meek, *The Quest for Celtic Christianity*, Handsel Press, Edinburgh, 2000, p.110.
211 Bede, *An Ecclesiastical History of the English People*, Book IV, Chapter 16.
212 Bede, *An Ecclesiastical History of the English People*, Book IV, Chapter 26.

26   The Land and the Law
213 Susan Oosthuizen, *Tradition and Transformation in Anglo-Saxon England: Archaeology, Common Rights and Landscape*, Bloomsbury Academic, 2013, p.186.
214 John Blair, 'Exploring Anglo-Saxon Settlement', *Current Archaeology*, 5 June 2014. https://www.archaeology.co.uk/articles/features/exploring-anglo-saxon-settlement.htm Consulted 26 November 2020.
215 Bede, *An Ecclesiastical History of the English People*, Book II, Chapter 3
216 John Blair, 'Exploring Anglo-Saxon Settlement'. https://www.archaeology.co.uk/articles/features/exploring-anglo-saxon-settlement.htm Consulted 28 November 2020.
217 Sometimes referred to as sunken-feature buildings.
218 The word *ealdorman* has evolved in two different directions: to describe both the aristocratic earl and the civic alderman.
219 Gildas, *De Excidio et Conquestu Britanniae*, Part II, Chapter 25.
220 Bede, *An Ecclesiastical History of the English People*, Book IV, Chapter 13
221 Ælfric of Eynsham, *Colloquy*.

27   Words and Images
222 Bede, *An Ecclesiastical History of the English People*, Book IV, Chapter 24.
223 David Crystal, *The Stories of English*, Penguin, 2005, p.34.
224 David Crystal, *The Stories of English*, p.34.

225 Thomas Carlyle, *On Heroes and Hero Worship,* James Fraser, 1841, p.189.
226 John Mitchell Kemble, *Saxons in England,* Longman, Green, Brown & Longmans, 1849, Vol.I, p.5.
227 J.M.D. Meiklejohn, *A New History of England, Part I: B.C. 55–A.D.1509,* Alfred M.Holden, 1899, p.18.
228 *Science.* https://www.sciencemag.org/news/2018/11/why-536-was-worst-year-be-alive. Consulted 5 December 2020.
229 Barry Cunliffe, *Britain Begins,* p.424.
230 Robin Fleming, *Britain after Rome,* pp.89–119.

28   The Third Wave

231 Asser, *The Life of King Alfred,* Chapter 14.
232 *Anglo-Saxon Chronicle,* entry for the year 829.
233 *Anglo-Saxon Chronicle,* entry for the year 830.
234 Alex von Tunzelmann, 'The Vikings: not for revisionist historians', *The Guardian,* 21 May 2009.
235 Charter of 792, quoted in Gordon Ward, 'The Vikings Come to Thanet', *Archaeologia Cantiana,* Vol.63, 1950, pp.57–62.
236 *Anglo-Saxon Chronicle,* entry for the year 793.
237 https://dokumen.tips/documents/alcuin-letter-to-bishop-higbald.html. Consulted 9 January 2021.

29   Kingdoms in the North

238 Winston Churchill, *A History of the English-Speaking Peoples,* Vol.I: The Island Race, p.263.
239 Neil Oliver, *A History of Scotland,* Weidenfeld & Nicolson, 2010, p.65.
240 For clarity, it should be noted that 'the Isle of Man' becomes 'Mann' when not qualified.
241 Mark Redknap, 'Viking Age Settlement in Wales: Some Recent Advances', *Transactions of the Honourable Society of Cymmrodorion,* 2005, Vol.12, 2006, pp.5–35.
242 A.W. Moore, 'Foreign Elements in the Manx Language', http://www.isle-of-man.com/manxnotebook/iomnhas/lm3p059.htm. Consulted 1 February 2021.
243 Athena T. Knudson, *Raiders from the North: Irish Enslavement during the Viking Age,* University of Colorado, 2016.
244 Alison Grant, 'Gaelic Place-Names: Viking Influence on the Gaelic Place-

Names of the Hebrides', https://www.thebottleimp.org.uk/2017/06/gaelic-place-names-viking-influence-on-the-gaelic-place-names-of-the-hebrides. Consulted 1 February 2021.
245 Edmund Gilbert et al., 'The genetic landscape of Scotland and the Isles', *Proceedings of the National Academy of Sciences,* No.38, Vol.116, September 2019, pp.19064–70.
246 'Did Vikings Kill the Native Population of Orkney and Shetland?' http://www.orkneyjar.com/history/vikingorkney/warpeace/part4.htm. Consulted 2 February 2021.
247 Peder Gammeltof, 'Shetland and Orkney Island-Names – A Dynamic Group', https://www.abdn.ac.uk/pfrlsu/documents/Gammeltoft,%20Shetland%20and%20Orkney%20Island-Names%20_%20A%20Dynamic%20Group%20.pdf.

30 Kingdoms in the South

248 Paul Holm, 'The Slave Trade of Dublin: Ninth to Twelfth Centuries', *Peritia,* Vol.5, 1986, pp.317–45.
249 *Anglo-Saxon Chronicle,* entry for 851.
250 Justin Pollard, *Alfred the Great,* John Murray, 2006, p.64.
251 *Anglo-Saxon Chronicle,* entry for 865.
252 *Anglo-Saxon Chronicle,* entry for 871.
253 Asser, *Life of King Alfred,* Chapter 50.

31 England

254 King Alfred, Preface to *St Gregory's Pastoral Care.*
255 Edward Augustus Freemen, *The History of the Norman Conquest,* 5 vols, 1867–79.
256 *Anglo-Saxon Chronicle,* entry for 886.
257 The *Anglo-Saxon Chronicle* entry for 883 which suggests that Ælfred's younger son, Æthelstan, and an ealdorman named Sigehelm, had besieged London in that year is probably misplaced and should be part of the 886 entry.
258 Justin Pollard, *Alfred the Great,* John Murray, 2006, p.224.
259 Some sources suggest 893.
260 Ælfred, Preface to *Pastoral Care.*
261 Asser, *Life of King Alfred,* Chapter 75.
262 Ælfred, *Soliloquies,* Book III.

263 G.Craig, 'Alfred the Great: a diagnosis', *Journal of the Royal Society of Medicine*, Vol.84, No.5, pp.303–5.
264 *Anglo-Saxon Chronicle*, entry for 924.
265 Sarah Foot, *Æthelstan: The First King of England*, Yale University Press, 2011, pp.115–17.
266 Sarah Foot, *Æthelstan: The First King of England*, p.233.

32 War and Peace and War

267 *Anglo-Saxon Chronicle*, entry for 934.
268 *Chronicle of John of Worcester*, entry for 934.
269 Sarah Foot, *Æthelstan: The First King of England*, p.3.
270 Sarah Foot, *Æthelstan: The First King of England*, p.213.
271 'The Battle of Brunanburh', lines 58–59.
272 Æthelweard, *Chronicon*, entry for 939. Æthelweard's chronology is at odds with accepted contemporary dates.
273 Michael Livingston ed., *The Battle of Brunanburh: A Casebook*, University of Exeter Press, 2011, pp.24–25.
274 *Anglo-Saxon Chronicle*, entry for 946.
275 *Sancti Dunstani Vita*, ed. William Stubbs, Memorials of St Dunstan, Longman & Co., 1874, pp.32–33.
276 Sir Frank Stenton, *Anglo-Saxon England*, OUP, 1971, p.371.
277 The name *Æthelred* translates as 'noble plan' or 'noble advice', while the adjective *unraed* – a pun on the name – means 'badly planned' or 'badly advised'.
278 J.M.D. Meiklejohn, *A New History of England*, Part I: *B.C. 55–A.D. 1509*. p.35.
279 Winston Churchill, *A History of the English-Speaking Peoples*, Vol.I: *The Island Race*, Cassell, 1956, p.107.
280 Sir Frank Stenton, *Anglo-Saxon England*, pp.375–76.
281 Nicholas Higham and Martin Ryan, *The Anglo-Saxon World*, p.348.

33 Beyond England I

282 *Chronicle of John of Worcester*, entry for 973.
283 *Chronicle of John of Worcester*, entry for 973.
284 Sitric Cáech, Gofraid ua Ímair, Amlaíb mac Gofraid, and Amlaíb Cuarán.

34 Dynasties and Directions

285 Winston Churchill, 'The Saxon Dusk', *A History of the English-Speaking*

Peoples, Vol.I: *The Island Race*, pp.104–19.
286 Wulfnoth may have given his name to the church of St Mary Woolnoth in London.
287 *Anglo-Saxon Chronicle,* entry for 1012.
288 *Anglo-Saxon Chronicle,* entry for 1014.
289 Winston Churchill, *A History of the English-Speaking Peoples,* Vol.I: *The Island Race,* p.110.
290 *Encomium Emmae Reginae,* ed. Alistair Campbell, Royal Historical Society, 1949, pp.32–33.
291 The sobriquet was a twelfth-century addition, but serves here to distinguish him from other Haralds in the story.
292 Sir Frank Stenton, *Anglo-Saxon England,* p.421.
293 *Anglo-Saxon Chronicle,* entry for 1040.
294 Ian Howard, *Harthacnut: The Last Danish King of England,* The History Press, 2008, p.208.
295 *Anglo-Saxon Chronicle,* entry for 1042.

35   Beyond England II

296 *Early Sources of Scottish History,* Volume I, ed. Alan Orr Anderson, Oliver & Boyd, 1922, pp.572–73.
297 *Anglo-Saxon Chronicle,* entry for 1031.
298 The twelfth-century *Chronicon ex chronicis* states that a man called Máel Coluim (Malcolm), whom it describes as the son of a King of the Cumbrians was installed in Strathclyde/Cumbria. This is unlikely to refer to a different Malcolm, but rather to be a slightly awkward reference to the soon-to-be Malcolm III, probably designed to emphasise that his father, Duncan, ruled Strathclyde/Cumbria as well as Scotland.
299 *Early Sources of Scottish History,* Volume I, ed. Alan Orr Anderson, pp.603–4.
300 *Annals of the Kingdom of Ireland,* p.831. https://archive.org/details/annalsofkingdom002ocleuoft/page/830/mode/2up. Consulted 26 July 2021.
301 John Davies, *A History of Wales,* Penguin, 1994, p.97.

36   Power Struggle

302 Marc Morris, *The Anglo-Saxons,* Hutchinson, 2021, pp.381–83.
303 Tom Licence, *Edward the Confessor,* Yale University Press, 2020, p.231.
304 Tom Licence, *Edward the Confessor,* p.245.

37 The Year of Change

305 J.M.D. Meiklejohn, *A New History of England*, Part I: B.C. 55–A.D.1509, pp.42–43.
306 Winston Churchill, *A History of the English-Speaking Peoples*, Vol.I: *The Island Race*, p.131.
307 https://www.bbc.co.uk/bitesize/guides/zsjnb9q/revision/8. Consulted 7 August 2021.
308 Simon Schama, *A History of Britain 1, At the Edge of the World*, BBC, 2000, p.84.
309 Simon Schama, *A History of Britain 1, At the Edge of the World*, p.89.
310 Having played on 'the battlefield' as a boy, and having walked every inch of the ground as a young teenager with maps and accounts of the battle in hand, I remain convinced that Senlac Hill is the most likely location.
311 Teresa Cole, *The Norman Conquest*, Amberley, 2018, 'Appendix I: Did Harold Die at Hastings? The Legend of the Hermit of Chester', pp.261–70.
312 *Anglo-Saxon Chronicle*, entry for 1066.
313 Teresa Cole, *The Norman Conquest*, p.208.
314 William E. Kapelle, *The Norman Conquest and the North: The Region and its Transformation 100–1136*, University of North Carolina Press, 1979, p.3.
315 *Anglo-Saxon Chronicle*, entry for 1137.

38 Transformation

316 The origin of the term is uncertain, but it does not mean that there were a hundred sub-divisions in each county.
317 *Anglo-Saxon Chronicle*, entry for 1085.
318 *The Metrical Chronicle of Robert of Gloucester*, ll.7499–7500, 7538, 7542–43. https://quod.lib.umich.edu/c/cme/AHB1378.0001.001/1:3.9?rgn=div2;view=fulltext. Consulted 19 August 2021.
319 https://www.britannica.com/place/United-Kingdom/The-Normans-1066-1154. Consulted 1 October 2021.

39 Scotland and the Isles

320 Kim Hjarder and Vegard Vike, *Vikinger i krig*, Spartacus, 2011, pp.284–85, claims that Hardrada took 1,000–2,000 Scottish warriors on board when he called on Malcolm III on his way south to meet Tostig, but the evidence for this is at best uncertain.
321 *Anglo-Saxon Chronicle*, entry for 1093.

322 Michael Lynch, *Scotland*, Pimlico, 1992, p.77.
323 *Anglo-Saxon Chronicle*, entry for 1093.
324 William Forbes Skene and Alexander MacBain, *The Highlanders of Scotland*, E.Mackay, 1902, pp.82–83.
325 Richard Oram, *David I, The King Who Made Scotland*, Tempus, 2004, p.46
326 Michael Lynch, *Scotland*, p.78.
327 Ed. Allan Orr Anderson, *Scottish Annals from English Chroniclers, A.D. 500 to 1286*, David Nutt, 1908, pp.221–22.
328 Ed. Allan Orr Anderson, *Scottish Annals from English Chroniclers, A.D. 500 to 1286*, p.239
329 Barbara E. Crawford, 'The Pawning of Orkney and Shetland: A Reconsideration of the Events of 1460–9', *The Scottish Historical Review*, Edinburgh University Press, Vol.48, No.145, pp.35–53.

40 Wales

330 John Davies, *A History of Wales*, p.102.
331 *Brut y Tywysogion (Chronicle of the Princes)*, ed. John Williams, Longman, Green, Longman and Roberts, 1860, p.219.
332 David Carpenter, *The Struggle for Mastery*, Penguin, 2003, p.322.
333 John Davies, *A History of Wales*, p.142.

41 Ireland

334 *Anglo-Saxon Chronicle*, entry for 1087.
335 Sean Duffy, *Brian Boru and the Battle of Clontarf*, Gill& Macmillan, Dublin, 2014, pp.15–16.
336 Michael Richter, *Medieval Ireland*, pp.127–28; Thomas Bartlett, *Ireland: A History*, p.34.
337 *Annals of Ulster*, entry for 1171. https://celt.ucc.ie/published/T100001A/index.html. Consulted 1 December 2021.
338 *Annals of the Four Masters*, ed. John O'Donovan, Dublin, 1849, p.1185. https://babel.hathitrust.org/cgi/pt?id=uc2.ark:/13960/t4xg9w70d&view=1up&seq=7&skin=2021. Consulted 11 December 2021.
339 Simon Schama, *A History of Britain 1: At the Edge of the World*, p.131.
340 Thomas Bartlett, *Ireland: A History*, p.37.
341 *The Parliamentary Register; Or, History of the Proceedings and Debates of the House of Lords and House of Commons*, J. Debrett, 1799, p.448.

Closing the Dig

342 Kate Ravilous, 'Neolithic Europe's Remote Heart', *Archaeology*, January/February 2013. https://www.archaeology.org/issues/61-1301/features/327-scotland-orkney-neolithic-brodgar. Consulted 20 October 2019.

343 Norman Davies, *The Isles*, pp.xxi–xlii; *Europe East and West*, Jonathan Cape, 2006, pp.83–88.

Sources

Adams, Douglas, *The Hitchhiker's Guide to the Galaxy*, 'Fit the Second'. BBC Radio 4, 15 March 1978.
Ælfred, *Preface to St Gregory's Pastoral Care*.
Æthelweard, *Chronicon*.
Alcuin, https://dokumen.tips/documents/alcuin-letter-to-bishop-higbald.html.
Alison, George, https://www.newscientist.com/article/2209691-hear-what-music-would-have-sounded-like-at-stonehenge-4000-years-ago.
Ammianus Marcellinus, *Rerum gestarum libri (The Chronicles of Events)*.
Anderson, Alan Orr, ed., *Early Sources of Scottish History*, Volume I. Oliver & Boyd, 1922.
Anderson, Allan Orr, ed., *Scottish Annals from English Chroniclers, A.D. 500 to 1286*. David Nutt, 1908.
Anglo-Saxon Chronicle.
Annales Cambriae.
Annals of the Kingdom of Ireland.
Appian, *The Civil Wars*.
Appleby, Andrew, http://orkneypottery.co.uk/prehistoric-pottery/neolithic-pottery-firings/.
Archaeology News Network, https://archaeologynewsnetwork.blogspot.com/2018/06/neolithic-henge-site-unearthed-in.html#K5h9ZvAtotR7PkBe.97.
Asser, *The Life of King Alfred*.
Atlas of Hillforts, https://hillforts.arch.ox.ac.uk/.
Avienus, *Ora Maritima*.
Bartlett, Thomas, *Ireland: A History*. Cambridge University Press, Cambridge, 2011.
Bede, *An Ecclesiastical History of the English People*.
Bentham, James, *The History and Antiquities of the Conventual & Cathedral Church of Ely*, Vol. 3. Stevenson, 1817.
Bertrand, Simone, *La Tapisserie de Bayeux*. Zodiaque, 1966.
Blair, John, 'Exploring Anglo-Saxon Settlement'. *Current Archaeology*, 5 June 2014.

Bolton, Timothy, *Cnut the Great*. Yale, 2017.
Brace, Selina et al., 'Ancient genomes indicate population replacement in Early Neolithic Britain'. *Nature, Ecology & Evolution*, 3, 2019.
Bridgman, Timothy P., 'Keltoi, Galatai, Galli: Were They All One People?' *Proceedings of the Harvard Celtic Colloquium*, Vol. 24/25. Harvard University, 2005.
Broderick, George, 'The Names for Britain and Ireland Revisited'. *Sonderdruck aus Beitrage zur Namenforschung*, Vol.44, Notebook 2, Universität Mannheim, 2009.
Brown, Michelle, *How Christianity Came to Britain and Ireland*. Lion Hudson, 2006.
Byrne, Ross P., et al., https://journals.plos.org/plosgenetics/article?id=10.1371/journal.pgen.1007152.
Calderwood, David, *The History of the Kirk of Scotland*, Volume 1. Wodrow Society, Edinburgh, 1843.
Cambridge Core, https://www.cambridge.org/core/journals/antiquity/article/development-of-the-pictish-symbol-system-inscribing-identity-beyond-the-edges-of-empire/4F09B9C943A1C29F226659A20BEC5248/core-reader.
Camden, William, *Britannia*, 1607.
Campbell, Alistair, ed., *Encomium Emmae Reginae*. Royal Historical Society, 1949.
Carlyle, Thomas, *On Heroes and Hero Worship*. James Fraser, 1841.
Carpenter, David, *The Struggle for Mastery*. Penguin, 2003.
Cassius Dio, *Roman History*.
Chadwick, Nora, *The Celts*. Penguin, 1971.
Chronicle of John of Worcester.
Chronicle of Prosper of Aquitaine.
Churchill, Winston, *A History of the English-Speaking Peoples*, Vol.I: *The Island Race*. Cassell, 1956.
Civilisations Disparues, http://www.civilisationsdisparues.com/pages/articles/les-plus-vieilles-roues-du-monde.html.
Clarkson, Tim, *Strathclyde and the Anglo-Saxons in the Viking Age*. John Donald, 2016.
Cole, Teresa, *The Norman Conquest*. Amberley, 2018.
Collingwood, R.G., *The Archaeology of Roman Britain*. Methuen & Co, 1930.
Craig, G., 'Alfred the Great: a diagnosis'. *Journal of the Royal Society of Medicine*, Vol.84, No.5.

Crawford, Barbara E., 'The Pawning of Orkney and Shetland: A Reconsideration of the Events of 1460-9'. *The Scottish Historical Review*, Edinburgh University Press, Vol.48, No.145.

Crystal, David, *The Stories of English*. Penguin, 2005.

Cunliffe, Barry, *Britain Begins*. OUP, 2012.

Cunliffe, Barry, *Danebury Hillfort*. The History Press, 2011.

Cunliffe, Barry, *Druids: A Very Short Introduction*. OUP, 2010.

Cunliffe, Barry, *The Extraordinary Voyage of Pytheas the Greek*. Penguin Books, 2002.

Current Archaeology, 'Mesolithic Timelords: A monumental hunter-gatherer "calendar" at Warren Field, Scotland'. *Current Archaeology*, 283, 5 September 2013.

Davies, John, *A History of Wales*. Penguin, 1994.

Davies, Norman, *Europe*. OUP, 1996.

Davies, Norman, *Europe East & West*. Jonathan Cape, 2006.

Davies, Norman, *The Isles*. Macmillan, 1999.

Davies, Norman, *Vanished Kingdoms*. Allen Lane, 2011.

De Barran, Caoimhín, 'Opinion: Our Celtic identity might not be what we think it is', https://www.thejournal.ie/readme/celts-ireland-4199945-Aug2018.

Dio Chrysostom, *Discourse* 49.

Diodorus Siculus, *Bibliotheca Historica*.

Douglas, David C., *William the Conqueror*. Yale, 1964.

Duffy, Sean, *Brian Boru and the Battle of Clontarf*. Gill & Macmillan, Dublin, 2014.

Eumenius, *Panegyric VI*.

Flavius Eutropius, *Breviarium Historiae Romanae*.

Fleming, Robin, *Britain after Rome*. Allen Lane, 2010.

Fletcher, Peter, 'Discussions of the Possible Origin of Europe's First Boats – 11,500 BP', http://www-labs.iro.umontreal.ca/~vaucher/History/Prehistoric_Craft/1031-3451-1-PB.pdf.

Foot, Sarah, *Æthelstan: The First King of England*. Yale University Press, 2011.

Forsythe, Wes, and Gregory, Niall, 'A Neolithic Logboat from Greyabbey Bay'. *Ulster Journal of Archaeology*, Third Series, Vol.66, 2007.

Freemen, Edward Augustus, *The History of the Norman Conquest*, 5 vols. 1867–79.

Frere, Sheppard, *Britannia*. Routledge & Kegan Paul, 1967.

Gammeltof, Peder, 'Shetland and Orkney Island-Names – A Dynamic Group'. https://www.abdn.ac.uk/pfrlsu/documents/Gammeltoft,%20Shetland

%20and%20Orkney%20Island-Names%20_%20A%20Dynamic%20Group%20.pdf.

Gilbert, Edmund, *et al.*, 'The Genetic Landscape of Scotland and the Isles'. *Proceedings of the National Academy of Sciences*, Vol.116, pp.19064–70, 17 September 2019.

Gildas, *De Excidio et Conquestu Britanniae*.

Giles, Reverend J.A., *Six Old English Chronicles, of Which Two Are Now First Translated from the Monkish Latin Originals*. Bell and Daldy, 1848.

Grant, Alison, https://www.thebottleimp.org.uk/2017/06/gaelic-place-names-viking-influence-on-the-gaelic-place-names-of-the-hebrides.

Andersen, H., and Niels, H., 'Causewayed Enclosures in Northern and Western Europa', https://www.academia.edu/20105549/Causewayed_enclosures_in_Northern_and_Western_Europa.

Harald the Smith, https://www.haraldthesmith.com/iron-smelting-part-iv-furnace-design/.

Hawkins, Gerald S., and White, John B., *Stonehenge Decoded*. Doubleday, 1965.

Herodian, *History*.

Herodotus, *Histories*.

Higgins, Charlotte, https://www.theguardian.com/uk/2012/aug/15/scotland-dna-study-project.

Higham, Nicholas, and Ryan, Martin, *The Anglo-Saxon World*. Yale, 2015.

Hjarder, Kim, and Vike, Vegard, *Vikinger i krig*. Spartacus, 2011.

Holm, Paul, 'The Slave Trade of Dublin: Ninth to Twelfth Centuries'. *Peritia*, Vol.5, 1986.

Hutton, Ronald, *Pagan Britain*. Yale, 2013.

Howard, Ian, *Harthacnut: The Last Danish King of England*. The History Press, 2008.

Jackson, Kenneth, 'Queen Boudicca?' *Britannia*, 10, p.255, 1979.

Jones, Dan, 'Neanderthals wore make-up and liked to chat'. *New Scientist*, 27 March 2008.

Julius Caesar, *Commentaries on the Gallic Wars*.

Kapelle, William E., *The Norman Conquest and the North: The Region and its Transformation 1000–1135*. University of North Carolina Press, 1979.

Kemble, John Mitchell, *Saxons in England*. Longman, Green, Brown & Longmans, 1849.

Kennedy, Maev, 'Arrival of Beaker folk changed Britain for ever, ancient DNA shows'. *The Guardian*, 22 February 2018.

Kenneth Clark, Sir Kenneth, *Civilisation: A Personal View*. BBC, 1969, Episode 1 'The Skin of our Teeth'.

Key, Michael John, *Edward the Elder*. Amberley, 2019.

Knudson, Athena T., *Raiders from the North: Irish Enslavement during the Viking Age*. University of Colorado, 2016.

Kohler, Timothy A. et al., 'Greater post-Neolithic wealth disparities in Eurasia than in North America and Mesoamerica'. *Nature,* Vol.551, 30 November 2017.

Krawiec, Kristina, *The Mesolithic to Bronze Age Landscape Development of the Trent–Derwent Confluence Zone at Shardlow Quarry*. Ph.D. thesis, University of Birmingham, 2012.

Leslie, S. et al., 'The fine-scale genetic structure of the British population'. *Nature,* 519, 2015.

Lhuyd, Edward, *Archaeologia Britannica*, 1707.

Licence, Tom, *Edward the Confessor*. Yale University Press, 2020.

Livingston, Michael, ed., *The Battle of Brunanburh: A Casebook*. University of Exeter Press, 2011.

Lubbock, Sir John, *Pre-Historic Times, As Illustrated by Ancient Remains, and the Manners and Customs of Modern Savages*. Williams & Norgate, 1865.

Lynch, Michael, *Scotland*. Pimlico, 1992.

Macdonagh, Michael, http://www.tii.ie/technical-services/archaeology/publications/archaeologymonographseries/Ch-2-MacDonagh.pdf..

Markus, Gilbert, *Conceiving a Nation*. Edinburgh University Press, 2017.

McCarter, Susan Foster, *Neolithic*. Routledge, 2007.

McClatchie, M. et al., 'Neolithic farming in north-western Europe: archaeobotanical evidence from Ireland'. *Journal of Archaeological Science*, 51, 2014.

McCormick, Finbar, 'The Horse in Early Ireland'. *Anthropozoologica* 42, 1.

McGrath, Matt, 'World's oldest bog body hints at violent past' https://www.bbc.co.uk/news/science-environment-24053119.

McHardy, Stuart, *A New History of the Picts*. Luath Press, 2010.

Meek, Donald E., *The Quest for Celtic Christianity*. Handsel Press, Edinburgh, 2000.

Meiklejohn, J.M.D., *A New History of England, Part I: B.C. 55–A.D.1509*. Alfred M.Holden, 1899.

Moffat, Alastair, *Arthur and the Lost Kingdoms*. Weidenfeld & Nicolson, 1999.

Moffat, Alastair, *The Wall*. Birlinn, 2009.

Moffat, Alastair, *The Borders*. Birlinn, 2007.

Moffat, Alistair, *Before Scotland*. Thames and Hudson, 2005.
Moffat, Alistair, *The Sea Kingdoms*. Harper Collins, 2002.
Moore, A.W., 'Foreign Elements in the Manx Language', http://www.isle-of-man.com/manxnotebook/iomnhas/lm3p059.htm.
Morris, John, 'The Date of St Alban'. *Hertfordshire Archaeology*, 1, 1968.
Morris, John, *The Age of Arthur*. Weidenfeld & Nicolson, 1973.
Morris, Marc, *The Anglo-Saxons*. Hutchinson, 2021.
Morris, James, 'Animal Ritual Killing: from Remains to Meanings'. https://www.academia.edu/226219/Animal_ritual_killing_from_remains_to_meanings.
Nennius, *Historia Brittonum*.
Noble, Gordon, and Evans, Nicholas, *The King in the North*. Birlinn, 2019.
Olalde, Iñigo, *et al.*, 'The Beaker Phenomenon and the Genomic Transformation of Northwest Europe'. https://www.biorxiv.org/content/biorxiv/early/2017/05/09/135962.full.pdf.
Oliver, Neil, *A History of Scotland*. Weidenfield & Nicolson, 2009.
Oosthuizen, Susan, *Tradition and Transformation in Anglo-Saxon England: Archaeology, Common Rights and Landscape*. Bloomsbury Academic, 2013.
Oram, Richard, *David I, The King Who Made Scotland*. Tempus, 2004.
Origen, *Homilies on Ezekiel* IV.
Orkneyjar, http://www.orkneyjar.com/history/vikingorkney/warpeace/part4.htm.
Oxford University Museum of Natural History, http://www.oum.ox.ac.uk/learning/pdfs/buckland.pdf..
Parker Pearson, M., *et al.*, 'The original Stonehenge? A dismantled stone circle in the Preseli Hills of west Wales'. *Antiquity*, Vol. 95, No. 379.
Parker Pearson, M., *et al.*, 'The origins of Stonehenge: on the track of the bluestones'. *Archaeology International*, 20, 2017.
Pezron, Paul-Yves, *Antiquité de la nation et la langue des Celtes, autrement appellez Gaulois*. 1703.
Pickrell, John, 'Unprecedented Ice Age Cave Art Discovered in U.K.' *National Geographic News*, 18 August 2004.
Pinter, Andrea, *Rivers Keep Many Secrets: Bronze Age Depositions of Human Remains in River and Settlement Contexts*. M.A. thesis, University of Amsterdam / VU University, 2016.
Pliny, *Natural History*.
Pollard, Justin, *Alfred the Great*. John Murray, 2006.

Polybius, *Histories*.
Pomponius Mela, *De Situ Orbis*.
Portable Antiquities Scheme.
   https://finds.org.uk/database/artefacts/record/id/512552.
Portable Antiquities Scheme.
   https://finds.org.uk/guides/bronzeage/objects/swords.
Price, Neil, *The Children of Ash and Elm*. Allen Lane, 2020.
Procopius, *De Belli*.
Proto-Indo-European Roots.
   https://tied.verbix.com/project/phonetics/word11.html.
Pryor, Francis, *Britain A.D.* Harper Perennial, 2005.
Pryor, Francis, *Britain B.C.* Harper Collins, 2003.
Pryor, Francis, *Seahenge*. Harper Collins, 2002.
Pryor, Francis, *Stonehenge*. Pegasus, undated.
Ravilous, Kate, 'Neolithic Europe's Remote Heart'. *Archaeology*, January/February 2013.
Redknap, Mark, 'Viking Age Settlement in Wales: Some Recent Advances'. *Transactions of the Honourable Society of Cymmrodorion 2005*, Vol.12, 2006.
Richards, Julian, *Stonehenge: The Story So Far*. Historic England, 2017.
Richter, Michael, *Medieval Ireland*. Gill & Macmillan, 2005.
Roberts, Alice, *The Celts: Search for a Civilization*. Heron Books, 2016.
Roche, Barry, https://www.irishtimes.com/news/call-for-1200-bc-hill-fort-to-be-secured-as-national-monument-1.957169.
Rowlands, Henry, *Mona Antiqua Restaurata*. 1723.
Schama, Simon, *A History of Britain*, '1. At the Edge of the World?' BBC, 2003.
Schiermeier, Quirin, 'Ancient DNA reveals how wheat came to prehistoric Britain'. *Nature*, 26 February 2015.
Science Daily,
   https://www.sciencedaily.com/releases/2009/08/090812104141.htm.
Science, https://www.sciencemag.org/news/2018/11/why-536-was-worst-year-be-alive.
Simms, Katharine, *From Kings to Warlords: The Changing Political Structure of Gaelic Ireland in the Later Middle Ages*. Boydell Press, 2000.
Skene, William Forbes, and MacBain, Alexander, *The Highlanders of Scotland*. E.Mackay, 1902.
Smith, Isobel, *Windmill Hill and Avebury*. Excavations by Alexander Keiller 1925–1939. OUP, 1965.

Smyth, Jessica, 'The house and group identity in the Irish Neolithic', *Proceedings of the Royal Irish Academy: Archaeology, Culture, History, Literature*, Vol. 111C, 2011.

Southern, Patricia, *Roman Britain*. Amberley, 2013.

Spotiswoode, John, *The History of the Church of Scotland: Beginning the Year of our Lord 203, and Continued to the end of the Reign of King James VI of Ever Blessed Memory*, Book 1. 1639.

Stanton, David *et al.*, 'Colonization of the Scottish islands via long-distance Neolithic transport of red deer (Cervus elaphus)'. *Proceedings of the Royal Society*, Series B, 6. April 2016.

Stenton, Sir Frank, *Anglo-Saxon England*. OUP, 1971.

Strabo, *Geography*.

Stubbs, William, ed., *Sancti Dunstani Vita, Memorials of St Dunstan*. Longman & Co., 1874.

Suetonius, *Life of Claudius*.

Tacitus, *Agricola*.

Tacitus, *Annals*.

Tertullian, *Adversus Judaeos*.

The Metrical Chronicle of Robert of Gloucester.

The Monthly Register, 3, January 1793.

The Parliamentary Register. J. Debrett, 1799.

Thom, Alexander, 'The megalithic unit of length'. *Journal of the Royal Statistical Society*, Series A 125, 1962.

Thompson, E.A., 'Zosimus 6.10.2 and the Letters of Honorius'. *The Classical Quarterly*, Vol.32, No.2, 1982.

Tipping, Richard, *et al.*, 'Moments of crisis: climate change in Scottish prehistory'. *Proceedings of the Society of Antiquaries of Scotland*, Vol. 142, 2012.

Toynbee, J.M.C., 'Christianity in Roman Britain'. *Journal of the British Archaeological Association*, Vol. 16, No.1, 1953.

Tunzelmann, Alex von, 'The Vikings: not for revisionist historians'. *The Guardian*, 21 May 2009.

Ward, Gordon, 'The Vikings Come to Thanet'. *Archaeologia Cantiana*, Vol.63, 1950.

Watts, Dorothy, *Religion in Late Roman Britain*. Taylor & Francis, 2002.

Williams, John, ed., *Brut y Tywysogion (Chronicle of the Princes)*. Longman, Green, Longman and Roberts, 1860.

Woods, David, 'Caligula's Seashells', *Greece & Rome*. Vol.47, No.1.

Woods, David, 'On the Alleged Letters of Honorius to the Cities of Britain'. *Latomus,* Vol.71, 2012.

Woodward, A., and Leach, P., 'The Uley Shrines: Excavation of a Ritual Complex on West Hill, Uley: Gloucestershire, 1977–79'. *English Heritage Archaeological Report,* 17, English Heritage, 1993.

Zosimus, *Historia Nova.*

Index of Places and Events

Aberconwy, Treaty of, 549
Aberdeen, 67, 96–97, 218, 529
Aberdyfi, Council of, 547
Abernethy, Treaty of, 522–23, 525. 538
Ailech, Kingdom of, 373–74
Aire Gap, 55–56
Airgialla, Kingdom of, 293, 438
Alba, 137, 369, 371–72, 374–75, 403
Albion (and related forms), 137–38, 140–41
Alnwick, 248, 253, 531
Alt Clud (*see also* Dumbarton Rock and Kingdom of Strathclyde), 244, 279, 285, 294, 303–5, 315–17, 327–29, 331, 350, 362–63, 369–70, 384
Alton, Treaty of, 517
Amesbury, 94, 98
Anglesey Sound, Battle of, 534, 541
Anglesey, 67, 159, 161, 167, 173, 178, 182, 193, 199–200, 206, 283, 365, 378, 384, 440–41, 445, 465, 477, 534, 544. 549–50
Antonine Wall, 214–15, 220, 301
Antrim, 278, 303, 438
Appledore, 398
Aquitaine, 104, 518
Argyll, 278–79, 294
Arklow, 264
Armagh, 293, 296, 471
Armorica, 23, 34, 42, 88–90, 104, 125, 143, 150, 158–59, 164, 188, 314, 385
Arran, Isle of, 303, 375
Ashdown, Battle of, 392
Ashington, Battle of, 450–51
Athelney, Isle of, 396–97, 406, 419
Avebury, 62, 74–79, 82, 85, 97–98, 115, 122, 142
Aveline's Hole, 27
Avenue, The (Stonehenge), 79
Avon, River, 54, 308
Aylesford, 286

Bainbridge, 217
Balbridie, 49
Balksbury, 124
Bamburgh, 308, 315, 336, 403, 411, 417, 462–63
Bann, River, 24, 159
Barnhouse Settlement, 80
Bath (Aquae Sulis), 233, 253–54, 313, 333
Battersea, 121, 157
Battle (East Sussex), 136, 498
Bayeux Tapestry, 479, 487, 492, 494–95, 497, 499
Beckhampton Avenue, 79
Bedford, 355, 403, 405
Bellaghmoon, Battle of, 439
Belmarsh, 57
Bend in the Boyne (sacred landscape), 79, 82
Benfleet, 398,
Berkhamsted, 500, 506, 521
Bernicia (*see also* Kingdom of Northumbria), 285, 308, 311, 315–17, 322, 324–25, 329, 372, 386, 403, 431
Bewcastle, 213, 253, 351
Birrens, 213
Black Isle, The, 306
Bodmin Moor, 106
Bodmin, 314
Bontnewydd, 17
Bosham, 487, 494
Bouldnor Cliff, 24–25, 33, 142
Boulogne, 185, 196, 457, 481, 483, 490, 501, 515
Bowness-on-Solway, 213, 233
Boyne, River, 33, 297, 364
Brancaster, 233, 267
Brecon, 540–41, 543, 547, 549
Brega, Kingdom of, 329, 362, 383–84
Bréifne, Kingdom of, 293, 438, 469, 473, 552–53

Index of Places and Events

Brigg, 39
Bristol Channel, 39, 99, 367, 405, 477, 502
Bristol, 54, 313, 385
British Camp, 131, 134
Brittany, 53, 74, 93, 97, 103–4, 130, 137–39, 154, 164, 184, 233, 314, 317–18, 363, 405, 410, 413, 415, 487, 494, 497, 513, 563
Brodgar, Ness of, 75, 80–81, 101–2, 129, 142, 560
Brodgar, Ring of, 74, 77, 80
Broighter Hoard, 41, 157
Bronocice, 55
Brú na Bóinne, *see* Bend in the Boyne
Brunanburh, Battle of, 343, 414–17, 431, 442, 467, 491
Brycheiniog, Kingdom of, 405, 408, 412, 441–42, 444
Bryn Celli Ddu, 67
Buellt, Kingdom of, 444
Bulverhythe, 497
Burrian, Broch of, 129
Bush Barrow, 97–98
Bute, Isle of, 99, 362
Buttington, 399
Byzantium, 29, 280, 314, 339, 350, 358, 363, 385, 414, 488, 492
Cadbury Castle, 131, 168
Cadiz (Gadir)+A237, 138, 162–63
Caerleon, 257–58, 318
Caernarfon, 253, 550
Caerwent, 233, 444
Caistor St Edmunds (Venta Icenorum), 227
Caithness, 375–76, 381, 413, 433–34, 436, 464–66, 536
Calais, 32, 518–19
Caledonia (and related forms), 146–47, 179–80, 217, 219, 236–37, 244–49, 255, 262–64, 271, 304
Callanish, 10, 77, 85, 97, 115, 122, 172
Cambourne, 317
Cambridge, 286, 393, 403, 405, 502

Camp Hill, 124
Campi Flegrei (volcano), 18
Camulodunum, *see* Colchester
Canterbury, 85, 122, 186, 222, 227, 311, 314, 319–20, 333, 336, 421, 424, 457, 478, 482–83, 500, 509–10, 516, 531
Cardiff, 199, 225
Carham, Battle of, 431–32
Carlingford Lough, 364, 438
Carlisle (Luguvalium), 206–7, 257–58, 263, 305, 315, 523, 529, 530
Carmarthen, 365, 542–43, 545, 547–48
Carn Brea, 62
Carnac, 74–75, 88, 90
Carolingian Empire, 359, 363, 388–89, 509
Carrawburgh, 253
Cashel, 110–11, 438, 468
Castlerigg Stone Circle, 82
Catraeth, Battle of, 316
Céide Fields, 47, 105
Ceredigion, 540, 542–46
Chelmsford, 2245
Chester (Deva Victrix), 206–7, 224, 233–34, 255, 399, 403, 435, 444, 499, 505, 530, 540, 542, 544
Chester, Battle of, 345
Chichester, 198, 222, 510
Chippenham, 384–85, 397
Christchurch, 400, 427
Circle 275, 74
Cirencester, 228, 251, 269, 313, 333, 397
Clashanimud, 110–11
Clifton, 121–22, 167
Clonard, 296–99, 384
Clonmacnois, 251
Clontarf, Battle of, 436, 463, 467, 471–72, 474, 491
Clyde, River, 44, 99, 207, 244, 283, 305, 328, 362, 370, 466, 535
Coilsfield, Battle of, 285
Colchester (Camulodunum), 189–91, 196–97, 200, 205, 222, 228, 252, 505

Coldrum Long Barrow, 68–69
Coll, Isle of, 434
Coneybury Henge, 75, 82
Connacht, Kingdom of, 293, 362 438–39, 472–73, 553, 556,
Conwy, Battle of, 441
Copa Hill, 92
Corbridge, 207, 210, 385, 430
Cork, 110–11, 157, 472, 474, 556–57, 382–83, 385, 436, 438, 472, 474, 556–57
Corlea Trackway, 92
Cornwall, 91, 139, 142, 152, 155, 159, 230, 281, 289, 291, 313–14, 317, 327, 425–26, 451, 471, 511, 562
County Down, 248
Craeb Telcha, Battle of, 438
Creswell Crags, 19–21, 30
Crickley Hill, 62
Cullen, 418
Cumbria, 52, 82, 153, 213, 253, 283–85, 332, 345, 351, 406, 408, 416–17, 430–32, 460, 511, 521–23, 528
Dál Riata, Kingdom of, 279, 294, 300–4, 306, 322, 327–28, 331, 350, 368–75, 384, 399, 429, 431
Danebury, 133–35, 168
Danelaw, The, 397, 403–5, 420, 427, 447, 449–50, 452
Danube, River, 34–35, 89, 123, 157–58, 195, 210, 215, 252, 270
Dartmoor, 106, 225
Deerhurst, Treaty of, 450–51
Deheubarth, Kingdom of, 408, 412, 442, 444–45, 476, 540, 543–46, 548–49
Deira (*see also* Kingdom of Northumbria), 308, 311, 316, 319, 322–35, 329
Denmark, 112, 251, 285, 287, 360–61, 378, 426, 447–48, 451, 454–58, 463, 481, 488, 490, 502, 520, 537
Derby, 403, 405
Derry, 278, 298, 303
Derwent, River, 38, 54, 121, 496
Deskford, 137

Devon, 18, 62, 100, 159, 230, 281, 312, 314, 396, 425–26, 511
Din Eidyn, *see* Edinburgh
Doggerland, 22, 25
Doncaster, 224, 312
Donegal, 471, 557
Dorchester (Dornovaria), 62, 188, 227, 361
Dorchester-on-Thames, 114, 325
Dorset Cursus, 63, 65
Dover, 32, 39, 55, 138, 185, 190–91, 228, 233, 333, 389, 483, 500–1, 505, 532
Dowris, 125
Dowth, 79
Dreghorn, 49
Droitwich, 113
Druimvargie, 23
Drumanagh, 180, 238
Drumturn Burn, 107
Dublin, 238, 362, 364, 369–70, 375, 378, 382–86, 408, 414–17, 434, 436–37, 439–40, 465, 467, 469–75, 477, 534, 553–56, 558
Dumbarton Rock (*see also* Alt Clud and Kingdom of Strathclyde), 244, 279, 304, 317, 363, 370, 375
Dumfries, 64, 66, 108, 129, 153, 157, 207, 351, 414, 532
Dumnonia, Kingdom of, 3130150 14, 318, 356, 367
Dun Nechtan, Battle of , 330
Dun Ringhill, 128–29
Dundalk, 364–65, 558
Dundurn, 329
Dunkeld, 430, 460–61, 525, 528
Dunnicaer, 247,
Dunottar, 329, 374, 413
Dunragit, 315
Dunstable, 168
Durham, 228, 460–61, 502, 522–53,
Durno, 208
Durrington Walls, 74, 79, 84
Durrow, 298, 300, 350

Dyfed, Kingdom of, 365, 403, 406, 408, 441–42, 444, 476–77, 540–43, 545
Dyrham, Battle of, 313, 315
Eamont Bridge, 408, 411, 442
Eartham Pit, 16
East Anglia (region), 11, 93, 106, 126, 146, 159, 199
East Anglia, Kingdom of, 307–11, 321–22, 325, 353, 355–57, 386, 390–92, 394, 397–99, 403–4, 426, 447, 455, 479, 481–82, 484–85, 501, 511
East Barns, 24
East Kennett Long Barrow, 79
Ebrauc, Kingdom of, 285, 308
Edercloon, 57
Edinburgh, 160, 207, 304, 316, 413, 413, 417, 431, 527, 529, 531
Egypt, 29–30, 108, 141, 149, 167, 270, 296–97
Eigg, Isle of, 306
Eildon Hill, 110, 131, 134, 207, 291
Eilean Dòmhnuill, 129
Elgin, 461, 529
Elmet, Kingdom of, 285, 315–17
Ely, 287, 478, 505, 510
Emain Macha, 136, 293, 296, 470–71
Ems, River, 104
Er Lannic, 74
Essex (region), 93, 188, 334, 398, 404–5, 426
Essex, Kingdom of, 309–12, 320–21, 352, 357, 387, 389, 397
Exeter (Isca Dumnoniorum), 199, 201, 203, 224, 393, 400, 502, 504
Far Northern Isles (*see also* Shetland), 23, 44, 53, 59, 66, 75, 126, 128
Fengate, 105, 118
Fermanagh, 557
Ferriter's Cove, 38, 42, 60
Fishbourne, 198, 237
Fiskerton, 121–22
Flag Fen, 118, 121–22, 167

Flanders, 421, 457, 481–82, 485, 489–90, 494
Folkestone, 426
Fort Augustus, 306
Fort Navan, *see* Emain Macha
Forteviot, 429–30
Forth—Clyde line, 147, 179, 207, 210, 214, 219, 245, 279, 345
Fortriu, 328–29, 369
Fulford, Battle of, 491, 495–97, 506
Fulham, 397
Gadir, *see* Cadiz
Gainsborough, 447–48
Galicia (Iberia), 42, 88, 104, 137–38, 314
Galicia (Poland), 150
Galloway, 66, 108, 129, 150, 153, 157, 207, 247, 263, 285, 298, 315, 317, 368, 375, 465, 522, 531, 533
Galway, 150, 180, 436, 473, 556
Gaul, 140–43, 146, 150, 154, 157, 171–73, 175, 177, 179, 181, 183–88, 190–91, 216, 219, 228, 230–32, 242, 250, 264, 268–72
Glasbury, Battle of, 476
Glasgow, 305, 535
Glastonbury, 419–20, 451, 509
Glenmama, Battle of, 470 475
Gloucester, 222, 224, 230, 233, 235, 269, 313, 333, 393, 404–5, 523, 545
Goat's Hole Cave, 7, 10, 19
Göbekli Tepe, 81
Godwin Ridge, 121
Gough's Cave, 19, 21, 27
Gower Peninsula, 7, 21, 377, 545
Graig Lwyd, 52–53
Great Glen, 96, 147, 208, 217, 235, 248, 430
Great Langdale, 52–53, 56
Great Orme's Head, 90, 377
Great Ouse, River, 37, 121, 405
Greater Cursus (Stonehenge), 63–64
Greenwich, 447, 450
Grime's Graves, 51

Guadalquivir Valley, 138, 162
Guirdil Bay, 52
Gwent, Kingdom of, 405, 408, 412 442, 444–45, 476, 540–41, 543
Gwynedd, Kingdom of, 283, 290, 305, 312, 316, 322, 365, 378, 403, 406 408, 412, 440–45, 464, 475–76, 501, 534, 539–46, 548–50
Hadrian's Wall, 145, 147, 179, 211–17, 219–21, 230, 233–34, 236–38, 243, 252–54, 261–63, 271–72, 275, 279
Hallaton, 168
Hallstatt Culture, 156–57, 162
Ham Hill, 199
Hambeldon Hill, 62
Happisburgh, 14–16, 560
Harrow Way, The, 55
Hastings, 233, 287, 498, 500, 515
Hastings, Battle of, 540, 491, 498–500, 506
Heavenfield, Battle of, 322
Hekla (volcano), 108, 113
Hembury, 62
Hengistbury Head, 9, 125, 127–28, 187–88, 191
Hereford, 353, 355, 405, 408, 414, 427, 476, 501, 510, 540, 543, 549
High Rochester, 213
Holyrood, 528, 537
Housesteads, 234
Howick, 24
Huelva, 104
Huly Hill, 160
Humber, River, 39, 56, 126, 197, 288, 311–12, 404, 406, 415, 447, 447, 495, 503–4
Huntingdon, 403, 501, 530
Hwicce, Kingdom of, 309, 312
Iberia, 22–3, 34–5, 42, 87–9, 98, 138, 149, 151, 153–54, 162–64, 180, 191, 225, 232–33, 251, 264, 314
Iceland, 108, 139, 297–98, 346, 355–61, 363, 466, 535
Ilkley, 217

Inchmarnock, Isle of, 99, 362
Invergowrie, 527
Inverness, 96–97, 300
Iona, Isle of, 179, 298, 300–1, 305, 320, 323–25, 362–63, 430, 462
Ipswich, 426
Iron Age Settlement Zones, 126–27
Islandbridge, Battle of, 385, 436
Islay, Isle of, 3034, 375, 533
Isle of Man (see also Halfway Isle), 130, 364, 375–79, 383–86, 415, 418, 434–46, 445, 461, 465–67, 471–72, 533–36, 554
Isle of Wight, 24, 199, 286, 288, 307, 309, 326, 426
Jarlshof, 128
Jedburgh, 528, 531
Jórvik (see also York), 13, 386, 391, 399, 403–8, 414–17, 427, 433–34, 436–37, 442, 447, 452, 474
Kells, 298, 301, 363
Kent (region), 55, 67, 105, 111, 126, 139, 146, 150, 159, 161, 188, 196, 233, 260, 286, 367, 386, 398, 426, 447, 457, 494, 515
Kent, Kingdom of, 286, 309, 311–12, 319, 321–24, 335–36, 340, 343–44, 352, 355–57, 361, 387, 389, 397
Kerry, 297–98, 557
Kiev, 449, 451, 486, 488, 492
Kilnsea, 39
Kingston-on-Thames, 407
Kinloch, 52
Kintyre, 30, 303, 375, 527, 533
Knap Hill, 62
Knowth, 67, 79
La Tène Culture, 156–62
Lambeth, Treaty of, 532
Lancaster, 224, 233
Land Bridge, 16–17, 22–25, 32–33, 38, 55
Laois, 298, 383, 557
Lawley, The, 124
Leicester, 222, 227, 403, 405, 416, 510

Leinster, 153, 264, 293–95, 297–98, 383–84, 433, 439–40, 469–75, 553–55
Lesser Cursus (Stonehenge), 63, 79
Lewes, Battle of, 548
Lewes, 117, 400, 509
Lewis, Isle of, 129, 172, 379, 533, 538
Liffey, River, 364, 382–83, 385
Limavady, 41
Limerick, 382, 385–86, 436–38, 468–69, 474, 556
Lincoln (Lindum Colonia), 201, 203, 222, 228, 233, 235, 252–53, 269, 333, 403, 405, 502, 510, 531
Lindholme, 57
Lindisfarne, 315, 323, 349–51, 361–62, 416
Lindsey, Kingdom of, 287, 309, 329, 367
Lismore, Isle of, 306
Little Isleham, 116–17
Liverpool, 45, 54, 124
Lizard Peninsula, 106
Llandeilo Fawr, Battle of, 550
Llyn Cerrig Bach, 159, 167, 193
Llyn Fawr, 124
Loch Bhorghastail, 129
Loch Olabhat, 129
Londinium, 200–1, 205, 333
London (see also Londinium), 16, 45, 54, 57, 122, 167, 175, 183, 187, 222, 228, 233, 235, 252, 257–58, 269, 273–74, 279, 311, 320, 333, 344, 352, 367, 392, 398, 402–3, 405, 426, 447, 449–51, 456–57, 476, 481, 483, 495, 498, 500–1, 510, 516, 527, 529
Londonderry, 557
Long Meg and her Daughters, 82
Longstones, The, 79
Lough Gill, 60
Lough Neagh, 438
Lowbury Hill, 168
Lullingstone, 260
Maes Howe, 67, 72, 77, 80, 82, 166
Magheraboy, 60–61
Maiden Castle, 62, 131–35, 199

Maldon, Battle of, 343, 405, 426
Malienydd, Kingdom of, 441, 444
Mann, see Isle of Man
Marden Henge, 74
Maritime Contact Zones, 37–38
Maryport, 234
Massalia, 139, 143, 172, 188
Mayburgh Henge, 82
Meath (Mide), Kingdom of, 293–94, 362, 438–40, 469–73, 556
Medway, River, 68, 196, 198
Mercia, Kingdom of, 307–10, 312–13, 322, 325–27, 329–31, 335–36, 341, 343–34, 352–57, 367, 391–94, 397–98, 405–8, 410, 421, 441–42, 447, 449–50, 452, 456, 476, 480, 485, 489
Meretun, Battle of, 392
Middlewich, 113
Migdale, 117
Milan, Edict of, 255, 257–58
Mold, 92
Mons Badonicus, Battle of, 288–90, 307, 313
Mons Graupius, Battle of, 161, 208–10, 220, 244
Montgomery, Treaty of, 549
Mooghaun, 110, 117, 119
Moray, 306, 329, 369, 376, 430, 433–34, 460–62, 520, 526, 529
Morgannwg, Kingdom of, 444–45, 476, 540–41
Mortlach, 306
Mount Batten, 125, 140
Mount Sandel, 23–24
Movilla, 298–99
Munster, 153, 293, 383, 433, 438–39, 467–73, 534, 551
Must Farm, 108–10, 118, 129
Nantes, 104
Narbonne, 160–61
Nene, River, 37, 287, 308
Netherby, 213
Nettleton Shrub, 259

Newbridge, 160
Newcastle-upon-Tyne, 211, 224, 233, 523
Newgrange, 55, 63–64, 66–67, 72, 79–80, 82, 96, 166, 238
Newstead (Trimontium), 207, 210–11, 214–15
Norfolk, 14, 51, 84, 157, 191, 287, 515
Normandy, 104, 125, 344, 415, 425, 433, 446–47, 451, 453, 456–59, 478–80, 484–88, 490–94, 498–99, 501, 507–9, 512–18, 521, 525, 530–31, 543, 546, 551–52
North Walney, 52
Northampton, 355, 403, 405, 489, 501, 531
Northern Isles (see also Orkney), 23, 35, 44, 66–67, 74, 80–81, 86, 130
Northey Island, 118
Northumbria, Kingdom of, 246, 303–13, 317, 322–25, 327–33, 336, 340–45, 350–52, 356–57, 362, 386, 391, 393–94, 398, 402–3, 406, 410–12, 416–17, 420–21, 430–31, 450–52, 455, 458, 461, 480, 489, 495–96, 501–3, 514, 521–23, 527, 531–32
Norway, 25, 344, 359–61, 376, 378, 413, 436, 447, 449, 455–57, 463, 465–67, 490, 492, 495, 533–37
Norwich, 227, 505
Nottingham, 391, 403, 405, 502
Offaly, 251, 350, 383, 557
Offa's Dyke, 353, 365, 403, 406, 441, 540
Old Montrose Cursus, 65
Orewin Bridge, Battle of, 550
Orkney (see also Northern Isles), 23, 44, 139, 152, 197, 247, 301, 329, 358, 363–64, 368, 375–78, 380–82, 413, 431–36, 463–67, 471, 495, 497, 515, 520, 524, 529, 533, 535–38
Oronsay, Isle of, 23–24, 300
Ostraige, Kingdom of, 293, 433, 439, 469, 473
Oswestry, 312, 544
Oxford, 29, 355, 447, 449, 456–58

Oxfordshire, 68, 112, 168, 188, 274, 332, 349, 352, 514
Paris, 228, 250, 390, 394
Paris, Treaty of, 518
Pas de Calais, 32, 93, 159, 185
Pegwell Bay, 187, 282, 320
Pembroke, 540–43, 545, 553, 555
Perranzabuloe, 317
Perth, 291, 429–30, 522, 529
Perth, Treaty of, 379, 538–39
Pevensey, 233, 309, 345, 484, 497, 515
Pictland, 301, 304–6, 320, 327–31, 368–39, 371–75, 384, 393
Picton, Treaty of, 549
Pocklington, 160
Portland, 367, 425
Portmahomack, 300, 305–6
Post Track, 56–57
Powys, Kingdom of, 365, 391, 408, 440–42, 444–45, 475–76, 540–42, 544–46, 548–49
Preseli Mountains, 76
Priddy Circles, 74
Rathgall, 110
Rathlin Island, 362–63
Ravenglass, 213
Renfrew, Battle of, 535
Rheged, Kingdom of, 285, 315–17, 328
Rhine, River, 22, 88–89, 93, 96, 101, 103, 132, 146, 150, 158–60, 183–84, 205, 230, 233, 252, 267–68, 271, 273, 275
Rhône, River, 104, 140
Rhône–Rhine Corridor, 88, 103, 164
Rhynie, 247
Richborough, 267, 273
Ridgeway, The, 55, 68, 98
Ripon, 323
Rochester, 55, 233, 320, 323, 367, 398, 510, 515
Rome, 140, 178, 183–205, 209–11, 215–226, 232, 237, 243, 246, 249, 251, 254–57, 262–63, 265–71, 273, 276–82, 295, 298, 305, 318–20, 322–26, 345, 349,

352, 387–88, 393, 396, 421, 441–42, 455, 461, 464, 473, 493, 561
Rosemarkie, 306
Ross Island, 90
Rum, Isle of, 52
Ruthwell, 341, 351
Salcombe, 100
Salisbury, 505, 510
Sanctuary, The, 79
Sanday, Isle of, 247
Sandwich, 386, 400, 426, 448, 457, 480
Schleswig-Holstein, 104, 307
Scone, 429–30, 525, 528
Scythia, 149, 157
Seahenge, 84, 86, 92, 97
Seaton, 55
Seine, River, 103–4, 146, 159–60, 184, 344, 390, 399, 433
Seisyllwg, Kingdom of, 365, 408, 441–42
Selsey Bill, 286, 309, 338, 509
Seven Sleepers, Battle of, 462
Severn, River, 54, 60, 126, 309, 313, 321, 327, 426, 445, 450, 540
Shannon, River, 54, 364, 437, 468–70
Shardlow, 121
Sheppey, Isle of, 365
Shetland (see also Far Northern Isles), 18, 44, 152, 181, 246, 301, 358, 363–64, 368, 375–76, 378, 380–82, 385, 432, 436, 464–66, 533, 536–38
Shrewsbury, 504–5, 539–40, 546, 550
Sicily, 40, 88, 172, 488
Silbury Hill, 79, 84, 86, 97
Silchester (Calleva Atrebatum), 189–90, 223
Silvertown, 57
Skara Brae, 80,
Skellig Michael, 297, 299
Skitten Mire, Battle of, 433
Skye, Isle of, 52, 128, 136, 303, 375, 533
Solway—Tweed line, 532
Solway—Tyne line, 179, 206, 210–11
Somme, River, 184

South Downs (flint mines), 50
Southampton Water, 39
Southampton, 45, 224, 333, 367, 425, 450, 457, 459, 325
Springfield Lyons, 111
St Albans (Verulamium, Verlamion), 189, 191, 200–1, 222, 230, 237, 257
St Andrews, 116–17, 119, 371, 375
St David's, 377, 440, 443, 445
Stainmore Gap, 55, 522–23
Stainmore, Battle of, 417, 433
Stamford Bridge, Battle of, 491, 496–97, 506
Stamford, 355, 403, 405
Stanton Drew, 82
Stanwell Cursus, 63
Star Carr, 24, 29–30, 33, 250
Stenness, Stones of, 74–75, 80, 85
Stirling, 283, 304, 522, 528–29, 531
Stonehenge, 7, 10, 63–64, 67, 73–79, 82–86, 94, 97–98, 115, 118, 122, 129, 166, 173–74, 182–83, 293
Stour, River, 309, 398
Stracathro, Battle of, 529
Strathclyde, Kingdom of (see also Alt Clud and Dumbarton Rock), 370–71, 373, 385, 393, 398, 403, 406, 408, 413–14, 416, 431–32, 460
Sussex (region), 233, 338, 426, 487, 494, 506, 509, 543
Sussex, Kingdom of, 286–87, 309–11, 323, 326, 352, 355–57, 387, 389, 397
Sutherland, 375–76, 381–82, 436, 536
Sutton Hoo, 311, 351
Swanscombe, 17
Swansea, 377, 440
Sweden, 358, 378, 451, 454, 486, 537–38
Sweet Track, 57, 118
Tamworth, 336, 404–5
Tara, Battle of, 469
Tara, Hill of, 57, 238, 241, 293–95, 434, 440
Tartessos, 138, 162–63

Tegeingl, Cantref of, 544–45
Tettenhall, 404
Thames, River, 14–16, 22, 37, 45, 54, 57, 68, 98, 105, 121–22, 157, 159, 167, 187–88, 196, 228, 286, 309, 311, 325, 352, 360, 367, 397, 403, 410, 421, 425, 450–1, 456, 478, 484, 500, 508
Thanet, Isle of, 282, 368, 425
The Isles, Kingdom of, 376–78, 417, 434–36, 463–67, 515, 533–36, 561
Thetford, 391
Thomond, Kingdom of, 467–68
Thornborough Henges, 74, 76–77, 86
Thwing, 111
Tievebulliagh, 52–53
Tinchebrai, Battle of, 517, 541
Tintagel, 290
Tipperary, 351, 383
Torksey, 393
Tormarten, 114
Tower of London, 16, 501, 505
Traprain Law, 110, 220, 262
Trent, Battle of, 329–30, 352
Trent, River, 37, 121, 308
Troyes, Treaty of, 518
Tweed, River, 207, 220, 430–31, 530–31
Tyne Gap, 55
Tyne, River, 55, 207, 211, 385, 393, 530
Tyninghame, 416
Tyrone, 557
Uley, 259
Ulster, Kingdom of, 293, 315, 469–74, 556
Ulva, Isle of, 23
Upton Lovell, 98
Verulamium/Verlamion, *see* St Albans
Vindolanda, 234, 243
Walbury, 124
Wandsworth, 157
Wareham, 393, 397, 424, 427
Warren Field, 27–28
Watchet, 425

Waterford, 382–86, 439, 468, 472–74, 552, 554–55
Waterloo, 121
Wayland's Smithy, 68–69, 82
Weald—Artois Incline, *see* Land Bridge
Wells, 421
Wessex (region), 78, 97–100, 103, 106
Wessex, Kingdom/Earldom of, 287, 307–13, 315, 318, 325–26, 335–38, 343, 346, 352–57, 361, 368, 386–94, 397–98, 400–7, 410, 413, 416–21, 442, 447, 449–55, 457, 478–86, 50–1, 516, 524
West Kennet Avenue, 79
West Kennet Long Barrow, 68, 79
Westminster, 478, 485, 489, 500, 502, 509–10, 527, 559, 560, 563
Wexford, 382, 385, 436, 439, 468, 472, 474, 534–35
Wharfe, River, 253
Whitby, 323, 325, 372, 509
Whithorn, 263, 298, 304
Wicklow, 92, 110, 136
Winchester, 222, 227, 332, 336, 389, 396, 400, 407, 409, 420–22, 447, 457, 477–78, 486, 488, 500, 509–10, 516
Windmill Hill, 62, 79
Windy Dido, 106
Woodbridge, 57
Woodhenge, 74, 79, 82, 84, 97, 168
Worcester, 458, 493, 510
Worcester, Treaty of, 547
Wormy Hillock, 74, 166
Wroxeter, 280
Yetholm, 112
York (Eboracum; *see also* Jórvik), 206–7, 218–19, 222, 224, 230, 252, 269, 283–85, 308, 322–33, 333, 336, 351, 386, 391, 403, 489, 495–97, 502–4, 509–10, 516, 522, 528, 532
York, Treaty of, 536
Yougal, 383

Index of Persons

Aaron, Saint, 257–58, 318
Adams, Douglas, 31
Adelfius of Lincoln, 258
Adomnán, Saint, 298, 300–01, 304, 306
Adrian IV, Pope, 555
Áed Find, King of Dál Riata, 331, 369
Áed Findliath, King of Ailech, 374
Áed mac Cináeda, 371–72
Ælfgifu, wife of King Æthelred, 446, 457, 459
Ælfgifu, wife of King Cnut, 451, 453, 455–58
Ælfgifu, wife of King Eadwig, 420–21
Ælfred (Alfred the Great), King of Wessex, 13, 335, 343, 353, 355, 361, 387–88, 391–403, 405, 407, 409, 418, 426–27, 442, 451-52, 479, 563
Ælfred (son of King Æthelred and Queen Emma), 451, 456–57, 479, 483–84
Ælfric of Eynsham, 338, 432
Ælfric, Ealdorman, 426–27
Ælfsige, Archbishop of Canterbury, 421
Ælle, founder of Sussex, 309, 311, 345
Ælle, King of Deira, 308
Ælle, usurper of Northumbria, 391
Æscwine, founder of Essex, 309
Æthelbald of Mercia, 331, 352, 355
Æthelbald of Wessex, 386–87, 389
Æthelbald, brother of King Ælfred, 400
Æthelberht, King of Kent, 309, 320–21, 333, 335, 387
Æthelberht, King of Wessex, 387, 389, 391
Æthelburg of Kent, 322
Æthelfirth, Archbishop of Canterbury, 616
Æthelfirth, King of Bernicia and Deira, 308
Æthelflaed of Mercia, 403–07, 413, 419, 442

Æthelheard of Wessex, 352
Æthelhelm, Archbishop of Canterbury, 407, 419
Æthelhelm, son of Æthelred of Wessex, 403
Æthelred (the Unready), King of England, 422–48, 432, 436, 446–54, 456, 478
Æthelred I of East Anglia, 353
Æthelred II of East Anglia, 353
Æthelred II of Mercia, Ealdorman, 397, 403–04
Æthelred of Wessex, 391–92, 403
Æthelric , King of Bernicia, 308
Æthelstan of Mercia, 329
Æthelstan, King of Wessex, 335, 402–03, 407–19, 253 426–27, 437, 442, 444, 474, 479, 520
Æthelstan, son of Æthelwulf, 386, 400
Æthelweard of Wessex, 452–53
Æthelweard, historian, 361, 415
Æthelwold, Bishop, 420, 422–23
Æthelwold, son of Æthelred of Wessex, 403–04
Æthelwulf, King of Wessex, 356, 386–89, 394
Agricola, 145, 161, 173, 179, 199, 205–10, 214, 218–21, 226, 237, 239–40, 243, 245, 412, 522
Aidan, Saint, 323
Ailill Molt of the Uí Néill, 293
Airgiallia (clan), 293
Alain of Brittany (Alan Twistedbeard), 413
Alban, Saint, 257
Albert, Prince, 338, 341, 563
Albinus, Decimus Clodius, 216–17
Alcuin, 351, 355, 362
Alemanni (tribe), 267–68, 273–75
Alexander I of Scotland, 528, 543

Alexander II of Scotland, 532, 536
Alexander II, Pope, 493–94, 508
Alexander III of Scotland, 536, 548
Alexander III, Pope, 477
Alhfrith, King of Northumbria, 323, 325
Allectus, 269
Alphege, Archibishop of Canterbury, 447
Alpín MacEchdach, King of Dál Riata, 368
Ambrosius Aurelianus, 288–89
Amlaíb Conung (Amlaíb mac Gofraid; Olaf Guthfrison), 369–71, 383–84, 414–16, 436–37, 439
Amlaíb Cuarán (Amlaíb mac Sitric; Olaf Sigtryggsson), 13, 416–17, 434, 469, 474–75
Ammianus Marcellinus, 272
Anarawd, son of Rhodri Mawr, 445, 476–77
Andrew of Wyntoun, 371–72
Angles (tribe), 9, 285, 287, 307–8, 313, 315–17, 319, 330, 332, 335, 370, 384, 415, 492
Anna, King of East Anglia, 325
Antoninus, Pius, Roman Emperor, 214
Aristotle, 172
Arne, Thomas, 396
Arnulf of Montgomery, 540, 551
Arthgal ap Dyfnwal, King of Strathclyde, 370
Arthur, King, 289–92, 563
Asser, 353, 355, 391–94, 396, 402
Atrebates (tribe), 188–90, 223, 226, 230
Aubrey, John, 7, 182
Augustine, Saint, 309, 311, 319–21
Augustus, Roman Emperor, 194
Auisle mac Gofraid, 369
Aurelian, Roman Emperor, 268
Avienus, 40, 137, 140–41
Bacsecg, 392
Baldwin V of Flanders, 481–82, 489–90
Beaduheard, 361
Bede, 256–57, 263, 277, 282, 285–86, 288–89, 300, 304, 311–12, 318, 321–22, 325–27, 329–30, 338, 343, 345, 362
Belgae (tribe), 145–46, 227
Beli I, King of the Picts, 329
Benedict III, Pope, 388
Benedict of Nursia, Saint, 418
Beorhtric, King of Wessex, 353, 355–56
Beorn Estrithsson, 479, 481–82
Beornwulf, King of Mercia, 356
Bernard of Clairvaux, 555
Bertha, Princess of the Franks, 319
Blake, William, 155
Boece, Hector, 262
Bolanus, Marcus Vettius, 205
Boudicca (Boadicea), Queen of the Iceni, 12, 173, 199–205, 208, 226–29, 291, 563
Boughton, Rutland, 291
Brehons (Irish lawgivers), 242
Brendan of Clonfert (Brendan the Navigator), Saint, 40, 44, 297–98
Brian Boru (Bóruma), 241, 467–73, 475, 534
Bridei I, King of the Picts, 300, 305
Bridei III, King of the Picts, 329–30
Bridei IV, King of the Picts, 330
Brigantes (tribe), 198–200, 205–7, 213–15, 217, 220, 225–26, 230
Buckland, William, 7–8
Burgred, King of Mercia, 391, 393
Burns, Robert, 345
Byrhthelm, Archbishop of Canterbury, 421
Cadell, son of Rhodri Mawr, 441–42
Cadwallon ap Cadfan, King of Gwynedd, 312, 322–23
Cadwallon of Gwynedd, 445
Cadwgan of Powys, 542
Caedmon, 343
Caedwalla of Wessex, 326, 387
Calderwood, David, 262
Caledonii (Caledonians; tribe), 146–47, 179, 217, 219, 244–46, 248, 265, 271

Calgacus, 161, 208, 244
Caligula, Roman Emperor, 190, 194
Cantii (Cantiaci; tribe), 188, 197, 199, 227
Caracalla, Roman Emperor, 217–20, 267
Carausius, usurper, 269
Carinus, Roman Emperor, 269
Carlyle, Thomas, 345
Cartimandua, Queen of the Brigantes, 198–200, 205, 226
Carvetii (tribe), 206, 214
Cassius Dio, 145, 147, 184, 190, 195, 198, 201, 216–18, 224, 244–45
Cassivellaunus, King of the Catuvellauni, 187, 189
Catan, Saint, 300
Catuvellauni (tribe), 186–87, 189–90, 196, 226
Causantín mac Áeda (Constantine II) of Scotland, 373–75, 403, 406, 408, 411, 413–15, 417, 429, 430
Causantín mac Cináeda (Constantine I) of Scotland, 13, 369–71
Ceawlin, King of Wessex, 287, 311, 313, 315
Celestine, Pope, 264
Cellach, Bishop, 372
Cenel nEógain of the Uí Néill, 293
Cennétig mac Lorcáin, 467–68
Cenwalh of Wessex, 325–26
Cenwold, Bishop, 410
Ceolwulf II of Mercia, 393, 441
Cerdic and Cynric, 282, 287, 307
Cerialis, Quintus Petrus, 201, 205–06
Cetwine of Wessex, 326
Chabrier, King of the Franks, 319
Chadwick, Nora, 151
Charlemagne, 351, 353–56, 387, 401
Charles de Valois, 518
Charles II of the West Franks, 344
Charles the Bald, 388, 390, 397, 400
Charles the Simple, 407, 410, 441
Charles VI of France, 518
Charles VII of France, 518

Charles, son of Charlemagne, 354
Chaucer, Geoffrey, 344, 378
Chrétien de Troyes, 290
Cicero, 7, 145, 185, 193, 203
Cináed MacAlpín (Kenneth MacAlpin), 13, 368–69, 371, 373–74, 429, 460
Claudius, Roman Emperor, 144, 173, 178, 191, 194–98, 200–01, 204, 205, 214, 222–24, 226, 231, 252, 267
Clonycavan Man, 169–70
Clydog of Dyfed, 406, 442
Cnut, King of England and Denmark, 448–58, 460–61, 463, 465, 479–81, 485–86, 506–7, 512–13, 517, 521
Coel Hen, 283–85, 315
Coenwulf, King of Mercia, 355–56
Colmán, Bishiop, 323
Columba, Saint, 294, 298–301, 303–06, 320, 323, 363, 430
Commius, King of the Atrebates, 189
Commodus, Roman Emperor, 215–16
Conall mac Comgaill, King of Dál Riata, 300
Connachta (clan), 293
Constantine I (the Great), Roman Emperor, 269–71
Constantine III of Scotland, 429
Constantine III, Roman Emperor, 275
Constantius I (Constantius Chlorus), Roman Emperor, 245, 269–71
Constantius II, Roman Emperor, 272
Copsig, 501–02
Corieltauvi (Corieltavi; Coritani; tribe), 191, 227
Cormac mac Cuillennáin, Saint, 439
Coroticus, ruler of Alt Clud, 304–05
Crassus, Marcus Licinus, 184
Crínan of Dunkeld, 460–61, 524,
Cunedda, 283
Cunobelin, King of the Catuvellauni, 189–91, 198
Curle, Alexander Ormiston, 262
Cuthwine, son of Ceawlin, 313

Cwichelm of Wessex, 325
Cynegils, King of Wessex, 312, 325
Cyngen ap Cadell, 365, 440–41
Cynon ap Clydno, ruler of Alt Clud, 316
Dafydd ap Llywelyn, 548–50
Dafydd ap Owain, 545
Dallán, Saint, 306
David I of Scotland, 528–30, 536
David, Saint, 318
Deane, John Bathurst, 182
Decantae (tribe), 248
Decianus, Catus, 20, 226
Deda and Mela, 282
Diarmait mac Cerbaill of the Uí Néill, 299
Didus, Aulus Gallus, 199
Diocletian, 255–58, 262, 267, 269–70
Diodorus Siculus, 138–40, 172, 175, 177, 179–80, 204, 243
Diogenes, Laertius, 172
Dionysius of Halicarnassus, 204
Diviciacus (Diviaticus), 171
Dobunni (tribe), 191, 226, 230
Domitian, Roman Emperor, 209–10, 206
Domnall mac Ailpín (Donald I) of Scotland, 13, 369
Domnall mac Causantín (Donald II) of Scotland, 373–75
Domnall mac Eimín, Mormaer of Mar, 472
Domnall mac Eógain, King of Strathclyde, 416
Domnall Ua Lochlain, 534
Domnall, son of Brian Boru, 471
Donald III of Scotland (Donald Bán), 525–27, 533, 461
Donnabán mac Cathail, 468
Donnán, Saint, 306, 320
Donnchad mac Dómnaill Clóen, 469–70
Drest VI, King of the Picts, 329
Druids, 144, 161, 171–83, 199, 204, 221, 224, 241–42, 189–200, 205, 225, 249, 262, 298, 560

Duncan I of Scotland, 460–61, 524
Duncan II of Scotland, 524–27
Dunnchadh mac Gilla Pátraic of Ostraige, 473
Dunstan, Archbishop of Canterbury, Saint, 419–24, 500
Durotriges (tribe), 188, 199, 227
Dyfnwal ab Owain of Strathclyde, 431–32
Eadbald, King of Kent, 321–22
Eadberht of Northumbria, 331
Eadberht Praen, 355
Eadfrith, Saint, 350
Eadgar, King of England, 421–24, 431–32, 434–46, 448, 450, 453
Eadmund, King of England, 415–17, 419–20, 431, 444
Eadred, King of England, 417, 420–21, 483
Eadric Streona, 446–47, 449–50, 452–53
Eadulf of Bamburgh, 460–61
Eadweard of Wessex, see Edward the Elder
Eadweard the Martyr, 402, 422–424
Ealdred I of Northumbria, 406, 408, 411
Ealdred, Archbishop of York, 486–87, 493, 500–01, 509
Eanflaed, 322–23
Eanred of Northumbria, 357
Eborius of York, 258
Ecgberht, Bishop, 330
Ecgberht, King of Wessex, 353, 356–57, 367, 386
Ecgfrith of Mercia, 354–55
Ecgfrith, King of Northumbria, 329–30
Echmarcach mac Ragnaill, 461, 465
Edgar of Scotland, 526–29, 533
Edgar the Ætheling, 486, 488–89, 500, 502, 504, 513, 521–22, 538
Edith Swan-Neck, 489, 499, 502
Edith, wife of Edward the Confessor, 479–80, 484–86, 489, 500
Edmund Ironside, son of Æthelred, 449–52, 486

Edmund, King of East Anglia, 390–92
Edmund, son of Harold Godwineson, 502, 551
Edric the Wild, 501, 504, 538–39
Edward (the Confessor), King of England, 402, 451, 458–59, 4612, 476–90, 492–93, 500–01, 505, 521, 524, 551
Edward I, King of England, 518, 549–50
Edward II, King of England, 518
Edward the Elder (Eadweard of Wessex), 335, 343, 400, 402–09, 413, 442
Edward, son of Malcolm III of Scotland, 523, 525–26
Edwin, brother of Leofric, Earl of Mercia, 476
Edwin, Earl of Mercia, 495–96, 500–02, 506
Edwin, King of Deira, 308, 311–12, 316–17, 322–23, 329
Einarr Rognvaldson (Torf-Einarr), 432–33
Eirik Blodøks, 413, 417–18, 433–34, 453
Eirik Hákonarson, 449, 452–53, 455, 463
Emma, Queen of England, 425, 446–47, 453–54, 456–59, 480, 506
Eochaid, King of Strathclyde, 373
Eóganachta (clan), 293, 438, 468, 472–73
Eóganan mac Óengusa, 368
Eorpwald, King of East Anglia, 321
Eowils of Jórvik, 404
Ephorus, 162
Eumenius, 245
Eustace II of Boulogne, 481, 483, 490, 501, 513
Fedelmid mac Crimthainn, 438
Fiachna, King of Ulster, 315
Finnian of Clonfert, Saint, 297–99
Finnian of Movilla, Saint, 297–99
Flaithbertach mac Inmainén, 439
Flaithbertach Ua Néill, 470–72
Flann Sinna, King of Meath, 374, 439
Flavius Aetius (Agitius), 282, 286
Flavius Eutropius, 197

Francis I of France, 519
Fraomarius, King of the Bucinobantes, 274
Frisians (tribe), 268, 285, 313, 332, 335
Galerius, Roman Emperor, 255
Gallienus, Roman Emperor, 255, 268
Geoffrey Gaimar, 396
Geoffrey of Monmouth, 278, 289, 290
Germanianus, son of Coel Hen, 285
Germanus of Auxerre, Saint, 257–58, 279
Geta, son of Emperor Severus, 217–19
Gilbert de Clare, 543–44, 549
Gildas, 202, 257, 277, 281–82, 288–89, 305, 318, 338, 345, 362
Giles, G.A., 202–03
Gilli, 434–35
Giric mac Dúngail, 371–75, 430
Gododdin (tribe; see also Votadini), 244, 279, 283, 285, 289, 304–05, 315–17, 328
Godred Crovan, 533, 535
Godred the Black, 535
Godwine, Earl, 452, 454–57, 459, 461, 479–86
Gofraid mac Arailt, King of the Isles, 434
Gofraid of Lochlann, 383
Gofraid ua Ímair, 386, 408, 414, 434, 436–37, 474
Golding, William, 31
Gormlaith ingen Muchada, 474–75
Gospatric, 502, 504
Goths (tribe), 268, 275
Gratian, Roman Emperor, 274
Gratian, usurper, 275
Gregory I (Gregory the Great), Pope, 319–21, 326, 343
Gruffudd ap Cynan of Gwynedd, 528, 534, 541–43, 464
Gruffudd ap Rhydderch of Gwent, 476
Gruffudd ap Rhys of Deheubarth, 543
Guinevere, 290–91
Gunn, William, 256–57

Guoremor (Vorimorus), King of Dumnonia, 281
Guthrum II of East Anglia, 405
Guthrum of Great Heathen Army, 392–94, 396–98, 401, 403, 441, 451–52
Gyrth Godwineson, 484–85, 499
Gytha, mother of Harold Godwineson, 499, 501–02
Hadrian, Roman Emperor, 211, 214, 228
Haesten, 398, 401
Hákon Eiríksson, 455, 463
Hákon, King of Norway, 413
Hakon, son of Sweyn Godwineson, 487–88
Hákon, Viking leader, 383
Halfdan of Great Heathen Army, 392–93, 398, 441
Halfdan of Jórvik, 404
Harald Bluetooth, King of Denmark, 425
Harald Fairhair, King of Norway, 374, 376, 413
Harald Hardrada (Harald Sigurdsson), 13, 462, 465, 489–90, 492, 495–98, 506, 520, 533
Harald Harefoot (Harald I of England), 456–58, 478, 487
Harald II of Denmark (brother of King Cnut of England), 448, 454
Harald Maddadson, 536–37
Harold Godwineson (Harold II), King of England, 13, 314, 476, 479, 481–85, 487–99, 506, 521–22, 538, 540 540, 551, 563
Harthacnut, King of England and Denmark, 454, 467–69, 483, 485, 488
Hecataeus of Abdera, 172
Hecataeus of Miletus, 150
Hengist and Horsa, 282, 286, 320, 345
Henry I, King of England, 454, 514–17, 528–29, 541–43, 551
Henry II, King of England, 517, 520, 530–31, 544–45, 551, 553–59
Henry II, King of France, 518

Henry III, Holy Roman Emperor, 481
Henry III, King of England, 517, 532, 547–49
Henry IV, King of England, 344, 512
Henry of Scotland, 529–30
Henry V, King of England, 518, 520
Henry VI, King of England, 518
Henry VII, King of England, 518
Henry VIII, King of England, 400, 479, 519
Herbert, Frank, 43
Herodian, 217–18
Herodotus, 138, 140, 142, 157, 161, 163
Hlodvir Thorfinnson, 433
Holder, Alfred, 138
Honorius, Roman Emperor, 265–66, 275–76
Hugh d'Avranches, 540–41
Hugh de Lacy, 556
Hugh Le Despenser, 518
Hugh of Mongomery, 534
Hussa, King of the Angles, 315
Hywel ab Edwin, 476
Hywel Dda (Hywel the Good), 442, 444–45, 448, 476–77
Hywel of Dyfed and Deheubarth, 406, 408
Iaroslav I (Yaroslav) of Kiev, 453, 486, 488
Iceni (tribe), 11–12, 191, 199–200, 226–27
Icil (Icel), leader of the Angles, 307–08
Ida, King of Bernicia, 308, 315
Idwal Foel (Idwal ap Anarawd), 406, 444–45
Imar of Limerick, 468
Indulf, King of Scotland, 417–18, 429, 431
Ine of Wessex, 338, 346, 387
Ingibjorg, 462, 524–25
Ingimund of Lewis, 532
Ingimund, Viking leader, 378
Ingres, Jean-Auguste-Dominique, 155
Innocent IV, Pope, 524, 548
Israel the Grammarian, 410
Jackson, Kenneth, 151

Index of Persons

James III of Scotland, 537
James VI and I, King of Scotland and England, 7, 560
John de Coucy, 556
John of Fordun, 261–62, 372
John of Salisbury, 555
John of Worcester, 432
John, King of England, 517, 531–32, 546–47, 556–57
Johnson, Samuel, 155
Jones, Inigo, 7
Judith, Queen of Wessex, 388–89
Julian (the Apostate), Roman Emperor, 256, 271–72
Julius Caesar, 7, 40, 143, 145–46, 149–50, 161, 171, 175, 177–79, 183–94, 203–04, 218–19, 223–24, 226, 237, 242, 245, 267, 320
Julius, Saint, 257–58, 318
Jutes (tribe), 282, 285–87, 313, 332, 335, 492
Keating, Geoffrey, 240
Kenneth II of Scotland, 429–31
Kenneth III of Scotland, 429
Kingsley, Charles, 292, 505
Laigin (clan) 293–94, 439
Lanfranc, Archbishop of Canterbury, 493, 509
Le Sueur, Jean-François, 155
Leo IV, Pope, 387–88
Leo IX, Pope, 483, 493
Leofwine Godwineson, 484–85, 499
Lhuyd, Edward, 154, 158, 262
Lindow Man, 169–70
Llywelyn ap Gruffudd, (Llywelyn II; Llywelyn the Last), 548–50
Llywelyn ap Merfyn, King of Powys, 444
Llywelyn ap Seisyll, King of Powys and Gwynedd, 475
Llywelyn mab Iorweth (Llywelyn the Great), 546–47
Ímar (Ímar ua Ímair; Ívarr the Boneless), 369, 384, 391, 396

Lollius Urbicus, 214, 243
Louis IX of France, 548
Louis VII, 554–55
Louis, Prince of France, 517, 532
Lubbock, Sir John, 4, 6
Lucius (legendary king), 256–57, 262
Lucius Alfenus Senecio, 217
Lucius Verus, Roman Emperor, 256
Lulach, 429, 462, 525
Lupus of Troyes, 258
Macbeth, 429, 460–62, 524–25
Maccus mac Arailt, 434, 436
MacKinnon, Donald, 151
Macpherson, James, 155
Madog ap Maredudd, 544–45
Madog ap Rhiryd, 542
Maeatae (tribe), 216–19, 246
Máel Coluim ap Dyfnwal (Malcolm of Cumbria), 432
Máel Muire, 374
Máel Sechnaill I, King of Meath, 383, 439
Máel Sechnaill II, (Máel Sechnaill mac Domnaill), King of Meath, 469–70, 472–75
Máel Snechtai, 461
Maerleswein, 502, 504
Magnentius, Flavius Magnus, 271–72
Magnus Godwineson, 502, 551
Magnus II, Earl of Orkney, 537
Magnus III (Magnus Barelegs), King of Norway, 527, 533–35, 541
Magnus Olafsson (Magnus I; Magnus the Good) King of Norway, 455, 457, 459, 465, 480–81, 488
Magnus VI, King of Norway, 536
Magnus, son of Harold Godwineson, 502, 551
Malcolm I of Scotland, 416–17, 430–31
Malcolm II of Scotland, 429, 431–33, 460–61, 464
Malcolm III of Scotland, 461–62, 490, 495, 513–14, 516, 520–27, 538
Malcolm IV of Scotland, 530, 535, 551

Mandubracius, 186–87, 237
Marcellus, Ulpius, 215, 217
Marcus Aurelius, Roman Emperor, 215, 256
Marcus, usurper, 275
Maredudd ab Owain, 445, 476–77
Margaret of Scotland, Saint, 502, 521–22, 524–26,
Margaret, Princess of Denmark, 537
Margaret, Queen of Norway and Denmark, 537
Martin of Tours, Saint, 263, 296, 319–20
Martin, John, 155
Mathgamain, 468
Matilda, Empress, 529, 543
Matilda, Queen, 502, 514
Maurice, Thomas, 182
Maximian, Roman Emperor, 269
Maximinus II, Roman Emperor, 255
Maximus, Magnus (Macsen Wledig), 274–75, 283, 314
Meiklejohn, John, 8, 265, 345, 422
Mendelssohn, Felix, 155
Merfyn Frych, King of Gwynedd, 290–91, 440
Merfyn, son of Rhodri Mawr, 442
Merlin (Myrddin), 169, 289
Meurig ap Dyfnwal, 441
Moluog, Saint, 306, 320
Morcar, Earl of Northumbria, 489, 495–96, 500–02, 505–06
Morgant Bwlch, 315
Muirchertach Ua Briain, 534, 551
Muirchertach, mac Néill, 436
Mungo (Kentigern), Saint, 305
Murchad mac Briain, 471–72, 475
Nechtan mac Der-Ilei, King of the Picts, 330–31, 372
Nechtan Morbet mac Erp, King of the Picts, 305
Nectaridus, 272
Nennius, 240, 256–57, 278, 282, 288–89, 290, 338

Nero, Roman Emperor, 200, 205, 254
Nest ferch Rhys, 542–43
Niall Glúndub, 385, 436
Niall Noigiallach (Niall of the Nine Hostages), 293, 298
Ninian, Saint, 262–63, 298, 304
O'Connell, Daniel, 467
Oda (Odo), Archbishop of Canterbury, 410, 416, 420–22
Odo of Bayeux, 501, 513, 515, 523
Óengus (Unust), King of the Picts, 331
Óengus of Moray, 529
Offa, King of Mercia, 327, 340, 352–56, 361, 387, 403, 4095
Olaf Haakonsson, King of Denmark and Norway, 537
Olaf II of Norway (Olaf Haraldsson), Saint, 455, 463–65,
Olaf III, King of Norway, 533
Olaf Sigtryggson (Amlaíb mac Sitruic), 463–65
Olaf, son of Harald Hardrada, 497
Olave the Red, 535
Old Groghan Man, 169–70
Olith, daughter of Malcolm II of Scotland, 434, 464
Orderic Vitalis, 498, 504, 515
Ordovices (tribe), 198, 206
Origen, 255
Orosius, Paulus, 197, 239, 343, 350
Osbeorn of Denmark, 503–04
Osberht of Northumbria, 391
Osmund, Saint, 509–10
Ostorius Scapula, Publius, 197–99, 227
Osulf of Northumbria, 417
Oswald, King of Bernicia and Deira, 308, 311–12, 322, 325, 328, 404
Oswiu, King of Northumbria, 308, 311–12, 317, 322–23, 325–26, 328
Otto I, Holy Roman Emperor, 410
Owain ap Cadwgan, 542–44
Owain ap Dyfnwal of Strathclyde (elder), 408, 413–15

610 Index of Persons

Owain ap Dyfnwal of Strathclyde (younger), 432
Owain ap Hywel, 445
Owain Foel of Strathclyde, 432
Owain Glyndŵr (Owen Glendower), 550
Owain, son of Urien, 316
Palladius, 264, 295, 299, 304
Parker, Matthew, Archbishop of Canterbury, 396
Patrick, Saint, 165, 181, 193, 258, 263–64, 295–96, 299, 304–05
Paulinus, 322–23
Paulus Catenus, 272
Peada, King of Mercia, 322
Peel, Robert, 467
Penda, King of Mercia, 312–13, 322, 325–26
Pertinax, Publius Helvius, Roman Emperor, 215–16
Petronius Turpilianus, Publius, 202, 204
Pezron, Paul-Yves, 154, 158
Philip de Braose, 556
Philip I of France, 513
Philip II of France, 517, 531
Philip IV of France, 518
Picts, 245–49, 255, 258, 263, 267, 271–72, 275, 280, 282–83, 285, 292, 300, 304–06, 328, 330–31, 368–75, 380, 384, 399, 431
Piran, Saint, 317
Platorius Nepos, Aulus, 211, 213
Plautius, Aulus, 195–98
Plegmund, Archbishop of Canterbury, 409
Pliny the Elder, 40, 140, 174, 176–77
Polybius, 204
Pompey the Great (Gnaeus Magnus Pompeius), 184
Pomponius Mela, 177, 179–80
Posidonius, 138, 177
Postumus, Poenius, 201
Postumus, Roman Emperor, 268
Prasutages, King of the Iceni, 199–200

Priscus Attalus, 265–66
Probus, Roman Emperor, 269
Procopius, 145, 213, 314
Prosper of Aquitaine, 264, 295
Ptolemy, 140, 147, 217, 239, 241, 244–45, 248, 380
Pytheas, 40, 139–40, 142–43, 150, 172, 177
Quintus Verianus, 199
Raedwald, King of East Anglia, 308, 311–12, 316, 320, 327
Ragnall mac Gofraid, 435
Ragnall ua Ímair, 385–86, 406
Ralph de Gael, 513
Ralph de Vexin, 482, 487
Restitutus of London, 258
Rhiainfellt, Princess of Rheged, 317
Rhodri Mawr, King of Gwynedd, 365, 378, 440–42, 448, 464, 477
Rhun ap Arthgal, King of Strathclyde, 370
Rhydderch Hael, ruler of Alt Clud, 305, 315
Rhys ap Tewdr, 540
Rhys, Sir John, 151, 248, 250
Ricberht, usurper in East Anglia, 321
Richard de Belmeis, 542
Richard de Clare (Strongbow), 543, 554–55, 557
Richard I, Duke of Normandy, 425
Richard I, King of England, 517, 530–341, 546
Richard II, Duke of Normandy, 425, 447, 458–59, 480
Richard III, Duke of Normandy, 459
Robert Curthose, 513–17, 523, 526, 541
Robert de Mowbray, 523, 526
Robert fitz Wimarc, 482, 498
Robert Fitzhammo, 541
Robert of Bellême, 515
Robert of Comines, 502
Robert of Gloucester, chronicler, 512
Robert of Jumièges, 482–83, 485–86, 493
Roger Mortimer, 549

Roger of Montogmery, 540–41
Rognvald Eysteinsson, 376
Rognvald, Earl of Orkney C.11th, 465
Rognvald, Earl of Orkney C.12th, 536
Rollo (Rolf the Walker, Hrólf the Ganger), 344, 432–33, 552
Rowlands, Henry, 182
Ruaidrí Ua Conchobair, 553–56
Saebert, King of Essex, 311–12, 320
Saxons (tribe), 7, 9, 68, 258, 271–72, 275, 279–80, 282, 285–86, 288, 313, 332, 335, 415, 464, 492, 506, 512, 551–52
Schubert, Franz, 155
Scott, Sir Walter, 155, 292
Scotti (tribe), 264, 272, 278–79, 295, 300, 303
Serf, Saint, 304–05
Setantii (Segantii; tribe), 215
Severus, Septimius, Roman Emperor, 216–19, 221
Sextus Aurelius Victor, 190
Sextus Julius Frontinus, 206
Shakespeare, William, 26, 189, 460, 518
Sigtrygg Silkbeard (Sigtrygg Olafsson), 436, 462–63, 470–70, 475
Sigurd Eysteinsson (Sigurd the Mighty), 376, 432
Sigurd Hlodvirsson (Sigurd the Stout), 376, 433–36, 456, 463–64, 466, 471–72
Sigurd, son of Magnus Barelegs, 533–36
Silures (tribe), 146–47, 198–99, 206
Simeon of Durham, 396, 415
Sitric Cáech (Sitric ua Ímair), 384–86, 406–08, 436–37, 474
Siward, Earl of Nortnumbria, 461–61, 480, 482, 484–86, 521, 524
Skuli, 433
Solinus, 40
Somerled, Lord of the Isles, 531, 535
Sotion of Alexandria, 172
Spotiswoode, John, 262
Stephen of Blois, 529–30, 543–44

Stigand, Archbishop of Canterbury, 480, 485–87, 493, 500–01, 509
Stilicho, 275
Strabo, 138, 140, 142, 162, 174, 177, 180, 191, 193, 195, 231, 243
Strongbow, see Richard de Clare
Stukely, William, 64, 182
Suetonius (historian), 177, 190, 197, 199
Suetonius Paulinus, Gaius (governor of Britain), 173, 178, 199–201
Suthen Bjornsdottir, 461
Swein Forkbeard, King of Denmark and England, 377, 425–27, 447–48, 450, 452, 485–86, 504
Sweyn Godwineson, 479, 481–85, 514
Sweyn II Estridsen, King of Denmark, 481, 490, 502, 504
Sweyn Knutsson, 455–56, 458
Tacitus, 7, 145–47, 149–50, 153, 173, 178–79, 193, 198–202, 205–10, 224, 244–45, 380
Taexali (tribe), 248
Taran mac Ainftech, King of the Picts, 330
Tasciovanus, King of the Catuvellauni, 189, 200
Tertullian, 255
Theodosius, Count (father of Emperor Theodosius), 273–74
Theodosius, Roman Emperor, 256, 274
Thietmar of Merseburg, 449
Thom, Alexander, 77
Thomas of Bayeux, Archbishop of Canterbury, 509
Thomsen, Christian Jürgensen, 3, 6
Thomson, James, 396
Thorfinn Sigurdsson (Thorfinn the Mighty), 464–67, 520, 524–25, 533, 535
Thorfinn Torf-Einarsson, 433
Thorgest, 383
Thorkell, 447–49, 452, 454–55
Tiberius, Roman Emperor, 194

Tigernán Ua Ruairc, 553–54
Timaeus, 40, 139–40, 172
Togidumnus (Cogidubnus), Tiberius Claudius, 198–99
Togodumnus, King of the Catuvellauni (see also Togidumnus), 191, 196, 198
Toland, John, 182
Tostig Godwineson, 476, 482, 484–85, 487, 489–90, 492, 495–97, 501, 506, 520–212
Tournel, Paul, 3
Trebellius Maximus, Marcus, 204–5
Túathal Techtmar, 237, 240
Turner, Sharon, 292
Tyndale, William, 410
Uhtred of Northumbria, 450
Uí Néill (clan), 241, 293–96, 298–300, 303, 329, 364, 373–74, 436, 438–40, 469–71, 474, 534, 551
Ulaid (clan), 293–95, 297–98, 303, 438, 470–71, 474
Ulf Jarl, 454–55
Urien, King of Rheged, 315–17
Ussher, Bishop James, 8
Vacomagi (tribe), 248
Venicones (tribe), 248
Vennemann, Theo, 141
Venutius, husband of Queen Cartimandua, 199, 205, 226
Verne, Jules, 43
Vespasian, Roman Emperor, 199, 205, 224, 227
Victoria, Queen, 202, 338, 341, 563

Vitellius, Roman Emperor, 205
Votadini (tribe; see also Gododdin), 211, 217, 220, 226, 243–44, 262, 279, 283
Waltheof of Northumbria, 501, 504, 513
Wells, H.G., 31
Wentworth, Lord, 519
Westropp, Hodder M., 4, 6
Wilfrid, Saint, 323, 328, 338
William Fitzosbern, 501, 540
William I (the Conqueror), King of England, 344, 479, 484–88, 490–95, 497–502, 504–10, 512–15, 517, 519–25, 538–40, 551
William I of Scotland, 530–31
William II (William Rufus), 514–16, 523, 525–27, 540–41, 551
William III, King of England, Ireland, and Scotland, 559
William of Malmesbury, 396, 415
William of Poitiers, 410
William of Warenne, 509
William Walcher, 523
Williams, Edward (Iolo Morganwg), 183
Wilson, Daniel, 3
Wulfhere of Mercia, 326, 329
Wulfhere, Ealdorman, 394–95
Wulfnoth, 446, 452
Wulfstan I, Archbishop of York, 416–17, 419
Wulfstan II, Archbishop of York, 453, 506
Yrfei, King of the Goddodin, 316
Zosimus, 265–66, 269, 275–76

www.ingramcontent.com/pod-product-compliance
Lightning Source LLC
Chambersburg PA
CBHW021823090426

42811CB00032B/1997/J